HOUSING LAW AND PRACTICE

HOUSING LAW AND PRACTICE

Gail Price LLB (Hons), LLM, Barrister

Published by

College of Law Publishing,
Braboeuf Manor, Portsmouth Road, St Catherines, Guildford GU3 1HA

© The University of Law 2014

All rights reserved. No part of this publication may be reproduced, stored in a retrieval system, or transmitted in any way or by any means, including photocopying or recording, without the written permission of the copyright holder, application for which should be addressed to the publisher.

Crown copyright material is licensed under the Open Government Licence v1.0.

British Library Cataloguing-in-Publication Data
A catalogue record for this book is available from the British Library.

ISBN 978 1 910019 04 7

Typeset by Style Photosetting Ltd, Mayfield, East Sussex
Printed in Great Britain by Polestar Wheatons, Exeter

Preface

This book is intended as an aid to students and practitioners of housing law. The book was designed to accompany the housing law and practice elective on the LPC, and attempts to address a perceived gap for an up-to-date, comprehensive text covering aspects of housing law identified for inclusion on the course.

In the interest of brevity, the masculine pronoun has been used throughout to include the feminine.

The law is generally stated as at 30 September 2013.

I would like to give particular thanks to Corin Barton, who wrote and updated the two homelessness chapters for the 2006 and 2007 editions.

GAIL PRICE

Contents

PREFACE		v
TABLE OF CASES		xi
TABLE OF STATUTES		xix
TABLE OF STATUTORY INSTRUMENTS AND CODES OF PRACTICE		xxvii
ABBREVIATIONS		xxxi

Chapter 1		INTRODUCTION TO HOUSING LAW AND PRACTICE	1
	1.1	Scope of housing law	1
	1.2	Property law aspects of housing law	1
	1.3	Public law aspects of housing law	2
	1.4	Areas covered in this chapter	2
	1.5	The categories of occupation for housing law purposes	3
	1.6	The impact of contract legislation on residential leases	5
	1.7	The impact of provisions in the HA 2004 on residential leases	6
	1.8	Further reading	8

Chapter 2		ASSURED AND ASSURED SHORTHOLD TENANCIES	9
	2.1	Introduction	9
	2.2	Assured tenancies	10
	2.3	Exclusions from assured tenant status	11
	2.4	Terms of an assured tenancy	13
	2.5	Security of tenure for assured tenants	16
	2.6	The grounds for possession	17
	2.7	Assured shorthold tenancies	24
	2.8	Tenancy deposit schemes for assured shorthold tenants	26
	2.9	Assured tenants of RSLs and PRPs	28
	2.10	Private sector assured tenants	33
	2.11	Further reading	33
		Summary	34

Chapter 3		RENT ACT REGULATED TENANCIES	35
	3.1	Introduction – Rent Act 1977	35
	3.2	Protected tenancies	36
	3.3	Exclusions from protected tenant status	36
	3.4	Security of tenure	37
	3.5	Rents under regulated tenancies	43
	3.6	Registered rents for housing association tenants	44
	3.7	Further reading	45
		Summary	45

Chapter 4		HOUSING AND HUMAN RIGHTS	47
	4.1	Introduction	47
	4.2	The rights relevant to housing law	47
	4.3	The effect of the main rights	48
	4.4	The courts' interpretation	48
	4.5	The scope for legal challenge to UK housing law	49
	4.6	Procedure for human rights claims	55
	4.7	Further reading	57
		Summary	57

viii Housing Law and Practice

Chapter 5	PUBLIC FUNDING AND COSTS IN HOUSING DISPUTES	59
5.1	Introduction	59
5.2	The levels of service available in housing disputes	61
5.3	The interrelationship between the different levels of service	64
5.4	The levels of contracts available for housing disputes	65
5.5	Financial eligibility	66
5.6	The statutory charge	69
5.7	Costs	69
5.8	Further reading	70
	Summary	70

Chapter 6	PUBLIC SECTOR HOUSING – SECURE TENANTS	71
6.1	Introduction	71
6.2	Housing allocation	72
6.3	Secure tenants – HA 1985, Pt IV	76
6.4	Non-secure tenancies	78
6.5	Introductory tenancies	80
6.6	Security of tenure	81
6.7	Grounds for possession	85
6.8	The rights and obligations of a secure tenant	89
	Summary	98

Chapter 7	DISREPAIRS	99
7.1	Introduction	99
7.2	The meaning of 'disrepair' and 'repair'	99
7.3	The contractual obligation	101
7.4	Obligations in tort	105
7.5	Civil remedies	107
7.6	Procedure for a civil claim	112
7.7	Public funding for civil disrepair claims	114
7.8	Public law obligations	115
7.9	Further reading	117
	Summary	118

Chapter 8	THE RIGHTS OF LONG LEASEHOLDERS	119
8.1	Introduction	119
8.2	Security on the expiry of a long lease	120
8.3	Exercising rights to acquire a greater interest in the property	121
8.4	Service charge and other issues in long leases	125
8.5	Statutory protection against forfeiture during long lease	128
8.6	Mortgage default and the rights of mortgagees	129
8.7	Further reading	132
	Summary	132

Chapter 9	PROTECTION FROM UNLAWFUL EVICTION AND HARASSMENT	135
9.1	Introduction	135
9.2	Civil causes of action	136
9.3	Civil remedies	140
9.4	Notice to quit	144
9.5	Civil procedure	145
9.6	Criminal sanctions	148
	Summary	150

Chapter 10	POSSESSION CLAIMS	151
10.1	Introduction	151
10.2	The scope of the rules in CPR, Part 55 and PD 55A and 55B	152
10.3	Starting the claim	153
10.4	Service of claims	156
10.5	The defendant's response	156

	10.6	The hearing	157
	10.7	Accelerated possession claims against assured shorthold tenants	157
	10.8	The possession orders	158
	10.9	Tolerated trespassers	164
	10.10	Challenging the possession order	166
	10.11	Warrants for possession	167
	10.12	Public funding and possession proceedings	168
	10.13	Checklist for possession claims	168
	10.14	Further reading	169
		Summary	169
Chapter 11		HOMELESSNESS I – THE LAW	173
	11.1	Introduction	173
	11.2	Eligibility for assistance	174
	11.3	Homelessness	176
	11.4	Priority need	180
	11.5	Intentional homelessness	184
	11.6	Local connection	187
	11.7	Duties towards homeless persons	190
	11.8	Further reading	196
		Summary	196
Chapter 12		HOMELESSNESS II – PROCEDURE	197
	12.1	Applications	197
	12.2	Enquiries	198
	12.3	Decisions	199
	12.4	Statutory reviews	199
	12.5	Appeals to the county court	202
	12.6	Judicial review	205
	12.7	Commissioners for Local Administration	209
	12.8	Further reading	211
		Summary	211

SUMMARIES – HOUSING LAW AND PRACTICE	213
Part I Summary – Security of Tenure	213
Part II Summary – Disrepair and Unlawful Eviction and Harassment	215
Part III Summary – Possession Claims	216
Part IV Summary – Homelessness	217
APPENDIX – LEGISLATION	219
Defective Premises Act 1972	221
Protection From Eviction Act 1977	223
Housing Act 1985	228
Landlord And Tenant Act 1985	259
Housing Act 1988	272
Environmental Protection Act 1990	300
Housing Act 1996	311
INDEX	341

Table of Cases

A

Abbey National Bank plc v Stringer [2006] EWCA Civ 338	131
Abbey National Mortgages v Bernard (1996) 71 P & CR 257, CA	162
Abbott v Bayley (2000) 32 HLR 72, CA	144
A-G v Fulham Corporation [1921] 1 Ch 440	203
Akram v Adam [2005] 1 All ER 741, CA	166
Alker v Collingwood Housing Association [2007] HLR 29, CA	107
Amaddio v Dalton (1991) 23 HLR 332, CA	41
American Cyanamid Co v Ethicon Ltd [1975] AC 396, HL	110, 141
Amoah v LB Barking and Dagenham [2001] All ER (D) 138	78
Amrit Holdings Co Ltd v Shahbakhti [2005] All ER (D) 37, CA	39
Andrews v Brewer (1998) 30 HLR 203, CA	10, 103
Anisminic Ltd v Foreign Compensation Commission [1969] 2 AC 147	203
Anufrijeva v Southwark LBC [2004] QB 1124, CA	50
Arogundade v Brent LBC (No 2) [2002] HLR 18, CA	168
Artesian Residential Investments Ltd v Beck [2000] QB 541, CA	16
Asghar v Ahmed (1984) 17 HLR 25, CA	142
Associated Provincial Picture Houses Ltd v Wednesbury Corporation [1948] 1 KB 223	203
Austin v Southwark LBC [2010] 3 WLR 144, UKSC	167
Ayari v Jethi (1992) 24 HLR 639, CA	141

B

Bah v UK [2011] ECHR 1448	55, 176, 183
Baker v MacIver and MacIver (1990) 22 HLR 328, CA	41
Banjo v Brent LBC [2005] EWCA Civ 292, CA	82, 120
Bank of Scotland v Hill [2002] EWCA Civ 1081	131
Bankway Properties Ltd v Penfold-Dunsford and Leech [2001] 1 WLR 1369, CA	14
Barclays Bank plc v O'Brien [1994] 1 AC 180, HL	130
Bardrick v Haycock (1982) 2 HLR 118, CA	13
Barnes v Gorsuch (1982) 43 P & CR 294, CA	13
Barrett v Lounova (1982) Ltd [1990] 1 QB 348, CA	102
Bassetlaw DC v Renshaw [1992] 1 All ER 925, CA	92
Bater v Greenwich LBC, Bater v Bater [1999] 4 All ER 944, CA	90
Begum (Nipa) v Tower Hamlets LBC [2000] 1 QB 133, CA	177
Begum (Runa) v Tower Hamlets LBC [2002] 2 All ER 668	203
Bevington v Crawford (1974) 232 EG 191, CA	37
Birmingham City Council v Ali [2009] 1 WLR 1506, HL	178, 193
Birmingham City Council v Ashton [2013] HLR 8, CA	161
Birmingham City Council v Walker [2007] 2 AC 262, HL	92
Boyland & Sons Ltd v Rand [2006] EWCA Civ 1860	163
Bracknell Forest BC v Green [2009] EWCA Civ 238	88
Bradbury v London Borough of Enfield [1967] 1 WLR 1311	204
Brew Brothers Ltd v Snax (Ross) Ltd [1970] 1 QB 612	101
British Anzani (Felixstowe) Ltd v International Marine Management (UK) Ltd [1980] QB 137	108, 160
British Oxygen v Minister of Technology [1971] AC 610	203
Brown v Brash [1948] 2 KB 247, CA	37
Brown v Liverpool Corporation [1969] 3 All ER 1345, CA	104
Buckland v UK [2013] HLR 2, ECtHR	49
Burton v Camden LBC [2000] 2 AC 399, HL	93

C

Cadogan Estates Ltd v McMahon [2001] AC 378, HL	39
Calabar v Stitcher [1984] 1 WLR 287, CA	110
Camden LBC v Alexandrou (No 2) (1998) 30 HLR 534, CA	93
Camden LBC v Goldenberg (1996) 28 HLR 727, CA	93
Camden LBC v Mallett (2001) 33 HLR 204, CA	23, 86

Caruso v Owen (1983) LAG Bulletin 106	138
Castle Vale Housing Action Trust v Gallagher (2001) 33 HLR 810, CA	20
CCSU v Minister for the Civil Service [1985] AC 374	203
Chapman v UK (2001) 10 BHRC 48	47, 50
Chasewood Park Residents Ltd v Kim [2010] EWHC 579 (Ch)	128
Chelsea Yacht and Boat Co Ltd v Pope [2001] 1 WLR 1941, CA	11
Church Commissioners for England v Meya [2006] HLR 4, CA	16
Clark v Grant [1950] 1 KB 104, CA	21
Clements v Simmonds [2002] EWHC 1652 (QB)	41
Cobstone Investments Ltd v Maxim [1985] QB 140, CA	39
Coney v Choyce [1975] 1 All ER 979	204
Congreve v Home Office [1976] 1 QB 629	203
Connors v UK [2004] 4 PLR 16	49, 51
Connors v United Kingdom 40 EHRR 189	52
Continental Property Ventures Inc v White [2006] 1 EGLR 85	126
Corby BC v Scott [2012] EWCA Civ 276	53, 56
Crawley BC v Sawyer (1987) 20 HLR 98, CA	77
Croydon LBC v Buston and Triance (1992) 24 HLR 36, CA	93
Cunningham v Birmingham CC (1998) 30 HLR 158, QBD	115
Curtis v London Rent Assessment Committee (No 2) [1999] QB 92, CA	43

D

Daejan Investments Ltd v Benson [2013] UKSC 14	127
Dame Margaret Hungerford Charity Trustees v Beazeley (1994) 26 HLR 269, CA	104
Davies v Peterson [1989] 1 EGLR 121, CA	42
De Falco v Crawley BC [1980] QB 460, CA	209
Dimes v Grand Junction Canal Proprietors (1852) 10 ER 301	203
Din v Wandsworth LBC [1983] 1 AC 657, HL	185
Doherty v Birmingham City Council [2009] 1 AC 367	52
Douglas-Scott v Scorgie [1984] 1 WLR 716, CA	103
Draycott v Hannells Lettings Ltd [2010] EWHC 217 (QB)	27
Drew-Morgan v Hamid-Zadeh (2000) 32 HLR 216, CA	19
Dudley & District Benefit Society v Emerson [1949] Ch 707, CA	18
Dunn v Bradford Metropolitan DC; Marston v Leeds City Council [2002] EWCA Civ 1137, CA	107

E

Eaton Square Properties Ltd v O'Higgins (2001) 33 HLR 771, CA	37
Edwards v Thompson (1990) 60 P & CR 222, CA	19
Ekinci v Hackney LBC [2001] EWCA Civ 776, CA	50
El Goure v Kensington and Chelsea RLBC [2012] EWCA Civ 670	181
El-Dinnaoui v Westminster City Council [2013] EWCA Civ 231	194
Eyre v McCracken (2001) 33 HLR 169, CA	101

F

F v Birmingham City Council [2007] HLR 18, CA	187
Fairmount Investments Ltd v Secretary of State for the Environment [1976] 1 WLR 1255	203
Fareham BC v Miller [2013] HLR 22, CA	53
Fennbend Ltd v Millar (1988) 20 HLR 19, CA	39
Fernandez v McDonald [2004] 1 WLR 1027, CA	145, 158
First National Bank v Achampong [2003] EWCA Civ 487	131
Forcelux Ltd v Binnie [2010] HLR 20	166
Francis v Brown (1998) 30 HLR 143, CA	144
Freeman v Islington LBC (2009) 24 EG 85, CA	91

G

Gallagher v Castle Vale Action Trust Ltd (2001) 33 HLR 72, CA	51, 86
Gent v De la Mare (1988) 20 HLR 199, CA	43
Ghaidan v Mendoza [2004] 2 AC 557, HL	54
Gibbons v Bury MBC [2010] EWCA Civ 327	201
GLC v Tower Hamlets LBC (1984) 15 HLR 54	115
Gofor Investments v Roberts (1975) 29 P & CR 366, CA	37
Guppys (Bridport) Ltd v Brookling [1984] 1 EGLR 29, CA	138, 142

H

Habinteg Housing Association v James (1995) 27 HLR 299, CA	106
Hackney LBC v Findlay [2011] HLR 15, CA	166
Hall v Wandsworth LBC; Carter v Wandsworth LBC [2004] EWCA Civ 1740, [2005] 2 All ER 192, CA	181, 201
Halsey v Milton Keynes NHS Trust [2004] 1 WLR 3002, CA	112
Hammersmith and Fulham LBC v Monk [1992] 1 AC 478, HL	89, 145
Hampstead Way Investments Ltd v Lewis-Weare [1985] 1 WLR 164, HL	38
Haniff v Robinson [1993] QB 419, CA	139, 143
Harler v Calder (1989) 21 HLR 214	144
Harouki v Kensington and Chelsea RLBC [2008] 1 WLR 797, CA	179
Harrow LBC v Johnstone [1997] 1 WLR 459, HL	89
Harrow LBC v Qazi [2004] 1 AC 983	52
Hilton v Plustitle Ltd [1989] 1 WLR 149, CA	36
Hodges v Blee [1987] 2 EGLR 119, CA	41
Holmes-Moorhouse v Richmond upon Thames LBC [2009] 1 WLR 413, HL	181
Holt v Reading BC [2013] EWCA Civ 641	89
Hopwood v Cannock Chase DC [1975] 1 WLR 373, CA	104
Horsham Properties Group Ltd v Clark [2009] 1 WLR 1255	129
Hounslow LBC v Pilling [1993] 1 WLR 1242, CA	89, 145
Hounslow LBC v Powell; Leeds City Council v Hall and Birmingham City Council v Frisby [2011] 2 WLR 287	53
Howard de Walden Estates Ltd v Les Aggio [2008] UKHL 44	124
Hughes v Borodex Ltd (2009) 26 EG 114	14
Hughes v Greenwich LBC [1994] 1 AC 170	79
Hussey v Camden LBC (1994) 27 HLR 5, CA	78

I

Irvine v Moran (1992) 24 HLR 1	103
Islington LBC v Uckac [2006] 1 WLR 1303, CA	87

J

James v UK (1986) 8 EHRR 123	48, 122

K

Kay v Lambeth LBC; Price v Leeds City Council [2006] 2 AC 465, HL; [2006] 2 WLR 570	52, 56
Keeves v Dean [1924] 1 KB 685	37
Kelsey Housing Association v King (1996) 28 HLR 270, CA	16
Kenny v Preen [1963] 1 QB 499, CA	136
King v Jackson (1998) 30 HLR 541, CA	143
Knowsley Housing Trust v McMullen [2006] HLR 43, CA	23, 160
Knowsley Housing Trust v White [2009] 1 AC 636	164

L

Laimond Properties Ltd v Al-Shakarchi (1998) 30 HLR 1099, CA	36
Laimond Properties Ltd v Raeuchle (2001) 33 HLR 113, CA	20
Lambeth LBC v Henry (2000) 32 HLR 874, CA	163
Lambeth LBC v Howard (2001) 33 HLR 58, CA	161
Lambeth LBC v Hughes (2002) 33 HLR 350, CA	168
Lambeth LBC v Johnston [2008] EWCA Civ 690	201
Lambeth LBC v Loveride [2013] HLR 31, CA	143
Landau v Sloane [1982] AC 490, HL	13
Lavender (H) & Son v Minister of Housing and Local Government [1970] 3 All ER 871	203
Lavender v Betts [1942] 2 All ER 72	136
Lee v Leeds City Council; Ratcliffe v Sandwell Metropolitan BC [2002] 1 WLR 1488, CA	54, 100, 107
Leeds City Council v Price [2005] 1 WLR 1825, CA	49
Lee-Parker v Izzet [1971] 1 WLR 1688	108
Leith Properties Ltd v Springer [1982] 3 All ER 731, CA	40
Lekpo-Bozua v Hackney LBC [2010] EWCA Civ 909	183
Lister v Lane & Nesham [1893] 2 QB 212, CA	100
Liverpool City Council v Irwin [1977] AC 239, HL	102, 103
Lomotey v Enfield LBC [2004] HLR 45, CA	186
London and Quadrant Housing Trust v Root [2005] HLR 28, CA	23
Love v Herrity (1991) 23 HLR 217, CA	140

Lower Street Properties Ltd v Jones (1996) 28 HLR 877, CA	26
Lubren v Lambeth LBC (1988) 20 HLR 165, CA	111
Lurcott v Wakely [1911] 1 KB 905, CA	100
Luton BC v Menni [2006] EWCA Civ 1880	79

M

Magill v Porter and Another [2002] 1 All ER 645	203
Makisi v Birmingham City Council [2011] EWCA Civ 355	201
Manchester City Council v Finn [2002] EWCA Civ 1998	167
Manchester City Council v Moran [2009] 1 WLR 1506	177
Manchester City Council v Pinnock [2010] UKSC 45	49
Manel v Memon (2001) 33 HLR 235, CA	24, 158
Mansfield DC v Langridge [2008] EWCA Civ 264	76
Mansukhani v Sharkey [1992] 2 EGLR 105, CA	41
Maswaku v Westminster City Council [2012] EWCA Civ 669	194
McAuley v Bristol City Council [1992] 1 QB 134, CA	102, 107
McCall v Abelesz [1976] QB 585, CA	136
McCann v United Kingdom 47 EHRR 913	52
McDonald v Fernandez [2004] 1 WLR 1027, CA	26
McDougall v Easington DC (1989) 21 HLR 310, CA	100
McGreal v Wake (1984) 13 HLR 107, CA	101
McIntyre v Hardcastle [1948] 2 KB 82, CA	41
McPhail v Persons, names unknown [1973] 3 All ER 393, CA	163
Mehta v Royal Bank of Scotland (1999) 32 HLR 45	143
Mellacher v Austria (1989) 12 EHRR 391, ECtHR	48
Melville v Bruton (1997) 29 HLR 319, CA	143
Miah v Newham LBC [2001] EWCA Civ 487	181
Miller v Eyo (1999) 31 HLR 306, CA	13
Minchburn Estates Ltd v Fernandez (1987) 19 HLR 29, CA	20
Moat Housing Group – South Ltd v Harris and Hartless [2005] EWCA Civ 287, [2005] HLR 33, [2006] QB 606, CA	22, 31, 51
Mohamed v Hammersmith and Fulham LBC [2002] 1 AC 547	188, 201
Mortgage Agency Services Number Two Ltd v Chater [2003] EWCA Civ 490	131
Mountain v Hastings (1995) 25 HLR 427, CA	17, 19, 161
Muir Group Housing Association Ltd v Thornley (1993) 25 HLR 89, CA	94
Mullaney v Maybourne Grange (Croydon) Management Co Ltd [1986] 1 EGLR 70	125
Mustafa v Ruddock (1998) 30 HLR 495, CA	18

N

National Coal Board v Thorne [1976] 1 WLR 543	116
Nessa v Chief Adjudication Officer [1999] 1 WLR 1937, HL	175
Niazi Services Ltd v Van der Loo [2004] 1 WLR 1254, CA	104
Noh v Hammersmith and Fulham LBC [2002] HLR 54, CA	198
North British Housing Association Ltd v Matthews [2005] 2 All ER 667, CA	20, 161
Notting Hill Housing Trust v Roomus [2006] 1 WLR 1375, CA	26
Nutting v Southern Housing Group Ltd [2004] EWHC 2982 (Ch)	14, 38, 91

O

O M Property Management Ltd v Burr [2013] HLR 29, CA	126
O'Brien v Robinson [1973] AC 912, HL	101
Oakley v Birmingham City Council [2001] AC 617, HL	115
Omar v Westminster CC [2008] EWCA Civ 421	201
Osei-Bonsu v Wandsworth LBC [1999] 1 All ER 265, CA	142, 143
Osmani v Camden LBC [2004] ECWCA Civ 1706, CA	181
Otter v Norman [1989] AC 129, HL	36
Oxford City Council v Bull [2011] EWCA Civ 609	185
Ozbek v Ipswich BC [2006] HLR 41, CA	189

P

Padfield v Minister of Agriculture [1968] AC 997	203
Parker v Camden LBC [1986] Ch 162, CA	109, 110
Pazgate Ltd v McGrath [1984] 2 EGLR 130, CA	40
Peabody Donation Fund Governors v Grant (1982) 264 EG 925, CA	91

Peabody Donation Fund v Higgins [1983] 1 WLR 1091, CA	93
Pike v Sefton MBC [2000] Env LR D31	115
Poplar HARCA Ltd v Donoghue [2002] QB 48, CA	48
Porter v Shepherds Bush Housing Association [2008] EWCA Civ 196	165
Postos v Theodotou [1991] 2 EGLR 93, CA	41
Proudfoot v Hart (1890) 25 QBD 42, CA	100, 103

Q

Quick v Taff Ely BC [1986] QB 809, CA	99, 104

R

R (A) v Lambeth LBC, R (Lindsay) v Lambeth LBC [2002] HLR 998, CA	75
R (Ahmad) v Newham LBC [2009] UKHL 14	74
R (Bernard) v Enfield London BC [2002] EWHC Admin 2282	50
R (Conville) v Richmond upon Thames LBC [2006] 1 WLR 2808, CA	196
R (Gilboy) v Liverpool City Council [2008] EWCA Civ 751	83
R (Joseph) v Newham LBC [2009] EWHC 2983	203
R (Khatun) v Newham LBC [2005] QB 37, CA	5
R (Lin) v Barnet LBC [2007] HLR 30, CA	73, 76
R (Maali) v Lambeth LBC [2003] All ER (D) 80	75
R (McCann) v Manchester Crown Court [2003] 1 AC 787, HL	32
R (McLellan) v Bracknell Forest BC [2002] QB 1129, CA	81
R (Morris) v Westminster City Council; R (Badu) v Lambeth LBC [2005] EWCA Civ 1184, [2006] 1 WLR 505	49, 50, 183
R (on the application of G) v Barnet London Borough Council [2004] 2 AC 208, HL	55
R (on the application of JL) v Secretary of State for Defence [2013] HLR 27, CA	53
R (on the application of Limbuela) v Secretary of State for the Home Department [2004] QB 1440, CA	55
R (on the application of Mohamed Ishaque) v Newham LBC, (2002) December 2002 Legal Action 22	206
R (on the application of Morris) v London Rent Assessment Committee [2002] EWCA Civ 276	121
R (on the application of Painter) v Carmarthenshire CC HBRB [2001] EWHC Admin 308	54
R (Paul-Coker) v Southwark LBC [2006] HLR 32	175, 203
R (Weaver) v London & Quadrant Housing Trust [2009] EWCA Civ 587	28
R (Weaver) v London & Quadrant Housing Trust [2010] 1 WLR 363, CA	48
R v Brent LBC, ex p Awua [1996] 1 AC 55, HL	177, 184, 185
R v Brent LBC, ex p O'Connor (1999) 31 HLR 923, QBD	206
R v Brent LBC, ex p Omar (1991) 23 HLR 446, QBD	193
R v Brent LBC, ex p Sadiq (2001) 33 HLR 525, QBD	206
R v Bristol CC, ex p Bradic (1995) 27 HLR 584, CA	182
R v Bristol CC, ex p Everett [1999] 1 WLR 1170, CA	115
R v Burke [1990] 2 All ER 385, HL	149
R v Camden LBC, ex p Mohammed (1997) 30 HLR 315, QBD	202, 206, 209
R v Camden LBC, ex p Pereira (1999) 31 HLR 317, CA	181
R v Cardiff CC, ex p Cross (1982) 6 HLR 1, CA	115
R v Chief Constable of Sussex, ex p International Trader's Ferry Ltd [1998] QB 477	203
R v Chiltern DC, ex p Roberts (1991) 23 HLR 387, QBD	197
R v Eastleigh BC, ex p Betts [1983] 2 AC 613, HL	188
R v Harrow LBC, ex p Fahia [1998] 1 WLR 1396, HL	185
R v ILEA, ex p Westminster City Council [1986] 1 WLR 28	203
R v Islington LBC, ex p Hinds (1996) 28 HLR 302, CA	199
R v Islington LBC, ex p Thomas (1998) 30 HLR 111, QBD	193
R v Kensington and Chelsea RLBC, ex p Ben-El-Mabrouk (1995) 27 HLR 564, CA	179
R v Kensington and Chelsea RLBC, ex p Byfield (1999) 31 HLR 913, QBD	206
R v Lambeth LBC, ex p Alleyne (1999) June 1999 Legal Action 23, CA	206
R v Lambeth LBC, ex p Carroll (1988) 20 HLR 142	198
R v Lambeth LBC, ex p Weir [2001] EWHC Admin 121; (2001) June 2001 Legal Action 26	199
R v Liverpool Crown Court, ex p Cooke [1997] 1 WLR 700	116
R v London Rent Assessment Panel, ex p Cadogan Estates [1998] QB 398	14
R v Newham LBC, ex p Khan and Hussain (2001) 33 HLR 29, QBD	179
R v Newham LBC, ex p Sacupima [2001] 1 WLR 563, CA	193
R v North Devon DC, ex p Lewis [1981] 1 WLR 328, QBD	186
R v Nottingham CC, ex p Costello (1989) 21 HLR 301, QBD	198
R v Oldham MBC, ex p Garlick [1993] AC 509, HL	198
R v Oxford CC, ex p Doyle (1998) 30 HLR 506, QBD	181
R v Rent Officer of West Sussex Registration Area, ex p Haysport Properties Ltd [2001] EWCA 237, CA	44

R v Secretary of State for the Environment, ex p Walters (1998) 30 HLR 328, CA	95
R v Secretary of State for the Home Department, ex p Daly [2001] 3 All ER 433	204
R v Stratford-upon-Avon DC, ex p Jackson [1985] 1 WLR 1319	207
R v Tower Hamlets LBC, ex p Begum [1993] AC 509, HL	198
R v Tower Hamlets LBC, ex p Subhan (1992) 24 HLR 541, QBD	193
R v Walsall MBC, ex p Price [1996] CLY 3068, QBD	182
R v Waveney DC, ex p Bowers [1983] 1 QB 238, CA	181
R v Waveney District Council, ex p Bowers (1982) The Times, 25 May, QBD	177
Rainbow Estates v Tokenhold [1998] 2 All ER 860	111
Rakhit v Carty [1990] 2 QB 315, CA	44
Ramdath v Daley [1993] 1 EGLR 82, CA	138
Ravenseft Properties Ltd v Davstone Holdings Ltd [1980] QB 12	100
Ravenseft Properties Ltd v Hall [2001] EWCA Civ 2034	25
Regalgrand Ltd v Dickerson & Wade (1996) 29 HLR 620, CA	143
Richmond Housing Partnership Ltd v Brick Farm Management Ltd [2005] EWHC 1650	124
Rimmer v Liverpool City Council [1985] QB 1, CA	105
Riverside Housing Association Ltd v White [2007] UKHL 20, [2007] HLR 31	14
Roberts v Hopwood [1925] AC 578	203
Ropaigelach v Barclays Bank plc [2000] 1 QB 263, CA	129
Royal Bank of Scotland v Etridge (No 2) [2002] 2 AC 773, HL	131

S

Saeed v Plustrade Ltd [2001] EWCA Civ 2011, CA	137
Sahardid v Camden LBC [2005] HLR 11, CA	75
Samin v Westminster City Council [2012] EWCA Civ 1468	176
Schnabel v Allard [1967] 1 QB 627, CA	144
Secretarial & Nominee Co Ltd v Thomas [2005] EWCA Civ 1008	36
Secretary of State for the Home Department, ex p Khawaja [1984] AC 74	203
Shala v Birmingham City Council [2007] EWCA Civ 624	203
Sharif v Camden LBC [2013] UKSC 10	177
Sheffield City Council v Hopkins [2001] All ER (D) 196, CA	167
Sheffield City Council v Shaw [2007] HLR 25, CA	160
Sheffield City Council v Smart; Central Sunderland Housing Co Ltd v Wilson [2002] HLR 639	51
Shepping v Osada (2001) 33 HLR 146, CA	19
Shine v English Churches Housing Group [2004] HLR 42, CA	110, 111
Short v Tower Hamlets LBC (1986) 18 HLR 171, CA	95
Slater v Lewisham LBC [2006] HLR 37, CA	194, 204
Smedley v Chumley & Hawke Ltd (1981) 261 EG 775, CA	101
Smith v Marrable (1843) 11 M & W 5	102
Solon South West Housing Association Ltd v James [2004] All ER (D) 328, CA	23, 160
Southwark LBC v Ince (1989) 21 HLR 504	115
Southwark LBC v McIntosh [2001] All ER (D) 133, Ch	105
Southwark LBC v Mills [2001] 1 AC 1, HL	136
Spath Holme Ltd v Chairman of Greater Manchester and Lancashire Rent Assessment Committee (1996) 28 HLR 107, CA	43
Spath Holme Ltd v UK, Application No 78031/01	43
St Brice v Southwark LBC [2002] 1 WLR 1537, CA	53
Stent v Monmouth DC (1987) 19 HLR 269, CA	100
Steven v Blaenau Gwent CBC [2004] HLR 54	106
Street v Mountford [1985] AC 809, HL	4
Sumeghova v McMahon [2003] HLR 26, CA	13, 139
Superstrike Ltd v Rodrigues [2013] EWCA Civ 669	28
Sykes v Harry [2001] QB 1014, CA	106

T

Tagro v Cafane [1991] 1 WLR 378, CA	140, 143
Taj v Ali (2001) 33 HLR 27, CA	163
Tan v Sitkowski [2007] EWCA 30	36
Tandon v Trustees of Spurgeons Homes [1982] AC 755, HL	121
Tanya Grand v Param Gill [2011] EWCA Civ 554	103
Thomas v Fryer [1970] 1 WLR 845, CA	41
Thurrock BC v West [2013] HLR 5, CA	53, 92
Torridge DC v Jones (1986) 18 HLR 107, CA	84

Tower Hamlets LBC v Begum [2005] EWCA Civ 340	195
Tower Hamlets LBC v Miah [1992] QB 622, CA	79
Tsyfayo v UK [2007] HLR 19	48

U

Ujima HA v Ansah (1997) 30 HLR 831, CA	11
Uratemp Ventures Ltd v Collins [2002] 1 AC 301, HL	10, 77, 138

V

Vella v Lambeth LBC [2006] HLR 12	115
Vine v National Dock Labour Board [1957] AC 488	203

W

Wainwright v Leeds City Council (1984) 270 EG 1289	101
Wallace v Manchester City Council (1998) 30 HLR 1111, CA	110
Waltham Forest LBC v Roberts [2005] HLR 2, CA	86
Waltham Forest LBC v Thomas [1992] 2 AC 198, HL	91
Wandsworth LBC v Michalak [2003] 1 WLR 617, CA	54, 91
Wandsworth LBC v Randall [2008] 1 WLR 359, CA	88
Warren v Keen [1954] 1 QB 15	102
Watchman v Ipswich BC [2007] EWCA 348	186
Welsh v Greenwich LBC (2001) 33 HLR 438, CA	101
West Kent HA v Davies (1999) 31 HLR 415, CA	23
West Kent Housing Association Ltd v Haycraft [2012] EWCA Civ 276	53
Westminster CC v Clarke [1992] 2 AC 288, HL	77
Westminster CC v Peart (1992) 24 HLR 389, CA	91
Westminster Corp v LNWR [1905] AC 426	203
Wragg v Surrey CC [2008] EWCA Civ 19	79
Wycombe Area Health Authority v Barnett (1982) 5 HLR 84	104

Y

Yemshaw v Hounslow London Borough Council [2011] 1 WLR 433	179
Yorkshire Bank plc v Tinsley [2004] 1 WLR 2380, CA	131

Table of Statutes

Access to Justice Act 1999 59
Administration of Justice Act 1970 129, 162
   s 36 162, 172
Administration of Justice Act 1973 129, 162
   s 8 162
   s 8(2) 172
Agricultural Holdings Act 1986 12
Anti-social Behaviour Act 2003 83
   Part 3 32
   ss 25A–25B 32
   ss 26A–25C 32
   s 28A 32
Anti-social Behaviour, Crime and Policing Bill 2013–14 22
   Part 5 20
Asylum and Immigration Act 1996 74, 175
   s 13(2) 175

Building Act 1984
   s 76 116

Children Act 1989 55
   s 17 55, 196
   s 20 182, 196
Civil Evidence Act 1968
   s 11 147
Civil Partnership Act 2004 11, 54
Commonhold and Leasehold Reform Act 2002 121, 124, 126, 128
   Part 1 (ss 1–70) 125, 132
   s 2(1)(a) 125
   s 3(1)(a)–(c) 125
   s 9 125
   Part 2 123, 132
   Part 2, Ch 1 ss 71–113 123
   s 72 123
   s 75 123
   s 79 123
   s 151 126
   s 166 129, 133
   s 167 128, 129, 133
   s 168 129, 133
   s 168(3) 129
   s 170 128, 133
   Schs 6–7 123
   Sch 11 127
      para 3 127
      para 4 127
Consumer Credit Act 1974 129, 133, 153, 162
   s 16 129
County Courts Act 1984
   s 38 109
   s 138 163, 172
Crime and Disorder Act 1998 144
   Part I (ss 1–27) 29, 32
   s 1 32, 93
   s 1(1)(a)–(b) 144
   s 1(3) 144

Crime and Disorder Act 1998 – *continued*
   s 1(7) 144
   s 1B 32
   s 1B(1) 144
Criminal Law Act 1977 148, 152
   s 6 149
   s 6(1) 149

Defective Premises Act 1972 106, 215, 221–2
   s 4 106, 110, 111, 112
   s 4(1) 106, 107
   s 4(3) 107
   s 4(4) 106, 107
   s 6(3) 106
   s 21 108
Domestic Violence and Matrimonial Proceedings Act 1976 89

Enterprise Act 2002
   Part 8 (ss 210–236) 6
Environmental Protection Act 1990 115, 118, 215, 300–10
   Part III (ss 79–85) 115
   s 79 115
   s 79(1) 116
   s 79(1)(a) 115
   s 79(1)(g) 115
   s 80 115
   s 80(1)–(5) 116
   s 81(3)–(4) 116
   s 82 112, 116
   s 82(7) 116
Equality Act 2010 76
   ss 4–13 76
   s 15 76
   s 15(1)–(2) 76
   s 19 76
   s 149 76

Family Law Act 1996 154, 167
   s 30 11
   s 45(2)(a) 31
Financial Services and Markets Act 2000 130, 153

General Rates Act 1967
   s 26(3)(a) 12

Homelessness Act 2002 71, 72, 73, 174, 207
Housing Act 1980 42, 77, 92
   s 89 158, 161
Housing Act 1985 2, 28, 44, 51, 71, 77, 165, 171, 213, 214, 228–58
   s 8 71
   s 27 95
   s 27AB 95
   s 27B 37
   Part IV (ss 79–117) 76, 95
   s 79 76, 78

Housing Act 1985 – continued
    s 79(2) 77, 78
    s 80 77, 78
    s 81 77
    s 82 81, 159
    s 82(1) 144
    s 82(3) 82
    s 82(4)(b) 83
    s 82A 30, 83
    s 83 81, 82, 84, 171
    s 83(1)(b) 84
    s 83A(1) 85
    s 83A(3)–(5) 85
    s 84 51, 85
    s 85 159
    s 85(2) 161, 167
    s 85(2)(b) 167
    s 85(4) 164, 167
    s 85A 22, 86, 160
    s 85A(2) 161
    s 86 82, 92
    s 86(1)(a) 82
    s 86A 90
    ss 87–106A 89, 90
    s 87 91, 92
    s 88 92
    s 89 92
    s 89(2) 91
    s 89(3)–(4) 79
    s 90 92
    s 90(3) 79, 92
    s 90(4) 79
    s 91 92
    s 91(1) 93
    s 91(2) 78, 79
    s 91(3) 93
    s 92 85, 87, 92
    s 93(2) 78, 79, 94
    s 94(2) 94
    s 96 94, 108
    s 97 94
    s 97(5) 94
    s 102 94, 95
    ss 103–105 94, 95
    ss 106–106A 94
    s 107A 77, 78
    s 107A(2) 78
    s 107B 77, 78
    s 107C 77, 81
    s 107D 77, 82, 171
    s 107D(5) 82
    s 107E 77
    s 107E(7) 82
    s 112 77
    s 113 91
    Part V (ss 118–188) 95
    ss 118–119 96
    s 121 96
    s 121A 96
    s 122 97
    ss 124–125 97
    s 125D 97
    s 131 97

Housing Act 1985 – continued
    s 138(2A) 96
    s 155 97
    s 155A 97
    s 156A 98
    s 160 97
    s 163A 97
    s 218A 29
    Part X (ss 324–329) 87, 88
    s 327 179
    ss 330–338 87
    Sch 1 79, 84
        para 4ZA 79
    Sch 2 22, 81, 82, 85
        Part I (grounds 1–8) 85
        ground 1 84, 85, 86, 93
        ground 2 84, 85, 86, 93, 96, 160
        ground 2A 23, 85, 86, 93
        ground 3 85, 93
        ground 4 85, 93
        ground 5 24, 85, 86, 87, 93
        ground 6 85, 87, 93
        ground 7 85, 87, 88
        ground 8 85
        Part II (grounds 9–11) 85, 87, 88
        ground 9 85, 87
        ground 10 85, 87
        ground 10A 85, 87
        ground 11 85, 87
        Part III (grounds 12–16) 85, 88
        ground 12 85, 88
        ground 13 85, 88
        ground 14 85, 88
        ground 15 85, 88
        ground 15A 88, 91
        ground 16 85, 88, 91
        Part IV 85, 89
        Part V 85
    Sch 3 92
    Sch 5 96
Housing Act 1988 2, 9, 10, 11, 13, 24, 28, 35, 37, 45, 77, 84, 120, 121, 123, 135, 165, 172, 213, 272–99
    s 1 10, 11, 24, 25, 34
    s 3 11
    s 5 10, 16, 25, 28, 159
    s 5(3)(d) 16
    s 6 16
    s 6A 29, 30
    s 6A(5)–(6) 30
    s 7 10, 16
    s 7(6) 16
    s 8 10, 16, 19, 21, 172
    s 8(1)(b) 16, 21
    s 8(2) 17, 19
    s 8(3) 17
    s 8(5) 17
    s 9 20, 159
    s 9(2) 167
    s 9(4) 164, 167
    s 9(6) 20, 161
    s 9A 20, 22, 160
    s 11 19, 21
    s 13 13, 14

Housing Act 1988 – *continued*
　s 13(5) 14
　s 14 13, 14
　s 15 13, 14, 15
　s 15(2) 14
　s 15A 29, 30
　s 16 13, 15, 105
　s 17 13, 14, 15, 19
　s 17(4)–(5) 14
　s 18 13, 15, 16
　s 19A 25, 158
　s 20 10, 24
　s 20(1) 24
　s 20(1)(a)–(c) 158
　s 20(2) 24, 25
　s 20(3)–(5) 25
　s 20A 25
　s 20A(4) 25
　s 20B 30
　s 20B(3) 30
　s 20C 31
　s 21 8, 10, 19, 25, 28, 34, 53, 157, 158, 159, 161, 172, 216
　s 21(1) 158
　s 21(1A) 26
　s 21(1B) 26
　s 21(2) 26
　s 21(4) 26, 30, 158
　s 21(4)(a) 158
　s 21(5) 26
　s 22 26
　s 27 137, 140, 141, 142, 143, 144, 215
　s 27(1)–(2) 140
　s 27(3) 140, 142, 144
　s 27(5) 144
　s 27(7)(a)–(b) 143
　s 27(8) 140, 142
　s 28 140, 142
　s 28(1) 142
　s 28(3) 143
　s 34 35, 36, 42
　s 34(1)(b) 36
　s 39 25
　s 45 10
　s 45(4) 16
　s 91(2) 29, 30
　s 93(2) 29, 30
　s 116 104
　Sch 1 11, 18, 33, 36, 120, 139
　　Part I (paras 1–13) 10, 34
　　para 10 12
　　para 12ZA 12
　　para 21 13
　　para 22 12–13
　Sch 2 16, 17, 33, 34, 120, 213
　　Part I (grounds 1–8) 17, 20, 161
　　ground 1 17, 21, 29, 42
　　ground 2 16, 17, 18, 21, 22, 42
　　ground 3–ground 5 17, 18, 21, 42
　　ground 6 17, 18, 21, 120
　　ground 7 17, 19
　　ground 8 16, 17, 19, 20, 41, 160, 161
　　Part II (grounds 9–17) 17, 20, 39, 85, 120
　　ground 9 17, 20, 21, 39

Housing Act 1988 – *continued*
　　ground 10 16, 19, 20, 21, 39
　　ground 11 16, 19, 20, 21
　　ground 12 16, 20, 21, 39
　　ground 13 16, 20, 21, 24, 40
　　ground 14 16, 17, 20, 22, 30, 39, 93, 160
　　ground 14A 23, 29
　　ground 14ZA 22
　　ground 15 16, 20, 24, 40
　　ground 16 17, 20, 24, 40, 120
　　ground 17 16, 20, 24
　　Part III 17, 20, 21
　　Part IV 17
　Sch 2A 25
　Sch 15 214
Housing Act 1996 10, 24, 25, 26, 50, 71, 86, 128, 165, 171, 175, 181, 182, 188, 199, 205, 311–39
　s 81 128, 172
　ss 96–100 24
　Part V (ss 124–158) 80, 81
　s 124 80
　s 125 80
　s 125A 80
　s 125B 80
　s 127 81, 159
　s 128 80, 81, 171
　ss 131–132 80
　s 133 80
　s 133(3) 79
　ss 134–137 80
　s 143 159
　s 143A 83
　s 143D 155
　s 143D(2) 52
　s 143E 83, 155, 171
　s 143E(3) 83
　s 143F 83
　s 145 85
　s 150 23
　s 153A 31, 83
　s 153A(1) 31
　ss 153B –153E 31, 83
　Part VI (ss 159–174) 72, 74, 194
　s 159(2) 72
　s 159(4B) 74
　s 159(5) 74
　s 160A 74, 75
　s 160ZA 74
　s 160ZA(2) 74
　s 160ZA(7)–(8) 75
　s 166A 73
　s 166A(2) 73
　s 166A(3) 73, 74, 75
　s 166A(4) 73
　s 166A(9)(c) 76
　s 166A(14) 75
　s 167(1) 73, 76
　s 167(1A) 73
　s 167(2) 73, 74, 75
　s 167(2B)–(2C) 75
　s 167(2ZA) 73
　s 167(4A)(d) 76
　s 167(8) 75

Housing Act 1996 – continued
  s 170 75
  Part VII (ss 175–218) 79, 174, 196, 197, 198, 217
  s 175 176, 177, 180, 184, 187
  s 175(1) 176
  s 175(1)(a)–(c) 178
  s 175(2) 177, 178
  s 175(3) 177, 178, 193
  s 175(4) 177, 179
  s 176 177, 178, 185, 192
  s 176(b) 177
  s 177 179
  s 177(1)–(1A) 179
  s 177(2)–(3) 179
  s 182 174
  s 183 197
  s 183(1) 197
  s 184 191, 199
  s 184(1)–(2) 191, 198
  s 184(3) 191, 199, 200
  s 184(3A) 191
  s 184(4) 191
  s 184(5)–(6) 191, 199
  s 184(7) 183
  s 185 176, 180, 184, 187, 198, 200
  s 185(1)–(3) 175
  s 185(4) 176, 183
  s 186(1) 175, 200
  s 188 193
  s 188(1) 191
  s 188(3) 191, 202
  s 189 184, 187
  s 189(1) 180
  s 189(1)(c) 181, 182
  s 189(2) 180
  s 190 191, 200
  s 190(2)(a)–(b) 196
  s 190(3) 195
  s 191 184, 200
  s 191(1) 184, 193
  s 191(2) 184, 187
  s 191(3) 184
  s 192 195, 200
  s 192(2)–(3) 195
  s 193 191, 192, 193, 194, 195, 200, 206
  s 193(2) 192, 193, 195
  s 193(3B) 183
  s 193(5)–(6) 194
  s 193(7) 194
  s 193(7A) 192
  s 193(7AA) 194, 195
  s 193(7AC) 195
  s 193(7AD) 191
  s 193(7B)–(7D) 192, 195
  s 193(7E) 192
  s 193(7F) 192, 194
  s 195 191, 200
  s 195(4A) 191
  s 195A 195
  s 196 200
  s 198 189, 190
  s 198(1) 200
  s 198(2) 189, 190

Housing Act 1996 – continued
  s 198(2A) 190
  s 198(3)–(4) 190
  s 198(5) 200
  s 199 74, 188, 190
  s 199(1) 188
  s 199(3)(b) 188
  s 200 200
  s 200(3)–(4) 200
  s 202 199, 202, 206
  s 202(1) 199
  s 202(2)–(3) 200
  s 203 199, 200
  s 203(3) 201
  s 203(4)–(5) 202
  s 203(8) 201
  s 204(1) 202
  s 204(2) 202
  s 204(2A) 202, 207
  s 204(2A)(a)–(b) 202
  s 204(3)–(4) 204
  s 204A 204
  s 204A(4) 204
  s 204A(6) 204
  s 206(1) 192
  s 206(1)(a) 192
  s 208(1) 193
  s 210(1)–(2) 192
  s 211 191
  s 218 83
Housing Act 2004 3, 6, 29, 87, 93, 97, 98, 118
  Part 1 (ss 1–54) 116, 215
  s 2 117
  ss 5–12 117
  s 30 117
  s 32 117
  Part 2 (ss 55–78) 6, 8
  ss 55–60 7
  s 72 7, 8
  s 73 7
  s 73(3) 8
  s 73(8)(a) 8
  s 74 7
  s 74(2) 8
  s 74(5) 8
  s 75 7, 8
  Part 3 (ss 79–100) 8, 33
  ss 79–83 8
  s 85 8
  Part 4 (ss 101–147) 8
  ss 101–104 8
  s 179 80
  ss 212–214 27
  s 215 27, 28
  s 215(2A) 28
  s 216 88
  s 254 6
  s 258 7
  Sch 10 27
  Sch 14 7
Housing and Planning Act 1986
  s 9(1) 85
Housing and Regeneration Act 2008 28, 164

Housing and Regeneration Act 2008 – *continued*
   s 297 33
   s 299 159, 165
   s 314 176
   Sch 11 159, 165
      Part 1 (paras 1–14) 164, 165
      Part 2 (paras 15–26) 165
   Sch 15 176, 183
Human Rights Act 1998 2, 47, 48, 146
   s 3 48, 56
   s 4 49
   s 6 48, 54, 203
   s 6(1) 56
   s 6(3)(b) 28
   s 6(5) 49
   s 7 55
   s 7(1)(b) 56
   s 8 209
   Sch 1 47

Immigration Act 1971 175
Immigration and Asylum Act 1999
   Part VI (ss 94–127) 12, 79

Jobseekers Act 1995
   s 26 67, 68

Landlord and Tenant Act 1927
   s 11(6) 15
   s 18 111
   s 19 14
Landlord and Tenant Act 1954 117, 120, 121
   Part I (ss 1–22) 120
   s 2 120
   Part II (ss 23–46) 12, 80, 138
   s 30(1)(f) 19
Landlord and Tenant Act 1985 126, 259–71
   s 8 102
   s 11 5, 94, 95, 99, 102, 103, 104, 105, 110, 117, 156, 215
   s 11(1) 102
   s 11(1)(a)–(c) 104
   s 11(1A) 104
   s 11(1A)(b) 104
   s 11(3) 104
   s 11(6) 105
   s 12 95, 101
   s 13 95
   s 13(1A) 103
   s 14 95, 103
   ss 15–16 95
   s 17 110
   s 18 126
   s 18(2) 126
   s 19 126
   s 20 126, 127
   s 20B 126
   s 20ZA 126, 127
   s 21 126
   s 21B 126
   ss 22–26 126
   s 27A 127
   Sch
      para 8 127

Landlord and Tenant Act 1987 121, 126
   Part I (ss 1-20) 122, 132
   ss 4–5 123
   s 10A 123
   s 12B 123
   Part II (ss 21–24B) 109, 123
   Part III (ss 25–34) 123, 132
   s 25(2) 123
   s 26 123
   s 27 123
   s 29 123
   Part IV (ss 35–40) 127
   s 35 125
   s 48 19, 160, 168
   s 58(1)–(2) 123
Law of Property Act 1925
   s 146 82, 111, 129, 172
   s 146(2) 163, 172
Leasehold Property (Repairs) Act 1938
   s 1 111
Leasehold Reform Act 1967 121, 122, 124, 132
   s 2(3) 121
   s 9(1) 122
   s 9(1A)–(1E) 122
   s 9A 122
   s 22 122
   Sch 3 122
Leasehold Reform, Housing and Urban Development Act 1993 121, 126
   Part 1 (ss 1-103) 124, 132
   s 5(2)(b) 124
   s 5(5) 124
   s 12A 124
   s 13 124
   Part 1, Chp 2 (ss 39-62) 124
   s 39(2) 124
   s 42 124
   Sch 6 124
   Sch 13
      Part II 125
Legal Aid, Sentencing and Punishment of Offenders Act 2012 70
   s 1 59
   s 4 60
   s 9 60
   s 10 60
   s 11 59
   s 12 59
   s 21 66
   s 26 69, 70
   s 144 5
   Sch 1
      Part 1 (paras 1–46) 59
         para 19 60
         para 22 60
         para 33 60
         para 33(1) 63
         para 33(1)(b) 115
         para 34 60
         para 35 60, 114
         para 35(4) 114
Limitation Act 1980 113
Local Government Act 1974 210

Local Government Act 2000
   s 2 196
Local Government and Housing Act 1989 25, 120, 121, 122
   s 186 120
   Sch 10 120
      para 3(1) 120
      para 3(3) 120
      para 10 120
Localism Act 2011 72, 77, 90, 109, 174
   s 148 194
   s 149 194
   s 150 71
   s 158 93
   s 159 93
   s 160 90
   s 161 14
   s 164 26
   s 178 28
   ss 180–182 109, 211
   Sch 14 93
   Sch 16 28

Matrimonial Homes Act 1967 154
Matrimonial Homes Act 1983 154
Mortgage Repossessions (Protection of Tenants etc) Act 2010 130, 162
   s 1(2) 162
   s 1(8) 162

National Assistance Act 1948
   s 21 50, 196

Occupiers' Liability Act 1957 106
   s 2 106

Police and Justice Act 2006 83
   s 23 32
   s 24 32
Powers of Criminal Courts (Sentencing) Act 2000 150
   s 130 116
Prevention of Social Housing Fraud Act 2013 30
   s 1 79
Protection from Eviction Act 1977 2, 135, 136, 145, 148, 152, 223–7
   s 1(1) 149
   s 1(2) 148
   s 1(3) 148, 149
   s 1(3A) 149
   s 1(3C) 149
   s 2 129, 135, 138, 150, 163, 172
   s 3 12, 135, 137, 138, 139, 150, 215
   s 3(1) 135
   s 3(2) 138
   s 3(2B) 138
   s 3A 12, 139, 150
   s 3A(2) 139
   s 3A(5)(a) 139
   s 5 135, 145, 150, 170, 171
   s 5(1) 4
   s 6 148, 149
   s 8 138
Protection from Harassment Act 1997 60, 148, 150, 152
   s 2 150

Protection from Harassment Act 1997 – *continued*
   s 2(1) 150
   s 3 137, 140, 141, 144, 150
   s 3(1) 150
   s 3(3) 144
   s 3(6) 150
   s 4 150
   s 4(1) 150
   s 5 150
   s 5(5) 150
   s 7(2) 150

Rent Act 1977 2, 9, 12, 15, 18, 25, 35, 37, 38, 45, 77, 86, 120, 121, 123, 143, 161, 178, 213, 214
   Part I (ss 1–26) 36
   s 1 10, 36
   s 2 37
   s 2(1) 38
   s 2(1)(a)–(b) 37
   s 3(1) 38
   s 3(2) 38, 105
   s 3(3)–(4) 38
   s 4 36
   s 5 36
   s 5A 36
   ss 6–14 36
   s 15 37, 44
   s 16 37
   s 18 35
   ss 22–24 36
   s 26 36
   Part III (ss 44–61) 43
   s 44 44
   s 49 44
   s 57 44
   Part IV (ss 62–75) 43
   s 67 43, 44
   s 67(3) 44
   s 70 43
   s 70(2) 43
   s 73 44
   Part VI (ss 86–97) 12, 44
   s 98 37
   s 100 159, 164
   s 100(2) 167
   s 100(4) 164, 167
   s 102 41
   Part IX (ss 119–128) 43
   s 148 105
   Sch 1
      Part I (paras 1–11A) 37
      para 2 38
      para 2(3) 38
      para 3(1) 38
      para 4 38
      para 6 38
   Sch 2
      para 4 13
   Sch 11
      paras 6–8 44
   Sch 15 37
      Part I 39
         Case 1 39

Rent Act 1977 – *continued*
    Case 2 39, 86
    Cases 3–7 40
    Case 8 39, 40, 41
    Case 9 39, 40, 41, 120
    Case 10 41
  Part II 39, 41
    Cases 11–12 42, 43
    Cases 13–18 42
    Case 19 42–3
    Case 20 43
  Part III 40
  Part V 42, 43
Rent (Agriculture) Act 1976 12, 18

Senior Courts Act 1981
  s 31(6) 206
  s 37(1) 109

Unfair Contract Terms Act 1977
  Sch 1
    para 1(b) 5

International legislation
European Convention on Human Rights and Fundamental
  Freedoms 1950 47, 183, 203, 204
  art 3 48, 51, 55
  art 6 47, 48, 49, 51, 53, 81, 83, 157, 166, 168
  art 6(1) 47
  art 8 47, 48, 49, 50, 51, 52, 53, 54, 55, 56, 57, 81, 83, 91,
    157, 158, 161, 183, 216
  art 8(1) 47, 49, 50, 81
  art 8(2) 48, 49, 51, 52, 54, 55, 57, 81, 90, 91
  art 14 47, 48, 50, 54, 91, 157, 183
  Protocol 1
    art 1 44, 47, 48, 122, 168
Universal Declaration of Human Rights 1948
  art 25(1) 47

Table of Statutory Instruments and Codes of Practice

Administration Charges (Summary of Rights and Obligations) (England) Regulations 2007 (SI 2007/1258) 127
Allocation of Housing and Homelessness (Eligibility) (England) (Amendment) Regulations 2009 (SI 2009/358) 176
Allocation of Housing and Homelessness (Eligibility) (England) Regulations 2006 (SI 2006/1294) 75, 175
    reg 6 175, 176
Allocation of Housing and Homelessness (Review Procedure) Regulations 1999 (SI 1999/71) 200
    reg 1(2)(b) 200
    reg 2 201
    reg 6(2)(a)–(b) 201
    reg 8(1)–(2) 201
    reg 9(1)–(2) 202
Allocation of Housing (Wales) Regulations 2003 (SI 2003/239) 75
Assured and Protected Tenancies (Lettings to Students) Regulations 1998 (SI 1998/1967) 12, 18
Assured Tenancies and Agricultural Occupancies (Forms) Regulations 1988 (SI 1988/2203) 24, 25
Assured Tenancies and Agricultural Occupancies (Forms) Regulations 1997 (SI 1997/194) 17, 24

Building Regulations 1991 (SI 1991/2768) 7

Civil Legal Aid (Costs) Regulations 2013 (SI 2013/611) 70
Civil Legal Aid (Financial Resources and Payment for Services) Regulations 2013 (SI 2013/480) 66
Civil Legal Aid (Merits Criteria) Regulations 2013 (SI 2013/104) 59, 62
    reg 11(4) 63
    reg 11(6) 63
    reg 13 61
    reg 14 61
    reg 18 62
    reg 32 61
    reg 39 63
    reg 40 63
    reg 40(1)(a)–(b) 63
    regs 41–45 63
    regs 53–56 66, 204
    regs 61–63 63
Civil Legal Aid (Procedures) Regulations 2012 (SI 2012/3098) 60, 65
    Part 1 (regs 2–15) 65
    Part 3 (regs 21–28) 65
    Part 4 (regs 29–49) 65
    reg 31 65
Civil Legal Aid (Statutory Charge) Regulations 2013 (SI 2013/503)
    regs 5–9 69
Civil Procedure Rules 1998 (SI 1998/3132)
    Part 3
        r 3.1 166
        r 3.1(2)(a) 207

Civil Procedure Rules 1998 – *continued*
    PD 4
        para 3.1 153
    Part 6
        r 6.2(1)(b) 166
    Part 7 55, 113, 145
    Part 8 145
        r 8.2 207, 208
    Part 13
        r 13.3 166
    Part 15 148
    Part 16 55, 146
        r 16.2(5) 146
        r 16.4 146, 154
        r 16.5 148
    PD 16 146
        paras 4.1–4.3 147
        paras 7.1–7.3 146
        para 8.1 147
        para 15 55
    Part 20 156
    Part 25 108, 147
    PD 25A 147
        para 2 147
        para 2.4 147
        para 3.3 147
        para 4 147
        para 4.4 147
        para 4.5 147
        para 5 147
    Part 26 113, 148
        r 26.6 113
        r 26.8 157
    Part 30
        r 30.3 55
    Part 32 113
    PD 32
        paras 17–19 113
    Part 36 69, 113
        r 36.10 113
        r 36.11 113
        r 36.14 113
        r 36.14(3)(d) 113
    Part 39 157
        r 39.2(3) 157
        r 39.2(3)(c) 157
        r 39.3 166
    PD 39
        para 1.5 157
    Part 44 69
        r 44.2 69
        r 44.2(4) 69
        r 44.2(5) 69
    PD 44 69
        para 9.8 69
    Part 45–Part 48 69
    Part 52 166, 204

Civil Procedure Rules 1998 – *continued*
  PD 52 204
  Part 54 55, 207
    r 54.2 208
    r 54.3 209
    r 54.5 206
    rr 54.7–54.8 208
    rr 54.11–54.12 208
    r 54.14 208
  PD 54
    para 5.6 208
    para 5.7 208
    para 5.9 208
    para 21 208
  Part 55 30, 150, 155, 168, 169, 216
    Section I 150
    Section II 150, 157
    Section III 152, 155
    r 55.1(a) 152
    r 55.3(2) 153
    r 55.3(4) 155
    r 55.5(2)–(3) 156
    r 55.6 156
    r 55.7 156
    r 55.8(4) 156
    r 55.8(6) 156
    r 55.9 157
    r 55.9(1) 157
    r 55.10 155
    r 55.10A 154
    r 55.12 157
    r 55.14 158
    r 55.16 158
    r 55.17 158, 166
    r 55.18 158
    r 55.19 166
    rr 55.20–55.28 155
  PD 55A 152
    para 1.3 153
    para 1.5 153, 156
    para 2 154
    para 2.3 154
    para 2.3A 154
    para 2.4 154
    para 2.4A 154
    para 2.4B 154
    para 2.5 154, 155
    para 2.5(4)–(6) 155
    para 2.5(8) 155
    para 2.6 155
    para 2.7 155
    para 3.2 156
    paras 5.3–5.4 157
    para 10.3 159, 164
  PD 55B 152, 154
  Part 65 30
    rr 65.14–65.19 155
    section I 32
    section IV 32
    section VII 33
  Sch 2, County Court Rules 147
    Ord.29
      r 1(2) 147

Civil Procedure Rules 1998 – *continued*
  Pre-action Protocol (Housing Disrepair) 112, 113, 114, 115, 215
    paras 3.2–3.3 112
    para 3.4 113
    para 3.5 112
    paras 3.6–3.7 113
  Pre-action Protocol (Judicial Review) 204, 205, 207
  Pre-action Protocol (Possession Claims based on Mortgage or Home Purchase Plan arrears in Respect of Residential Property) 130, 153, 162
  Pre-action Protocol (Possession Claims based on Rent Arrears) 152, 153, 160, 161, 168, 216
Commonhold Regulations 2004 (SI 2004/1829) 125

Displaced Persons (Temporary Protection) Regulations 2005 (SI 2005/1379) 12, 79

Financial Services and Markets Act 2000 (Regulated Activities) Order 2001 (SI 2001/544)
  art 25A 130
  art 61 130
Flexible Tenancies (Review Procedures) Regulations 2012 (SI 2012/695) 78, 82

Homeless Persons (Priority Need for Accommodation) (England) Order 2002 (SI 2002/2051) 182
Homeless Persons (Priority Need for Accommodation) (Wales) Order 2001 (SI 2001/607) 182
Homelessness (Suitability of Accommodation) (England) Order 2003 (SI 2003/3326) 192
Homelessness (Suitability of Accommodation) (England) Order 2012 (SI 2012/2601) 192
Homelessness (Suitability of Accommodation) Order 1996 (SI 1996/3204) 179, 192
Housing Health and Safety Rating System (England) Regulations 2005 (SI 2005/3208) 116
Housing (Right of First Refusal) Regulations 2005 (SI 2005/1917) (England) 98
Housing (Right of First Refusal) Regulations 2005 (SI 2005/2680) (Wales) 98
Housing (Right to Buy) (Prescribed Form) (Amendment) (England) Regulations 2007 (SI 2007/784) 97
Housing (Right to Manage) (England) Regulations 2012 (SI 2012/1821) 95
Housing (Tenancy Deposits) (Prescribed Information) Order 2007 (SI 2007/797) 27
Housing (Wales) Measure 2011
  Part 1 96

Introductory Tenancies (Review of Decisions to Extend a Trial Period) (England) Regulations 2006 (SI 2006/1077) 81
Introductory Tenants (Review) Regulations 1997 (SI 1997/72) 80

Landlord and Tenant (Notice of Rent) (England) Regulations 2004 (SI 2004/3096) 129
Landlord and Tenant (Notice of Rent) (Wales) Regulations 2005 (SI 2005/1355) 129

Notice to Quit (Prescribed Information) Regulations 1988 (SI 1988/2201) 145

Rent Acts (Maximum Fair Rent) Order 1999 (SI 1999/6) 43
Rent Repayment Orders (Supplementary Provisions) (England) Regulations 2007 (SI 2007/572) 7
Rights of Re-entry and Forfeiture (Prescribed Sum and Period) (England) Regulations 2004 (SI 2004/3086) 128

Secure Tenancies (Notices) Regulations 1987 (SI 1987/755) 84
Secure Tenants of Local Housing Authorities (Right to Repair) Regulations 1994 (SI 1994/133) 94
  Sch 109
Service Charges (Consultation Requirements) (England) Regulations 2003 (SI 2003/1987) 126
Service Charges (Summary of Rights and Obligations and Transitional Provision) (England) Regulations 2007 (SI 2007/1257) 126–7

Unfair Terms in Consumer Contracts Regulations 1999 (SI 1999/2083) 5, 6, 14, 16
  regs 3–5 5
  reg 6(2) 5, 14
  reg 7 5
  regs 10–14 6

EU secondary legislation
Directive 93/13/EEC 5

Codes and guidance

Allocation of Accommodation: Choice Based Lettings Code of Guidance (2008) 72
Allocation of Accommodation: Code of Guidance (2002) 72, 73, 74, 75
Allocation of Accommodation; guidance for LHAs in England 2012 (England Code) 72, 73, 74, 75

DCLG Tolerated Trespassers Guidance for social landlords 164
  paras 13–14 165
  paras 27–28 164

FSA Mortgages: Conduct of Business Rules 130

Homelessness Code of Guidance for Local Authorities 174, 177, 181, 186, 189, 198, 199
  para 6.15 198
  para 6.16 199
  para 6.20 198
  para 6.21 199
  para 8.5 177
  para 8.6 177
  para 8.29 179
  para 10.5 180
  para 10.6 181
  para 10.8 181
  para 10.15 181
  para 10.16 182
  para 10.18 182
  para 10.30 182
  para 10.42 182
  para 11.9 187
  para 11.11 185
  para 11.20 185
  para 11.25 187
  para 11.28 186
  para 18.10 189
  paras 18.13–18.14 189
  para 18.16 189
  para 18.22 189
  Annex 10
    para 1 175
  Annex 18 188

LC Guidance 61, 65
  para 6.2 61
  para 6.3 64
  para 6.4 64
  para 6.9 61
  para 6.15 62
  para 6.16 62
  para 12 114
  para 12.6 114
  para 12.7 61
  para 12.10 114
Local Authority Agreement 189
  para 4.1 188, 189

Abbreviations

ADR	alternative dispute resolution
AIA 1996	Asylum and Immigration Act 1996
AJA 1999	Access to Justice Act 1999
AJAs 1970 and 1973	Administration of Justice Acts 1970 and 1973
ASBO	anti-social behaviour order
CADA 1998	Crime and Disorder Act 1998
CCA 1984	County Courts Act 1984
CFA	conditional fee agreement
CLRA 2002	Commonhold and Leasehold Reform Act 2002
Code of Guidance	Code of Guidance on the Allocation of Accommodation
CPR	Civil Procedure Rules 1998
DCLG	Department for Communities and Local Government
DPA 1972	Defective Premises Act 1972
EPA 1990	Environmental Protection Act 1990
FCA	Financial Conduct Authority
FSA	Financial Services Authority
HA	Housing Act
HAT	housing action trust
HCA	Homes and Communities Agency
HHSRS	Housing Health and Safety Rating System
HMO	house in multiple occupation
Homelessness Code of Guidance	Homelessness Code of Guidance for Local Authorities
HRA 1998	Human Rights Act 1998
IPO	interim possession order
LGHA 1989	Local Government and Housing Act 1989
LAA	Legal Aid Agency
LHA	local housing authority
LPA 1925	Law of Property Act 1925
LRA 1967	Leasehold Reform Act 1967
LRHUDA 1993	Leasehold Reform, Housing and Urban Development Act 1993
LSC	Legal Services Commission
LTA	Landlord and Tenant Act
OFT	Office of Fair Trading
PD	Practice Direction
PEA 1977	Protection from Eviction Act 1977
PRPs	private registered providers of social housing
RA 1977	Rent Act 1977
RSL	registered social landlord
SQM	Specialist Quality Mark
TMO	tenant management organisation
UTCCR 1999	Unfair Terms in Consumer Contracts Regulations 1999

CHAPTER 1

INTRODUCTION TO HOUSING LAW AND PRACTICE

1.1	Scope of housing law	1
1.2	Property law aspects of housing law	1
1.3	Public law aspects of housing law	2
1.4	Areas covered in this chapter	2
1.5	The categories of occupation for housing law purposes	3
1.6	The impact of contract legislation on residential leases	5
1.7	The impact of provisions in the HA 2004 on residential leases	6
1.8	Further reading	8

LEARNING OUTCOMES

After reading this chapter you will be able to:
- understand the scope of housing law
- explain the different types of statutory regimes that deal with residential tenancies
- describe the categories of housing occupation
- understand the effect of an unfair term in residential leases
- explain the licensing provisions for HMOs.

1.1 SCOPE OF HOUSING LAW

Housing law is concerned with aspects of property law, as well as with aspects of public law. The property law comprises, in particular, residential landlord and tenant law. The public law covers the obligations of local authorities to uphold housing standards in their areas, to take action against owners who harass residential occupiers and to provide housing or ensure that housing is made available for certain categories of people. It is true to say that the division is not absolute, and there are many grey areas and areas of overlap.

1.2 PROPERTY LAW ASPECTS OF HOUSING LAW

In the area of residential landlord and tenant law, housing law is concerned with the basic contractual rights between the parties, as well as with the many statutory provisions which regulate those rights. Statute has intervened to prevent occupiers losing their homes, to provide security and rent control, and to impose obligations relating to the condition of dwellings.

There are at present three distinct statutory regimes providing varying levels of security for residential tenants. Each of these regimes stems from the basic common law contractual relationship of landlord and tenant. As indicated in the table below, two of the statutory regimes are in the private sector, ie where the landlord is not a public body per se. The third relates to tenancies granted by a public body, usually a local housing authority (LHA). However, this basic division becomes blurred as a result of the court regarding certain types of 'private sector' landlords as quasi-public bodies (see **2.9** and **4.4.1**).

Types of residential tenancies created from freehold or leasehold estates

Private sector	Public sector
Standard contract tenancy (ie exclusive possession of dwelling house) Not within statutory regime, eg high rent **Rent Act-regulated tenancy** Gives security, succession rights and rent control, but no new ones after 15 January 1989 **Assured or assured shorthold tenancy (HA 1988)** Since 15 January 1989. Assured tenants given security and some succession rights	**Secure tenancy (HA 1985)** Gives security, succession rights and right to buy, etc

This book starts with the most recent statutory regime to offer protection to residential tenants. This is examined in **Chapter 2**, which looks at assured tenancies under the Housing Act (HA) 1988. **Chapter 3** then considers the Rent Act (RA) 1977 and the security and rent control provisions that apply to regulated tenancies. In **Chapter 6**, the security given to public sector tenants is discussed at length. The chapter starts by looking at the allocations criteria that local housing authorities (LHAs) have to apply in selecting their tenants. All these provisions are within the Housing Act (HA) 1985 as amended.

On a less detailed basis, the statutory security offered to long leaseholders is also considered in **Chapter 8**. There are a number of different statutory provisions applicable here and only an outline is given.

The relationship of landlord and tenant normally carries obligations to keep the premises in repair. The common law and statutory obligations are considered in the context of disrepairs in **Chapter 7**. **Chapter 9** looks at the remedies available to an occupier who has been harassed by his landlord. It also covers the notice provisions necessary to terminate a periodic tenancy, as these provisions come within the broad remit of the Protection from Eviction Act (PEA) 1977. Related to this too are provisions which provide compensation for breach of the occupier's right of occupation contained in the HA 1988. **Chapter 10** looks at the procedural provisions relating to possession proceedings to terminate a residential occupancy.

1.3 PUBLIC LAW ASPECTS OF HOUSING LAW

In the public law area, LHA obligations to uphold housing standards are considered briefly in the context of disrepair in **Chapter 7**. The criminal sanction that is available against owners who harass their residential occupiers is discussed in **Chapter 9**, although it is fair to say that the chapter focuses more on the civil sanctions that an occupier could use against the harasser. **Chapters 11** and **12** focus on the law and procedure that obliges LHAs to assist homeless applicants in their areas. The two chapters not yet mentioned, namely **Chapters 4** and **5**, deal with the pervasive issues in housing law. The provisions therefore impact on LHAs as landlords and in the performance of their duties as public bodies. **Chapter 4** considers in general terms the impact of the Human Rights Act (HRA) 1998 on housing law. It is fair to say that this has had an effect in both the property and public law sectors, but more particularly where public bodies (eg LHAs) are involved. **Chapter 5** looks at the public funding issues in housing law.

1.4 AREAS COVERED IN THIS CHAPTER

In this chapter an outline of the general categories of residential occupancy will be given. It is these basic common law categories on which the various statutory regimes have been superimposed. The statutory regimes considered in the chapters which follow therefore start from one or other of these basic categories. The different categories or forms of occupancy also often overlap with different forms of ownership or interest in property. Also briefly considered is the impact on residential leases of legislative provisions contained in contract regulations and the licensing scheme for houses in multiple occupation in the HA 2004.

1.5 THE CATEGORIES OF OCCUPATION FOR HOUSING LAW PURPOSES

1.5.1 Owner-occupiers

The term 'owner-occupier' can relate to two forms of legal estates in land: freehold and leasehold. In one context it really only relates to a freehold estate, where the occupier has outright and absolute ownership of the dwelling by owning the fee simple absolute in possession. Except in the area of mortgage repossession and housing conditions, housing law does not generally deal with owner-occupiers who have a freehold estate of their dwellings. Brief reference is made to a new category of freehold ownership, the commonhold in **Chapter 8** (see **8.3.2.6**).

1.5.1.1 Leasehold estates

A long leaseholder of a dwelling is often thought of as, and certainly considers himself as, the owner-occupier of his dwelling. The lease will have been created out of the freehold estate, or out of another longer leasehold estate in the land. Where the leasehold estate is created out of another leasehold estate, the original lease will be known as the head lease and the later lease is called a sub-lease. The leaseholder or sub-leaseholder is given exclusive possession of the dwelling either by himself or jointly with one or more other persons. Joint tenants will hold one lease and have collective rights and responsibilities in relation to the leased premises. The leaseholder, subject to the terms of the lease, can assign (sell) his estate or create shorter lease terms (sub-lets) out of it.

The exclusive possession granted will be for a defined period – a term of years absolute. The long leaseholder will have the grant of an estate that exceeds 21 years. It is quite common in, residential leases, for the grant to have been for a term of 99 or more years. The significant difference between this estate and a freehold estate, however, is that the leasehold estate is a wasting or diminishing asset. At the end of the agreed term, at common law, the right to possession again belongs to or reverts to the freeholder or the estate holder from whom the lease was granted.

As is the case with a freeholder, a long leaseholder is often able to acquire his estate in the property only with the assistance of a mortgage or legal charge – a loan secured on the property. This legal interest in the property can creates its own problems if the borrower or mortgagor gets into financial difficulties and is unable to keep up with the mortgage or other payments. Common problems in relation to these issues are considered in the context of long leaseholders in **Chapters 8** and **10**.

1.5.2 Tenancies

Strictly speaking, a tenancy is a leasehold estate in land. The tenant has exclusive possession of the dwelling for a short fixed period, or on a periodic basis. There is no legal distinction between the grant of a term of six months and one of 99 years. The terms 'tenant' and 'leaseholder' or 'lessee' are interchangeable, and often used as such in statutes. However, generally the term 'lessee' is used to refer to a long leaseholder and 'tenant' to those occupying under a shorter period of occupation.

In practice, and as a result of the many different statutory regimes with different levels of protection, short and periodic leases are often treated very differently from long leases. To begin with, the formalities required to create a short tenancy and a 99-year term are very different. Also, a person is highly unlikely to get a mortgage to finance a short lease of residential property. Short leases cannot be registered at Land Registry as legal estates in land, as can long leases. There are terms statutorily implied into residential leases to protect tenants of short and periodic leases. These provisions are not available to long leaseholders. A long leaseholder is normally responsible for the upkeep of his dwelling, unlike a short leaseholder of a dwelling. In practice, therefore, for housing law purposes, the residential occupier of a long leasehold estate is more properly regarded as an owner-occupier, separate and distinct from the residential occupier of a periodic or short-term lease of property.

1.5.2.1 The notice requirement for periodic tenancies

There is also a difference between a fixed-term tenancy and a periodic tenancy in the way that they are terminated. At common law, a fixed-term tenancy expires at the end of the term, the period agreed at the beginning. On the other hand, a periodic tenancy – which may be weekly, monthly, quarterly, six-monthly or yearly – will go on from period to period unless or until terminated by one of the parties serving the appropriate notice to quit, or the tenant surrendering and the landlord accepting surrender of the tenancy.

The length of the notice at common law depends either on what the parties agreed or, failing that, on the length of the tenancy. In all except a yearly tenancy, the length of notice was the same as the length of the period. For a yearly tenancy, however, the length of notice was and is six months. In all cases, unless agreed otherwise, the notice must expire at the end of a period. So, for example, if a weekly tenancy was granted on a Monday, notice needed to be of at least one week, ending at midnight on a Sunday. However, for residential tenancies, the provisions in s 5(1) of the PEA 1977 now stipulate a minimum period of notice of four weeks to terminate a periodic tenancy (see **9.4.1** on length of notice).

For tenancies subject to one of the statutory regimes that will be considered in the following chapters, the common law position has been replaced by specific provisions to terminate the tenancy. Nonetheless, the common law position remains relevant for tenancies which are not within any of the statutory regimes. The common law notice provisions are also still relevant for notice to quit given by tenants who are within the statutory regimes and for certain types of notices given by landlords within the statutory regime (see **2.5.1.1** and **6.6.5**).

1.5.3 Licences

A licensee is someone with a contractual right to occupy land. The licensee will not have a legal estate in the property. The licence is a personal right which cannot be assigned in the way that a lease, at common law, can be. However, the key distinction between a lease and a licence is that of exclusive possession. A tenant has the right to exclude all others from his premises during the continuation of the tenancy; a licensee generally does not (see *Street v Mountford* [1985] AC 809, HL).

For residential occupiers, the significance of the distinction between a lease and a licence has become almost academic as a result of changes in the statutory security offered. Under previous statutory regimes, extensive security and rent protection were offered to residential tenants but not to licensees (see **3.2**). As a result, landlords were keen to avoid granting tenancies and went to great lengths to draft agreements which purported to create licences. In the private sector, landlords can now obtain market rents on new lets and can regain possession without difficulty from assured shorthold tenants (see **2.7**). Thus there is little incentive to try to avoid creating a tenancy. In the public sector, the statutory regime offers equal protection to both residential tenants and licensees, provided the qualifying conditions are met (see **6.3**).

1.5.4 Trespassers

In housing law, there are two distinct categories of trespassers:

(a) a person who never had permission to be on the land, ie who came onto it as an initial trespasser;

(b) a person who had permission and the permission has expired or been terminated, but where the owner allows or tolerates the continued occupation of the premises by the trespasser – previously known as a 'tolerated trespasser'.

1.5.4.1 Initial trespassers

The term 'trespass' in this category is closely related to that in tort law, and has the same meaning. A trespasser is someone who is interfering with someone else's possession of land. As noted at **1.5.1** above, both freehold and leasehold estates relate to possession, either absolute or exclusive. In housing law, a trespasser in this category is someone who interferes with that possession by taking up residence without the owner's consent. In modern terminology, such trespassers are known as 'squatters'. The way in which the owner can regain possession against such a person is very different from the procedure necessary for regaining possession against a tolerated trespasser. By s 144 of the Legal Aid, Sentencing and Punishment of Offenders Act 2012, it is now a criminal offence for an initial trespasser to squat in residential buildings. Conviction can lead to imprisonment for a term of up to 51 weeks or a fine of up to £5,000 (see **10.3.5**).

1.5.4.2 Tolerated trespassers

In this second category are persons who were originally tenants of the dwelling, but whose leases terminated. Where the landlord allowed the previous tenant to continue in occupation, despite his no longer having a legal estate, the previous tenant was known as a tolerated trespasser. As a result of legislative amendments, this type of trespasser will no longer exist for most types of residential tenancies (see further **10.9**).

1.6 THE IMPACT OF CONTRACT LEGISLATION ON RESIDENTIAL LEASES

Traditionally, as leases were contracts relating to land, the standard consumer contract provisions were deemed, or expressly ruled, to be inapplicable to them (eg Unfair Contract Terms Act 1977, Sch 1, para 1(b)). However, the Unfair Terms in Consumer Contracts Regulations (UTCCR) 1999 (SI 1999/2083), introduced as a result of a European harmonisation Council Directive 93/13/EEC, have been held to apply to certain residential leases.

1.6.1 Applicability of the Unfair Terms in Consumer Contracts Regulations 1999 to residential leases

Leases made under contracts entered into after 1 July 1995 where:

(a) the grant is by a landlord who acts for purposes relating to his trade, business or profession;

(b) the tenant is an individual who acts as a consumer;

(c) the allegedly unfair terms have not been individually negotiated by the parties; and

(d) those terms do not reflect mandatory statutory or regulatory provisions (eg, s 11 of the LTA 1985 (see **7.3.3.2**)

are caught by the provisions in the UTCCR 1999.

1.6.1.1 The effect of an unfair term

A term will not be binding on the tenant if it is unfair. A term will be regarded as unfair if, contrary to the requirements of good faith, it causes a significant imbalance in the parties' rights and obligations under the contract to the detriment of the consumer (see UTCCR 1999, regs 3–5). The assessment of fairness of a term will not relate to the premises demised or the rent payable, although there is a general requirement, which applies to these key terms too, that terms be written in plain, intelligible language (UTCCR, 1999, regs 6(2), 7).

In R (Khatun) v Newham LBC [2005] QB 37, CA, it was held that the UTCCR 1999 applied to contracts for the disposal of an interest in, or rights of occupation over, land. In that case one of the issues was whether they applied to LHAs. It was held that they did, as an LHA was a 'seller or supplier' and the claimants in the case, prospective tenants, were consumers within the meaning of the UTCCR 1999. Thus the provisions will apply in many residential cases where the landlord operates his letting as a business.

1.6.1.2 The Office of Fair Trading Guidance

The OFT has issued Guidance on unfair terms in tenancy agreements, the latest version of which was published in September 2005. The OFT has regulatory and enforcement powers in relation to unfair terms, given to it in the UTCCR 1999, regs 10–14 and in the Enterprise Act 2002, Pt 8. In its extensive Guidance, the OFT lists examples of unfair terms in leases and groups them into categories. They include terms which exclude liability for disrepair arising out of statutory provisions 'as far as the law permits'. Terms have also unlawfully excluded liability for personal injury, for the state of the premises and for poor services provided by the landlord. Other terms have put obligations on the tenant which strictly belong to the landlord, or have imposed unreasonable interest and charges on the tenant. Yet another group of terms unfairly restricts the tenant from being able to assign or sub-let his tenancy.

The Guidance relates primarily to assured and assured shorthold tenancies, although the OFT refers briefly to LHA and RSL tenancies, and recognises, as a result of the *Khatun* case, that they are also within the UTCCR 1999. The 127-page Guidance can be found on the OFT website at www.oft.gov.uk.

1.7 THE IMPACT OF PROVISIONS IN THE HA 2004 ON RESIDENTIAL LEASES

A number of the changes that will impact directly on residential tenancies have only relatively recently been fully implemented. These include a licensing scheme for landlords who let houses in multiple occupation (HMOs); a discretionary licensing scheme for landlords with properties in problem areas or with anti-social tenants; and new fitness standards and enforcement provisions for residential properties. A brief outline of their effect is given below.

In addition, there are provisions affecting the right to buy, provisions for secure tenants and the extension of the period for introductory tenancies (see **Chapter 6**). Those provisions are dealt with in the relevant chapters of this book.

1.7.1 Licensing provisions for HMOs

In 2008 it was estimated that there were over 236,000 HMOs in England. The licensing provisions in Pt 2 of the HA 2004 (fully in force in England from 6 April 2006 and in Wales from 16 June 2006) are designed to deal with only a fraction of these.

The provisions provide a new definition of HMOs, and require landlords of certain types of HMOs to be mandatorily licensed. The aim of the provisions is to provide greater protection for the health, safety and welfare of people who occupy HMOs. There is also provision for discretionary or selective licensing schemes for HMOs that are not within the mandatory scheme.

The Register of Licensed Houses in Multiple Occupation estimates that there are approximately 56,000 mandatory licensable HMOs in England under these licensing provisions. In a number of these premises, there are problems of overcrowding, inadequate facilities, poor fire safety and unscrupulous management. The occupiers of these premises suffer poor living conditions as a result. Very often the tenants occupy under assured shorthold tenancies, so that they have no real security of tenure (see **2.7**).

1.7.1.1 HMOs defined

By s 254 of the HA 2004, an HMO will include:

(a) any building (house, hostel or flat) in which two or more households share basic amenities;

(b) any converted building containing one or more units which are not self contained accommodation; and

(c) any converted building which contains self-contained flats, which do not meet the 1991 Building Regulation Standards and where more than one-third of the flats are let on short leases.

'Household' is defined in s 258 to include a single person, a family, a co-habiting couple, and other categories to be prescribed by regulations (eg, carers and those cared for), who occupy the building as their only or main residence. Thus a hotel would not normally be an HMO (unless used to accommodate residents, say, homeless families), but a hostel may be.

However, Sch 14 goes on to exclude from the definition of HMOs, buildings controlled or managed by public bodies, registered providers of social housing (PRPs) and RSLs; buildings provided by educational establishments or other specified persons for student lettings; buildings occupied by religious communities; buildings occupied by only two persons who form two households; and buildings which are owner-occupied with up to two lodgers.

1.7.1.2 The requirement for mandatory licensing of HMOs

Any HMO which meets the four following conditions will require a licence (HA 2004, s 55 and proposed regulations):

(a) the HMO must have three stories or more;
(b) it must be occupied by five or more persons;
(c) the persons form two or more households; and
(d) the persons have to share facilities.

The licence is valid for five years. In deciding whether to grant the licence, the LHA will have to decide, amongst other things, whether the landlord is a fit and proper person, and whether the management arrangements for the property are satisfactory. Local authorities will have to keep a register of licensed HMOs.

In addition, ss 56 to 60 give LHAs the power to extend the licence scheme to the whole of or to specified parts of their areas for HMOs not within the mandatory category. So, for example, an LHA may extend the licence scheme to a specified area which contains HMOs of two storeys, occupied by four persons. However, the LHA would have to be satisfied that the management of the specified HMOs was causing problems and that licensing the HMOs was in accordance with its housing strategy.

1.7.2 Consequences of failure to obtain a licence

It is an offence to fail to obtain a licence for an HMO where it is a requirement to do so. On conviction, magistrates can impose fines of up to £20,000 (HA 2004, s 72). However, it is the provisions in ss 73 to 75 which may benefit certain tenants of unlicensed HMOs.

It is often the case that the tenants who occupy the worst housing are those in the lowest income category. Many of these tenants obtain housing benefit to assist them with their rent payments. Where such tenants are on housing benefit and occupy unfit housing, a complaint to a LHA may yield some relief. If the HMO is one that should be licensed and is not, the LHA has the power not only to prosecute but, additionally or alternatively, to recover any housing benefit that has been paid, by making an application to a residential property tribunal for a rent repayment order (ss 73–75 and the Rent Repayment Orders (Supplementary Provisions) (England) Regulations 2007 (SI 2007/572)).

Where an occupier has paid for his accommodation, he can also apply to recover rent payment for any unlicensed period. Unfortunately for occupiers, they will be able to apply only where the landlord has already been convicted of an offence under s 72, or where a rent repayment order has been made in favour of the LHA in relation to housing benefit paid on part of the

HMO (s 73(8)(a)). If the landlord has been convicted under s 72, the tribunal has to make the repayment order on an application by an LHA, whereas it has a discretion to do so if there has been no conviction (s 74(2), (5)).

The landlord will also be prohibited from obtaining a mandatory order for possession against the tenant following service of a notice under s 21 of the HA 1988 (see **2.8.3**) while the premises remain unlicensed (HA 2004, s 75). Unfortunately the tenant will not be excused from paying the rent for unlicensed premises. He may be able to recover rent paid, but will not be entitled to refuse to pay the rent (s 73(3)).

1.7.3 Selective licensing of houses

Part 3 of the HA 2004 contains licensing provisions similar to those in Pt 2. The provisions here are applicable to certain private sector houses in areas designated by the LHA for selective licensing. The houses will be those that are occupied under a single tenancy, or under multiple tenancies in respect of different dwellings (HA 2004, s 79). Factors that may influence designation include an area suffering significant and persistent problems caused by anti-social behaviour, where the private sector landlords are not dealing adequately with the problems (s 80). Subject to further preconditions, consultation and approval (see HA 2004, ss 81–83), LHAs will require licensing of all houses in a designated area unless otherwise excluded or exempt (s 85).

One important objective behind this provision is to oblige private sector landlords to take a more responsible approach to management. As a condition of granting the licence, landlords may have to undertake to impose relevant anti-social behaviour clauses in their tenancy agreements. They may need to be more selective as to whom they grant new tenancies, and they will have to be more efficient in taking action against anti-social tenants.

Failure to license under Pt 3 will have similar consequences to failure under Pt 2 (see **1.7.2**), including large fines on conviction and rent repayment orders on application to a residential property tribunal.

1.7.4 Management orders

Local housing authorities have powers in Pt 4 of the HA 2004 to make management orders (interim and final) to take control of HMOs and Pt 3 premises (selective licensing). This will occur where, for example, the premises are not licensed, despite being required to be so, and the LHA has identified a need to protect the health, safety or welfare of the occupiers of the property (HA 2004, ss 101–104).

1.8 FURTHER READING

The following texts discuss in detail the areas covered in this introductory chapter:

S Garner and A Frith, *A Practical Approach to Landlord and Tenant* (7th edn, 2013)
J McQueen, *A Guide to Landlord and Tenant Law* (2nd edn, 2009)
S Cottle, *Housing Law Handbook* (2009)

CHAPTER 2

Assured and Assured Shorthold Tenancies

2.1	Introduction	9
2.2	Assured tenancies	10
2.3	Exclusions from assured tenant status	11
2.4	Terms of an assured tenancy	13
2.5	Security of tenure for assured tenants	16
2.6	The grounds for possession	17
2.7	Assured shorthold tenancies	24
2.8	Tenancy deposit schemes for assured shorthold tenants	26
2.9	Assured tenants of RSLs and PRPs	28
2.10	Private sector assured tenants	33
2.11	Further reading	33
	Summary	34

LEARNING OUTCOMES

After reading this chapter you will be able to:

- explain the key differences between assured and assured shorthold tenancies
- list the mandatory and discretionary grounds for possession
- understand the structured discretion in relation to discretionary Ground 14 for anti-social behaviour
- explain the powers available to PRPs and RSLs to deal with anti-social behaviour
- advise on the operation of the tenancy deposit scheme.

2.1 INTRODUCTION

Since the implementation of the HA 1988, assured and assured shorthold tenancies together have become the largest category of residential lettings. A large number of assured tenancies have come into existence as a result of large-scale voluntary transfers of public sector housing (of tenants who were formerly secure tenants) to what were formerly registered social landlords (RSLs). In England RSLs will in future be known as private registered providers of social housing (PRPs) or social housing landlords. The RSL regime continues, however, in Wales (see **2.9**).

Today HA 1988 tenancies account for about 40% of the rented sector, while public sector secure tenants account for about 35% (see **Chapter 6**). In the purely private sector the market is dominated by assured shorthold tenancies, while RSLs grant mainly assured tenancies. Tenancies regulated under the Rent Act 1977 (see **Chapter 3**) account for only about 4% of the rented sector.

Nearly all new residential tenancies outside the public sector, granted after 15 January 1989, when the HA 1988 came into force, are subject to the provisions of the 1988 Act and will be assured or assured shorthold tenancies if they satisfy the qualifying conditions. The basic requirements for the two types of tenancies are the same. In particular, the provisions in s 1 of the HA 1988 defining the requirements necessary for an assured tenancy, s 5 in relation to security of tenure, s 7 orders for possession, and s 8 notice requirements apply equally to assured and assured shorthold tenancies. Perhaps the key distinction today is the additional mandatory method to terminate an assured shorthold tenancy in s 21 of the HA 1988. For assured shorthold tenancies created pre-Housing Act 1996, there are other important differences (see **2.7.1**).

This chapter will follow the structure of the legislation and start with consideration of the requirements necessary to create an assured tenancy. The special position of RSL and now PRP assured tenants is also considered. The requirements in relation to an assured shorthold tenancy and the new rights acquired by tenants are discussed at **2.7** and **2.8** below.

2.2 ASSURED TENANCIES

Section 1 of the HA 1988 provides that a tenancy under which a dwelling-house is let as a separate dwelling will be an assured tenancy if and so long as:

(a) the tenant or each joint tenant is an individual; and

(b) the tenant or at least one joint tenant occupies the dwelling as his only or principal home; and

(c) the tenancy is not excluded by Pt I of Sch 1 to the HA 1988 from becoming an assured tenancy.

The wording of this provision is very similar to that in s 1 of the RA 1977, which has had exhaustive case law adjudicating on each part of the definition. What has become clear is that there must be a tenancy. Licences are not within the provisions of the HA 1988.

2.2.1 'Let as'

The purpose of the letting must be as a dwelling-house.

> **CASE EXAMPLE**
>
> In *Andrews v Brewer* (1998) 30 HLR 203, CA, the claimant let an eight-bedroom property, previously used as a guest house and rated for business purposes, to the defendant on an assured shorthold tenancy. It was a term of the letting that the defendant would not use the property other than as a private dwelling-house. The defendant, in breach of the covenant, used the premises for business purposes and resisted a possession claim on the basis that the s 20 notice, required to be served by the claimant (see **2.7.1**), was defective, so that the defendant had a business tenancy. It was held that, in considering whether a property is 'let as a dwelling-house' for the purposes of s 1 of the HA 1988, the primary consideration was the agreement, not the nature of the property or the use to which it was put. The landlord obtained an order for possession.

2.2.2 Separate dwelling-house

By s 45 of the HA 1988, a dwelling-house can be a house or a part of a house. This will clearly include a flat, or rooms within a flat or a house, or perhaps even an hotel. In *Uratemp Ventures Ltd v Collins* [2002] 1 AC 301, HL, it was held that a dwelling-house could be just one room in an hotel, with or without cooking facilities. In the leading judgment given by Lord Millett, he stated:

> In both ordinary and literary usage, residential accommodation is 'a dwelling' if it is the occupier's home (or one of his homes). It is the place where he lives and to which he returns and which forms part of the centre of his existence. Just what use he makes of it when living there, however, depends on his mode of life. No doubt he will sleep there and usually eat there; he will often prepare at least some of his meals there. But his home is not the less his home because he does not cook there but prefers to eat out or bring in ready-cooked meals. It has never been a legislative requirement that cooking facilities must be available for a premises to qualify as a dwelling.

However, to be a separate dwelling, the tenant must have exclusive use of some accommodation. Living accommodation includes living room, bedroom and kitchen, but not a bathroom or toilet. Joint tenants are regarded as a single entity and so it is no problem for joint tenants to share. Where an individual has exclusive occupation of any accommodation (eg, his bedroom) but also, under the terms of his tenancy, shares living accommodation (eg, living room, kitchen) with another person or persons, none of whom is his landlord, s 3 provides that the separate accommodation will be regarded as a dwelling-house let on an assured tenancy.

Exclusive occupation of a dwelling that is not a part of the land will not be a dwelling-house within the assured tenancy regime. Thus, a houseboat, even where gas, electricity, water, telephone and sewage services are connected, will not be a dwelling-house for these purposes (*Chelsea Yacht and Boat Co Ltd v Pope* [2001] 1 WLR 1941, CA). The dwelling must be real property, not a chattel.

2.2.3 Only or principal home

'If and so long as' the tenant occupies the dwelling-house as his only or principal home, he will be an assured tenant. Case law has established that in order to maintain that a property is the only or principal home, there must be outward signs that the house can be occupied as a home (eg, furniture, personal effects) and an intention on the part of the tenant, if he is not physically present, to return to the home.

> **CASE EXAMPLE**
>
> In *Ujima HA v Ansah* (1997) 30 HLR 831, CA, the defendant, who had an assured tenancy from the claimant, let out the flat on an assured shorthold tenancy. The claimant sought possession of the flat on the basis that the defendant had lost his assured tenant status. The defendant argued that he had left furniture in the flat and intended to return. It was held that the matter had to be looked at objectively. On that basis, the defendant showed no outward signs of the property remaining his principal home as he had left no personal belongings in it. The furniture, left by the defendant in the flat, could be construed as being consistent with the sub-letting, particularly since the defendant was able to obtain almost four times the amount of rent from the sub-tenant as that which he had to pay for his assured tenancy. It was also clear that the defendant could not easily regain occupation of the property while the sub-tenancy was in existence.

If the dwelling-house was the matrimonial home and the spouse or civil partner who is the sole tenant leaves the property, the non-tenant spouse or civil partner who remains in occupation will be deemed to occupy on behalf of the absent tenant while the marriage or civil partnership lasts (Family Law Act 1996, s 30, as amended by the Civil Partnership Act 2004).

2.3 EXCLUSIONS FROM ASSURED TENANT STATUS

Schedule 1 to the HA 1988 lists the categories of tenancies that, even though they may satisfy the definition in s 1 (see **2.2** above), cannot be assured. They are:

(a) subject to certain exceptions, tenancies entered into before, or pursuant to a contract made before, the HA 1988 came into effect on 15 January 1989;

(b) high-value premises, ie where the rateable value for pre-1 April 1990 lettings exceeded £1,500 in Greater London or £750 elsewhere; or where a letting on or after 1 April 1990 has an annual rent exceeding £25,000 in Wales and, from 1 October 2010, £100,000 in England;

(c) tenancies at no or low rent, ie where no rent is payable or where for pre-1 April 1990 lettings the rent was less than two-thirds the rateable value of the dwelling-house on 31 March 1990; or for lettings on or after 1 April 1990, the rent payable in Greater London is £1,000 or less a year, or £250 or less a year elsewhere;

(d) business tenancies to which Pt II of the Landlord and Tenant Act (LTA) 1954 applies;

(e) licensed premises for the sale and consumption of intoxicating liquors;

(f) tenancies of agricultural land where agricultural land (as defined in s 26(3)(a) General Rates Act 1967), exceeding two acres, is let together with the dwelling-house;

(g) tenancies of agricultural holdings where the dwelling-house is comprised in an agricultural holding (within the meaning of the Agricultural Holdings Act 1986) or farm business and is occupied by the person responsible for control of the farming or management of the holding;

(h) lettings to students who are pursuing or intend to pursue a course of studies and where the letting is provided by a specified educational institution. The institutions specified are universities and colleges listed in the Assured and Protected Tenancies (Lettings to Students) Regulations 1998 (SI 1998/1967) as amended;

(i) holiday letting, where this is the purpose of the letting;

(j) resident landlords – see **2.3.1**;

(k) lettings by public bodies, ie the Crown, local authorities etc;

(l) a tenancy provided by a private landlord for asylum-seekers under Pt VI of the Immigration and Asylum Act 1999;

(m) a tenancy provided by a private landlord for persons with temporary protection under the Displaced Persons (Temporary Protection) Regulations 2005 (SI 2005/1379);

(n) a family intervention tenancy granted by a registered provider of social housing or an RSL who has complied with the requirements in para 12ZA of Sch 1; and

(o) a protected tenancy under the RA 1977; a housing association tenancy within Pt VI of the RA 1977; a secure tenancy; and a protected occupier within the Rent (Agriculture) Act 1976.

2.3.1 Resident landlord lettings

This is perhaps the most important exclusion from assured tenant status, not least because the Department for Communities and Local Government (DCLG) Housing Statistics for 2007/08 indicate that there were some 127,000 resident landlord lettings. The Government has offered tax incentive schemes, in the form of tax-free rental income up to £4,250, to encourage people to let out spare rooms in their homes. The exclusion is designed to encourage owner-occupiers and tenants with space in their homes to let it out to tenants (or lodgers), safe in the knowledge that those tenants will not obtain any security which would prevent the landlord being able to obtain their removal without too many procedural difficulties. The landlord protection goes beyond just depriving the tenant of security. In addition, tenants who share accommodation with resident landlords are excluded from the requirement that the landlord has to obtain a court order to evict them from the property (see ss 3 and 3A of the PEA 1977 and **9.2.2.5** on excluded tenancies and licences).

2.3.1.1 Occupation by the landlord of a dwelling in the same flat or building

The provision is quite detailed in stipulating the conditions necessary for the resident landlord exclusion to apply. By para 10 of Sch 1, where a landlord, who occupies a dwelling-house as his only or principal home, lets out a part of the flat which he occupies or a part of the building in which his dwelling-house is situated to a tenant, then that tenant will not be an assured tenant.

What the provisions make clear is that if the landlord owns a purpose-built block of flats, and he occupies one flat in the building as his dwelling-house and lets out the others to tenants, the exclusion from assured tenant status will not apply to the tenants of those flats. A purpose-built block of flats is defined as a building which as constructed contained, and it contains, two or more flats which form part only of the building, and which is separated horizontally from another dwelling-house which forms part of the same building (Sch 1, para

22). In *Barnes v Gorsuch* (1982) 43 P & CR 294, CA, it was held that a Victorian house converted into a number of flats was not 'a purpose built block of flats' within the statutory provision (there are identical provisions in RA 1977, Sch 2, para 4 – see **3.3**).

'Building' is not defined in the HA 1988, and so it will be a question of fact in each case. In *Bardrick v Haycock* (1982) 2 HLR 118, CA, it was held that a two-storey extension, built and occupied by the landlord and connected to the side of a house, but with no means of internal communication with the house and with its own front door, was not part of the same building so as to make the landlord a resident landlord to the tenants who occupied flats in the house.

2.3.1.2 Continuous occupation by the landlord as his only or principal home

The landlord must continue to occupy the dwelling-house as his only or principal home throughout the duration of the tenancy for the exclusion to apply. If he ceases to so occupy, the tenant will obtain assured tenant status. However, if the letting was by joint landlords, so long as there is occupation which satisfies the requirement by any one of them throughout the continuation of the tenancy, this will be sufficient. Joint landlords can thus change who is occupying the dwelling as their only or principal home, without the tenant gaining security.

The same criteria as stated at **2.2.3** above for tenants apply when deciding whether the occupancy is of the landlord's only or principal home. This issue was tested in *Sumeghova v McMahon* [2003] HLR 26, CA, where the landlord spent every night sleeping in the house in which he had let a room to the claimant. However, he spent most of his days and ate all his meals at an adjoining property occupied by his adult children. It was held that the landlord satisfied the requirement of a resident landlord in respect of the house. The place where a person sleeps, while not decisive, was held to be extremely important in determining the principal place of residence.

The landlord exclusion did not apply where a tenant was granted an assured tenancy and was not told that the landlord reserved the right to re-enter and share the accommodation in a way which would affect the assured status of the tenant (*Miller v Eyo* (1999) 31 HLR 306, CA).

The landlord's continuous residence requirements are qualified somewhat where the building is sold or vests in another individual, or in trustees or the landlord's personal representative after his death. There are various periods of disregard, from 28 days to two years depending on the circumstances, to enable a new owner to take up residence if he is so inclined. During the periods of disregard, a possession order cannot be obtained against the tenant, other than an order which might be made if the tenancy was an assured tenancy (HA 1988, Sch 1, para 21). However, if the tenancy is a periodic tenancy, a valid notice to quit can terminate it, and the owner will then be able to obtain possession of the dwelling-house at the end of the relevant period of disregard (see *Landau v Sloane* [1982] AC 490, HL).

2.4 TERMS OF AN ASSURED TENANCY

Statutory intervention as to the terms of an assured tenancy is fairly limited. The landlord and tenant are free to agree most of the terms as they see fit. However, by ss 13 to 18 of the HA 1988, there are some terms implied in relation to rent increases, assignment and succession for periodic assured tenancies; a general requirement in relation to access for repairs; and a statutory right for lawful assured sub-tenants' tenancies to continue on the termination of their landlord's interest.

2.4.1 Rent increases for periodic assured tenants

The rent set by private sector landlords will normally be what the market can bear, ie the market rent. Assured tenants of RSLs and PRPs are in a more fortunate position, as their rents are, on average, below those in the private sector for similar properties (see **2.7.1**). Tenancy agreements with RSLs usually have an express term dealing with how the rent is to be increased. Where there is such a provision, the landlord must ensure that the correct rent increase procedure is followed. If not, the rent may not be lawfully due (see *Riverside Housing Association Ltd v White* [2007] UKHL 20, [2007] HLR 31).

If a landlord has not included a rent review clause (a provision for the rent to be increased) in an assured periodic tenancy agreement then, by s 13 of the 1988 Act, in order to increase the rent he ought to serve a prescribed notice to commence a rent increase procedure. The landlord should propose a rent which, if the tenant considers it to be excessively above current market rents in the area, the tenant can refer to a rent assessment committee which has the power to determine a market rent for the property (s 14). However, the provisions recognise that the parties are free to vary the rent terms by agreement, without recourse to the notice procedures (s 13(5)). If a rent assessment committee determines an open market rent in excess of £100,000 per annum, the tenancy will cease to be assured (see *R v London Rent Assessment Panel, ex p Cadogan Estates* [1998] QB 398 and *Hughes v Borodex Ltd* (2009) 26 EG 114).

In effect, there is little, if any, rent control for assured tenants, unless the terms of the original agreement on rent increases can be challenged as being fictitious or repugnant (see *Bankway Properties Ltd v Penfold-Dunsford and Leech* [2001] 1 WLR 1369, CA).

The provisions in ss 13 and 14 do not apply to fixed-term assured tenants. There the parties are bound by the terms of their agreement, unless they can be challenged as being unfair contract term, under the UTCCR 1999 (which would probably be unlikely in light of reg 6(2)).

2.4.2 Implied term as to assignment and sub-letting for periodic assured tenants

In the absence of an express provision in the terms of a periodic assured tenancy agreement dealing with the tenant's right to assign or sub-let, s 15 of the HA 1988 implies into the agreement a term that the tenant cannot assign or sub-let without the landlord's consent. The landlord does not have to be reasonable in deciding to refuse consent, as s 15(2) specifically excludes the general provision in s 19 of the LTA 1927 which would otherwise require the landlord to be reasonable in exercising his discretion.

The provision applies to all periodic tenancies which do not have an express term. It also applies to all statutory periodic tenancies, whether or not there was an express term in the original fixed-term agreement.

2.4.3 Succession rights for certain periodic assured tenancies

The succession provisions for tenancies granted by PRPs created after 1 April 2012, when s 161 of the Localism Act 2011 came into force, are somewhat different to those which apply to assured tenancies generally prior to that date.

2.4.3.1 Succession rights for certain periodic assured tenancies

The unamended provisions of s 17 of the HA 1988 still apply to all tenancies created before 1 April 2012 and to non-PRP landlords who grant assured tenancies after that date.

By s 17 of the HA 1988, the spouse or civil partner of a sole tenant to an assured periodic tenancy can succeed to the assured tenancy. The only condition to be satisfied is that the spouse or civil partner was occupying the dwelling-house as his or her only or principal home immediately before the tenant's death.

A person who was living with the tenant as his or her spouse or civil partner is also eligible to succeed (s 17(4)). The requirement that the successor must have been 'living with' the deceased is fairly strictly construed. In *Nutting v Southern Housing Group Ltd* [2004] EWHC 2982 (Ch), it was held that to be treated as a spouse the relationship had to be an emotional one entailing a lifetime of commitment, rather than one of convenience, friendship, companionship or the living together of lovers. The relationship must be openly and unequivocally displayed to the outside world. If there is more than one person eligible under the provisions, they can agree who will succeed or, failing that, the county court will decide (s 17(5)).

The right of succession will not be available where the deceased was himself a successor tenant. 'Successor tenant' is widely defined to include:

(a) where the deceased succeeded under the s 17 provisions;
(b) where he was originally one of two or more joint tenants of the property and became the sole tenant by survivorship;
(c) where the deceased derived the tenancy under the will or intestacy of a previous tenant; or
(d) where he was a successor to the assured tenancy as a result of the RA 1977 succession provisions (see **3.4.1.3**).

The succession provisions do not apply to fixed-term assured tenancies. On the death of a fixed-term tenant, the normal rules will apply with the tenancy passing under the deceased tenant's will or intestacy. This will also be the case for an assured periodic tenancy where there is no one eligible to succeed under the s 17 provisions. However, in that instance, the landlord will have a mandatory ground for possession (see **2.6.1.7**).

2.4.3.2 Succession rights for periodic or fixed-term assured tenants of PRP landlords

By s 17 of the HA 1988 as amended, succession is possible on the death of a sole tenant. The succession can be in relation to:

- a periodic tenancy or a fixed-term tenancy of not less than two years;
- granted by a PRP landlord in England on or after 1 April 2012.

The successor can be:

- a spouse or civil partner occupying the dwelling as his or her only or principal home; or
- a person who was living with the tenant as a spouse or civil partner.

Or, if there is no spouse or civil partner and provided there are terms in the tenancy agreement to that effect, succession can be to a person other than a spouse or civil partner who meets the terms of the tenancy agreement.

2.4.4 Implied term for access to repair

Implied in every assured tenancy by s 16 of the HA 1988, whether fixed-term or periodic, is an obligation for the tenant to allow the landlord access to the dwelling-house and reasonable facilities to carry out any repairs he is entitled to do. This provision is in addition to and goes beyond the implied term in s 11(6) of the LTA 1985, which only allows the landlord access to view the condition and state of repair of the premises (see **7.3.4**).

2.4.5 The rights of sub-tenants to a continuation of their tenancy

Depending on the status of a head landlord, by s 18 of the HA 1988 a sub-tenant will be entitled to have his tenancy continue after the termination of his landlord's interest. This provision modifies the common law rule, which provides that a sub-tenancy is determined by operation of law whenever the superior leasehold interest from which it derives comes to an end.

There are three conditions to be satisfied for the provision to apply:

(a) the dwelling-house must be lawfully let on an assured tenancy;
(b) the landlord of the assured tenant is himself a tenant under a superior tenancy; and
(c) the superior tenancy has come to an end.

The provision will apply only if the landlord is not an exempt landlord, ie one who could not grant an assured tenancy (eg, an LHA). The provision does not appear unduly harsh to the landlord given that, under s 15 of the HA 1988 (see **2.4.2** above), the landlord can arbitrarily refuse permission to sub-let, or include an express term in the lease to that effect. However, the provisions in the UTCCR 1999 may need to be taken into account, as may the views of the OFT on absolute prohibitions on assignment (see **1.6.1.2**). Where it is applicable, the effect of s 18 is that if the landlord does allow a tenant to sub-let, he will not be able to obtain vacant possession of the property on the termination of the original tenancy. The sub-tenant will have security of tenure under the provisions in s 5 of the HA 1988.

2.5 SECURITY OF TENURE FOR ASSURED TENANTS

Security is provided in s 5 of the HA 1988, which states that an assured tenancy cannot be brought to an end by the landlord, except by obtaining a court order for possession and execution of the order in accordance with the provisions in the Act. The landlord therefore cannot terminate a periodic assured tenancy by a notice to quit. However, the tenant is free to terminate the tenancy by surrender or notice to quit, as the case may be.

Where the term of a fixed-term assured tenancy has expired, or the landlord has exercised a right to determine the term, the tenant will continue as a statutory periodic tenant on terms broadly similar to those under the previous fixed-term tenancy. Section 5(3)(d) provides that the periodic tenancy will be determined by the frequency with which the rent was last payable under the fixed-term tenancy. In *Church Commissioners for England v Meya* [2006] HLR 4, CA, a one-year tenancy was granted at rent of £17,680 per annum payable by 'equal quarterly payments in advance on the usual quarter days'. It was held that the tenant had a quarterly periodic tenancy. This will be the case unless the tenant is granted another tenancy of the dwelling-house by the landlord, or the terms are varied in accordance with s 6 of the HA 1988.

Forfeiture of a fixed-term assured tenancy, in the conventional sense of terminating the tenancy, will not be possible (s 45(4); and see *Artesian Residential Investments Ltd v Beck* [2000] QB 541, CA). The landlord may be able to obtain a court order to terminate a fixed-term tenancy where he has reserved a specific right to terminate in the tenancy agreement (whether by way of a forfeiture clause, a provision for re-entry or otherwise). The specific reason for forfeiting the tenancy must be within one of the limited grounds permitted by s 7(6) of the HA 1988. These are Grounds 2, 8, 10 to 15 inclusive, and 17 of Sch 2 (see **2.6** below).

If the landlord has failed to reserve the right to terminate the fixed-term tenancy on one or more of these specific grounds then he will not be able to terminate the tenancy during the term, regardless of the tenant's breach of obligation.

The court cannot make an order for possession of an assured tenancy except on one or more of the grounds set out in Sch 2 to HA 1988 (s 7), and proceedings for possession cannot be entertained unless the landlord has served a notice of proceedings for possession in accordance with s 8.

2.5.1 Notice provisions

By s 8 of the HA 1988, the landlord or at least one joint landlord must serve notice on the tenant in accordance with the provisions in the section before the court can consider a claim for possession. This notice is referred to as a 'section 8 notice'. However, in most cases the court has a discretion to dispense with the notice requirement if it considers it is just and equitable to do so (s 8(1)(b)).

> **CASE EXAMPLE**
>
> In *Kelsey Housing Association v King* (1996) 28 HLR 270, CA, the court exercised its discretion to dispense with the s 8 notice. The tenant was unsuccessful in his appeal that he was prejudiced by a lack of notice of the fault. In weighing all the factors – including the fact that the tenant had had many months' notice of the nature of the allegations of nuisance and had put in a defence to the claim; the impact on the neighbours of his behaviour; and that he had delayed for months in objecting to the lack of notice – the Court of Appeal held that the tenant had not been prejudiced.

The discretion to dispense with notice applies to all the grounds for possession except Ground 8 (s 8(5); see **2.6.1.8**).

The notice is required to be in a prescribed form, or substantially to the same effect as stipulated in Form 3 of the Assured Tenancies and Agricultural Occupancies (Forms) Regulations 1997 (SI 1997/194). The notice should make clear that the landlord is intending to take possession proceedings to terminate the tenancy on one or more of the grounds specified in Sch 2 to the HA 1988. The notice should give details of the ground specified by giving particulars, so that the tenant understands fully what the fault is and what action, if any, he can take to avoid a possession order (see *Mountain v Hastings* (1995) 25 HLR 427, CA). The tenant should also be informed in the notice of the earliest date when the landlord may begin possession proceedings and that they cannot begin later than 12 months from the date of service of the notice (s 8(3)). The court can give leave to alter or add to the grounds specified in a notice that has already been served on the tenant (s 8(2)).

2.5.1.1 Notice period

The landlord can begin proceedings immediately after service of the s 8 notice if the ground or one of the grounds for possession is Ground 14 (anti-social behaviour).

For Grounds 1, 2, 5, 6, 7, 9 and 16, the notice period from service to the commencement of the proceedings must be at least two months, or the equivalent period that would be required for that tenancy under a notice to quit, whichever is the longer. If, for example, the tenancy was a quarterly periodic tenancy, in the absence of express agreement to the contrary, the minimum notice would be three months (see **1.5.2.1** for common law notice periods).

For all other grounds, the notice period from service to commencement of proceedings must be at least two weeks. If the landlord commences proceedings within the notice period, the tenant may be able to challenge the validity of the proceedings, but this will be subject to the court's discretion to dispense with the notice requirements (see **2.5.1** above).

2.6 THE GROUNDS FOR POSSESSION

The grounds for possession are set out in Sch 2 to the HA 1988. Schedule 2 is divided into four parts.

Part I contains the grounds for possession which, if established by the landlord, will automatically entitle him to an order for possession. These are referred to as the mandatory grounds for possession – Grounds 1–8.

Part II contains grounds which, if established by the landlord, will result in a possession order being made only if the court is satisfied that it is reasonable to make a possession order in the circumstances.

Part III deals with the availability of suitable alternative accommodation for the purposes of Ground 9 (see **2.6.2.2**); and Part IV covers notices relating to recovery of possession.

Only Pts I, II and III are discussed below.

2.6.1 Part I – The mandatory grounds for possession

2.6.1.1 Ground 1 – recovery by owner occupier or future occupier

This ground applies in two situations:

(a) where an owner occupier wants to let out his property; and
(b) where an owner buys a property with the intention to reside in it at some future date but wishes to let it out in the meantime.

In either case the owner should have given written notice at the beginning of the tenancy to the assured tenant that possession might be sought on this ground. The court does have discretion to dispense with the notice if it considers it just and equitable to do so (see *Mustafa v Ruddock* (1998) 30 HLR 495, CA). Where the landlord is a joint owner, one of them can apply under this ground.

Under category (a), the landlord, or at least one joint landlord, must have occupied the dwelling as his only or principal home at some point before it was let out. Under category (b), the landlord, or at least one joint landlord, must show that he requires possession of the property for occupation as his or his spouse's or civil partner's only or principal home.

The ground does not apply to a landlord who bought the property after the assured tenancy was created (ie, bought the reversion). Neither will it be applicable to landlords who are legal persons as opposed to individuals. Thus RSLs and PRPs would not be able to use this ground.

2.6.1.2 Ground 2 – recovery by mortgagees

This ground applies where the property is subject to a mortgage which existed before the assured tenancy was granted and the mortgagor has not kept up with the mortgage payments. Ground 2 entitles a mortgagee to obtain possession for the purpose of sale with vacant possession, provided the tenant had written notice before the tenancy was created or the court decides that it is just and equitable to dispense with notice. Ground 2 envisages the landlord granting the assured tenancy with the consent of the mortgagee. If the assured tenancy is in breach of the mortgage terms then the mortgagee will be able to obtain possession outside this ground as the illegal tenancy will not be binding on the mortgagee (see *Dudley & District Benefit Society v Emerson* [1949] Ch 707, CA).

2.6.1.3 Ground 3 – recovery of out-of-season holiday lettings

This ground allows premises that would otherwise be used for holiday lettings to be let out on assured tenancies, presumably out of season. However, for the ground to apply the landlord must have given written notice to the tenant before the start of the tenancy and the dwelling-house must have been occupied under a holiday letting within the period of 12 months before the start of the assured tenancy.

2.6.1.4 Ground 4 – recovery of student accommodation

This ground enables specified education institutions (as listed in the Assured and Protected Tenancies (Lettings to Students) Regulations 1998 (SI 1998/1967) as amended) to recover possession of premises which were let out on an assured tenancy for a fixed term not exceeding 12 months. This is provided the landlord served written notice at the beginning of the tenancy that possession could be recovered on this ground and the premises had been let out as a student let within Sch 1 to the HA 1988 (see **2.3** at (h)) within the preceding 12 months.

2.6.1.5 Ground 5 – recovery of premises for a minister of religion

Where the landlord has given written notice at the beginning of the assured tenancy that the dwelling-house is held for the purpose of being available for occupation by a minister of religion as a residence from which to perform his duties then, provided the court is satisfied that possession is required for this purpose, the landlord can obtain possession under this ground.

2.6.1.6 Ground 6 – recovery for redevelopment

This ground applies where a landlord, who did not acquire his interest for money or money's worth after the tenancy was created, wishes to demolish, reconstruct or carry out substantial works to the whole or a substantial part of the dwelling-house and cannot do so without obtaining possession. This ground will not apply to an assured tenancy which arose as a result of succession under the RA 1977 (see **3.4.1.3**) or similar provision in the Rent (Agriculture) Act 1976.

The landlord must establish that possession is necessary and that he is ready to proceed with the redevelopment. The ground is similar to one available to landlords of business tenants under s 30(1)(f) of the LTA 1954. Case law relating to the redevelopment ground for business tenants makes clear that the landlord must have not only a settled intention, but also the means and ability to carry out the redevelopment (see *Edwards v Thompson* (1990) 60 P & CR 222, CA).

If the landlord is an RSL, PRP or charitable housing trust, the ground can be used by a superior landlord. This provision enables RSLs, PRPs and charitable housing trusts to use 'short life' premises to provide accommodation, in the knowledge that when development is ready to proceed, possession can be obtained on this ground.

The tenant will be entitled to his reasonable removal expenses if possession is obtained under this ground (HA 1988, s 11).

2.6.1.7 Ground 7 – recovery on the death of a periodic tenant

Where an assured periodic tenant, a statutory periodic tenant, or a fixed term tenant in England dies and his tenancy passes under his will or on intestacy (rather than under s 17 – see **2.4.3**), the landlord will be able to obtain possession against the new tenant provided he commences proceedings within 12 months of the date of death, or within 12 months of becoming aware of the death (as determined by the court). Proceedings commence with the issue of a court claim, not the s 8 notice (see *Shepping v Osada* (2001) 33 HLR 146, CA).

Accepting rent from the new tenant will not be regarded as creating a new tenancy, unless the landlord has agreed in writing to changes in the terms of the tenancy.

2.6.1.8 Ground 8 – recovery for serious rent arrears

The landlord will be able to recover possession against an assured tenant who pays rent weekly or fortnightly, if he satisfies the court that, both at the date of the service of a s 8 notice and the date of hearing, at least eight weeks' rent is unpaid. In the case of a tenancy where the rent is payable monthly, at least two months' rent must be unpaid; and for a tenancy where the rent is payable quarterly, at least one quarter's rent must be more than three months in arrears.

The rent must, however, be rent lawfully due from the tenant. A provision in s 48 of the LTA 1987 provides in effect that rent is not to be treated as lawfully due from the tenant of a dwelling-house if the landlord has not provided the tenant with details of a name and address at which notices may be served. In *Drew-Morgan v Hamid-Zadeh* (2000) 32 HLR 216, CA, it was held that providing those details in a notice under s 21 of the HA 1988 (seeking possession of an assured shorthold tenancy – see **2.8.3**) was sufficient, and the landlord did not have to state in addition that the tenant could serve notice there.

Ground 8 is one of the most controversial possession grounds in the 1988 Act as, for the first time in all the statutory regimes, rent arrears is a mandatory ground for possession. It is one of three grounds for possession based on rent arrears available to the landlord of an assured tenant. The other two grounds (Grounds 10 and 11) are discretionary (see **2.6.2.3** and **2.6.2.4** below). There is nothing to stop a landlord seeking possession on all the rent arrears grounds in the alternative (as happens in practice).

The mandatory provisions are strictly construed by the court. As indicated above, the landlord must have served a valid s 8 notice. In *Mountain v Hastings* (1995) 25 HLR 427, CA, a possession order granted on the basis of Ground 8 arrears was set aside as the s 8 notice was held invalid. The notice did not give sufficient particulars to the tenant, and it was held that the discretion in s 8(2) to allow the landlord to add to or alter the notice applied only to an otherwise valid notice, so was not applicable to the landlord in this case.

The delay in the payment of housing benefit cannot be used by a tenant as a defence to this ground. Nor will the court grant an adjournment of the hearing, in such cases, to enable the payment of housing benefit to be made so as bring the arrears below the amount for the ground to apply. This is because the court does not have the extended discretion to adjourn or suspend in mandatory cases (HA 1988, s 9(6)) (see *North British Housing Association Ltd v Matthews* [2005] 2 All ER 667, CA and **10.8.2**). However, if the tenant has a legitimate counter-claim against the landlord, an adjournment may be possible. For example, if the tenant had a counter-claim for disrepair, where the amount of compensation likely to be awarded on the counter-claim could be used to cancel out the arrears or to reduce it below the mandatory ground limit, then an adjournment to the possession proceedings could be obtained. This is because it could be argued that the court would not then be satisfied under s 9(6) that the landlord was entitled to possession under Ground 8 until the counter-claim had been tried (per Dyson LJ in *North British Housing Association Ltd v Matthews*, above).

2.6.1.9 Proposed new mandatory ground

The Government has introduced in Pt 5 of the Anti-social Behaviour, Crime and Policing Bill 2013–14 an additional mandatory ground for possession in Pt I of Sch 2 to the HA 1988. This will be for repeated anti-social behaviour by a tenant or a person residing in or visiting the dwelling-house of the tenant (see DCLG paper, *Strengthening Powers of Possession for Anti-social Behaviour*, May 2012). Although there is already a discretionary ground for possession for anti-social behaviour (see **2.6.2.7**), the Government believes that PRPs should have the option to pursue a mandatory ground in more serious cases.

2.6.2 Parts II and III – The discretionary grounds for possession

Even where the landlord makes out one of the grounds listed below (Grounds 9–17), the court will not make an order for possession unless it considers it reasonable to do so.

2.6.2.1 Reasonableness

The court has an extended discretion under s 9 of the HA 1988, in relation to these discretionary grounds, to adjourn the proceedings, or to stay, postpone or suspend any possession order made.

The burden of proof to show that it is reasonable to make the order is on the landlord. The landlord is expected to plead any relevant circumstances he wants the court to take into account in exercising its discretion in his favour, otherwise the court may not consider those circumstances (see Chadwick LJ in *Laimond Properties Ltd v Raeuchle* (2001) 33 HLR 113, CA).

The court will consider all relevant factors at the date of the hearing. The factors and the emphasis given to them may vary according to the ground of possession being claimed. The relevant factors can include the length of time the tenant has occupied the property; the interests of the landlord and neighbours; the reasons for the breach occurring and the chances of it recurring; and, in rent arrears cases, the rental payment history and the conduct of the parties. For RSLs and PRPs, another factor also now relevant in rent arrears cases will be whether there has been compliance with the Protocol for Possession Claims based on rent arrears (see **10.2.1**).

For nuisance claims under Ground 14, s 9A of the HA 1988 has introduced a 'structured discretion' to be applied by the court when deciding whether a possession order should be made (see **2.6.2.6**). The tenant will have a right to appeal if the trial judge fails to consider the issue of reasonableness, or if he fails to consider any relevant factors or considers irrelevant factors, where the landlord is claiming on one or more of the discretionary grounds (see *Minchburn Estates Ltd v Fernandez* (1987) 19 HLR 29, CA, and *Castle Vale Housing Action Trust v Gallagher* (2001) 33 HLR 810, CA).

2.6.2.2 Ground 9 – availability of suitable alternative accommodation

The court may order possession if the landlord is able to show that suitable alternative accommodation is available for the tenant, or will be available when the possession order takes effect.

Part III of Sch 2 to the HA 1988 defines the requirements for this ground to apply. In the very fortunate but unlikely event that the landlord obtains a certificate from the LHA that it will provide the tenant with suitable alternative accommodation, this will be conclusive evidence that suitable alternative accommodation will be available for the tenant if the court makes a possession order. In the absence of such a certificate, the landlord will need to provide or find accommodation which provides adequate security of tenure and which is suitable to the tenant's needs. Neither an assured shorthold tenancy, nor a tenancy which can be terminated under Grounds 1 to 5 (see **2.6.1** above) will be deemed to provide adequate security.

The alternative accommodation must be suitable for the tenant's needs as regards proximity to place of work, and either:

(a) similar as regards rental and extent to the accommodation provided by a LHA to people with similar needs to those of the tenant; or

(b) reasonably suitable to the means and needs of the tenant and his family as regards extent and character.

Once the court is satisfied that the accommodation is suitable, it must decide whether it is reasonable to make an order for possession. If the landlord obtains possession under this ground, as with Ground 6 (see **2.6.1.6** above), the tenant is entitled to his reasonable removal expenses (HA 1988, s 11).

2.6.2.3 Ground 10 – recovery for rent arrears

This ground for possession will be established if the landlord can show that both at the date of issue of proceedings and at the date of service of the s 8 notice, the tenant was in arrears with rent lawfully due. If the court dispenses with the need for notice under s 8(1)(b) (see **2.5.1** above), the only requirement to be met is that there were arrears at the issue of proceedings.

2.6.2.4 Ground 11 – recovery for persistent delay in paying rent

Where there is evidence that the tenant persistently delays paying rent which is lawfully due, the landlord will have satisfied this ground, even if there are no arrears at the start of the possession proceedings.

It is unlikely that the court would order possession on this ground or Ground 10 in isolation if the tenant is not actually in arrears at the date of trial. However, if there is a pattern of combined breaches, the court may be inclined to exercise its discretion to make a postponed order for possession on condition that the tenant complies with the terms of the tenancy in the future.

2.6.2.5 Ground 12 – recovery for breach of obligation

This ground will be satisfied if the tenant breaches an express or implied obligation of the tenancy. However, the court is unlikely to exercise its discretion to make a possession order if the breach is not a serious one. Nor will the court exercise its discretion where the lease can be forfeited but the landlord has waived the breach by accepting rent after becoming aware of it or by some other indication (see *Clark v Grant* [1950] 1 KB 104, CA).

2.6.2.6 Ground 13 – recovery due to deterioration of the dwelling-house or common parts

If the landlord can establish that the condition of the dwelling-house, or any of the common parts, has deteriorated owing to acts of waste by, or neglect or default of, the tenant or any other person residing in the dwelling-house, then he will have satisfied the requirement of this ground. Where the acts of waste, or neglect or default were committed by a lodger or sub-tenant, the landlord must also show that the tenant has not taken such steps as he ought reasonably to have taken for the removal of that person.

2.6.2.7 Ground 14 – recovery for nuisance, annoyance or criminal activity

There are three distinct situations where the landlord can use this ground. It is available where the tenant, or a person residing in or visiting the dwelling-house:

(a) has been guilty of conduct causing or likely to cause a nuisance or annoyance to a person residing, visiting or otherwise engaging in a lawful activity in the locality; or

(b) has been convicted of using the dwelling-house, or allowing it to be used, for immoral or illegal purposes; or

(c) has been convicted of an indictable offence committed in, or in the locality of, the dwelling-house.

Ground 14 has become the second most common ground (after rent arrears) on which RSLs and PRPs (and LHAs using Ground 2, an identical ground, in Sch 2 to the HA 1985; see **6.7.1**) seek possession. However, it is a long way behind rent arrears claims, not least because both public sector landlords, PRPs and RSLs can rely on other methods to deal with anti-social tenants (see **2.9.4**).

As a consequence of the riots which took place in various cities in England in 2011, the Government proposes to extend this discretionary ground to cover convictions of tenants or members of their household for offences committed at the scene of a riot wherever that took place in the UK (see Anti-social Behaviour, Crime and Policing Bill 2013–14, cl 91, introducing a new Ground 14ZA).

The existing provision goes beyond the activities of the tenant. Anti-social conduct by the tenant's family, friends and associates could result in an eviction. As mentioned at **2.6.2.1** above, s 9A has introduced a 'structured discretion' for the courts to consider when deciding whether it is reasonable to make a possession order under this ground.

The structured discretion

Since 30 June 2004 (for England) and 30 September 2004 (for Wales), the courts have been required by the provisions in s 9A of the HA 1988 (and also, for secure tenants, almost identical provisions in s 85A of the HA 1985 for possession under Ground 2; see **6.7.1.2** below) to consider in particular:

(a) the effect that the nuisance or annoyance has had on persons other than the person against whom the order is sought;

(b) any continuing effect the nuisance or annoyance is likely to have on such persons; and

(c) the effect that the nuisance or annoyance would be likely to have on such persons if the conduct is repeated.

In Moat Housing Group – South Ltd v Harris and Hartless [2005] HLR 33, CA, Brooke LJ, giving the judgment of the Court of Appeal, noted that the provision does not do much more than codify the existing case law, with a greater emphasis on the matters referred to in the section. What was made clear in the case was that the s 9A provisions are not the only provisions to consider under Ground 14. The court is still bound to take account of all relevant considerations. In this case, an outright possession order was made against a mother and her four children, aged between 6 and 14, as a result of nuisance and threats caused by the mother and two of her children, as well as by her non-resident partner.

In considering whether the trial judge had taken account of all the relevant factors when exercising her discretion, the Court of Appeal held that she had not as, amongst other things, the interest of the family, and in particular the two relatively blameless children, warranted some attention. Brookes LJ highlighted the fact that they had a right to respect for their home under human rights law, and it was important that procedural fairness was observed before their home was taken away. However, after reconsidering the issue of reasonableness, the Court of Appeal upheld the possession order in part, taking account of the seriousness of the conduct of the defendant, her partner and two of her children. The nuisance had involved vandalism, graffiti, littering, bullying, swearing and threats to other residents. Nonetheless, instead of an outright order, the Court suspended the order on condition that there were no further breaches or nuisance.

Where the tenant or members of his family have been guilty of racially abusing neighbours, the court takes a firm line and is more inclined to make an outright possession order rather than a suspended order (see *West Kent HA v Davies* (1999) 31 HLR 415, CA, and *Solon South West Housing Association Ltd v James* [2004] All ER (D) 328, CA).

> **CASE EXAMPLES**
>
> An outright possession order was upheld in *London and Quadrant Housing Trust v Root* [2005] HLR 28, CA. In that case the nuisance related to litter and noise, caused by a car repair business being run from the front garden of the tenanted property, in breach of the terms of the tenancy. There was also evidence of threats and verbal abuse when neighbours complained about the noise. On the facts, the Court of Appeal was satisfied that an outright possession order was appropriate, taking account of the defendant's conduct and attitude about the breaches of her tenancy agreement.
>
> In *Knowsley Housing Trust v McMullen* [2006] HLR 43, CA, the tenant appealed against a suspended possession order made against her. The tenant argued that the nuisance was mainly committed by her 19-year-old son whom, for various reasons, including the tenant's own disability, she was unable to control. Her son's behaviour included abuse, harassment and intimidation of neighbours. He had damaged the neighbours' property and homes, caused noise nuisance, set vehicles alight, and thrown bricks and iron bars at motor vehicles. It was held that the tenant's inability to control her son, who was still living with her, was a factor which counted against her. It could influence the court to grant an outright possession order or a postponement on terms which relate to the son's behaviour.

(See also **10.8.1.2** for further examples of the exercise of the discretion in anti-social possession claims.)

2.6.2.8 Ground 14A – recovery because of domestic violence

This ground is available only to RSLs, PRPs or charitable housing trust landlords where a dwelling-house was occupied by a married couple or civil partners, or by a couple living together as spouses or civil partners, and one (or both) of the partners is a tenant of the property. The landlord can seek possession if one partner has left as a result of violence or threats of violence by the other towards that partner or a member of that partner's family who was living with the partner immediately before the partner left. The court may grant possession if satisfied that that partner is unlikely to return.

The court must be satisfied that the landlord has served notice of the proceedings for possession on the partner who has left the home, or that it has taken reasonable steps to do so, or that it is just and equitable to dispense with the notice requirements (see HA 1996, s 150).

This ground is identical to Ground 2A in Sch 2 to the HA 1985 for secure tenants (see **6.7.1.3**). In *Camden LBC v Mallett* (2001) 33 HLR 204, CA, it was held that the domestic violence ground would not be satisfied unless the real and effective reason the partner left was because of the domestic violence. It was not sufficient that it was one of a number of causes for her to leave.

2.6.2.9 Ground 15 – recovery because of furniture deterioration

Where furniture has been provided for use under the tenancy, the landlord will establish this ground if he can show that the furniture has deteriorated owing to ill-treatment by the tenant or any other person residing in the dwelling-house. As with Ground 13 (see **2.6.2.6**), where the ill-treatment was committed by a lodger or sub-tenant, the landlord must also show that the tenant has not taken such steps as he ought reasonably to have taken for the removal of that person.

2.6.2.10 Ground 16 – recovery from former employee

Where the landlord was the employer of the tenant and the tenancy was granted in consequence of that job then, when the employment has terminated, the landlord is entitled to regain possession of the property. It is not necessary for the landlord to show that he needs the property for another employee, although this may influence the court in exercising its discretion on reasonableness.

2.6.2.11 Ground 17 – recovery for false statements

The landlord will be able to recover under this ground if the tenant, or a person acting at the tenant's instigation, knowingly or recklessly made a false statement which induced the landlord to grant the tenancy. This ground is identical to that in Ground 5 in Sch 2 to the HA 1985 (see **6.7.1.4**).

2.7 ASSURED SHORTHOLD TENANCIES

Assured shorthold tenancies are a particular type of assured tenancy. As such they have to meet all the pre-conditions of an assured tenancy in s 1 of the HA 1988, and not be subject to any of the exclusions mentioned at **2.3** above. The key distinction between the two types of tenancies relates to the level of security of tenure given. Assured shorthold tenancies have extremely limited security of tenure. In essence, provided the proper procedure is followed, a landlord can regain possession of the premises after six months (see **2.7.3**).

The requirements for the creation of an assured shorthold tenancy have changed since implementation of the HA 1988. The initial requirements were that an assured shorthold tenancy had to be granted for a fixed term of at least six months and that a prescribed notice had to be served by the landlord before the start of the tenancy. However, following amendment to the HA 1988 by ss 96 to 100 of the HA 1996, there is no longer a requirement either for a pre-tenancy notice, or for an initial fixed term. When looking at the status of an assured shorthold tenant, it is important to ascertain whether the tenancy is subject to the pre- or post-HA 1996 regime, as different provisions apply.

2.7.1 Assured shorthold tenancies pre-HA 1996

An assured tenancy will be subject to the provisions in s 20 of the HA 1988 if it was entered into before 28 February 1997 (the date the HA 1996 provisions came into effect). Under s 20(1), to be an assured shorthold tenancy, the tenancy must have been granted for a fixed term of at least six months, with the landlord not being able to terminate it within that time (other than as he would be able to do for a fixed-term assured tenant, see **2.5**). Most importantly, the landlord must have served on the prospective tenant a notice in accordance with s 20(2), before the assured tenancy was entered into, stating that the tenancy was to be an assured shorthold tenancy. The notice was required to be in accordance with, or substantially to the same effect as, Form 7 in the Assured Tenancies and Agricultural Occupancies (Forms) Regulations 1988 (SI 1988/2203) (since revoked by SI 1997/194).

The notice requirement has generated a lot of case law, as an invalid notice has the effect of creating an assured tenancy instead of an assured shorthold tenancy. In *Manel v Memon* (2001) 33 HLR 235, CA, the tenant successfully resisted a possession claim on the basis that she had an assured tenancy, not an assured shorthold tenancy, as the s 20(2) notice served on her by the landlord was defective. The notice failed to include important advice to the tenant that was required by the Regulations. However, in *Ravenseft Properties Ltd v Hall* [2001] EWCA Civ 2034, it was held that the sole question to ask in determining the validity of a notice was whether, despite any errors or omissions, the notice was substantially to the same effect as a correct notice in serving the statutory purpose of informing the tenant of the special nature of an assured shorthold tenancy. Although on the facts of the case there had been an error in the notice, in that it gave an incorrect commencement date, it was held that the notice achieved its purpose and was valid.

A landlord who granted an assured tenancy before 28 February 1997 cannot grant an assured shorthold tenancy to the same tenant immediately after (s 20(3)). By s 20(4), where a landlord, on the termination of an assured shorthold tenancy granted before 28 February 1997, granted another tenancy of the property to the same tenant, that tenancy would be an assured shorthold tenancy unless the landlord served a notice specifically stating that it was not to be a shorthold tenancy (s 20(5)).

2.7.2 Assured shorthold tenancies post-HA 1996

The position discussed in **2.7.1** above is reversed for assured shorthold tenancies created on or after 28 February 1997 (unless made pursuant to a contract made before that date). Subject to certain exceptions listed in Sch 2A to the HA 1988, a tenancy which satisfies the conditions in s 1 of the 1988 Act will be an assured shorthold tenancy (s 19A). One of the exceptions in Sch 2A applies where the landlord serves a notice on the tenant informing him that the tenancy is not to be an assured shorthold tenancy, or if there is a term in the tenancy agreement to that effect. This would most commonly be the case for tenancies granted by RSLs or PRPs. The schedule also recognises that secure tenancies which become assured (normally as a result of stock transfer by an LHA) would not be shorthold. Also excluded are tenancies which arise on the ending of long leases under the Local Government and Housing Act (LGHA) 1989 and by way of family member succession under the RA 1977 (HA 1988, s 39) (see **8.2.1** and **3.4.1.3**).

Assured shorthold tenancies no longer have to be fixed-term or made in writing. To help address this vacuum for post-HA 1996 tenants, s 20A entitles such tenants, where they do not already have the information, to apply to their landlords in writing, requesting written details relating to:

(a) the commencement date of the tenancy;
(b) the amount of and date of payment for the rent;
(c) any rent review terms; and
(d) if the tenancy is fixed-term, the length of the fixed term.

It is a summary offence punishable by fine for the landlord, unless he has a reasonable excuse, to fail to respond to such a request within 28 days of receipt (s 20A(4)).

2.7.3 Recovery of possession of assured shorthold tenancies

The essential difference between an assured and an assured shorthold tenancy is that there is no real security of tenure for assured shorthold tenants. The relevant provision which effects this is s 21 of the HA 1988. The provisions in s 5, as considered above at **2.5**, also apply to assured shorthold tenants. However, in addition s 21 enables the landlord to obtain a mandatory order for possession of the premises once the appropriate notice provisions have been complied with (see below). This overriding provision enables the landlord to obtain a possession order without any fault of the tenant once the proper notice has been served.

2.7.3.1 Fixed-term assured shorthold tenancies

A mandatory order for possession can be obtained on the expiry of a fixed-term tenancy. The only conditions to be satisfied are that the landlord has not granted a new fixed term which is still in existence, and he has served on the tenant two months' written notice that he requires possession of the property. The notice does not have to be in any prescribed form and can be given before the fixed term expires (s 21(2)). The court does not have the power to dispense with this notice.

For new fixed-term assured shorthold tenancies granted by PRPs after 2 April 2012, s 164 of the Localism Act 2011 has added s 21(1A) and (1B) into the HA 1988. The provisions provide that where the tenancy is a fixed-term tenancy for a term certain of not less than two years, the court may not make an order for possession of the dwelling-house let on the tenancy unless the landlord has given to the tenant not less than six months' notice in writing:

(a) stating that the landlord does not propose to grant another tenancy on the expiry of the fixed-term tenancy; and

(b) informing the tenant of how to obtain help or advice about the notice and, in particular, of any obligation of the landlord to provide help or advice.

2.7.3.2 Periodic assured shorthold tenancies

For periodic tenancies, the notice must specify the date the landlord requires possession. This must be the last day of a period of the tenancy. The notice must be of two months' duration, or, if longer, the notice period that would be required to terminate that tenancy by notice to quit (s 21(4)). If the wrong date is specified in the notice it will not be valid and the court will not be able to grant a possession order. However, if no date is specified the notice may still be valid, provided appropriate words are used. In *Lower Street Properties Ltd v Jones* (1996) 28 HLR 877, CA, it was held that words to the effect 'at the end of the period of your tenancy which will end after the expiry of two months from the service upon you of this notice' were sufficient to satisfy s 21(4). Kennedy LJ stated that those were a form of words which met the requirement because the tenant knew or could easily ascertain the date referred to.

The last date of the tenancy is strictly construed, however. In *McDonald v Fernandez* [2004] 1 WLR 1027, CA, the periodic assured shorthold tenancy ran from the fourth day of the month to the third day of the following month. It was held that a s 21(4) notice which stated that possession was required on the fourth day of the month, was invalid, as that was not the last day of the period of the tenancy but the day after. (See also *Notting Hill Housing Trust v Roomus* [2006] 1 WLR 1375, CA.)

By s 21(5), an order for possession in relation to a post-HA 1996 assured shorthold tenancy cannot take effect earlier than six months from the beginning of the original tenancy. Thus both pre- and post-HA 1996 tenancies are subject to the same, limited six-month security against a s 21 possession claim.

2.7.4 Rent referral to a rent assessment committee

By s 22 of the HA 1988, an assured shorthold tenant can refer an excessive rent to a rent assessment committee either during the initial term of a fixed term, or within the first six months of a periodic tenancy. However, the committee will have jurisdiction only if there are sufficient comparables in the same area as the applicant's dwelling and the rent is deemed to be significantly higher than those others. Not surprisingly, given the limited security available, few references have been made under this provision.

2.8 TENANCY DEPOSIT SCHEMES FOR ASSURED SHORTHOLD TENANTS

It is fairly common practice for private sector landlords to require a security deposit on the granting of a new tenancy. The amount is not prescribed but is generally between one and three months' rent for the property. If the tenant has looked after the property and is not otherwise in breach of any terms, he should have his deposit returned to him at the end of the tenancy. In many cases, however, tenants have complained that the landlord has unlawfully failed to return the deposit.

To deal with this problem, provisions in ss 212 to 215 of and Sch 10 (as amended) to the HA 2004 introduced a tenancy deposit scheme for deposits taken from assured shorthold tenants after 6 April 2007. The provisions aim to safeguard tenancy deposits paid in connection with shorthold tenancies and also facilitate the resolution of disputes arising in connection with such deposits. A further aim is to ensure that where the tenant is not at fault, the deposit is returned to him within 10 days of the end of the tenancy.

2.8.1 The authorised schemes

The provisions operate by requiring deposits, which can only be money and no other property, to be dealt with in accordance with an authorised scheme (HA 2004, s 213). There are two types of schemes: one is custodial and the other is insurance based. The custodial scheme requires the landlord to pay the deposit into a designated account held by a scheme administrator. There is one such scheme at present, the Deposit Protection Service. This is a free-to-use scheme available online or by postal service. It is open to private landlords and letting agents. Details of the scheme may be accessed at www.depositprotection.com.

There are two insurance schemes. One is provided by Tenancy Deposit Solutions Ltd: see www.mydeposit.co.uk. The other is provided by The Dispute Services Limited (TDS Ltd): see www.tds.gb.com. With these insurance schemes, the landlord retains the deposit. He has to pay the scheme operators a premium for their service, which may be required in the event of a dispute. If there is a dispute at the end of the tenancy, over whether and how much deposit should be returned to the tenant, the landlord will be required to transfer the deposit to the scheme administrator until the parties agree or the matter is resolved at court.

Both the custodial scheme and the insurance schemes make available alternative dispute resolution mechanisms to resolve any dispute.

There are various obligations imposed on a landlord. The first is that within 30 days of receiving a deposit the landlord must enter it into a government designated tenancy deposit scheme and provide the tenant with prescribed information. The prescribed information includes providing the tenant with the name and address of the scheme administrator and the procedures to be followed for return of the deposit at the end of the tenancy and also if a dispute arises (see the Housing (Tenancy Deposits) (Prescribed Information) Order 2007 (SI 2007/797)).

2.8.2 Orders and sanctions where non-compliance

There are a number of compliance requirements and sanctions imposed on the landlord. If the landlord fails to comply with the initial requirements of a scheme, or has failed to give the tenant relevant information, an application can be made to the county court by the tenant or the person who paid the deposit on behalf of the tenant. The court may order the deposit holder to repay the deposit, or to pay the deposit as required under a custodial scheme. If the applicant is a former tenant (ie he no longer has the relevant tenancy), the court has a discretion to order the person holding the deposit to repay all or part of it to the applicant within 14 days. In addition, the landlord may be ordered to pay between one and three times the deposit amount to the applicant within 14 days of the order being made (HA 2004, s 214) (see *Draycott v Hannells Lettings Ltd* [2010] EWHC 217 (QB)).

Nevertheless, there is also a sanction on the landlord for as long as there is non-compliance with the provisions. The sanction is that the landlord will not be able to serve a HA 1988, s 21 notice to terminate the tenancy where he remains in breach of any of the relevant provisions. This includes failure to hold the deposit in accordance with an authorised scheme, failing to comply with the initial requirements of such a scheme and failing to serve the tenant with relevant information in the prescribed form (HA 2004, s 215).

If the landlord returns the full deposit, or an agreed lesser amount, to the tenant, or a compensation claim brought by the tenant for non-compliance with a scheme has been compromised, then the landlord will be able to serve a valid s 21 notice (HA 2004, s 215(2A)).

The provisions are not retrospective in relation to deposits paid before the relevant sections came into force. However, if a new tenancy of the same property with the same parties arises after the coming into force of these provisions and a deposit continues to be held from the previous tenancy, then the provisions will apply to the new tenancy and also to the deposit.

> **CASE EXAMPLE**
>
> In *Superstrike Ltd v Rodrigues* [2013] EWCA Civ 669, a one-year fixed-term tenancy was granted to R on 8 January 2007 and a one-month deposit paid. As this was three months before the tenancy deposit provisions came into force, the landlord was not required to and did not protect the deposit under any scheme. On the expiry of the fixed term in January 2008 the landlord did not renew the tenancy. Consequently, by s 5 of the HA 1988, a new statutory periodic tenancy arose on the same terms as the previous fixed-term tenancy. In June 2011 the landlord served a s 21 notice requiring possession. It was held that the landlord was not entitled to possession, as the legislation required the tenant's deposit to be held in accordance with an authorised scheme no later than the end of January 2008. Since it was not so held, the landlord was not entitled to serve a notice under s 21 in June 2011.

2.9 ASSURED TENANTS OF RSLS AND PRPS

Assured tenants of RSLs and PRPs are in many ways in a much better position than assured tenants of private sector landlords; they enjoy many of the benefits available to public sector tenants. In others ways, though, it could be said that they may be at a slight disadvantage. However, for most tenants the advantages probably outweigh the disadvantages.

RSLs and PRPs are businesses established to provide social housing on a not-for-profit basis. They are set up in various forms, for example as trusts and co-operatives, but most are set up as housing associations. Although they are strictly speaking private organisations, they are registered with a public body. This used to be the Housing Corporation. The Housing Corporation was abolished in December 2008 by provisions in the Housing and Regeneration Act 2008. Its regulatory functions over RSLs were transferred to a new body, the Tenant Services Authority (TSA). The system of 'registered social landlords' continued only in Wales.

The TSA was abolished from 31 March 2012 and its functions transferred to a new Regulation Committee of the Homes and Communities Agency (HCA) (see Localism Act 2011, s 178 and Sch 16). From 1 April 2012 the new regulator has general supervision over English RSLs (now PRPs) and other bodies who choose to register, including for-profit organisations as well as over 180 LHAs that still have a housing stock.

On a practical level, as social landlords, RSLs and PRPs operate almost as quasi-public bodies. This is reinforced by the fact that until the enactment of the HA 1988, most of their tenants were secure tenants within the provisions of the HA 1985. The decision in R *(Weaver) v London & Quadrant Housing Trust* [2009] EWCA Civ 587 would seem to confirm this. It was held that RSLs are public authorities for judicial review purposes and also within s 6(3)(b) of the HRA 1998 when performing housing management functions (see **4.4.1**).

However, the vast majority of RSL and PRP tenants are now assured tenants within the provisions of the HA 1988. Having said that, a number of RSLs have introduced a probationary scheme for new tenants. This is a means of controlling anti-social behaviour. The new tenant is given not an assured tenancy but a starter tenancy. A starter tenancy is effectively an assured shorthold tenancy (see **2.7**). A starter tenancy will last for 12 months, after which it automatically becomes an assured tenancy unless terminated before then.

The HCA has issued a new regulatory framework effective from 1 April 2012 that is applicable to all providers of social housing. The framework details seven standards for social housing in England.

Three are 'economic standards', namely value for money, governance and financial viability, and rent. The economic standards apply to PRPs only and the regulator will take a proactive role in regulating these.

The remaining four standards are 'consumer standards'. These are more directly applicable to tenants. The regulator will take a more reactive form of regulation for the consumer standards and will only intervene if there is serious mismanagement by a social landlord. The consumer standards are applicable to all social housing providers.

2.9.1 Advantages of having a regulatory framework

The advantages lie not in the benefits conveyed by the HA 1988, but in the additional rights conveyed to PRP assured tenants by the regulatory framework.

The four consumer standards are as follows:

(a) *Tenant involvement and empowerment.* This covers matters such as customer service, choice and complaints.

(b) *Home.* This includes minimum expectation on matters of repairs, maintenance and quality of accommodation. Social housing providers should ensure that their homes meet the Government's Decent Homes Standard by 31 December 2010.

(c) *Tenancy.* This deals with fair and transparent allocations and mutual exchange of appropriate tenure. In addition to periodic tenancies, PRPs can now grant five-year (or, exceptionally, two-year) fixed-term assured shorthold tenancies.

(d) *Neighbourhood and community.* This deals with management issues including preventing and tackling anti-social behaviour.

Assured and assured shorthold tenants of landlords not registered with the HCA do not have the benefit of these regulatory provisions over their landlords.

2.9.2 Certain disadvantages affecting security and freedom

The potential disadvantage to being an RSL or PRP assured tenant lies in the possible grounds for possession and other action that can be taken only by RSLs or PRPs, not by private sector landlords with assured tenants. While an RSL or PRP cannot obtain possession on, for example, mandatory Ground 1 (owner-occupier or future occupier, see **2.6.1.1**), an assured tenant of an RSL or PRP may be at risk of a possession claim under Ground 14A (domestic violence, see **2.6.2.8**) whereas assured and assured shorthold tenants of non-registered landlords would not be.

In addition, an RSL or PRP (in line with LHAs and Housing Action Trusts (HATs) – see **2.9.4** and **6.8**) has powers to take proceedings to obtain injunctions and orders against its tenants for anti-social behaviour. These powers are within a wider framework of policies which LHAs, PRPs and RSLs, as well as the police, are required to have for dealing with anti-social behaviour in their areas (see, eg, 218A of the HA 1985 and Pt I of the Crime and Disorder Act (CADA) 1998).

However, the provisions for selective licensing introduced by the HA 2004 (see **1.7.4**) impose obligations on non-registered private sector landlords that may oblige them to start taking a firmer line in dealing with anti-social tenants.

Prevention of Social Housing Fraud Act 2013

In order to deal with the problem in England of PRP assured tenants sub-letting the whole of their home for profit, the Prevention of Social Housing Fraud Act 2013 introduces a new criminal offence of unlawful sub-letting of an assured tenancy. Conviction could lead to imprisonment and/or a fine. An unlawful profit order can also be made by the court to recover the profit made by the tenant from unlawfully sub-letting the property. Similar provisions apply to the unlawful sub-letting of LHA secure tenancies (see **6.4.1**).

The Act also amends the Housing Act 1988 to add a new s 15A. This provides that where a PRP tenant, in breach of the terms of the tenancy, sub-lets the whole of the property, the tenancy will cease to be an assured tenancy and cannot subsequently become an assured tenancy. This provision brings PRP assured tenancies in line with a similar provision for secure tenants in ss 91(2) and 93(2) (see **6.4.1**).

2.9.3 Demoted tenancies as a result of a demotion order

Since 30 June 2004 (for England) and 30 April 2004 (for Wales), an RSL or PRP assured tenant may also lose his assured status and have his tenancy demoted as a result of anti-social behaviour or unlawful use of the premises (see **6.6.2**). The provisions, introduced in ss 6A and 20B of the HA 1988 by the Anti-social Behaviour Act 2003, enable RSLs and PRPs to control the behaviour of anti-social tenants without necessarily taking possession action.

The process is instigated by an RSL or PRP serving notice on the tenant, giving particulars of the conduct for which the order will be sought and indicating that proceedings will not begin before two weeks have expired or after 12 months. However, the court can dispense with the notice requirement if it considers it just and equitable to do so (HA 1988, s 6A(5), (6)). The provisions are similar to those introduced for secure tenants, who are demoted under s 82A of the HA 1985 (see **6.6.2**).

In practice, although there are separate procedures to obtain a demotion order in CPR, Part 65, it is quite common for an RSL to apply for a possession order relying on Ground 14 (see **2.6.2.7**), and in the claim to indicate that an application for a demoted tenancy would be an alternative application, should the court not be minded to make a possession order. In such cases the procedure in CPR Part 55 applies (see **Chapter 10**). On Form N5 (claim form for possession of property), the claimant has to indicate whether anti-social behaviour is in issue and whether a demoted tenancy is being applied for.

The effect of a demotion order on an assured tenant

A demoted tenancy is a demoted assured shorthold tenancy and will remain so for a period of one year (HA 1988, s 20B). During this time it is in effect an assured shorthold tenancy (see **2.7** above). It will revert to being an assured tenancy at the end of this period, unless the landlord has in the meantime commenced possession proceedings as a result of the tenant's further misbehaviour. Unlike the position with demoted secure tenants (see **6.7.1**), there is no statutory provision entitling the demoted assured shorthold tenant to a review before any possession proceedings are commenced against him. However, it is not uncommon for social landlords such as PRPs and RSLs to have a review procedure included in their assured tenancy agreements.

The result of such proceedings is to continue the demoted tenancy until the proceedings are withdrawn or determined in favour of the tenant. If no proceedings are commenced within six months of notice being given then the demoted assured shorthold tenancy will revert to being an assured tenancy if more than a year has expired since the demotion order was made (s 20B(3)). If the landlord does commence proceedings, provided a two-month notice of possession proceedings is served (see s 21(4) at **2.7.3**), the landlord will be entitled to possession without the need to prove a ground for possession.

Under s 20C of the HA 1988, a demoted assured shorthold tenant in England who was previously granted a fixed-term shorthold tenancy for a term certain of not less than two years will (provided the landlord serves notice to that effect on him before the expiry of the demotion period) on the ending of the one-year demotion period obtain a fixed-term assured shorthold tenancy of at least two years.

2.9.4 Anti-social behaviour injunctions

In addition RSLs, LHAs and non-profit registered providers (relevant landlords) can apply for various injunctions to control the behaviour of anti-social individuals on their estates under ss 153A to 153E of the HA 1996. On an application by a relevant landlord, the court can grant an injunction against anti-social behaviour. Anti-social behaviour is defined in s 153A, as amended, as conduct which is capable of causing nuisance or annoyance to any person, and which directly or indirectly relates to or affects the housing management functions of a relevant landlord. The provisions are designed to protect residents of the relevant landlord, other residents in the neighbourhood and housing workers who have to come into the area, although it is immaterial where the forbidden conduct occurs; it can be conduct anywhere (s 153A(1)).

A power of arrest can be attached to the injunction, which gives the police the ability to arrest, without warrant, any person who is in breach of the order. The injunction can prevent the person from entering or being in any premises, or in any area specified in the order (s 153C). By s 153E, an application can be made for this injunction without notice to the person against whom it is to be issued, if the court considers that it is just and convenient to do so, and a power of arrest may be attached to this too. The provisions are common to LHA secure tenancies (see **6.6.2.3** below).

In *Moat Housing Group – South Ltd v Harris and Hartless* [2006] QB 606, CA, the landlord applied for and obtained a without notice injunction against the defendants which, amongst other things, required the second defendant to leave her home and thereafter not to enter within a defined area of the property. The order was stated to be effective for six months, although there was a hearing set for the following week. The order had a power of arrest attached and the defendant was ordered to leave the property by 6 pm that day.

On the defendants' appeal against the granting of a without notice injunction with such draconian terms, the Court of Appeal gave comprehensive guidance to county court judges as to how to deal with such cases. Their Lordships adopted the guidance given in s 45(2)(a) of the Family Law Act 1996 for similar applications. It was held that only in exceptional circumstances – for example, where there is a risk of significant harm to some person or persons, attributable to the conduct of the defendant if the order is not made immediately – should a without notice order be granted. In those circumstances the order must not be wider than is necessary and proportionate as a means of avoiding the apprehended harm.

On the facts of the case it was held appropriate to make the order restricting the defendants causing nuisance or annoyance to others, but not to order the second defendant out of her home and excluding her from the surrounding areas. It was also held that a power of arrest should be attached to a without notice order only where the court is satisfied that the defendant has used or threatened violence towards a resident or housing worker, and there is a likelihood of one or more of them suffering significant harm without such a power being attached to the order.

Advice was also given on the service of such orders. It was held that the court should generally require the order to be served at a reasonable time of day, eg between 9 am and 4.30 pm on a weekday. Guidance was also given to the landlord. It was stated that great care should be taken by the claimant in the drafting of witness statements in support of without notice relief, which were seriously deficient in this case. As a lot of the anti-social behaviour by the defendants was attributable to two of their children, it was held that every landlord should be alert to intervene creatively at a far earlier stage than occurred here, in order to do everything possible to avoid recourse to eviction, not least because of the human rights aspects.

The procedure for applying for an anti-social behaviour injunction is contained in CPR, Part 65, Section I.

2.9.5 Anti-social behaviour orders

This is another controlling provision available to social landlords. Part I of the CADA 1998, as amended, makes provision for anti-social behaviour orders (ASBOs). An ASBO can be made against any person aged 10 or over, if he has acted in an anti-social manner. 'Anti-social' is defined here to mean in a manner that caused or was likely to cause harassment, alarm or distress to one or more persons not of the same household as himself, and the order is necessary to protect relevant persons from further such acts by him (CADA 1998, s 1).

Applications are normally made to a magistrates' court. Although an ASBO is a civil order, a criminal standard of proof applies. 'Non-profit registered providers of social housing' (amongst other bodies) can apply for ASBOs in county court proceedings too, for example as a part of possession proceedings (CADA 1998, s 1B). A relevant landlord can also apply to be joined to proceedings in which it is not otherwise involved in the county court, or to have an anti-social person joined to the proceedings, solely for the purpose of obtaining an ASBO against an anti-social person (CADA 1998, s 1B). The court has a wide discretion as to the restrictions that may be placed in an ASBO. The ASBO remains effective for a minimum period of two years.

The unfortunate defendants in *Moat Housing Group – South Ltd v Harris and Hartless* (see **2.7.4** above), in addition to everything else, had an ASBO made against them restraining their conduct for a period of four years. The Court of Appeal, applying the principles stated in an earlier House of Lords decision (R *(McCann) v Manchester Crown Court* [2003] 1 AC 787, HL), held that there was not the evidence of 'persistent and serious anti-social behaviour' on the part of the defendants here (as opposed to two of their children – against whom no order was made) which is required before it would be necessary to make an ASBO. The Court therefore allowed the appeal on this point and the order was set aside. Guidance was also given on the procedure to follow in making such an order.

The procedure for applying for an ASBO in the county court is contained in CPR, Part 65, Section IV.

2.9.6 Parenting contracts and orders

The Police and Justice Act 2006, ss 23 and 24 amended Pt 3 (adding ss 25A, 25B, 26A, 26B, 26C and 28A) of the Anti-social Behaviour Act 2003 to insert new provisions further to control anti-social behaviour. From 29 June 2007, relevant landlords can further control anti-social behaviour of children by entering into a parenting contract with a parent of a child or young person, where there is reason to believe that the child or young person has engaged, or is likely to engage, in anti-social behaviour. An RSL or a non-profit registered provider must show that such behaviour directly or indirectly relates to or affects its housing management functions.

In the parenting contract the parent agrees to comply with what is required to ensure better behaviour by the child or young person. It could, for example, be to ensure that the child is at home between certain hours in the evening. The contract can include an obligation to attend counselling or guidance sessions. A failure to abide by the terms of the contract or to agree to a parenting contract could prompt an application for a parenting order.

Relevant landlords can also apply for a parenting order against a parent of a child or young person, where there is reason to believe that the child or young person has engaged in anti-social behaviour. As with a parenting contract, an RSL or a non-profit registered provider must also show that such behaviour directly or indirectly relates to or affects its housing management functions. The RSL or non-profit registered provider must also consult with the local authority in whose area the child or young person in question resides or appears to reside.

The order will be made if the court is satisfied that the child or young person has engaged in anti-social behaviour and it is appropriate to make the order to prevent further such behaviour. The order can require the parent to comply with certain requirements. This may include counselling or guidance programmes for up to three months. The order can last for up to 12 months. Breach of the order can lead, on conviction, to a fine of up to £1,000.

Application for parenting orders may be made either to a magistrate's court, or, in certain cases where proceedings are already begun, to a county court. One might expect that such orders would most often be applied for in the county court, in existing proceedings to obtain possession and/or an injunction or ASBO against the parent or child.

The procedure for applying for a parenting order in the county court is contained in CPR, Part 65, Section VII.

2.9.7 Family intervention tenancies

A tool made available to social landlords is the family intervention tenancy, introduced by s 297 of the Housing and Regeneration Act 2008. This enables RSLs, PRPs and LHAs to offer family intervention tenancies in circumstances where the tenant is likely to be evicted on the grounds of anti-social behaviour or in the opinion of the landlord could have been so evicted (see **6.6.2.3**). This option differs from simply demoting the tenant as there is a rehabilitation element to it. The tenant is offered and has to agree to the provision of behaviour support services.

The tenant will not have an assured tenancy – it will be an excluded tenancy under Sch 1 to the HA 1988. As a result there will be no security of tenure. It will be possible to terminate family intervention tenancies by notice to quit without the need to prove any grounds in Sch 2 to the HA 1988. However, before a family intervention tenancy can be agreed to by a tenant, the landlord must comply with strict notice requirements which include an explanation on the lack of security. The tenant must enter the tenancy agreement voluntarily. Family intervention tenancies are designed to be used where intensive support is being or will be delivered to households during the tenancy.

The aim is to offer support for the duration of the tenancy which is likely to be at least six to 12 months and may be longer. At the end of the agreed period, a decision should be taken by the landlord as to whether the tenant is offered a tenancy with more security or whether possession should be sought.

2.10 PRIVATE SECTOR ASSURED TENANTS

Whilst assured tenants of RSLs and PRPs are susceptible to a wide range of controlling measures against anti-social behaviour, which protect the majority and deal with a 'problem' minority (see **2.9.2–2.9.7**), private sector assured and assured shorthold tenants have so far been free of this level of intervention by their landlords. However, the selective licensing provisions in Pt 3 of the HA 2004 may, if used effectively by LHAs, put private sector landlords in a similar position to RSLs and PRPs when dealing with anti-social tenants (see **1.7.3**).

2.11 FURTHER READING

S Garner and A Frith, *A Practical Approach to Landlord and Tenant* (7th edn, 2013)

> **SUMMARY**
>
> - There are two types of assured tenancies in the HA 1988:
>   - assured tenancies; and
>   - assured shorthold tenancies.
> - The two tenancies have the same requirements in s 1 of the HA 1988 that the tenant is an individual and occupies the dwelling as his only or principal home and that none of the exclusions in Pt I of Sch 1 to the HA 1988 applies. Both are subject to the discretionary and mandatory provisions for possession set out in Sch 2 to the HA 1988.
> - The key distinction between the two is that assured tenancies have full security of tenure and assured shorthold tenancies do not because of the mandatory right to recover possession contained in s 21 of the HA 1988. In addition, the tenancy deposit scheme applies only to assured shorthold tenancies.
> - Assured tenancies are legally private sector tenancies. Non-registered private landlords usually grant assured shorthold tenancies because they give them the benefit of the mandatory right of recovery of possession in s 21.
> - RSLs and PRPs are social providers of housing that generally grant assured tenancies. However, many PRPs and RSLs initially grant 'starter tenancies', which are in effect assured shorthold tenancies, for the first year of a new tenancy, so they have the option to use s 21 if the tenant turns out to be undesirable for whatever reason.
> - The courts treat some RSLs and PRPs as quasi-public bodies when they are performing their housing management functions. This is partly because many RSLs and PRPs have received substantial public funding to assist them to provide social housing. Also, they have powers similar to LHAs to deal with anti-social tenants. For example, they can obtain:
>   - demotion orders;
>   - ASBOs;
>   - parenting orders;
>   - family intervention tenancies.

CHAPTER 3

Rent Act Regulated Tenancies

3.1	Introduction – Rent Act 1977	35
3.2	Protected tenancies	36
3.3	Exclusions from protected tenant status	36
3.4	Security of tenure	37
3.5	Rents under regulated tenancies	43
3.6	Registered rents for housing association tenants	44
3.7	Further reading	45
	Summary	45

LEARNING OUTCOMES

After reading this chapter you will be able to:

- understand the background to the Rent Act provisions
- explain what a regulated tenancy is
- describe the effect of rent registration.

3.1 INTRODUCTION – RENT ACT 1977

Rent Act regulated tenants have enjoyed the longest period and most comprehensive form of statutory protection of all the statutory regimes relating to residential tenancies. The provisions were introduced as a temporary measure during the First World War (in 1915), at a time when the vast majority of dwellings, in fact 90%, were privately rented rather than owner occupied, and public sector housing was non-existent.

The original aim of the first piece of legislation was to control the rent increases which were taking place as a result of housing shortages in industrial areas. The rent increases were causing civil unrest, and this led to rent strikes at a time when what was needed at home was stability and a focus on the production of munitions for the war. Security of tenure was a necessary adjunct to rent control to avoid further unrest.

What was initially a temporary measure went (depending on the party in government) through various stages of decontrol and then re-introduction of control on rent levels, culminating in the RA 1977. Under that Act, controlled rents, a much stricter form of rent control, became regulated rents. This later form of rent control lends its name to the two types of regulated tenancies as defined in s 18 of the RA 1977, namely protected and statutory tenancies. Protection was by no means universal but was dependent on whether the property was within the relevant rateable value limits and not otherwise excluded.

The DCLG statistics for 2008 indicate that there are only about 120,000 Rent Act regulated tenancies still in existence. This number is diminishing year by year as, with the exception of a few transitional provisions, no new regulated tenancy could be created on or after 15 January 1989 when the HA 1988 came into force (see **2.1** and HA 1988, s 34).

In this chapter the present provisions, contained in the RA 1977, are briefly considered, and where overlaps with the assured tenancy provisions occur, reference is made back to **Chapter 2**.

3.2 PROTECTED TENANCIES

Under s 1 of the RA 1977, a protected tenancy is one where a dwelling-house is let as a separate dwelling. The dwelling can be a house, or a part of a house. As with assured tenancies, there must be a tenancy, not a licence (see **1.5.3**), of a separate dwelling (see **2.2.2**). Premises let for mixed business and residential purposes will not be premises let as a separate dwelling. This will be so even where the tenant has occupied the premises for residential purposes only for a number of years (see *Tan v Sitkowski* [2007] EWCA 30). Unlike assured tenancies, however, there is no requirement that the tenant occupy the dwelling as his only or principal home to be protected. In addition, there is no requirement that the tenant be an individual, so a company could have a protected tenancy (*Hilton v Plustitle Ltd* [1989] 1 WLR 149, CA).

As with assured tenancies, s 22 of the RA 1977 provides that where a tenant has exclusive possession of a part of a property but shares other accommodation with another person or persons, none of whom is his landlord, the shared accommodation will be regarded as a dwelling let on a protected tenancy. The tenant can also sub-let part of the dwelling without compromising his protected tenant status in relation to the whole (s 23).

Although protected tenancies cannot generally be created on or after 15 January 1989, s 34 of the HA 1988 does have some transitional provisions designed to stop regulated tenancies which existed before that date losing protection. So, for example, if a tenancy is granted post-15 January 1989 and immediately before the grant the tenant was a protected (or statutory) tenant of that landlord, then the new tenancy will be protected under the RA 1977 even if it is of a different property (HA 1988, s 34(1)(b) and *Laimond Properties Ltd v Al-Shakarchi* (1998) 30 HLR 1099, CA). The same is true if a new tenancy is granted to joint tenants, where only one of them was immediately before a protected tenant of the landlord and the other was not (see *Secretarial & Nominee Co Ltd v Thomas* [2005] EWCA Civ 1008).

3.3 EXCLUSIONS FROM PROTECTED TENANT STATUS

The provision in s 1 of the RA 1977 (see **3.2**) is subject to the rest of Pt I of the Act, and ss 4 to 16 and s 24 qualify and exclude certain types of tenancies from protected tenant status. Of the 15 exclusions in those sections, 11 of them (namely ss 4, 5, 6, 8 to 14 and 24) have been broadly reproduced in Sch 1 to the HA 1988 as exclusions from assured tenancy status too. The exclusions that are similar are listed here; see **2.3**, (b)–(k), for further details:

(a) high-value premises (s 4);
(b) tenancies at low or no rent (s 5);
(c) tenancies of agricultural land (ss 6, 26);
(d) lettings to students (s 8);
(e) holiday lettings (s 9);
(f) tenancies of agricultural holdings (s 10);
(g) licensed premises (s 11);
(h) resident landlords (s 12);
(i) lettings by public bodies (ss 13, 14); and
(j) business tenancies (s 24).

The other exclusions from protected tenant status are:

(k) certain qualifying shared ownership leases, eg, granted by Housing Associations (s 5A);
(l) payment for board (ie, meals) or attendance (ie, services) where this formed a substantial part of the rent payment. Substantial for these purposes simply means not de minimis (see *Otter v Norman* [1989] AC 129, HL; s 7);

(m) landlord's interest belonging to a housing association, the Housing Corporation or a charitable housing trust (s 15); and

(n) landlord's interest belonging to a housing cooperative within the meaning of s 27B of the HA 1985 (s 16).

These four exclusions, while taking a tenancy outside the protection of the RA 1977, are not excluded under the HA 1988, and in fact most assured tenancies are granted by housing association landlords.

3.4 SECURITY OF TENURE

A protected tenancy is a contractual tenancy subject to the normal rules of landlord and tenant. If a fixed-term tenancy, it will expire or terminate at the end of the fixed term. If a periodic tenancy, it will expire or terminate at the end of the relevant valid notice period (see **1.5.2.1**). Thus the security provided under the RA 1977 operates in a different way to that of assured tenancies, where a court order is required to terminate the tenancy. The security provisions in the RA 1977 are contained in s 2 and s 98.

By s 2(1)(a), on the termination of a protected tenancy, the person who immediately before was the protected tenant of the dwelling will be the statutory tenant, if and so long as he occupies the dwelling as his residence.

The second security provision, s 98, provides that a court shall not make an order for possession of a dwelling let on a protected or statutory tenancy unless the provisions of that section and Sch 15 are satisfied. Each of the security provisions is considered in more detail below.

3.4.1 Statutory tenancies

It is clear from the wording of s 2 of the RA 1977 that it is a necessary prerequisite to becoming a statutory tenant that the tenant must be an individual capable of occupying the dwelling, even though this was not necessary in order to have protected tenant status (*Eaton Square Properties Ltd v O'Higgins* (2001) 33 HLR 771, CA; see **3.2**). By s 2(1)(b) and Pt I of Sch 1 to the RA 1977, the statutory security can be given not just to the original tenant, but also to his spouse and/or other family member on the death of the original tenant (see **3.4.1.3**).

3.4.1.1 Statutory tenant status

A statutory tenancy, unlike the protected tenancy that preceded it, is not an interest in land but is a personal right – what has been called a 'status of irremovability' for as long as the tenant continues to occupy the dwelling as a residence (*Keeves v Dean* [1924] 1 KB 685). However, the courts have been generous in their interpretation of continued residence, even where the tenant has been absent for considerable periods of time. The requirement is that the tenant should have an intention to return and display outward signs of that intention. It has been held that leaving furniture in the dwelling may be sufficient outward evidence of the intention to return (*Brown v Brash* [1948] 2 KB 247, CA).

> **CASE EXAMPLES**
>
> In *Bevington v Crawford* (1974) 232 EG 191, CA, a tenant spent only 10 days each year in his rented flat in Harrow, with his furniture and belongings left there. He spent nine months of the year working in France, where he rented another flat. It was held that he still occupied the Harrow flat as his residence in England and had security under the RA 1977.
>
> Similarly, in *Gofor Investments v Roberts* (1975) 29 P & CR 366, CA, it was held that a family living abroad for up to 10 years, but who displayed an intention to return, continued to occupy the dwelling for what could be considered a reasonable period.

However, the tenant must occupy the dwelling as a residence, not just use it as a base.

> **CASE EXAMPLE**
>
> In *Hampstead Way Investments Ltd v Lewis-Weare* [1985] 1 WLR 164, HL, a tenant spent five nights each week in a rented flat, to avoid disturbing his wife and children as he worked unsociable hours. He made very little use of the flat otherwise. He ate all his meals and spent the other two nights of the week in a house half a mile away, where his wife and family lived. It was held that the tenant could not be said to occupy the flat as a residence and so was not a statutory tenant within s 2(1).

3.4.1.2 Terms of the statutory tenancy

The statutory tenant occupies the dwelling under the terms and conditions of the original contractual tenancy, in so far as they are consistent with the provisions of the Act (RA 1977, s 3(1)). Implied into that contract, if not already expressed, will be a requirement that the statutory tenant give the landlord access to carry out repairs (s 3(2)), and that the tenant give at least three months' notice to quit, unless a shorter time is stipulated in the original contract (s 3(3)). However, the landlord does not have to serve a notice to quit on the statutory tenant, before obtaining a court order for possession (s 3(4)).

3.4.1.3 Succession to a statutory tenancy

On the death of the regulated tenant, any spouse or civil partner who was residing in the dwelling-house immediately before the tenant's death, or a person who was living with the tenant as a spouse or civil partner, will become the statutory tenant of the property (RA 1977, Sch 1, para 2, as amended) (see *Nutting v Southern Housing Group* [2004] EWHC 2982 (Ch) on 'living with', as discussed at **2.4.3**). The successor will remain a statutory tenant for as long as he or she continues to occupy the dwelling as his or her residence. This category of successor tenant is known as the 'first successor' (RA 1977, Sch 1, para 4).

If there is no surviving spouse or equivalent then a member of the tenant's family who was residing with the tenant for the two years up to the date of death may succeed to the tenancy. However, the succession will be to an assured tenancy of the dwelling (RA 1977, Sch 1, para 3(1), as amended; and see **Chapter 2**).

It is also possible for there to be a second succession. Where a person who was residing with the first successor for the two years immediately before his death was related to the first successor and the original tenant (eg, a child of the original tenant and the first successor), that person will be entitled to an assured tenancy of the dwelling by succession (RA 1977, Sch 1, para 6, as amended; and see **Chapter 2**).

If there is more than one person eligible to succeed to a statutory tenancy, either as a first or as a second succession, the parties can decide who will succeed, or failing agreement the court will decide (RA 1977, Sch 1, paras 2(3) and 3(1), as amended).

It can be seen that only a spouse or civil partner can succeed to a statutory tenancy. Other family members, whether they succeed directly from the original tenant or follow on from the successor spouse (the first successor), will obtain only an assured tenancy by succession. Regulated tenancies will thus cease after the original tenant and any spouse or equivalent have died. However, regulated tenancies could still be with us, in ever-decreasing numbers, for some considerable time into the 21st century.

3.4.2 Limitations on recovery of possession

The landlord will be able to recover possession from a RA 1977 regulated tenant only if he can bring the claim within one of three distinct categories:

(a) he is offering the tenant suitable alternative accommodation and the court considers it reasonable to make a possession order;

(b) he is claiming under one of the Cases listed in Pt I of Sch 15 to the RA 1977, he has established the Case and the court considers it reasonable to make a possession order; or

(c) he is claiming under one of the Cases listed in Pt II of Sch 15 to the RA 1977 and he has established the Case. In this instance the court must make a possession order.

3.4.2.1 Suitable alternative accommodation

This basis of claim is the same as that in Ground 9 for assured tenants (see **2.6.2.2**). The alternative tenancy, where a secure tenancy is not on offer from the LHA, can be either a protected tenancy, other than one under which the landlord might recover possession of the dwelling under Pt II Cases, or a tenancy where the tenant is afforded security reasonably equivalent to that enjoyed by a regulated tenant (eg, an assured tenancy). The courts are very sympathetic to tenants who have occupied their rented properties for a number of years. This is so even where the tenant owns property of his own nearby, of which he could arguably obtain possession and move into (see *Fennbend Ltd v Millar* (1988) 20 HLR 19, CA; *Amrit Holdings Co Ltd v Shahbakhti* [2005] All ER (D) 37, CA).

3.4.2.2 Reasonableness test

The same criteria apply as for assured tenants – see **2.6.2.1**.

3.4.2.3 Cases in RA 1977, Sch 15, Pt I

The Cases listed in Pt I are similar to a number of those in Pt II of Sch 2 to the HA 1988 (see **2.6.2**). Both Parts are concerned with situations where the court may order possession if it considers it reasonable to do so. With the exceptions of Cases 8 and 9, the Cases in Pt I could be described as fault-based Cases, as the tenant has usually done something wrong, and it is this that gives the landlord the basis on which to seek possession.

Case 1 – recovery for rent arrears or breach of obligation

This Case has, in effect, two basis of claim: one is rent arrears; the other is breach of obligation. For assured tenants, these would be Grounds 10 and 12 respectively (see **2.6.2.3** and **2.6.2.5**). In *Cadogan Estates Ltd v McMahon* [2001] AC 378, HL, a statutory tenant became bankrupt. Although there was no term in the lease that he must not become bankrupt, the landlord had reserved a right to forfeit the lease if he did. It was held that the forfeiture clause created a condition that the tenant did not become bankrupt, which he had breached. This was held to be within Case 1 and a possession order was made.

Case 2 – recovery for nuisance, annoyance or criminal activity

This Case is much narrower in its scope than Ground 14 for assured tenants (see **2.6.2.7**). Here, the basis of claim is limited to the activities of the tenant only. It does not extend to others residing with the tenant, or to visitors who cause a nuisance or annoyance to adjoining occupiers.

The area of annoyance appears much narrower too. However, despite the much narrower definition of 'adjoining occupiers', rather than 'the locality', it was held in *Cobstone Investments Ltd v Maxim* [1985] QB 140, CA, that adjoining occupiers did not mean 'contiguous' but would extend to any premises sufficiently close or related so as to be affected by the nuisance.

Another difference is that in Case 2 the tenant must actually have caused a nuisance or annoyance. It does not extend to the 'likelihood' of causing nuisance or annoyance. However, it is enough that the tenant is convicted of using the dwelling for illegal or immoral purposes. The provision does not qualify the conviction by requiring it to be for an indictable offence.

Case 3 – recovery due to deterioration of the dwelling-house

Save that this provision does not extend to the common parts, it covers the same area as Ground 13 for assured tenants (see **2.6.2.6**).

Case 4 – recovery because of furniture deterioration

This Case is the same as Ground 15 for assured tenants (see **2.6.2.9**).

Case 5 – recovery from tenant who has given notice to quit

This Case will apply where the landlord has contracted to sell, or has taken other steps as a result of the tenant having given notice to quit, and so would be seriously prejudiced if he did not regain possession.

Case 6 – recovery for assignment or sub-letting of the whole of the dwelling without the landlord's consent

This Case is date sensitive. Not all tenants will be affected in the same way. An adviser would need to check when the tenancy commenced and see whether it is caught by the particular date provision.

> **CASE EXAMPLE**
>
> In *Pazgate Ltd v McGrath* [1984] 2 EGLR 130, CA, on the death of a protected tenant, his executors executed a vesting assent transferring the tenancy to the deceased tenant's daughter-in-law who lived in the flat. This was despite a prohibition in the tenancy agreement against assignment. In the subsequent possession claim under this Case, it was held that it was reasonable to make a possession order, as the assignee who occupied the flat could become a statutory tenant whereas the deceased tenant could not have done as he did not reside in the flat.

This Case will apply even where the tenant is, at common law, permitted lawfully to assign. This will be the case where the tenancy agreement does not specifically restrict it (see *Leith Properties Ltd v Springer* [1982] 3 All ER 731, CA).

Case 7 – repealed

Case 8 – recovery from former employee

This Case is similar to Ground 16 for assured tenants (see **2.6.2.10**).

Case 9 – recovery for occupancy by the landlord or other family member

This Case will apply where the landlord did not become the landlord by purchasing his interest in the property and he reasonably requires possession so that the dwelling can be occupied as a residence by either:

(a) himself; or
(b) any adult child of the landlord; or
(c) a parent of the landlord; or
(d) a parent of his spouse or civil partner.

In deciding whether to make a possession order, the court is required to consider whether greater hardship would be caused by granting the order than by refusing it (RA 1977, Sch 15, Pt III). The burden of proving greater hardship is on the defendant.

This Case has given rise to a substantial amount of case law, not least in recent years. There have been several recent cases looking at a number of different issues, including greater hardship, the eligibility of the proposed occupier and whether the landlord became a landlord by purchase.

In *Baker v MacIver and MacIver* (1990) 22 HLR 328, CA, it was held that on the evidence, the landlord was financially better off and had the opportunity of suitable alternative protected premises, which the tenant did not. On this basis, the Court of Appeal took the unusual step of overturning the county court judge's findings of greater hardship in favour of the landlord and allowed the tenant's appeal against the possession order.

The Court of Appeal was not, however, prepared to find the decision of the trial judge perverse in *Hodges v Blee* [1987] 2 EGLR 119, CA. There, the tenant, a man of 57 who was on housing and supplementary benefits, had occupied the flat for 15 years. He had two large dogs to which he was attached. The evidence was that he would not be entitled to be re-housed by the LHA. Against this was the claim to occupy as a residence of the landlord's two adult sons, who were in good jobs but had unsatisfactory accommodation. The Court indicated that it might have come to a different conclusion on greater hardship, but would not interfere with the judge's decision to give possession to the landlord.

In *Mansukhani v Sharkey* [1992] 2 EGLR 105, CA, it was held that where parents had transferred their interest in a flat to their son, but subject to his covenanting to pay off the mortgage on the property, he was not a landlord by purchase and so could rely on Case 9 to obtain possession of the flat. However, in *Amaddio v Dalton* (1991) 23 HLR 332, CA, the claimant had been an employee of the previous owner of the property, R, who had had only a life interest in the property. On R's death she expressed the wish that the claimant be offered the property for its market value and, if he wished to buy it, that it be paid for out of her estate. It was held that the claimant was a landlord by purchase and so could not rely on Case 9 against the statutory tenant in occupation of one of the flats at the property. However, where one joint beneficiary to a property buys out the others, this will not result in there being a landlord by purchase (see *Thomas v Fryer* [1970] 1 WLR 845, CA).

In *Postos v Theodotou* [1991] 2 EGLR 93, CA, the issue was whether the natural son of one only of two joint landlords was within Case 9. It was held, adopting a purposive construction of the provision, that he was, even though both joint landlords would need to show that they required possession for their own occupation (see *McIntyre v Hardcastle* [1948] 2 KB 82, CA).

Where, however, the landlord obtains possession under this Case or Case 8 by misrepresentation or concealment of material facts, s 102 of the RA 1977 entitles the tenant to be compensated on a tortious basis. In *Clements v Simmonds* [2002] EWHC 1652 (QB), the statutory tenant recovered £60,000 compensation for loss of her statutory tenancy when the landlady recovered possession under Case 9 and then two weeks later put the property on the market and sold it for £1,250,000.

Case 10 – recovery for over-charging a sub-tenant of the dwelling

Where a regulated tenant has sub-let part of the dwelling and rent has been registered in relation to the dwelling, the tenant will risk possession under this Case if he charges in excess of the fair rent which has been registered for that part (see **3.5.1** for fair rents).

3.4.2.4 Cases in RA 1977, Sch 15, Pt II

Part II of Sch 15 contains Cases for which, if established by the landlord, the court must order possession. Unlike the position with assured tenants, where Ground 8 (serious rent arrears) is a mandatory ground for possession, there are no fault-based Cases for possession in this Part. All 10 Cases in Pt II require the tenant to have had advance written notice that possession could be obtained under one of these Cases.

Case 11 – recovery by owner occupier

This Case is similar to the first part of Ground 1 for assured tenants (see **2.6.1.1**). It is limited to an owner occupier who gave written notice of intention to resume occupation at the beginning of the tenancy. However, as with assured tenants, the court can dispense with the notice if it considers it just and equitable to do so.

In *Davies v Peterson* [1989] 1 EGLR 121, CA, the landlord obtained possession under Case 11, on the basis that he wished to reside in the dwelling whenever he visited London. The landlord normally lived and worked abroad. The trial judge had exercised his discretion to dispense with the written notice requirement, as the landlord had given the tenant oral notice of his intention.

There are additional alternate provisions for obtaining possession in Sch 15, Pt V – for example, that possession is required not for the owner but for a member of his family who lived with him when he last occupied the dwelling, or the owner has died and the dwelling is required for a member of his family who was residing with him at the time of his death. It is under Pt V that the equivalent of Ground 2 (recovery by mortgagee) is also available (see **2.6.1.2**).

Case 12 – recovery for occupation as a retirement home

This Case is similar to the second part of Ground 1 for assured tenants (see **2.6.1.1**). However, Case 12 is somewhat more restricted, as the purpose is stated to be for retirement. As above, the court can dispense with notice, and there are additional alternate provisions for obtaining possession in Sch 15, Pt V.

Case 13 – recovery of out-of-season holiday lettings

This Case is identical to Ground 3 for assured tenants (see **2.6.1.3**).

Case 14 – recovery of student accommodation

This Case is identical to Ground 4 for assured tenants (see **2.6.1.4**).

Case 15 – recovery of premises for a minister of religion

This Case is identical to Ground 5 for assured tenants (see **2.6.1.5**).

Cases 16, 17 and 18 – recovery of premises to let to agricultural employees

These three Cases all relate to agricultural workers being let premises, where they were given written notice at the beginning of the tenancy that possession might be required under the particular Case.

Case 19 – recovery from a protected shorthold tenant

This Case relates to tenancies that can no longer be created and most of which have probably expired. Protected shorthold tenancies were the intermediate category between fully regulated and assured shorthold tenancies. They had the benefit of the fair rent system (see **3.5.1**), but no security after expiry of the fixed term. Introduced by the HA 1980 (and since repealed), they were for fixed terms of between one and five years. After expiry the landlord was entitled to possession under this Case, provided the appropriate written notice was served at least three months before expiry of the term or an anniversary of the term.

By s 34 of the HA 1988, no new protected shorthold tenancies can be created, and any new tenancy granted by the same landlord to the same tenant after 15 January 1989 will be an assured shorthold tenancy. For any tenant who was granted a protected shorthold tenancy and who has not been granted a new tenancy since 15 January 1989, but simply holds over, the landlord will need to follow the procedure in this Case to obtain possession (see *Gent v De la Mare* (1988) 20 HLR 199, CA).

Case 20 – recovery for occupation by a member of the regular armed forces

This Case is intended to achieve the same objective as Cases 11 and 12, except it specifically relates to an owner who was a member of the regular armed forces when he acquired the dwelling and when he let it to the tenant. As with Cases 11 and 12, written notice must have been given to the tenant at the beginning of the tenancy that possession could be obtained to enable the owner to occupy the dwelling as a residence. However, here too the court has a discretion to dispense with the requirement for written notice. The alternative provisions for obtaining possession in Sch 15, Pt V, apply here too.

3.5 RENTS UNDER REGULATED TENANCIES

Parts III and IV of the RA 1977 set out the provisions dealing with the process for and effect of registration of a fair rent on a dwelling. Supporting anti-avoidance provisions in Pt IX make it an offence to charge a premium for the grant, renewal, continuance or assignment of a protected tenancy. Paradoxically, the main reason for the introduction of Rent Act legislation, ie to fix affordable rents, has been rendered almost redundant as a direct result of the availability in large numbers of assured shorthold tenancies in the residential market.

3.5.1 Determination of a fair rent

The basis for determining a fair rent involves taking account of all relevant circumstances, including the age, character, locality and state of repair of the dwelling, and any furniture provided. Disregarded is any deterioration or improvement of the dwelling attributable to the tenant (RA 1977, s 70).

The most significant assumption made in s 70(2) is that supply equals demand, so that a fair rent should not include any scarcity value. A rent officer, who, under s 67, is the person to whom application for a determination is made, must assume that supply equals demand in assessing a fair rent.

In *Spath Holme Ltd v Chairman of Greater Manchester and Lancashire Rent Assessment Committee* (1996) 28 HLR 107, CA, it was held that various methods could be used in assessing a fair rent. This could include the use of comparable fair rents and comparable assured tenancy rents in the area. However, as more and more residential properties have become available for letting since the introduction of assured and assured shorthold tenancies, in many areas there is now no scarcity of accommodation. As a result, landlords repeatedly argued to rent assessment committees, when challenging a determination made by a rent officer (see **3.5.2** below), that there should be no reduction to take account of a non-existent scarcity value. Landlords argued that the fair rent, according to the s 70 criteria, should be the market rent. This argument succeeded in *Curtis v London Rent Assessment Committee (No 2)* [1999] QB 92, CA, where the distinction between a fair rent and a market rent was successfully challenged as an artificial one.

However, Parliament responded very quickly with the introduction of the Rent Acts (Maximum Fair Rent) Order 1999 (SI 1999/6). The aim of this provision is to reduce the impact on fair rents that decisions like *Curtis* would otherwise have on them. The Order limits the maximum rent increase to RPI plus 7.5% on a first re-registration, and subsequent increases are limited to RPI plus 5%. It is clear from these developments that the gap between 'fair' rents and 'market' rents will diminish over time.

The claimant in the *Spath Holme* case was so upset by the introduction of the 1999 Order that it took its case to the European Court of Human Rights in *Spath Holme Ltd v UK*, Application No 78031/01. However, it was unsuccessful in its challenge that the 1999 Order was an infringement of its rights under Article 1 of the First Protocol (peaceful enjoyment of possessions) (see **4.2.4**).

3.5.2 Effect of registration

By s 67 of the RA 1977, either the tenant or the landlord (or both together on a joint application) can apply to a rent officer, using the prescribed form, to register a fair rent for the property. Once registered that rent is the maximum rent that can be charged for that dwelling, unless an objection is raised by the landlord and/or the tenant. Schedule 11, paras 6, 7 and 8 make provision for any objection to the rent officer's determination to be referred to a rent assessment committee. The committee has the power to confirm the fair rent, or to make its own determination.

If the tenancy is still a contractual tenancy and the contractual rent is higher than the rent now registered for the dwelling, the tenant does not have to pay anything above the registered rent from the date of registration (s 44). However, where the registered rent is higher than the contractual rent, something that is not unheard of, the landlord can serve a notice of increase, in the prescribed form, on a periodic tenant to increase the rent to the higher registered figure (s 49). This will have the effect of terminating the contractual tenancy. For a fixed-term tenant, the landlord will have to wait until the term has expired before he can increase the rent to the registered amount.

The registered rent is binding on the parties and on future tenancies of the property until there is a re-registration (s 67(3)) or a cancellation of the registered rent (s 73). This will be so even if the rent was registered on the basis of an unfurnished dwelling and the property is subsequently let as a furnished dwelling (see *Rakhit v Carty* [1990] 2 QB 315, CA).

If it transpires, as it did in *Rakhit v Carty*, that the contractual rent the tenant has been paying exceeds a previously registered rent on the dwelling, the tenant can recover any excess for a period of up to two years (RA 1977, s 57).

3.5.3 Basis for re-registration

The rent cannot be re-registered for a period of two years, unless there has been a change in the condition of the dwelling-house that justifies a re-application within that time (s 67(3)).

> **CASE EXAMPLE**
>
> In *R v Rent Officer of West Sussex Registration Area, ex p Haysport Properties Ltd* [2001] EWCA 237, CA, a rent was determined taking account of the fact that the premises were seriously unfit and subject to a local housing authority repairs notice. Within a month of the registration the landlord had carried out the necessary works and re-applied for a new fair rent. On appeal against the rent officer's decision that there was no change in the condition of the premises to warrant a re-evaluation of the rent, the Court of Appeal held that the carrying out of repairs which transformed the house from one that was unfit into one fit for human habitation must be regarded as a change in the 'condition' of the premises sufficient to warrant reconsideration of the rent.

3.6 REGISTERED RENTS FOR HOUSING ASSOCIATION TENANTS

Although housing association tenants were excluded from protected tenant status by s 15, Pt VI of the RA 1977 provided that housing association tenants could have a fair rent under the rent registration system. This provision is applicable to residential housing association tenancies that existed prior to 15 January 1989. Most of these were also secure tenancies under the HA 1985 provisions. Thus secure tenants of many RSL and PRP landlords enjoy public sector secure status, as well as the benefits of regulated rents under Pt VI of the RA 1977.

3.7 FURTHER READING

M Barnes et al, *Hill and Redman's Law of Landlord and Tenant*

SUMMARY

- Rent Act tenancies are regulated tenancies because they are subject to a regulated rent.
- Regulated tenancies can be:
    (a) protected, ie during the contractual period of the tenancy; or
    (b) statutory – the status of irremovability that continues the tenancy after the contractual period has terminated.
- The exclusions from Rent Act protection and the grounds for possession have similarities with those for assured tenancies.
- No new Rent Act tenancy can be created after 15 January 1989 when the HA 1988 came into effect and introduced the assured tenancy regime.

CHAPTER 4

HOUSING AND HUMAN RIGHTS

4.1	Introduction	47
4.2	The rights relevant to housing law	47
4.3	The effect of the main rights	48
4.4	The courts' interpretation	48
4.5	The scope for legal challenge to UK housing law	49
4.6	Procedure for human rights claims	55
4.7	Further reading	57
	Summary	57

LEARNING OUTCOMES

After reading this chapter you will be able to:

- explain the relevant ECHR provisions applicable to housing law
- understand the concepts of margin of appreciation and proportionality
- explain the situations in which human rights challenges have been successful in housing law cases
- describe the procedure for dealing with Article 8 challenges in the county court.

4.1 INTRODUCTION

While many provisions of international human rights treaties recognise housing as a fundamental right (eg, Article 25(1) of the Universal Declaration of Human Rights 1948), the European Convention for the Protection of Human Rights and Fundamental Freedoms 1950 (the Convention), most of which is now a part of UK law, does not. In *Chapman v UK* (2001) 10 BHRC 48, a decision in the European Court of Human Rights (ECtHR), it was held that Article 8 of the Convention does not give a right to be provided with a home. Even before that decision a large part of the Convention had been incorporated into UK law, implemented by the Human Rights Act (HRA) 1998, which came into force on 2 October 2000.

4.2 THE RIGHTS RELEVANT TO HOUSING LAW

The provisions of the Convention incorporated into UK law are contained in Sch 1 to the HRA 1998. The provisions that would normally be relevant to housing law disputes are Articles 6, 8 and 14, plus Article 1 of the First Protocol.

Article 6
Right to a fair trial

1. In the determination of his civil rights and obligations ... everyone is entitled to a fair and public hearing within a reasonable time by an independent and impartial tribunal established by law. Judgment shall be pronounced publicly but the press and public may be excluded from all or part of the trial in the interest of morals, public order or national security in a democratic society ...

Article 8
Right to respect for private and family life

1. Everyone has the right to respect for his private and family life, his home and his correspondence.

2. There shall be no interference by a public authority with the exercise of this right except such as is in accordance with the law and is necessary in a democratic society in the interests of national security, public safety or the economic well-being of the country, for the prevention of disorder or crime, for the protection of health or morals, or for the protection of the rights and freedoms of others.

Article 14

Prohibition of discrimination

The enjoyment of the rights and freedoms set forth in this Convention shall be secured without discrimination on any ground such as sex, race, colour, language, religion, political or other opinion, national or social origin, association with a national minority, property, birth or other status.

Article 1

The First Protocol

Protection of property

Every natural or legal person is entitled to the peaceful enjoyment of his possessions. No one shall be deprived of his possessions except in the public interest and subject to the conditions provided for by law and by the general principles of international law.

The preceding provisions shall not, however, in any way impair the right of a State to enforce such laws as it deems necessary to control the use of property in accordance with the general interest or to secure the payment of taxes or other contributions or penalties.

4.3 THE EFFECT OF THE MAIN RIGHTS

It can be seen that the main substantive right is in Article 8, the right to respect for one's home. It is, however, a qualified right, in that justified interference from the State is permissible. The right given under Article 1 of the First Protocol is even more limited, in that the State can deprive an individual of this right if it serves the general interest. (See *James v UK* (1986) 8 EHRR 123, freeholder's complaint about rights of long leaseholders to enfranchise; and *Mellacher v Austria* (1989) 12 EHRR 391, ECtHR, landlord complaint about statutory rent control. In both cases the complaint was not upheld.) Article 6 is a procedural provision which ensures that where a person's civil rights, which includes Convention rights, are at risk, proper procedure must be followed and a fair hearing given to the person (see *Tsyfayo v UK* [2007] HLR 19). Article 14 does not stand alone but needs to be based on the infringement of some other Convention right.

Another provision worth mentioning here is Article 3 of the Convention (the prohibition of torture), which provides that no one shall be subjected to torture, or to inhuman or degrading treatment or punishment. It is a provision that has been successfully pleaded by destitute asylum seekers (see **4.5.7**).

4.4 THE COURTS' INTERPRETATION

4.4.1 Compatability with Convention rights

Section 3 of the HRA 1998 provides that so far as it is possible to do so, primary legislation and subordinate legislation must be read and given effect in a way which is compatible with the Convention rights. Section 6 makes it unlawful for a public authority to act in a way which is incompatible with a Convention right. A court of law is included in the definition of 'public authority', as is any person with functions of a public nature, which would include LHAs and, in certain situations, perhaps an RSL or PRP (see *Poplar HARCA Ltd v Donoghue* [2002] QB 48, CA).

In *R (Weaver) v London & Quadrant Housing Trust* [2010] 1 WLR 363, CA, it was held that an RSL may be treated as a public body within the HRA 1998 when performing its management functions. The factors which influenced the decision were:

(a) the RSL's work was subsidised by the State, here in the form of capital grants;

(b) the RSL was granted special intrusive powers by law, such as the power to apply for an anti-social behaviour order;

(c) the RSL was working closely with local government to help the LHA achieve its duties under the law both with voluntary transfers and housing applicants from the LHA's waiting list; and

(d) the RSL was providing a public service of a type which the Government would normally provide, ie, providing housing at below market rents.

The Court of Appeal held that the key question in the case was whether the act of termination was a private or public act within s 6(5) of the HRA 1998. Lord Justice Elias went on to state that:

> In my judgment the Trust is a hybrid public authority and the act of terminating a tenancy is not a private act. It does not necessarily follow, however, that every RSL providing social housing will necessarily be in the same position as the Trust. The determination of the public status of a body is fact sensitive. For example, a potentially important difference is that apparently some RSLs have not received any public subsidy at all, and arguably – and I put it no higher than that – their position could be different.

Where a court cannot interpret legislation in a way which is compatible with the Convention rights, a declaration of incompatibility may be made by the court (HRA 1998, s 4). This has occurred in two housing law cases (R (Morris) v Westminster City Council; R (Badu) v Lambeth LBC [2005] EWCA Civ 1184, [2006] 1 WLR 505 (see **4.5.1** for the facts of this case), and Leeds City Council v Price [2005] 1 WLR 1825, CA (see **4.5.5** for a discussion relating to this case)).

In addition, the ECtHR has found UK housing law to be incompatible with Convention rights in Connors v UK [2004] 4 PLR 16 (see **4.4.2**) and in Tsyfayo v UK (see **4.3** above), which was concerned with an Article 6 violation in a housing benefit dispute.

4.4.2 The margin of appreciation given to national legislature in housing matters

Housing law affects social and economic policies in society, and consequently the ECtHR and (now) the UK courts have held that the legislature must be given a wide margin of appreciation (ie, a large amount of discretion). In Connors v UK [2004] 4 PLR 16, the court restated that in spheres such as housing, which play a central role in the welfare and economic policies of modern societies, it will respect the legislature's judgement as to what is in the general interest, unless that judgement is manifestly without reasonable foundation. However, where the right at stake is crucial to the individual's effective enjoyment of intimate or key rights (eg, respect for private and family life under Article 8 of the Convention), the margin of appreciation will be narrower.

In Connors, gypsies were evicted from a site they had occupied for about 15 years, after their licence to occupy was terminated. They were given no opportunity to argue the legitimacy of the right to terminate the licence and their application for judicial review was refused. The ECtHR held that their Article 8 rights had been violated as there had not been adequate procedural safeguards. The lack of any requirement to establish proper justification for the serious interference with the applicant's rights was not proportionate to the legitimate aim that had been pursued. See also Buckland v UK [2013] HLR 2, ECtHR.

4.5 THE SCOPE FOR LEGAL CHALLENGE TO UK HOUSING LAW

The persistence of housing lawyers in repeatedly challenging areas of UK housing law considered to be an infringement of human rights has finally resulted in a significant victory. For many years the courts had taken a rather conservative view and, in many cases, not found UK housing law to be incompatible with Convention rights. In some areas Article 8(1) was recognised as being engaged, but the courts held that there had been no violation of the right as the interference was justifiable under Article 8(2). The decision in Manchester City Council v Pinnock [2010] UKSC 45 now establishes that the Article 8 Convention right may be raised as a defence in housing law cases where a social landlord seeks possession and the occupier is at risk of losing his home (see **4.5.3.2**).

Outlined below are some of the areas of housing law where challenges have been made.

4.5.1 Homelessness

In *Chapman v UK* (2001) 10 BHRC 48, the ECtHR restated the point, made in earlier cases, that Article 8 does not give a right to be provided with a home. The provisions of the HA 1996, providing for certain categories of people who are homeless (see **Chapter 11**), go beyond what is required by the Convention. As a result, it would normally be difficult successfully to challenge the operation of the homelessness provisions under Article 8. This is illustrated in *Ekinci v Hackney LBC* [2001] EWCA Civ 776, CA. The applicant claimed a breach of Article 8 when the LHA refused to recognise him as being in priority need on the basis that his 17-year-old wife was a dependent child. Pill LJ stated (at [16] and [17]):

> Article 8(1) does not require applicants with child spouses to be given priority over applicants with adult spouses or over other categories of applicant. To find in favour of the applicant would undoubtedly 'promote [his] private life and privacy', but to hold that he does not have the priority over other applicants which he claims does not involve the lack of the respect contemplated by Article 8(1).

However, it would appear that if there is unjustifiable discrimination in the way in which the housing provisions operate, the court is more likely to find a violation of Article 8. In *R (Morris) v Westminster City Council; R (Badu) v Lambeth LBC* [2005] EWCA Civ 1184, [2006] 1 WLR 505 the claimant was able successfully to challenge the homelessness provision on the basis of a failure to promote family life. The claimant and her daughter, of whom the claimant had sole care, came to the UK from Mauritius as visitors. The claimant subsequently successfully applied for British citizenship for herself, but it was thought at that time that her daughter was not eligible, so she remained a Mauritius national. The claimant applied to the defendant LHA as a homeless person. Her application was refused on the basis that she was not in priority need. Her daughter's immigration status, as a person from abroad, was such that the claimant could not rely on it to establish priority (see **11.2.1** on the status of persons from abroad).

The claimant alleged unjustifiable infringement of her Article 8 right and discrimination in breach of Article 14. The Court held that the relevant provisions of the HA 1996 were intended to promote family life and so engaged Article 8. This made Article 14 potentially applicable. The claimant's treatment was different to others on the basis of national origin. Although the difference in treatment was intended to pursue legitimate aims, the judge was of the view that it was unlikely those aims would be achieved, and on that basis the difference in treatment was not justified. As a result the LHA's decision amounted to an infringement of the claimant's right under Article 14 to enjoy without discrimination respect for her family life under Article 8. The Court upheld a declaration of incompatibility.

(See also **4.5.6** for other discrimination challenges.)

4.5.2 Duty to provide a suitable home

Whilst accepting the principle in *Chapman v UK* (see **4.5.1** above) to be correct, the Court of Appeal in *Anufrijeva v Southwark LBC* [2004] QB 1124, CA, agreed that once a duty to provide accommodation did arise, an LHA could be in breach of Article 8 of the Convention if it failed to provide a suitable home. This was the case in *R (Bernard) v Enfield London BC* [2002] EWHC Admin 2282, where a duty to provide accommodation had arisen under s 21 of the National Assistance Act 1948 as a consequence of the claimant's physical disabilities. Sullivan J held that the LHA was liable in damages to the claimant for breach of Article 8, when it left the claimant and her family residing in degrading conditions for 20 months. Lord Woolf CJ in *Anufrijeva* stated (at p 1140):

> Sullivan J was correct to accept that Article 8 is capable of imposing on a State a positive obligation to provide support. We find it hard to conceive, however, of a situation in which the predicament of an individual will be such that Article 8 requires him to be provided with welfare support, where his predicament is not sufficiently severe to engage Article 3 [degrading treatment, as was nearly the case

in Bernard though on the facts the judge held that Article 3 had not been infringed]. Article 8 may more readily be engaged where a family unit is involved. Where the welfare of children is at stake, Article 8 may require the provision of welfare support in a manner which enables family life to continue.

4.5.3 Possession claims

In this field it would appear that it will be only in rare cases that the courts will uphold a challenge to the housing authority's right to seek possession when it has followed the procedural provisions of the housing legislation and, as held in *Pinnock*, has acted reasonably and proportionately. However, it is important that proper procedures are followed. The procedural process in Article 6 should be observed in possession claims to avoid successful challenges on those grounds. This was made clear in *Moat Housing Group – South Ltd v Harris* [2005] EWCA Civ 287, CA, where the Court held, citing *Connors v UK* [2004] 4 PLR 16, that Convention jurisprudence makes clear that the right to respect for a home has inherent in it the principle that procedural fairness will be observed before the home is taken away.

4.5.3.1 LHA seeking possession after terminating tenancy on discretionary ground

Where possession is being sought under one of the discretionary grounds (see **6.7**), which give the court the power to decide whether or not an order should be made, the defendant has extremely limited, if any, grounds for complaint of an Article 8 violation, as held in *Gallagher v Castle Vale Action Trust Ltd* (2001) 33 HLR 72, CA. In that case, the claimant appealed against a 28-day possession order, terminating her secure tenancy of 15 years as a result of anti-social behaviour by members of her household. The Court allowed her appeal on the basis that the trial judge had failed to consider the possibility of suspending the order. The Court also held, however, that the Convention right added nothing to the requirement of reasonableness contained in the 1985 Act, or to the court's approach to such cases (see **2.6.2.1** above on reasonableness).

The point was made clear beyond doubt by Lord Neuberger in *Manchester City Council v Pinnock* (see **4.5** above) at paras 55 and 56:

> [N]o order for possession can be made against a secure tenant unless, inter alia, it is reasonable to make the order. Any factor which has to be taken into account, or any dispute of fact which has to be resolved, for the purpose of assessing proportionality under Article 8(2), would have to be taken into account or resolved for the purpose of assessing reasonableness under section 84 of the [HA 1985]. Reasonableness under that section, like proportionality under Article 8(2), requires the court to consider whether to order possession at all, and, if so, whether to make an outright order rather than a suspended order, and, if so, whether to direct that the outright order should not take effect for a significant time.
>
> It therefore seems highly unlikely, as a practical matter, that it could be reasonable for a court to make an order for possession in circumstances in which it would be disproportionate to do so under Article 8.

4.5.3.2 LHA or PRP seeking possession in non-discretionary cases

Even where an occupier does not enjoy the full security and safeguards granted to secure tenants in the HA 1985 (see **Chapter 6**), which gives the court the discretion to decide whether or not a possession order should be made, until recently the courts had been reluctant to limit the margin of appreciation given to LHAs in dealing with their housing stock.

There are a number of situations in which an LHA may seek possession where the court does not have discretion. For example, this would be the case in relation to temporary accommodation given to a homeless applicant (see **11.7.3** and **11.7.5**). The tenant has no security of tenure and so a notice to quit will terminate the tenancy (see *Sheffield City Council v Smart; Central Sunderland Housing Co Ltd v Wilson* [2002] HLR 639).

Another example would be the case where one joint tenant has terminated the joint tenancy by serving the landlord with a valid notice to quit (see **6.8.1**). The remaining joint tenant has no legal right to remain in the property and would be a trespasser against whom, legally, an LHA would be entitled to possession (see *Kay v Lambeth LBC; Price v Leeds City Council* [2006] 2 AC 465, HL).

A third example is where an LHA has the right to possession against a demoted (see **6.6.3**) or an introductory tenant (see **6.5.3**) once the procedural process has been complied with (see *Manchester City Council v Pinnock*, **4.5** above).

Until *Manchester City Council v Pinnock*, the Supreme Court had maintained that it was not open to a defendant to have the proportionality of the LHA's actions, based on the defendant's personal circumstances, taken into account in any of these cases. However, in this historic decision a nine-member UK Supreme Court departed from its own previous decisions in three cases – namely, *Harrow LBC v Qazi* [2004] 1 AC 983, *Kay v Lambeth LBC* (above) and *Doherty v Birmingham City Council* [2009] 1 AC 367 – and decided that Article 8 defences can be raised in possession proceedings in the county court.

Lord Neuberger, who gave the judgment of the Court in *Pinnock*, stated (at para 45):

> [T]he following propositions are now well established in the jurisprudence of the European court:
>
> (a) Any person at risk of being dispossessed of his home at the suit of a local authority should in principle have the right to raise the question of the proportionality of the measure, and to have it determined by an independent tribunal in the light of Article 8, even if his right of occupation under domestic law has come to an end: *McCann v United Kingdom* 47 EHRR 913, para 50; *Zehentner v Austria* given 16 July 2009, para 59; ...
>
> (b) A judicial procedure which is limited to addressing the proportionality of the measure through the medium of traditional judicial review (ie, one which does not permit the court to make its own assessment of the facts in an appropriate case) is inadequate as it is not appropriate for resolving sensitive factual issues: *Connors v United Kingdom* 40 EHRR 189, para 92; *McCann v United Kingdom* 47 EHRR 913, para 53; *Kay v United Kingdom*, paras 72–73.
>
> (c) Where the measure includes proceedings involving more than one stage, it is the proceedings as a whole which must be considered in order to see if Article 8 has been complied with: *Zehentner v Austria*, para 54.
>
> (d) If the court concludes that it would be disproportionate to evict a person from his home notwithstanding the fact that he has no domestic right to remain there, it would be unlawful to evict him so long as the conclusion obtains – for example, for a specified period, or until a specified event occurs, or a particular condition is satisfied.
>
> Although it cannot be described as a point of principle, it seems that the European court has also franked the view that it will only be in exceptional cases that Article 8 proportionality would even arguably give a right to continued possession where the applicant has no right under domestic law to remain: *McCann v United Kingdom* 47 EHRR 913, para 54; *Kay v United Kingdom*, para 73.

In applying these principles to domestic law in situations where the court does not have discretion, Lord Neuberger continued (at para 57):

> The implications of Article 8 being potentially in play are much more significant where a local authority is seeking possession of a person's home in circumstances in which domestic law imposes no requirement of reasonableness and gives an unqualified right to an order for possession. In such a case the court's obligation under Article 8(2), to consider the proportionality of making the order sought, does represent a potential new obstacle to the making of an order for possession.

The *Pinnock* case related to a possession claim under s 143D(2) of the HA 1996 against a demoted tenant (see **6.6.3**). A demotion order had been obtained against the tenant (P) because of a long history of crime, nuisance and harassment by P's five children. The criminal and anti-social behaviour continued after the demotion order was made, and the landlord sought possession. P argued that he should not lose his home of over 30 years because of the behaviour of his children who no longer lived at the property. The Supreme Court decided that the demoted tenancy regime was compatible with Article 8. Section 143D(2) should be read as allowing the court to exercise the powers which are necessary to consider, and where appropriate to give effect to, any Article 8 defence raised by a defendant in possession proceedings. Applying proportionality to the facts, the Supreme Court decided that the possession order made against the defendant should stand, as it was proportionate on the facts of that case.

In *Hounslow LBC v Powell; Leeds City Council v Hall and Birmingham City Council v Frisby* [2011] 2 WLR 287, a seven-member Supreme Court applied the principles in *Pinnock* to possession claims defended by a homeless applicant whose tenancy had been terminated by the LHA (Powell) and two introductory tenants against whom the LHAs were seeking possession (Hall and Frisby).

In giving judgment in *Powell*, Lord Hope reinforced what had been said in *Pinnock*. Lord Hope stated (at para 33):

> The court will only have to consider whether the making of a possession order is proportionate if the issue has been raised by the occupier and it has crossed the high threshold of being seriously arguable. The question will then be whether making an order for the occupier's eviction is a proportionate means of achieving a legitimate aim. But it will, of course, be necessary in each case for the court first to consider whether the property in question constitutes the defendant's 'home' for the purposes of Article 8. This is because it is only where a person's 'home' is under threat that Article 8 comes into play (Pinnock, para 61).

CASE EXAMPLE

In *West Kent Housing Association Ltd v Haycraft* [2012] EWCA Civ 276, the landlord served a s 21 HA 1988 notice on its starter tenant (H) and obtained a court order for possession. H challenged the possession order citing breach of his Article 8 rights. The background facts were that a vulnerable neighbour had made an allegation of indecent exposure against H, which was investigated by the landlord and the police. There were further allegations of nuisance made against him. The landlord started possession proceedings. However, at H's instigation, the landlord carried out a formal review of the decision to end his tenancy. A hearing panel concluded that H was guilty of the indecent exposure and upheld the decision to seek possession.

The Court of Appeal held that the trial judge was right to grant the possession order without hearing evidence, as it was clear on the facts that it was a case that could not succeed and so should not take up valuable court time.

(See also *Corby BC v Scott* [2012] EWCA Civ 276; *Fareham BC v Miller* [2013] HLR 22, CA; *Thurrock BC v West* [2013] HLR 5, CA.)

4.5.3.3 Warrants for possession

Once an outright possession order is granted, if the occupier does not vacate the property, a warrant for possession needs to be obtained from the court (see **10.11**). With a suspended possession order, the owner can apply for possession as soon as the terms of any suspension have been breached. In *St Brice v Southwark LBC* [2002] 1 WLR 1537, CA, it was held that there was no breach of either Articles 6 or 8 of the Convention when the LHA enforced the suspended possession order it had obtained, because the tenant had not complied with the terms of the suspension. The claimant's civil rights had been dealt with fairly at the possession hearing, and the application for the warrant was simply an administrative act to give effect to the earlier judicial process.

However, exceptionally, Article 8 may be raised at the enforcement stage where there has been a fundamental change in the personal circumstances of the defendant after a possession order has been made but before its enforcement. In *R (on the application of JL) v Secretary of State for Defence* [2013] HLR 27, CA, although JL had raised an Article 8 defence at the possession hearing, the case was heard pre-*Pinnock* so the defence was not allowed. In these exceptional circumstances, JL was allowed to raise an Article 8 defence at the enforcement stage. The Court made clear that generally, if the issue of proportionality under Article 8 was considered by the court at the possession hearing, or if the occupier failed to raise proportionality at that hearing, it would be an abuse of process for the occupier to challenge the decision to enforce the possession order on the basis that eviction would be disproportionate.

4.5.4 Succession claims

Article 14 of the Convention, in conjunction with Article 8, was successfully used in this field in *Ghaidan v Mendoza* [2004] 2 AC 557, HL, where it was held that there was no justification for the difference in treatment between heterosexual and same-sex couples. In this case, however, the House of Lords did not make a declaration of incompatibility, as the majority felt able to interpret the legislation so as to bring it into line with the Convention. In any event, the Civil Partnership Act 2004 has now addressed the discrepancy in many areas of housing law, where same-sex couples were not accorded equal treatment.

4.5.5 Housing conditions

Tenants of a LHA who tried to argue that their landlord was in breach of Article 8 in failing to remedy design defects which rendered their premises unfit for human occupation, were again frustrated by the construction given to housing legislation by the UK courts. In *Lee v Leeds City Council* [2002] 1 WLR 1488, CA, the Court of Appeal was very reluctant to find that the landlords had breached the tenants' human rights. The facts in this case concerned premises, let to secure tenants, which were structurally sound but which suffered from severe condensation, mildew or mould, due to design defects. The tenants contended that the premises were unfit for human habitation or a statutory nuisance, and required the landlords to install a new heating system to deal with the mould.

Chadwick LJ (with whom Tuckey LJ and Sir Murray Stuart-Smith agreed) held that s 6 of the HRA 1998 could impose on a local authority landlord an obligation to take steps to ensure that the condition of a dwelling-house which it has let for social housing is such that the tenants' Convention right under Article 8 is not infringed. However, in deciding whether the condition of the dwelling-house is such that the tenants' Convention right has been infringed, regard must be had to the fair balance that has to be struck between the competing interests of the individual and of the community as a whole:

> The steps required to ensure compliance with 'respect' for private and family life must be determined in each case by having due regard to the needs and resources of the community and of individuals. And, in striking the balance between the resources of a local housing authority (and the need to meet other claims upon those resources) and the needs of the individual tenant, regard must be had to ... the democratically determined priorities. ([2002] 1 WLR 1488, at p 1507)

It was clear on the facts of *Lee v Leeds* that it had not been shown that there had been a breach of the duty, but Chadwick LJ was clear that in an appropriate case there could be a breach.

4.5.6 Discrimination and the right to family life

Although there have been two notable successful challenges using Articles 8 and 14 of the Convention (see *R (on the application of Morris) v Westminster City Council* at **4.5.1** and *Ghaidan v Mendoza* at **4.5.4**), it is not the case that this combined challenge will always lead to success.

In *R (on the application of Painter) v Carmarthenshire CC HBRB* [2001] EWHC Admin 308, although Articles 8 and 14 were engaged, the claimant was unsuccessful in establishing an unjustifiable infringement. The relevant housing benefit rules disentitled the claimant from getting any housing benefit because he was living with someone (his landlady) with whom he had had a close relationship. The discrimination was held justified under Article 8(2). The discrimination was also held justified in *Wandsworth LBC v Michalak* [2003] 1 WLR 617, CA, when the claimant did not fall within the category of relatives eligible to succeed to a secure tenancy on the death of the tenant (see **6.8.2.1** – family definition and human rights). See also *Bah v UK* [2011] ECHR 1448.

4.5.7 Other areas of challenge

Claimants have tried to challenge the LHA using other statutory provisions which engage Article 8.

> **CASE EXAMPLES**
>
> In *R (on the application of G) v Barnet London Borough Council* [2004] 2 AC 208, HL, it was argued that s 17 of the Children Act 1989 – which imposes a general duty on local social services authorities to safeguard and promote the welfare of children in need within their area and, so far as necessary, provide a range and level of services appropriate to those needs – put a specific duty on the local authority to provide housing for the child and his family. To do otherwise, it was argued, would infringe Article 8. The House of Lords held that the general duty in s 17 was not intended to be enforceable by individuals. Although social services could, as a part of their function, provide accommodation, the provision of residential accommodation to house a child in need so that he could live with his family was not the principal or primary purpose of the legislation. Housing was the function of the LHA. The 1989 Act was felt to be in compliance with Article 8(2).
>
> In *R (on the application of Limbuela) v Secretary of State for the Home Department* [2004] QB 1440, CA, allegedly destitute asylum seekers, ineligible for normal housing or other State assistance, were successful in claiming that to refuse them assistance under immigration legislation amounted to infringement of Article 3 of the Convention. The Court of Appeal held that intense physical or mental suffering, or humiliation of a degree sufficient to break moral or physical resistance, would engage Article 3. However, it was not necessary for an asylum seeker to show the actual onset of severe illness or suffering. If the evidence was that severe suffering was imminent, he would have done enough to show that he was verging on the necessary degree of severity. Because there were over 600 similar claims outstanding, the Court was of the view that the Secretary of State had a duty to assist, and the policy in operation was unlawful as violating Article 3.

4.6 PROCEDURE FOR HUMAN RIGHTS CLAIMS

By s 7 of the HRA 1998, any victim of an unlawful act can bring proceedings in the appropriate court or tribunal, or rely on the Convention right in any legal proceedings. For housing law issues, a claim may be brought in the High Court or a county court, unless the claim is by way of judicial review or in relation to a judicial act, where it should be started in the High Court. The Civil Procedure Rules, Part 7 (claims) or Part 54 (judicial review) would normally apply (see **12.6.3** for the judicial review procedure under CPR Part 54).

The Civil Procedure Rules, Part 16 and PD 16, para 15 deal with the requirements of a statement of case in making a human rights infringement claim. The provision provides that full details need to be given, including precise details of the Convention rights infringed. Details of the relief sought should also be given, including whether a declaration of incompatibility or damages are required.

Very often, Convention infringement issues arise in proceedings brought by the LHA in the county court, which has jurisdiction to deal with most housing disputes. Where, as has frequently happened in such cases there is the chance that a declaration of incompatibility may be made, the county court does not have power to make such a declaration. Only the High Court, Court of Appeal or Supreme Court (formerly the House of Lords) may do so. In such cases, CPR, r 30.3 allows the matter to be transferred to the High Court to be resolved.

4.6.1 Article 8 issues in county court possession proceedings

In *Kay v Lambeth LBC; Price v Leeds City Council* [2006] 2 WLR 570, the House of Lords stated that in future possession proceedings it would not be necessary for an LHA to plead or prove in every case that domestic law complies with Article 8. The assumption will be that it does. It will only be in highly exceptional cases that a seriously arguable challenge can be made. This could be on the basis that the relevant law is incompatible with the Convention, or that the procedural means available to challenge the decision by the owner to evict him are inadequate. The county court should decide the issue summarily on the basis of an affidavit or particulars in the defendant's defence, and either proceed to make a possession order or, where an HRA 1998, s 3 issue is raised, consider whether it may be appropriate to refer the proceedings to the High Court instead of dealing with the matter itself.

The House of Lords stated that the authority for the county court to deal with the Article 8 challenge was to be found in s 7(1)(b) of the HRA 1998, which provides:

> (1) a person who claims that a public authority has acted (or proposes to act) in a way which is made unlawful by section 6(1) (ie in a way which is incompatible with a Convention right) may ...
>
> (b) rely on the Convention right or rights concerned in any legal proceedings, but only if he is (or would be) a victim of the unlawful act.

The view of the House of Lords in *Kay v Lambeth LBC* was expressly approved in *Manchester City Council v Pinnock* (see **4.5** above) (at para 81). Lord Neuberger stated at para 74:

> Where it is required in order to give effect to an occupier's Article 8 Convention rights, the [county] court's powers of review can, in an appropriate case, extend to reconsidering for itself the facts found by a local authority, or indeed to considering facts which have arisen since the issue of proceedings, by hearing evidence and forming its own view.

This view was expressly approved in *Hounslow LBC v Powell* (see **4.5.3.2**) as being applicable in all possession claims brought by a public body.

4.6.2 Guidance on county court approaches to dealing with Article 8 challenges

In his decision in *Corby BC v Scott* [2012] EWCA Civ 276, Lord Neuberger addressed the present practice in the county courts when Article 8 challenges are raised. He stated:

> [36] So far as procedural issues are concerned ... there appears to have been no initial judicial consideration as to whether Ms Scott had raised a sufficiently strong Article 8 proportionality argument to go to a hearing. Further, we were told that there was no consistency of approach in different county courts as to how to proceed when a tenant raises an Article 8 proportionality point in possession proceedings. In some courts, the case is automatically listed for a hearing on the merits of the point; in other courts, the case remains in the usual housing possession list, and is then (depending on the court):
>
> (i) adjourned for fuller consideration;
>
> (ii) automatically re-listed for a hearing;
>
> (iii) briefly considered and then either rejected or adjourned as under (i) or re-listed as under (ii).
>
> [37] Although we were asked to do so, it does not appear to me to be appropriate for us to give firm guidance on the procedure to be adopted in possession cases where the tenant raises Article 8. We simply do not have the information available to give such guidance. Different courts may have good reasons for adopting slightly different practices ...
>
> [39] The only specific point I would make is to emphasise the desirability of a judge considering at an early stage (normally on the basis of the tenant's pleaded case on the issue) whether the tenant has an arguable case on Article 8 proportionality, before the issue is ordered to be heard. If it is a case which cannot succeed, then it should not be allowed to take up further court time and expense to the parties, and should not be allowed to delay the landlord's right to possession. I accept, however, that it may well be that even that cannot be an absolute rule.

4.7 FURTHER READING

J Watson and M Woolf, *Human Rights Act Toolkit* (2008)

> **SUMMARY**
> - The human rights provisions do not entitle a person to be provided with a home.
> - However, if a public body provides a home, it must be suitable.
> - Article 8 is engaged whenever a public body seeks to terminate an occupier's right to possession; however, in most cases the termination may be justifiable under Article 8(2).
> - Article 8 may be engaged if there is unjustifiable discrimination in the treatment of a housing applicant.
> - The county courts should deal summarily with Article 8 challenges that have no arguable case on proportionality.

CHAPTER 5

Public Funding and Costs in Housing Disputes

5.1	Introduction	59
5.2	The levels of service available in housing disputes	61
5.3	The interrelationship between the different levels of service	64
5.4	The levels of contracts available for housing disputes	65
5.5	Financial eligibility	66
5.6	The statutory charge	69
5.7	Costs	69
5.8	Further reading	70
	Summary	70

LEARNING OUTCOMES

After reading this chapter you will be able to:
- list the areas of housing law within the new scope for legal aid
- understand the basis upon which legal aid is granted
- explain the standard and special criteria to be met for legal aid in housing law cases
- describe the financial eligibility requirements for legal aid.

5.1 INTRODUCTION

Housing disputes can, subject to the financial means of the litigant, be financed by public funds. A financially eligible client will be able to apply to a legal service supplier (which does not always have to be a solicitor) for legal aid. For 13 years legal aid was administered by the Legal Services Commission (LSC) under provisions in the Access to Justice Act (AJA) 1999. However, as from 1 April 2013, the Ministry of Justice now administers legal aid.

5.1.1 New provisions for the administration of legal aid

Part 1 of and Sch 1 to the Legal Aid, Sentencing and Punishment of Offenders Act 2012 ('the 2012 Act') has introduced radical changes to the way legal aid is administered. The changes include the abolition of the LSC and a limitation on the scope of legal aid available in housing law cases.

Section 1 of the 2012 Act provides that the Lord Chancellor has a duty to secure the availability of civil and criminal legal aid. An executive agency within the Ministry of Justice, known as the Legal Aid Agency (LAA), now administers the delivery of legal aid services in England and Wales. The Lord Chancellor has designated a civil servant to be the Director of Legal Aid Casework ('the Director'). He has statutory responsibility for taking decisions (described as 'determinations': s 12) on legal aid in individual cases.

Regulations made under provisions in ss 11 and 12 of the 2012 Act stipulate the criteria the Director has to follow in determining whether an individual qualifies for legal aid. The main regulations are the Civil Legal Aid (Merits Criteria) Regulations 2013 (SI 2013/104) ('the

Merits Regulations') and the Civil Legal Aid (Procedures) Regulations 2012 (SI 2012/3098) ('the Procedure Regulations'). In carrying out his functions, the Director must have regard to guidance issued by the Lord Chancellor (see Lord Chancellor's Guidance under section 4 of Legal Aid, Sentencing and Punishment of Offenders Act 2012 – 'the LC Guidance').

The 2012 Act sets out the new limits of legal aid in housing law matters (s 9 and Sch 1, paras 33–36). This new limited scope is effective from 1 April 2013. Legal aid is limited to matters relating to:

- possession of the home (other than mortgage possession)
- eviction from the home (including unlawful eviction)
- seeking repairs to rented accommodation where the disrepairs pose a serious risk of harm to health or safety
- homelessness assistance for persons who are homeless or threatened with homelessness
- injunctions under the Protection from Harassment Act 1997 in the context of housing and ASBO matters in the county court.

Mortgage possession of a home is also eligible for legal aid, but under the category of 'debt' rather than 'housing'.

> **EXAMPLE OF LIMIT UNDER NEW SCOPE**
>
> Under the former LSC criteria, legal aid would have been available to a tenant who had left a property in serious disrepair and who was now suing primarily for compensation for having had to live in those conditions. Under the new scope, legal aid will not be available to bring a claim for damages only as a result of disrepair in the home.

Legal aid will also be available to challenge public bodies by bringing claims for judicial review and breach of Convention rights (s 9 and Sch 1, paras 19 and 22)(see **12.6.7**).

The Lord Chancellor can vary the list by adding or removing categories. He also has the power to award legal aid for a case not within the list if it is 'exceptional', in that it will involve a breach of an individual's human rights or EU law (s 10).

The Lord Chancellor's Exceptional Funding Guidance (Non-Inquests) at para 57 gives an example of factors that may be considered in a housing case that would not normally be within scope:

> In applications relating to out of scope housing disrepair claims the following matters may be particularly relevant:
>
> Where the applicant is seeking to claim damages, what is the level of damages sought? Do they include damages to compensate for items of particular importance to the applicant, such as damage to important medical equipment?
>
> To what extent is expert evidence necessary to resolve disputes concerning the allegations of disrepair, the medical effects of disrepair or the nature of remedial work required?

To obtain legal aid for housing law work that is within the new limited scope, a client will need to find a firm that is contracted to provide housing law services by the LAA, and sign a form to obtain the relevant level of service. In housing disputes three different levels of service are available: Legal Help, Help at Court and Legal Representation. Each of these will be considered in more detail at **5.2** below.

For housing law, a contract between the legal aid provider and the LAA determines the categories of housing law work and the levels at which it can be provided. There are two types of contracts for housing, namely 'Controlled Work' (see **5.4.1**) and 'Licensed Work' (see **5.4.2**).

5.2 THE LEVELS OF SERVICE AVAILABLE IN HOUSING DISPUTES

5.2.1 Legal Help

Regulation 13 of the Merits Regulations defines Legal Help as:

the provision of civil legal services other than—
(a) acting as a mediator or arbitrator;
(b) issuing or conducting court proceedings;
(c) instructing an advocate in proceedings;
(d) preparing to provide advocacy in proceedings; or
(e) advocacy in proceedings.

Initial advice and assistance with legal problems may be given, but Legal Help does not cover the issue or conduct of court proceedings, nor advocacy before any court or tribunal. The LC Guidance (at para 12.7) indicates that Legal Help would be appropriate, for example, in the early stages of a within scope disrepair case to fund expert reports so that the merits of the claim can be investigated.

Regulation 32 of the Merits Regulations lists two criteria to be met before Legal Help will be provided:

(a) that it is reasonable for the individual to be provided with legal help; and
(b) the sufficient benefit test.

5.2.1.1 Reasonableness

Legal Help may be provided only if it is reasonable for the matter to be funded by legal aid, having regard to any other potential sources of funding. There are upper costs limits on the amount that a service provider can recover for Legal Help. Unless authorised by the LAA to exceed the limit, any work done in excess of that amount will not be paid for.

5.2.1.2 Sufficient benefit test

Legal Help may be provided only where there is sufficient benefit to the client, having regard to the circumstances of the matter, including the personal circumstances of the client, to justify work or further work being carried out. The LC Guidance (at para 4.2.13) indicates that this is primarily a test of whether a reasonable, private, paying individual of moderate means would pay for the legal advice and assistance. While the test is not a particularly difficult one for most clients to satisfy initially, it does need to be kept under review by the service provider throughout the case. If it becomes apparent that it is not worth continuing the provision of legal service because the sufficient benefit test is no longer being met, then the service provider must stop working on the case.

5.2.2 Help at Court

Regulation 14 of the Merits Regulations defines Help at Court as:

the provision of any of the following civil legal services at a particular hearing—
(a) instructing an advocate;
(b) preparing to provide advocacy; or
(c) advocacy.

This covers informal advocacy, usually by way of mitigation at court. It allows a solicitor or an adviser to speak on behalf of a person at certain court hearings, without formally acting for that person in the whole proceedings. The LC Guidance (at paras 6.2 and 6.9) states that Help at Court allows the provision of advocacy at a particular hearing but not generally in the proceedings. It gives a typical example of possession proceedings where the client has no defence to the possession claim but seeks to influence the discretion of the court in relation to postponing possession or suspending eviction.

The following criteria must be met:

(a) the criteria for Legal Help (see **5.2.1** above), which also apply to an application for Help at Court; and
(b) the nature and circumstances of:
   (i) the proceedings;
   (ii) the particular hearing; and
   (iii) the individual,
   are such that advocacy is appropriate and will be of real benefit to that individual.

5.2.3 Legal Representation

Legal Representation may take the form of Investigative Representation or Full Representation.

Regulation 18 of the Merits Regulations defines Legal Representation as:

> the provision of civil legal services, other than acting as a mediator or arbitrator, to an individual or legal person in particular proceedings where that individual or legal person—
> (a) is a party to those proceedings;
> (b) wishes to be joined as a party to those proceedings; or
> (c) is contemplating issuing those proceedings.

Investigative Representation is defined as:

> legal representation which is limited to the investigation of the strength of the contemplated proceedings and includes the issuing and conducting of proceedings but only so far as necessary—
> (a) to obtain disclosure of information relevant to the prospects of success of the proceedings;
> (b) to protect the position of the individual or legal person applying for investigative representation in relation to an urgent hearing; or
> (c) to protect the position of the individual or legal person applying for investigative representation in relation to the time limit for the issue of the proceedings.

Full Representation is defined as legal representation other than Investigative Representation.

5.2.3.1 Investigative Representation

Investigative Representation cannot be granted to a person who considers that proceedings may be brought against him or who might be involved in some other way. It is available only where prospects of success are unclear. The LC Guidance (at para 6.15) states that once sufficient work has been carried out to determine the prospects of success criterion, the provider should report this to the Director who will consider whether Investigative Representation should be withdrawn or whether the certificate should be extended to Full Representation.

5.2.3.2 Full Representation

Full Representation enables a client to be represented in court if taking or defending proceedings. It includes litigation and advocacy services, steps preliminary or incidental to proceedings, and help to effect a compromise to avoid or bring to an end any proceedings. It does not include the provision of mediation or arbitration (but this does not prevent help being given in relation to mediation or arbitration, or the payment of a mediator's or an arbitrator's fees as a disbursement) (LC Guidance, para 6.16).

5.2.3.3 Criteria for Legal Representation

The Merits Regulations outline the criteria to be met for Legal Representation. There are different criteria to be met depending on whether the claim is a housing-specific or public law claim (ie homelessness and judicial review).

The housing-specific criteria in regs 61–63 indicate which of the general or standard merits criteria apply to Legal Representation.

General and standard criteria

The relevant general criteria are set out in regs 39–45 of the Merits Regulations. Regulation 39 applies the standard criteria to all types of Legal Representation in housing cases. Regulation 39 provides:

> An individual may qualify for legal representation only if the Director is satisfied that the following criteria are met—
>
> (a) the individual does not have access to other potential sources of funding (other than a conditional fee agreement) from which it would be reasonable to fund the case;
>
> (b) the case is unsuitable for a conditional fee agreement;
>
> (c) there is no person other than the individual, including a person who might benefit from the proceedings, who can reasonably be expected to bring the proceedings;
>
> (d) the individual has exhausted all reasonable alternatives to bringing proceedings including any complaints system, ombudsman scheme or other form of alternative dispute resolution;
>
> (e) there is a need for representation in all the circumstances of the case including—
>
>   (i) the nature and complexity of the issues;
>
>   (ii) the existence of other proceedings; and
>
>   (iii) the interests of other parties to the proceedings; and
>
> (f) the proceedings are not likely to be allocated to the small claims track.

In addition, reg 11(4) provides that the criteria in reg 11(6) have to be satisfied before an applicant can qualify for legal services. These relate to the conduct of the applicant. Examples of conduct which could disqualify an applicant from entitlement to legal aid is his being a vexatious litigant or one who fails to report a change of financial circumstances.

Specific criteria for housing law disputes

There are three different specific criteria to be met for Legal Representation in housing disputes, depending on the issue to which the matter relates (see Merits Regulations, regs 61–63).

For Full Representation in relation to court orders for possession, only reg 39 of the general merits criteria (above) needs to be satisfied. In addition, the Director must be satisfied that:

(a) the individual has a defence to the claim;

(b) the prospects of success are very good, good, moderate or borderline; and

(c) the proportionality test is met (reg 61).

In possession claims and mortgage possession claims, Legal Representation is likely to be refused unless there is a substantive defence to the claim. It will be refused for the accelerated possession procedure, and is unlikely to be granted for cases where arrears are not in dispute and a suspended possession order in rent or mortgage cases is the likely order that will be made.

For Full Representation in other housing matters (unlawful eviction, harassment or repair claims), the criteria are the same as for court orders for possession set out above; but in addition, if the prospects for success are only borderline, the case must be of significant wider public interest or a case with overwhelming importance to the individual (reg 62).

The third type of Legal Representation subject to the specific criteria in reg 63 relates to determinations for Investigative Representation in relation to unlawful eviction cases (see Sch 1, Pt 1, para 33(1) to the 2012 Act). In such cases, reg 39 (above) and reg 40(1)(a) and (b) apply. Regulation 40(1)(a) and (b) relate to the prospects of success being unclear so that substantial investigative work is necessary to determine the prospects, but there being reasonable grounds for the Director to believe that the outcome of the investigation will result in a determination for Full Representation.

In addition, if the individual's claim is primarily a claim for damages or other sum of money in which the likely damages do not exceed £1,000, the case must be of significant wider public interest. Where such damages or money claim form part of a multi-party action, only the lead claim within that action is capable of being a case of significant wider public interest.

Legal Representation may be refused if there has been no letter before action in a claim for harassment and wrongful eviction, unless justified on the facts.

Public law claims – criteria in homelessness and judicial review claims

The Merits Regulations deal with Legal Representation for homelessness and judicial review claims as public law claims. The criteria for these are contained in regs 53–56. They are broadly similar to the standard, general and specific criteria outlined above.

Legal Representation will not be granted in homelessness or judicial review claims unless the matter appears to be susceptible to challenge, the client has exhausted all available remedies, and the LHA has been notified of the proposed litigation and given a reasonable opportunity to respond. Here, a letter before action should always be sent.

5.2.4 Housing Possession Court Duty Scheme

As part of a package of measures designed to try to help people in financial difficulties as a result of the financial crisis, the Government and the former LSC have provided assistance under this scheme. The scheme continues under the LAA. A client who is a tenant in eviction proceedings or a mortgagor (borrower) facing repossession of his home as a result of mortgage arrears, may be able to get free legal advice and representation in court on the day of the hearing under the Housing Possession Court Duty Scheme.

Under the Scheme, a duty solicitor can give on-the-day advice and advocacy to clients who have a hearing listed at court. This service is available to clients irrespective of eligibility under means and merits tests (see **5.2.1** and **5.5**).

The scheme can be a source of last-minute help for someone who has not had legal advice before the hearing. It is provided in many county courts in England and Wales. Legal advisers who provide this duty scheme at court are required to have a 2013 Standard Civil Contract for Housing and Debt with the LAA. The Duty Scheme is not within the Procedures Regulations (see reg 14).

5.2.5 Civil Legal Advice

In addition, clients eligible for legal aid can get telephone advice on housing law matters from the Civil Legal Advice Service. Details of the service can be found at www.gov.uk/civil-legal-advice.

5.2.6 Telephone Gateway Service

Although the telephone advice service (**5.2.5** above) is not mandatory for clients with housing law problems, a new mandatory Telephone Gateway Service operates for clients accessing debt advice, unless the particular client is exempt. This mandatory service would apply to clients facing possession claims due to mortgage arrears.

5.3 THE INTERRELATIONSHIP BETWEEN THE DIFFERENT LEVELS OF SERVICE

Paragraphs 6.3 and 6.4 of the LC Guidance give clarification of the interrelationship between the different levels of service for housing. They state:

Part 1 of the Procedure Regulations defines the different levels of service that may be provided. The levels of service may be provided as Controlled Work (Part 3 of the Procedure Regulations) or Licensed Work (Part 4).

The way in which the form of civil legal service is provided is important as this affects who may determine the application. The power to determine most applications for Controlled Work will, for example, be delegated to the provider. In the majority of cases, however, applications for Licensed Work must be made to the Director and will only be delegated where emergency representation is required. Once the Director has made a determination a certificate will be issued.

5.4 THE LEVELS OF CONTRACTS AVAILABLE FOR HOUSING DISPUTES

5.4.1 Controlled Work

The Procedures Regulations outline the procedure to be followed by providers in relation to Controlled Work. In housing cases, it relates mainly to Legal Help and Help at Court (see **5.2.1** and **5.2.2**). This contract work is described as 'controlled' because, for any given local area, the LAA invites tenders from service providers and awards contracts based on the amount of funds available and the local needs for housing law services in that area. This is work carried out under the Standard Civil Contract, for which a separate application to the LAA is not required.

The scheme operates by granting delegated authority to specified individuals in the contract firm to take certain decisions on behalf of the LAA. This is known as 'delegated functions' (formerly under the LSC as 'devolved powers'). For Controlled Work, the authorisation may be exercised in any category that the specified individuals are authorised to perform under the contract. A quality-mark person, generally a partner, will have the authority to sign a funding form for the work to be undertaken.

To obtain authorisation, the quality-mark partner will have demonstrated that the firm has met the Specialist Quality Mark (SQM) or Lexcel standard required to be eligible to get the contract. For housing law practitioners who wish to obtain an SQM or Lexcel standard for contract work, they have to demonstrate that they can meet the criteria in a number of areas of housing law.

A client who wishes to obtain Legal Help or Help at Court has to find a firm or supplier who holds a contract, and he also has to satisfy the financial eligibility requirements (see **5.5**).

5.4.2 Licensed Work

Legal Representation for housing law claims is not funded within the Controlled Work category (see **5.4.1**) but within the Licensed Work category. Every application for Licensed Work must be made in writing to the LAA, providing details prescribed in reg 31 of the Procedures Regulations.

Unlike the position with Controlled Work, there is no set budget or control of Licensed Work. The LC Guidance states that if the prospects of success of the potential claim are clear and all other criteria for Full Representation are satisfied, a certificate covering Full Representation may be granted, but this will usually be limited by the LAA to the early stages of proceedings, further enquiries and research, and settlement negotiations with the potential opponent (para 6.9).

If a certificate is granted, the service provider will obtain payments on account to cover certain costs and disbursements during the progress of the claim. At the conclusion of the case, the final bill will, depending on its size, be assessed either by the LAA or by the court.

A client who wishes to obtain Legal Representation can apply to a firm that holds a Controlled Work contract and has an authorised litigator. The client will also have to satisfy the financial eligibility requirements (see **5.5**).

5.5 FINANCIAL ELIGIBILITY

The provisions dealing with financial eligibility are now in s 21 of the 2012 Act and regulations made under it, ie the Civil Legal Aid (Financial Resources and Payment for Services) Regulations 2013 (SI 2013/480). The LAA has also issued guides, namely, the Guide to Determining Financial Eligibility for Controlled Work and Family Mediation April 2013 v1 ('the FE Guide') and the Guide to Determining Financial Eligibility for Certificated Work – April 2013 v1 ('the FECW Guide').

There are both capital and income limits beyond which a client will not be eligible for assistance with legal funding from the LAA. From 1 April 2013, the capital limit for Legal Help, Help at Court and Legal Representation in housing matters is £8,000. If a client has disposable capital above this sum, no funding will be provided unless the LAA considers that the probable costs would exceed the contribution payable.

A client who is in receipt of income support, income-based jobseekers' allowance, income-related employment and support allowance, guarantee or universal credit will automatically qualify on income eligibility for all levels of service. This is referred to as the 'passporting benefit'. However, capital eligibility must be assessed in all cases.

For clients with a gross income above the relevant limit (see **5.5.3**), funding will be refused without the need to carry out a full assessment. Once a client is within the financial eligibility limit, he will be entitled to LAA funding for all levels of service. For Legal Help and Help at Court, the client does not have to make any contributions for the service provided; it is only for Legal Representation that, subject to the level of capital and income, the client may be expected to make a contribution. Even where a client does not have to pay a contribution, the statutory charge may apply (see **5.6** below).

5.5.1 Disposable capital

Disposable capital is calculated by taking account of various items and discounting or ignoring others (see Step 7 at **5.5.3** below). A client with disposable capital of £8,000 or less will be eligible for funding if his disposable income is also below the relevant limit.

5.5.2 Disposable income

The income limit for legal funding varies according to the number of children a client has. If a client has no children, or up to four children, and a gross income above £2,657 per month, he will not be eligible for legal funding. The eligibility limit on income increases by £222 for each additional child above four. After deduction of all allowable deductions and expenses from gross income (see **5.5.3**, Step 4), a client who has a monthly disposable income above £733 will not be eligible for LAA funding.

5.5.3 Guide to assessing financial eligibility for housing services

The LAA has provided a step-by-step guide (Keycard 49) to help a service provider to assess the financial eligibility of a client for legal services relating to non-contributory Controlled Work. This is available on the website at www.justice.gov.uk. The FECW Guide (at paras 4–7) gives detailed guidance on legal aid eligibility and the levels of contribution for Legal Representation. An adapted version of the Keycard, incorporating eligibility for Legal Representation, specifically for housing clients, is shown below:

Step 1: Identify whether the client has a partner whose means should be included in the assessment (see reg 16 and section 4.2 of the FE Guide).

Step 2: Identify clients in receipt of a passporting benefit in order to determine whether the client automatically satisfies the gross and disposable income limits.

Clients in receipt (either directly or indirectly) of passporting benefits are eligible on income grounds for all levels of service.

Step 3: Work out the client's monthly gross income (where not passported).

Add together the client's monthly gross income (ie before tax) and that of his/her partner, if appropriate. Income includes:

(a) earnings or profits from business;
(b) maintenance payments;
(c) pensions;
(d) certain welfare benefits;
(e) income from savings and investments;
(f) dividends from shares;
(g) monies received from friends and relatives;
(h) student grants and loans.

Income excludes the full amount of any of the following welfare benefits:

(a) attendance allowance;
(b) council tax benefit;
(c) housing benefit;
(d) social fund payments;
(e) disability living allowance;
(f) constant attendance allowance;
(g) invalid care allowance;
(h) severe disablement allowance;
(i) exceptionally severe disablement allowance;
(j) any war pensions;
(k) independent living fund payments;
(l) fostering allowance (to the extent it exceeds the relevant dependant's allowance);
(m) back to work bonus under s 26 of the Jobseekers Act 1995;
(n) payments made under the Earnings Top-up Scheme and payments under the Community Care Direct Payment Scheme.

Step 4: Work out deductible allowances and expenses.

Deduct the following from monthly income:

(a) income tax and National Insurance Contributions;
(b) maintenance payments made;
(c) £45 for client and/or partner in receipt of salary or wage;
(d) child-care expenses incurred because of employment or self-employment;
(e) housing costs, ie:
    (i) rent or mortgage repayments (less any housing benefit), although the amount allowed if the client has no dependants is limited to £545,
    (ii) endowment policy premiums (if paid in connection with a mortgage),
    (iii) actual costs of accommodation if the client is neither a tenant nor an owner-occupier;
(f) fixed amounts for each dependent relative (adult and child) living with the client. The monthly allowances for dependants are:
    (i) partner – £177.50,
    (ii) dependants aged 15 or under – £285.13,
    (iii) dependants aged 16 or over – £285.13.

Step 5: Work out the client's monthly disposable income.

Monthly gross income (see Step 3) minus deductions (see Step 4) gives the monthly disposable income.

Step 6: Does the monthly disposable income qualify the client for funding?

For all levels of service, the client will not get funding if his disposable income exceeds the relevant limits. Clients with monthly disposable income between £316 and £733 will be required to make regular contributions towards their legal aid for Legal Representation (see FECW Guide, Appendix 2).

Step 7: Work out capital.

Add together all the capital of the client (and partner, if appropriate). Capital includes:

(a) all land and buildings other than the client's home, including interests in timeshares, and the market value of the client's home in excess of £100,000, after allowing for any outstanding mortgage but only up to £100,000 (a maximum of £100,000 is allowed in respect of all mortgages on all the client's properties);
(b) money in the bank, building society, Post Office, premium bonds, National Savings certificates, etc;
(c) investments, stocks and shares;
(d) money that can be borrowed against the surrender value of insurance policies;
(e) money value of valuable items, eg a boat, caravan, antiques, jewellery (but not wedding or engagement rings, or (usually) the client's car);
(f) money owed to the client;
(g) money due from an estate or a trust fund;
(h) money that can be borrowed against business assets.

Capital does not include:

(a) loans or grants from the Social Fund;
(b) back to work bonus under s 26 of the Jobseekers Act 1995;
(c) home contents, eg (unless exceptionally valuable) furniture and household effects;
(d) personal clothing;
(e) personal tools and equipment of trade;
(f) payments under the Community Care Direct Payment scheme;
(g) the first £100,000 of savings, valuable items or property the ownership of which is the specific subject of the court case.

The sum of all the items that can be included as capital is the client's total disposable capital.

Step 8: Does the disposable capital qualify the client for funding?

Sums above £8,000 will render the client ineligible for funding. An individual whose disposable capital exceeds £3,000 is required to pay a contribution of either the capital exceeding that sum or the likely maximum costs of the funded service, whichever is the lower.

Where the client has been approved for LAA funding for Legal Representation, it will be on the basis that he may be liable to pay the legal costs incurred in the case under the funding certificate. Payment could be made by the client by way of contributions out of capital and/or income, and/or by way of a statutory charge (see **5.6** below). The application form (CIVAPP1) requires the client to acknowledge that his legal representative has explained the statutory charge to him.

5.6 THE STATUTORY CHARGE

The client will need to be warned of the risk of the statutory charge applying to any sums recovered as a result of Legal Representation. The statutory charge does not apply in housing cases at Controlled Work level (see **5.4.1**). However, when property is recovered or preserved in proceedings in which a client received legal aid, a statutory charge will arise in favour of the LAA, unless there are regulations that provide otherwise (see Civil Legal Aid (Statutory Charge) Regulations 2013 (SI 2013/503), regs 5–9). This would not generally be an issue for tenants in possession proceedings, as the tenant would not normally have any equity value in the property. However, where a mortgage borrower with the benefit of legal aid funding successfully preserves his home, the charge will arise unless any costs recovered from the unsuccessful mortgage lender cover the sums expended by the LAA Fund.

The Lord Chancellor has discretion to waive the statutory charge for public interest reasons, where he considers it equitable to do so (Civil Legal Aid (Statutory Charge) Regulations 2013, reg 9). Where damages are awarded to a client, eg in a harassment and illegal eviction claim, the statutory charge will apply to the damages recovered, to the extent that the client's legal representative's costs are not recovered from the losing party. For example, the court may make an award limiting the amount that the losing party has to pay.

5.7 COSTS

5.7.1 General rules

The general rules on the award of costs at the end of a court hearing are contained in CPR, r 44.2, which gives the court a discretion as to whether costs are payable by one party to another, the amount of costs and when they are to be paid. If the court decides to make a costs order, the general rule is that the unsuccessful party will be ordered to pay the costs of the successful party, but the court may make a different order.

Rule 44.2(4) provides that in deciding what order (if any) to make about costs, the court must have regard to all the circumstances, including:

(a) the conduct of all the parties;
(b) whether a party has succeeded on part of his case, even if he has not been wholly successful; and
(c) any payment into court or admissible offer to settle made by a party which is drawn to the court's attention (whether or not made in accordance with Part 36).

Conduct can include conduct both before and during the proceedings. The extent to which the parties followed any relevant pre-action protocol is a particularly important factor. The reasonableness of pursuing or contesting a particular allegation or issue, the manner in which a party has conducted himself, and whether a successful claimant exaggerated his claim in whole or in part are all relevant factors (CPR, r 44.2(5)). The reader is directed to CPR, Parts 44 to 48 and PD 44 General Rules about Costs, which detail the basis of assessment, relevant factors and other matters relating to costs.

5.7.2 Costs and legal aid funding

Where the client has received legal aid funding, the normal provisions may not apply. For example, a summary assessment of costs cannot be made by the court where the client is LAA-funded (PD 44, para 9.8).

Where a legal aid-funded client loses his case, subject to the court's discretion (see **5.7.1**), he would usually be ordered to pay the costs of the winning party. However, s 26 of the 2012 Act imposes a costs protection, which limits to a reasonable amount the sum that the client can be ordered to pay. The costs protection is available only for Legal Representation, not Legal Help or Help at Court. The factors to determine the reasonable costs where there is costs protection will include the financial resources of all the parties to the proceedings, and their conduct in connection with the dispute to which the proceedings relate.

In deciding the costs order in s 26 cases, the court can initially consider the costs position as if the losing party were not legally aided. It may then decide to order the losing party to pay a small part of the costs that would have been awarded against him, or award costs of a set amount (which may be the full or a lesser amount) but add a proviso that the costs order cannot be enforced without the court's permission.

Regulations made under s 26 impose further conditions and limitations on who can benefit from costs protection and when, and also detail the circumstances in which the Lord Chancellor may be required to pay the costs of the non-funded party (see Civil Legal Aid (Costs) Regulations 2013 (SI 2013/611)).

Where costs protection does not apply, the court can award costs in the normal way.

5.8 FURTHER READING

V Ling and S Pugh, *Legal Aid Handbook 2013/14*

SUMMARY

- The Legal Aid, Sentencing and Punishment of Offenders Act 2012 has abolished the LSC and restricts the areas for which legal aid will be available in housing law cases.
- Legal aid is available for Legal Help, Help at Court and Legal Representation in housing law cases that are within scope, subject to the client meeting the means and merits requirements.
- Free legal aid may be available, under the Housing Possession Court Duty Scheme, to a client defending a possession claim at court who has had no legal advice before and regardless of his financial position.
- Legal advisers providing legal aid must be subject to a contract with the LAA to provide Controlled Work or Licensed Work.
- A client who has no children, or no more than four children, with disposable capital of £8,000 or less and gross income of no more than £2,657 per month will meet the financial eligibility requirements for legal aid in housing cases.

CHAPTER 6

Public Sector Housing – Secure Tenants

6.1	Introduction	71
6.2	Housing allocation	72
6.3	Secure tenants – HA 1985, Pt IV	76
6.4	Non-secure tenancies	78
6.5	Introductory tenancies	80
6.6	Security of tenure	81
6.7	Grounds for possession	85
6.8	The rights and obligations of a secure tenant	89
	Summary	98

LEARNING OUTCOMES

After reading this chapter you will be able to:

- understand the legal basis for housing allocation schemes
- explain the categories of housing applicants who should be given reasonable preference for housing allocation
- describe the different types of tenancies that an LHA can grant
- list the options open to an LHA to deal with anti-social behaviour
- list the grounds for possession
- explain the rights and obligations of secure tenants.

6.1 INTRODUCTION

Although home ownership is perceived to be the most desirable form of tenure, not everyone is in a position to own their own home. For those who are not, perhaps the next best form of tenure now is to have a secure tenancy in the public sector. Such a tenancy provides a high level of security of tenure, coupled with below-market rents, thanks to government subsidy designed to keep social housing affordable. The main statutory provisions in this area are contained in the HA 1985, the HA 1996 and the Homelessness Act 2002.

By s 8 of the HA 1985, LHAs have a duty to consider housing needs in their areas, with a view to providing further housing. They do not have to provide housing themselves, though, where a shortage is identified. Historically, LHAs did provide a large amount of housing in their areas, but in more recent years government policy has been such that LHAs have been divesting themselves of their housing stock, either under the Right to Buy scheme given to secure tenants, or through large-scale voluntary transfers to RSLs.

The Localism Act 2011, s 150 now requires all LHAs in England to have published by 15 January 2013 a 'tenancy strategy' for their area. LHAs must have regard to the tenancy strategy when exercising any of their housing management functions. The strategy will include:

(a) the kinds of tenancies they grant;

(b) the circumstances in which they will grant a tenancy of a particular kind;
(c) where they grant tenancies for a term certain, the lengths of the terms; and
(d) the circumstances in which they will grant a further tenancy on the coming to an end of an existing tenancy.

6.1.1 Issues concerning how secure tenancies are allocated

In order to become a secure tenant, a person needs to apply to an LHA for housing accommodation. In many areas the demand for public sector housing is greater than the amount of accommodation available, so not every applicant will be successful.

Due to serious criticism of the way in which some LHAs exercised their wide discretion in allocating limited housing stock to applicants, the Government introduced Pt VI of the HA 1996. This was a radically different system to that which existed before. It was designed to make LHA procedures – either when allocating an applicant a secure tenancy, or when nominating an applicant to be an assured tenant of an RSL or PRP – more consistent, fair and transparent. The provisions of Pt VI of the HA 1996 were substantially amended by the Homelessness Act 2002.

The Localism Act 2011 introduced further changes for housing allocation in England (see **6.2**).

6.1.2 The provision of secure tenancies

Secure tenancies are provided primarily by LHAs and HATs, although there are pre-1989 RSL tenancies that enjoy secure tenant status (see **6.3.2**). In some areas, the LHAs have transferred their housing stock to one or more RSLs by way of large-scale voluntary stock transfer. In such cases the tenants cease to be secure and become assured tenants of the RSLs and now PRPs, retaining many, if not all, of the rights that they previously enjoyed as secure tenants (see **6.8**). Even where an LHA has transferred its housing stock to an RSL, the LHA still has responsibility for its statutory housing duty, which involves a strategic responsibility for meeting its area's housing needs.

In exercising their allocation powers, LHAs in Wales are required to have regard to the revised Code of Guidance on the Allocation of Accommodation ('the Code of Guidance'), issued in 2002 by the Secretary of State, as well as the Allocation of Accommodation: Choice Based Lettings Code of Guidance issued in 2008 ('the 2008 Code').

In England, a new code of guidance has replaced all the codes mentioned above that are still applicable in Wales. The Allocation of Accommodation: guidance for LHAs in England 2012 ('the England Code') is to be taken into account by all LHAs in England when exercising their functions under Pt VI of the HA 1996.

In this chapter we consider the allocations provisions before examining the statutory provisions applicable to secure tenant status and the rights that go with it.

6.2 HOUSING ALLOCATION

The provisions in Pt VI of the HA 1996, as amended, require LHAs to consider housing allocation as one of the tools for combating homelessness and assisting other vulnerable people in their area. Allocation is defined in s 159(2) as when an LHA:

(a) selects a person to be a secure or introductory tenant of housing accommodation held by it;
(b) nominates a person to be a secure or introductory tenant of housing accommodation held by another person; or
(c) nominates a person to be an assured tenant of housing accommodation held by a PRP or RSL.

The amendments in the Homelessness Act 2002 are designed to:

(a) facilitate the introduction of choice-based letting allocation schemes, which offer new applicants and existing tenants a more active role in choosing their accommodation. The view is that this will ensure sustainable tenancies and settled communities, as tenants are more likely to look after properties they have chosen to live in;

(b) ensure wide access to social housing for applicants, by removing blanket exclusions of certain categories and obliging LHAs to consider all applicants, not just those with a local connection to their areas;

(c) introduce reasonable preference categories based on housing need, with existing social tenants being equally eligible for consideration; and

(d) ensure free assistance to those likely to have difficulty applying for housing.

6.2.1 Allocation schemes

Local housing authorities are required to have an allocation scheme for determining priorities, and for defining the procedures to be followed in allocating housing accommodation (HA 1996, s 166A (England); s 167(1) (Wales)). Both the England Code and the Code of Guidance make clear that the 'procedure' includes all aspects of the allocation process, including the people, or descriptions of people, by whom decisions are taken. It is essential that the scheme reflects all the housing authority's policies and procedures, including information on whether the decisions are taken by elected members, or by officers acting under delegated powers. An allocation scheme that does not explain clearly all aspects of the procedures to be followed in allocating accommodation will be held invalid (*R (Lin) v Barnet LBC* [2007] HLR 30, CA).

Under s 166A(2) (England) and s 167(1A) (Wales) of the 1996 Act, the scheme must include a statement of the housing authority's policy on offering eligible applicants a choice of accommodation, or the opportunity to express preferences about the accommodation offered to them. Even where no choice can be offered, eg for lack of enough housing, LHAs have to address this point and take a policy decision on it. The scheme must also be framed in such a way as to ensure that reasonable preference is given to certain classes of people. The categories have been revised by the 2002 Act.

6.2.1.1 Reasonable preference

In framing its allocation scheme so as to determine priorities in the allocation process, an LHA must ensure that reasonable preference is given to the following categories of people, as set out in s 166A(3) (England) and s 167(2) (Wales) of the HA 1996:

(a) people who are homeless (unless a restricted case, see s 166A(4) (England) and s 167(2ZA) (Wales) and **11.4.7**);

(b) people who are owed certain homelessness duties (see **11.7**);

(c) people occupying insanitary or overcrowded housing, or otherwise living in unsatisfactory housing conditions;

(d) people who need to move on medical or welfare grounds; and

(e) people who need to move to a particular locality in the district of the LHA, to avoid hardship (to themselves or to others).

Being granted reasonable preference will not necessarily put an applicant at the top of the housing list. In *R (Lin) v Barnet LBC* [2007] HLR 30, CA, it was held that the duty to give a reasonable preference merely requires the giving of a 'reasonable head start'. The claimant, a homeless applicant, was placed in private sector temporary accommodation by Barnet. She challenged the housing allocation policy of Barnet because she was allocated only 10 points for her homelessness. With that, there was little chance that she would become eligible for council accommodation until the lease on the temporary accommodation expired after 10 years. Dyson LJ stated that:

> Preference should not be confused with prospects of success. Prospects of success depend on many factors, of which the most material is the fact that the demand for accommodation greatly exceeds the supply. It is quite possible for a lawful scheme to give reasonable preference to a person within section 167(2) and for that person never to be allocated Part VI housing.

In R (Ahmad) v Newham LBC [2009] UKHL 14, the House of Lords opined that the factors identified in s 167(2) (now s 166A(3) for England) did not require an LHA to have a scheme which was capable of operating cumulatively. Once reasonable preference was given, priority between applicants could be decided solely on waiting time.

The England Code and the Code of Guidance have now framed their guidance to LHAs following the *Ahmad* interpretation of how a scheme can operate.

6.2.1.2 Additional preference

Additional preference may be given to people who fall within the reasonable preference categories set out at **6.2.1.1** above, who have urgent housing needs. For example, people exposed to domestic violence, or to racial or homophobic harassment which amounts to violence or threats of violence, or those who need to move for urgent medical reasons.

In England, additional preference should also be given to current and former service persons who fall within the reasonable preference categories and who have an urgent housing need, if such a person:

(a) is serving in the regular forces and suffering from a serious injury, illness or disability which is attributable (wholly or partly) to the person's service;

(b) formerly served in the regular forces;

(c) has recently ceased, or will cease to be entitled, to reside in accommodation provided by the Ministry of Defence following the death of that person's spouse or civil partner who has served in the regular forces and whose death was attributable (wholly or partly) to that service; or

(d) is serving or has served in the reserve forces and is suffering from a serious injury, illness or disability which is attributable (wholly or partly) to the person's service.

6.2.1.3 Other factors that may be taken into account

While reasonable preference must be given to those who come within the above categories, other factors may be taken into account too, for example financial resources, behaviour and the local connection of the applicant. (Local connection is defined in s 199 of the HA 1996 (see **11.6.1**).) However, LHAs must be careful that such factors do not discriminate against any ethnic group (see **6.2.5**). Both the England Code and the Code of Guidance also allow LHAs to go outside the reasonable preference categories in order to fill hard-to-let vacant properties.

6.2.2 Eligibility of applicants

In principle, most applicants are eligible and can apply for housing. Existing tenants of LHAs wishing to transfer (HA 1996, s 159(4B) (England) and s 159(5) (Wales)) will be eligible within the provisions of Pt VI only if they are in the reasonable preference category (see **6.2.1.1**). However, in considering housing applications, LHAs are required by s 160ZA(2) (England) and s 160A (Wales) of the 1996 Act to ascertain if an applicant is to be excluded from allocation as ineligible because he is subject to immigration control within the meaning of the Asylum and Immigration Act 1996. The Secretary of State, exercising his powers to make regulations under s 160ZA and s 160A of the HA 1996, has prescribed that certain persons from abroad who are subject to immigration control are nonetheless eligible for housing allocation, and other categories of persons are deemed ineligible (see Allocation of

Housing and Homelessness (Eligibility) (England) Regulations 2006 (SI 2006/1294) as amended, and Allocation of Housing (Wales) Regulations 2003 (SI 2003/239)).

In England, subject to the immigration ineligibility provisions, LHAs have a new power to decide on what classes of persons are, or are not, qualifying persons for the allocation of social housing (s 160ZA(7)).

Under s 160ZA(8), the Secretary of State may by regulations—

(a) prescribe classes of persons who are, or are not, to be treated as qualifying persons by LHAs in England; and

(b) prescribe criteria that may not be used by LHAs in England in deciding what classes of persons are not qualifying persons.

Local housing authorities must give written notification, with reasons for their decision, to any applicant they decide is ineligible or not a qualifying person.

A person who is not being treated as a qualifying person may (if he considers that he should be treated as a qualifying person) make a fresh application to the LHA for an allocation of housing accommodation.

In Wales, an LHA may treat an applicant as ineligible for housing if it is satisfied that he, or a member of his household, has been guilty of unacceptable behaviour serious enough to make him unsuitable to be its tenant (HA 1996, s 160A). Such an applicant would also have no preference status in any allocation scheme (HA 1996, s 167(2B), (2C)).

By s 170 of the HA 1996, RSLs and PRPs are required to cooperate with LHAs that request their assistance in offering accommodation to people with priority under the LHA's allocation scheme. It is often the case that RSLs aand PRPs use the LHA's housing list or register to allocate housing to people. Some LHAs enjoy full nomination rights to local RSL and PRP housing stock. This will be particularly so where the LHA has transferred all its housing stock to the RSL. In other cases LHAs may have only limited nomination rights to local RSL and PRP housing stock.

6.2.3 Challenging the operation of the allocation schemes

By s 166A(14) (England) and s 167(8) (Wales) of the HA 1996, an LHA should not allocate housing except in accordance with its allocation scheme. An LHA which allocates housing without following its allocation scheme, or whose allocation scheme does not give reasonable preference to the categories of people listed in s 166A(3) (England) and s 167(2) (Wales) (see **6.2.1.1**), will be open to challenge. This was the case in R (A) v Lambeth LBC, R (Lindsay) v Lambeth LBC [2002] HLR 998, CA, where the scheme did not identify applicants who qualified under more than one category and so had a greater need than others. In trying to redress the situation, Lambeth tried to alter the targets and quotas in its scheme. Lambeth's allocation scheme was held to be unlawful as it did not secure the statutory preference required by s 167(2). In addition, in altering targets and quotas the authority deviated from the scheme as published, in breach of s 167(8), which was also unlawful.

In *Sahardid v Camden LBC* [2005] HLR 11, CA, the LHA's housing scheme entitled an applicant with a child over 5 years old to be eligible for a two-bedroom property. When, on a review of the applicant's challenge to the offer of a one-bedroom flat (at a date when her son was over 5 years old), the LHA upheld the offer as being reasonable, it was successfully challenged for not following its own policy.

It will also be unlawful to plead administrative excuses for failing to change an unlawful scheme so that an applicant can be allocated to the correct preference category to entitle him to priority housing (see R (Maali) v Lambeth LBC [2003] All ER (D) 80).

An allocation scheme which does not fully explain how an applicant can earn accommodation points may be challenged as invalid. In R (Lin) v Barnet LBC [2007] HLR 30, CA (see **6.2.1.1** above), a homeless applicant placed in private sector temporary accommodation could obtain 300 points if the landlord terminated the private sector lease. However, the allocation scheme did not provide information as to when and for how long the 300 points would be available. To this extent it was held that the allocation scheme did not comply with s 167(1) and was invalid.

6.2.4 Review of allocation decisions

An applicant has the right to request an internal review of any decision with which he is dissatisfied (HA 1996, s 166A(9)(c) (England) and s 167(4A)(d) (Wales)). If the applicant is still unhappy with the outcome of a review, he can make a claim for judicial review of the LHA decision, as did the applicants in the cases mentioned in **6.2.3** above.

6.2.5 Discrimination issues

Both the England Code and the Code of Guidance emphasise the need to ensure that local lettings policies do not discriminate on racial or other equality grounds. Local housing authorities will have to have regard to the Equality Act 2010. The Act consolidates, harmonises and extends in part what were a number of different statutory regimes dealing with discrimination in relation to disability, race, sex and sexual orientation amongst a range of protected characteristics. These characteristics are defined in ss 4–12 of the Act. The Act prohibits certain conduct against the protected characteristics. These include both direct (s 13) and indirect (s 19) discrimination.

The disability discrimination provision in s 15 (in force from 1 October 2010) of the Act provides:

(1) A person (A) discriminates against a disabled person (B) if—
  (a) A treats B unfavourably because of something arising in consequence of B's disability, and
  (b) A cannot show that the treatment is a proportionate means of achieving a legitimate aim.
(2) Subsection (1) does not apply if A shows that A did not know, and could not reasonably have been expected to know, that B had the disability.

Section 149, which came into force on 5 April 2011, places a duty on public sector bodies, which could include RSLs and PRPs as persons who are not public authorities but who exercise public functions as determined in *Weaver* (see **4.4.1**).

The duty in s 149, referred to as the public sector equality duty, provides:

(1) A public authority must, in the exercise of its functions, have due regard to the need to—
  (a) eliminate discrimination, harassment, victimisation and any other conduct that is prohibited by or under this Act;
  (b) advance equality of opportunity between persons who share a relevant protected characteristic and persons who do not share it;
  (c) foster good relations between persons who share a relevant protected characteristic and persons who do not share it.

6.3 SECURE TENANTS – HA 1985, PT IV

A tenant who is allocated accommodation by an LHA or HAT may, provided all the requirements are met, be a secure tenant. Section 79 of the HA 1985 provides that a tenancy or licence (other than a licence granted as a temporary expedient to a trespasser) under which a dwelling-house is let as a separate dwelling, is a secure tenancy at any time when the landlord condition and the tenant condition are satisfied. This will be the case even where the LHA states otherwise (see *Mansfield DC v Langridge* [2008] EWCA Civ 264). The letting may be for a fixed term, or it may be periodic. However, a non-exclusive licence to occupy a dwelling will not be a secure tenancy (see *Westminster CC v Clarke* [1992] 2 AC 288, HL). In addition, s 79(2) provides that certain types of lettings, which would otherwise satisfy the conditions for security, will not be secure (see **6.4**).

From 2 April 2012, LHAs have the option of granting a new form of secure tenancy, called the 'flexible tenancy'. This was implemented by the Localism Act 2011, introducing new provisions into the HA 1985, ss 107A–107E (see **6.3.4**).

6.3.1 Let as a separate dwelling

By s 112 of the HA 1985, a dwelling-house can be a house or a part of a house, and can include up to two acres of non-agricultural land with it. The principles from the decision in *Uratemp Ventures Ltd v Collins* [2002] 1 AC 301, HL (albeit a case relating to an assured tenancy, see **2.2.2**) are applicable here. A separate dwelling can consist of one room, if the tenant has exclusive possession of it and it is his home.

6.3.2 Landlord condition

The landlord can be:

(a) a local authority;
(b) a new town corporation;
(c) a HAT;
(d) an urban development corporation (HA 1985, s 80);
(e) a Mayoral development corporation; or
(f) in certain situations, the HCA, the Greater London Authority or the Welsh minister.

Secure tenancies were introduced by the HA 1980 and, prior to the 1988 Act, the Housing Corporation, housing associations and charitable trusts were also landlords within this provision. As a consequence, tenancies still in existence that were granted by these bodies prior to 15 January 1989 (when the HA 1988 came into effect, see **2.1**) continue to enjoy secure tenant status with RSLs and PRPs. However, new tenants of RSLs and PRPs cannot be secure tenants under these provisions.

6.3.3 Tenant condition

The tenant must be an individual who occupies the dwelling-house as his only or principal home (HA 1985, s 81). Where there is a joint tenancy, each of the joint tenants must be an individual and at least one of them must occupy the dwelling-house as his only or principal home.

There have been a number of cases concerned with the issue of whether the premises were occupied as the tenant's only or principal home. The provision for secure tenants is rather stricter than that for a statutory tenant under the RA 1977, where occupation as a residence is sufficient (see **3.4**). Despite this much narrower provision in the HA 1985, the courts have continued to be very liberal in their interpretation of what is a person's only or principal home.

> **CASE EXAMPLES**
>
> In *Crawley BC v Sawyer* (1987) 20 HLR 98, CA, the tenant was out of occupation for two years. He had disconnected the electricity and gas supplies, but continued to pay rent. He told the LHA that he intended to buy a home with his girlfriend, with whom he had been living for the period. The LHA served notice to quit on the basis that the tenancy had ceased to be secure. Shortly after the notice to quit on his tenancy had expired, the tenant returned to the property having broken up with his girlfriend. It was held that the tenant's residence with his girlfriend had been on a temporary basis, and the LHA property had remained his principal home throughout the period.

> In *Hussey v Camden LBC* (1994) 27 HLR 5, CA, the tenant allowed someone else to occupy his tenanted property while he was absent for months at a time over a four-year period. It was held that whilst the tenant might have lost his security during the periods of absence, he had regained his secure status by going back into possession before expiry of a notice to quit served by the LHA. The tenant therefore had security at the relevant time. (This liberal interpretation is thought to turn on the words in s 79, 'at any time when', which suggest that there may be times when the tenant may not have security (see **6.3** above).

A long period of enforced absence was also discounted in *Amoah v LB Barking and Dagenham* [2001] All ER (D) 138. The court held that leaving furniture in the property, and arranging for a relative to look after the property and pay the rent on it while the tenant was serving a 12-year prison sentence, was sufficient evidence of the tenant's intention to return and of the property remaining his principal residence. However, where a tenant parts with possession or sub-lets the whole of the dwelling, his secure status is lost for good (see HA 1985, ss 91(2) and 93(2), and **6.4.1** below).

6.3.4 Secure flexible tenancies

As mentioned at **6.3**, LHAs now have a power to grant flexible tenancies under s 107A of the HA 1985 instead of or in addition to the normal periodic secure tenancies.

Under s 107A(2), a flexible tenancy is a secure tenancy if:

(a) it is granted by an LHA (or other landlord within s 80 HA of the 1985) in England for a term certain of not less than two years; and

(b) before it was granted, the person who became the landlord under the tenancy served a written notice on the person who became the tenant under the tenancy stating that the tenancy would be a flexible tenancy.

Written notice that a flexible tenancy will be created can be served on:

(a) new tenants of the LHA;

(b) an introductory tenant notifying him, prior to the start of the introductory tenancy, that at the end of the introductory period he will become a secure flexible tenant (see **6.5**);

(c) a family intervention tenant who was previously a secure flexible tenant (see **6.6.3.3**); and

(d) a demoted tenant who was previously a secure flexible tenant (see **6.6.2**).

Review of a flexible tenancy

The person served with a written notice has 21 days, or such longer time as the LHA agrees, to request a review of the decision. However, the only basis of challenge is that the length of the term does not accord with a policy of the prospective landlord as to the length of the terms of the flexible tenancies it grants (s 107B).

The Flexible Tenancies (Review Procedures) Regulations 2012 (SI 2012/695) set out the procedure for such reviews. This gives the applicant a right to request an oral hearing.

6.4 NON-SECURE TENANCIES

By s 79(2) of the HA 1985, certain tenancies may cease to be secure and others are excluded from security altogether.

6.4.1 Tenancy ceasing to be secure

There are two situations in which a tenancy may cease to be secure:

(a) where, on the death of a periodic or fixed term secure tenant, there is no one eligible to succeed to the secure tenancy, or no one with family or matrimonial rights under property adjustment orders (see HA 1985, ss 89(3) and (4) and 90(3) and (4));

(b) where the secure tenant has assigned or sub-let the whole of the property (see HA 1985, ss 91(2) and 93(2); and *Luton BC v Menni* [2006] EWCA Civ 1880).

A new criminal offence of unlawful sub-letting of a secure tenancy has been introduced by s 1 of the Prevention of Social Housing Fraud Act 2013 (see **2.9.2**).

6.4.2 Exclusions from secure status

Schedule 1 to the HA 1985 lists the categories of tenancies that are excluded from secure tenant status. A few of these are identical to those excluded under the regulated tenancy and assured tenancy regimes (see **Chapters 2** and **3**), but the majority are unique to the public sector. The exclusions are:

(a) a long tenancy, ie a tenancy granted for a term of more than 21 years (see **1.5.1.1**). Although expressed differently, this is similar to the exclusion in **2.3** (tenancies at low rent), as often a premium is paid on the grant of a long lease;

(b) an introductory tenancy, or one which has ceased to be an introductory tenancy as a result of disposal on death to a non-qualifying person (HA 1996, s 133(3)), or the tenant or joint tenants ceasing to occupy the property as his/their only or principal home, or a demoted tenancy (see **6.5** for introductory tenancies and **6.6.2** for demoted tenancies);

(c) where the tenant is an employee of the landlord or another public body, and occupies the premises as a requirement of his employment contract to enable him better to perform his duties. The onus is on the landlord to show that this exemption applies as there are many qualifications within the schedule (see *Hughes v Greenwich LBC* [1994] 1 AC 170, HL; *Wragg v Surrey CC* [2008] EWCA Civ 19);

(d) where the dwelling-house is on land acquired for development and is being used by the landlord pending development;

(e) accommodation given to a homeless person under Pt VII of the HA 1996 (see **11.7.5**);

(f) a family intervention tenancy granted by an LHA who has complied with the requirements in para 4ZA of Sch 1;

(g) accommodation provided for asylum seekers under Pt VI of the Immigration and Asylum Act 1999;

(h) accommodation provided to someone under the Displaced Persons (Temporary Protection) Regulations 2005 (SI 2005/1379), which relate to certain categories of asylum seekers given exceptional leave to enter the UK;

(i) temporary accommodation provided to a non-resident of the district to enable him to work in the district or its surrounding area and to find permanent accommodation there;

(j) short-term arrangements where the landlord has leased the premises from a non-public owner for use as temporary accommodation (see *Tower Hamlets LBC v Miah* [1992] QB 622, CA);

(k) temporary accommodation provided to non-secure tenants during works to their own homes;

(l) the tenancy of an agricultural holding where the tenant is the person responsible for management of the holding;

(m) the tenancy of premises licensed for the supply and consumption of alcohol on the premises, eg a pub;

(n) student lettings to enable a student to attend a designated course at an educational establishment, provided the student has prior notice of this exception from protection;

(o) business tenancies (see **2.3** at (d));

(p) a licence to occupy an almshouse, granted by an almshouse charity.

The status of the above non-secure tenancies will be governed by the general law of landlord and tenant, unless some other statutory regime applies (eg, the provisions in Pt II of the LTA 1954 for business tenants).

If the tenancy is for a fixed term then it will terminate on expiry of the term. If it is a periodic tenancy, it will be terminable on the expiry of the appropriate notice to quit served by the landlord (see **9.4**). In the cases of *Crawley BC v Sawyer* and *Hussey v Camden LBC* (see **6.3.3**), the landlords had served notice to quit on the tenants in the belief that the tenancies had ceased to be secure.

6.5 INTRODUCTORY TENANCIES

Part V of the HA 1996 was introduced in response to a general perception that public sector landlords were often faced with difficult, anti-social tenants and/or bad rent payers who would gain security of tenure, which made it difficult to obtain possession against them subsequently. Local housing authorities (and HATs) can elect to operate this regime. It enables them to offer non-secure tenancies and licences for a trial period of one year initially, which can be extended to 18 months if the landlord so elects.

Where an election for this system is made and a new periodic tenancy is created, with the relevant landlord and tenant conditions for a secure tenancy being met, an introductory tenancy will arise (HA 1996, s 124). As indicated at **6.4.2** above, an introductory tenant will not be secure and so the security of tenure provisions will not apply to him. Provided the landlord follows the correct procedures for terminating an introductory tenancy, the court will be obliged to make a possession order. The provisions do not apply to a new tenancy granted to an existing secure tenant, or to an assured (but not an assured shorthold) tenant of an RSL or PRP.

6.5.1 Rights of introductory tenants

For the one-year or 18-month (if extended) trial period, apart from the absence of security of tenure, the introductory tenant has some of the rights enjoyed by a secure tenant: his family can enjoy the right of succession, and he has the right to repairs and to consultation on housing management issues that secure tenants have. However, he does not have the right to buy, to take lodgers, to sub-let, to improve, to exchange or to vote on transfer to a new landlord (HA 1996, ss 131 to 137). These are all additional rights enjoyed by secure tenants (see **6.8** for tenants' rights and obligations).

6.5.2 Extension of an introductory tenancy

As noted above, an introductory tenancy will last for one year initially, provided the landlord and tenant conditions applicable for secure tenants continue to apply (HA 1996, s 125). If, however, the tenant's conduct during this test period gives the landlord reason to do so, it can, on giving the tenant at least eight weeks' notice prior to the expiry of the first year, extend the trial period by a further six months (HA 1996, ss 125A and 125B, as amended by s 179 of the HA 2004).

6.5.3 Termination of an introductory tenancy

At the end of the 12-month trial period (or 18-month, if extended), the introductory tenant will become a secure tenant unless the landlord has commenced proceedings for possession. The landlord must serve a notice on the tenant informing him of its intention to bring proceedings and the reasons for doing so. The notice must specify when proceedings may be begun, and this must not be earlier than the date the landlord could proceed after service of a notice to quit. The tenant should be informed of his right to request a review (HA 1996, s 128). The Introductory Tenants (Review) Regulations 1997 (SI 1997/72) set out the procedure for such reviews. The tenant also has the right to request a review of a decision to extend the initial 12-month trial period to 18 months (see Introductory Tenancies (Review of Decisions to Extend a Trial Period) (England) Regulations 2006 (SI 2006/1077)).

The court must grant the landlord possession of the premises if the notice procedure in s 128 of the HA 1996 is correctly followed (s 127). As the tenant has no security of tenure under s82 of the HA 1985, the court will have no discretion to decide whether or not to make a possession order. In such cases an outright order for possession is likely to be made (see **10.8**).

6.5.4 Introductory tenancies and human rights issues

The legitimacy of the introductory tenancy regime was challenged as being in breach of Articles 6 and 8 of the European Convention on Human Rights in R *(McLellan) v Bracknell Forest BC* [2002] QB 1129, CA, by tenants who were being evicted under the provisions in Pt V of the HA 1996. It was held that although Article 8(1) was engaged, Article 8(2) justified the eviction. Further, that although the review procedure involved a determination of the tenants' civil rights, and therefore Article 6 was engaged, the procedure, together with judicial review that was available in principle, provided adequate safeguards against unfairness and/or infringement of their Convention rights. Accordingly, the scheme was not incompatible with Article 6 either.

The decision of the Supreme Court in *Hounslow LBC v Powell; Leeds City Council v Hall and Birmingham City Council v Frisby* makes clear that not only is the introductory tenancy regime compatible with Convention rights, but there are also sufficient safeguards for an occupier who is contesting a possession claim (see **4.5.3.2** and **4.6**).

6.6 SECURITY OF TENURE

The security provision is contained in s 82 of the HA 1985. It provides that a landlord can end a secure tenancy only by obtaining a court order for possession and the execution of the order. There are three categories of orders that the court (normally a county court) can make on the application of a landlord. They are:

(a) an order for possession, which will not be granted unless the landlord follows the notice requirements stipulated in s 83 of the HA 1985, or the court dispenses with them, and the court is satisfied that one of more of the possession grounds in Sch 2 to the HA 1985 is made out (see **6.7** for the grounds for possession); or

(b) an order for demotion, which terminates the secure tenancy if the court finds there has been anti-social behaviour (see **6.6.3**); or

(c) an order terminating a fixed-term secure tenancy so that a periodic tenancy arises instead.

A secure tenant who wishes to terminate his tenancy can do so by surrender, or by serving a valid notice to quit on his landlord (see **9.4**). The orders which a landlord can obtain are discussed in further detail below.

Although the tenant of a fixed-term tenancy would not, at common law, be able to terminate the tenancy by notice to quit, s 107C of the HA 1985 makes it a term of every flexible tenancy that the tenant can terminate his tenancy. This can be done by the tenant serving a written notice on the landlord, giving at least four weeks' notice from the date of service of the notice. The parties can agree to dispense with the notice requirements. The notice will be effective only if the tenant is not in arrears of rent and there is no other material breach of a term of the tenancy.

6.6.1 Termination by an LHA of a fixed-term secure tenancy

A fixed-term secure tenancy may be terminated by an LHA in a number of ways, but this will not entitle the LHA to possession. The fixed term may be terminated under s 82(3) of the HA 1985 by way of the LHA exercising a forfeiture provision in the agreement. However, the notice provisions of s 146 of the Law of Property Act (LPA) 1925 may be applicable, and the tenant would have the right to apply for relief (see **8.5.3.1** for the notice procedure under s 146 of the LPA 1925). Alternatively, there may be a re-entry provision in the tenancy agreement. In either case, if the court makes an order to terminate the fixed term on a specified date, a statutory periodic tenancy will arise after that date (HA 1985, s 86). In order to obtain possession of the property, the LHA has to follow the notice provisions in s 83 of the 1985 Act and claim for forfeiture or re-entry, as well as one of the grounds for possession in Sch 2.

A statutory periodic tenancy will also arise where the fixed term has come to an end by effluxion of time (HA 1985, s 86(1)(a)). This will be the case unless the LHA grants the tenant another fixed term, or a periodic secure tenancy of the same dwelling-house. The periodic tenancy will be on the same terms as the original tenancy, except for the re-entry or forfeiture provisions. A long lease which was never secure cannot become a statutory periodic tenancy under s 86 (see *Banjo v Brent LBC* [2005] EWCA Civ 292, CA).

6.6.2 Termination by an LHA of a flexible tenancy

In addition to the statutory grounds for possession available to a landlord in Sch 2 to the HA 1985 (see para **6.7**), the landlord has a mandatory right to possession against a flexible tenant on expiry of the fixed term of a flexible tenancy.

By s 107D, a court must make an order for possession if three conditions are satisfied:

(a) The flexible tenancy has come to an end and no further secure tenancy (whether or not a flexible tenancy) is for the time being in existence, other than a secure tenancy that is a periodic tenancy (whether or not arising by virtue of s 86).

(b) The landlord must have given the tenant not less than six months' written notice:
    (i) stating that the landlord does not propose to grant another tenancy on the expiry of the flexible tenancy;
    (ii) setting out the landlord's reasons for not proposing to grant another tenancy; and
    (iii) informing the tenant of the tenant's right to request a review of that proposal and of the time within which the review must be made.

(c) The landlord has given the tenant not less than two months' written notice stating that it requires possession.

The two-month notice may be given before or on the day on which the tenancy comes to an end (s 107D(5)).

The tenant has 21 days to request a review after service of the six-month notice. The Flexible Tenancies (Review Procedures) Regulations 2012 (SI 2012/695) apply to any review proceedings. The landlord must give written notice of its review decision, and if the decision is adverse to the tenant then it must give reasons (s 107E(7)).

A court can refuse to grant a possession order if the landlord has not carried out a tenant's request for a review or the decision on the review is otherwise wrong in law.

6.6.3 Demoted tenancies

6.6.3.1 Grounds for a demotion order

An LHA, HAT, PRP or RSL can apply to a county court for a demotion order to terminate a secure tenancy, on the basis that the tenant, or a person residing in or visiting the dwelling-house, has engaged in or threatened to engage in anti-social behaviour, or is using the premises for unlawful purposes (HA 1985, s 82A). Anti-social behaviour is defined in the Anti-social Behaviour Act 2003 as 'conduct which is capable of causing nuisance or annoyance to any person and which directly or indirectly relates to or affects the housing management functions of a relevant landlord'. The court must not make a demotion order unless it considers that it is reasonable to do so (HA 1985, s 82(4)(b)).

6.6.3.2 The effect of a demotion order terminating a secure tenancy

The effect of the order in terminating the secure tenancy is that it terminates the tenant's right to buy and security of tenure status. The demoted tenancy, for LHA and HAT secure tenants, is one to which s 143A of the HA 1996 applies. The consequence of this is that, provided the landlord follows the mandatory notice and review procedures in ss 143E to 143F, the court must make a possession order. The notice procedure requires the tenant to be given detailed reasons why a possession order is being sought. This will almost certainly be because the tenant has continued his anti-social behaviour, or has breached some other term of the tenancy.

The notice should also state the date proceedings may start. This date cannot be earlier than the date that would need to be given to terminate under a notice to quit (HA 1996, s 143E(3)). The tenant has a right to request a review of the decision to seek possession within 14 days of receipt of the notice.

The tenant will become a secure tenant once more if the landlord does not seek to terminate the demoted tenancy within one year from the demotion order being made.

As with introductory tenancies (see **6.5**), the legitimacy of the demoted tenancy possession procedure was challenged as being in breach of Articles 6 and 8 of the Convention. The Court in R (Gilboy) v Liverpool City Council [2008] EWCA Civ 751 held that there was no distinguishing feature of the demoted tenancy scheme which would allow the reasoning in McLellan (see **6.5.4**) not to apply in this case. The legislative intention was clearly to replicate the introductory tenant scheme, and such differences as there were between that and the demoted scheme would not be a ground for distinguishing McLellan. This has been upheld in both the Pinnock and Powell Supreme Court judgments (see **4.5.3.2** and **4.6**).

6.6.4 The policy for dealing with anti-social behaviour

The demoted tenancy provision is designed to deal with existing anti-social tenants, just as the introductory tenancy provisions (see **6.5**) deal with new anti-social tenants. These are just two ways in which public sector landlords can seek to control anti-social tenants.

6.6.4.1 Anti-social behaviour injunctions

In addition, the Anti-social Behaviour Act 2003 introduced ss 153A to 153E of the HA 1996, which enable an LHA, HAT, RSL or a non-profit registered provider to obtain an anti-social behaviour injunction, an injunction against immoral and unlawful use of premises, or an injunction against breach of tenancy agreement. The Police and Justice Act 2006 substituted a new s 153A (see **2.9.4**). These injunctions can carry with them a power of arrest for breach. The landlords are required to draw up and publish policies and procedures for dealing with anti-social behaviour (HA 1996, s 218) so that relevant parties may be fully aware of what to expect when infringement occurs. (See **2.9.4** and **2.9.5** for examples of cases where RSLs have made applications for anti-social behaviour injunctions and orders.)

6.6.4.2 Parenting contracts and orders

The provisions in the Police and Justice Act 2006 on parenting contracts and parenting orders are available to local authorities generally to control anti-social behaviour in their area. Local housing authorities will clearly be able to use these provisions against anti-social tenants (see **2.9.6**).

6.6.4.3 Family intervention tenancies

As with RSLs and PRPs, another tool available to LHAs is the ability to offer family intervention tenancies in circumstances where a tenant is likely to be evicted on the grounds of anti-social behaviour or in the opinion of the landlord could have been so evicted. The provision operates in a similar way to those under the HA 1988 (see **2.9.7** for further details).

A tenant with a family intervention tenancy will not be a secure tenant and will have no security of tenure while he holds a family intervention tenancy as it is specifically excluded in Sch 1 to the HA 1985 (see 6.4.2(f)). After the period agreed for the tenancy has expired, the tenant could once again become a secure tenant or, if he was not a secure tenant before, be granted a secure tenancy if he has been receptive to and has benefited from the support given. The aim of the tenancy is to provide the family with support to help rehabilitate them. The lack of security is supposed to work as an incentive to persuade the tenant to comply with the support network. If the tenant fails to comply, the ultimate sanction is that the LHA can obtain a possession order against him.

6.6.5 The notice requirements before possession or termination can be claimed against secure tenants

Before an LHA (or HAT) can start possession proceedings, it must first have served a notice seeking possession, unless the court considers it just and equitable to dispense with this requirement (see HA 1985, s 83(1)(b)).

The notice requirements in s 83 of the HA 1985 require the LHA to serve a notice in the prescribed form (see Secure Tenancies (Notices) Regulations 1987 (SI 1987/755), as amended), specifying and giving details of the ground for seeking possession. The notice should also state either the date after which proceedings could start (this applies to an application for a demotion order too), or, where one of the grounds specified is for nuisance or other anti-social behaviour (Ground 2, see **6.7.1.2** below), the date the tenant is to give up possession of the property. In either case, the date specified should not be earlier than the date on which the tenancy could have been brought to an end by a notice to quit (see **9.4.1**). Where Ground 2 is one of the grounds for seeking possession, the notice must also state that possession proceedings may start immediately.

> **EXAMPLE**
>
> A secure tenant was granted a monthly periodic tenancy which started on the 10th of the month. Some time later, the LHA served a notice seeking possession due to the tenant's rent arrears (Ground 1). The notice was served on 1 February. The earliest date after which the LHA can start proceedings will be 10 March, not 1 March. This is because 10 March is the first day after the expiry of the notice on 9 March, the last day of the monthly term. If there was provision in the tenancy agreement allowing for a minimum notice period of four weeks, the four weeks would still need to end on 9 March in the absence of express agreement to the contrary (see **9.4.1**).
>
> If the notice also included a claim for anti-social behaviour (Ground 2) then the LHA could start proceedings for possession immediately. The relevant date specified in the notice here would be the date for the tenant to give up possession. This date could not be earlier than 10 March unless once again there was express provision in the tenancy agreement allowing for the minimum notice period of four weeks, ending at any time.

Minor inaccuracies in the notice will not invalidate it. However, it is important to include details of the ground for possession in a way that makes clear to the tenant what he has done wrong and to enable him to remedy it if possible. In *Torridge DC v Jones* (1986) 18 HLR 107, CA, a notice which simply told the tenant that 'The reasons for taking this action are non payment of rent', without any further details, was held invalid.

The notice will cease to be valid 12 months after the specified date. If the LHA wanted to start possession proceedings after the specified date, it would have to issue a new notice, as the court must not allow proceedings to commence on the basis of an expired notice (HA 1985, s 83A(1)). Where one of the grounds for possession relates to domestic violence (Ground 2A, see **6.7**), the landlord must satisfy the court that it has taken reasonable steps to serve a notice on the non-tenant partner who has left, informing her (usually) of the proceedings and the basis for them (HA 1985, s 83A(3)–(5)).

These provisions apply equally to flexible tenancies where the landlord is not relying on the mandatory ground at the expiry of the fixed period (see **6.6.2**).

6.7 GROUNDS FOR POSSESSION

The court will not make an order for possession unless the landlord satisfies the court that one or more of the grounds listed in Sch 2 to the HA 1985 has been made out (s 84). Schedule 2 divides the grounds into three parts. Part I covers the fault grounds (Grounds 1–8), where the court may order possession once the ground is made out, if it considers it reasonable to do so. In fact there are now nine grounds in Pt I, as s 145 of the HA 1996 introduced a new Ground 2A (domestic violence). Part II comprises Grounds 9–11, which give the court the power to make a possession order if suitable alternative accommodation is available for the tenant. There are four grounds here, as s 9(1) of the Housing and Planning Act 1986 added Ground 10A (redevelopment schemes), and the related Pt V to Sch 2. Part III contains Grounds 12–16, where the court may make a possession order if it considers it reasonable to do so and suitable alternative accommodation is available.

The criteria for the suitability of any alternative accommodation to be provided in Pts II and III are set out in Pt IV of Sch 2 (see **6.7.4**).

6.7.1 Part I – Grounds 1–8

The first six grounds in Pt I (Grounds 1–5 below) are in very similar terms to those already considered for assured tenants in Pt II of Sch 2 to the HA 1988 (discretionary grounds) (see **2.6.2**), and so will not be discussed in great detail here. In brief, the Pt I grounds are as follows:

Ground 1 – Rent arrears or breach of some other term of the tenancy.

Ground 2 – Nuisance or annoyance, or conviction for using premises for immoral or illegal purposes by the tenant or a person residing in or visiting the dwelling.

Ground 2A – Domestic violence by a resident partner causing the victim to leave.

Ground 3 – Waste, neglect or default, causing deterioration to the dwelling-house or the common parts of the building, by the tenant or a person residing in the dwelling.

Ground 4 – The ill-treatment of furniture by the tenant or a person residing in the dwelling-house.

Ground 5 – False statement made to obtain the tenancy.

Ground 6 – Premium taken on a s 92 assignment of the tenancy.

Ground 7 – The conduct of the tenant of, or a person residing in, an employment-linked dwelling is such as to make their continued occupation inappropriate.

Ground 8 – Possession of premises occupied while works are completed on the original premises let to the tenant under a secure tenancy.

6.7.1.1 Rent arrears (Ground 1)

Of the thousands of possession orders made against LHA tenants every year, the vast majority relate to rent arrears claims (see **10.2.1**). The next most significant ground is anti-social behaviour (Ground 2). However, possession orders on this ground are a long way behind those for rent arrears. Nonetheless, the Government amended Ground 2 in the HA 1996 to broaden its scope, the previous definition having been more in line with the RA 1977 provisions (see Case 2 at **3.4.2.3**).

6.7.1.2 Anti-social behaviour (Ground 2)

This ground is now subject to the provisions in s 85A, which has introduced the structured discretion for the courts to apply in anti-social behaviour cases (see **2.6.2.7**). However, the courts have always taken a firm line in anti-social behaviour cases, as in *Gallagher v Castle Vale Action Trust Ltd* (2001) 33 HLR 72, CA, where the judge at first instance made an outright order against a secure tenant. The order was made against the tenant because of the anti-social behaviour of her daughter and the daughter's boyfriend, both of whom had resided at the property. On appeal it was held that the judge had failed to take account of the fact that the tenant, Mrs Gallagher, had not committed a nuisance, and the daughter and boyfriend had, before the possession hearing, moved out of the dwelling. These were factors, the Court of Appeal held, which should have influenced the judge to exercise his discretion against making an outright order, not least because of human rights considerations (see **4.5.3.1**). See **10.8.1.2** for further examples of the exercise of the discretion in anti-social behaviour cases.

6.7.1.3 Domestic violence (Ground 2A)

Ground 2A, the domestic violence ground, was introduced by the HA 1996 to deal with the all too common situation where the abused partner is driven from the home, leaving the abuser with the benefit of the secure tenancy. Where the parties are joint tenants, or the tenancy is in the sole name of the victim, a notice to quit given to the landlord by that party would give the landlord the ability to take possession proceedings against the person who remains in occupation (see **6.8.1** below). However, if the tenancy was in the sole name of the abuser, this option was not, until Ground 2A, available.

This ground is designed to enable public sector landlords to manage their housing stock more effectively. However, the courts have applied a strict interpretation of the ground before they will grant an order here (see *Camden LBC v Mallett* (2001) 33 HLR 204, CA; **2.6.2.8**).

6.7.1.4 False statements (Ground 5)

There have been a number of reported cases dealing with false statements under Ground 5. The courts have not always been keen to grant a possession order simply because of the tenant's deception. Other factors are taken into consideration, for example the risk that the tenant and any children may become homeless.

In *Waltham Forest LBC v Roberts* [2005] HLR 2, CA, the Court had to consider whether or not there had been a misrepresentation. The appellant was relying on Grounds 1 and 5 in seeking possession against the respondent. The respondent was a former LHA employee. She had been granted a secure tenancy after she falsely claimed that she did not own or receive any rental income from any property. The respondent also applied for and obtained housing benefit for the secure tenancy. When the appellant discovered that the respondent and her son did own and were receiving rental income on another property, it sought to recover the overpayments of housing benefit and commenced possession proceedings on Grounds 1, for rent arrears, and 5, for the false statement which induced the appellant to grant the tenancy. The trial judge was of the view that the appellant had created the arrears by wrongfully withdrawing the housing benefit, and that there was no inducement as the appellant had granted the secure tenancy in the discharge of its obligation to a retiring employee.

The Court of Appeal, in allowing the appeal, held that the judge had taken the wrong approach. The materiality of the misstatement was relevant, and here the respondent's ownership of a property was material, especially as it affected the appellant in the discharge of its public functions. Once materiality was established, it was a fair inference of fact that the false statement operated on the appellant's mind. The inducement was made out. On the rent arrears claim, the Court stated that as no challenge by way of judicial review had been made against a review board's finding that the respondent had not been entitled to housing benefit, the appellant's reclaiming of it was not wrongful and the respondent was, as a result, in arrears. Both grounds were therefore made out. The case was remitted to consider the issue of whether it would be reasonable to make an order for possession.

In *Islington LBC v Uckac* [2006] 1 WLR 1303, CA, one of the defendants had lied to the LHA to obtain a secure tenancy. He then assigned the tenancy to his wife. When the LHA discovered the fraud, they tried to obtain possession under Ground 5. However, it was held that Ground 5 could not be used, as possession could be sought only against the person to whom the tenancy was granted.

6.7.1.5 Unlawful assignment (Ground 6)

Ground 6 is concerned with the abuse of one of the limited circumstances in which secure tenants are allowed to assign their tenancies. Section 92 of the HA 1985 allows secure tenants, subject to obtaining their landlord's consent, to assign by way of mutual exchange with another secure tenant or an RSL or PRP assured tenant (see **6.8.2.2**, right to assign). If a premium (ie a fine or other like sum, or any other pecuniary consideration in addition to the rent) is paid by either party then it becomes a ground for possession against them, and against any successor who is a family member of the original assigning tenant if he still resides in the property.

6.7.1.6 Misconduct (Ground 7)

Ground 7 relates to a dwelling-house, situated within the curtilage of primarily non-housing property held by the landlord, which was let to the tenant or his predecessor as a result of employment with the landlord or some other public body, where the tenant or a person residing in the dwelling has been guilty of conduct incompatible with the tenant being allowed to remain.

6.7.2 Part II – Grounds 9–11

Few challenges have been made by tenants under the four grounds in this Part. Consequently, other than Ground 9 which may be affected by provisions in the HA 2004, the grounds are merely listed here.

Ground 9 – Overcrowding of the dwelling-house within Pt X (ss 324–329) of the HA 1985, where the occupier is guilty of an offence.

Ground 10 – Demolition or reconstruction of the premises, which requires the landlord to have possession of the property.

Ground 10A – The dwelling-house is situated in an area subject to an approved redevelopment scheme, and the landlord wishes to dispose of the property in accordance with that scheme.

Ground 11 – Where continued occupation by the tenant would conflict with the charity landlord's objectives (this provision does not apply to an LHA).

6.7.2.1 Overcrowding (Ground 9)

Under the present provisions, which have been criticised as being outdated, an offence will be committed if the landlord or an occupier of a dwelling causes or permits it to be overcrowded (see HA 1985, ss 324–338). Overcrowding occurs if the occupancy of the property breaches either a room standard, or a space standard. The room standard prohibits persons over the age of 10, and of the opposite sex, sharing the same room unless they are living together as a couple. The space standard relates to the number of rooms and the floor area, with regulations providing a detailed process for calculation of the measurement. According to the size of the room, a permitted maximum number of persons are allowed to occupy it. Children under the age of 1 year do not count for these purposes. If they are between the age of 1 year and under 10, they count as a half person. The maximum number of occupants for a large room is two (which could be four children between the age of 1 year and under 10). The HA 2004 (s 216) has given a discretionary power to the Secretary of State (or the National Assembly for Wales) to make alternative provisions to determine whether a dwelling is overcrowded for the purposes of Pt X of the 1985 Act.

6.7.3 Part III – Grounds 12–16

The grounds for possession in Pt III are as follows:

Ground 12 – An employment-related tenancy is required for a new employee. This, rather like Ground 7 (see **6.7.1.6**), relates to a dwelling-house situated within the curtilage of primarily non-housing property held by the landlord, and let to the tenant or his predecessor as a result of employment with the landlord or some other public body. Here, however, the employment of the present occupier has ceased and the landlord requires the dwelling for a new employee.

Ground 13 – A specially designed dwelling-house is required for a disabled person, where the present tenant does not require accommodation of this kind.

Ground 14 – The dwelling-house is required by a housing association or housing trust for a special housing needs occupant, where the present occupant is not such a special needs occupant, or he has been offered a secure tenancy of other premises by an LHA.

Ground 15 – The dwelling-house is required for a special needs occupant where a social service or special facility is provided in close proximity. The tenant does not have those special needs and the landlord requires the property for someone who does.

Ground 15A – In England, the dwelling-house is under-occupied by a successor tenant who is not the spouse or civil partner of the original tenant to a periodic or fixed-term tenancy. The landlord must act to obtain possession within a specified period of more than six months but less than 12 months after the relevant date. This date is either the date of the original tenant's death or, where the court permits, the date the landlord became aware of the death.

Ground 16 – In Wales, the dwelling-house is under-occupied by a successor tenant who is not the spouse or civil partner of the original tenant (see *Wandsworth LBC v Randall* [2008] 1 WLR 359, CA). The landlord must act to obtain possession within a specfied period of more than six months but less than 12 months of the relevant date. The date is either the date of the tenant's death or the date the landlord became aware of the death.

Even where one of Grounds 12 to 16 is made out, the landlord must show that suitable alternative accommodation will be available for the tenant before the court will consider whether it is reasonable to make an order for possession. In *Bracknell Forest BC v Green* [2009] EWCA Civ 238, the Court found that suitable alternative accommodation was available, but refused to exercise its discretion in favour of the LHA's Ground 16 claim. As with Pt II, few challenges to possession have been made under these grounds.

In *Wandsworth LBC v Randall*, the LHA sought possession under Ground 16 against a successor tenant. The LHA argued that the successor's sole occupancy of a four-bedroom house was too large for his needs. He was offered a one-bedroom flat instead. However, after the notice seeking possession was served, the mother and young sister of the successor tenant moved into the house with him. The Court held that the composition of the family for the purposes of Ground 16 was not fixed at the date of the succession but was to be determined as at the date of the hearing. The hearing date was also the relevant date for other cases in Pt II and Pt III where the court had to be satisfied that suitable accommodation would be available for the tenant.

6.7.4 Suitable alternative accommodation

The provisions in Pt IV of Sch 2 to the HA 1985 are slightly different from those for tenants in the private sector (see **2.6.2.2** and **3.4.2.1**). In particular, the LHA cannot 'self-certificate' itself as providing suitable alternative accommodation. The court will decide whether any alternative secure or assured tenancy being offered is suitable to the needs of the tenant and his family. Paragraph 2 of Sch 2 lists the factors to consider in making that determination. The character of the property is not, unlike the provisions for regulated and assured tenants, specifically mentioned. The factors are:

(a) the nature of the accommodation which it is the practice of the landlord to allocate to persons with similar needs;

(b) the available accommodation's distance from the place of work or education of the tenant and of any members of his family;

(c) its distance from the home of any member of the tenant's family if proximity to it is essential to that member's or the tenant's well-being;

(d) the needs (as regards extent of accommodation) and means of the tenant and his family;

(e) the terms on which the accommodation is available and the terms of the secure tenancy;

(f) if furniture was provided by the landlord for use under the secure tenancy, whether furniture is to be provided for use in the other accommodation and, if so, the nature of the furniture to be provided.

In *Holt v Reading BC* [2013] EWCA Civ 641, it was held that the expression 'suitable alternative accommodation' was broad enough to include accommodation identified by reference to its essential characteristics. It might not always be necessary to identify a specific property before an order for possession was made. On occasion, considering the particular circumstances of the case, it might be appropriate for the court to specify what should be included in the alternative property and make a conditional order for possession subject to a time limit for the landlord to comply with the order.

6.8 THE RIGHTS AND OBLIGATIONS OF A SECURE TENANT

Security of tenure, as outlined in **6.6** above, is arguably the most significant right that a secure tenant has. However, Pt IV (ss 87–106A) of the HA 1985 contains a number of further rights that can be enjoyed by a secure tenant. Before considering the statutory provisions, mention is made here of the tenant's common law right to terminate his tenancy.

6.8.1 Tenant's right to terminate the tenancy

As mentioned at **6.6**, the tenant has the common law right to terminate the tenancy either by surrendering the tenancy, or, if a periodic tenant, by serving a notice to quit on the landlord. Notice to quit by a periodic secure tenant is most commonly used by a joint tenant, often the victim of domestic abuse, to enable her (usually) to become eligible for re-housing by the LHA in another property. The notice, even though from one joint tenant, if validly served, will terminate the tenancy, and the LHA will then be able to take possession proceedings against the person remaining in occupation as a trespasser with no security of tenure (see *Hammersmith and Fulham LBC v Monk* [1992] 1 AC 478, HL; *Hounslow LBC v Pilling* [1993] 1 WLR 1242, CA).

The human rights aspect to this process has been challenged in a number of cases, as discussed in **Chapter 4**. The potential for this right to terminate to cause problems in other overlapping areas of law which impact on the relationship between the parties is rather sadly illustrated in a number of cases concerned with family and domestic violence law.

In *Harrow LBC v Johnstone* [1997] 1 WLR 459, HL, the husband obtained an injunction in ex parte proceedings under the Domestic Violence and Matrimonial Proceedings Act 1976, to restrain his wife from using violence and abuse against him. The wife applied for separate housing, but as the LHA was not prepared to grant two tenancies to the same family unit, the wife served a notice to quit terminating the joint tenancy of the family home, in which the husband continued to reside. At first instance and in the Court of Appeal it was held that the wife and LHA were in breach of the injunction and in contempt of court for bringing possession proceedings when they were aware of the terms of the order. However, the House of Lords decided that as the notice to quit had terminated the tenancy, there was no contempt. The injunction was concerned only with the exercise of rights under the tenancy, not with its continued existence. It could not be said that Harrow, in carrying out its statutory duty, was in contempt of court.

In *Bater v Greenwich LBC, Bater v Bater* [1999] 4 All ER 944, CA, the wife served a notice to terminate the joint tenancy, with the intention of frustrating her husband's attempt to exercise his right to buy. (The notice, in terminating the secure tenancy, also terminated the right to buy.) The Court of Appeal held that it had no jurisdiction under family law legislation to set aside a unilateral notice to terminate a joint tenancy by one of the two joint tenants in a matrimonial dispute. Such a notice is not a disposition of property. There was, however, a suggestion by one of the judges in the case that if the court was aware of the intention to serve the notice before it was served, it might be able to intervene.

The position now, following the Supreme Court judgments in *Pinnock* and *Powell*, is that the remaining joint tenant will need to raise an Article 8 defence in any possession claim brought by the LHA, and it will then be for the LHA to demonstrate to the satisfaction of the court that the interference with the remaining joint tenant's right to his home is proportionate within Article 8(2) of the Convention (see **4.5.3.2** and **4.6**).

6.8.2 Additional statutory rights in HA 1985, Pt IV

The additional rights set out in Pt IV of the HA 1985, sometimes referred to as the 'Tenant's Charter', may be listed as the rights to:

(a) succession;
(b) assign in certain cases;
(c) take lodgers and sub-let a part of the dwelling-house;
(d) have repairs carried out;
(e) carry out improvements; and
(f) be consulted on housing management matters.

Each right is considered briefly below.

6.8.2.1 The right to succeed

Following the amendments introduced by the Localism Act 2011, the succession provisions vary for secure tenancies in England that existed before the implementation of s 160 of that Act on 2 April 2012, and for secure tenancies created on and after that date.

The position in England for tenancies created on or after 2 April 2012

For new secure tenancies created in England on or after 2 April 2012, one succession to a secure tenancy is allowed to a person who occupied the dwelling-house as his only or principal home and who was the tenant's spouse or civil partner, or who was living with the tenant as if he was a spouse or civil partner. No other person has an automatic right to succession. However, if a tenancy agreement provides for succession by others, in the absence of a qualifying spouse or civil partner, then effect will be given to that succession (HA 1985, s 86A).

The position in Wales and for tenancies created in England before 2 April 2012

When the secure tenant dies, one succession to a secure tenancy is allowed to a person who occupied the dwelling-house as his only or principal home at the time of the tenant's death

(HA 1985, s 87). If the tenant was married or had a registered civil partner, his spouse or civil partner has priority to succeed to the tenancy (s 89(2)). If the tenant was not married, or his spouse or civil partner was not in occupation, another member of his family may be eligible to succeed if that person had resided with the tenant for the 12-month period which led up to the tenant's death. In *Freeman v Islington LBC* (2009) 24 EG 85, CA, it was held that mere physical presence is not enough to amount to 'residing with' the tenant. The residence does not need to have been in the same dwelling-house throughout the 12-month period (see *Waltham Forest LBC v Thomas* [1992] 2 AC 198, HL).

The 12-month period of residence as the only or principal home was generously interpreted in *Peabody Donation Fund Governors v Grant* (1982) 264 EG 925, CA. The defendant, who up until mid-1979 lived with her two children, her mother and step-father in Salisbury, began to spend increasing amounts of time in London with her ailing father, a secure tenant. By 1980, the defendant spent four nights each week at her father's flat in London, keeping her clothes and books there. On the father's death in June 1981, the defendant claimed the right to succeed to his tenancy. It was held the defendant had satisfied the burden of showing that she had resided with the deceased for the requisite period, during which the flat was her principal home.

If the LHA considers that the dwelling house is too large for the needs of the successor tenant, Ground 15A or Ground 16 may be used to try to obtain possession of that property from the successor tenant. The LHA must be able to offer suitable alternative accommodation to the successor (see **6.7.3** and **6.7.4**). The alternative accommodation would usually be smaller than the original property. However, it must be suitable to the needs of the successor tenant as it stands at the date of trial (see *Wandsworth LBC v Randall* (2008) at **6.7.3**).

'Family' definition and human rights

A member of the person's family is defined in s 113 to include those living together as husband and wife or civil partners, as well as parents, grandparents, children, grandchildren, siblings, uncles, aunts, nephews and nieces. Relationships of the half blood, step-children and illegitimate children are included. The list does not extend to include cousins.

Living together as husband and wife was taken very literally in *Westminster CC v Peart* (1992) 24 HLR 389, CA. It was held that the parties had to demonstrate, by their conduct, a settled intention to be regarded as husband and wife throughout the 12-month period. Merely living together in the same household was not sufficient to meet this requirement (see also *Nutting v Southern Housing Group Ltd* [2004] EWHC 2982 (Ch) at **2.4.3**).

In *Wandsworth LBC v Michalak* [2003] 1 WLR 617, CA, the landlord sought possession of premises where the secure tenant had died. The defendant alleged that the LHA landlord had, in breach of Articles 8 and 14 of the Convention (see **4.2** above), infringed his human rights by not respecting his home. The LHA was seeking to evict him from accommodation he had been residing in for several years. The defendant, a cousin of the deceased tenant, contended that he should be entitled, under s 87 of the HA 1985, to succeed to the secure tenancy as a member of the deceased tenant's family. The defendant had been in occupation of the premises for more than 12 months at the time of the tenant's death. Treating him differently from other family members, the defendant contended, amounted to unjustified discrimination.

It was held that the defendant did have an Article 8 right and was being treated differently from other, closer family members in a similar situation. Interference with the defendant's Article 8 right would be justified under Article 8(2), though, unless there was unjustified discrimination. The Court of Appeal took a very structured approach to dealing with the Article 14 point. The Court asked and answered four questions, which in essence sought to establish whether, on the facts, the defendant had a Convention right that had been breached in that he was treated differently from others in a comparable position. If so, was the difference in treatment justifiable? The Court of Appeal held that it was for the proper democratic process to determine the allocation of limited public resources, not for the courts to examine individual cases. On that basis, there had been no discrimination against the defendant. He was not entitled to succeed to the tenancy. See also *Thurrock BC v West* [2013] HLR 5, CA.

'Successor' defined

There will be no entitlement to succeed if the tenant was himself a successor. Unfortunately, s 88 of the HA 1985 gives a very broad definition of who is to be treated as a successor. There are seven different categories. These are:

(a) where the deceased was a successor to a periodic tenancy under s 89;

(b) where the deceased was a joint tenant who became the sole tenant. In *Bassetlaw DC v Renshaw* [1992] 1 All ER 925, CA, it was held that the deceased has to become the sole tenant under the same tenancy for this exclusion to apply. If the joint tenancy is terminated and a new sole tenancy granted, the succession right will not have been exhausted. In *Birmingham City Council v Walker* [2007] 2 AC 262, HL, it was held that this exclusion would apply only if the deceased had succeeded to a secure tenancy. Where, as here, the successor had succeeded to the tenancy in 1969 by right of survivorship and only subsequently became a secure tenant when the HA 1980 came into effect, these provisions did not apply and her son could succeed to the secure tenancy;

(c) where the tenancy arose as a periodic tenancy on the termination of a fixed term (under s 86), and the fixed tenancy was granted to some other person, or jointly to the deceased and some other person;

(d) where the deceased became a tenant as a result of an assignment (although there are some matrimonial provisions and mutual exchange exceptions);

(e) where the tenancy was vested in the deceased on the death of the previous tenant (eg, as the result of a property adjustment order in matrimonial proceedings (s 90(3));

(f) where the tenancy was previously an introductory tenancy and the deceased was a successor to the introductory tenancy;

(g) where a former successor tenant is given a new tenancy within six months of the old one, by the same landlord and/or of the same dwelling (unless the new agreement states otherwise).

If there is no one eligible to succeed to a secure tenancy, the LHA will, in the case of a periodic tenancy, have to serve notice to quit. This will properly terminate what would have become a common law periodic tenancy. The LHA is then able to take possession proceedings against anyone still in occupation of the property, as was the case in *Wandsworth LBC v Michalak* (above).

Where a fixed-term secure tenancy vests in someone not eligible to succeed to the secure tenancy under ss 87 to 90, the tenancy will cease to be secure. However, the tenancy cannot be terminated by the LHA without some provision in the tenancy agreement being breached by the new non-secure tenant. In such a case the landlord may have a right to re-enter or forfeit. If the fixed-term secure tenancy vests in someone eligible to succeed, the tenancy will remain secure.

6.8.2.2 Right to assign

Assignment as a general concept is prohibited for secure tenants (HA 1985, s 91). However, there are three situations in which assignment is permitted. They are as follows:

(a) An assignment by way of exchange (s 92) with another secure tenant or an assured RSL tenant. This will be subject to the written consent of the landlord, which cannot be withheld except on specified grounds in Sch 3 to the HA 1985. Originally 10 grounds were specified, covering objections such as an outright possession order having already been made against the secure tenant or proposed assignee; possession proceedings having commenced on one of the fault-based grounds in Pt I (Grounds 1–6); the accommodation being too big or not reasonably suitable to the needs of the proposed assignee; and so on.

In June 2005, the HA 2004 introduced a new ground of objection in Sch 3, Ground 2A. This allows the landlord to object on the ground of the anti-social behaviour of the tenant, the proposed assignee or a person living with either of them, which has led to the landlord applying for possession on the nuisance ground (Ground 2 of Sch 2 to the HA 1985, or Ground 14 of Sch 2 to the HA 1988) (see **2.6.2.7**), for a demotion order or an anti-social behaviour injunction under one of several statutory provisions (see **2.9.3** and **2.9.4**) or for an anti-social behaviour order under s 1 of the CADA 1998 (see **2.9.5**).

Provisions in ss 158, 159 of and Sch 14 to the Localism Act 2011 deal with exchanges where one party is a flexible tenant or fixed term assured shorthold tenant. Instead of mutual exchange, the transfer will be effected by surrender and re-grant of the tenancies.

(b) An assignment as part of a property adjustment order in matrimonial or civil partnership proceedings, or financial relief against parents in children's proceedings (HA 1985, s 91(3)).

(c) An assignment to a person who would be qualified to succeed the tenant if the tenant were to die immediately before the assignment. The assignment must be properly executed in a deed, or there must be a written, signed agreement for it to be effective (see *Camden LBC v Alexandrou (No 2)* (1998) 30 HLR 534, CA and *Croydon LBC v Buston and Triance* (1992) 24 HLR 36, CA).

> **CASE EXAMPLE**
>
> In *Camden LBC v Goldenberg* (1996) 28 HLR 727, CA, the issue was whether a grandson was eligible on the residence basis to have the dwelling assigned to him. Mrs G, an old lady, executed a deed of assignment of her flat, transferring it to her grandson in late 1992. She then moved into a nursing home. Although he had resided with her at her flat since 1991, there was a 10-week period when he moved out, having married, and was living elsewhere. The LHA argued that this broke his period of continued occupation and so he was not eligible. It was held that the grandson satisfied the residence requirement, having demonstrated an intention to return. The assignment was valid.

A tenant who assigns in breach of these provisions is in breach of a term of the tenancy; but more seriously, he will risk the tenancy ceasing to be secure (see **6.4**). As a result, the landlord can, on the service of a valid notice to quit, regain possession of the property. However, a tenant who assigns in breach of the terms of his tenancy agreement against any assignment, but within the allowable provisions, will effect a valid assignment. The assignee will have security of tenure, although he may be exposed to a possession claim on Ground 1 (breach of a term of the tenancy) (see *Peabody Donation Fund v Higgins* [1983] 1 WLR 1091, CA).

Attempts to use other methods to achieve the same result have also failed.

> **CASE EXAMPLE**
>
> In *Burton v Camden LBC* [2000] 2 AC 399, HL, an outgoing joint tenant, by a deed of release, transferred her interest in the property to the remaining tenant of their three bedroom flat. The remaining tenant then sought a declaration that she had become the sole tenant and should be entitled to housing benefit to cover the whole. It was held that the release was not effective because of the prohibition on assignment in s 91(1); the form of words chosen – 'release' rather than 'assignment' – would not defeat this as the effect was to achieve the same result.

6.8.2.3 Right to take lodgers and to sub-let part of the dwelling-house

The tenant has a right to take lodgers at any time. In addition, subject to obtaining the landlord's consent, which should not be unreasonably withheld (HA 1985, s 94(2)), the tenant can sub-let part of the dwelling. What he should not do is part with possession of, or sub-let, the whole of the dwelling-house. If a tenant does part with the whole, he will lose his secure status and will not be able to regain it (HA 1985, s 93(2)). In *Muir Group Housing Association Ltd v Thornley* (1993) 25 HLR 89, CA, the landlords served notice to quit and obtained possession against former secure tenants, who lost their security when they sub-let the whole of the dwelling-house on an assured shorthold tenancy.

6.8.2.4 Right to repair

Secure and introductory tenants have the right to have certain types of repair works carried out within a set time, or to be entitled to compensation if the works are not done (HA 1985, s 96). Regulations made under s 96 detail the type of repair works and the relevant procedure (see Secure Tenants of Local Housing Authorities (Right to Repair) Regulations 1994 (SI 1994/133), as amended).

The Regulations provide that prescribed repair works costing up to £250 should be completed by the LHA, depending on the type of disrepair, in either one, three or seven days. Examples of prescribed works that should be completed within one working day are works remedying total loss of electrical power or water supply; an unsafe power or lighting socket, or an electrical fitting; total or partial loss of gas supply; a blocked flue to an open fire or a boiler; total or partial loss of space or water heating in the cold months of the year; the only working toilet in the dwelling-house not flushing; leaking from a water or heating pipe, a tank or cistern; and an insecure external window, door or lock.

The scheme has been heavily criticised as being overly complex, with the need to serve a number of forms and counter-notices, and minimal compensation when the LHA fails to comply. It is regarded as conveying fewer rights than other provisions and, in terms of according a remedy, is less effective than taking legal proceedings for disrepair under, say, s 11 of the LTA 1985 (see J Luba, *Repairs: Tenants' Rights* (4th edn, 2010)).

6.8.2.5 Tenant's improvements

It is an implied term that a secure tenant will not make any improvements without the written consent of his landlord (HA 1985, s 97). The landlord must not unreasonably withhold its consent. Improvement is defined as any alteration in, or addition to, the dwelling-house or the LHA's fixtures and fittings, and any addition or alteration connected with the provision of services. It also includes the erection of a wireless or television aerial and the carrying out of external decoration. Consent may be given after the works have been done.

In certain situations a qualifying tenant may be entitled to compensation on the secure tenancy coming to an end. The compensation is payable where the improvements have increased the value of the property. The sum is calculated using a prescribed formula, but the compensation cannot exceed £3,000.

Flexible tenancies are excluded from these provisions (HA 1985, s 97(5)).

6.8.2.6 The right to consultation on housing management matters

This raft of rights is contained in ss 102 to 106A of the HA 1985. These rights operate most effectively when the tenants work as a group rather than as individuals. Two cases serve to illustrate the point.

> **CASE EXAMPLES**
>
> In *R v Secretary of State for the Environment, ex p Walters* (1998) 30 HLR 328, CA, the applicant sought judicial review of a sale and leaseback scheme entered into by the LHA, on the basis that the consultation process was seriously flawed. The Court of Appeal found that the LHA had not followed the correct consultation procedure for the demolition of a housing estate, and also that the decision made was wrong in law. However, the Court refused the applicant the remedy sought as, amongst other things, he was only one tenant, the effect on his personal rights would be minimal and the clear majority of tenants were in favour of the scheme.
>
> By contrast, in *Short v Tower Hamlets LBC* (1986) 18 HLR 171, CA, the Court upheld the right of the tenants (as a group) to bring county court proceedings for injunctive relief to stop the implementation of any decision which required consultation but about which they had not been consulted.

By s 102 of the HA 1985, the terms of a secure tenancy can be varied only by:

(a)   agreement between the parties; or

(b)   notice under s 103.

If the change relates to rent (or services, facilities, rates or tax), the variation must be in accordance with the terms of the tenancy agreement or an agreement to vary.

Prior to the s 103 notice, a preliminary notice needs to be served on the tenants, setting out the proposed changes and what their effect will be, and inviting the tenants to comment within a specified time. The s 103 notice needs to be served on the tenant, giving not less than four weeks' notice, or the rental payment period (if longer), before the proposed variation is to take effect. Although couched in individual landlord and tenant terms, a sole tenant will find it difficult to resist any changes that an LHA wishes to impose, whereas a body of tenants, acting through a representative, is likely to be far more effective.

Section 104 requires an LHA to publish and keep up to date information regarding secure tenancies, explaining in simple terms the provisions of Pts IV and V of the HA 1985 and ss 11 to 16 of the LTA 1985. Every secure tenant is entitled to a copy of this at the commencement of his tenancy and a further copy of any updates.

Section 105 required an LHA to maintain such arrangements as it considers appropriate to enable those of its secure tenants who are likely to be substantially affected by a matter of housing management to which this section applies:

(a)   to be informed of the LHA's proposals in respect of the matter; and

(b)   to make their views known to the LHA within a specified period.

The LHA must consider any representations made by the tenant before making any decision on the matter. A matter is one of housing management if the LHA considers that it relates to the management, maintenance, improvement or demolition of dwelling-houses let by the authority under secure tenancies, or to the provision of services or amenities in connection with such dwelling-houses, but not to rent or other charges.

6.8.3 Right to manage

Another collective right, not within Pt IV of the 1985 Act, is the right to manage. By s 27 of the HA 1985, an LHA can enter into management agreements with another person to manage its estates, or to take over some of its management functions. By s 27AB, tenants can, if they form themselves into a tenant management organisation (TMO), serve written notice on their LHA to commence a procedure that will lead to them having the right to manage themselves (see Housing (Right to Manage) (England) Regulations 2012 (SI 2012/1821)). In 2009, there were over 230 TMOs already established. They range in size from as few as 12 properties to as many as 9,760. The TMOs cover an estimated 84,000 homes in England. Most of them are in London, with Lambeth having 17 and Southwark 14 TMOs throughout their areas.

6.8.4 Right to buy – HA 1985, Pt V

The provisions relating to the right to buy are contained in Pt V (ss 118–188) of the HA 1985, as amended, most recently by the HA 2004. The right is available to LHA and HAT secure tenants, and to pre-1989 secure tenants of non-charitable RSLs. A preserved right to buy is retained by RSL and PRP assured tenants who were previously secure tenants, but who were transferred to their new landlord by their LHA.

The Government, in response to perceived abuse of the right to buy provisions by some tenants who, after a short period of ownership, would sell at substantial profits, and also by tenants who buy to frustrate the LHA management functions, introduced substantial amendments, affecting the eligibility, discount and repayment requirements, as well as introducing a new right of first refusal to the landlord.

6.8.4.1 Eligibility to exercise right to buy

A secure tenant whose tenancy commenced before 18 January 2005, provided he is not within one of the exceptions to eligibility in Sch 5 to the HA 1985, will acquire the right to buy once he has been a secure tenant for two years. For a secure tenant whose tenancy commenced after that date, the period is increased to five years before the tenant will become eligible to exercise his right to buy (HA 1985, s 119).

If the tenancy is of a house and the LHA owns the freehold, the secure tenant can buy the freehold. If the LHA does not own the freehold, or if the tenancy is not of a house (eg, divided horizontally, with other property above and/or below), then the tenant may buy a long lease of the property, normally for a term of 125 years at an annual ground rent of £10. For joint tenancies, all joint tenants or one joint tenant can exercise the right, provided that if only one joint tenant is involved, he occupies the dwelling as his only or principal home (HA 1985, s 118).

6.8.4.2 Suspension of right to buy

The right to buy cannot be exercised where a possession order has been made against the tenant, or if he is an un-discharged bankrupt or has a bankruptcy petition pending against him (HA 1985, s 121). A new s 121A further provides that the landlord can petition the court where the tenant, or someone residing with him or visiting the property, is guilty of anti-social behaviour or of using the premises for illegal purposes. The court can, if it considers it reasonable to do so, issue a suspension order for a specified period, during which the tenant will not be able to exercise his right to buy. The landlord can apply for a suspension order at a late stage in the conveyancing procedure for the right to buy (s 138(2A)). The new provisions also enable the landlord to suspend the conveyance if it has commenced proceedings for a demotion order (see **6.6.2**) or a Ground 2 possession order (see **6.7.1.2**).

These provisions are specifically designed to strengthen the landlord's management powers and are aimed at anti-social tenants who previously were able to purchase the property under the right to buy provisions, before the landlord could obtain a possession order against them.

An LHA in Wales may, on application to the Minister for Wales, be able to obtain suspension of the right to buy in its area for up to five years. This will be possible if, after consultation, it concludes that the housing pressure in the area is such that the conditions for suspension are met (see Housing (Wales) Measure 2011, Pt 1 (Suspension of the Right to Buy and Related Rights)).

6.8.4.3 The discount

A big incentive used to encourage millions of secure tenants to exercise their right to buy is the discount on the purchase price offered to eligible tenants. The market value of the property is discounted by a percentage depending on how long the tenant has had secure tenant status. For a tenant with secure status before 18 January 2005, the price the tenant pays will effectively be the market value less, for houses, a discount of 32%, plus 1% for each complete year in excess of the two-year period the tenant has been a secure tenant; so, for a secure tenant of 10 years, a 40% discount. The discount for houses goes up to a maximum of 60%. For leases, the discount begins at 44% and then increases by 2% for each complete year over two years that the tenant had secure status, up to a maximum of 70%. For a tenant who obtained his secure status after 18 January 2005, in line with the new five years' eligibility period, the discounts have increased for a house and flat to, respectively, 35% and 50% initially, up to the same maximum in each case.

Regulations have been made under s 131 of the HA 1985 to set a cap on the maximum discount available. From 2 April 2012 the maximum discount is £75,000 across England, with the exception of the London boroughs where the maximum discount is £100,000.

6.8.4.4 Exercise of right to buy

In a straightforward transaction, the tenant commences the process by serving a s 122 written notice on his landlord. The notice needs to be in the form prescribed by the Housing (Right to Buy) (Prescribed Form) (Amendment) (England) Regulations 2007 (SI 2007/784). The tenant can withdraw the notice at any time up to completion. The landlord should respond within four weeks either admitting the tenant's right to buy, or denying it with reasons (s 124). If the landlord admits the right, a second notice must be served by it within eight weeks for a freehold, or 12 weeks for a leasehold, setting out the all the terms, including the purchase price (s 125). The tenant then has 12 weeks to respond either stating an intention to continue with the purchase, or withdrawing the claim (s 125D). Needless to say, the process is often not smooth, and challenges can arise, and have arisen, at every stage of the process, as is evidenced by the large number of cases in this area of housing law (see, eg, N Madge and C Sephton, *Housing Law Casebook* (5th edn, 2012)).

6.8.4.5 Repayment of the discount on early sale

It had previously been the case that if the tenant sold the property within three years of purchase, he would have to repay the discount on a sliding scale of one-third for each year within the three-year period. The HA 2004 amended s 155 of the HA 1985 to increase the repayment period to five years. Section 155A has changed the basis of the repayment, so that it is now a percentage of the price obtained on first sale, equal to the percentage discount the tenant got, but with the amount reducing by one-fifth for each complete year that passes after the grant and before the disposal. The idea is that the tenant will not be able to take all the benefits of the property increase.

> **EXAMPLE**
>
> If the tenant obtained a 40% discount on a £100,000 home and then sold it in year two for £150,000, he would have to repay £150,000 x 40% x 4/5 = £48,000.

Any deferred resale agreement – that is, where the tenant, during the discount period, agrees to sell the property after the expiry of the discount period – will, unless an exempt disposal (see HA 1985, s 160 – eg disposal as a result of death or intestacy), be treated as if it was a sale within the period (HA 1985, s 163A).

6.8.4.6 Right of first refusal for the landlord

A provision in the HA 2004 introduces a covenant into every right to buy sales agreement, requiring an owner who wishes to sell the property within the first 10 years after the conveyance or grant of the property, first to offer it back to the landlord (HA 1985, s 156A). Regulations have been made detailing the procedure for the operation of this covenant (see Housing (Right of First Refusal) Regulations 2005 (SI 2005/1917 (England) and SI 2005/2680 (Wales)).

SUMMARY

- LHAs have to draw up housing strategies to which they should have regard when dealing with housing management issues.
- Housing management issues can include their allocations policy and the types of tenancies they will grant.
- Reasonable preference has to be given to certain categories of applicants for housing accommodation.
- A housing applicant may challenge an LHA's refusal to allocate him housing.
- LHAs generally grant secure tenancies that give security of tenure. The courts have a wide discretion whether to grant a possession order in most of the grounds for possession available to an LHA.
- LHAs can elect to operate:
  - an introductory tenancy scheme giving no security of tenure; and/or
  - a flexible tenancy scheme granting fixed-term secure tenancies that give the landlord a mandatory right to possession at the end of the term.
- LHAs as social landlords have wide powers to deal with anti-social behaviour, including obtaining ASBOs, ASBIs, demotion orders, parenting orders and family intervention tenancies.
- Secure tenants have many rights, including the right to succeed, assign, take lodgers and the right to buy.

CHAPTER 7

Disrepairs

7.1	Introduction	99
7.2	The meaning of 'disrepair' and 'repair'	99
7.3	The contractual obligation	101
7.4	Obligations in tort	105
7.5	Civil remedies	107
7.6	Procedure for a civil claim	112
7.7	Public funding for civil disrepair claims	114
7.8	Public law obligations	115
7.9	Further reading	117
	Summary	118

> **LEARNING OUTCOMES**
>
> After reading this chapter you will be able to:
>
> - understand the difference between disrepair and improvement
> - describe the implied terms in s 11 of the LTA 1985
> - list the obligations on a landlord in tort
> - explain the civil remedies open to a tenant against a landlord in breach of his repairing obligations
> - outline the Disrepair Protocol
> - list the public law obligations on an LHA in relation to unfit premises.

7.1 INTRODUCTION

This chapter outlines the different bases upon which one party, in housing law normally the tenant, can obtain a remedy when his property is in disrepair. Tenants seem almost spoilt by the number of options available. However, this does not seem to prevent many tenants living in conditions of serious disrepair, which can often lead to stress and damage to physical health. The potentially huge outlay that may be involved in remedying a defect means that the party responsible often seeks to argue that an obligation to repair has not arisen in this instance.

In residential lettings on periodic or short-term tenancies, the main obligation to carry out repairs is usually on the landlord. The obligation could arise in contract – either by way of an express term in the tenancy agreement, or implied by common law or statute – in tort, or by virtue of public law. In this chapter we examine each of those obligations, starting first with a consideration of what amounts to disrepair.

7.2 THE MEANING OF 'DISREPAIR' AND 'REPAIR'

7.2.1 Disrepair

For premises to be in disrepair there must be some deterioration in the physical state of the premises from an earlier point (*Quick v Taff Ely BC* [1986] QB 809, CA).

Design defects which cause condensation, damp and mould to the extent that the property becomes unfit, will not amount to disrepair if there is no damage to the property requiring it to be repaired. In *Lee v Leeds City Council; Ratcliffe v Sandwell Metropolitan BC* [2002] 1 WLR 1488, CA, it was held that such an interpretation was not an infringement of the tenant's human rights. However, if the design defect causes damage to the property, as, for example, where rainwater penetration as a result of a design defect causes a front door to rot, then the most effective repair work may be to address the design defect (*Stent v Monmouth DC* (1987) 19 HLR 269, CA).

7.2.2 Repair

The meaning of the term 'repair' in a covenant has caused much litigation over the years. How wide or extensive is the obligation? Does it involve renewal, replacement or improvement to the property? In *Lister v Lane & Nesham* [1893] 2 QB 212, CA, Lord Esher MR said of a tenant's covenant to repair, 'a covenant to repair a house is not a covenant to give a different thing from that which the tenant took when he entered into the covenant. He has to repair that thing which he took; he is not obliged to make a new and different thing ...'.

In *Lurcott v Wakely* [1911] 1 KB 905, CA, it was held that repair can include the replacement or renewal of a part of the house: 'It will not cover the rebuilding of a house which has tumbled down, but, so long as the house exists as a structure, "repair" imports an obligation to replace part of it which has deteriorated.'

The covenant must also be construed in the context of the property that it relates to. For old houses, the age of the property can qualify the meaning of the covenant. What might be required to keep an old house in good condition as an old house, will be different from what is expected to keep a new house in good condition as a new house. In *Proudfoot v Hart* (1890) 25 QBD 42, CA, it was held that the obligation to keep in or leave in repair had to take into account the age, character and locality of the house. One would not expect the house to be in the same condition as when it was let, nor in perfect repair.

It is often baldly stated that an obligation to repair does not include an obligation to carry out improvements. This is really putting the matter too simply, as it has been stated judicially that repairs, properly so called, inevitably involve an element of renewal and improvement. In *Ravenseft Properties Ltd v Davstone Holdings Ltd* [1980] QB 12, it was held that repairs could include improvement. There, the whole of the stone cladding on the face of a building needed to be removed and replaced by new cladding. The new cladding incorporated expansion joints which had not previously been there. This was necessary to prevent the danger that had become apparent, of the stone cladding falling off the walls. It was held that this work was capable of amounting to repair. In reality, it is the extent of the necessary works, the cost of the works relative to the state of the premises, the character and the locality of the premises which are the factors that will be considered in deciding whether the works amount to repair or improvement. If the works are deemed to be improvement, they will be outside the normal repairing obligation.

7.2.2.1 The tests to determine repair or improvement

In *McDougall v Easington DC* (1989) 21 HLR 310, CA, Mustill LJ considered the differing interpretations from earlier cases of what could amount to repairs as opposed to improvement, and came to the conclusion that:

> in my opinion, three different tests may be discerned, which may be applied separately or concurrently as the circumstances of the individual case may demand, but all to be approached in the light of the nature and age of the premises, their condition when the tenant went into occupation, and the other express terms of the tenancy:
>
> (i) whether the alterations went to the whole or substantially the whole of the structure or to only a subsidiary part;
>
> (ii) whether the effect of the alterations was to produce a building of a wholly different character from that which had been let;

The provision applies to all weekly, monthly or yearly periodic tenancies and fixed-term tenancies, provided the period granted is for less than seven years. Leases that were granted for a term of less than seven years initially, for example a monthly periodic tenancy, which actually last for more than seven years, are within the provision. So most, if not all, assured, secure and regulated tenancies have the benefit of this implied term. In addition, from 1 April 2012, s 11 also applies to fixed-term assured or secure tenancies of seven years or more granted by PRPs and LHAs respectively (LTA 1985, s 13(1A)).

As mentioned at **7.2.2.2**, the obligation on the landlord will not arise under s 11 until the landlord has notice of the defect in relation to premises let to the tenant.

In *Andrews v Brewer* (1998) 30 HLR 203, CA, the tenants made a counterclaim, in the possession action against them, for £22,000 they had spent on repairs. They claimed the repairs related to the LTA 1985, s 11 landlord's obligation. The Court dismissed the counterclaim on the basis that, as no appropriate notice had been given to the landlord, there was no obligation on him to do or pay for the repairs under s 11.

Certain categories of tenancies, for example business and agricultural tenancies, are excluded from the provision (LTA 1985, s 14).

To keep in repair/and proper working order

In *Proudfoot v Hart* (1890) 25 QBD 42, CA, Lord Esher stated that it was established law that an obligation to 'keep in repair' meant putting the property into repair, even if it was not in repair at the time the tenancy commenced, and then keeping it in that state.

The obligation to keep the installations in proper working order extends to addressing design defects in them if they do not work properly. As stated by Lord Edmund-Davies in *Liverpool City Council v Irwin* [1977] AC 239, HL, the wording of the section 'presupposes that at the inception of the letting the installation was "in proper working order" and that if its design was such that it did not work "properly" the landlord is in breach'.

Structure and exterior

The structure can include the walls, the roof of a house and its foundations. Where the dwelling-house is a flat or a part only of a building, the structure may not be so extensive. So, for example, the structure of a ground-floor flat will not include the roof over the top flat. However, in deciding what is part of the structure and exterior, one must apply the ordinary meaning of those words, not what is actually let to the tenant. In *Douglas-Scott v Scorgie* [1984] 1 WLR 716, CA, the tenant had a letting of the top flat in a block. The roof was held to be part of the structure or exterior of the tenant's dwelling, even though it was conceded by the tenant that the roof was not part of the property that had been let to her.

The structure goes beyond just the load-bearing elements. It can include external windows and doors. However, quite how far the structure goes is open to debate. In *Irvine v Moran* (1992) 24 HLR 1, it was held that 'the structure of a dwelling-house consists of those elements of the overall dwelling-house which gives it its essential appearance, stability and shape. The expression does not extend to the many and various ways in which the dwelling-house will be fitted out, equipped, decorated and generally made to be habitable'. In that case it was held not to extend to internal plaster. In *Tanya Grand v Param Gill* [2011] EWCA Civ 554, Rimmer LJ reviewed earlier authorities on this issue, including *Irvine v Moran*. He concluded:

> In the days when lath and plaster ceiling and internal partition walls were more common than now, the plaster was, I should have thought, an essential part of the creation and shaping of the ceiling or partition wall, which serve to give a dwelling house its essential appearance and shape. I would also regard plasterwork generally, including that applied to external walls, as being ordinarily in the nature of a smooth constructional finish to walls and ceilings, to which the decoration can then be applied, rather than a decorative finish in itself. I would therefore hold that it is part of the structure.

In *Quick v Taff Ely BC* [1986] QB 809, CA, it was held that the structure and exterior of a 1970s-built house were not in disrepair as a result of severe condensation which caused the house to be virtually uninhabitable in winter. The condensation was caused by lack of insulation around the concrete window lintels, sweating from the single-glazed metal-framed windows, and inadequate heating. There was no evidence of any damage or want of repair in the metal windows, in the concrete lintels, or in any other part of the structure and exterior of the house occupied by the tenants. The problem was caused by a design defect, which, in the absence of disrepair, was not a breach of s 11.

The exterior is the external part of the dwelling, and can include the path and steps which give access to a house (*Brown v Liverpool Corporation* [1969] 3 All ER 1345, CA); but it has been held not to extend to access to the backyard, or the backyard or garden itself (*Hopwood v Cannock Chase DC* [1975] 1 WLR 373, CA).

Installations

This obligation relates to the condition of pipes, wiring, tanks, boilers, radiators or other space-heating installations. It covers their mechanical condition, and does not require the landlord to lag pipes against bursting in unusually cold weather (*Wycombe Area Health Authority v Barnett* (1982) 5 HLR 84).

Standard of repair

As with the general interpretation of repairing obligations (see **7.2.2**), s 11(3) of the LTA 1985 provides that in determining the standard of repair required, the age, character and prospective life of the dwelling-house, and the locality in which it is situated, should be taken into account. In *Dame Margaret Hungerford Charity Trustees v Beazeley* (1994) 26 HLR 269, CA, it was held that taking into account, amongst other things, the age and character of the premises, the cost of complete replacement and the relatively low income available, the landlords were not in breach of their obligation to keep the roof of the tenant's dwelling in repair. The landlords had carried out only running repairs rather than complete repair to the roof. On the evidence, the trial judge held that this was what was appropriate to effect proper repair to the roof.

Extension of the landlord's obligation beyond the dwelling-house

The landlord's repairing obligation has been extended for tenancies entered into on or after 15 January 1989. This is for tenancies of a dwelling-house which forms part only of a building. Section 116 of the HA 1988 has inserted s 11(1A) into the LTA 1985, to extend the obligation to repair the structure and exterior in s 11(1)(a) to any part of the building in which the landlord has an estate or interest.

In relation to the obligations in s 11(1)(b) and (c) regarding the installations in the dwelling-house, s 11(1A)(b) extends them to installations which, directly or indirectly, serve the dwelling-house and which either form part of any part of the building in which the landlord has an estate or interest, or are owned by the landlord or under his control.

> **CASE EXAMPLE**
>
> In *Niazi Services Ltd v Van der Loo* [2004] 1 WLR 1254, CA, the defendant had a sub-lease of the flat from the claimant. The claim was brought for arrears of rent which the defendant had withheld in protest at the claimants' failure to remedy various problems at the flat. The problems included inadequate water pressure in the flat. This meant that there was no water supply in the flat at certain times of the day. In addition, for a period of four months, there was no lighting on the stairs in the common parts of the building. The water problem was due to the restaurant having installed a larger take-off pipe in the lower part of the building which, when water was being used by the restaurant, adversely affected the supply to the defendant's flat. In the claimants' action to recover the rent, the defendant

> counter-claimed for damages for the disrepair in breach of s 11 of the LTA 1985 as amended. It was held that the claimants were not liable for these particular disrepairs as they were not in parts of the building in which they had an estate or interest, ownership or control.

7.3.3.3 Section 11 and the common problem of damp

It is apparent that there are many houses where damp is an intrusive and serious cause of damage and discomfort, if not more serious complaint, for the tenants. Section 11 of the LTA 1985 has not proved to be an effective tool to address this problem, as illustrated in *Quick v Taff Ely BC* (see **7.3.3.2**) and more recent cases.

> **CASE EXAMPLE**
> In *Southwark LBC v McIntosh* [2001] All ER (D) 133, Ch, the tenant had been using a storage cupboard, designed to store dry goods, for drying her laundry. As a result, severe damp and condensation had built up after about a year. The tenant complained to her landlord but nothing was done for over five years. When the matter was finally dealt with by the landlord, the tenant sued for compensation for the period she had lived with the inconvenience. The judge at first instance held that had the landlord investigated, it would have discovered the problem and would have minimised, if not prevented, the discomfort suffered by the tenant during the period. It was held on appeal that the landlord was not in breach of the implied obligation in s 11. That section did not imply a duty on the landlords to tell the tenant how to use a storage cupboard. Lightman J held, applying *Quick v Taff Ely BC*, that a landlord is not liable under the covenant merely because there is the most serious damp in the premises. The tenant needed to establish either that the damp arises from a breach of the covenant (ie physical damage to the structure or exterior of the premises), or that damp has itself caused damage to the structure or exterior and that this damage has caused the damp complained of.

7.3.4 Statutory implied terms on the tenant

By s 11(6) of the LTA 1985, in return for the tenant having a right to certain repairs, implied into the tenant's agreement is the obligation that the tenant will allow the landlord, or any person authorised by him in writing, to enter the tenanted property to view its condition and state of repair. The obligation is subject to the landlord giving 24 hours' notice to view at a reasonable time of the day.

In addition, implied into every assured tenancy is an obligation that the tenant will allow the landlord access and all reasonable facility to carry out any repairs which he is entitled to do in the dwelling-house (HA 1988, s 16). The same is true for statutory and protected tenants under ss 3(2) and 148 of the RA 1977.

7.4 OBLIGATIONS IN TORT

The obligations in tort do not generally give a tenant the right to require repairs to be carried out. What they sometimes provide is a remedy for any injury or damage suffered as a result of the disrepair of the premises.

7.4.1 Common law

The courts have been reluctant to find liability in nuisance or negligence against a landlord of unfurnished premises, unless he was also the designer or builder of the premises. In *Rimmer v Liverpool City Council* [1985] QB 1, CA, the landlords were held liable when a tenant was injured as a result of a design defect in the property. However, the Court made it clear that there would normally be no duty of care to a tenant arising out of the state of the premises when they were let. There was liability in this case because of the general duty owed to all persons who may be affected by design or construction defects in a property.

This principle was reinforced in *Habinteg Housing Association v James* (1995) 27 HLR 299, CA, where it was held that the landlords were not liable in nuisance or negligence for failing to remedy cockroach infestation in the tenant's flat, in the absence of any evidence that the infestation emanated from premises retained by them.

In *Steven v Blaenau Gwent CBC* [2004] HLR 54, CA, the defendant landlords refused a tenant's request to put window locks on her property to prevent her daughter opening those windows and falling out. The defendants felt that the risk of residents being trapped in a fire as a result of locked windows was a real one, and for that reason the policy was not to instal locks. There was no duty, even though the defendants subsequently put locks on the window after the tenant's daughter had fallen out of it.

7.4.2 Occupiers' Liability Act 1957

Where the landlord retains possession of, and therefore control over, parts of a building (eg, the common parts of a block of flats), he may be liable if the state of repair of those parts results in the tenant, or some other person on the premises, suffering injury. The landlord, under s 2 of the Occupiers' Liability Act 1957, has a common duty to take such care as in all the circumstances of the case is reasonable, to see that the visitor will be reasonably safe in using the premises for the purposes for which he is permitted to be there.

7.4.3 Defective Premises Act 1972

Section 4 of the Defective Premises Act (DPA) 1972 imposes a duty of care on landlords in two distinct situations. The first duty arises because of landlords' repairing obligation. The second duty may arise as a consequence of some right of the landlord to carry out maintenance or repairs.

7.4.3.1 Duty arising out of a repairing obligation

In s 4(1) of the DPA 1972, where a landlord has an express or implied duty to maintain or repair the premises, a duty is owed to anyone (ie, not just the tenant) who one might reasonably expect would be affected by defects in the state of the premises. The landlord is required to take such care as is reasonable in all the circumstances, to protect all persons and their property from any harm arising out of a 'relevant defect'. Relevant defects relate to acts or omissions by the landlord which amount to a failure to carry out the repairing or maintenance obligation. The duty is owed where the landlord knows (by whatever means), or ought to have known, of the relevant defect. The landlord cannot exclude or modify the duty (DPA 1972, s 6(3)).

> **CASE EXAMPLE**
>
> In *Sykes v Harry* [2001] QB 1014, CA, the landlord was held to be in breach of s 4 when the tenant suffered carbon monoxide poisoning from a defective gas fire. The landlord was liable even though the obligation to repair arose out of s 11 of the LTA 1985 (see **7.3.3.2**), and he was held not to be in breach of that provision as he had no notice of the defect. The landlord was, however, aware of the need for the gas fire at the premises to be serviced regularly. He was also aware that the tenant was not having it serviced. It was held that this knowledge put him under a duty to act reasonably. He had failed to so act in not servicing the fire himself, or checking with the tenant as to the state of the gas fire.

7.4.3.2 Duty arising out of right to repair

Section 4(4) of the DPA 1972 is a more controversial provision, as it appears to impose an obligation where none existed, simply because the landlord has reserved to himself a power to enter the premises to carry out works of maintenance or repair. The effect of s 4(4) is well summed up by Chadwick LJ in *Lee v Leeds City Council; Ratcliffe v Sandwell Metropolitan BC* [2002] 1 WLR 1488, CA. He states that s 4(4)

> extends liability under s 4(1) to certain defects in the state of the premises which do not arise from the landlord's failure to carry out his repairing obligations. It does so by introducing a statutory hypothesis. A landlord who is not otherwise under an obligation to carry out works of maintenance or repair of a particular description is to be treated, for the purposes of s 4(1) and (3) but for no other purpose, as if he were under an obligation to carry out works of maintenance and repair of that description if the terms of the tenancy (expressly or impliedly) give him 'the right to enter the premises to carry out that description of maintenance or repair of the premises'. So, for example, a landlord who is not otherwise under an obligation to carry out works of repair and maintenance to the garden but who has a right to enter for the purpose of carrying out such works if he chooses will be treated, for the purposes of s 4(1) and (3) of the Act, as if he were under an obligation to carry out such works; with the consequence that he owes a duty to take reasonable care to see that the tenant or other person who might reasonably be expected to be affected by defects in the state of the garden is reasonably safe from personal injury caused by such a defect arising from lack of repair or maintenance (see *McAuley v Bristol City Council* [1992] 1 QB 134, CA).

McAuley v Bristol City Council illustrates the severity of this provision from the landlord's perspective. The tenancy agreement contained a clause requiring the tenant to give the landlord entry for any purpose which might be required from time to time by the landlord. Although liable to repair the structure and exterior, the landlord's repairing obligation did not extend to the garden. It was held, however, that the clause giving the landlord access was sufficient to activate s 4(4) and imposed a duty under s 4(1). The result was that the landlord was liable when the tenant fell from a defective concrete step, of which the landlord was aware, and broke her ankle.

In *Lee v Leeds City Council; Ratcliffe v Sandwell Metropolitan BC*, however, the tenants were not successful in trying to use s 4(4) to oblige their landlords to remedy design defects in the premises which caused serious condensation and mould but no damage to the structure. The Court made it clear that there had to be disrepair for the provision to give rise to liability.

Despite the lack of success of the argument in *Lee v Leeds City Council*, the tenants in *Dunn v Bradford Metropolitan DC; Marston v Leeds City Council* [2002] EWCA Civ 1137, CA, felt they had a stronger case for applying s 4(4) of the DPA 1972, to require their landlords to carry out works to remedy a design defect. The tenants argued that as the tenancy agreement entitled the landlord to enter to carry out repairs 'and improvement works', s 4(4) applied to impose an obligation to correct a design defect that caused injury to the tenants. Chadwick LJ, who again gave the leading judgment, was not persuaded that the right of entry to execute improvement works led to the conclusion that the landlords were under a duty to maintain the premises in 'a reasonable condition', or to prevent (by improvement) any material deterioration of condition that affected the enjoyment of the premises. This, he held, would require interpreting the words in the section to go beyond maintenance or repair, which, he felt, was not the intention of Parliament.

There was a similar outcome in *Alker v Collingwood Housing Association* [2007] HLR 29, CA. It was held that the landlords did not owe a duty under s 4(4) to keep the premises in a safe condition. The tenant was unable to recover when, on pushing the front door to the property, her hand went through the glass panel. The panel was made of ordinary annealed glass rather than safety glass, but had not been damaged or broken before the accident. The door, although a safety hazard, was not in disrepair.

7.5 CIVIL REMEDIES

There are a number of remedies open to a tenant whose landlord has failed to carry out his repairing obligations. Which remedy a tenant pursues may depend to a large extent on the type of tenancy he has. For an assured shorthold tenant of a private sector landlord, for example, a successful claim to have repairs done by the landlord may quickly end in a s 21 notice to terminate the tenancy. A self-help remedy may have a similar result. Legal advisers should be careful to warn such tenants of the dangers of pursuing their repair rights.

The remedies available to a tenant may include:

(a) self-help – set off;
(b) the right to repair scheme (public sector);
(c) appointment of a receiver/manager (private sector);
(d) complaint to an ombudsman (independent or local government);
(e) injunction;
(f) specific performance; or
(g) damages.

The remedies available to a landlord are discussed at **7.5.8** below.

7.5.1 Self-help – set off against the rent

A tenant can rely on either common law or equity to set off the costs of repairs against future rent payments. While the common law rules are very strict, requiring certainty about the sum recoverable, the equitable principle in *Lee-Parker v Izzet* [1971] 1 WLR 1688 allows a tenant to recover against a landlord in breach of an express or implied obligation to repair. The tenant must ensure that the landlord's obligation has arisen by his having been given notice of the disrepair. He must also ensure that the disrepair does fall within the scope of the landlord's repairing obligation. In addition, the tenant should ensure that only the proper cost of repair is being deducted, perhaps by obtaining several estimates for the works and using the lowest.

It may be appropriate, for the sake of certainty, for the tenant to obtain a declaration from the county court under CPR Part 25, to say that the landlord is in breach, before proceeding with the work.

If a declaration is not obtained and the landlord tries to sue for possession on the basis of non-payment of rent, the tenant can counter-claim for the cost of the repairs and damages for any other loss suffered (*British Anzani (Felixstowe) Ltd v International Marine Management (UK) Ltd* [1980] QB 137).

7.5.2 Right to repair scheme (public sector)

For public sector tenants with minor repairs, the right to repair provisions in s 96 of the HA 1985 may be applicable (see **6.8.2.4**). The LHA must be notified of a prescribed defect at the property that is within its express or implied repairing obligations. Provided the cost of repairing the prescribed defect does not exceed £250, and the LHA has a housing stock of at least 100 properties, it will be obliged to appoint a contractor to carry out the repairs within a specified period of between one and seven days, depending on the nature of the defect. There is a list of some 20 prescribed defects in the Schedule to the Secure Tenants of Local Housing Authorities (Right to Repair) Regulations 1994 (SI 1994/133). If the works are not carried out within the specified time, the tenant may be entitled to compensation up to a maximum amount of £50.

Although the range of defects is very broad – from minor matters such as a door entryphone not working, the only toilet not flushing, or the loss of water supply or electric power, through to rotten timber flooring and a leaking roof – the low financial limit on the cost of repairing the defect means that the right will not be available in serious or major cases of disrepair. There is also a rather cumbersome notice procedure to be followed on the appointment of a contractor to do the works. Tenants of RSLs and PRPs can benefit from similar schemes, although the way in which they apply varies from one RSL or PRP to another.

7.5.3 Appointment of a receiver/manager in the private sector

Where the landlord has persistently neglected to carry out repairs to the property, and either he cannot be traced or the repairs require urgent attention, an application can be made to the court to appoint a receiver. A receiver will be appointed if the court is satisfied that it is just and convenient to do so (Senior Courts Act 1981, s 37(1); County Courts Act 1984, s 38). The court refused to apply this remedy against a LHA in *Parker v Camden LBC* [1986] Ch 162, CA.

For private sector residential tenants in a block consisting of two or more flats, Pt II of the LTA 1987, as amended, provides an alternative remedy. Where the landlord persistently fails to maintain the block and fails to respond to a notice warning him of an application being made under these provisions, the tenants can apply to a leasehold valuation tribunal for the appointment of a manager.

7.5.4 Complaint to the Housing Ombudsman

From 1 April 2013, complaints in England about the state of repair of tenancies granted by social landlords, as well as other landlord and tenant matters, should be made to the Housing Ombudsman (see ss 180–182 of the Localism Act 2011). Complaints can be made to the Housing Ombudsman if it could be said that the failure amounts to maladministration which is causing, or has caused, injustice. The Housing Ombudsman has the power to investigate and make recommendations or determinations. However, the procedure can be slow, and it may sometimes take more than a year to complete a determination.

The provisions in the 2011 Act introduce a 'democratic filter' into the process that did not exist before. After exhausting the landlord's internal complaints procedure, a complaint will need to be referred by a designated person to the Housing Ombudsman in order for it to be 'duly made'. The designated person can be:

(a) a member of the House of Commons;
(b) a Councillor (a member of the local housing authority for the district in which the property concerned is located); or
(c) a designated tenant panel.

A 'designated tenant panel' means a group of tenants recognised by a social landlord for the purpose of referring complaints against the social landlord. However, a direct referral may duly be made without resort to the designated person process where:

(a) any internal complaints procedure has been exhausted and eight weeks have passed since then; or
(b) the Housing Ombudsman is satisfied that a designated person:
  (i) has refused to refer the complaint to a Housing Ombudsman under an approved scheme; or
  (ii) has agreed to the complaint being made otherwise than by way of referral by a designated person,
  and the refusal, or agreement, is in writing, or the Ombudsman is satisfied that it has been confirmed in writing.

The Secretary of State will have a power to make regulations to provide that the Housing Ombudsman may apply to a court or a tribunal in order that a determination he makes against a social landlord may be made enforceable as if it were a court decision.

The provisions in the Localism Act 2011 are not yet applicable in Wales. Tenants of LHAs in Wales can complain to the Local Government Ombudsman for Wales (see **12.7**).

7.5.5 Interim injunction

An interim injunction may be applied for in exceptional circumstances where the court is satisfied that there is an immediate need for the work to be done for example, because there is a real risk to health. The order should be specific as to what works need to be done, as held in *Parker v Camden LBC* [1986] Ch 162, CA, applying a stricter test than that in *American Cyanamid Co v Ethicon Ltd* [1975] AC 396, HL, see **9.3.1.1**). The landlord will be in contempt of court if he fails to comply with the terms of an injunction.

7.5.6 Specific performance

By s 17 of the LTA 1985, the court may make an order of specific performance against a landlord in breach of his obligation to keep in repair a dwelling, or any part of the premises in which the dwelling is comprised. The order is available not just for s 11 repairs, but for any repairing covenant to repair, maintain, renew, construct or replace any property. The court can apply the order regardless of any equitable rule which would otherwise restrict the scope of the remedy, eg because the landlord would not be able to get an order against the tenant, or the tenant is in rent arrears. Failure to comply with this order is also a contempt of court.

7.5.7 Damages

The basis for compensation will depend on whether the claim is in contract for breach of the express or implied covenant to repair, or whether it is for a tortuous breach, such as, for example, breach of s 4 of the DPA 1972. Until recently it was thought that entirely different factors came into consideration. However, recent case law has set out general guidelines.

7.5.7.1 Contractual measure

In contract, the tenant may have a claim for general and special damages as a result of the disrepair. It was held in *Calabar v Stitcher* [1984] 1 WLR 287, CA, that the basis of compensation is to restore the tenant to the position he would have been in had there been no breach of the express or implied covenant to repair. This may include, where appropriate, the cost of alternative accommodation, the cost of any relevant repairs carried out by the tenant and compensation for living in deteriorating conditions. This last head of compensation could include general discomfort, inconvenience and ill-health suffered by the tenant as a result of the breach.

The amount of compensation payable for personal injury and ill-health suffered as a result of disrepair will depend upon the severity of the claim. Reference may be made to various sources, eg *Guidelines for the Assessment of General Damages in Personal Injury Cases* (Judicial Studies Board, 10th edn, 2010), *Encyclopaedia of Housing Law*, vol 1, para 1-2327.3, table (for county court cases), and 'Repairs' round-up in *Legal Action*.

In *Wallace v Manchester City Council* (1998) 30 HLR 1111, CA, it was held that the proper sum to compensate a tenant for the distress and inconvenience resulting from the landlord's failure to repair, might be ascertained in several ways. The first might be by a notional reduction in the rent on the dwelling. Secondly, a global award might be made for discomfort and inconvenience. The third method would be a mixture of the previous two methods. Morrit LJ held that, contrary to the previous perception of practitioners, a court was not bound to assess damages separately under the first and second methods. He went on to caution that where a global award was made, a judge would be well advised to cross-check his prospective award by reference to the rent payable for the period equivalent to the duration of the landlord's breach, so as to avoid over- or under-assessments through failure to give proper consideration to the period of the landlord's breach of obligation or the nature of the property.

In *Shine v English Churches Housing Group* [2004] HLR 42, CA, the Court recognised *Wallace v Manchester City Council* as the leading case on the subject of damages for disrepair. The Court of Appeal in *Shine* recognised that the guidelines of Morrit LJ in the earlier case should not be applied in a mechanistic or dogmatic way. It was also accepted that there may be cases in which the level of distress or inconvenience suffered by the tenant may require an award in excess of the rent payable. However, the Court held that if an award of damages for stress and inconvenience as a result of a landlord's breach of the implied covenant to repair is to exceed the level of the rental payable, clear reasons need to be given by the court for taking that course and the conduct of the landlord must warrant such an award.

For a tenant who gives up occupation of the premises and sells or sub-lets it, as a result of the disrepair, the amount of compensation will be the diminution in the sale price or the rent recovered as a result of the disrepair (*Wallace v Manchester City Council* (above)).

7.5.7.2 Tort measure

The guidelines given in *Wallace v Manchester City Council* (see **7.5.7.1**) apply equally to tort claims. In that case, the tenant's two children were also claimants, claiming under s 4 of the DPA 1972 (see **7.4.3**) for illness and discomfort caused by the disrepair. Morrit LJ did not distinguish the basis of compensation, and appeared to apply the same criteria, giving an award of £2,000 to each of the children for the tort breach.

7.5.7.3 Duty to mitigate loss

The tenant may have his damages reduced if he has failed to take reasonable steps to mitigate his loss. In *Lubren v Lambeth LBC* (1988) 20 HLR 165, CA, it was held that the tenant's failure to accept two offers of alternative accommodation to enable repairs to be carried out, did not amount to a failure to mitigate and so would not affect the award of damages, as the refusal was not made capriciously.

However, in *Shine v English Churches Housing Group* [2004] HLR 42, CA, the tenant's damages were substantially reduced for a two and a half year period, when he failed to vacate his flat to enable the repairs to be carried out and repeatedly refused the offer of alternative accommodation. The Court effectively awarded only 25% of the rental for this period, despite the fact that the premises were in very poor condition throughout. It attributed that period of discomfort primarily to the claimant's failure to mitigate his loss by accepting alternative accommodation for the period of repair, which would have been a much shorter duration of nine months.

7.5.8 Remedies available to a landlord

Although the obligation to repair in short leases is usually on the landlord, the tenant in a fixed-term lease for over seven but less than 21 years sometimes has certain obligations to maintain and repair the premises. Where the tenant has an obligation to repair, the landlord will be able to seek redress. Briefly, his remedies may include:

(a) self-help (subject to reservation of the right, either in the lease or by statute, to enter and do repair works that the tenant ought to have done);

(b) damages;

(c) forfeiture/possession proceedings; or

(d) specific performance.

The landlord will be able to recover the lower of the cost of repair or diminution in value by way of damages. If the premises are to be demolished or altered so as to render any repair valueless, no damages will be recoverable (LTA 1927, s 18).

Whether the landlord is seeking damages or forfeiture, he will be obliged to follow the strict procedural requirements in s 146 of the LPA 1925 and, if applicable, s 1 of the Leasehold Property (Repairs) Act 1938, which are designed to reduce the risk to the tenant of paying substantial damages or losing his tenancy.

Specific performance may be available to a landlord against a tenant in disrepair, in rare circumstances (see *Rainbow Estates v Tokenhold* [1998] 2 All ER 860).

7.6 PROCEDURE FOR A CIVIL CLAIM

The Pre-action Protocol for Housing Disrepair Cases, which may be found at the Department for Constitutional Affairs website at www.justice.gov.uk, sets out the procedure to be followed in certain disrepair claims. It is primarily for tenants who are bringing disrepair claims against their landlords. Its stated aim is to encourage the early exchange of information between the parties, to provide a clear framework in which to attempt an early and appropriate resolution of the issues. Court action is to be treated as a last resort. The specific aims are:

(a) to avoid unnecessary litigation;
(b) to promote speedy and appropriate repairs;
(c) to ensure that tenants receive any compensation to which they are entitled;
(d) to promote good pre-litigation practice; and
(e) to keep costs down.

Tenants are under an obligation to ensure the landlord is aware of the disrepair – an essential point, as a duty does not normally arise unless the landlord is so aware. The Protocol specifically encourages tenants to consider alternatives to litigation, such as alternative dispute resolution (ADR), right to repair, the Housing Ombudsman or the Local Government Ombudsman for Wales and local authority environmental health officers, as possible options, depending on the type of tenancy. However, a party should not be forced into arbitration or ADR (see *Halsey v Milton Keynes NHS Trust* [2004] 1 WLR 3002, CA).

A failure to comply with the Protocol could lead to adverse cost penalties, and the LAA may also refuse a certificate for Legal Representation where the Protocol has not been observed (see **7.7**).

7.6.1 The Protocol procedure

The Protocol applies to disrepair claims and any related personal injury claims arising out of the express and implied repairing obligations, and to tort disrepair claims (eg s 4 of the DPA 1972, common law nuisance and negligence), but not to disrepair counter-claims or set offs in other proceedings (most usually in possession claims brought by the landlord against the tenant), nor to statutory nuisance claims brought under s 82 of the EPA 1990 (see **7.8.1.2**). A claim may be brought by a tenant, or by a family member.

The Protocol procedure, which may be found at www.justice.gov.uk, requires the tenant to send an Early Notification Letter, or, if the matter is more urgent, a Letter of Claim to the landlord. The tenant's contact details and the address of the property (if different) should be given. The defects should be itemised, in a schedule if appropriate. Any previous notification given to the landlord of the need for repairs should also be listed. The tenant should, if the repairs are serious enough to warrant it, propose that an expert be appointed, and disclose to the landlord any relevant documents that he has. The tenant should request evidential information from the landlord, such as copies of notifications of disrepair, inspection reports or repair works to the property, and authorisation that the documents be released to the tenant's representative where appropriate. A Letter of Claim, if sent instead or subsequently, will, in addition, detail the effect of the defects on the tenant and any special damages (paras 3.2 and 3.3).

The landlord is required to respond within 20 working days, sending the information requested and indicating whether a single joint expert will be agreed or not. The landlord should indicate whether he admits liability and, if so, in relation to which defects. He should give a full schedule of works with start and completion dates, and outline any offer of compensation. Where the landlord disputes liability, reasons should be given. The landlord will be in breach of the Protocol if he does not respond within the given time frame (para 3.5).

If an expert is necessary, an inspection by a single joint expert, or, where the parties do not agree, a joint inspection, should take place within 20 working days of the landlord's response letter. The inspection should produce a schedule of works, detailing the defects and a timetable for any works required. In urgent cases, for example where an interim injunction will be sought, an earlier inspection may be necessary (para 3.6).

Where the claim is settled without litigation on terms which justify bringing the original claim, the landlord will pay the tenant's reasonable costs (para 3.7).

The point is made at para 3.4 of the Protocol that the procedure does not extend the normal limitation period for commencing claims. For disrepair claims, the limitation period (where no latent defects are involved) would normally be six years from the date of a breach of contract or damage being suffered in tort, where no claim is being made for personal injury. The limitation period where personal injury is being claimed is three years from the date of injury, or later knowledge of it (see Limitation Act 1980, as amended).

Annexes to the Protocol very usefully have, amongst other things, draft examples of Early Notification Letters, Letters of Claim and a Letter of Instruction to Expert.

7.6.2 Commencing proceedings

If the Protocol procedures do not result in settlement, the tenant will be obliged to start proceedings. The Civil Procedure Rules 1998, Part 7 will apply (see **9.5.1**). The relevant claim form will be Form N1 with particulars of claim and relevant documents to be relied on. Full particulars of the disrepair and loss suffered should be stated. If appropriate, any medical evidence should be pleaded, and all verified by a statement of truth.

Any witness statement to be submitted as evidence that will be put forward at trial should comply with CPR, Part 32 and PD 32, paras 17–19. Full details need to be given of the history of the disrepair and complaints and a detailed description of any damage suffered by person or property.

Part 26 of the CPR determines to which track the case will be allocated, depending on the value of the claim. The case will be allocated to the small claims track if the value of the claim is not more than £10,000 and any personal injury damages claim is not more than £1,000.

By CPR, r 26.6, if a residential tenant is seeking an order for the landlord to carry out repairs or other works to the premises, and the claim is for works with a value of not more than £1,000 and damages of not more than £1,000, the case will be allocated to the small claims track. However, if the value of the claim in that situation is over £1,000, and for claims valued over £10,000 but below £25,000, allocation will be to the fast track. For claims over £25,000, or if the trial is likely to last more than one day, the case will be allocated to the multi-track.

7.6.3 Part 36 offers

Either the claimant or the defendant can propose a settlement of the dispute on terms before trial. If the parties agree to settle in the form stipulated in CPR, Part 36 then the claim will be stayed and the claimant will be entitled to costs up to the date of service of acceptance (CPR, rr 36.10 and 36.11).

If the claimant refuses an offer from the defendant and is awarded less at trial, he could be ordered to pay the defendant's costs from the last date for acceptance of the offer, unless the court considers it would be unjust to so order (CPR, r 36.14). If the claimant's offer is refused by the defendant and the claimant does better at trial, the court may order that the claimant recover costs on an indemnity basis and interest on those costs, as well as on any sum awarded from the latest date that the defendant could have accepted the offer. An additional amount, of up to £75,000, can also be awarded (CPR, r 36.14(3)(d)).

7.7 PUBLIC FUNDING FOR CIVIL DISREPAIR CLAIMS

From 1 April 2013, Legal Representation will be available to commence a disrepair claim only where the disrepairs pose a serious risk of harm to health or safety in rented accommodation (see **5.1**).

The scope of legal aid for disrepair claims is set out in para 35 of Pt 1 of Sch 1 to the 2012 Act ('Risk to health or safety in rented home'). The LC Guidance, at para 12, details relevant factors to which the Director must have regard when deciding whether the claim is within the housing law scope. It states (at paras 12.2 and 12.3):

> Paragraph 35 of [Sch 1 to] the Act brings within the scope of legal aid civil legal services provided to an individual in relation to the removal or reduction of a serious risk of harm to the health or safety of the individual or relevant member of the individual's family where—
> a)   the risk arises from the deficiency in the individual's home,
> b)   the individual's home is rented or leased from another person, and
> c)   the services are provided with a view to securing that the other person makes arrangements to remove or reduce the risk.
>
> 'Deficiency' is defined in paragraph 35(4) of [Sch 1 to] the Act as 'any deficiency, whether arising as a result of the construction of a building, an absence of maintenance or repair, or otherwise'. This definition, as well as covering deficiencies in the home arising from lack of maintenance and lack of repair, will include poor design of a home that leads to a risk to health, such as condensation or dampness. (See **7.8.1**.)

At para 12.6 the LC Guidance states that civil legal services will be granted where there is a credible allegation that the disrepair poses a serious risk to the health or safety of the client or a relevant member of his family. Adequate information explaining the nature of the alleged disrepair and the risk to the client's health must be provided in all applications. Except in urgent cases, the Pre-action Protocol must be followed.

The LC Guidance at para 12.10 gives a non-exhaustive list of the factors that may be taken into account by the Director in order to determine whether the 'serious risk' requirement is met. These are:

(a)   whether the deficiency has already resulted in harm to the applicant or a relevant member of his family;

(b)   whether, as a result of the deficiency, an existing health condition is exacerbated (eg, where an applicant who has asthma is living in a damp home, or where an applicant who has rheumatism is living in a home with no heating);

(c)   whether the applicant or relevant family members affected by the deficiency are in a high-risk age group, such as the elderly and very young children, and therefore more susceptible to any deficiency;

(d)   whether the applicant is vulnerable due to a disability. For example, a leaking roof which causes flooring to be damp may be viewed as significantly more serious if the applicant has particular mobility problems, or where important medical equipment is placed in jeopardy as a result of the deficiency;

(e)   whether there are relevant environmental conditions. For example, broken heating may be a much more serious deficiency during the winter;

(f)   whether there are multiple deficiencies which could, taken cumulatively, be of greater seriousness than individually. For example, damp conditions combined with a broken window could exacerbate the health risks associated with excess cold;

(g)   whether a single deficiency poses multiple risks. For example, a roof in a state of disrepair could lead to hazards of excess cold, structural collapse, damp and mould, etc;

(h)   whether a deficiency affects rooms or areas that are shared. This may be a relevant factor if, for example, risks of infection could be increased in shared areas where disrepair is not dealt with;

(i)   whether the expert instructed under the Housing Pre-Action Protocol reports that the deficiency is likely to deteriorate further in the near future;

(j)   whether the local authority has already identified hazards which arise from deficiencies in the home, eg under the Housing Health and Safety Rating System.

Subject to the client's meeting the merits and financial eligibility criteria (see **5.2.3.3** and **5.5**), legal aid may be available to raise a counter-claim by way of defence to a rent arrears possession claim (2012 Act, Sch 1, Pt 1, para 33(1)(b)).

Damages-only claims as a result of disrepair are now out of scope for legal aid. However, it is open to the client to use a conditional fee agreement (CFA) to finance a damages-only disrepair claim.

7.8 PUBLIC LAW OBLIGATIONS

Under the Environmental Protection Act (EPA) 1990 and the housing legislation, local authorities often have a duty to act against owners of unfit premises within their areas. Unfortunately for secure tenants of premises owned by a LHA, the courts will not order the authority to take action against itself (R v Cardiff CC, ex p Cross (1982) 6 HLR 1, CA).

7.8.1 Environmental Protection Act 1990, Pt III

Under ss 79 and 80 of the EPA 1990, a local authority has a duty to carry out inspections of its area, or to investigate complaints of statutory nuisance in its area and, where it finds such, to serve an abatement notice on any person responsible for premises which are in such a state as to be prejudicial to health or a nuisance.

Premises will be prejudicial to health if they are injurious, or likely to cause injury to health. This can include actual and potential, mental and physical ill-health. In R v Bristol CC, ex p Everett [1999] 1 WLR 1170, CA, it was held that the term 'injury to health' in s 79(1)(a) related to the threat of disease, vermin or serious dampness which affects the occupier's health. It did not apply where the state of the premises was such that there was a likelihood of an accident causing personal injury. So, in Cunningham v Birmingham CC (1998) 30 HLR 158, QBD, it was held that a tenant who claimed that her kitchen was too small and dangerous because she had an autistic son fascinated with doors, did not have premises which were prejudicial to health. Objectively, there was no statutory nuisance. Again, in R v Bristol CC, ex p Everett (above), it was held not to apply where a steep staircase made it difficult for the tenant, who had a bad back, to get up and down stairs. In Oakley v Birmingham City Council [2001] AC 617, HL, it was held that premises were not prejudicial to health within the provisions in s 79 where the only toilet in the flat had no wash basin and the adjacent kitchen sink had to be used instead.

Serious dampness and mould growth due to inadequate ventilation can cause premises to be prejudicial to health (see GLC v Tower Hamlets LBC (1984) 15 HLR 54). However, if the problem is due to the tenant's not being prepared to pay for the cost of adequate heating, there will be no statutory nuisance (see Pike v Sefton MBC [2000] Env LR D31).

It was at one point thought that noise penetration into a dwelling as a result of inadequate sound insulation could be 'prejudicial to health and thus constitute a statutory nuisance' (Southwark LBC v Ince (1989) 21 HLR 504). However, in Oakley v Birmingham City Council (above), both Lord Hoffman and Lord Millett doubted the legality of Ince. In Vella v Lambeth LBC [2006] HLR 12 it was held that the lack of adequate sound insulation in a dwelling did not make it prejudicial to health or a nuisance under s 79(1)(a). The provisions in s 79(1)(a) and s 79(1)(g) (which deals with noise nuisance) were explained by Mr Justice Poole. Section 79(1)(a) deals with the 'state' of the premises. It is concerned with unwholesome conditions such as noxious matter that could cause ill-health or disease. Section 79(1)(g), however, deals with an 'activity' – noise emitted from premises. It is the activity, the emission of noise, which must be prejudicial to health or a nuisance.

The term 'nuisance' is not defined in the EPA 1990 and so has the common law meaning. It can either be a public nuisance which affects the comfort or quality of life of the public generally, or a private nuisance where the activities on neighbouring premises interfere with the use and enjoyment of the tenant's property and have an effect on his health. The problem needs to come from an external source, not arise in the tenant's property (*National Coal Board v Thorne* [1976] 1 WLR 543).

7.8.1.1 Enforcement by local authority

An aggrieved private sector, PRP or RSL tenant can complain to the local authority's Environmental Health Department, or the authority may discover a statutory nuisance as a result of its own inspection under s 79(1) of the EPA 1990. If satisfied that the provisions apply to the tenant's case, the authority must serve an abatement notice (EPA 1990, s 80(1)), specifying the works to be done and the time limits for compliance. The notice should be served on the person responsible for the nuisance, or, in cases where there are structural defects, on the owner of the premises (s 80(2)). In disrepair cases the tenant will be looking for a notice which requires the abatement of the statutory nuisance, and which requires the appropriate works and other necessary steps to achieve that end (s 80(1)).

The person on whom the notice is served can appeal to a magistrates' court within 21 days (EPA 1990, s 80(3)). However, if there is no appeal or action to carry out the works, the person commits a criminal offence punishable by fine (s 80(4)). If convicted, a compensation order can also be made against the person responsible for the statutory nuisance, under the court's powers in s 130 of the Powers of Criminal Courts (Sentencing) Act 2000. The magistrates' court has a discretion to make awards of up to £5,000. However, it has been made clear that where details of the nuisance have been properly pleaded, the compensation should not relate to a period more than six months before the complaint was made, or prior to the date of the expiry of a statutory notice if longer (see *R v Liverpool Crown Court, ex p Cooke* [1997] 1 WLR 700).

The local authority has the power to do the works itself where an abatement notice has not been complied with, and recover the expenses in default (EPA 1990, s 81(3), (4)). Alternatively, it may bring High Court proceedings against a person in default (s 80(5)). In an extreme case, the local authority has the power under s 76 of the Building Act 1984 to carry out the works itself after serving notice on the person responsible for the condition, stating its intention to remedy the nuisance. This will be done only where the authority believes that the normal abatement process would cause an unreasonable delay.

7.8.1.2 Enforcement by application to a magistrates' court

Any LHA, PRP, RSL, or private sector tenant, or other person suffering from a statutory nuisance can, under s 82 of the EPA 1990, commence proceedings directly against the landlord or other person responsible for the problem. The complainant must give at least 21 days' written notice of intention to bring proceedings in the magistrates' court (s 82(7)). If the court is satisfied that a nuisance exists, it must make an order requiring abatement and may also fine the defendant. A compensation order can be made in this instance too, at the discretion of the magistrates (see **7.8.1.1**).

7.8.2 Public funding for statutory nuisance claims

Legal aid may be available for complaints under s 82 of the EPA 1990 if the condition of the property poses a serious risk of harm to the health and safety of a tenant or a member of his family (see **5.2.3.3** and 7.7).

7.8.3 Improvement notices or prohibition orders under the HA 2004

Provisions in Pt 1 of the HA 2004, and accompanying regulations (see the Housing Health and Safety Rating System (England) Regulations 2005 (SI 2005/3208)), use a hazard-based system for assessing the condition of residential premises and how to deal with them. The provisions came into effect in England on 6 April 2006. The provisions introduce a Housing Health and Safety Rating System (HHSRS), which looks at the whole dwelling and allocates a numerical score, according to the likely effects that a number of hazards may have on the occupiers of the dwelling. There are 29 listed categories of hazards in the HHSRS. They range from damp and mould growth, through to structural collapse and failing elements. The hazards are divided into four main groups, namely: physiological requirements; psychological requirements; protection against infection; and protection against accidents.

An LHA will be required to inspect to see whether the condition of premises in its area poses hazards that fall into either category 1 or category 2. A category 1 hazard (s 2) is defined as dwellings which score over 1,000 points on the HHSRS; category 2 hazards will relate to dwellings which score below 1,000 points. The LHA will be required to take enforcement action in relation to dwellings with category 1 hazards. A range of options is available, depending on the nature of the hazard. Two options relevant to dwellings in serious disrepair could be service of an improvement notice on the person responsible to remedy the hazard, or service of a prohibition order to stop the premises being used either absolutely or by particular persons, dependent on the risk of serious harm to them. There are similar options for dwellings with category 2 hazards, but there the LHA has only a power to act, not a duty (ss 5–12). The recipient of the notice will have a right of appeal to the First-tier Tribunal (Property Chamber) (Residential Property) within the relevant time limit. For an improvement notice, the relevant time limit is 21 days. For a prohibition order, the time limit is 28 days. Failure to comply with an improvement notice or prohibition order, or to lodge an appeal within the relevant time, will amount to an offence punishable by fine (ss 30, 32).

It is hoped that these new regulatory provisions, coupled with the licensing requirements for houses in multiple occupation (HMOs) (see **1.7.1**), will address the serious issues of disrepair and unfitness that are often common for private sector tenants occupying HMOs.

7.9 FURTHER READING

J Luba, D Forster and B Prevatt, *Repairs: tenants' rights* (4th edn, 2010)

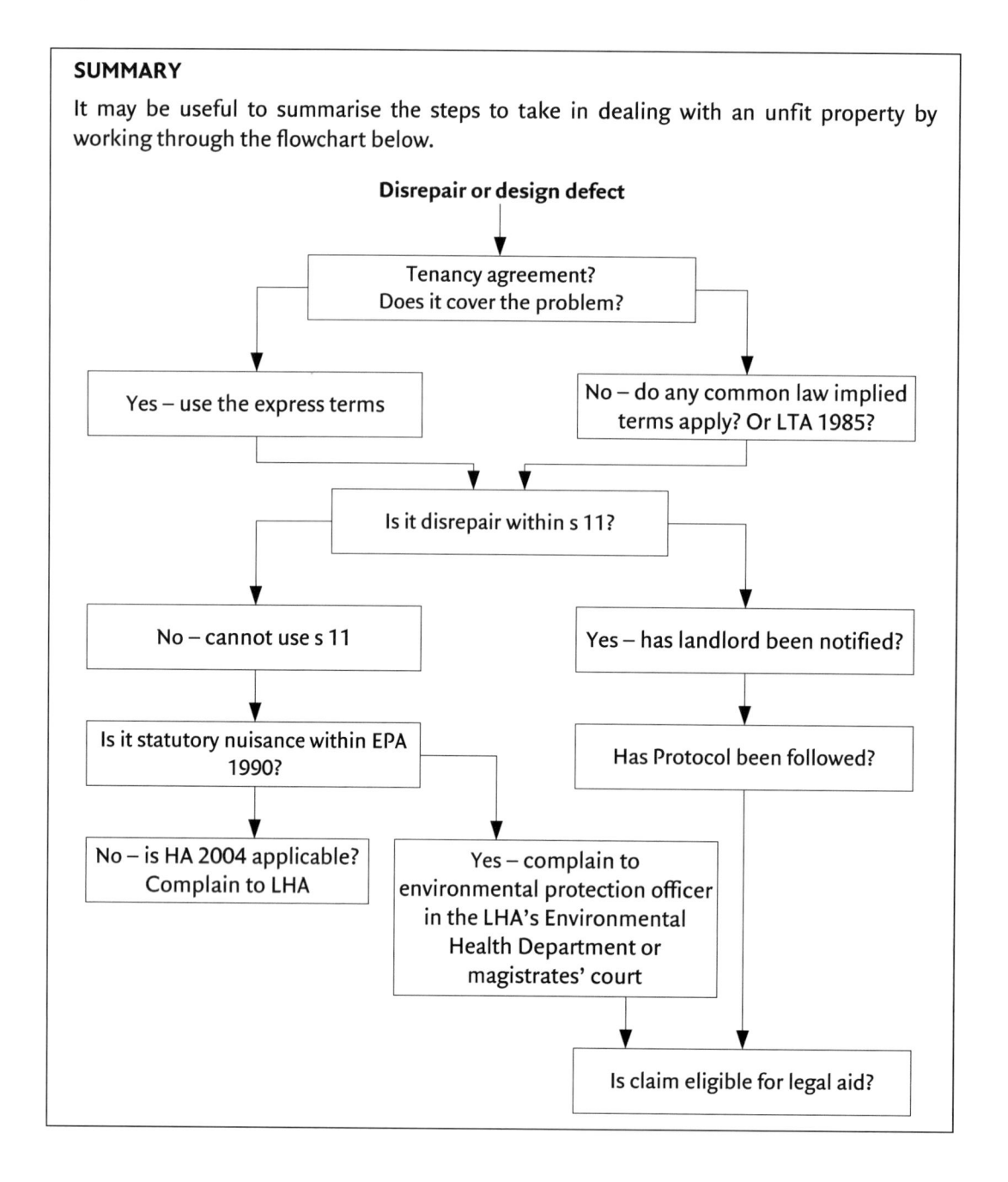

SUMMARY

It may be useful to summarise the steps to take in dealing with an unfit property by working through the flowchart below.

Disrepair or design defect
↓
Tenancy agreement? Does it cover the problem?
- Yes – use the express terms
- No – do any common law implied terms apply? Or LTA 1985?

↓

Is it disrepair within s 11?
- No – cannot use s 11
  - Is it statutory nuisance within EPA 1990?
    - No – is HA 2004 applicable? Complain to LHA
    - Yes – complain to environmental protection officer in the LHA's Environmental Health Department or magistrates' court
- Yes – has landlord been notified?
  - Has Protocol been followed?

↓

Is claim eligible for legal aid?

CHAPTER 8

The Rights of Long Leaseholders

8.1	Introduction	119
8.2	Security on the expiry of a long lease	120
8.3	Exercising rights to acquire a greater interest in the property	121
8.4	Service charge and other issues in long leases	125
8.5	Statutory protection against forfeiture during long lease	128
8.6	Mortgage default and the rights of mortgagees	129
8.7	Further reading	132
	Summary	132

LEARNING OUTCOMES

After reading this chapter you will be able to:

- explain the options open to a leaseholder to acquire a greater interest in the property
- describe the reasonableness requirements in relation to service charges and administration charges
- list the various statutory restrictions on a landlord's ability to forfeit the lease of a tenant who is in breach of the terms of the tenancy
- outline the limited protection available to a mortgage borrower in arrears with mortgage payments.

8.1 INTRODUCTION

A long lease is generally defined as the grant of a term of over 21 years. Residential long leases are normally granted for a term of 99 or 125 years. They are a form of ownership of residential property for which the leaseholder will have paid a large premium, usually with the assistance of a loan or mortgage. Thereafter, the leaseholder normally pays a very low annual ground rent on the property. Long leases can be granted for houses; historically these were building leases where the tenant undertook construction of the house on the leased land. However, for more recent grants, the property is invariably a flat – a dwelling-house within a larger building with other dwellings and/or other premises. As a result, long leaseholders often pay a service charge for upkeep of the common parts and structure of the building, in addition to their ground rent.

In this chapter, we consider some of the issues that may arise as a result of this form of ownership of a dwelling-house. We look briefly at the security that long leaseholders may have when their leases terminate. In addition, we briefly consider the rights they have to improve their holding or interest in the property. The chapter then examines issues that frequently arise when a service charge is payable, such as disputes over the reasonableness of the charge, the works, etc. Also considered are matters in relation to mortgage repossession or forfeiture of the lease. The chapter focuses on some of the more common situations in connection with long leaseholders, and does not attempt to give an in-depth account of what are substantive areas of land law and landlord and tenant law. The reader is referred to more detailed information on these areas at the end of the chapter (see **Further reading** at **8.7**).

8.2 SECURITY ON THE EXPIRY OF A LONG LEASE

The provisions in Pt I of the LTA 1954, and s 186 of and Sch 10 to the LGHA 1989, provide security for residential long leases which run their full term and expire without the tenant having exercised a right to acquire a greater interest in the property, or, more recently, where an extended term has expired.

These provisions were introduced in recognition of the apparent injustice that would otherwise be caused where long leases expired and the tenant was left with nothing after having paid a premium on the property, or having built the house on the land some 99 years before. This was considered particularly incongruous, as periodic and short leasehold tenants could enjoy full security and fair rents under the Rent Act provisions.

The provisions operate by continuing the long tenancy automatically at the end of the term, unless, as is invariably the case, the landlord takes steps either to terminate the lease or to convert it to an assured tenancy (see LGHA 1989, Sch 10, para 3(1)). The landlord will have every incentive to take action as the continuation tenancy is on the same terms as the long lease, including the payment of a very low ground rent (Sch 10, para 3(3)).

8.2.1 Assured tenant security under LGHA 1989

Since 15 January 1999, if the landlord takes steps to convert the long lease, the leaseholder of a qualifying long lease which expires having run its full term will normally be entitled to remain in occupation of the dwelling as an assured periodic tenant under the HA 1988. The tenant will thus be paying a market rent for continued occupation of his dwelling, which can be fixed by agreement or, failing that, assessed by a rent assessment committee (LGHA 1989, Sch 10, para 10).

In order to determine whether the long lease is a qualifying one, certain conditions have to be met. The first is that the lease must be a long lease at a low rent (see **2.3** at (c) for definition of low rent). If the lease was created before, or pursuant to a contract made before, 1 April 1990, the qualifying condition would be that the long lease would have been a RA 1977 protected tenancy but for the rent being a low rent. In other words, the rateable value of the property would need to be within the RA 1977 limits for the appropriate time and none of the other RA 1977 exclusions would apply (LTA 1954, s 2; see **Chapter 3**).

For leases created on or after 1 April 1990, the qualifying conditions are that the lease would be an assured tenancy under the HA 1988 were it not for the low rent. In other words, none of the other exclusions in Sch 1 to the HA 1988 should apply (see **2.3**). So, for example, the long leaseholder of a LHA would not qualify under these provisions as lettings by public bodies are specifically outside the protection of both the RA 1977 and HA 1988 (see *Banjo v Brent LBC* [2005] EWCA Civ 292; also **2.3** at (k) and **3.3** for tenancies excluded from protection).

8.2.2 Limits to the assured tenant security under LGHA 1989

There are provisions in Sch 10 to the LGHA 1989 that make it possible for the landlord to terminate the lease at the term date by service of a notice to resume possession, stipulating the reason. The landlord can rely on a number of the grounds for possession in Sch 2 to the HA 1988, namely: Ground 6 (recovery for redevelopment) or an equivalent provision; Pt II discretionary grounds (except Ground 16) (see **2.6.2**); or the equivalent of Case 9 in Sch 15 to the RA 1977 (see **3.4.2.3**).

Most qualifying tenants will try to obtain a better right before their long leases expire. However, it sometimes happens that leases do expire and the security provisions that were in the LTA 1954, and which are now in the 1989 Act (see above), come into play. The security provisions in the LGHA 1989 are not quite as generous for the tenant as the earlier provisions in the LTA 1954, which conveyed RA 1977 protection.

8.2.3 When an assured tenancy under LGHA 1989 will not arise

> **CASE EXAMPLE**
>
> In R *(on the application of Morris) v London Rent Assessment Committee* [2002] EWCA Civ 276, the long lease on a flat in Cadogan Place, London SW1 expired in 1995. The landlords served a notice proposing a statutory tenancy that would have been within the protection of the RA 1977, which would have been a statutory tenancy subject to a fair rent (see **3.5**). Fortunately for the landlords, through no fault of their own, the notice was served on the original leaseholder rather than on the present tenant (a very late assignee). As a result, the 1995 notice was invalid. The landlords served another notice on the correct tenant in June 1999. As this was after 15 January 1999, an assured tenancy was proposed, but at a rent of £46,800 per annum. The tenant challenged this before a rent assessment committee, which fixed a rent of £32,496 per annum. As this sum was over the £25,000 originally set in England for assured tenants within the protection of the HA 1988 (see **2.3** at (b)), the tenant was without any security on the expiry of the long lease. It was held that the rent assessment committee was not bound to fix a rent that was within the assured tenancy limit.

8.3 EXERCISING RIGHTS TO ACQUIRE A GREATER INTEREST IN THE PROPERTY

A long leaseholder can, provided he satisfies the relevant eligibility requirement, exercise one of the rights to enfranchise available in the Leasehold Reform Act (LRA) 1967, the LTA 1987, the Leasehold Reform, Housing and Urban Development Act (LRHUDA) 1993, or the Commonhold and Leasehold Reform Act (CLRA) 2002. The provisions apply to enable the long leaseholder of a house or flat to acquire an extended lease, or the freehold in certain circumstances.

8.3.1 The right to enfranchise the freehold of a house

The LRA 1967, as amended, gives long leaseholders of certain houses the right to acquire the freehold, or an extended lease (of an additional 50 years) of the house. The LRA 1967, as originally enacted, restricted the right to an extended lease or enfranchisement to houses with low rateable values and where a low ground rent was paid. However, after considerable amendments by a number of legislative provisions, ending with the CLRA 2002, the position now is that the right to enfranchise is, subject to limited exclusions, available to almost any long leaseholder of a house.

8.3.1.1 The conditions for enfranchisement

There are still some conditions to be met before the right will apply. The first condition is that the tenancy must be a long lease (ie a term certain exceeding 21 years). The second is that the leaseholder must have had the lease for at least two years before starting the enfranchisement procedures, although this requirement can be slightly different, eg requiring residence, for certain long leaseholders of houses under a business tenancy.

The third condition is that the leaseholder must have a lease of a 'house', which cannot be a building which is not structurally detached and has a material part above or below a part of the structure which is not comprised in the house (LRA 1967, s 2(3)). In other words, flats are excluded. However, apart from this, 'house' is generously defined to include any building that is designed or adapted for living in. It can apply to a building which has been divided into flats or maisonettes, or which has uses other than as a dwelling (see *Tandon v Trustees of Spurgeons Homes* [1982] AC 755, HL).

The procedure for enfranchisement is commenced by the leaseholder serving a notice in accordance with the provisions in s 22 of and Sch 3 to the LRA 1967 and accompanying regulations.

8.3.1.2 Factors relating to the purchase price

There are certain assumptions made in calculating the purchase price. For example, it is assumed that the landlord is selling the freehold subject to the existing tenancy, with the same rights and burdens but without the right to enfranchise. Long leaseholders who qualify under the original provisions relating to low rateable values are at an advantage, in that they can have both an extended lease, at no premium, and can also enfranchise. The purchase price is also calculated in a way which is very much to the leaseholder's advantage, as it assumes a lease extension of 50 years if the right has not already been exercised, and no account is taken of the fact that it is the tenant who is buying the freehold – so the 'marriage value' (ie, the extra value of the freehold if merged with the leasehold estate) is disregarded (LRA 1967, s 9(1)). This can result in the tenant paying a very low purchase price for the freehold.

For leases which have come within the provisions of the LRA 1967 as a result of later amendments, the provisions are not so generous. So for houses with higher rateable values, high rents, or where the leaseholder now has the ability to enfranchise during the 50-year extension period (not originally in the LRA 1967), the position now is that where the unexpired term of the lease is 80 years or less, the marriage value is taken account of but half is given to the tenant (LRA 1967, ss 9(1A)–(1E)). Where the unexpired term is over 80 years, the marriage value is ignored. The assumption is also that at the end of the term the tenants would be paying a market rent for the property as assured tenants under the LGHA 1989 provisions. In certain cases the landlord can also be compensated for loss and diminution in value of other property as a result of the sale or lease extension (LRA 1967, s 9A).

8.3.1.3 Human rights challenge

The provisions of the LRA 1967 have been challenged by a landlord as constituting unjust expropriatory legislation which breaches Article 1 of the First Protocol to the Convention (see **4.2**). However, the ECtHR held in *James v UK* (1986) 8 EHRR 123 that the compulsory transfer of property from one person to another may constitute a legitimate means for promoting the public interest, even where the community at large had no direct use or benefit of the property taken. It was also held that the legitimate objectives of public interest could justify reimbursement for the expropriation at less than market value.

8.3.2 The rights of long leaseholders of flats

Long leaseholders of flats have gone from having no right to acquire a greater interest in their home, to now having a whole raft of options, right up to a type of freehold ownership. Legislative provisions from 1987 through to 2002 have given them the right of first refusal, the right to be granted a new lease of the flat or collectively to acquire the freehold, and, lastly, the right to create a commonhold interest of the building in which the flat is situated. All these provisions are concurrently available. A brief outline of each is given below.

8.3.2.1 Tenants' right of first refusal

Part I of the LTA 1987, as amended, gives certain qualifying tenants of flats the right of 'first refusal' when their landlord wishes to dispose of his interest in the building. The provision is not directed specifically at long leaseholders, although they are within its scope.

The right will apply where:

(a) a building consists of two or more flats and at least 50% of the internal floor area (ignoring common parts) is for residential purposes; and

(b) more than 50% of the flats are occupied by qualifying tenants.

Qualifying tenants are negatively defined by specifically excluding certain types. Amongst the exclusions are business tenants, service tenants and assured tenants. Thus, by default, RA 1977 regulated tenants, tenants outside the HA 1988 (eg, because of high rent payment) and long leaseholders can be qualifying tenants. Secure tenants of social landlords will not qualify, as LHAs, PRPs and RSLs are exempt from the provisions (LTA 1987, s 58(1)). In addition, a building with a resident landlord may also be excluded. This will be the case if he is the landlord of a non purpose-built block of flats and he has occupied one of the flats as his only or principal residence for the last 12 months (LTA 1987, s 58(2)).

Where a landlord proposes to make a relevant disposal (as defined in s 4 of the LTA 1987), he is required to follow the statutory procedure, which requires him to serve notice on the qualifying tenants, giving them the right to buy that interest if they so desire (s 5). There are criminal sanctions if the landlord fails to follow the provisions (s 10A), and the tenants may still be able to exercise their right against the purchaser (s 12B).

8.3.2.2 Compulsory acquisition of the landlord's interest

Part III of the LTA 1987 gives qualifying tenants of flats (for these purposes long leaseholders (s 26)) the ability to apply to the court for an order compulsorily to acquire a neglectful landlord's interest. However, in this Part, the qualifying tenants must occupy at least two-thirds of the total number of flats in the premises (s 25(2)).

The right will arise if the tenants have gone through the process in Pt II of the LTA 1987, which involves the appointment of a manager by a leasehold valuation tribunal because of the landlord's failure, amongst other things, to manage the premises properly, or where he has imposed unreasonable service charges (see **7.5.3** and **8.4.3**). The provisions apply if the landlord continues to be in breach of his management obligations, despite a manager having been appointed under Pt II two years before the court application. The court may make an acquisition order if all the relevant conditions have been satisfied (s 29). However, before the court makes an order, two-thirds of the qualifying leaseholders have to go through a procedure requiring service of a notice on the landlord, giving him details of their complaint and giving him a reasonable time to remedy the problems (s 27).

It is questionable whether tenants will want to utilise the rather protracted and uncertain procedures in Pts II and III of the LTA 1987 in light of the new right to manage conveyed by Pt 2 of the CLRA 2002 (see **8.3.2.3** below).

8.3.2.3 The right of long leaseholders to manage their buildings

Part 2, Ch 1 (ss 71–113 and Schs 6 and 7) of the CLRA 2002 has, since 30 September 2003 for England and 30 March 2004 for Wales, given long leaseholders of flats the right to manage their buildings after setting up a right to manage company. They will be able to do so without having to prove that the landlord was not managing properly and without the need to pay compensation.

The right is not universal but restricted to self-contained premises with two or more flats, where qualifying tenants occupy at least two-thirds of the total number of flats in the premises (CLRA 2002, s 72). Certain premises will not count, however, eg: buildings where more than 25% of the internal floor area is for non-residential use; premises consisting of not more than four units (for residential or business use) with a resident landlord; and LHA-owned premises (see Sch 6). The qualifying tenant has a much narrower definition here than under Pt I of the LTA 1987 (those with the right of first refusal, see **8.3.2.1**). Here a qualifying tenant is essentially a lawful long leaseholder of a residential lease (s 75).

Any claim to the right must be made through the right to manage company giving a claim notice to the landlord or manager of the premises (see s 79).

8.3.2.4 The right of long leaseholders to collective enfranchisement

Part I (ss 1–103) of the LRHUDA 1993, as amended, has, from 1 November 1993, given rights to enfranchise, similar to those available to leaseholders of houses under the LRA 1967, to long leaseholders of flats. The rights are available to qualifying tenants of certain premises.

The criteria for qualifying tenants and premises, as amended by the CLRA 2002, are similar to those in relation to qualifying tenants with the right to manage (see **8.3.2.3**), save that there are a couple of additional qualifications. One is that if a tenant has a long lease of three or more flats in the premises, he will not be a qualifying tenant of any of them (LRHUDA 1993, s 5(5)). The second qualification is under s 5(2)(b), where a long leaseholder of a flat will not be a qualifying tenant if his immediate landlord is a charitable housing trust and the flat forms part of the housing accommodation provided by it in pursuit of its charitable purposes.

> **CASE EXAMPLE**
>
> In *Richmond Housing Partnership Ltd v Brick Farm Management Ltd* [2005] EWHC 1650, an LHA transferred two blocks of flats to a charitable housing trust. In one block, two-thirds of the tenants held on long leases, having exercised their right to buy as former secure tenants (see **6.8.4**). The other tenants were assured tenants of the trust. It was held that s 5(2)(b) did not prevent the long leaseholders of the block of flats being qualifying tenants eligible to exercise their right to enfranchise, as the long leaseholders' flats did not form part of the trust's housing accommodation provided in pursuit of its charitable purposes.

Qualifying tenants have the right, subject to various conditions being met, either collectively to acquire the freehold of their flats, or individually to acquire the grant of an extended lease (90 years) (see **8.3.2.5**). The amended provisions (in LRHUDA 1993, s 12A and not yet in force) provide that to enfranchise collectively, notice must be given to the reversioner by a right to enfranchise (RTE) company made up of qualifying tenants. The provisions at present (in LRHUDA 1993, s 13) allow the qualifying tenants, who must own not less than half the total number of flats in the premises, to serve the initial notice themselves, giving details of the nominee purchaser(s) who will act on their behalf.

The purchase price is calculated on a similar basis to house enfranchisement under the amended system applicable for higher value properties (see **8.3.1.2**). This effectively gives the freeholder the market value of his interest in the property. Account is taken of the value of the freehold interest, the marriage value, and any compensation due to the freeholder for losses caused to other property belonging to him which may be affected as a result of the enfranchisement. As with houses, there will be no marriage value if the leases have over 80 years unexpired. However, where the leases have 80 years or less to run, the landlord will get 50% of any marriage value (see LRHUDA 1993, Sch 6).

8.3.2.5 The right of a long leaseholder to an extended lease

A qualifying tenant will have the right to acquire a 90-year extension to the present lease. He may wish to do so, for example, where there are not enough qualifying tenants for them collectively to enfranchise. For this right, a qualifying tenant is as defined above for collective enfranchisement (see **8.3.2.4**), but without the s 5(5) qualification (ie, here the tenant can own any number of flats in the building). The provisions are contained in Pt I, Ch, 2 (ss 39–62), LRHUDA 1993. A pre-condition to eligibility is that the tenant must have been a long leaseholder of the flat for the last two years (s 39(2)). As with the procedure for the exercise of other rights, the process is started by the tenant serving an initial notice in accordance with the provisions in s 42.

The lack of restriction on the number of flats that can be held by a qualifying tenant means that a head lessee will have the right to an individual lease extension under these provisions (*Howard de Walden Estates Ltd v Les Aggio* [2008] UKHL 44).

As with other acquisitions, the premium for the extension will take account of marriage value and compensation for the landlord's loss, in addition to any diminution in the value of the landlord's interest in the flat as a result of the lease extension (see LRHUDA 1993, Sch 13, Pt II).

8.3.2.6 The right to register a commonhold ownership

Part 1 (ss 1–70) of the CLRA 2002 introduced, from 27 September 2004, the commonhold ownership. This enables a group of existing leaseholders to convert to a commonhold tenure. It also allows new developments of flats and other units to be built on a commonhold, rather than leasehold, basis. The main benefit will be that flat owners will have a permanent instead of a wasting asset, as commonholds are a form of freehold ownership of land. In addition, the management and consultation structures are simpler than those that now operate for residential leasehold blocks under the provisions considered above.

The leaseholders, in agreement with the freehold owner of the premises, will need to form a commonhold association, which is a private company limited by guarantee. The Commonhold Regulations 2004 (SI 2004/1829) provide details of the rules for operation of the commonhold and the constitution of the association. It is through this association that the interests of the unit holders will operate, and the association will be the registered proprietor of the freehold estate in the common parts of the premises. Membership of the association will comprise the unit holders or leaseholders of the flats. Each unit holder will be entitled to be registered as the proprietor of the freehold estate in the unit at Land Registry (CLRA 2002, s 9).

However, long leaseholders will not be able to convert to a commonhold interest without the consent of the freehold owner of the building, as registration of a commonhold interest can be done only by, or with the consent of, the freehold owner, as well as with the consent of every long leaseholder and charge holder (ss 2(1)(a), 3(1)(a), (b), (c)). It may be the case that long leaseholders would have to go through the lengthy process of collective enfranchisement before they could start the process of creating a commonhold. This may prove one step too far in the absence of unanimity amongst the leaseholders.

8.4 SERVICE CHARGE AND OTHER ISSUES IN LONG LEASES

It is fairly standard in long leases of flats for the landlord to have included a clause requiring the leaseholder to contribute to the costs of providing maintenance, repairs to the overall structure of the building and any common parts, insurance and other services. At common law, if a landlord does not impose an obligation on the leaseholder to pay for such services, or if the works he has completed go beyond what is reserved in the lease, then he cannot demand payment for them (see *Mullaney v Maybourne Grange (Croydon) Management Co Ltd* [1986] 1 EGLR 70).

It is, however, now possible for an application to be made to the Property Chamber of the First-tier Tribunal (leasehold valuation). Application can be made for the lease of a flat to be varied to remedy any deficiency in the provisions in the lease. This can include provisions relating to repairs, maintenance or payment of charges (see LTA 1987, s 35).

There will be an element of service charge in the rent that periodic tenants of flats pay to their landlords, whether it is a secure, an assured or a regulated tenancy. In periodic residential leases, however, unless the service element is substantial, the landlord normally does not break down the rental payment, or, indeed, have a variable charge for services. The legal issues that arise in relation to service charges most commonly occur when a variable charge is made for services, separate from any rental payment for the premises. This may occur in short and periodic tenancies, but it is much more common in long leases.

As a result of Government concerns that some landlords were abusing the management duties and not providing proper services, or were making unreasonable demands for the services that they did provide, a number of statutory provisions have been introduced to protect tenants of residential leases. The main provisions are now in the LTAs 1985 and 1987, as amended by the LRHUDA 1993, HA 1996 and, most recently, CLRA 2002. The provisions set the criterion of reasonableness as the basis on which landlords can demand payment for services provided.

8.4.1 Exclusions from protection of service charge provisions in LTA 1985

Under s 26 of the LTA 1985, for LHA tenants, the provisions in ss 18 to 25 relating to service charges and information will apply only to long leases granted by an LHA. Thus secure tenants will not have the benefit of these provisions, but tenants of flats who exercise their right to buy and obtain 125-year leases with service charges payable are within the LTA 1985.

8.4.2 Service charge defined

By s 18 of the LTA 1985, as amended, 'service charge' is defined to mean a variable amount payable by a tenant of a dwelling as part of, or in addition to, the rent, which is payable, directly or indirectly, for services, repairs, maintenance, improvements or insurance, or the landlord's costs of management. The landlord will be able to recover relevant costs for any of the defined items only if he has reserved the right to do so in the lease.

Section 18(2) defines relevant costs as the costs or estimated costs incurred or to be incurred by or on behalf of the landlord in connection with the matters for which the service charge is payable. Unless given advance written notice, a tenant will not be liable to pay a service charge that relates to relevant costs incurred more than 18 months before the demand was served on the tenant (s 20B). In *O M Property Management Ltd v Burr* [2013] HLR 29, CA, it was held that costs are incurred when demand for payment is submitted by the supplier or when payment is made, not when the liability to pay arose. The provisions then go on to regulate the basis upon which the landlord can charge for services for which he has reserved the right to charge in the lease.

In making a demand for service charges, the landlord is required by s 21B to provide the leaseholder with a summary of rights and obligations. The contents of this summary have been prescribed by regulations which came into force on 1 October 2007 (see Service Charges (Summary of Rights and Obligations and Transitional Provision) (England) Regulations 2007 (SI 2007/1257)). A leaseholder may withhold payment of a service charge which has been demanded from him if the landlord has not provided the summary as prescribed.

8.4.3 Reasonableness and consultation

The amount that the landlord can recover for the services provided is regulated by s 19 of the LTA 1985. This restricts the landlord's ability to recover service charges by limiting it to services that are reasonably incurred, and only for works and services provided to a reasonable standard. In *Continental Property Ventures Inc v White* [2006] 1 EGLR 85, it was held that repair costs had not been reasonably incurred by the landlords. The repair works could have been covered by a guarantee without any further cost to the tenant. As a result, the tenant did not have to pay the service charge which related to those works.

Before a landlord can carry out building or repair works to the premises above a certain value, or enter into long-term management contracts, he is now required, as a result of amendments made by the CLRA 2002, s 151 and regulations, to go through an extensive consultation process with the tenants. The works are defined as qualified works where tenants would be required to pay more than £250 each. The management contracts are defined as qualifying long-term agreements for which tenants would have to pay more than £100 in any accounting period, which is usually a year. A failure to follow the consultation procedures without having obtained a dispensation from the Property Chamber of the First-tier Tribunal, could result in the landlord being restricted in the amount he can recover from the tenant for the works or the service (see LTA 1985, ss 20, 20ZA; Service Charges (Consultation Requirements

(England) Regulations 2003 (SI 2003/1987); *Daejan Investments Ltd v Benson* [2013] UKSC 14 (see **8.4.5**).

8.4.4 Administration charges

Landlords are now also subject to controls in the amount they can charge for administrative tasks relating to the lease. An administration charge is defined in Sch 11 to the CLRA 2002, to include amounts payable for the grant of approvals under the lease, the provision of documentation or for actions taken by the landlord in relation to (alleged) breaches of covenant.

A variable administration charge will be payable only to the extent that it is reasonable, and a leaseholder can challenge a fixed administration charge, or any formula for calculating the charge, as being unreasonable by application to a leasehold valuation tribunal (see **8.4.5** and Sch 11, para 3).

In making a demand for payment of the charge, the landlord must provide the leaseholder with a summary of his rights and obligations in relation to the charge as prescribed by regulations (see Administration Charges (Summary of Rights and Obligations) (England) Regulations 2007 (SI 2007/1258)). The leaseholder will be entitled to withhold payment if the landlord does not provide him with a summary of his rights and obligations (see CLRA 2002, Sch 11, para 4).

8.4.5 Disputes and leasehold valuation tribunals

Where disputes arise, the Property Chamber of the First-tier Tribunal now has extensive jurisdiction to resolve them. It has the power to determine whether or not service charges are payable and the amount that is to be paid by the leaseholder, and to decide any question relating to reasonableness. The Tribunal has jurisdiction whether or not a payment has been made, but not on a matter that has been agreed by the tenant, or where it has been or is being dealt with elsewhere (eg, by a court or arbitration) (LTA 1985, s 27A). The Tribunal does not, however, have the power to order repayment of any money found not to be payable.

The jurisdiction extends to issues relating to whether insurance premiums should be paid by the landlord or the tenant, and, where the tenant is obliged to insure with an insurer approved by the landlord, deciding whether an alternative insurer can be used (see LTA 1985, Sch, para 8, as amended).

The Tribunal can also rule on the reasonableness of administration charges. Its jurisdiction includes dealing with issues over the reasonableness of variable as well as fixed administration charges (CLRA 2002, Sch 11, para 3). It has the power to vary lease terms that are defective, including matters relating to repairs, insurance, buildings or installations in the lease (see LTA 1987, Pt IV).

The Tribunal can also dispense with the consultation provisions in ss 20 and 20ZA of the LTA 1985 (see **8.4.3**). It is quite common for LHAs to apply for this dispensation where the works relate to buildings with long leaseholders. These leaseholders are former secure tenants who have exercised their right to buy (see **6.8.4**).

Private sector landlords can also apply under s 20ZA for a dispensation from the consultation provisions. The Tribunal may grant dispensation if it is reasonable to do so. In *Daejan Investments Ltd v Benson* [2013] UKSC 14, the landlords, Daejan, had carried out extensive and very expensive repair works to a block of leasehold flats. They had not properly complied with some of the procedural steps in the consultation provisions. Five long leaseholders argued successfully at the Tribunal and the Court of Appeal stage that they should each have to pay only the maximum of £250 (a total of £1,250) rather than the £280,000 total sum demanded by Daejan as the service charge for the works. The leaseholders claimed they had been prejudiced by Daejan's failure to consult properly, so it would not be reasonable to grant a dispensation. However, the Supreme Court, in allowing Daejan's appeal and granting the dispensation, gave guidance on the correct approach that the Tribunal should take in such cases.

The Court opined that the purpose of the consultation process was to protect leaseholders from paying for inappropriate works or paying more than was appropriate. The Tribunal should focus on how any breach of the consultation provisions had affected those matters. Dispensation should normally be granted if the failure to consult had not affected those matters. If the leaseholders felt they were prejudiced by the landlord's failure to consult, the factual burden was on them to identify some relevant prejudice. The Tribunal could grant dispensation on terms that could include the landlord agreeing to reduce the recoverable costs of the works and/or paying the leaseholders' reasonable costs of the dispensation application. Daejan offered, and the Court accepted as reasonable, a reduction of £50,000 to the total sum demanded, as no specific prejudice had been proved. The landlord also had to pay the leaseholders' legal costs.

8.5 STATUTORY PROTECTION AGAINST FORFEITURE DURING LONG LEASE

Provisions introduced by the HA 1996 and the CLRA 2002 have ensured that residential leaseholders are now effectively protected against what were perceived to be the overly aggressive management policies that some landlords used in the past to force tenants to pay rent or other charges. A landlord would often commence action to terminate a tenant's lease, even where there was an on-going dispute over the amount due or payable.

8.5.1 Restriction on termination for failure to pay service charges

It used to be the case that if a leaseholder failed to pay a disputed service charge, the landlord could and would commence forfeiture proceedings (ie, to terminate the lease) as a means of forcing compliance.

The provisions in s 81 of the HA 1996, as amended by the CLRA 2002, s 170, have severely restricted the ability of landlords to do this in future. The provisions apply to any tenancy agreement relating to dwellings which has a forfeiture clause, not just to long leases. Termination here includes service of a s 146 notice (see **8.5.3.1**). A landlord may not exercise a right of re-entry or forfeiture for failure by a tenant to pay a service charge or an administration charge, unless the tenant agrees the charge, or it has been finally determined by the appropriate tribunal or the court and 14 days have elapsed since the final determination.

8.5.2 Restriction on termination for failure to pay small amounts for short periods

Further protections, which came into effect early in 2005, have given additional assistance to long leaseholders. A landlord who has granted a long lease of a dwelling cannot in certain cases exercise a right of re-entry or forfeiture for non-payment of rent, service charges or administration charges (or a combination of them) unless certain conditions are met (CLRA 2002, s 167). The conditions are that the unpaid amount must exceed £350, or, alternatively, the unpaid amount must have been outstanding for three years (see Rights of Re-entry and Forfeiture (Prescribed Sum and Period) (England) Regulations 2004 (SI 2004/3086)). The landlord will not be able to take action if the rent is not lawfully due, and further provisions now impose new conditions on a landlord in relation to rent payment on long leases of dwellings.

8.5.2.1 Requirements to notify long leaseholders that rent is due

A long leaseholder will not be liable to pay rent for the dwelling unless the landlord has given him notice in the prescribed form. Thus the landlord will not be able to terminate the lease for rent that is not lawfully due as a result of non-compliance with these provisions (see *Chasewood Park Residents Ltd v Kim* [2010] EWHC 579 (Ch)). The notice must specify the amount due, the date of payment and further prescribed information, which includes notice of the restrictions in s 167 on forfeiture for small amounts or for short periods (see CLRA 2002, s 166 and Landlord and Tenant (Notice of Rent) (England) Regulations 2004 (SI 2004/3096) and Landlord and Tenant (Notice of Rent) (Wales) Regulations 2005 (SI 2005/1355)).

8.5.3 Restriction on service of a s 146 notice before breach is determined

Since 28 February 2005, a landlord under a long lease of a dwelling has been required to satisfy further conditions in addition to those already in existence, before he can terminate the lease. By s 168 of the CLRA 2002, a landlord may not serve a notice under s 146 of the LPA 1925 (restriction on forfeiture) in respect of a breach of covenant or condition (other than non-payment of rent), unless the tenant has admitted the breach, or the appropriate tribunal, a court or an arbitral tribunal has finally determined that the breach occurred. The landlord cannot serve the s 146 notice until 14 days after final determination (CLRA 2002, s 168(3)).

8.5.3.1 The s 146 notice procedure

The s 146 procedure is applicable to all breaches, except non-payment of rent, for which the landlord reserves the right to terminate the lease. The provisions require the landlord to serve a notice detailing the alleged breach which has occurred. The notice must give the tenant the opportunity to remedy the breach if it is capable of remedy, and finally require the tenant to make compensation in money for the breach.

Only if the tenant fails to remedy and/or compensate as appropriate within a reasonable time, will the landlord be able to terminate the lease. If the breach cannot be remedied (eg, assigning the lease without consent) then the landlord will be able to terminate the lease without waiting for the breach to be remedied.

The notice procedure is designed to give a tenant the opportunity to avoid the lease being terminated as a result of the breach.

8.6 MORTGAGE DEFAULT AND THE RIGHTS OF MORTGAGEES

Over two-thirds of all owner-occupiers have a mortgage on their homes, ie a loan the repayment of which is secured on the property. Long leaseholders (or indeed a freeholder) with financial difficulties often find themselves at risk of losing their homes. The risk comes not just from their landlords, in the case of long leaseholders who fail to make service charge or other payments, but also from mortgagees or lenders, to whom a substantial amount is often owed.

8.6.1 The need for a possession order

It is not necessary for most lenders to obtain a possession order to take possession of the property (see *Ropaigelach v Barclays Bank plc* [2000] 1 QB 263, CA and *Horsham Properties Group Ltd v Clark* [2009] 1 WLR 1255). This is unlike the position for a landlord, who would normally be restricted by s 2 of the PEA 1977 (see **9.2.2.5**). The exception, where lenders have to follow a very protracted procedure to obtain possession through the court, relates to loans regulated by the Consumer Credit Act 1974, as amended, in relation to credit agreements. Most banks and building societies that make loans to facilitate the purchase of the premises will not come within the 1974 Act, as they will be exempt by virtue of the provisions in s 16 of that Act.

In practice, however, lenders do seek possession orders against residential borrowers. In 2012, there were 33,900 mortgage repossessions, according to statistics issued by the Council of Mortgage Lenders. In the same year, over 59,000 mortgage possession claims were started, with over 44,000 possession orders made (see DCA Statistics at www.justice.gov.uk). In such possession proceedings, the court has a discretion to offer relief if the borrower can realistically raise funds to repay the loan (AJAs 1970 and 1973; see **10.8.3** for an outline of the extent of the discretion).

8.6.1.1 Limited protection for unauthorised tenants

It is a standard term in most owner-occupier mortgages that the borrower is prohibited from renting out the property either absolutely, or without the lender's consent. However, it is not uncommon for owners to rent out their property in breach of the mortgage deed. If the owner then falls into arrears and the lender commences possession proceedings, until 2010 the unauthorised tenant had no rights against the lender. The unauthorised tenant could be evicted at very short notice.

The Mortgage Repossessions (Protection of Tenants etc) Act 2010, which came into force on 1 October 2010, addresses this problem (see **10.8.3.1**).

8.6.1.2 New mortgages and new procedures

For certain residential mortgages created after 31 October 2004, the Financial Services and Markets Act 2000 gave the Financial Services Authority (FSA) (now the Financial Conduct Authority (FCA)) power to regulate how lenders deal with borrowers in arrears. The provisions apply to 'regulated mortgage contracts'. These are contracts where the borrower is an individual who is taking out a loan on property of which at least 40% is occupied, or will be occupied, by him or a member of his family, and the lender is taking a first legal mortgage over the property (see Financial Services and Markets Act 2000 (Regulated Activities) Order 2001 (SI 2001/544), art 25A and art 61).

The FSA (now FCA) has issued rules governing what lenders should do with borrowers in arrears. Essentially the provisions require lenders to use possession claims as a last resort only where all other reasonable efforts to assist the borrower have failed. Instead lenders should have procedures and policies designed to help borrowers who get into difficulty with repayments. The help could include changing payment dates, or extending the mortgage term (see FSA Mortgages: Conduct of Business (MCOB) Rules).

8.6.1.3 Mortgage pre-action protocol

A Pre-Action Protocol for Possession Claims based on Mortgage or Home Purchase Plan Arrears in Respect of Residential Property was introduced for possession claims in the county courts with effect from 19 November 2008 (see **10.2.2**). The Protocol gives clear guidance on what the courts expect lenders and borrowers to have done prior to a claim being issued. The Protocol does not alter the parties' rights and obligations. In effect there are no sanctions against a mortgagee who does not follow the Protocol. However, statistical evidence from the Council of Mortgage Lenders suggests a fall in the number of possession claims being made since the Protocol was introduced.

8.6.2 Challenges to the rights of the mortgagee (lender)

It is sometimes the case that borrowers are able to resist the loss of their homes by successfully challenging the validity of the loan agreement, relying on contractual defects in the agreement, for example misrepresentation or undue influence by the lender directly, or, more usually, that the lender has constructive notice of the defect caused by some other party to the agreement.

This has often happened where a wife acts as surety for her husband when he takes out a second mortgage on the family home. If the lender does not take steps to ensure that the wife has given full and informed consent, and that she has not been pressured or misled into the transaction, then the lender will not be able to enforce the security against her if her husband subsequently defaults on the mortgage – as often happens.

8.6.2.1 The case law

In *Barclays Bank plc v O'Brien* [1994] 1 AC 180, HL, a husband misled his wife into agreeing to take out a second mortgage on their family home for the purpose of his business activities. The bank was held to have constructive notice of the misrepresentation and undue influence as the wife was in effect a second party to the loan. There was no obvious advantage to her in agreeing to the mortgage. It was held that the bank, given the relationship between the borrowers and the lack of commercial benefit to the wife, was under an obligation to ensure that the wife was made fully aware of the consequences of the loan and had independent legal advice before agreeing to the mortgage.

The significance of this decision was explained in *Royal Bank of Scotland v Etridge (No 2)* [2002] 2 AC 773, HL. Here there were eight separate appeals relating to mortgage repossessions as a result of the borrowers having defaulted on their mortgages. Seven of the appeals involved mortgage repossession claims, where the wives alleged that possession should not be granted because there had been undue influence and/or misrepresentation by their husbands. They argued that the banks should be treated as having had constructive notice of the impropriety despite being aware that a solicitor had acted for the wife in each of the transactions. In the eighth case, the wife was suing the solicitor who gave her advice.

In lengthy opinions, the House of Lords gave guidance on actions that should be taken by the lender and any solicitor involved in such transactions. Their Lordships advised that where a bank was put on enquiry by a transaction which, on its face, appeared not to be to the financial advantage of one party, and where there were risks to that party in acting as a surety, the bank would be required to take reasonable steps to satisfy itself that the surety understood the practical implications of the transaction. This did not require the bank to have a private meeting with the surety but would ordinarily be met by confirmation from a solicitor acting for the surety that the surety had been advised appropriately. Their Lordships went on to outline the type of advice the solicitor should give. They made clear that the advice did not require him to veto the transaction, nor did the solicitor have to act exclusively for the surety if there was no conflict in him acting for more than one party to the transaction. The solicitor's role was not a formality but one requiring him to give detailed advice about the transaction, and the consequences of it for the surety.

The case law in this area has not abated after the decision in *Etridge*. In *Bank of Scotland v Hill* [2002] EWCA Civ 1081, another mortgage repossession case involving a wife standing surety for her husband's loan, it was held that the bank had discharged its duty of inquiry. The bank had received a standard form confirmation from the surety's solicitor stating that Mrs Hill had received independent legal advice. However, in *First National Bank v Achampong* [2003] EWCA Civ 487, it was held that the bank had not taken sufficient action to avoid having constructive notice of any undue influence, when a husband and wife executed a legal charge over their home in order to raise funds for other family members. The Court held that it was not enough that the bank knew that the wife had a solicitor acting for her on the charge, as that did not definitely ensure that the nature of the risks she was taking had been made clear to her. If the bank knew that the solicitor had been instructed to advise her independently, that would have been sufficient.

In *Mortgage Agency Services Number Two Ltd v Chater* [2003] EWCA Civ 490, it was held that in a mortgage possession claim against a mother and son, although the mother had established that there had been undue influence by her son, she had not established that the bank should have been put on inquiry as to any equitable wrong. There had been a joint application for the loan. The purpose of the loan had been stated as 'purchase', and there was nothing to suggest that the loan was exclusively for the son's purposes. In such a situation the lender was not obliged to make further enquiries.

In *Yorkshire Bank plc v Tinsley* [2004] 1 WLR 2380, CA, it was held that where a mortgage was voidable for undue influence, any new mortgage which substituted, even if over a different property, but between the same lender and borrower, was tainted by the original undue influence and was thus legally ineffective against the misled party.

In *Abbey National Bank plc v Stringer* [2006] EWCA Civ 338, the lenders were left without any security. Mrs Stringer had been told by the first mortgagees that she would not be given a mortgage on her own as the lenders did not view her as a good security risk. This was despite a substantial deposit which she had saved, and her intention and ability to make the mortgage repayments herself. At the lenders' suggestion, Mrs Stringer purchased her home in the joint names of herself and her then 19-year-old son.

Six years later, her son took out a second mortgage on the property with the claimant mortgagees. It was clear to the claimant that the money raised from the loan was for the son to invest in a business venture. Mrs Stringer, who was illiterate and could speak little English, was persuaded to sign the mortgage agreement without its content or effect being explained to her.

It was held on these facts that the son had no beneficial interest in the property. His name on the title deeds was purely to enable his mother to obtain the first mortgage. In addition, in getting her to sign the second mortgage agreement, there had been undue influence on her by her son. The claimant accepted that it had constructive notice of this and so Mrs Stringer was not bound by the mortgage agreement.

8.6.2.2 Public funding for undue influence claims

Subject to the applicant's financial status, Legal Representation may be available, under the debt rather than housing category, to defend a mortgage possession claim where there are allegations of undue influence or misrepresentation, as these would be substantive defences to the possession claim (see **5.1** and **5.6**, and **10.12**).

8.7 FURTHER READING

J Luba, N Madge and D McConnell, *Defending Possession Proceedings* (7th edn, 2010)
N Madge and C Sephton, *Housing Law Casebook* (5th edn, 2012)
S Garner and A Frith, *A Practical Approach to Landlord and Tenant* (7th edn, 2013)

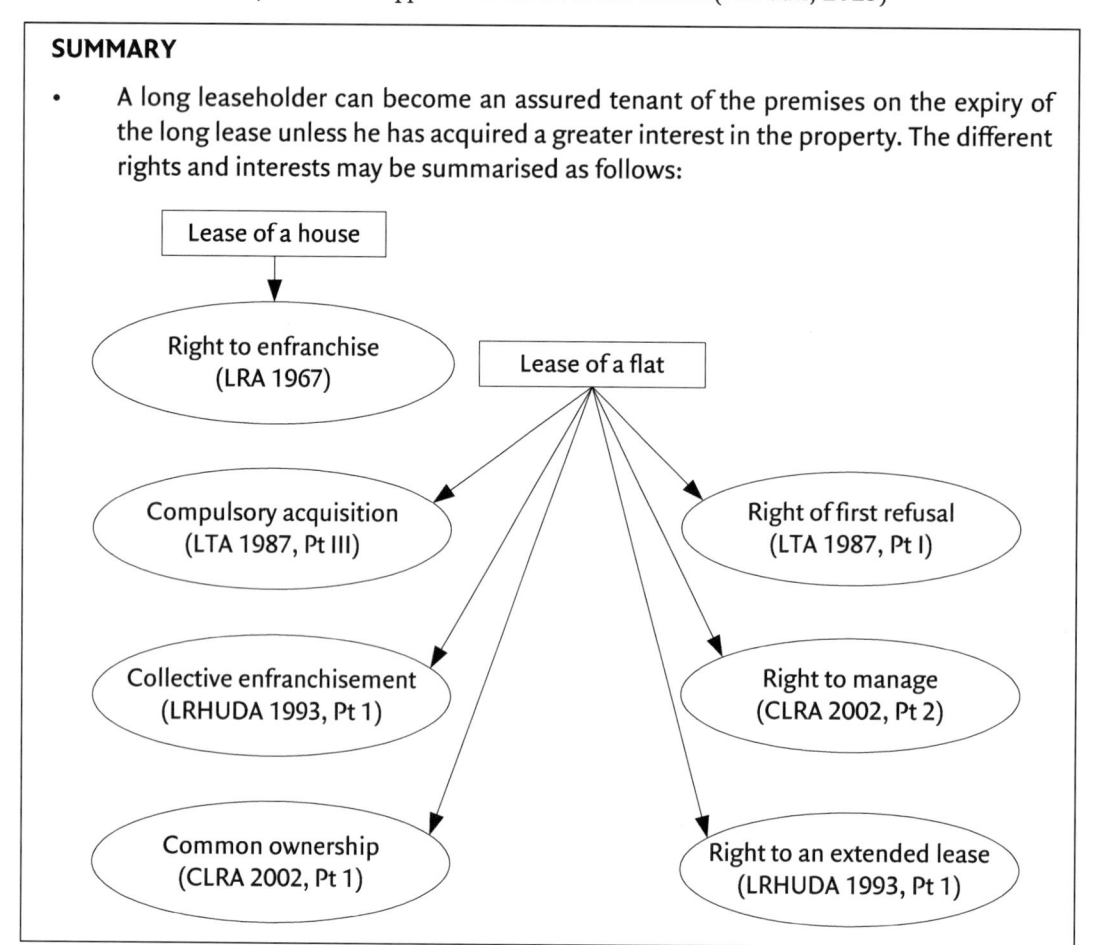

SUMMARY

- A long leaseholder can become an assured tenant of the premises on the expiry of the long lease unless he has acquired a greater interest in the property. The different rights and interests may be summarised as follows:

Lease of a house
→ Right to enfranchise (LRA 1967)

Lease of a flat
→ Compulsory acquisition (LTA 1987, Pt III)
→ Right of first refusal (LTA 1987, Pt I)
→ Collective enfranchisement (LRHUDA 1993, Pt 1)
→ Right to manage (CLRA 2002, Pt 2)
→ Common ownership (CLRA 2002, Pt 1)
→ Right to an extended lease (LRHUDA 1993, Pt 1)

- The obligation to pay a service charge or an administration charge is subject to the requirement of reasonableness in the LTA 1985, as amended.
- There are a number of provisions designed to protect tenants in breach against termination of their lease or tenancy. The restrictions against forfeiture by a landlord in the CLRA 2002 may be summarised as follows:

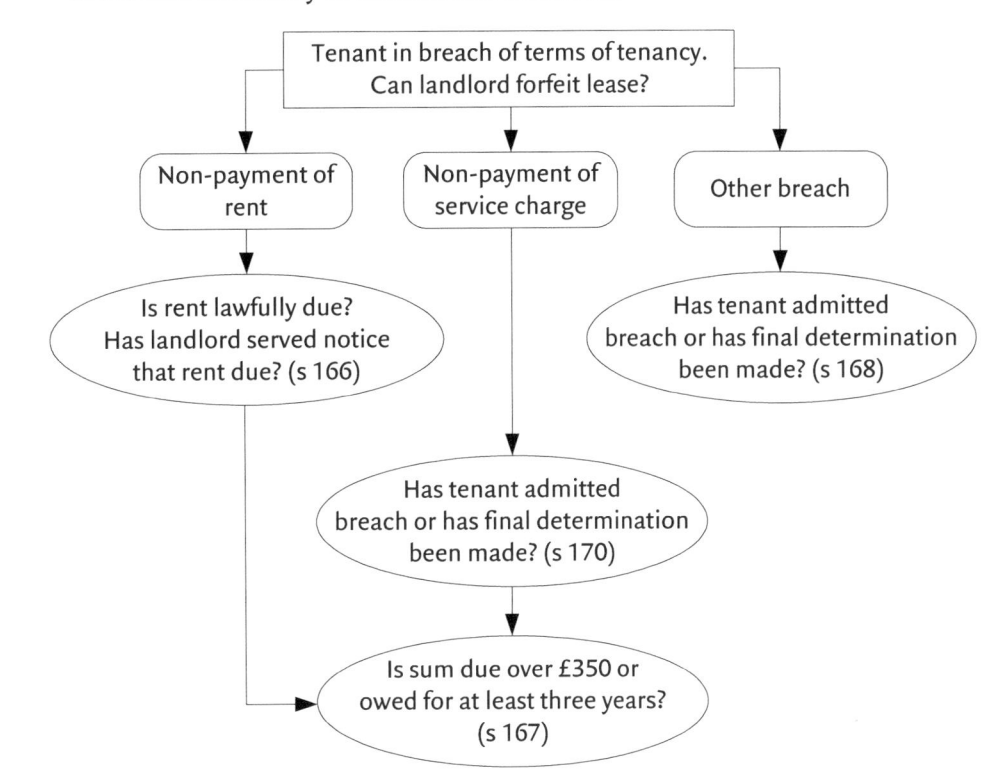

```
                    Tenant in breach of terms of tenancy.
                    Can landlord forfeit lease?
         ┌──────────────────┬──────────────────┐
         ▼                  ▼                  ▼
   Non-payment of     Non-payment of       Other breach
       rent           service charge
         │                  │                  │
         ▼                  │                  ▼
  Is rent lawfully due?     │           Has tenant admitted
  Has landlord served notice│           breach or has final determination
  that rent due? (s 166)    │           been made? (s 168)
         │                  ▼
         │           Has tenant admitted
         │           breach or has final determination
         │           been made? (s 170)
         │                  │
         │                  ▼
         │           Is sum due over £350 or
         └─────────► owed for at least three years?
                           (s 167)
```

- At common law, a mortgage lender can repossess a property when the borrower is in breach of the mortgage agreement without the need to go to court.
- The position is different for mortgages regulated by the Consumer Credit Act 1974 and for 'regulated mortgage contracts' regulated by the FCA.
- A mortgage pre-action protocol gives guidance on the procedure to follow when a borrower is in arrears with mortgage payments.
- Some borrowers are able to challenge the validity of a loan agreement when there has been undue influence of which the lender was or ought to have been aware.

CHAPTER 9

PROTECTION FROM UNLAWFUL EVICTION AND HARASSMENT

9.1	Introduction	135
9.2	Civil causes of action	136
9.3	Civil remedies	140
9.4	Notice to quit	144
9.5	Civil procedure	145
9.6	Criminal sanctions	148
	Summary	150

LEARNING OUTCOMES

After reading this chapter you will be able to:

- outline the contractual and tortious claims that may be brought against a landlord by a tenant who has been harassed or unlawfully evicted
- list and describe the different types of damages that may be awarded
- explain the notice provisions in s 5 of the PEA 1977
- outline the Civil Procedure Rules applicable to such claims
- describe the criminal sanctions available in unlawful eviction and harassment cases.

9.1 INTRODUCTION

This chapter looks at the civil causes of action available to tenants and other residential occupiers against a landlord who breaches their right to remain in occupation, or who interferes with their enjoyment of the property. Also briefly considered are the main criminal sanctions that can be brought against landlords and other persons who interfere with the occupier.

In the mid-1960s, legislation was introduced to protect residential occupiers against eviction without due process and against harassment from their landlords or anyone acting on the landlords' behalf. The legislation was primarily a criminal measure, imposing sanctions for unlawful eviction or harassment. It was hoped that it would prevent the ruthless harassment and eviction of tenants by their landlords, prompted in large part by the deregulation of the private rented sector. The actions of some came to be known as 'Rachmanism', after one particular landlord who used extreme measures to evict Rent Act protected tenants. This was during a period of decontrol of the rented sector.

The main provisions are now contained in the Protection from Eviction Act 1977 (PEA 1977), as amended by various housing provisions, in particular the HA 1988. The 1977 Act makes it unlawful, without a court order, to try to obtain possession of certain premises let as a dwelling, against an occupier who continues in occupation of the dwelling (PEA 1977, ss 2 and 3(1)).

Despite the existence of s 3 of the PEA 1977 (which is very limited in its application, see **9.2.2.5**), until the HA 1988, the most effective civil remedies available to an evicted or harassed occupier were in the common law areas of contract and tort, by actions such as breach of the covenant of quiet enjoyment and trespass to land and property. Local authorities who have the power to prosecute landlords under the PEA 1977, more often than not did not do so. The occupiers most in need of help were often too ill-informed of their rights, or not able, financially, to pursue the appropriate action against unlawful harassment and eviction. Legal funding is not available to pursue criminal proceedings, although it is available for civil claims. In any event, the remedy most likely to address the occupier's needs when unlawfully evicted or harassed is generally in the civil area.

9.2 CIVIL CAUSES OF ACTION

Although the criminal sanctions pre-date the statutory civil remedies, in practice residential occupiers find the civil causes of action more immediately accessible and appropriate when seeking a remedy.

There is no neat structure to the remedies available. They consist of a combination of common law and statutory provisions. At common law, there are, potentially, a number of different causes of action available in both contract and tort law. In addition, housing law and criminal law statutes have created new and distinct tort causes of action.

9.2.1 Contract claims

A residential tenant may have a claim against his landlord in contract in three areas:

(a) breach of the covenant of quiet enjoyment;
(b) derogation from grant; and
(c) breach of some other contractual term.

Breach of any of these rights will give rise to a cause of action. Unless special damages are claimed, or particulars of distress, discomfort or inconvenience stated, only nominal damages will be awarded in addition to any injunctive remedy claimed.

9.2.1.1 Breach of the covenant of quiet enjoyment

Even where a tenancy agreement is silent, the law will imply into the contract an obligation on the landlord not to interfere with the tenant's lawful possession of the property. Any eviction of the tenant whilst the tenancy agreement has not been lawfully terminated is clearly a breach of this covenant (see *Lavender v Betts* [1942] 2 All ER 72).

In addition, any acts of harassment of the tenant by the landlord, which fall short of actual eviction, may amount to a breach. In *Kenny v Preen* [1963] 1 QB 499, CA, the landlord was held to have breached the covenant by sending threatening letters, removing the tenant's belongings, repeatedly knocking on the tenant's door and shouting threats. In *McCall v Abelesz* [1976] QB 585, CA, it was stated (obiter) that a landlord who allowed the gas and electricity supply to be cut off was not only in breach of an implied term in the contract (see **9.2.1.3**), but also in breach of the covenant of quiet enjoyment.

However, the covenant cannot be used to oblige the landlord to improve the state of the property as let, so as to provide the tenant with something beyond what was originally granted. For example, in *Southwark LBC v Mills* [2001] 1 AC 1, HL, it was held that the covenant did not require the landlord to insulate premises against noise from neighbours.

9.2.1.2 Derogation from grant

This is another obligation implied into a tenancy agreement. In this instance the implied term is that the landlord will not act in a way which undermines the rights he has given to the tenant; in effect, he must not derogate from his grant. This provision may not have as wide an application as the covenant of quiet enjoyment, because it is most likely to arise, or become an issue, where the landlord has retained occupation of premises adjoining those let to the tenant (for example, the passageway outside the room or flat let to the tenant), or where he has let premises to other tenants with rights which directly conflict with those given to the tenant.

If the landlord uses premises retained by him in such a way that it has an adverse effect on the tenant's property, for example blocking a passageway over which the tenant has a right of way so as to prevent access to the tenant's property, this would amount to a breach of the obligation. However, as with the covenant of quiet enjoyment, this covenant cannot be used to oblige the landlord to repair or improve the premises (*Southwark LBC v Mills*, see **9.2.1.1**).

> **CASE EXAMPLE**
>
> In *Saeed v Plustrade Ltd* [2001] EWCA Civ 2011, CA, a tenant had a lease of a flat, together with a right in common with others to park her car in an area designated for parking when space was available. The landlords were held to have derogated from their grant by preventing the tenant, for over three years, from parking her car in the car park because refurbishment works were being carried out to the property.

9.2.1.3 Breach of other contractual terms

There may be other express or implied terms in the tenancy agreement, or indeed, unlike for the above causes of action, in a licence agreement to occupy premises. In *McCall v Abelesz* (see **9.2.1.1**), Lord Denning MR was in no doubt that the tenant had the right to sue for breach of the implied term that the landlord would continue to supply gas and electricity to the premises for as long as the tenancy continued.

9.2.2 Tort claims

The two most obvious causes of action that could arise in general tort law are trespass to land and nuisance (see **9.2.2.1** and **9.2.2.2**). In some cases, the person bringing the claim does not need to have a tenancy agreement. Any right to exclusive occupation which is interfered with in such a way as to give rise to a claim in tort will be sufficient. As such, references to the person making the claim will be to the claimant or the occupier.

If the landlord has interfered with the occupier's possessions, a cause of action for trespass to goods may arise (see **9.2.2.3**). This will be the case provided the occupier is able to produce evidence satisfactory to the court of the value of the possessions that have been lost. If the landlord has used or threatened violence against the occupier, a cause of action for trespass to the person may also be available (see **9.2.2.4**).

Unlike the position with contract law, the occupier can also claim for aggravated and exemplary damages. Aggravated damages are awarded to compensate the occupier for injury to his proper feelings of dignity and pride, and for aggravation generally, whereas exemplary damages are awarded in order to punish the defendant (see **9.3.2.4** and **9.3.2.5**).

Also of relevance for illegally evicted or harassed occupiers are the three statutory torts under which an occupier may claim, namely:

(a) breach of statutory duty under s 3 of the PEA 1977;

(b) for the tort of unlawful eviction under s 27 of the HA 1988; and

(c) for breach of s 3 of the Protection from Harassment Act 1997.

These are discussed at **9.2.2.5** to **9.2.2.7** below.

9.2.2.1 Trespass to land

Any occupier with a right to exclusive possession of premises can maintain a cause of action against any unlawful entry onto the premises. A landlord, or any other person, who enters without permission is committing a trespass. The trespass could take the form not just of unlawful entry, but also of placing or throwing things onto the land.

The tort is actionable without proof of damage; however, where damage has been caused, the occupier can also claim for aggravated and exemplary damages. In *Lavender v Betts* (see **9.2.1.1**), the landlord unlawfully entered the tenant's premises and removed the doors and windows, making it very uncomfortable for her to remain. The tenant was successful in obtaining aggravated damages for this trespass.

9.2.2.2 Nuisance

Any occupier with exclusive possession of land may have a right to bring a claim in nuisance if he can establish an unreasonable interference with his use or enjoyment of the land by the defendant. Typical examples include excessive noise, such as loud music for long periods, or shouting and screaming, building works or leaking water. In *Guppys (Bridport) Ltd v Brookling* [1984] 1 EGLR 29, CA, exemplary damages were awarded to tenants whose landlord was held responsible for the nuisance caused when the tenants' electricity and water supplies were disconnected and their toilet facilities removed.

9.2.2.3 Trespass to goods

If, in the course of unlawful eviction or harassment of an occupier, his possessions are damaged or taken by the trespasser, the occupier may have a cause of action for trespass to goods or conversion. In *Caruso v Owen* (1983) LAG Bulletin 106, a tenant recovered damages for the tort of wrongful interference with goods when the landlord burnt his belongings, thinking he had abandoned them. In *Ramdath v Daley* [1993] 1 EGLR 82, CA, the Court awarded damages for the tenant's goods, which went missing when he was illegally evicted from the property.

9.2.2.4 Trespass to person

It is not uncommon in harassment cases for the occupier to be threatened with, or to suffer, actual violence by the trespasser. In such cases, a claim for trespass to person in either assault (threats) and/or battery (intentional, direct, unlawful physical force against the occupier) is possible. In *Ramdath v Daley* (see **9.2.2.3**), the tenant was compensated for the brutal way in which he was evicted from the property; and also for threats of violence made against him.

9.2.2.5 Breach of statutory duty – PEA 1977, s 2 and s 3

Section 2 of the PEA 1977 makes it unlawful for a landlord with a right to forfeit a lease of a dwelling, to do so without obtaining a court order, while any person is lawfully residing in the premises or any part of them. It would seem that if the tenant is no longer in residence, the landlord can exercise his right to re-enter peaceably; however, this option is not available where someone is still lawfully residing in the dwelling.

Section 3 of the PEA 1977 is designed to give protection to certain occupiers who are not otherwise covered by statutory provisions. The section makes it unlawful for an owner otherwise than by court proceedings to try to regain possession of certain dwellings where the tenancy/licence has ended but the occupier has not left. An 'occupier' is defined in s 3(2) and (2B) of the PEA 1977 to mean any person lawfully residing in the premises, or part of them, at the termination of the former tenancy or licence. Dwellings have recently been fully defined in *Uratemp Ventures Ltd v Collins* [2002] 1 AC 301 (see **2.2.2**).

Breach of s 3 gives rise to a cause of action which is limited as to the number of potential claimants who can rely on it. This is because it does not apply to statutorily protected or excluded tenancies.

Statutorily protected tenancies

Statutorily protected tenancies are listed in s 8 of the PEA 1977, and include not only most of the residential and agricultural regimes subject to statutory control, but also what would normally be regarded as business tenancies within Pt II of the LTA 1954. The type of premises that might be caught by this provision would be, for example, shop premises let with residential accommodation above.

These statutorily protected tenancies are excluded from s 3 of the PEA 1977 because those statutory regimes provide adequate protection for the tenants.

While the former tenant is still in occupation, s 3 of the PEA 1977 will apply to him. In *Haniff v Robinson* [1993] QB 419, CA, a statutory tenant who had had a possession order made against her, was evicted by her landlord before an order for execution could be enforced by the court bailiffs. It was held that the tenant had a cause of action by virtue of s 3 of the PEA 1977 and could recover damages (see **9.3.2.6**, 'The amount of damages relative to the security lost').

Excluded tenancies and licences

Section 3A of the PEA 1977 defines excluded tenancies/licences to include occupiers sharing accommodation with a resident landlord/licensor; sharing with a member of the landlord/licensor's family where the landlord occupies other accommodation in a converted building; holiday lets; tenancies/licences granted as a temporary expedient to trespassers; or where no consideration is given for the right to occupy. In addition, certain accommodation provided under immigration and asylum legislation is excluded, as is hostel accommodation granted on licences where the licensor is a public body.

The category of excluded tenancies that has most often given rise to landlord and tenant disputes is the resident landlord exclusion. A resident landlord must occupy the premises which include the shared accommodation, as his only or principal home. Shared accommodation will include the common use of areas such as bathroom/toilet, kitchen and living rooms. It does not include the use of a storage area or staircase, passage or corridor or other means of access (PEA 1977, s 3A(5)(a)).

> **EXAMPLE – WHEN A TENANCY WILL NOT BE EXCLUDED WITHIN s 3A**
>
> L owns a large Victorian house that has been converted into four self-contained flats. L occupies one flat and lets out the other three flats to three tenants, A, B and C. L is not a resident landlord within s 3A of the PEA 1977, as he occupies a separate self-contained flat. The landlord would have to regain possession of each flat through court proceedings as required by s 3 of the PEA 1977. (Although note that L would be a resident landlord within Sch 1 to the HA 1988, so that A, B and C would not be assured tenants within that Act.)

> **CASE EXAMPLE**
>
> In *Sumeghova v McMahon* [2003] HLR 26, CA, the landlord occupied two rooms in a house as a bedroom and living room. This was a temporary arrangement while he was waiting for his adult children to vacate an adjoining property. The landlord ate his meals and spent most of his time in the adjoining property with his children. The landlord granted the claimant a tenancy of a room in the house where he slept. When the landlord evicted the claimant from her room, she sued under s 3 of the PEA 1977, claiming unlawful eviction, and was successful at first instance. However, the landlord successfully appealed on the basis that the claimant was an excluded tenant under s 3A(2) of the PEA 1977. It was held that the landlord was a resident landlord. The Appeal Court, in reversing the decision of the trial judge, held that where a person sleeps, whilst not decisive, was of the most enormous importance in influencing where a person's principal home was. On the facts of this case, as the landlord never slept at any property other than the shared house, that was his principal home. This was so even though it was only a temporary arrangement and he intended shortly to move permanently into the adjoining property.

9.2.2.6 Section 27 of the HA 1988

The provision in s 27 makes it an actionable tort for a landlord or his agent:

(a) unlawfully to deprive, or
(b) unlawfully to attempt to deprive

a residential occupier of his occupation of the whole or a part of the premises. It is also actionable, knowing or having reasonable cause to believe that the conduct is likely to have this effect, to do acts likely to interfere with the peace or comfort of the residential occupier or members of his household, or persistently to withdraw or withhold services reasonably required for the occupation of the premises as a residence, with the consequence that the residential occupier gives up occupation of the premises (s 27(1), (2)).

An occupier so unlawfully deprived can claim damages under s 27(3) against the landlord. However, the occupier will not be able to claim damages under s 27(3) unless he permanently gives up or loses possession. Permanent reinstatement must not have taken place either as a result of the landlord reconsidering his behaviour, or as a result of a court order having been obtained. In *Tagro v Cafane* [1991] 1 WLR 378, CA, the Court held that the occupier had not been reinstated by her landlord when she was handed keys which no longer fitted the lock to a room that had been wrecked. The measure of damages is dealt with in s 28 of the HA 1988 (see **9.3.2.6** below).

A landlord who has deprived an occupier can plead the defence in s 27(8) of the HA 1988, that he believed and had reasonable cause to believe that the occupier had given up residence, or that he had reasonable grounds for doing the acts or withdrawing or withholding services to the tenant.

9.2.2.7 Section 3 of the Protection from Harassment Act 1997

This Act was designed to deal with harassment in general, not just harassment in the housing field. It mainly introduced new criminal offences in this area. However, it also provides a civil remedy for victims, where the offence of harassment has been made out. The offence is committed, and therefore a claim can be made, where a person pursues a course of conduct which amounts to harassment and which he knows, or ought to know, amounts to harassment of the other (see **9.6.3**). A claim for an injunction and/or damages can be brought by any occupier against anyone, including a landlord, who commits the offence.

9.3 CIVIL REMEDIES

Where an occupier has been unlawfully evicted, his primary concern will often be to obtain re-entry to the property. Where he has been and continues to be harassed, his concern will be to stop the harassment continuing. An injunction is the appropriate remedy to deal with these matters. Damages may also be available, either contractual and/or tortious, to cover any loss of property, or loss of rights. In certain cases an anti-social behaviour order (ASBO) may be appropriate.

9.3.1 Injunctions

As a discretionary remedy, the court will not award an injunction where damages would be an adequate remedy. Where the occupier has been unlawfully evicted and wishes to regain entry to his property, obtaining an injunction should not prove difficult, provided there are no obstacles, such as, for example, the property having been re-let to another person, or where the displaced occupier has done something to disqualify him from this remedy. In *Love v Herrity* (1991) 23 HLR 217, CA, the displaced tenants were denied injunctive relief against the landlord as he, thinking the tenants had vacated the premises, had re-let to a third party.

Injunctions are a final remedy. However, in unlawful eviction and harassment cases, the occupier often needs more immediate relief. This can be achieved by applying for an interim injunction. In *Love v Herrity*, the applicant had applied for an interim injunction, before the full trial of the matter, to try to regain entry to the property.

9.3.1.1 Interim injunctions

An application may be made for an interim injunction to be granted, before there has been a full hearing of the case. It will be appropriate to make such an application when the occupier has been illegally evicted and a wait of weeks or months until full trial would defeat the object of the remedy required immediately. It might also be appropriate where the occupier wishes to stop on-going harassment, for example, to require that the harasser stop abusing him, or to reconnect services that have been disconnected.

An interim injunction will be granted only where the applicant satisfies the requirements laid down in *American Cyanamid Co v Ethicon Ltd* [1975] AC 396, HL:

(a) that there is a serious issue to be tried between the parties;
(b) if the applicant succeeded at trial, that he would not be sufficiently compensated by an award of damages; and
(c) that the balance of convenience lies in favour of granting the injunction now, to restore or maintain the status quo, rather than on awaiting the outcome of the full trial.

If an interim order is made, it is usual for the applicant to give an undertaking to compensate the respondent if it transpires, at the full trial, that the applicant was not entitled to the order.

An interim application can be made either with notice to the other side, or, in certain circumstances, without notice. A without notice application will be appropriate where the matter is urgent, for example, where the landlord has changed the locks on the entrance to the occupier's premises and immediate relief is required to enable him to regain entry. In *Ayari v Jethi* (1992) 24 HLR 639, CA, the landlord locked the claimant out of her flat on a Friday evening. The claimant was able to issue proceedings on the Monday and obtain an ex parte injunction, enabling her to regain possession of the property the following day (Tuesday).

9.3.2 Damages

There are several different types of damages that may be claimed by a harassed or an evicted occupier. The list will vary according to whether the claim is contractual only, or also based in tort. The damages may be nominal, general, special, aggravated or exemplary. In addition, there may be claims available for statutory damages under s 27 of the HA 1988, or under s 3 of the Protection from Harassment Act 1997 (see **9.3.2.6** and **9.3.2.7** respectively).

9.3.2.1 Nominal damages

Nominal damages will be a small sum, perhaps £5, awarded where the claimant has not suffered any damage but the court accepts that he had a right to bring the claim. The occupier may in fact be more concerned with obtaining an injunction rather than damages, as the primary relief in the situation at hand.

9.3.2.2 General damages

General damages comprise an unliquidated amount to cover losses, which can include loss of the right to occupy, or any physical injury and inconvenience. In *Ayari v Jethi* (see **9.3.1.1**), the claimant received £1,250 general damages for being kept out of her property for four nights.

9.3.2.3 Special damages

Special damages are awarded for liquidated losses. They can cover replacement costs for goods lost or destroyed by the defendant, or the cost of reasonable alternative accommodation for the occupier whilst unlawfully evicted. In *Ayari v Jethi* (see **9.3.1.1**), the claimant recovered £11,472 plus interest for the loss of her belongings.

9.3.2.4 Aggravated damages

Aggravated damages and exemplary damages (below) are available only for certain tort claims, not for breach of contract. Aggravated damages are awarded to compensate the claimant for injury to his feelings, or for any outrage or distress caused to him. They are particularly appropriate where an occupier has been unlawfully evicted in distressful and abusive circumstances. In *Asghar v Ahmed* (1984) 17 HLR 25, CA, the claimant was awarded aggravated damages of £500 to compensate him for injured feelings and distress caused by the ruthless way in which the landlord changed the locks, placed the claimant's belongings in the garden of the premises and refused to let him back in, even after he had obtained an injunction.

9.3.2.5 Exemplary damages

Exemplary damages, unlike aggravated damages, are a punitive award made against a defendant to teach him that tort does not pay. They are properly awarded where the evidence suggests that the defendant calculated to make a profit over and above any compensation that would be payable to the claimant. As with aggravated damages, it is most appropriate in cases of unlawful eviction. In *Guppys (Bridport) Ltd v Brookling* [1984] 1 EGLR 29, CA (see **9.2.2.2** above), the claimants received £1,000 each in exemplary damages for the landlord's blatant disregard for their rights in furtherance of his own interests. An award of £1,000 in exemplary damages was also made in *Asghar v Ahmed* (see **9.3.2.4**).

9.3.2.6 Sections 27 and 28 of the HA 1988

Section 27 of the HA 1988 gives a statutory basis for claiming damages in tort where a residential occupier has been unlawfully and permanently deprived of all, or any part, of his premises. This statutory claim has been available to any occupier permanently displaced since 9 June 1988, against a landlord or any person acting on his behalf who unlawfully deprives the residential occupier of any premises in whole or part, or does acts, as indicated in **9.2.2.6** above, to give rise to the civil claim. Section 27(3) provides that the defaulting landlord has to compensate the occupier for the loss of his right to occupy his residence. The measure of damages is covered in s 28 of the 1988 Act.

Defence to a s 27 claim

The landlord has a defence to a claim of unlawful eviction (in HA 1988, s 27(8)), that he either believed or had reasonable cause to believe that the residential occupier had ceased to reside in the premises, or, where the claim relates to the doing of acts or the withdrawal or withholding of services, that he had reasonable grounds for doing these things. A landlord who relied on an invalid notice to quit from one departing joint tenant could not rely on this defence in *Osei-Bonsu v Wandsworth LBC* [1999] 1 All ER 265, CA (and see **9.4.2** for valid notice to quit).

Measure of damages in s 28

The basis of assessment

> is the difference in value, determined as at the time immediately before the residential occupier ceased to occupy the premises in question as his residence, between:
>
> (a) the value of the interest of the landlord in default determined on the assumption that the residential occupier continues to have the same right to occupy the premises as before that time; and
>
> (b) the value of that interest determined on the assumption that the residential occupier has ceased to have that right. (HA 1988, s 28(1))

In effect, the provision is designed to ensure that the landlord does not profit from his wrongdoing. His interest is valued at the date the occupier left, taking the value as it was when the occupier was in occupation against the value of it with the occupier out of occupation. The valuation is made on the assumption that the sale would be made in an open market to an independent purchaser, the property having no development benefits attached to it (HA 1988, s 28(3)).

Following the decision in Lambeth LBC v Loveride [2013] HLR 31, CA, it seems that an LHA that unlawfully evicts its tenant may not have to pay s 28 compensation. In that case, the LHA successfully argued that in applying the correct basis of assessment in s 28 to an evicted secure tenant, account could be taken of the fact that the secure tenancy was vulnerable to being converted to an assured tenancy on sale to a private landlord. On this basis, the tenant's rights would have no adverse effect on the value of the LHA's interest. This is because a private purchaser would pay the same for the building with the flat subject to an assured tenancy as it would pay for it with the flat empty.

Reduction of damages

The damages may be reduced or mitigated, at the discretion of the court, if the occupier's conduct (or that of anyone living with him) was such that it would not be appropriate to award full compensation, or if the occupier unreasonably refused an offer of reinstatement before proceedings were begun (or it would have been an unreasonable refusal, had he not obtained alternative accommodation beforehand) (HA 1988, s 27(7)(a), (b)).

In Regalgrand Ltd v Dickerson & Wade (1996) 29 HLR 620, CA, Aldous LJ made it clear that the proper approach to be used when considering mitigating damages under s 27(7)(a) of the Act, was to look at the tenant's conduct in the light of the surrounding facts. In doing so, he reduced the damages from £12,000 to £1,500 to take account of the tenants unjustifiably withholding their rent and not giving the landlord notice of continued problems with their flat. In Osei-Bonsu v Wandsworth LBC [1999] 1 All ER 265, CA, it was held that the tenant's illegal eviction was the culmination of an unbroken chain of events starting with his violence towards his wife. This was conduct within the mitigation provisions of s 27(7)(a), justifying a £20,000 reduction in the damages, from £30,000 to £10,000.

Any offer of reinstatement by the landlord under s 27(7)(b) must be genuine. In Tagro v Cafane [1991] 1 WLR 378, CA (see **9.2.2.6**), the offer of keys to a broken door and a wrecked bedroom that was no longer fit for the claimant to occupy was in no way a genuine offer to reinstate. In Mehta v Royal Bank of Scotland (1999) 32 HLR 45, it was held that temporary reinstatement, of some 11 days, under an interim order which was subsequently discharged, did not amount to reinstatement so as to deprive the claimant of s 27 compensation.

The amount of damages relative to the security lost

The greater the security of tenure that the occupier enjoys, the greater will be the compensation payable. Hence, a RA 1977 tenant will be awarded a higher level of compensation than an assured shorthold tenant. In Haniff v Robinson [1993] QB 419, CA, an RA 1977 statutory tenant was awarded £26,000 damages under s 27 when she was unlawfully evicted from the tenanted property.

In Melville v Bruton (1997) 29 HLR 319, CA, however, an award of £15,000 to an evicted assured shorthold tenant was set aside on appeal. The Court held that the valuation evidence had wrongly assumed vacant possession throughout the property, when in fact there were other tenants in occupation. The eviction of the claimant had not resulted in an increase in value of the landlord's premises. The claimant recovered instead £500 common law damages for inconvenience, discomfort and distress.

In King v Jackson (1998) 30 HLR 541, CA, an award of £11,000 was set aside as the assured shorthold tenant had given notice to quit and had only six days of her tenancy left when she was unlawfully evicted. The claimant was awarded £1,500 instead.

However, an assured shorthold tenant was awarded £6,750 damages under s 27, as well as £2,050 for breach of the covenant of quiet enjoyment, when his landlord wrongfully re-let the tenant's room while he was away on holiday, and then threatened and intimidated him on his return so that the tenant felt obliged to leave (see *Abbott v Bayley* (2000) 32 HLR 72, CA).

Double recovery not permitted

It is not possible to recover damages for the same loss both under s 27(3) and under the head of general damages in s 27(5). Section 27(5) provides that the statutory provision in s 27 does not affect the enforcement of any other liability in respect of the occupier's loss of the right to occupy against the landlord. Although both causes can be claimed for, normally an award under s 27(3) will be made where it is appropriate, that is, that the residential occupier has ceased to occupy the premises within the meaning of the provisions. In *Francis v Brown* (1998) 30 HLR 143, CA, it was held that the damages award under s 27 was exhaustive, and the claimant was not entitled to an additional award of exemplary damages against the landlady.

9.3.2.7 Section 3 of the Protection from Harassment Act 1997

This provision does not add greatly to the armoury of remedies that an occupier already has against his landlord. However, s 3(3) does allow the victim of harassment to claim specifically for anxiety caused by the harassment and, because it is not housing-specific, it is a remedy available to anyone, not just a tenant or residential occupier.

9.3.3 Anti-social behaviour orders

The CADA 1998 (as amended) gives local authorities, the police, PRPs and RSLs the power to apply to a magistrates' court (s 1(3)), or in on-going county court proceedings (s 1B(1)), for an ASBO against anyone aged 10 or over who acts in a manner that causes, or is likely to cause, harassment, alarm or distress to one or more persons not of the same household as the offender (s 1(1((a)). The court must be satisfied that such an order is necessary to protect the victim from further anti-social acts (s 1(1)(b)).

This provision is in the nature of a civil procedure to control persistent anti-social behaviour in local areas. It is designed to be used to deal with vandals, drug abusers, and racist and homophobic offenders who make life uncomfortable for others. An ASBO will last for a minimum of two years (s 1(7)), and if breached without reasonable excuse, will lead to criminal prosecution. It is more commonly used by landlords in the context of controlling anti-social tenants (see **2.9.5** and **6.7.1.2** on anti-social behaviour)

9.4 NOTICE TO QUIT

At common law, a notice to quit is required to terminate a periodic tenancy. There are now a number of statutory provisions, for example in s 82(1) of the HA 1985, which provide that a landlord's notice to quit is ineffective to terminate certain types of tenancies. For periodic tenancies that are terminable by a notice to quit, the length of notice and its form depend on the frequency of the rental payments, or on the terms agreed in the tenancy agreement.

9.4.1 Length of notice

At common law the length of notice would depend, in the absence of express agreement to the contrary, on the length of the tenancy: a weekly tenancy would be terminable by one week's notice; a monthly tenancy by a month's notice; a yearly tenancy by six months' notice. The notice would need to terminate the tenancy on the last day of the period, unless the tenancy agreement stipulated otherwise. So, if a weekly tenancy commenced on a Monday, it would need to be terminated on the Sunday at midnight (see *Schnabel v Allard* [1967] 1 QB 627, CA). If a monthly tenancy began on the 3rd of the month, it would need to terminate at midnight on the 2nd of the month (see *Harler v Calder* (1989) 21 HLR 214). At common law, the courts have recognised as valid a notice terminating a tenancy on the anniversary of the term, so, using the examples above, terminating the weekly tenancy which began on a Monday on a Monday, and terminating the monthly tenancy which began on the 3rd of the month, on the 3rd of the later month. As stated by Hale LJ in *Fernandez v McDonald* [2004] 1 WLR 1027, CA:

> It may be possible to give a notice to quit which expires on either day, but that is not because there are two last days: it is because the last day ends at midnight and the first day of the new period begins thereafter and that is the first day on which possession can be required.

Section 5 of the PEA 1977 imposes a minimum period of notice and requires certain information to be given when terminating premises let as a dwelling. It applies to both tenancies and licences created before or after the passing of the PEA 1977, but not to excluded tenancies or licences (see **9.2.2.5**) created after the passing of the Act. The provision states that a notice served by either a landlord or a tenant will not be valid unless it is given in writing and contains such information as may be prescribed, and is given at least four weeks before it is due to take effect. This minimum period of four weeks is less than the minimum period required at common law to terminate a monthly or yearly tenancy, and so would not be sufficient to terminate those periodic tenancies, unless the agreement provides otherwise.

9.4.2 Prescribed information in notices served by a landlord

The prescribed information for a licensor's or landlord's notice is contained in the Notice to Quit (Prescribed Information) Regulations 1988 (SI 1988/2201). The aim is to ensure that a tenant or licensee is aware of his legal right not to be forced out of the property without a court order, even after the notice has expired. The tenant or licensee must also be informed of the fact that he can obtain advice from a solicitor, the Citizens' Advice Bureau, a Housing Aid Centre or a rent officer. The notice should further inform the tenant or licensee that the Legal Aid Scheme may help with the cost of obtaining legal advice.

9.4.3 Notice to quit by a tenant

Although notice from a tenant or licensee terminating his right to occupy also has to be in writing, no prescribed information has to be included. It is possible for one joint tenant to terminate the joint tenancy by service of a valid written notice to quit. This can be done without the consent or knowledge of the other tenant. The notice must, however, comply with the minimum notice provisions in s 5 of the PEA 1977 (see **9.4.1**). The landlord will not have a discretion to accept a shorter notice period (*Hounslow LBC v Pilling* [1993] 1 WLR 1242, CA).

The service of notice by one joint tenant is a device often employed by abused wives as a means of terminating their existing joint tenancy with their public sector landlord, on condition that they are then given a new tenancy elsewhere in their sole name. This was the outcome of *Hammersmith and Fulham London Borough Council v Monk* [1992] 1 AC 478, HL, where the House of Lords confirmed an earlier decision in the Court of Appeal which held that joint tenancies could be terminated in this way (see **6.8.1** for tenant's right to terminate).

However, following the decisions in *Pinnock* and *Powell* (see **4.5.3.2** and **6.8.1**), this option may not be so easily available to public sector tenants.

9.5 CIVIL PROCEDURE

The Civil Procedure Rules (CPR), Part 7 and Part 8 govern the appropriate procedure to be followed when commencing a claim. As CPR, Part 8 relates to claims where there are no substantial disputes of fact, it would normally not be applicable to a claim of unlawful eviction or harassment.

Set out below is the procedure involved in commencing a claim for unlawful eviction or harassment.

9.5.1 CPR, Part 7

Proceedings are usually commenced in the county court. In any event, unless the claim for damages exceeds £25,000, the proceedings cannot normally be started in the High Court.

There may be serious funding issues or cost penalties for the claimant, if proceedings are commenced unnecessarily in the High Court.

The claimant will need to complete Form N1, which includes, or should have attached to it, the particulars of the claim. However, before the claim is issued in the county court, the claimant will need to be advised on the most appropriate basis on which to make the claim. There will need to be careful consideration and progression of the case to ensure that the CPR are not breached, as cost or interest penalties could result.

9.5.2 Public funding

Unlawful eviction and harassment claims are within the types of claim for which legal aid may be available for Legal Representation at court. See **5.2.3.3** and **5.5** for the merit and financial eligibility criteria that would need to be satisfied to obtain Legal Representation.

9.5.3 Commencing proceedings

If the clients' problems are not resolved by mediation or otherwise, the legal adviser will need to commence proceedings. In addition to Form N1 with the particulars of claim, consideration should be given to whether, if an injunction is one of the remedies sought, an interim application for an injunction is appropriate. This may be necessary where there has been an illegal eviction and the occupier needs to regain entry to the property, or where severe harassment of the occupier is continuing. If such an application is necessary, Form N16A will also need to be completed (see **9.5.3.3**).

9.5.3.1 Claim Form N1

Part 16 of the CPR sets out the contents of the claim form. This should include details of the parties to the claim, a concise statement of the nature of the claim and the remedy sought by the claimant. However, under CPR, r 16.2(5), the court has a discretion to grant any remedy to which the claimant is entitled. The form also requires information to be given on whether there are any issues under the Human Rights Act 1998, as well as a statement of value, indicating the amount of any damages claimed. This last requirement is to assist the court when deciding on allocation to the appropriate track.

9.5.3.2 Particulars of claim

Rule 16.4 of the CPR requires that the particulars of claim contain a concise statement of the facts, as well as details of any interest claimed and any aggravated, exemplary or provisional damages (the last for personal injury claims). The facts need to be detailed enough to give the court a clear indication of the basis of the claim and that the claimant has a genuine cause of action.

Further information – injunctions

The Practice Direction to Part 16 (PD 16) details further information that should be included in the particulars. For example, if an injunction is required, relating to the use and enjoyment of any land, details of the land and whether the injunction relates to residential premises must be given (PD 16, para 7.1).

Further information – trespass to goods and written agreements

Where a claim includes a claim for recovery of goods, a statement showing the value of the goods must be given (PD 16, para 7.2). If there is a tenancy or other written agreement on which the claimant is relying, a copy must be attached to the particulars of claim and the original produced at trial (PD 16, para 7.3).

Further information – personal injury

If the claimant is claiming for personal injury as, for example, a result of trespass to the person, full details must be pleaded, including the claimant's date of birth and brief details of the personal injury. If medical evidence is being relied on, a written report needs to be attached to the particulars of claim, as well as (if claimed) a schedule detailing any past and future expenses and losses (PD 16, paras 4.1–4.3).

Further information – criminal convictions

The claimant may want to rely on evidence of the defendant's criminal conviction in relation to any assault or battery, harassment or illegal eviction allegations being made in the claim. In such cases, s 11 of the Civil Evidence Act 1968 will apply. In the particulars of claim details will need to be given of the type of conviction, the court that convicted and the issue in the claim to which the conviction relates (PD 16, para 8.1).

9.5.3.3 Interim injunction application – Form N16A

This form requires the claimant to indicate whether proceedings have already begun, or whether the application is under a statutory provision. The term of the order sought, whether mandatory or restraining, must be clearly set out.

Part 25 of the CPR and the accompanying Practice Direction (PD 25A) detail the requirements for this application. Practice Direction 25A, at para 2, makes clear that the date, time and place of the hearing must be given in the application notice, and service must be made not less than three days before the hearing date. Evidence in support of the application must be served with the notice. The evidence here would normally be in the form of a witness statement which sets out the facts on which the claim relies, including all the material facts of which the court needs to be made aware (PD 25A, para 3.3).

Paragraph 2.4 provides that whenever possible a draft of the order sought should be filed with the application notice, together with a disk containing the draft. The disk should be in a format compatible with the word processing software used by the court, so that the court officer can make any amendments easily and to facilitate the speedy preparation and sealing of the order.

Urgent or without notice applications

In cases of illegal eviction or serious harassment, it may be necessary to make an urgent or without notice application. Practice Direction 25A, para 4 details the procedure to be followed in such situations. If a claim has already been issued, the application notice, evidence in support and a draft order should be filed with the court two hours before the hearing, if this is possible. If an application is made before the application notice has been issued, a draft order should be provided at the hearing, and the application notice and evidence in support filed with the court on the same or the next working day, or as ordered by the court. The respondent should be notified unless secrecy is essential.

If a claim form has not yet been issued, undertakings must be given to do so immediately, unless the court indicates otherwise, and the claim served with the order (PD 25A, para 4.4). The injunction hearing is normally dealt with at court. However, in particularly urgent cases, for example where the court offices are closed, an application can be made by telephone provided the applicant is acting by counsel or a solicitor. The lawyer will then need to give undertakings to file the appropriate documents and fees on the same day or the next working day (PD 25A, paras 4.5 and 5).

Service of injunction order and hearing

To be effective, the injunction order needs to be served on the respondent(s) named in the order. Service can be done personally, or by the court. If the applicant wants to apply for committal of the respondent for any breach of the order, Ord 29, r 1(2) of the County Court Rules (CCR) (CPR, Sch 2) requires that the applicant will have to prove that the respondent was served personally with a copy of the order.

At the return date on an injunction application, the court will decide, on the evidence given by the parties. The court can decide to dismiss the application, make an order or accept an undertaking from the respondent to observe the terms of the application until full trial of the matter.

9.5.3.4 Defence

Part 15 of the CPR details the procedure for the defendant to follow if he wishes to defend the claim. The defendant will (unless extensions of time are agreed or ordered) need to file a defence 14 days after service of the particulars of claim. Alternatively, if he files an acknowledgement of service, he has up to 28 days after the particulars of claim are served to file his defence.

Rule 16.5 stipulates what must be contained in the defence. The defendant will need to state which allegations are denied and the reasons for doing so, which are admitted, and which he is unable to admit or deny but requires the claimant to prove (for example, allegations of loss or damage).

Once the defence is filed, CPR Part 26 determines the procedure for an allocations questionnaire, unless dispensed with, a directions hearing and whether disclosure, witness statements and expert evidence are needed.

9.6 CRIMINAL SANCTIONS

Depending on which statutory provision is being used, the police, or the local authority, may have power to commence criminal proceedings. Alternatively, it is open to the victim to bring a private prosecution.

The PEA 1977 created three distinct offences: one of harassment and two relating to unlawful eviction. However, what became apparent very quickly was that the legislation was not being enforced by local authorities, the bodies given the power to prosecute under s 6 of the PEA 1977, with the level of enthusiasm and commitment that had been envisaged. Relatively few complaints have been made under the PEA 1977 and there have been even fewer prosecutions (see D Cowan, 'Harassment and Unlawful Eviction in the Private Rented Sector – a Study of Law In (–) action' [2001] 65 Conv 249).

The Criminal Law Act 1977 and the Protection from Harassment Act 1997 have wider application than housing law alone, and may also assist an occupier with further criminal sanctions or, as indicated at **9.2.2.7**, with civil remedies.

Set out below are the various statutory provisions under which criminal proceedings may be brought as a result of unlawful eviction or harassment.

9.6.1 Protection from Eviction Act 1977

There are three distinct offences created by the PEA 1977, designed to protect occupiers of residential premises from unlawful eviction or harassment:

(a) Unlawful eviction under s 1(2) of the PEA 1977. It is an offence for any person unlawfully to deprive, or attempt to deprive, the residential occupier of any premises of his occupation of the premises or any part of it. It is a defence to show that the person believed, and had reasonable cause to believe, that the residential occupier had ceased to reside in the premises.

(b) Harassment by anyone under s 1(3) of the PEA 1977. It is an offence for any person, with the intent to cause the residential occupier to give up occupation of the premises or any part of it, or to refrain from exercising any rights or pursue any remedy in respect of the premises, to do acts likely to interfere with the peace or comfort of the residential occupier, or members of his household. It is also an offence under this provision, persistently to withdraw or withhold services reasonably required for the occupation of the premises as a residence.

(c) Harassment by the landlord or his agent under s 1(3A) of the PEA 1977. It is an offence for the landlord or his agent, without reasonable grounds, to do acts likely to interfere with the peace or comfort of the residential occupier or members of his household. Here too, persistently to withdraw or withhold services reasonably required for the occupation of the premises as a residence is an offence. In relation to the offences under s 1(3A), the landlord or agent must know, or have reasonable cause to believe, that the conduct is likely to cause the residential occupier to give up the occupation of the whole or part of the premises, or to refrain from exercising any right or pursue any remedy in respect of the whole or part of the premises. The landlord offence is almost identical to the other harassment offence in s 1(3), except that whereas there must have been intention to commit the offence in s 1(3), a subjective intention on the part of the landlord is not necessary for s 1(3A) landlord offence.

9.6.1.1 Meaning of 'residential occupier' and 'landlord'

'Residential occupier' is widely defined in s 1(1) of the PEA 1977 to mean:

> a person occupying the premises as a residence, whether under a contract or by virtue of any enactment or rule of law giving him the right to remain in occupation or restricting the right of any other person to recover possession of the premises.

The 'landlord' for the purposes of s 1(3A), is defined in s 1(3C) to include not only the occupier's immediate landlord but any superior landlord as well.

9.6.1.2 Dealing with the offences

All the offences are triable either summarily or on indictment, with the penalty on indictment being an unlimited fine and/or imprisonment for up to two years.

Although successful prosecutions have been brought for unlawful eviction, leading, in more serious cases, to sentences of imprisonment, the police have not been keen to institute proceedings under these provisions. Similarly, local authorities generally are not keen to prosecute using their power under s 6 of the PEA 1977, preferring to focus on mediation. Where prosecutions have been brought successfully, the punishment has often tended to be limited to a small fine.

> **CASE EXAMPLE**
>
> In R v Burke [1990] 2 All ER 385, HL, the landlord, on being convicted of harassment under s 1(3), was fined £250 on each of two counts. He committed acts such as padlocking the toilet door and storing furniture in the bathroom (there were alternative, but less convenient bath and toilet facilities at the property). He also disconnected the front door bell's link to the tenant's floor. He had also tried to get his tenants to apply to the council for housing. The landlord appealed on the basis that as none of these acts constituted an actionable civil wrong, he should not have been convicted. However, the House of Lords unanimously dismissed his appeal.

9.6.2 Criminal Law Act 1977, s 6(1) – violent entry to premises

There are a number of offences under this Act relating to a person entering and remaining on property. However, the provision most appropriate to use against a landlord who has harassed an occupier is s 6. This section makes it an offence for any person, without lawful authority, to use or threaten violence in order to secure entry to any property, knowing that there is someone present on those premises at the time who is opposed to the entry. It does not matter whether the violence is directed against the property or the person. Prosecutions may be brought by the CPS. This offence carries a maximum penalty on summary conviction of six months' imprisonment and/or a fine of up to £5,000.

9.6.3 Protection from Harassment Act 1997

This Act was passed to deal with all types of harassment, not just those relating to housing. It focuses on a course of conduct by the defendant that amounts to, and which the defendant knows or ought to know amounts to, harassment. Four new offences were created under the Act:

(a) harassment (s 2(1));
(b) putting people in fear of violence (s 4(1));
(c) breach of an injunction order made in civil proceedings under s 3(1) (s 3(6)); and
(d) breach of a restraining order made in connection with a s 2 or s 3 offence (s 5(5)).

Harassing a person is defined in s 7(2) to include alarming the person or causing him distress. A course of conduct in relation to a single person must involve conduct on at least two occasions in relation to that person. One incident will not be enough to constitute an offence against a single person. What is considered to be the less serious offence of harassment under s 2 is punishable by six months' imprisonment or a fine of up to £5,000. The more serious offence under s 4, of harassment leading to fear of violence, carries the same penalty for summary conviction but, on indictment, a maximum penalty of five years' imprisonment and/or an unlimited fine. Under s 5, a court can make a restraining order to protect a victim. The penalty for breach of such an order is the same as for the s 4 offence. The same penalties are also available for the offence of breaching an injunction under s 3.

9.6.4 Compensation orders in criminal proceedings

The Powers of Criminal Courts (Sentencing) Act 2000 provides that where a defendant is convicted of an offence, the court can order him to pay up to £5,000 in compensation to the victim for any personal injury, loss or damage resulting from that offence or any other offence taken into consideration when sentencing the defendant. However, any sums received here would be deducted from an award in subsequent civil proceedings, where compensation is given in relation to the same loss.

SUMMARY

Civil claims

- A victim of unlawful eviction or harassment may have claims in contract and/or tort.
- Remedies of injunction and/or damages are available.

Due process under the PEA 1977

- Court proceedings are required for re-entry or forfeiture against an occupied dwelling (s 2).
- Court proceedings are required to regain possession against certain former tenants who hold over after their tenancy has terminated (s 3).
- Certain tenancies are excluded from due process (s 3A).
- A landlord's notice to quit will be valid only if it is in writing, gives a minimum of at least four weeks, notice, and contains the prescribed information (s 5).

Criminal sanctions

- The PEA 1977 creates three offences to protect against unlawful eviction or harassment.
- The Criminal Law Act 1977 creates an offence against violent entry to premises.
- The Protection from Harassment Act 1997 creates four offences to protect against harassment that might help in a housing context.

CHAPTER 10

POSSESSION CLAIMS

10.1	Introduction	151
10.2	The scope of the rules in CPR, Part 55 and PD 55A and 55B	152
10.3	Starting the claim	153
10.4	Service of claims	156
10.5	The defendant's response	156
10.6	The hearing	157
10.7	Accelerated possession claims against assured shorthold tenants	157
10.8	The possession orders	158
10.9	Tolerated trespassers	164
10.10	Challenging the possession order	166
10.11	Warrants for possession	167
10.12	Public funding and possession proceedings	168
10.13	Checklist for possession claims	168
10.14	Further reading	169
	Summary	169

LEARNING OUTCOMES

After reading this chapter you will be able to:

- understand the procedure for possession claims
- list and explain the different possession orders
- outline the possible challenges to a possession order
- explain the matters to check in possession claims.

10.1 INTRODUCTION

Possession claims are claims for the recovery of possession of land. The one thing that all occupiers of premises leased from a landlord have in common, whether they be weekly periodic tenancies or long leaseholders, is that their landlord has the power, if the relevant circumstances exist, to terminate, or to get a court to terminate, their right to occupy the premises. In the case of residential occupiers, in most (but not all) cases, the landlord will need a court order to effect termination to give him the right to regain possession of the premises. In 2012 there were over 150,000 possession claims issued by landlords in the county court in England and Wales. Landlords were successful in obtaining over 100,000 possession orders.

Although freehold owners do not have this threat hanging over them, they are not entirely free of the risk of losing their right of occupation if they have a mortgage on their property and any of the mortgage terms are breached. The most serious breach, of course, would be to fail to make regular mortgage repayments. In such cases the mortgagee will seek to obtain possession of the premises, normally with a view to selling the property to recover the loan, plus the outstanding arrears of interest payments. For 2012 over 59,000 mortgage possession claims were started and over 44,000 orders were made.

In this chapter, we look at the procedure that will need to be followed by a landlord or mortgagee when seeking possession of premises. Also briefly considered is the procedure to be followed by an owner seeking to recover possession against trespassers occupying the land. The provisions are contained in CPR, Part 55 and PD 55A and 55B. Part 55 is divided into three sections: Section I contains the general rules which apply in most cases; Section II is concerned with accelerated possession claims of property let on an assured shorthold tenancy (see **10.7**); Section III relates to interim possession orders (see **10.3.5**). The protocols for possession claims based on rent arrears and for mortgage arrears are also considered.

10.2 THE SCOPE OF THE RULES IN CPR, PART 55 AND PD 55A AND 55B

The rules apply to claims brought in five distinct categories:

(a) by a landlord (or former landlord);
(b) by a mortgagee;
(c) by a licensor (or former licensor);
(d) against a trespasser; and
(e) by a tenant seeking relief from forfeiture.

The rules, which came into force on 15 October 2001, apply to claims begun on or after that date. The rules apply to a possession claim, which is a claim for the recovery of possession of land, including buildings or parts of buildings (CPR, r 55.1(a)).

10.2.1 Pre-action Protocol for Possession Claims based on Rent Arrears

Possessions claims based on rent and mortgage arrears form the vast majority of possession cases brought in the courts each year. In an effort to reduce those numbers, a Pre-action Protocol for Possession Claims based on Rent Arrears was introduced. The Protocol came into effect on 2 October 2006. The Protocol is directed at social landlords, defined to include LHAs, RSLs, PRPs and HATs. Its aim is to encourage more pre-action contact between landlords and tenants, and to enable court time to be used more effectively where claims are based solely on rent arrears. The Protocol does not apply to long leases or claims for possession where there is no security of tenure.

Social landlords are now required to take all reasonable steps to avoid litigation. The landlord is required to contact the tenant as soon as reasonably possible after he falls into arrears. The landlord should discuss the cause of the arrears, the tenant's financial circumstances, his benefit entitlement and possible repayment of the arrears. Where the tenant is found eligible, the landlord should offer to assist him in any claim for housing benefit.

The Protocol requires social landlords to comply with guidance issued by the Housing Corporation or the Department for Communities and Local Government. If the landlord decides to take possession proceedings, the tenant should be provided with an up-to-date rent statement no later than 10 days before the hearing as well as disclosure of the landlord's knowledge of the tenant's housing benefit position. The landlord is also required to inform the tenant of the hearing, and advise the tenant to attend the hearing, and keep a record of such advice.

The Protocol specifically provides that possession proceedings should not be started where arrears are increasing due to housing benefit delays rather than the tenant being at fault in not making payment for sums not covered by housing benefit. Where proceedings are started, the court may require proof from the parties of efforts to resolve the dispute by discussion and negotiation beforehand. A claim may be adjourned, struck out or dismissed (unless brought solely on mandatory grounds), or alternatively there may be costs penalties if the landlord unreasonably fails to comply with the terms of the Protocol. Tenants who fail to comply may have it taken into consideration as a factor in deciding whether an order for possession should be made.

10.2.2 Pre-Action Protocol for Possession Claims based on Mortgage or Home Purchase Plan Arrears in Respect of Residential Property

This Protocol, effective from 19 November 2008, has similar objectives to the Rent Arrears Protocol. Its aim is to ensure mortgagees (referred to in the Protocol as 'lenders') and mortgagors ('borrowers') act fairly and reasonably with each other in dealing with arrears. It also aims to encourage more pre-action contact between the parties to try to enable them to reach agreement and, if not, to enable court time to be used more efficiently.

The Protocol applies to arrears on:

(a) first charge residential mortgages and home purchase plans regulated by the FSA under the Financial Services and Markets Act 2000;

(b) second charge mortgages over residential property and other secured loans regulated under the Consumer Credit Act 1974 on residential property; and

(c) unregulated residential mortgages.

The Protocol applies to possession claims which include a money claim as well.

Detailed guidance is given to the lender in the Protocol as to information it should provide and steps it should take in order to try to avoid a possession claim. There are also obligations on a borrower to act reasonably in facilitating an agreement. Where a lender decides that a possession claim is inevitable, the lender is required to give the borrower notice of the reasons for this decision five days before starting proceedings.

10.3 STARTING THE CLAIM

Possessions claims will normally be brought in the county court for the district in which the land is situated. Only in exceptional circumstances will a possession claim start in the High Court, for example where there are complicated disputes of fact, points of law of general importance, or where, in claims against trespassers, there is a substantial risk of public disturbance or serious harm to persons or property which properly requires immediate determination (PD 55A, para 1.3). If a claim is started in the High Court, CPR, r 55.3(2) requires the claimant to file with his claim form a certificate stating the reasons for bringing the claim in that court, and have it verified by a statement of truth. There will be cost penalties if a claim is inappropriately brought in the High Court.

10.3.1 The appropriate claim form

The claimant is required to use the appropriate claim form and particulars of claim form (PD 55A, para 1.5). The claim forms are:

N5 – claim form for possession of property;

N5A – claim form for relief against forfeiture; and

N5B – claim form for possession of property (accelerated procedure) (assured shorthold tenancy).

A claimant may use a single claim form to start all claims which can be conveniently disposed of in the same proceedings, so possession claims can include other issues too (eg, rent arrears).

10.3.2 The particulars of claim

The claimant is required to use the relevant particulars of claim form, which must be filed and served with the claim form. The forms are (PD 4, para 3.1):

N119 – particulars of claim for possession (rented residential premises);

N120 – particulars of claim for possession (mortgaged residential premises); and

N121 – particulars of claim for possession (trespassers).

Rule 16.4 of the CPR sets out the general contents of the particulars of claim (see **9.5.3.2** for an outline of the contents). In addition, PD 55A, para 2 gives further guidance on the contents of different types of possession claims. In general, the particulars of claim in any possession proceedings must:

(a) identify the land to which the claim relates;
(b) state whether the claim relates to residential property;
(c) state the grounds on which possession is claimed;
(d) give full details of any mortgage or tenancy agreement; and
(e) give details of every person who, to the best of the claimant's knowledge, is in possession of the property.

10.3.3 Additional requirements for residential property

With tenancies of residential property, where the claim includes a claim for non-payment of rent, PD 55, para 2.3 stipulates that the particulars of claim must set out:

(a) the amount due at the start of the proceedings;
(b) a schedule of the dates when the arrears of rent arose, all amounts of rent due, the dates and amounts of all payments made, and a running total of the arrears;
(c) the daily rate of any rent and interest;
(d) any previous steps taken to recover the arrears of rent with full details of any court proceedings; and
(e) any relevant information about the defendant's circumstances, in particular details of whether he is on social security benefits and whether any benefit payments are made direct to the claimant.

In addition, if the claimant wishes to rely on a history of arrears which is longer than two years, he should state this in his particulars and exhibit a full (or longer) schedule to a witness statement (PD 55A, para 2.3A).

If the claimant knows of any person (including a mortgagee) entitled to claim relief against forfeiture as underlessee, the particulars of claim must state the name and address of that person; and the claimant must file a copy of the particulars of claim for service on him (PD 55A, para 2.4).

If the claim for possession relates to the conduct of the tenant or relies on a statutory ground or grounds for possession, the particulars of claim must state details of the conduct alleged and specify the ground or grounds relied on (PD 55A, para 2.4A and 2.4B).

A provision in CPR, r 55.10A and PD 55B enables claimants who are seeking possession based solely on the grounds of rent arrears or mortgage arrears to be able to issue the claim online in certain specified county courts.

10.3.4 Possession claims by mortgagees

With possession claims brought by a mortgagee in relation to residential property, PD 55A, para 2.5 states that the particulars of claim must also set out:

(a) whether a land charge of Class F, or a notice under the Matrimonial Homes Act 1967 or 1983 respectively has been registered, or a notice under the Family Law Act 1996 (if any of the provisions apply, the claimant will have to serve notice of the claim on the persons on whose behalf the registration or notice was entered);
(b) the state of the mortgage account, including the amount of the advance, any periodic repayments and interest, and the amount needed to redeem the mortgage, including the costs of doing so;

(c) if the mortgage is a regulated consumer credit agreement, the total amount outstanding; and

(d) the rate of interest payable and any changes since commencement of the mortgage, immediately before any arrears accrued and at the commencement of proceedings.

As with rent arrears (see **10.3.3**), if the claim is brought for mortgage arrears, PD 55A, para 2.5 requires the particulars of claim to set out in a schedule the dates when the arrears arose, all amounts due, the dates and amounts of all payments made, and a running total of the arrears. As with rent arrears claims, there are similar requirements to detail benefits provisions and previous steps taken by the claimant to recover the arrears (PD 55A, para 2.5(6) and (8)). In addition, further details relating to regulated consumer credit loans are required (see PD 55, para 2.5(4), (5)).

By CPR, r 55.10, where a mortgagee is seeking possession of residential property, he must send a notice to the LHA, to any registered proprietor (other than the claimant) of a registered charge over the property and to the property addressed to 'the tenant or the occupier' within five days of receiving notification of the hearing by the court, giving details of the claim and the hearing. The claimant will need to produce at the hearing a copy of the notice and evidence of service.

10.3.5 Possession claims against trespassers

A trespasser for these purposes is someone who entered or remained on the land without the consent of a person entitled to possession of that land. It does not include a tenant or sub-tenant whose tenancy has terminated. For claims against trespassers where the claimant does not know the name of the trespasser, the claim must be brought against 'persons unknown' in addition to any named defendants (CPR, r 55.3(4)). The particulars of claim against trespassers must state the claimant's interest in the land, or the basis of his right to claim possession, and the circumstances in which it has been occupied without licence or consent (PD 55A, para 2.6).

In certain situations, a claimant who has an immediate right to possession of the property and who acted promptly (ie, within 28 days) on discovering the presence of the trespassers (as defined above) on the land, can use the provisions in Section III to obtain an interim possession order (IPO) against the trespasser (CPR, rr 55.20–55.28). The IPO requires the defendant to vacate the property within 24 hours of the service of the order. It is an offence for the defendant to fail to leave the premises as required by the order. A full hearing of the claim will be made not less than seven days thereafter, and if the claimant was not justified in his claim, the defendant will be entitled to reinstatement and damages.

10.3.6 Possession claims in relation to demoted tenancies by a HAT or LHA

With possession claims against demoted tenants by a HAT or an LHA under s 143D of the HA 1996 (see **6.6.3**), the particulars of claim must have attached to them a copy of the notice to the tenant served under s 143E of the 1996 Act (PD 55A, para 2.7).

There are amended procedures in CPR, Part 55 where the landlord is seeking a demotion order in the course of possession proceedings.

Where the landlord is seeking only a demotion order, the relevant procedure is that in CPR, rr 65.14–65.19 (Proceedings relating to anti-social behaviour and harassment) and claim form N6. This is a procedure similar to that in CPR, Part 55.

10.3.7 The hearing date

The court will fix a date for the hearing when it issues the claim form. This will normally be for not less than 28 days, and the standard period for the hearing not more than eight weeks, from the date of issue of the claim form. For claims against trespassers, shorter periods are applicable.

10.4 SERVICE OF CLAIMS

The defendant must be served with the claim form and particulars of claim not less than 21 days before the hearing date. Any witness statements to be used must be verified by a statement of truth, and must be filed and served at least two days before the hearing (CPR, r 55.8(4)). However, the time limits are different for claims against trespassers in occupation of residential property. In such cases the trespasser must be served with the claim form, particulars of claim and any witness statements not less than five days before the hearing (CPR, r 55.5(2), (3)).

If the defendant or persons for whom he is responsible have assaulted, or threatened to assault, the claimant, or its staff or residents in the locality, or there are reasonable grounds for fearing such an assault to person or property, the court may exercise its powers to shorten the time periods given in CPR, r 55.5(2) and (3) (PD 55A, para 3.2).

The court can arrange for service, or the claimant may choose to arrange service of the documents. If the claimant serves the claim form and particulars of claim, he must produce a certificate of service at the hearing (CPR, r 55.8(6)). For claims against trespassers where there are 'persons unknown', CPR, r 55.6 provides particular procedures for service, which includes pinning copies of the documents to the main door of the property, putting copies in transparent envelopes through the letter box and attaching copies to stakes erected in visible places on the land.

10.5 THE DEFENDANT'S RESPONSE

The defendant should be sent not only the claim form, but also the defence form together with explanatory notes. The defence form will vary according to the status of the defendant. The relevant forms are (PD 55A, para 1.5):

N11 – defence form;

N11B – defence form (accelerated possession procedure) (assured shorthold tenancy);

N11M – defence form (mortgaged residential premises); and

N11R – defence form (rented residential premises).

The defendant does not need to acknowledge service of the claim. Trespassers do not need to file a defence. For a non-trespass defendant, if he intends to defend the claim, he should file a defence within 14 days of service of the claim. However, failure to do so will not stop him being able to participate at the hearing, but there may be cost penalties against the defendant as a result (CPR, r 55.7). A default judgment cannot be obtained in a possession claim, as the court has to be satisfied that the landlord has made out his claim before an order can be made (see **10.6**).

Most of the defence forms are fairly prescriptive; however, the defendant will have the opportunity to dispute the claim at the appropriate point. Typical defence points could include challenging the claim on the basis that the landlord has not made out the claim because, say, he has not served the appropriate notice, or there are no arrears.

Very often, the defendant may have a counter-claim. Often this relates to a claim for damages for disrepair of the premises under s 11 of the LTA 1985 (see **7.3.3.2**), or for breach of the covenant of quiet enjoyment (see **9.2.1.1**). Where this is the case, CPR, Part 20 applies. These counter-claims should be included as part of the defence document to avoid the need to obtain the court's permission to bring a counter-claim. The defendant will need to give full particulars of the counter-claim.

10.6 THE HEARING

Part 39 of the CPR contains miscellaneous provisions in relation to hearings. The provisions take into account the requirements of Article 6 of the Convention (to have a public hearing), as well as Articles 8 and 14 (to respect private life and correspondence, and not to be discriminatory in interfering with Convention rights). Rule 39.2(3) gives a judge discretion to decide whether to conduct a hearing in public or private. One of the factors to take into account in deciding whether to hear a case in private is if the hearing involves confidential information, including that relating to personal financial matters (CPR, r 39.2(3)(c)). Practice Direction 39, para 1.5 gives rent arrears and mortgage arrears repossession claims as examples of claims within CPR, r 39.2(3)(c). As a result, most possession claims are now heard in private, whether they relate to mortgage possession claims (which always were private hearings) or rent arrears possession claims (which previously were not).

At the hearing, or at any adjourned hearing, the court may either decide the claim or give case management directions. Where there is a genuine dispute with substantial grounds of challenge, the directions will include the allocation of the claim to a track, or directions to enable a track to be allocated.

The court will allocate a possession claim to the small claims track only if all the parties agree. When this happens, the claim is treated for costs purposes as if it were a fast track claim, except that the court will have a discretion over trial costs and must not exceed the amount that would be recoverable if the value of the claim was up to £3,000 (CPR, r 55.9). Rule 26.8 and the related Practice Direction give guidance on the factors to consider when deciding the track for a particular claim. In addition, CPR, r 55.9(1) gives additional factors to take into account for a possession claim. The size of the arrears, the importance of the defendant retaining possession and of the claimant obtaining it, as well as the conduct of the defendant, are all additional relevant factors.

County courts often include a large number of possession claims in each day's listing on the basis that the vast majority will be undefended. The courts tend to adopt a system where possession claims by registered social landlords are listed together, while private sector landlord claims and mortgage repossession claims are listed separately. As many defendants often do not attend at the hearing of the claim, the lists are disposed of in private very efficiently. However, the court must be satisfied in each case that the grounds for possession are made out, that the appropriate notice, be it notice to quit or notice seeking possession, was served and, where the court has a discretion, that it is reasonable to make the possession order.

Where the case is actually heard, up-to-date evidence on benefits, arrears, etc should be provided to the court. If evidence given in a witness statement is disputed and the maker of the statement is not at the hearing, the court will normally adjourn the hearing so that oral evidence may be given (PD 55A, paras 5.3 and 5.4).

10.7 ACCELERATED POSSESSION CLAIMS AGAINST ASSURED SHORTHOLD TENANTS

Section II of CPR, Part 55 deals with a speedy process for possession claims against assured shorthold tenants. The claim must be started in the county court for the district in which the property is situated and brought under s 21 of the HA 1988, provided certain conditions are met. The conditions are that (CPR, r 55.12):

(a) the tenancy was entered into on or after 15 January 1989;
(b) the only purpose of the claim is to recover possession and no other claim (eg rent arrears) is being made;
(c) the tenancy did not immediately follow an assured tenancy which was not an assured shorthold tenancy;

(d) the tenancy fulfilled the conditions provided by s 19A or s 20(1)(a) to (c) of the HA 1988 (see **2.7.1** and **2.7.2**);

(e) there is a written agreement in relation to this or a previous tenancy of the property; and

(f) a notice under s 21(1) or s 21(4) of the HA 1988 was given to the tenant (see **2.7.3**).

This procedure can also be used against a demoted assured shorthold tenant (see **2.9.3**). In such cases, only the conditions in (b) and (f) above will apply. The claim procedure will be as stated earlier (see **10.3.1**).

10.7.1 Defence to accelerated possession claim

If a tenant wishes to oppose the claim or seek a postponement of possession, he must file a defence (in Form N11B) within 14 days after service of the claim form (CPR, r 55.14). If the defendant fails to file a defence within the time stipulated, the claimant may file a written request for a possession order. Where a defence is filed, the court sends a copy to the claimant and the case is referred to a judge, who can make an order for possession without requiring the attendance of the parties if satisfied that the claim is well made out. Where he is not so satisfied, he can set a hearing date and case management directions can be made, or he can strike out the claim if it discloses no reasonable grounds for bringing the claim (CPR, rr 55.16 and 55.17). The claimant can apply to restore the claim within 28 days after being served with the order and reasons for striking out the claim.

The landlord needs to comply with the strict procedural requirements to ensure he has made out his case for possession under s 21 of the HA 1988. If relevant notice has not been served or the notice is defective, the claim will fail. In *Manel v Memon* (2001) 33 HLR 235, CA, a case concerned with a pre-HA 1996 tenancy, the s 20 notice served on the tenant prior to the commencement of her assured shorthold tenancy did not contain the notes of advice that were set out in Form 7, eg there was no information advising of the need to take legal advice. It was held that the notice was not substantially to the same effect as Form 7 (see **2.7.1**) and therefore was invalid. In *Fernandez v McDonald* [2004] 1 WLR 1027, CA, the landlord was again frustrated. It was held that the landlord's notice under s 21(4)(a) of the HA 1988 was invalid when it did not give the last day of the period of the tenancy, as required by s 21, but the day after (see **2.7.3**). The landlord's claim was dismissed. The landlord will also defeat his aim if he includes a claim for arrears of rent in this accelerated procedure.

10.7.2 Postponement of possession

Where the defendant seeks postponement of the possession order on the ground of exceptional hardship, a hearing will be held unless the claimant has indicated that he would not object to postponement of possession. The judge has a discretion under s 89 of the HA 1980, if satisfied that exceptional hardship would be caused by requiring possession to be given up by the date in the order (normally within 14 days), to set a date up to six weeks after the making of the order (CPR, r 55.18). The Supreme Court in *Powell* (2011) (see **4.5.3.2**) declined to rule s 89 of the HA 1980 incompatible with Article 8 of the Convention.

10.8 THE POSSESSION ORDERS

The type of order that a judge may make once the claimant has established a case for possession, will very much depend on the nature of the defendant's occupancy of the premises and whether he comes within any of the statutory schemes which give the court discretion in this area. Where the court has the power to exercise its discretion, it may decide that it will not make a possession order at all. Instead the proceedings may be adjourned generally, either with or without terms (see **10.8.1**).

Possession orders may be:

(a) immediate, to take effect forthwith. This is the order that would normally be made against a trespasser (see **10.8.5**);

(b) outright (or absolute), to take effect within 14 days unless exceptional hardship is claimed (when an order may be postponed as outlined at **10.7.2**). This is the order that would normally be made against an occupier who has no security of tenure (eg an assured shorthold tenant) or where the claimant has a mandatory right to possession (see **10.8.2**);

(c) suspended. This order is commonly used where the court has discretion. An order is commonly made relying on Form 28 and ordering possession within 28 days suspended on terms that the defendant complies with certain conditions. If the defendant breaches the terms, the claimant may apply for a warrant of execution (see **10.8.1** and **10.8.6.1**);

(d) postponed on terms. Form N28A grants possession postponed on terms. No date for possession is specified in the order. A date will be fixed by the court following an application by the claimant.

Where the order has been postponed on terms, the claimant will only be entitled to apply to court for a possession date if the tenant has breached the payment terms of the order and the claimant has complied with the procedure in para 10.3 of PD 55A. The procedure requires advance written notice, of between 14 days and three months before the application, to be given to the tenant of the claimant's intention to apply for an order fixing a date for possession. The written notice must:

(a) state the claimant's intention to apply for an order;

(b) state the current arrears;

(c) state how the defendant has failed to comply with the order;

(d) request a reply from the defendant within seven days agreeing or disputing the arrears; and

(e) inform the defendant of his right to apply to the court for a further postponement of the date for possession or to stay or suspend enforcement.

If the defendant agrees with the arrears stated, he must explain why payments have not been made in his reply. If he disputes the figure, he must provide details of payments or credits made.

In practice many county court judges used Form N28A when granting possession orders against assured and secure tenants.

This is now the position for landlord terminations of secure, assured, introductory and demoted tenancies as a result of s 299 of and Sch 11 to the Housing and Regeneration Act 2008 which has amended s 82 of the HA 1985, ss 5 and 21 of the HA 1988 and ss 127 and 143 of the HA 1996. Under the amended provisions, a landlord who wishes to terminate one of these tenancies must obtain a court order for possession and, unless the tenant leaves before, have the order executed (ie, obtain a warrant for possession and have court bailiffs evict the tenant) (see further **10.8.6.3** and **10.9**).

The application of these different types of orders is considered below in the context of the type of occupation of the defendants.

10.8.1 Discretionary grounds for possession

The provisions of s 100 of the RA 1977, s 85 of the HA 1985 and s 9 of the HA 1988 all give the court generous powers in relation to certain claims for possession against regulated, secure or assured tenants, where the court can decide whether it is reasonable to make an order for possession (ie the discretionary grounds for possession). The court has a wide discretion to adjourn the possession proceedings, or, if a possession order is made, to stay or suspend execution of the order, or to postpone the date of possession for such period as the court thinks fit (see **10.8.6** below).

10.8.1.1 Discretion in rent arrears cases

Rent arrears claims are by far the most common possession claims. Apart from the mandatory Ground 8 for assured tenants (see **2.6.1.8**), the court normally has a discretion to decide whether or not to make a possession order where rent arrears have been established.

For the arrears to have been established, the landlord must show that rent was lawfully due and unpaid. Care should be taken to ensure that the rent is lawfully due. For example, if the landlord has not supplied the tenant with an address for service of notices, as required by s 48 of the LTA 1987, rent (as well as any service charge and administration charge) will not be treated as being due.

The tenant may have a legitimate counter-claim to the arrears, which, if successful, may cancel the arrears (see *British Anzani (Felixstowe) Ltd v International Marine Management (UK) Ltd* [1980] QB 137 and **7.5.1** for set off in possession claims).

In deciding whether it is reasonable to make an order, where the arrears have been established, the court should have regard to the history of events, the tenant's past payment record, his behaviour with any previous arrears and the reasons for the present arrears. Compliance with the Pre-action Protocol for Possession Claims based on rent arrears will be an important factor for the court to consider in claims brought by social landlords (see **10.2.1**). Housing statistics from the DCLG indicate that the majority of LHA, PRP and RSL tenants claim housing benefit. Many of these tenants suffer as a result of delays in the processing of their housing benefit claims.

10.8.1.2 Discretion in anti-social behaviour possession claims

Claims for nuisance are fast becoming the second biggest category of possession claims. The structured discretion introduced in s 9A of the HA 1988 and s 85A of the HA 1985 (see **2.6.2.7** on Ground 14 and structured discretion for assured tenants, and **6.7.1.2** for Ground 2 secure tenants) has given the courts a more codified manner of exercising their discretion.

The courts were already taking a firm line in nuisance cases, however, particularly where there were allegations of violence and racist abuse. In *Solon South West Housing Association Ltd v James* [2004] All ER (D) 328, CA, the Court upheld an immediate possession order where the defendants had a two-year history of terrorising their neighbourhood. The evidence the trial judge relied on was based in large part on hearsay evidence. This was accepted because of the reluctance of witnesses to come forward for fear of reprisals. Other relevant factors in making the decision were the impact a suspended order might have on the neighbours and the fact that the defendants had been unrepentant about their behaviour.

In *Knowsley Housing Trust v McMullen* [2006] HLR 43, CA (see **2.6.2.7**), the fact that an ASBO already existed against the tenant's son, who was mainly responsible for the anti-social behaviour, was a factor taken into account in deciding what order to make. It was held that the existence of the ASBO did not prevent the Court making a possession order. However, it influenced the Court to make a suspended possession order rather than an outright order against the tenant.

Nevertheless, in *Sheffield City Council v Shaw* [2007] HLR 25, CA, the landlord did not get the outright order for possession that it was expecting. The defendant had become obsessed with the 12-year-old daughter of a neighbour, and over a period of years had stalked and harassed her, even threatening to kill her. The defendant was convicted for this harassment, and an ASBO and a restraining order were made against him, both of which he breached. At trial the defendant apologised for his behaviour and evidence was given that with psychiatric help he was capable of reform. The judge took this evidence into account and made a suspended possession order. The landlord appealed on several grounds, one of which was that insufficient weight had been given to the fear and apprehension of the victim.

The landlord relied on the decision in *Lambeth LBC v Howard* (2001) 33 HLR 58, CA, where it was held that an outright order was appropriate despite the tenant's good behaviour in the year leading up to the trial. Sedley LJ stated that the outright order was appropriate as, 'even if the tenant were to return next door and commit no acts of harassment in the future, the shadow of the past is too heavy upon the present'. The Court, in dismissing Sheffield City Council's appeal, held that the proposition that historic conduct could be so bad as to produce in a victim apprehension for the future that could not be dispelled, and that past conduct should outweigh future optimism, was not established as a principle.

It is interesting to note that the defendant in *Lambeth LBC v Howard*, despite his subsequent good behaviour, had refused to acknowledge the harm caused by his conduct. By contrast, in *Sheffield City Council v Shaw*, the defendant, after being in denial for many years, had come to realise, with the benefit of psychiatric help, the effect his behaviour must have had on his victims, and had apologised for it.

In *Birmingham City Council v Ashton* [2013] HLR 8, CA, it was held that although the court might not be mandated to take account of the factors in s 85A(2) (ie, the structured discretion – see **2.6.2.7**) in considering whether to suspend an order for possession, they were factors highly relevant to the exercise of the judgment to be made in relation to the power to suspend under s 85(2). Also, that the onus was on the party seeking to have the benefit of a suspended order to provide cogent evidence to show that the anti-social behaviour would not, or would be unlikely to, recur.

10.8.2 Mandatory grounds for possession

If the claimant makes out a case for a mandatory ground for possession against regulated tenants under the RA 1977, and against assured or assured shorthold tenants under Pt I of Sch 2 to the HA 1988 or s 21 of the HA 1988, the court does not have the generous powers available for the discretionary grounds. An outright order for possession will be made and the provisions of s 89 of the HA 1980 will apply (see **10.7.2**). However, the claimant will not get an order for possession if the relevant ground has not been properly made out, or if the appropriate procedure has not been observed, as in *Mountain v Hastings* (1995) 25 HLR 427, CA, where an invalid s 8 notice defeated the landlord's possession claim (see **2.6.1.8**).

Where the landlord can make out a mandatory ground for possession at the hearing date, the court does not have the power to adjourn the hearing for the purpose of enabling the tenant to avoid the ground for possession. This was held to be the case in *North British Housing Association Ltd v Matthews* [2005] 2 All ER 667, CA. The case involved four co-joined appeals by assured tenants, who were all in arrears with their rent payments as a result of delays in the payment of housing benefits. The respective landlords all served s 8 notices, relying on Ground 8 of Sch 2 to the HA 1988, a mandatory ground for possession. At the possession hearings the tenants had applied for an adjournment that would have allowed them to reduce their arrears below the Ground 8 threshold limits so as avoid the mandatory possession orders. The Court of Appeal upheld the trial judge's decision that it would be wrong to exercise his discretion in that way, as it would undermine the provisions in s 9(6) of the HA 1988. The Court recognised that there might be exceptional circumstances where an adjournment could be made, for example where the tenant had a legitimate defence to the claim for possession. However, maladministration by the housing benefit authority was not considered to be such an exceptional circumstance.

While the Pre-action Protocol for Possession Claims based on Rent Arrears (see **10.2.1**) will help many tenants avoid possession claims as a result of rent arrears, it may not help tenants in cases similar to *North British Housing Association Ltd v Matthews*. The exception in the Protocol for claims on mandatory grounds would suggest that the outcome in future such disputes is likely to be the same. However, PRPs that bring such claims would be at risk of cost penalties where they disregard the Protocol and commence proceedings against tenants whose arrears are due solely to housing benefit delays after proper applications have been made. In addition, following the Supreme Court judgments in *Pinnock* and *Powell*, a tenant in a situation similar to those in the *Matthews* case could raise an Article 8 and/or an unreasonableness defence against a social landlord (see **4.5.3.2**).

10.8.3 Possession orders against mortgagors

At common law the mortgagee has an immediate right to possession of the mortgaged property. It is normal for there to be a term in the mortgage agreement that entitles the mortgagee to exercise his right of possession as soon as the mortgagor breaches an important term of the mortgage. However, for residential mortgages, the court has statutory powers under the AJAs 1970 and 1973, or, if it is a regulated agreement, under the Consumer Credit Act 1974, to grant some relief.

Under s 36 of the AJA 1970, as amended by s 8 of the AJA 1973, the court may exercise similar powers to those available in connection with the discretionary grounds for possession under the statutory regimes considered at **10.8.1**. The court can adjourn the possession proceedings, or stay or suspend execution of the order, or postpone the possession date if it appears to the court that it is likely that the mortgagor will be able to pay off the arrears, as well as the current sums due on the mortgage, within a reasonable period. However, the courts cannot suspend an order under s 36 if there is no prospect of the borrower reducing the arrears (see *Abbey National Mortgages v Bernard* (1996) 71 P & CR 257, CA). The Mortgage Pre-action Protocol is designed to help reduce the number of possession claims brought by mortgagees (see **10.2.2**).

Where the Consumer Credit Act 1974 applies, the court has wider powers, which can include rescheduling the repayments and, in some cases, rewriting the agreement. (The detailed and complex provisions of the Consumer Credit Act 1974 and related regulations are beyond the scope of this book.)

10.8.3.1 Postponed possession orders against unauthorised tenants

The Mortgage Repossessions (Protection of Tenants etc) Act 2010, which came into force on 1 October 2010, enables unauthorised tenants to apply to court to postpone the date for delivery of possession when their home is being repossessed because their landlord has defaulted on the mortgage on the property (see **8.6.1.1**). Section 1(8) of the Act defines an unauthorised tenant as a tenant who has entered into a tenancy agreement with a landlord which does not give them any rights against their landlord's mortgage lender. Although the agreement is valid between tenant and landlord, it is not binding against the lender.

Where the lender is seeking a possession order, he must send notice of the claim to the property (see **10.3.4**). The unauthorised tenant can apply to the court to postpone the date of any possession order made. The court may postpone the date by which the tenant must leave by up to two months (s 1(2)). In deciding whether to exercise the discretion to postpone, the court can take into account the tenant's circumstances, including whether there are any rent arrears or anti-social behaviour. Alternatively, if a tenant did not apply to the court when the possession order was made, the tenant may apply direct to the lender to agree not to enforce the possession order for two months. If the lender does not agree, the tenant may apply to the court to grant a stay or suspension of the order for up to two months.

The court has the power to make any postponement, stay or suspension of the possession proceedings conditional on the tenant making payments to the lender in return for the tenant's occupation of the property.

10.8.4 Possession as a result of forfeiture of a long lease

A long leaseholder may be exposed to possession proceedings where he defaults on terms in his lease. This could be either for non-payment of ground rent or service charges, or for breach of some other important term (see **8.5**). The county court and High Court both have distinct powers to grant relief, but proceedings in relation to residential premises are normally brought in the county court. Section 2 of the PEA 1977 requires forfeiture proceedings against a person in occupation of residential premises to be by way of court proceedings (see **9.2.2.5**).

The county court has powers under s 138 of the County Courts Act (CCA) 1984 as amended, in relation to forfeiture for rent arrears, or under s 146(2) of the LPA 1925 in relation to other breaches, to grant relief against forfeiture (see **8.5.3** for details of the s 146 notice procedure). For rent arrears claims, under s 138 of the CCA 1984 the court's powers include the ability to suspend a possession order for at least four weeks to give the lessee the chance to pay off the arrears. Even if the lessee defaults on this and a possession order is granted to the lessor, the lessee may still be able to apply for relief up to six months after possession has been granted. For breaches other than arrears of rent, s 146(2) of the LPA 1925 gives the court the power to grant relief on whatever conditions it thinks fit.

If the court does grant relief, it will do so having taken account of the nature and seriousness of the breach, the conduct of the parties, the value of the property and the extent of any damage caused by the breach, as well as the losses that will be suffered by the tenant if relief is not granted. The court can impose terms as to costs, expenses, damages, compensation, penalty or otherwise, including the granting of an injunction to restrain any like breach in the future (LPA 1925, s 146(2)).

10.8.5 Possession orders against trespassers

Possession orders against trespassers, as defined at **10.3.5**, usually take immediate effect. This will be the case where the claimant has not previously obtained an interim possession order (see **10.3.5**). The court is bound to make an immediate order unless the claimant agrees otherwise; it has no discretion to suspend the order, or to give time to vacate on the basis of exceptional hardship (*McPhail v Persons, names unknown* [1973] 3 All ER 393, CA; *Boyland & Sons Ltd v Rand* [2006] EWCA Civ 1860).

10.8.6 Suspended and postponed orders for possession

10.8.6.1 Suspended orders

A suspended order for possession was, until recently, the most common type of order made against tenants in rent arrears. The court imposed conditions on the tenant for the payment off of any rent arrears. Form N28 was used, which gave a date for possession but purported to suspend the effect of the date given for possession in the order for as long as the tenant met the conditions. The intention was that the tenancy continued in existence so long as the tenant met the conditions imposed (see **10.8**).

10.8.6.2 Postponed orders

The courts will usually make a postponed order for possession if the tenant is able to continue to pay the current rent plus an amount off the arrears within a reasonable time (see **10.8**). The courts appear to view the issue of reasonable time according to whether the landlord is a social landlord or a private sector landlord. In *Lambeth LBC v Henry* (2000) 32 HLR 874, CA, the Court held that a suspended order to pay £1.85 per week off arrears of £2,375 which would take over 23 years to be satisfied was not an unreasonable length of time. Peter Gibson LJ said public sector landlords were extremely conscious of the hardship that would be caused if they stood on their strict legal rights. He stated that it was the practice of the courts to be merciful and to give tenants a realistic opportunity to pay off the arrears even if it takes a considerable period of time.

However, in *Taj v Ali* (2001) 33 HLR 27, CA, a RA 1977 possession claim, the trial judge made a suspended order in relation to arrears of £14,500 on the basis of current rent of £49 plus £5 per week off the arrears. Even without taking account of the further interest that would accrue on this debt, it would have taken more than 55 years for the debt to be paid off. The Court of Appeal held that the wide discretion given to the court in s 100 of the RA 1977 and other similar provisions was one that must be exercised judicially, and suspending possession for an indefinite period that 'stretched into the mists of time' did not meet this requirement. An outright order for possession was substituted for the suspended order.

10.8.6.3 Breach of suspended or postponed possession orders

As a result of the amendments outlined at **10.8**, secure, assured, introductory and demoted tenancies will not now be capable of terminating as a result of a court order until the order is executed (unless the tenant has given up possession before that date). The DCLG has issued 'Tolerated Trespassers Guidance for social landlords'. The changes as they affect the outcome of certain possession orders are explained at paras 27 and 28 of the non-statutory guidance:

> On commencement of Part 1 of Schedule 11, it will no longer be necessary for landlords to use the N28A form and the two stage procedure so far as avoidance of creating tolerated trespasser status is concerned. Landlords may therefore wish to revert to asking the court to make an order using the N28 form, which grants the landlord possession on a specified date but suspends execution of the order on terms. However, the option of using the N28A form will remain.
>
> There may be benefits to both landlords and tenants of using N28A. For tenants, it means that they will be given notice of the landlord's intention to proceed to eviction, and the leave of the court is required before the possession order can be enforced. For landlords, it means that they will avoid the risk of a claim for unlawful eviction, should it later be found that they were not entitled to a warrant for possession (for example, if the tenant is able to show that the alleged breach of the possession order did not in fact occur).

In principle, it is still possible for suspended orders to be made in a slightly amended Form N28. If the tenant complies with the terms of the postponed or suspended order and pays off all the arrears, or indeed complies with any other condition imposed, the court has the power to discharge or rescind any possession order made (see RA 1977, s 100(4); HA 1985, s 85(4); and HA 1988, s 9(4)).

If, on the other hand, the tenant breaches the terms imposed then, for tenants against whom a suspended possession order was made, the tenancy will continue for as long as the tenant remains in occupation. However, the landlord can apply for a warrant to be issued without giving notice to the tenant (see **10.11**).

For tenants against whom a postponed possession order was made under the new procedure in para 10.3 of PD 55 (see **10.8**), the tenancy will continue unless the claimant makes an application to the court (on payment of a without notice application fee) to obtain a date for possession. The court will then specify the next working date as the possession date, without a hearing. However, here, notice must be given to the tenant who can admit or dispute the alleged breach. If there is no dispute or the breach is proved, the claimant is then able to enforce the possession order by applying to the court to issue a warrant of possession (see **10.11**).

10.9 TOLERATED TRESPASSERS

Until the House of Lords decision in *Knowsley Housing Trust v White* [2009] 1 AC 636 in relation to assured tenants, and the provisions in the Housing and Regeneration Act 2008 (see **10.8**), it was the case that a tenancy could terminate when a possession order was made.

The status of a tenant who remained in occupation could change to that of a 'tolerated trespasser' in various situations. Examples included:

(a) where the claimant had obtained an outright order for possession but then allowed the defendant to remain in occupation instead of applying for a warrant of possession;

(b) where a tenant had breached the terms of a suspended order and the tenancy had terminated as a result, but the 'tenant' remained in occupation; and

(c) where a warrant for possession was suspended or stayed.

The occupier was said to be in a state of limbo – neither tenant nor trespasser. He no longer had any contractual or statutory rights, and subsequent agreements with the landlord to pay off arrears would not, as indicated in a number of cases, change his status.

10.9.1 The effect of being a tolerated trespasser

As a tolerated trespasser, the ex-tenant had no contractual rights on which to maintain a claim against the landlord. There was no contractual basis for a claim for breach of the covenant to repair (see *Porter v Shepherds Bush Housing Association* [2008] EWCA Civ 196). The rights that go with certain tenancies – for example, the right to buy, to assign or to succession – were not available to a tolerated trespasser.

10.9.2 Reforms

There had been considerable criticism of the status of tolerated trespassers, not least because of the unclear and unsatisfactory state in which it left former tenants. Legislation has made provisions to address the problem. Section 299 of and Sch 11 to the Housing and Regeneration Act 2008 introduce amendments to the Housing Acts 1985, 1988 and 1996.

As the Tolerated Trespassers Guidance explains at paras 13 and 14:

> Part 1 of Schedule 11 (paragraphs 1–14) amends the 1985, 1988 and 1996 Housing Acts to provide that, where a possession order is made against a secure, assured, introductory or demoted tenant, the tenancy will end on the date on which the order for possession is executed (that is to say, when the court bailiff evicts the tenant) unless the tenant gives up possession of the property before that date. Together the provisions ensure that no tolerated trespassers will be created after the commencement date for Schedule 11.
>
> The provisions do not affect the position where the tenant voluntarily gives notice to quit or surrenders the tenancy. Where notice to quit is served, the tenancy will end once the notice period has elapsed or possibly on an earlier date if this is accepted by the landlord. The date on which a surrender is effective will depend on the facts of the case.

The Tolerated Trespassers Guidance explains that while Part 1 of Sch 11 to the 2008 Act prevents the creation of any new tolerated trespassers, Part 2 (paras 15–26) restores tenancy status to existing tolerated trespassers. It does this by granting new tenancies to former secure, assured, introductory and demoted tenants who became tolerated trespassers before the commencement date, so long as they meet specified conditions.

The conditions are that:

(a) the home condition is met, namely, that the dwelling house is the ex-tenant's only or principal home on the commencement date, and has been throughout the termination period, ie the period during which the occupant was a tolerated trespasser (alternatively, where the ex-tenant has been evicted and is absent from the property at the commencement date but is subsequently able to return to it because the warrant of eviction is set aside);

(b) the ex-landlord is entitled to let the dwelling-house; and

(c) the ex-landlord and ex-tenant have not in the meantime entered into a new tenancy.

The new tenancies are subject to any subsisting possession order that was still active against the original tenancy. The terms and conditions of the new tenancy will in general be the same as those of the original tenancy, except the rent will be the mesne profits that the tenant was paying at the commencement date or, if lower, the rent that is payable on existing tenancies of that type. New introductory and demoted tenancies will run for one year from the grant of the new tenancy.

10.10 CHALLENGING THE POSSESSION ORDER

It is possible for a tenant against whom a possession order has been made to challenge it in a number of ways. Application may be made to set aside the order, provided the conditions to do so are met; an appeal against the making of the order could be lodged; or application could be made to stay or suspend. Each of these is considered below.

10.10.1 Application to set aside the possession order

A defendant who did not attend the hearing may make application to set aside the possession order. Application can be made under CPR, r 3.1. However, the requirements in CPR, r 39.3 will be applied by analogy. Rule 39.3 will apply provided the defendant:

(a) acted promptly on becoming aware of the order;

(b) had a good excuse for not attending the hearing; and

(c) has a reasonable prospect of success at a reconvened trial.

If, as sometime happens, the tenant did not attend the hearing because he was led to believe, by his landlord, that it would not be necessary, then the court may accept this as a good reason for not having attended. The effect of a possession order being set aside is that the tenancy is restored as if an order had never been made.

All three requirements must be met before the courts will set a possession order aside, even where breach of Article 6 of the Convention (that the defendant did not have a fair trial) is pleaded.

In *Forcelux Ltd v Binnie* [2010] HLR 20, the Court of Appeal held that CPR, r 3.1 was wide enough to give the court power to set aside a possession order if, in its discretion, it considered that the interests of justice demanded it. This appeared to negate the requirement to satisfy the three-stage test in CPR, r 39.3. However in *Hackney LBC v Findlay* [2011] HLR 15, CA, it was held that in the absence of some unusual and highly compelling factor such as in *Forcelux* (where a long leaseholder would have lost a valuable asset for failure to pay a modest ground rent), a court that was asked to set aside a possession order under r 3.1 should, in general, apply the requirements of r 39.3 by analogy.

> **CASE EXAMPLE**
>
> In *Akram v Adam* [2005] 1 All ER 741, CA, the defendant, a protected tenant, applied to have set aside a possession order made against him in his absence. He alleged that he had not received the claim form, particulars of claim and notification of the hearing date, which had been sent to him by first-class post as permitted under CPR, r 6.2(1)(b). He argued that the right to notification was a fundamental principle of law, and even where service had been effected in accordance with the rules, the judgment should still be set aside as it would otherwise be incompatible with the right to a fair trial under Article 6 of the Convention. The Court of Appeal held that where there was proper service, the judgment could be set aside only as a matter of discretion (CPR, r 13.3), and on the facts of the case, as the defence had no merit, it would have been pointless to set the judgment aside. Article 6 of the Convention had not been breached as, in the absence of a defence with a real prospect of success or some other compelling reason for a trial, it did not require the parties and the court to indulge in an expensive and time-consuming charade.

An accelerated possession order made under CPR, r 55.17 can also be set aside or varied by CPR, r 55.19 either on an application by a party within 14 days of service of the order, or on the court's own initiative.

10.10.2 Appeal against a possession order

If a defendant cannot meet the requirement necessary to set aside a possession order (eg, because he did attend the hearing), he could try to appeal the order. By CPR, Part 52, a party can appeal to a circuit judge after having obtained permission from the district judge who heard the case or, failing this, from a circuit judge. The application is made on Form N161.

The tenant will need to show that there is a real prospect of the appeal succeeding, or that there is some other compelling reason why the appeal should be heard, for example that the judge has made an error of law or has not applied the law correctly in making the order. This may be difficult where the judge exercised his discretion in making the order. Notice needs to be filed within 21 days of the date of order. An application may need to be made, pending any appeal, to stay the possession order so that the landlord cannot execute it.

10.10.3 Stay, suspension or discharge of possession orders

For possession orders made as a result of the judge exercising his discretion, application can be made under s 85(2) of the HA 1985, s 9(2) of the HA 1988 or s 100(2) of the RA 1977, as appropriate, using Form N244, at any time before execution of the possession order, to stay or suspend execution of the order, or to postpone the date of possession. Application may be made by the former tenant, or by a non-tenant spouse, or former spouse or civil partner who has home rights under the Family Law Act 1996 and remains in occupation of the premises.

Application may also be made by the personal representative of a deceased tenant. In *Austin v Southwark LBC* [2010] 3 WLR 144, UKSC, it was held that the fact that the secure tenant had died did not deprive the court of its jurisdiction to exercise the power conferred on it by s 85(2)(b) of the HA 1985 to postpone the date of possession under a possession order. It was open to the applicant, as the personal representative of the person who had been served with a claim for possession, to apply for the date for possession to be postponed and thus revive the secure tenancy. The applicant had been living with his brother, the deceased tenant, for more than a year and so would now be eligible to succeed to the revived tenancy (see **6.8.2.1**).

Application would normally be made by the defendant, but the claimant may also apply to vary the terms of a suspended order if, for example, new facts suggest that a suspended possession order should be replaced by an outright order (see *Manchester City Council v Finn* [2002] EWCA Civ 1998).

If the conditions in a postponed or suspended possession order are complied with, the tenant may apply for the order to be discharged or rescinded (see HA 1985, s 85(4); HA 1988, s 9(4); RA 1977, s 100(4)).

10.11 WARRANTS FOR POSSESSION

A warrant for possession may be applied for by the claimant where a possession order has been obtained but the tenant remains in possession of the property.

The claimant can apply for a warrant of possession using Form N325. He can do this without the leave of the court at any time up to six years after the date of the possession order. No notice to the defendant is necessary in the county court unless the original order specified that no warrant was to be issued without the leave of the court. Once granted, the warrant will be valid for 12 months and be subject to renewal by the court.

The warrant for possession will be enforced by the court bailiffs, who have the power to evict everyone on the premises. The bailiffs normally give advance notice to the defendant and any other occupants of the property of when the execution of the warrant will take place, using Form N54. They also usually notify the defendant that an application may be made to the court to suspend the warrant. Under the various statutory provisions – namely, s 85(2) of the HA 1985; s 9(2) of the HA 1988; or s 100(2) of the RA 1977 – the court has the discretion to stay or suspend the warrant before execution. On an application by the defendant for a stay or suspension of the warrant of execution, it is open to the landlord to object to any such application by bringing new evidence to court, even if it relates to issues not before the court at the original hearing when the possession order was made (see *Sheffield City Council v Hopkins* [2001] All ER (D) 196, CA).

In *Arogundade v Brent LBC (No 2)* [2002] HLR 18, CA, the claimant had her claim for disrepair struck out and was debarred from defending a counter-claim by the defendant for possession of the property, because of her failure, for more than six months and despite repeated applications by the defendant, to put in a defence to the counter-claim. The claimant applied for the suspension of the warrant of execution of the possession order that subsequently had been obtained by the defendant. This was to enable the claimant to petition the House of Lords on the basis of a breach of her right to a fair trial under Article 6 of the Convention as well as of Article 1 of the First Protocol (right to property) (see **Chapter 4**). The Court of Appeal dismissed her application as being misconceived.

10.11.1 Oppression in the execution of a warrant

Once the warrant has been executed, the tenant is no longer able to rely on the statutory provisions mentioned above to undo the execution of the warrant; although if a late application to set aside the possession order is allowed, any warrant, whether or not executed, would fall with the setting aside of the possession order. Failing this, an executed warrant for possession can be set aside only if the defendant can show that it was obtained by fraud, or there has been an abuse of process or oppression in its execution.

It is difficult to define precisely what will amount to oppression, but maladministration by an LHA landlord comes within the category.

> **CASE EXAMPLE**
>
> In *Lambeth LBC v Hughes* (2002) 33 HLR 350, CA, the defendant was held to have made out a case of oppression when he established that he had received misleading advice from the court and was also misled as to the procedures that were available to him by the LHA landlord. He was led to believe by the LHA that payment in full of all the rent arrears would be required in order to avoid eviction, and he was wrongly led to believe, by the court, that eviction papers had not been issued. This was deemed to be unfair and sufficiently oppressive for the executed warrant to be set aside.

10.12 PUBLIC FUNDING AND POSSESSION PROCEEDINGS

As was discussed at **5.4.2**, unless there is a substantive defence to a possession claim, a defendant would normally obtain only Legal Help or Help at Court and not Full Representation.

The former LSC, in its aim to develop new and more responsive ways of delivering legal services to clients in need, introduced the Housing Possession Court Duty Schemes in a number of county courts in England to provide emergency assistance at court to people facing eviction proceedings. The Schemes operate without applying the normal rules relating to financial eligibility for the clients (see **5.2.4**).

10.13 CHECKLIST FOR POSSESSION CLAIMS

Legal advisers, whether representing the landlord or the tenant, should check that:

(a) the correct notice was served on the tenant to terminate the tenancy or to seek possession – with the correct time frame, according to the relevant statutory regime;

(b) the ground for possession is properly made out (for example, that arrears of rent are lawfully due and s 48 of the LTA 1987 has been complied with);

(c) in rent arrears only claims, brought by social landlords, the Pre-action Protocol for Possession Claims based on Rent Arrears has been complied with;

(d) the correct claim form and particulars of claim have been completed, giving all the relevant details as required in CPR Part 55, including a statement of truth;

(e) the defendant has/does not have a valid counter-claim (for example, breach of the covenant to repair);
(f) the claim has been issued in the correct court;
(g) service on the tenant was effected not less than 21 days before the hearing date (five days for trespassers);
(h) if a possession order is made, there are/are no grounds on which the tenant or landlord can challenge the order or the execution of any warrant for possession.

10.14 FURTHER READING

J Luba, N Madge and D McConnell, *Defending Possession Proceedings* (7th edn, 2010)
N Madge and C Sephton, *Housing Law Casebook* (5th edn, 2012)

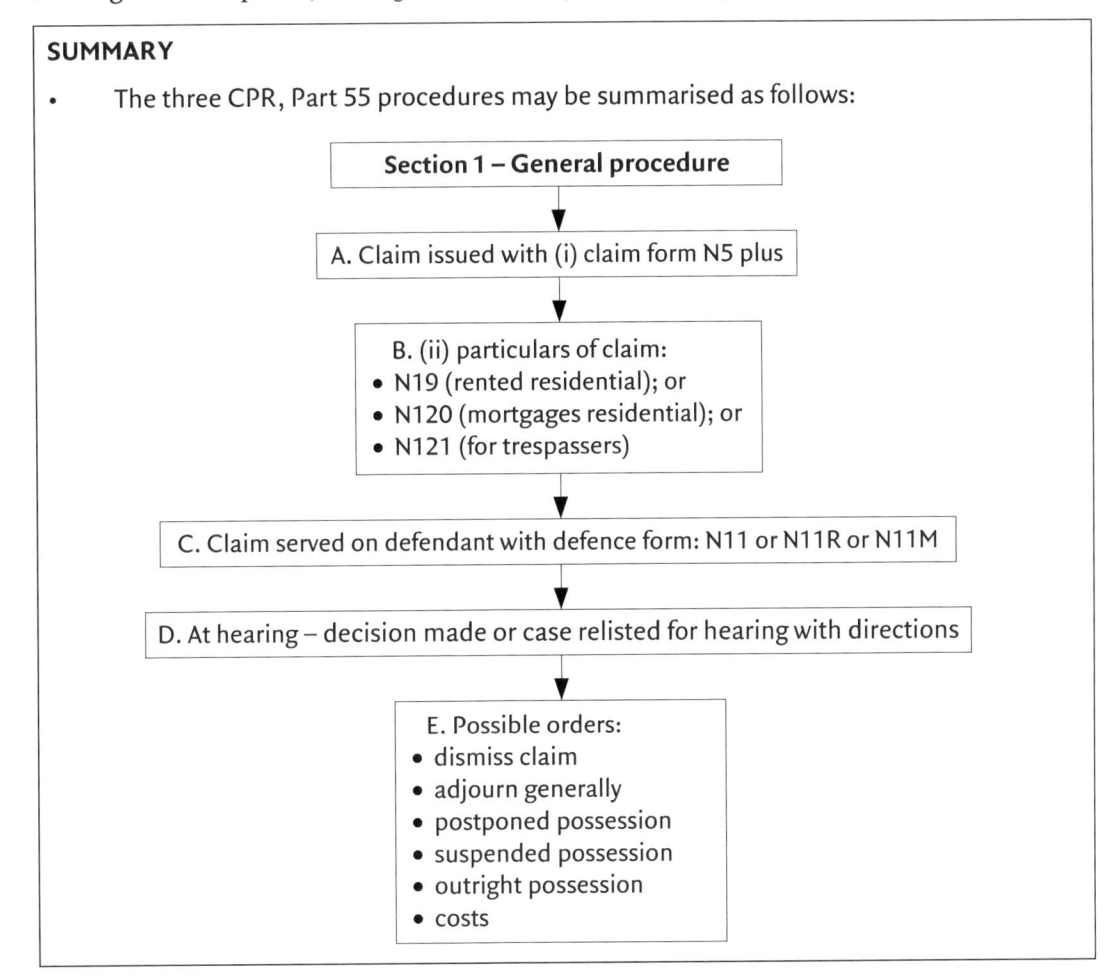

SUMMARY

- The three CPR, Part 55 procedures may be summarised as follows:

Section 1 – General procedure

↓

A. Claim issued with (i) claim form N5 plus

↓

B. (ii) particulars of claim:
- N19 (rented residential); or
- N120 (mortgages residential); or
- N121 (for trespassers)

↓

C. Claim served on defendant with defence form: N11 or N11R or N11M

↓

D. At hearing – decision made or case relisted for hearing with directions

↓

E. Possible orders:
- dismiss claim
- adjourn generally
- postponed possession
- suspended possession
- outright possession
- costs

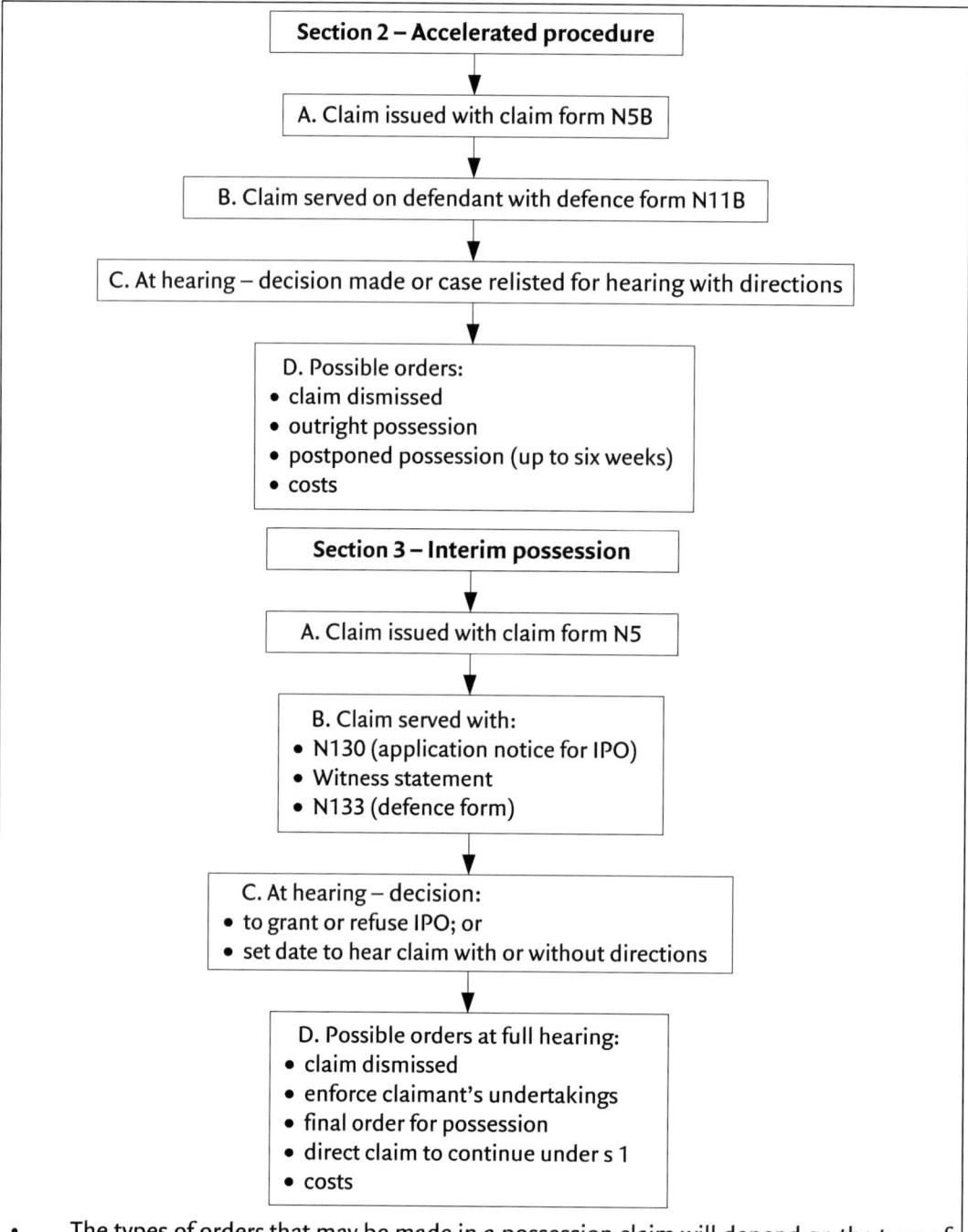

```
Section 2 – Accelerated procedure
            │
            ▼
A. Claim issued with claim form N5B
            │
            ▼
B. Claim served on defendant with defence form N11B
            │
            ▼
C. At hearing – decision made or case relisted for hearing with directions
            │
            ▼
D. Possible orders:
   • claim dismissed
   • outright possession
   • postponed possession (up to six weeks)
   • costs

Section 3 – Interim possession
            │
            ▼
A. Claim issued with claim form N5
            │
            ▼
B. Claim served with:
   • N130 (application notice for IPO)
   • Witness statement
   • N133 (defence form)
            │
            ▼
C. At hearing – decision:
   • to grant or refuse IPO; or
   • set date to hear claim with or without directions
            │
            ▼
D. Possible orders at full hearing:
   • claim dismissed
   • enforce claimant's undertakings
   • final order for possession
   • direct claim to continue under s 1
   • costs
```

- The types of orders that may be made in a possession claim will depend on the type of tenancy or other occupancy of the premises. This may be summarised as follows:

Type of tenancy or occupation	Notice required before proceedings?	Possible order if claim made out	Occupier's status after order
Contractual tenancy outside statutory regimes	Generally yes if periodic tenancy – PEA 1977, s 5. Notice to quit (min 4 weeks)	Outright – 14 days or up to 6 weeks (exceptional hardship)	Trespasser

Type of tenancy or occupation	Notice required before proceedings?	Possible order if claim made out	Occupier's status after order
Rent Act protected tenancy	Yes if periodic tenancy – PEA 1977, s 5. Notice to quit (min 4 weeks)	Tenant will become statutory tenant if still in occupation – see Rent Act statutory tenancy	
Rent Act statutory tenancy	No – see above	If mandatory ground – outright – 14 days or up to 6 weeks (exceptional hardship). If discretionary – suspended or postponed order on terms or outright	Trespasser or tenancy continues if terms of suspended order kept
Introductory tenancy (HA 1996)	Yes – HA 1996, s 128. Notice of proceedings for possession (min 4 weeks)	Outright – 14 days or up to 6 weeks (exceptional hardship)	Introductory tenant until leave or evicted
Secure periodic tenancy (HA 1985)	Yes – HA 1985, s 83. Notice of proceedings for possession (min 4 weeks unless Ground 2 claim where no minimum)	Discretionary – suspended or postponed order on terms or outright	Secure tenant until leave or evicted
Secure flexible tenancy (HA 1985)	Yes – as above if Sch 2 Ground or if terminating fixed term – HA 1985, s 107D (6 months and 2 months)	If discretionary – Sch 2 – suspended or postponed order on terms or outright. If terminating fixed term – mandatory ground – outright – 14 days or up to 6 weeks (exceptional hardship)	Secure flexible tenant until leave or evicted
Demoted tenancy (HA 1996)	Yes – HA 1996, s 143E. Notice of proceedings for possession (min 4 weeks)	Outright – 14 days or up to 6 weeks (exceptional hardship)	Demoted tenant until leave or evicted

Type of tenancy or occupation	Notice required before proceedings?	Possible order if claim made out	Occupier's status after order
Assured tenancy (HA 1988)	Yes – HA 1988, s 8. Notice of proceedings for possession (various lengths of notice – none, 2 weeks to 2 months)	If discretionary – Sch 2 – suspended or postponed order on terms or outright. If mandatory ground – outright – 14 days or up to 6 weeks (exceptional hardship)	Assured tenant until leave or evicted
Assured shorthold tenancy (HA 1988)	Yes – as above if Sch 2 Grounds – HA 1988, s 8. Notice of proceedings for possession (various lengths of notice – none, 2 weeks to 2 months or mandatory s 21 notice – minimum 2 months)	As above – if discretionary – Sch 2 – suspended order on terms or outright. If mandatory ground – outright – 14 days or up to 6 weeks (exceptional hardship)	Assured shorthold tenant until leave or evicted
Forfeiture of long lease (PEA 1977, s 2)	Yes if not for rent arrears – LPA 1925, s 146 – giving reasonable time for tenant to remedy breach	Relief – LPA 1925, s 146(2). HA 1996, s 81 for service charge arrears. County Court Act 1984, s 138 for rent arrears – court has discretion to grant relief on terms	Lease continues if relief given and terms kept. If no relief – outright possession order made – tenant will become trespasser
Mortgage repossession	Not required for borrower [but see now Protocol procedures and notice to unauthorised tenants]	Adjourn/stay/ suspend/ postpone/ possession – AJA 1970, s 36. Provided borrower likely to be able to repay [AJA 1973, s 8(2)]	Ownership continues if no outright order made, otherwise borrower becomes trespasser
Trespasser (squatter)	No	Immediate	Trespasser

CHAPTER 11

HOMELESSNESS I – THE LAW

11.1	Introduction	173
11.2	Eligibility for assistance	174
11.3	Homelessness	176
11.4	Priority need	180
11.5	Intentional homelessness	184
11.6	Local connection	187
11.7	Duties towards homeless persons	190
11.8	Further reading	196
	Summary	196

LEARNING OUTCOMES

After reading this chapter you will be able to:

- understand the legal definition of homelessness
- outline and explain the criteria for an applicant to be owed a duty under the homelessness provisions
- explain when local connection is relevant in homelessness cases
- list the different duties owed by LHAs to homeless applicants, depending on their homelessness status.

11.1 INTRODUCTION

This chapter will outline the law relating to homeless persons, and will deal with the help provided by LHAs to those who find themselves homeless.

11.1.1 Who is homeless?

Although this might seem a fairly obvious question to ask, the answer is far from straightforward in a legal context. Most visibly, there are 'rough sleepers' who live in shop doorways, hostel accommodation or night-shelters. A significant number of rough sleepers have a history of mental health problems, or alcohol or drug dependency. Many, particularly the young, are at risk from abuse or prostitution.

In addition to rough sleepers, there are also homeless families, occupying bed and breakfast accommodation or temporary housing, or staying with relatives in overcrowded conditions. These families may have lost their previous accommodation through debt or relationship breakdown, or may never have had their own home.

In addition to homeless families, there are many single homeless people who cannot afford their own accommodation and find themselves sleeping on a friend's floor, or staying with family in overcrowded conditions.

Lastly, there are people, who, although they have accommodation, cannot really call it a 'home' in any meaningful sense. This would include sick or disabled persons who cannot cope in their present accommodation, or people living in seriously dilapidated properties. It would also include people subjected to violence within the home, or to racial or other harassment from neighbours.

The problem of homelessness is, therefore, both diverse and complex. The response of successive Governments, through legislation, has been selective. Because of the cost and resource implications involved in helping the homeless, there is no automatic right to assistance. The approach has been to limit the help offered to those deemed to be 'in priority need', while the less needy receive only advice and assistance. The responsibility for helping those in priority need has been placed upon LHAs, while those not entitled to assistance are reliant upon housing charities and voluntary organisations.

From a legal perspective, therefore, it is crucially important to know what type of statutory duties exist and to whom they are owed. Before considering these in detail, it is useful to have an overview of the relevant legislative provisions.

11.1.2 The legislation in outline

The main piece of legislation dealing with homeless persons is Pt VII of the HA 1996, as amended by the Homelessness Act 2002 and the Localism Act 2011. This sets out who is eligible for assistance and what duties are owed to eligible persons. It also sets out a statutory review scheme for applicants who are refused assistance and, ultimately, provides for an appeal to the county court.

The Act is supplemented by various codes of guidance, the most relevant of which is the Homelessness Code of Guidance for Local Authorities (the 'Homelessness Code of Guidance') to which LHAs are required to 'have regard' (HA 1996, s 182). There is also a supplementary Homelessness Code issued in August 2009 to give specific guidance on how LHAs should exercise their homelessness functions in deciding whether applicants are intentionally or unintentionally homeless, having lost their homes because of difficulties in meeting mortgage commitments.

11.1.3 The role of the lawyer

Homeless applicants may seek advice from a solicitor about a wide range of issues. Common problems include the following matters:

(a) *Initial application.* The client may be about to make an initial application for assistance and may be seeking guidance on whether he is eligible and, if so, what duties are owed by the LHA.

(b) *Initial refusal.* The client may have already made an application which has been refused. In such circumstances, advice will be required to enable the client to seek a review of the refusal to provide assistance.

(c) *Refusal on review.* The client may already have requested a review of the refusal to provide assistance. Where that review has been unsuccessful, the client will require advice about whether he has grounds to appeal to the court.

(d) *Suitability of temporary accommodation.* The client may have been provided with temporary accommodation by the LHA under its housing duties, but may not regard the accommodation as suitable for his needs. Legal advice will be required as to the extent of the duties on LHAs to provide suitable accommodation, including consideration of whether the actual accommodation provided is suitable.

The issues referred to above are not intended to be exhaustive, although they are illustrative of the range of problems that arise in relation to typical homelessness cases. It is now necessary to look at the legislative provisions in more detail.

11.2 ELIGIBILITY FOR ASSISTANCE

In order to make an application to an LHA for assistance as a homeless person, an applicant must be 'eligible for assistance'. Most applicants will be eligible, but problems may arise in relation to 'persons from abroad' and those not 'habitually resident' in the UK.

The eligibility provisions are complex and require cross-reference to a number of other Acts and various sets of regulations beyond the scope of this chapter. The following is a brief summary of the provisions. If eligibility is an issue, careful consideration of the applicant's immigration position and the relevant statutory provisions will be necessary.

11.2.1 Persons from abroad

Section 185(1) of the HA 1996 provides that a person is not eligible for assistance if he is a person from abroad who is ineligible for housing assistance. Section 185(2) goes on to state that a person who is subject to immigration control within the meaning of the Asylum and Immigration Act (AIA) 1996 is not eligible for housing assistance unless he is of a class prescribed by regulations made by the Secretary of State. Section 185(3) provides that the Secretary of State may make provision by regulations as to other persons who are to be treated as persons from abroad who are ineligible for assistance.

The effect of these provisions is to create two categories of persons from abroad who are not eligible for assistance:

(a) s 185(2) excludes from assistance those subject to immigration control, unless they are re-qualified by regulations made by the Secretary of State;

(b) s 185(3) excludes those who, while not subject to immigration control, are nevertheless excluded by regulations.

11.2.1.1 Subject to immigration control

The term 'subject to immigration control' is defined in s 13(2) of the AIA 1996 as meaning a person who, under the Immigration Act 1971, requires leave to enter or remain in the United Kingdom (whether or not such leave has been given). Those not requiring leave to enter or remain include British citizens.

Generally, persons subject to immigration control are ineligible for homeless assistance. However, the Allocation of Housing and Homelessness (Eligibility) (England) Regulations 2006 (SI 2006/1294), as amended, provide a list of persons who, despite being subject to immigration control, are nevertheless re-qualified as eligible. These include recognised refugees, those granted exceptional leave to enter or remain in the UK whose leave is not subject to a requirement that they can maintain and accommodate themselves without recourse to public funds, and those who sought asylum in the UK before 3 April 2000 who are still awaiting a decision on their asylum claim. (Asylum seekers who applied after that date are ineligible for assistance under the HA 1996. Furthermore, even asylum seekers who applied before 3 April 2000 are excluded if they have some accommodation available to them, however temporary (HA 1996, s 186(1).)

11.2.1.2 Habitual residence

The second class of person deemed ineligible for assistance are those in respect of whom regulations have been passed declaring them to be ineligible. This is the case with those not 'habitually resident' within the UK (Allocation of Housing and Homelessness (Eligibility) (England) Regulations 2006, reg 6 (**11.2.1.1** above)). In practice, this affects applicants arriving in or returning to the UK during the two-year period prior to making their application (Homelessness Code of Guidance, Annex 10, para 1).

In order to be eligible for assistance, such applicants must be habitually resident in the UK, the Channel Islands, the Isle of Man or the Republic of Ireland (the 'Common Travel Area'). Habitual residence is a question of fact and depends on all the circumstances of the case. Relevant considerations include where one intends to reside, the length and continuity of residence, and family, social and work connections (see *Nessa v Chief Adjudication Officer* [1999] 1 WLR 1937, HL; *R (Paul-Coker) v Southwark LBC* [2006] HLR 32).

Special provisions waiving the normal habitual residence requirements for British citizens and British nationals returning from Zimbabwe were introduced into the 2006 Regulations as a result of amendments in SI 2009/358.

Workers from the EU and their family members are entitled to assistance without having to prove habitual residence (Allocation of Housing and Homelessness (Eligibility) (England) Regulations 2006, reg 6). However, an applicant from a Member State who is permanently unable to work will not be eligible for assistance (see *Samin v Westminster City Council* [2012] EWCA Civ 1468).

11.2.2 Partially eligible households

It is sometimes the case that certain family members are eligible for assistance and others are not. For example, a couple may have different immigration status from one another, or children have different status from their parents. In certain cases, ineligible members of the household cannot be taken into account by the LHA when deciding whether an applicant is homeless, threatened with homelessness or in priority need (HA 1996, s 185(4)).

It used be the case that the disregard of ineligible members applied to all homelessness applicants. However, as a result of amendments to s 185 introduced by s 314 of and Sch 15 to the Housing and Regeneration Act 2008, the disregards no longer apply in the case of an applicant for housing assistance who is a British citizen, a Commonwealth citizen with a right of abode in the UK, or an EEA or Swiss national exercising an EU Treaty right to reside in the UK. However, applicants who are persons with refugee status, persons who have humanitarian protection or persons with exceptional or indefinite leave to enter or remain will still be subject to the disregards in s 185(4).

(See **11.4.7** below in relation to priority need and the discussion there of *Bah v UK* [2011] ECHR 1448.)

```
                    Is the applicant eligible for assistance (HA 1996, s 185)?
                                    │                    │
                                    ▼                    ▼
                                   Yes                   No
                                    │                    │
                                    ▼                    ▼
              Consider whether the applicant       No duty is owed
              • is homeless
              • is in priority need
              • is unintentionally homeless
              • has a local connection
```

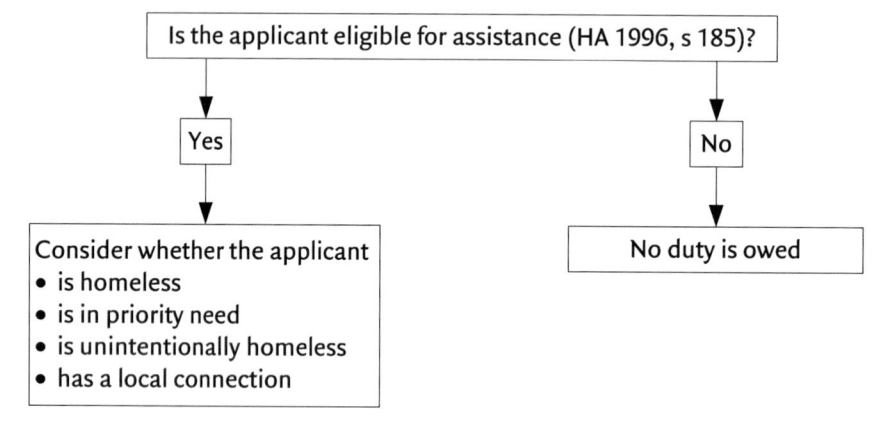

Figure 11.1 – Summary

11.3 HOMELESSNESS

11.3.1 The statutory definition

Local housing authority duties towards eligible applicants arise when a person is homeless or threatened with homelessness, as defined by s 175 of the HA 1996. Section 175(1) provides that a person is homeless if he has no accommodation for his occupation, in the UK or elsewhere, which he:

(a) is entitled to occupy by virtue of an interest in it or by virtue of a court order; or

(b) has an express or implied licence to occupy; or

(c) occupies by virtue of any enactment or rule of law giving him the right to remain in occupation.

A person may also be homeless if he has accommodation but cannot secure entry to it, or, where it is a moveable structure, has nowhere to place it and reside in it (s 175(2)).

Furthermore, a person shall not be treated as having accommodation unless it is accommodation which it would be reasonable for him to continue to occupy (s 175(3)).

A person is threatened with homelessness if it is likely that he will become homeless within 28 days (s 175(4)).

All these provisions are discussed in further detail below.

11.3.2 Accommodation

The first question that arises under s 175 is what is meant by the term 'accommodation'. Generally, the usual meaning is given to the word (R v Brent LBC, ex p Awua [1996] 1 AC 55), but the courts have found that there will be some types of property which will not constitute accommodation. An example of this is a night shelter (R v Waveney District Council, ex p Bowers (1982) The Times, 25 May, QBD). In Manchester City Council v Moran [2009] 1 WLR 1506, the House of Lords considered whether women's refuges were 'accommodation' within s 175. Their Lordships decided that it would not be reasonable for a woman who had left her home because of domestic or other violence and found a temporary haven in a women's refuge to continue to occupy her place there indefinitely. Consequently, the applicant remains homeless. As a result, it became unnecessary to decide whether a refuge could be 'accommodation' within the meaning of the Act. Residents of night shelters may be considered homeless, despite the fact that they have some form of temporary accommodation available to them.

Section 176 of the HA 1996 provides that accommodation shall be regarded as available for a person's occupation only if it is available for occupation by him together with:

(a) any other person who normally resides with him as a member of his family; or
(b) any other person who might reasonably be expected to reside with him.

The Homelessness Code of Guidance provides that 'member of his family' includes 'those with close blood or marital relationships and cohabiting partners' (including same-sex partners) (para 8.5), while 'any other person' might include, for example, a housekeeper or a companion for an elderly or disabled person, or children who are being fostered by the applicant (para 8.5).

Section 176(b) also refers to those who may not have been living as part of the household at the time of the application but whom it would be reasonable to expect to reside with the applicant. The question of whether a person might reasonably be expected to reside with the applicant is a question for the LHA to consider. The Homelessness Code of Guidance provides that persons who normally live with the applicant but are unable to do so because there is no accommodation in which they can all live together, should be included in the assessment (para 8.6).

The accommodation must also be accessible in both a practical and a legal sense (Begum (Nipa) v Tower Hamlets LBC [2000] 1 QB 133, CA). Practical accessibility includes whether the person can physically access the property, while legal accessibility concerns whether the person has a right to access the property.

It should be noted that it is not just accommodation in the UK that is taken into account when considering whether someone is homeless. The LHA will look at accommodation anywhere in world (see Begum (Nipa) v Tower Hamlets LBC, referred to above, where the applicant was held not to be homeless because she had accommodation available to her in Bangladesh in her father-in-law's house, in which it was reasonable for her reside).

In Sharif v Camden LBC [2013] UKSC 10, it was held that two adjoining flats offered to S, one to be occupied by S and her minor sister and the other for her father, for whom she cared, satisfied the provision in s 176. The word 'accommodation' was not to be equated with 'unit of accommodation'. The statutory test could be satisfied if the two units were so located that they enabled the family to live together in practical terms.

11.3.3 Basis of occupancy

In order to have accommodation, a person must have some form of right to reside in the property. Section 175(1)(a)–(c) of the HA 1996 set out the situations in which a person will be treated as having a right to occupy.

11.3.3.1 Right to occupy under an interest or an order of the court

This includes those with a legal interest in property, such as an owner or a tenant. It also includes those with an equitable interest, such as the husband or wife of an owner, who would have rights by virtue of the marriage. Those with rights under a court order would again include spouses, who could be given rights during family court proceedings.

11.3.3.2 An express or implied licence to occupy

This covers those with an interest falling short of a tenancy, known as a 'licence to occupy', which may be either express or implied. It would include lodgers or people sharing flats or houses, or children living with their parents.

11.3.3.3 Occupation under an enactment or rule of law

This includes persons who have had rights of occupation conferred by statute. An example would be a statutory tenant under the RA 1977. In order to retain such protection, continued occupation is required (ie, the right will be lost if the person moves out of the accommodation).

11.3.4 Securing entry and moveable structures

A person with accommodation may nevertheless be homeless if he cannot secure entry into the property, or, in the case of a moveable structure, such as a caravan or houseboat, has nowhere to site or moor it (HA 1996, s 175(2)).

A person may not be able to secure entry to a property if he has been locked out illegally by his landlord. If someone has been unlawfully evicted from his home, the LHA would usually require him to take steps to enforce his legal right to re-entry. However, this may be futile in certain circumstances, such as where the landlord is likely to re-evict again. In such situations, although the landlord will be committing a criminal offence, it may not be possible to enforce the right to re-entry, and the LHA may decide that the person is homeless without requiring him to take legal proceedings against the landlord.

11.3.5 Reasonableness to continue to occupy

A person will not be treated as having accommodation unless it is accommodation which it would be reasonable to continue to occupy (HA 1996, s 175(3)). This subsection applies only to accommodation that is already occupied by the applicant, and does not include other accommodation which may be available to the applicant but which he does not actually occupy.

In *Birmingham City Council v Ali* [2009] 1 WLR 1506, HL, the House of Lords decided that s 175(3) was looking to the future as well as to the present, and accommodation that might be unreasonable for persons to occupy for a long period might be reasonable for them to occupy for a short period. The LHA was entitled to decide that the families were homeless because it would not be reasonable for them to remain in their current accommodation indefinitely. However, the LHA could then leave them there for the short term. It would be a question of fact whether the period was too long.

The question of reasonableness is dealt with in s 177 of the HA 1996, which sets out a number of circumstances in which it will not, or may not, be reasonable to continue to occupy accommodation.

11.3.5.1 Violence

It is not reasonable for a person to continue to occupy accommodation if it is probable that this will lead to domestic violence or other violence against him, or against a person who normally resides with him as a member of his family or any other person who might reasonably be expected to reside with him (HA 1996, s 177(1)).

'Violence' means violence from another person, or threats of violence from another person which are likely to be carried out. Such violence is 'domestic' if it is from a person associated with the victim (HA 1996, s 177(1A)). The Supreme Court in *Yemshaw v Hounslow London Borough Council* [2011] 1 WLR 433 has interpreted domestic violence to include physical violence, threatening or intimidating behaviour and any other form of abuse which, directly or indirectly, may give rise to the risk of harm. In deciding on a particular case, the test to be applied is the view of the objective outsider, applied to the particular facts, circumstances and personalities of the people involved.

11.3.5.2 General housing circumstances in the area

In determining whether it would be reasonable to continue to occupy accommodation, regard may be had to general circumstances prevailing in relation to housing conditions in the district of the LHA to which the applicant applies for assistance (HA 1996, s 177(2)). This covers issues such as the physical condition of the property and the level of overcrowding. However, even if a property was deemed unfit for human habitation, the occupant will not necessarily be considered homeless if, for example, the LHA is taking steps to deal with the state of repair of the property (see *R v Kensington and Chelsea RLBC, ex p Ben-El-Mabrouk* (1995) 27 HLR 564, CA).

In *Harouki v Kensington and Chelsea RLBC* [2008] 1 WLR 797, CA, the tenant, H, had a tenancy of a three-bedroom flat which she occupied with her husband and five children. The accommodation was found to be overcrowded (see **6.7.2.1**). It was deemed fit for occupation by only five and a half persons. The family counted as six. There was some overcrowding which amounted to an offence under s 327 of the HA 1985. H applied as homeless to her LHA. The LHA decided, and its decision was upheld in the Court of Appeal, that having regard to the general circumstances relating to housing in the district, it would be reasonable for H to continue to occupy the accommodation. It was not so overcrowded that it was unreasonable for H and her family to continue to occupy it.

11.3.5.3 Other specified circumstances

The Secretary of State may specify other circumstances in which it is to be regarded as reasonable or not reasonable for a person to continue to occupy accommodation (HA 1996, s 177(3)). One such specified circumstance is the question of whether the accommodation is affordable for the applicant (Homelessness (Suitability of Accommodation) Order 1996 (SI 1996/3204)). The Homelessness Code of Guidance states that affordability must be considered in all cases (para 8.29).

11.3.6 Threatened with homelessness

A person is threatened with homelessness if he will become homeless within 28 days (HA 1996, s 175(4)). This means that if an applicant approaches a LHA for assistance within the 28-day period, it should start making enquiries into his case. The applicant should not be required to wait until he actually becomes homeless. This is often of great practical significance for applicants, since LHAs will often try to defer their enquiries until a later stage, but this would be unlawful (*R v Newham LBC, ex p Khan and Hussain* (2001) 33 HLR 29, QBD).

```
┌─────────────────────────────────────────────┐
│ Is the applicant eligible for assistance (HA 1996, s 185)? │
└─────────────────────────────────────────────┘
        │                           │
        ▼                           ▼
      ┌─────┐                   ┌─────┐
      │ Yes │                   │ No  │
      └─────┘                   └─────┘
        │                           │
        ▼                           ▼
┌──────────────────────┐      ┌──────────────┐
│ Is the applicant     │      │ No duty is owed │
│ homeless             │──┐   └──────────────┘
│ (HA 1996, s 175)?    │  │
└──────────────────────┘  │
        │                 │
        ▼                 ▼
      ┌─────┐           ┌─────┐
      │ Yes │           │ No  │
      └─────┘           └─────┘
        │                 │
        ▼                 ▼
┌──────────────────────┐  ┌──────────────┐
│ Consider whether the │  │ No duty is owed │
│ applicant            │  └──────────────┘
│ • is in priority need│
│ • is unintentionally │
│   homeless           │
│ • has a local        │
│   connection         │
└──────────────────────┘
```

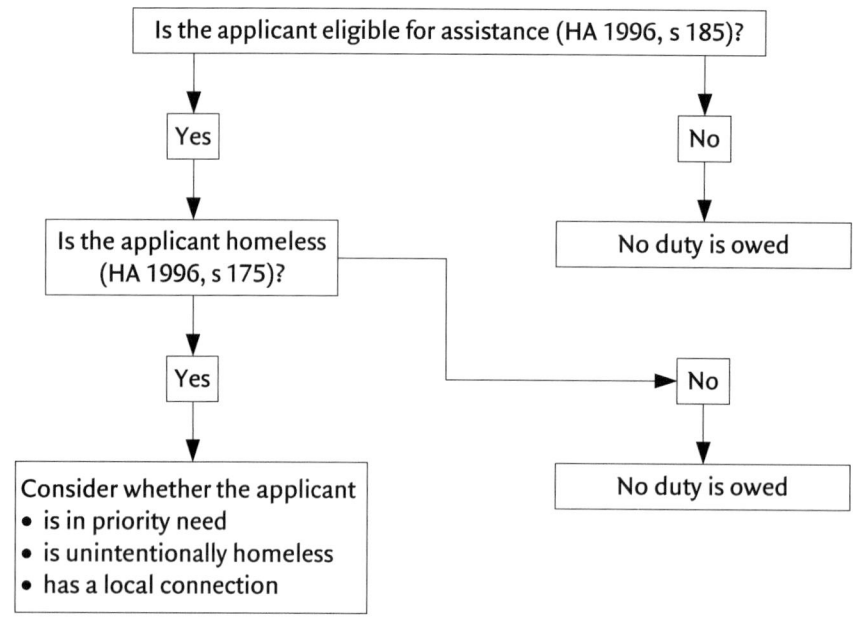

Figure 11.2 – Summary

11.4 PRIORITY NEED

In addition to being eligible for assistance and homeless within the meaning of the statute, in order to obtain housing an applicant must also be in priority need. This means that not all homeless persons will actually qualify for help from an LHA. The effect of the legislation is to target the assistance at those deemed to be most in need of the limited help available. Homeless applicants who are not in priority need will generally be offered only 'advice and assistance' (see **11.7** for more detail).

11.4.1 Who is in priority need?

Priority need is defined in s 189(1) of the HA 1996. The section provides that the following persons have a priority need for accommodation:

(a) a pregnant woman, or a person with whom she resides or might reasonably be expected to reside;

(b) a person with whom dependent children reside or might reasonably be expected to reside;

(c) a person who is vulnerable as a result of old age, mental illness or handicap or physical disability or other special reason, or with whom such a person resides or might reasonably be expected to reside;

(d) a person who is homeless or threatened with homelessness as a result of an emergency such as flood, fire or other disaster.

Section 189(2) goes on to provide that the Secretary of State may, by order, specify further descriptions of people as having a priority need for accommodation.

11.4.2 Pregnant women

Confirmed pregnancy at any stage will place a woman in priority need. Under the Homelessness Code of Guidance (para 10.5), if a pregnant woman suffers a miscarriage or terminates her pregnancy during the assessment process, the housing authority should consider whether she may continue to be in priority need as a result of some other factor, for example as a result of 'some other special reason' (see **11.4.4** below). Note that a person who resides with a pregnant woman, or who might reasonably be expected to reside with her, such as the father of the baby, will also be in priority need.

11.4.3 Dependent children

In the case of dependent children, it is important to note that it is not the children themselves who are in priority need but the person with whom they reside or might reasonably be expected to reside. The Homelessness Code of Guidance states (para 10.6) that actual residence with some degree of permanence or regularity is required, rather than a temporary arrangement. The children must also be dependent (either financially or otherwise) upon the applicant and not on some other person.

The HA 1996 does not define 'dependent children', but the Homelessness Code of Guidance provides that housing authorities may wish to treat as dependent all children under 16 years of age and all children aged 16 to 18 who are in, or about to begin, full-time education or training, or who for other reasons cannot support themselves and who live at home (para 10.7). The case of *Miah v Newham LBC* [2001] EWCA Civ 487, (2001) June 2001 LAG Bulletin 25, CA, confirms that this covers children under 19 and does not exclude children from the time they reach their 18th birthday.

The children need not be the applicant's own children and could include, for example, foster children (para 10.8).

Where parents are separated, there may be a residence order indicating with which parent the children will live. If there is no residence order, the LHA has to decide which parent has residence on the facts of the case. It will only be in very exceptional cases that a child might be considered to reside with both parents. See, for example, the case of *R v Oxford CC, ex p Doyle* (1998) 30 HLR 506, QBD, where a father with a joint residence order and children residing with him from Thursday to Monday each week, was held not to be in priority need. See also *Holmes-Moorhouse v Richmond upon Thames LBC* [2009] 1 WLR 413, HL, and *El Goure v Kensington and Chelsea RLBC* [2012] EWCA Civ 670.

11.4.4 Vulnerability

Vulnerability in this context has been defined as, when homeless, being less able to fend for oneself than an ordinary homeless person, so that injury or detriment would have resulted when a less vulnerable person would be able to cope without harmful effect (*R v Camden LBC, ex p Pereira* (1999) 31 HLR 317, CA). This has become known as the 'Pereira test' and requires a two-stage approach (*R v Waveney DC, ex p Bowers* [1983] 1 QB 238, CA). In the first place the authority must decide whether or not the applicant is vulnerable and, secondly, if so, whether his vulnerability arises from any of the reasons set out in s 189(1)(c) of the HA 1996 (see **11.4.4.1** to **11.4.4.3** below).

When assessing vulnerability, the authority must consider the applicant's ability to fend for himself if he were to be living on the street (*Osmani v Camden LBC* [2004] ECWCA Civ 1706, CA). The authority should take into account any medical or other evidence presented by the applicant, but it is ultimately for the authority to decide whether the applicant is vulnerable (*Osmani v Camden LBC* above). However, should the authority decide against the applicant, it should explain its reasons for rejecting any evidence provided (*Hall v Wandsworth LBC; Carter v Wandsworth LBC* [2004] EWCA Civ 1740).

The grounds of vulnerability are set out in s 189(1)(c) and are as follows.

11.4.4.1 Old age

The Homelessness Code of Guidance states that old age alone is not sufficient to make someone vulnerable, but that it may be that, as a result of old age, a person would be less able to fend for himself or herself. The Code goes on to provide that all applications from the over-60s should therefore be carefully considered (para 10.15).

11.4.4.2 Mental illness, learning or physical disability

The Code uses slightly different wording from s 189(1)(c), referring to learning disability rather than mental handicap. It provides (para 10.16) that LHAs should have regard to the nature and extent of the illness or disability, the relationship between the illness or disability and the applicant's housing difficulties, and factors such as drug or alcohol misuse.

There are special provisions relating to applicants discharged from psychiatric hospitals, and particular duties to coordinate their care and housing needs.

Local housing authorities have to look at individual circumstances and seek appropriate medical evidence including, where necessary, in circumstances where the applicant suffers from a disability or long-term acute illness (para 10.18).

11.4.4.3 Some other special reason

When determining whether a person may be vulnerable for some other special reason, housing authorities must have regard to the facts and circumstances of the particular case (Homelessness Code of Guidance, para 10.30).

11.4.5 Emergency or other disaster

Flood and fire are examples of qualifying types of emergency, but are not exhaustive. The event must be both an emergency and a disaster, and must involve some form of physical damage or threat of damage to the property rendering it uninhabitable. This would exclude, for example, the situation where someone had been unlawfully evicted, which would not constitute an emergency for these purposes (R v Bristol CC, ex p Bradic (1995) 27 HLR 584, CA).

The event must also be sudden. For example, see R v Walsall MBC, ex p Price [1996] CLY 3068, QBD, where a property became infested with vermin and had its utilities cut off over a period of weeks. This was held not to constitute an emergency within the meaning of the HA 1996 as it did not occur suddenly.

Applicants have a priority need by reason of emergency whether or not they have children or are vulnerable for any reason (para 10.42).

11.4.6 Other categories of priority need

Other categories of priority need have been added by regulation. These are slightly different depending upon whether the application is made in England or in Wales. The Homeless Persons (Priority Need for Accommodation) (England) Order 2002 (SI 2002/2051) governs the position in England, while the Homeless Persons (Priority Need) (Wales) Order 2001 (SI 2001/607) governs the position in Wales.

The England Order adds the following additional categories of priority need:

(a) 16- and 17-year-olds (except care leavers or those owed a duty under s 20 of the Children Act 1989 who are the responsibility of Social Services);

(b) young people under 21 (except students) who were in care at any time between the ages of 16 and 18);

(c) persons who are vulnerable because of their institutional background, ie care leavers aged over 21, vulnerable former members of the armed forces, and vulnerable former prisoners; and

(d) those vulnerable due to fleeing violence.

The Welsh Order adds the following additional categories:

(a) 18 to 20-year-olds (if previously in care, or if they are at particular risk of sexual or financial exploitation);

(b) 16- and 17-year-olds;

(c) persons fleeing domestic violence or threatened domestic violence;

(d) persons leaving the armed forces (who have been homeless since leaving the forces); and

(e) former prisoners (who have been homeless since leaving custody).

11.4.7 Priority need and non-eligible persons

Generally speaking, persons who are not eligible for assistance because of their immigration status (see **11.2** above) cannot be taken into account for the purposes of assessing priority need (HA 1996, s 185(4)). The effect of this is that an eligible applicant without priority need cannot acquire priority need from an ineligible person. So, for example, an eligible applicant whose priority need was based on the fact that a disabled person resided with him could not acquire priority need from the disabled person if that person was ineligible for assistance.

It used to be the case that an eligible British parent could not acquire priority need by reliance upon an ineligible dependent child. This was held to be incompatible with Article 8 of the European Convention of Human Rights (right to respect for private and family life) in the jointly considered cases of R (Morris) v Westminster City Council; R (Badu) v Lambeth LBC [2005] EWCA Civ 1184, [2006] 1 WLR 505, CA. The provisions in the HA 1996 have been amended by Sch 15 to the Housing and Regeneration Act 2008 to address this issue. Where a duty is owed to an applicant who is found to be homeless and to have a priority need only by reliance on a household member who is a 'restricted person' (see below), the application will be known as a 'restricted case' (s 193(3B)). In a restricted case, the duty owed to such an applicant may be discharged in a more limited way than in relation to an eligible applicant whose priority status is not dependent on a restricted person (see **11.7.5.1** and *Lekpo-Bozua v Hackney LBC* [2010] EWCA Civ 909).

A restricted person is defined in s 184(7) of the HA 1996 as someone who requires leave to enter or remain in the UK and does not have it, or a person who does have the required leave but that leave was granted on the condition that the person would have no recourse to public funds.

Human rights challenge

The difference in the treatment of non-British applicants on the eligibility and priority status of their dependants was unsuccessfully challenged in *Bah v UK* [2011] ECHR 1448.

The applicant (B), an asylum-seeker from Sierra Leone, was given indefinite leave to remain in the UK in 2005. In 2007 her 11-year-old son joined her and was given leave to remain on condition that he did not have recourse to public funding. Shortly after, B applied to Southwark LHA as homeless. The LHA found B unintentionally homeless but not in priority need, as, due to the conditions of his entry and his immigration status, her son was not an eligible person. However, the LHA helped her to find accommodation in the private sector.

B complained to the European Court of Human Rights that there had been a violation of her rights under Articles 8 and 14 of the Convention. She had been treated differently based on the nationality of her son. The Court held that it was justifiable to distinguish between those who relied for priority need status on a person who was in the UK on condition that they had no recourse to public funds, and those who did not. Given that B had never actually become homeless and that, had she been accorded priority need, she would most likely have been housed in temporary private accommodation until a social tenancy became available, the differential treatment to which she was subjected was reasonably and objectively justified by the need to allocate fairly the available social housing between different categories of claimants and was not disproportionate to the legitimate aim pursued. Accordingly, there had been no breach of Article 14, taken in conjunction with Article 8.

Flowchart

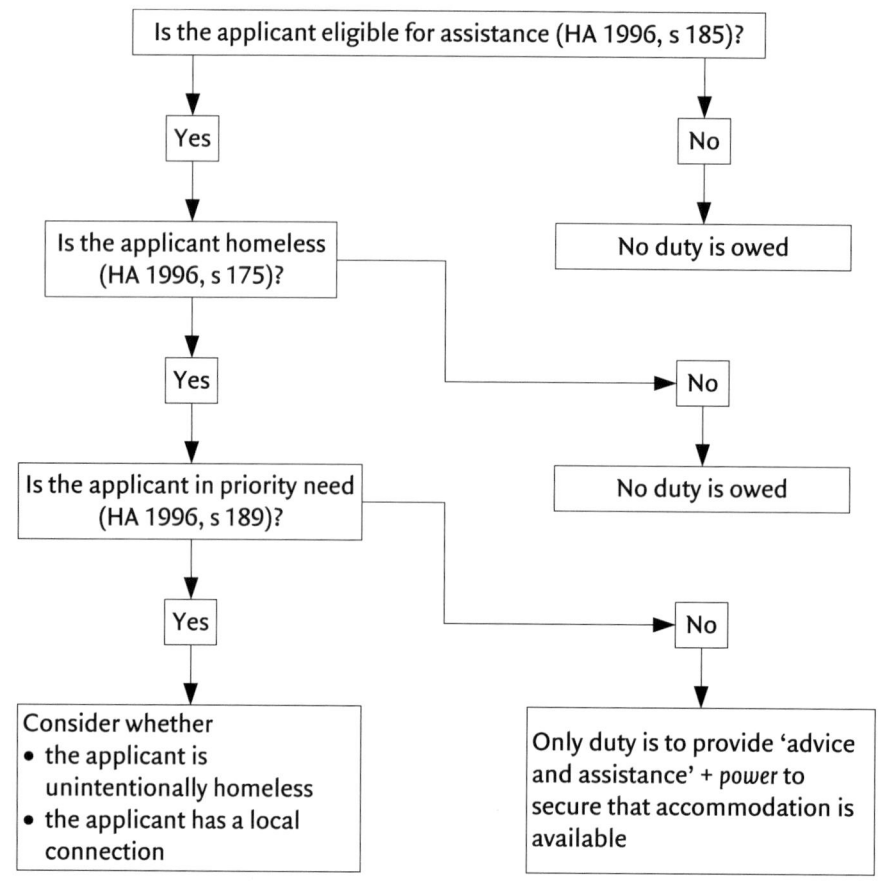

- Is the applicant eligible for assistance (HA 1996, s 185)?
  - Yes → Is the applicant homeless (HA 1996, s 175)?
    - Yes → Is the applicant in priority need (HA 1996, s 189)?
      - Yes → Consider whether
        - the applicant is unintentionally homeless
        - the applicant has a local connection
      - No → Only duty is to provide 'advice and assistance' + *power* to secure that accommodation is available
    - No → No duty is owed
  - No → No duty is owed

Figure 11.3 – Summary

11.5 INTENTIONAL HOMELESSNESS

In addition to being eligible for assistance, homeless and in priority need, applicants must also not be intentionally homeless. This is dealt with in s 191 of the HA 1996 and essentially excludes applicants who have made themselves homeless.

Section 191(1) provides that a person becomes homeless intentionally if he deliberately does or fails to do anything, in consequence of which he ceases to occupy accommodation which is available for his occupation and which it would have been reasonable for him to continue to occupy. Section 191(2) provides that an act or omission in good faith on the part of a person who was unaware of any relevant fact shall not be treated as deliberate.

Section 191(3) goes on to provide for a further situation in which intentional homelessness may arise, namely where a person enters into an arrangement under which he is required to cease to occupy accommodation which it would have been reasonable for him to continue to occupy, and the purpose of the arrangement was to enable him to become entitled to assistance as a homeless person and there is no other good reason why he is homeless.

11.5.1 The meaning of 'intentionality'

For an applicant to be found intentionally homeless, he must have deliberately done something or failed to do something which led to the loss of accommodation. The provision applies only to accommodation which an applicant loses, and not to some other accommodation which he might have been able to move into. The accommodation must have been available for the applicant's occupation and it must have been reasonable for him to continue to occupy the accommodation (R v Brent LBC, ex p Awua [1996] 1 AC 55, HL).

11.5.2 Deliberate act or omission

Intention requires a deliberate act or omission. The Homelessness Code of Guidance (para 11.20) provides various examples of deliberate acts or omissions which might lead to the loss of accommodation. These include:

(a) where someone chooses to sell his home in circumstances where he is under no risk of losing it;

(b) where someone loses his home through wilful and persistent refusal to make rent or mortgage payments;

(c) where someone significantly neglects his affairs having disregarded sound advice from qualified persons;

(d) voluntary surrender of adequate accommodation in this country or abroad which it would have been reasonable to continue to occupy;

(e) eviction due to anti-social behaviour, or nuisance/harassment or violence to others;

(f) eviction due to violence or threats of violence by the applicant towards another person; and

(g) where someone leaves a job with tied accommodation, where it would have been reasonable for him to continue in the employment and reasonable to continue to occupy the accommodation.

11.5.3 In consequence

The accommodation must be lost in consequence of the deliberate act or omission. In *Oxford City Council v Bull* [2011] EWCA Civ 609, a father (B) was held intentionally homeless when he lost the tenancy of a single room after he allowed his three children to move in with him. The Court found that there was no need for the children to move in with B. It was reasonable for him to continue to occupy the single room. That property was 'available' within the meaning of s 176. By his own deliberate conduct B had created a situation in which he was forced to leave that property.

The Homelessness Code of Guidance provides that this is a matter of cause and effect (para 11.11). It is possible for the cause of the intentional homelessness to persist even though the applicant might have had other accommodation in the interim. For example, if an applicant were to give up a flat voluntarily and move in with family members, if he were asked to leave the family home, the housing authority could look back to the act of giving up the flat when considering the question of intention.

The housing authority will be concerned with how the applicant's last settled accommodation came to be lost (*R v Brent LBC, ex p Awua* [1996] 1 AC 55, HL). For example, see *Din v Wandsworth LBC* [1983] 1 AC 657, HL, where the applicants left rented accommodation as a result of rent arrears. They moved in with relatives, but were then forced to leave that accommodation. The council could look back to the circumstances in which the applicants left the rented flat and were able to conclude that they had become homeless intentionally from that accommodation.

In order to be considered unintentionally homeless, an applicant who has deliberately lost accommodation will have to 'break the chain of intentionality'. This could be achieved, for example, by a period in settled (as opposed to temporary) accommodation after the loss of accommodation, and before any subsequent application for assistance as a homeless person (*Din v Wandsworth LBC*, above).

In the case of *Awua* (above), the House of Lords left open the question of whether the 'chain' could be broken in ways other than obtaining settled accommodation. In the subsequent case of *R v Harrow LBC, ex p Fahia* [1998] 1 WLR 1396, HL, it was made clear that there could be a supervening event (such as a marriage breakdown) which meant that the original cause of intentional homelessness was no longer operative.

> **CASE EXAMPLE**
>
> In *Watchman v Ipswich BC* [2007] EWCA 348, the chain of intentionality was not broken when the applicant's husband lost his job. The family had a history of debt problems, including rent arrears. Despite this, they decided to buy their home under the right-to-buy scheme. They obtained a mortgage under which the monthly repayments were significantly higher than the rent on the property had been. When, a few months later, the husband lost his job, the family fell into arrears with the mortgage repayments. The mortgagee obtained possession and the applicants applied as homeless. The Court of Appeal held that the substantial cause of this family's homelessness was their own act in taking out the mortgage, rather than the husband's losing his job. This was because it was deemed inevitable that the family would fall into mortgage arrears, and the loss of the job simply accelerated that process.

11.5.4 Reasonable to continue to occupy

See **11.3.5** above.

11.5.5 Entering into a collusive arrangement

The final means by which a person may become homeless intentionally is where he enters into an arrangement that results in him becoming homeless from accommodation which it would have been reasonable for him to continue to occupy. This applies where the purpose of the arrangement was to facilitate an application for assistance as a homeless person.

This may arise in at least two situations. The first is where friends or relatives collude with an applicant in order to make him homeless. The second situation is where a tenant colludes with a landlord over the tenant's eviction, with a view to then applying as homeless. In such circumstances, if collusion can be shown and there is no other good reason why the applicant is homeless, he will have been taken to have made himself intentionally homeless.

> **CASE EXAMPLE**
>
> In *Lomotey v Enfield LBC* [2004] HLR 45, CA, the applicant was found to have colluded in the loss of her home. She and her brother had jointly bought a flat in 1990. Eleven years later she applied to Enfield LBC to join the housing needs register. The applicant was informed that she was not eligible because she was a joint owner of the flat. Three months later the applicant surrendered her interest in the flat, for no consideration, to her brother. Some two weeks later he gave her notice to quit. The applicant was held intentionally homeless because of collusion.

The Homelessness Code of Guidance provides that 'other good reason' would include overcrowding, or an obvious breakdown in the relationship between the parties (para 11.28). Where circumstances such as these exist, intentional homelessness should not be inferred.

11.5.6 Conduct of the parties

Where more than one person is eligible to apply for assistance as a homeless person, for example both partners in a couple, an issue may arise as to whose conduct is relevant to the issue of intentionality. For example, where one partner has been involved in conduct which would undoubtedly result in a finding of intentional homelessness, couples may arrange for the other partner to make the application. However, the courts have held that housing authorities may consider whether the 'innocent' party acquiesced in the conduct (*R v North Devon DC, ex p Lewis* [1981] 1 WLR 328, QBD). If so, they will still be entitled to make a finding of intentional homelessness even if the 'innocent' party makes the application. Conversely, the Homelessness Code of Guidance makes it clear that there may be circumstances where one member of a household acted against the wishes and/or without the knowledge of another member, so that a finding of intentionality may not be appropriate (para 11.9).

11.5.7 Acts or omissions in good faith

Following s 191(2) of the HA 1996, acts or omissions in good faith, where someone was genuinely unaware of a relevant fact, must not be regarded as deliberate. The Homelessness Code of Guidance gives as an example (para 11.25) the situation where someone gave up accommodation in the belief that he had no legal right to occupy the property. Another example would be where an applicant fell into rent arrears and lost accommodation, whilst unaware that he might have qualified for welfare benefits to help with the rent. In *F v Birmingham City Council* [2007] HLR 18, CA, it was held that wilful ignorance or shutting one's eyes to the obvious was not an act or omission in good faith.

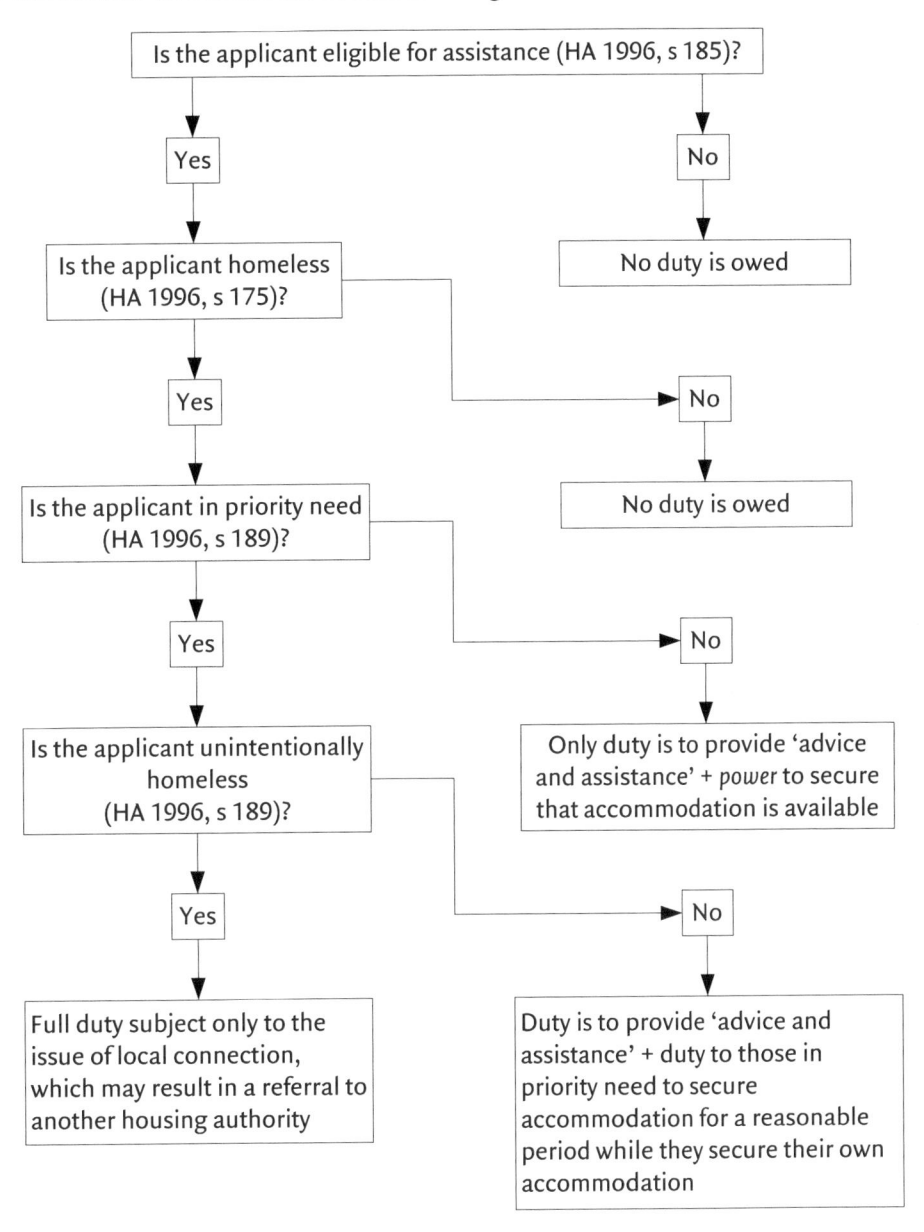

```
                Is the applicant eligible for assistance (HA 1996, s 185)?
                           │                              │
                          Yes                            No
                           │                              │
                Is the applicant homeless        No duty is owed
                   (HA 1996, s 175)?
                    │              │
                   Yes             No
                    │              │
           Is the applicant in priority need    No duty is owed
                   (HA 1996, s 189)?
                    │              │
                   Yes             No
                    │              │
        Is the applicant unintentionally   Only duty is to provide 'advice
                   homeless                 and assistance' + power to secure
                (HA 1996, s 189)?           that accommodation is available
                    │              │
                   Yes             No
                    │              │
        Full duty subject only to the      Duty is to provide 'advice and
        issue of local connection,         assistance' + duty to those in
        which may result in a referral to  priority need to secure
        another housing authority          accommodation for a reasonable
                                           period while they secure their own
                                           accommodation
```

Figure 11.4 – Summary

11.6 LOCAL CONNECTION

Once an applicant has satisfied all of the requirements referred to above, a full housing duty will be owed (see **11.7** below). However, where an applicant has no local connection with the housing authority to which he has applied, the housing authority has the discretion to refer the applicant to another authority with which the applicant does have a local connection. The onus of establishing a local connection rests on the applicant (R v Eastleigh BC, ex p Betts [1983] 2 AC 613, HL).

In order to regulate referrals between authorities, the Local Authority Agreement (Annex 18 of the Homelessness Code of Guidance) has been drawn up, which provides guidance on how issues of local connection should be resolved.

11.6.1 The meaning of 'local connection'

'Local connection' is defined in s 199 of the HA 1996. A person has a local connection with the district of a housing authority if (s 199(1)):

(a) he is, or was, normally resident there of his own choice;
(b) he is employed there;
(c) he has family associations there; or
(d) there are special circumstances.

11.6.2 Normal residence

The concept of 'normal residence' is clearly open to interpretation. Generally speaking, it will be satisfied by residence within a housing district of six months out of the last 12 months, or three years out of the last five (Local Authority Agreement, para 4.1). The use of such an approach has judicial approval, but the courts have also made it clear that housing authorities should also have regard to the particular circumstances of the applicant's case (R v Eastleigh Borough Council, ex p Betts [1983] 2 AC 613, HL).

Residence must be 'of choice', so that, for example, prisoners or those detained in psychiatric hospitals will not establish residence of choice in the area in which they are detained (s 199(3)(b)).

Where an applicant is placed in temporary accommodation during the course of a homeless application (and any subsequent review), this may constitute normal residence for the purpose of establishing a local connection.

> **CASE EXAMPLE**
>
> In Mohamed v Hammersmith and Fulham LBC [2002] 1 AC 547, the applicant, having become separated from her husband during the civil war in Somalia, came to the UK with her two small children. For the next four years she lived mainly in Ealing. In January 1998, her husband came to the UK. He lived with a friend in Hammersmith and Fulham LBC for a period of four months. The couple were then reunited and applied to Hammersmith and Fulham as homeless. They were placed in temporary accommodation, but were informed in July 1998 that they had no local connection with that borough and that they were to be referred to Ealing. The couple challenged the decision and the case reached the House of Lords, who held that occupation of interim accommodation within the borough to which the applicant applied could constitute normal residence and could be taken into account as evidence of a local connection.

11.6.3 Employment

The statute does not specify that full-time employment is required to establish a local connection, so it would be possible for part-time employment to be sufficient. However, it would need to be of more than a temporary or casual nature.

11.6.4 Family associations

The HA 1996 does not define what is meant by 'family associations', but there is guidance in the Local Authority Agreement (para 4.1) which provides that a local connection can be established if an applicant or a member of his or her household has parents, adult children, brothers or sisters currently residing in the housing authority district in question. These family members must themselves have been living in the relevant area for a period of five years.

In *Ozbek v Ipswich BC* [2006] HLR 41, CA, it was held that it was not just near relatives, such as parents, siblings or children, that could suffice to establish local connection. Other relatives, such as a cousin with whom the applicant had a close bond, could be sufficient. However, the existence of two brothers in an area for a period of only 18 months was held to be, given the five-year period in the guidance, too short a period to establish local connection.

It is possible to imagine extended families or step-families, where the definition in the Local Authority Agreement may not be appropriate. In such cases, housing authorities should be encouraged to take into account any representations made by the applicant, and not close their minds to the question of whether there was a valid family association.

11.6.5 Special circumstances

There is no statutory definition of 'special circumstances' but, again, there is guidance contained in the Local Authority Agreement and the Homelessness Code of Guidance. The Local Authority Agreement (para 4.1) refers to ex-prisoners or hospital patients who wish to return to an area where they were brought up or had lived for a considerable length of time in the past. The Homelessness Code of Guidance also refers to ex-prisoners (para 18.16) and to the example of those who need to be near special medical or support services which are available only in a particular district (para 18.10).

11.6.6 No local connection

It is possible that there may be applicants with no local connection to any housing district. In such circumstances, the duty to secure accommodation will rest with the housing authority that has received the application (Homelessness Code of Guidance, para 18.22).

11.6.7 Local connection with two or more housing authorities

Where an applicant has a local connection with more than one housing district, it is not open to the authority to which he applies to refer the applicant to the other authority if he has a local connection with the authority to which he applies (Homelessness Code of Guidance, para 18.13). However, it is open to the authority to request assistance from the other housing authority, as part of securing that accommodation is made available to the applicant.

Where an applicant has a local connection with more than one housing district and no local connection with the authority to which he applies, that authority may wish to take into account the applicant's preference as to which authority to refer him to (Homelessness Code of Guidance, para 18.14).

11.6.8 When can a referral be made?

A housing authority has discretion to refer to another authority on the basis of local connection. It need not do so in any particular case, although such is the pressure on housing authorities that they will generally wish to refer elsewhere when they can.

Section 198 of the HA 1996 governs when a housing authority may refer an applicant to another authority. In order for a referral to take place, the following conditions must be satisfied (s 198(2)):

(a) neither the applicant nor any person who might reasonably be expected to reside with him has a local connection with the district to which the application has been made;

(b) the applicant or a person who might reasonably be expected to reside with him has a local connection with the district to which they are to be referred; and

(c) neither the applicant nor any person who might reasonably be expected to reside with him will run the risk of domestic violence in that other district.

Section 198(2A) also provides that the referral conditions are not met if:

(a) the applicant or anyone reasonably expected to reside with him has suffered violence (other than domestic violence) in the district of the other authority; and

(b) it is probable that the return to the district of the victim will lead to further violence of a similar kind against him.

Section 198(3) provides that for the purposes of s 198(2) and (2A), 'violence' means:

(a) violence from another person; or

(b) threats of violence from another person which are likely to be carried out;

and violence is 'domestic violence' if it is from a person who is associated with the victim.

See **11.3.5.1** for the meaning of 'domestic violence' as set out in *Yemshaw v Hounslow LBC*.

Lastly, s 198(4) provides for the situation where an applicant applies to a housing authority for assistance and is placed outside of the authority's area as a result of that application. Should the applicant make a new application to the housing authority in whose district he has been placed, that authority can refer him back to the first authority if the second application is made within five years of when accommodation was made available under the first application.

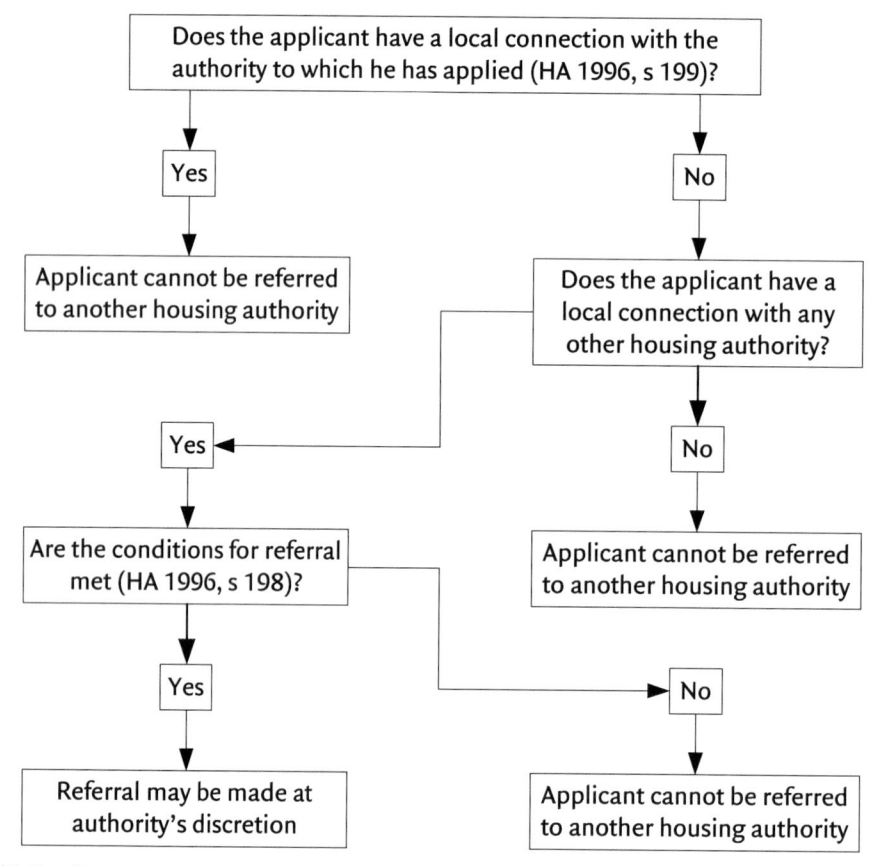

Figure 11.5 – Summary

11.7 DUTIES TOWARDS HOMELESS PERSONS

Local housing authorities have a number of duties imposed on them in relation to homeless applications. Some of these duties apply during the course of an application, for example the duty to make enquiries, reach decisions, provide accommodation pending a decision and to protect homeless persons' possessions. Other duties arise once a decision has been reached, and depend upon the finding made by the LHA. For example, different duties arise depending upon whether an applicant has been found to be in priority need or unintentionally homeless. The duties may be summarised as follows.

11.7.1 Duty to make enquiries

Section 184(1) of the HA 1996 provides that if a LHA has reason to believe that an applicant may be homeless or threatened with homelessness, it shall make such inquiries as are necessary to satisfy itself:

(a)   whether he is eligible for assistance; and

(b)   if so, whether any duty, and if so what duty, is owed to him.

Section 184(2) provides that the LHA may make inquiries whether the applicant has a local connection with another housing authority in England, Wales or Scotland.

11.7.2 Duty to make and notify decisions

Section 184(3) of the HA 1996 provides that, on completing its inquiries, the LHA shall notify the applicant of its decision and, so far as any issue is decided against the applicant, inform him of the reasons for its decision.

In restricted cases, the LHA has an additional notification duty under s 184 (3A) to:

(a)   inform the applicant that its decision was reached on that basis;

(b)   include the name of the restricted person;

(c)   explain why the person is a restricted person; and

(d)   explain the effect of s 193(7AD) or (as the case may be) s 195(4A).

If the authority has notified, or intends to notify, another housing authority under the local connection provisions, it shall at the same time notify the applicant of that decision and inform him of the reasons for it (HA 1996, s 184(4)).

Any notice given under s 184(3) or s 184(4) must also inform the applicant of his right to request a review of the decision and of the time within which a review must be requested (HA 1996, s 184(5)). (See **12.4** for details of statutory reviews.)

Notice given under s 184 is required to be given in writing and, if not received by the applicant, shall be treated as having been given to him if it is made available for collection at the authority's office for a reasonable period (s 184(6)). This provision is necessary as an applicant may be 'of no fixed abode', and it may therefore be difficult for the LHA to send notification by post.

11.7.3 Duty to provide accommodation pending enquiries

Section 188(1) of the HA 1996 provides that if the LHA has reason to believe that an applicant may be homeless, eligible for assistance and in priority need, it shall secure that accommodation is available for his occupation pending a decision on his application. This is an interim duty and ends when the authority's decision is notified to the applicant, even if the applicant requests a review of an adverse decision (HA 1996, s 188(3)). The LHA may provide accommodation pending a review decision, but is not obliged to do so (HA 1996, s 188(3)).

11.7.4 Duty to protect property

Section 211 of the HA 1996 requires LHAs to take reasonable steps to prevent loss or damage to an applicant's property. This duty arises where the authority is under a duty to provide interim accommodation pending a decision, or where a duty has arisen under s 190, s 193 or s 195 of the HA 1996. In practical terms this duty is usually met by LHAs placing applicants' furniture and possessions into storage while they are in temporary accommodation.

11.7.5 Duties towards successful applicants

Where an applicant has been found to be eligible for assistance, homeless, in priority need and unintentionally homeless, a full housing duty will arise under s 193 of the HA 1996. The extent of the duty for applicants who are not restricted cases (see **11.4.7**) is that the LHA shall secure that accommodation is available for occupation by the applicant's household (HA 1996, ss 176 and 193(2)) until the duty ceases in accordance with s 193.

It is important to note that the duty is to secure accommodation and not necessarily to provide accommodation from within the LHA's own stock. Section 206(1) of the 1996 Act provides that a local housing authority may discharge its housing functions towards a successful applicant only in the following ways:

(a) by securing that suitable accommodation provided by the LHA is made available to him;

(b) by securing that he obtains suitable accommodation from some other person; or

(c) by giving him such advice and assistance as will secure that suitable accommodation is available from some other person.

If the LHA uses its own accommodation under s 206(1)(a), the tenancy will not be secure, ie the property will be let on a non-secure basis until the homeless applicant is provided with permanent accommodation through the usual allocations provisions. This is to avoid the problem of homeless applicants 'leapfrogging' other people in housing need who have been registered, probably for a number of years, on the council's waiting list.

In a restricted case, the LHA is required, so far as possible, to bring its duty to secure accommodation to an end by ensuring that an offer of accommodation for a period of at least 12 months in the private rented sector is made to the applicant. If such an offer is made, the duty is discharged whether or not the applicant accepts the offer (s 193(7A)–(7F)).

11.7.5.1 Suitability of accommodation

Section 210(1) of the HA 1996 provides that, when determining suitability, the LHA shall have regard to issues such as slum clearance, overcrowding and the use of houses in multiple occupation. The intention of this section is to require the LHA to think carefully before using such accommodation, but it does not prevent the authority from using unfit or overcrowded properties, or houses in multiple occupation.

Section 210(2) of the 1996 Act provides that the Secretary of State may by order specify:

(a) circumstances in which accommodation is or is not to be regarded as suitable for a person; and

(b) matters to be taken into account or disregarded in determining whether accommodation is suitable for a person.

An example of an order made under s 210(2) is the Homelessness (Suitability of Accommodation) (England) Order 2003 (SI 2003/3326), which provides that bed and breakfast accommodation will not be regarded as suitable for families or pregnant women, except where there is no other accommodation available, and even then only for a maximum period of six weeks. Other issues include affordability of accommodation (see the Homelessness (Suitability of Accommodation) Order 1996 (SI 1996/3204)).

The Homelessness (Suitability of Accommodation) (England) Order 2012 (SI 2012/2601) gives further guidance to LHAs on the matters to be taken into account in determining whether accommodation is suitable for a person. These include:

(a) where the accommodation is situated outside the district of the LHA, the distance of the accommodation from the district of the authority;

(b) the significance of any disruption which would be caused by the location of the accommodation to the employment, caring responsibilities or education of the person or members of the person's household;

(c) the proximity and accessibility of the accommodation to medical facilities and other support which:

(i) are currently used by or provided to the person or members of the person's household, and

(ii) are essential to the well-being of the person or members of the person's household; and

(d) the proximity and accessibility of the accommodation to local services, amenities and transport.

Section 208(1) of the HA 1996 provides that, so far as reasonably practicable, the authority must secure that accommodation is made available in its district rather than elsewhere.

The issue of suitability has been widely litigated by homeless persons. They are likely to spend a considerable period of time in the accommodation provided as a result of their homeless application, while they await permanent rehousing through the usual allocations procedure. For this reason, it is crucial that any accommodation provided is suitable for their needs.

Although applicants get very little choice as to the accommodation they are offered, the courts have shown a willingness to apply certain minimum standards. See, for example, the case of *R v Newham LBC, ex p Sacupima* [2001] 1 WLR 563, CA, where the issue of location was considered relevant. The applicants approached Newham Council in London for assistance as homeless persons. They were provided with interim s 188 accommodation in a bed and breakfast hotel in Great Yarmouth. The LHA was found to have failed to consider the effect of the location of the hotel on matters such as the education and employment needs of the applicants and their children.

See also the case of *R v Tower Hamlets LBC, ex p Subhan* (1992) 24 HLR 541, QBD, where the court quashed a decision to place Bengali applicants on an estate where an independent study had shown a high level of racial harassment.

However, applicants cannot usually chose a particular type of property (see, for example, *R v Islington LBC, ex p Thomas* (1998) 30 HLR 111, QBD, where an applicant was unsuccessful in her attempts to obtain a property on a 'street' rather than on an estate due to her mental health needs and history of violent sexual assault on a previous estate. Contrast this with the case of *R v Brent LBC, ex p Omar* (1991) 23 HLR 446, QBD, where a refugee who had fled torture and imprisonment in Somalia successfully challenged the offer of a cockroach-infested basement flat with high windows, which reminded her of a prison.

In *Birmingham City Council v Ali and Others* [2009] 1 WLR 1506, HL, the applicants had been found to be homeless by reason of the severely overcrowded conditions in which they lived. The LHA nonetheless left them in that accommodation and placed them in a waiting list band which meant they would remain in their unsuitable accommodation for a considerable period. The applicant challenged this as unlawful, claiming the LHA was in on-going breach of its s 193 duty.

The House of Lords, reversing the Court of Appeal decision, decided that 'suitability' for the purpose of s 193(2) did not imply permanence or security of tenure, and an authority could satisfy its full housing duty under the provision by providing temporary accommodation. Their Lordships stated that, as with s 175(3) (see **11.3.5**), ss 191(1) and 193(2) were looking to the future as well as to the present, and accommodation that might be unreasonable for a person to occupy for a long period might be reasonable for him to occupy for a short period.

However, their Lordships decided that it was unlawful for the LHA to leave such families where they were until a house became available under the LHA's allocation scheme, as the present accommodation might become unsuitable long before then. Their Lordships also upheld the Court of Appeal's view that the LHA's allocation policy distinction was unlawful if and to the extent that it gave preference to people in one type of temporary accommodation which was no less satisfactory than the accommodation in which homeless families were left temporarily in their original home. See also *El-Dinnaoui v Westminster City Council* [2013] EWCA Civ 231.

11.7.5.2 Cessation of the duty

The duty under s 193 of the HA 1996 continues until one of the events described in the section occurs. Amendments introduced by ss 148 and 149 of the Localism Act 2011 mean that from 9 November 2012, cessation of the duty differs for applicants in England and Wales. The changes introduced by the Act have come into force for England, but the unamended provisions continue to apply in Wales.

For England, s 193(5) provides that the s 193 duty will cease if the applicant refuses an offer which the LHA is satisfied is suitable for him. The offer of accommodation must not be an offer of accommodation under Pt 6 or a private rented sector offer. Also, the LHA must notify the applicant that it regards itself as ceasing to be subject to the duty under s 193. This applies only if the authority has advised the applicant of the possible consequences of refusal and of his right to request a review of the suitability of the accommodation.

For Wales, s 193(5) provides that the s 193 duty will cease if the applicant refuses an offer which the authority is satisfied is suitable for him, and the authority notifies him that it regards itself as having discharged the duty under s 193. This applies only if the authority has advised the applicant of the possible consequences of refusal and of his right to request a review of the suitability of the accommodation. Section 193(7AA) contains similar provisions in relation to restricted cases.

In *Maswaku v Westminster City Council* [2012] EWCA Civ 669, it was held that the LHA had properly advised M of the consequences of refusal when it informed her that:

> By giving you a suitable temporary home we have discharged our housing duty. Under current circumstances, we are not required to offer you anywhere else to live. So if you refuse the offer, you will have to find your own accommodation unless you successfully challenge our decision.

The LHA was not required to spell out in the letter to M the possibilities of eviction, her right to make a fresh application or the loss of priority on the waiting list.

Section 193(6) applies equally to England and Wales. It provides that the LHA shall cease to be subject to the duty under s 193 if the applicant:

(a) ceases to be eligible for assistance;
(b) becomes homeless intentionally from the accommodation made available for his occupation;
(c) accepts an offer of accommodation under Pt VI of the HA 1996 (ie, through the usual allocation of housing provisions);
(d) accepts an offer of an assured tenancy (other than an assured shorthold) from a private landlord; or
(e) otherwise voluntarily ceases to occupy as his only or principal home the accommodation made available for his occupation.

Section 193(7) provides that the LHA shall also cease to be subject to the duty if the applicant, having been informed of the possible consequences of refusal (or, for England, acceptance) and of his right to request a review of the suitability of the accommodation, refuses a final offer of accommodation under Pt VI of the HA 1996. The LHA must be satisfied both that the Pt VI accommodation offered is suitable for the applicant and that it is reasonable for him to accept the offer (s 193(7F)). In *Slater v Lewisham LBC* [2006] HLR 37, CA, it was held that these were two distinct considerations to be satisfied by the LHA. Accommodation that was suitable for the applicant might not be reasonable to be accepted.

When deciding whether it is reasonable for an applicant to accept an offer of accommodation, the authority must have regard to all the applicant's personal circumstances, his needs, and his hopes and fears. Taking account of those subjective factors, the decision-maker must then apply an objective test to determine whether it is reasonable for the applicant to accept the offer; the test is whether it is reasonable for the particular applicant to accept the offer of the particular accommodation. However, *Tower Hamlets LBC v Begum* [2005] EWCA Civ 340 has established that an LHA would be obliged to consider a renewed application from such an applicant at a future date if there had been a change in circumstances that was more than trivial.

For Wales, s 193(7B) provides that, in a case which is not a restricted case, an authority shall cease to be subject to the duty under s 193 if the applicant accepts a qualifying offer of an assured shorthold tenancy. This covers the situation where a LHA works with a private landlord to arrange for the provision of privately rented accommodation let on an assured shorthold basis. Section 193(7C) makes it clear that, in a case which is not a restricted case, an applicant is free to refuse an offer of an assured shorthold tenancy. Section 193(7D) sets out the qualifying conditions that must be met in order to protect the applicant, such as the provision of a written statement informing the applicant that he is not obliged to accept the offer, but that the s 193 duty will cease if he does so.

In England, LHAs can discharge their full housing duty to any applicant under s 193 of the HA 1996 by the offer of a private rented sector tenancy (s 193(7AA) as amended). Section 193(7C) has been repealed for England. The LHA will have discharged its duty by the offer of a suitable private sector tenancy, whether the applicant accepts or refuses the offer.

The private rented sector offer is the same as for restricted case accommodation (see **11.7.5**), namely a private sector assured shorthold tenancy, approved by the LHA, for a fixed term of at least 12 months (HA 1996, s 193(7AC)).

If the applicant becomes unintentionally homeless again within two years of accepting a private rented sector offer, he will be automatically eligible under s193(2) (duty on LHA to secure accommodation), regardless of the applicant's priority need status at that time (HA 1996, s 195A).

11.7.6 Duties towards applicants without priority need

The statutory provisions make a distinction between applicants without priority need who are not intentionally homeless, and applicants without priority need who are intentionally homeless.

Section 192 of the HA 1996 governs those not in priority need who are unintentionally homeless. The LHA must provide such an applicant with advice and assistance in any attempts he may make to secure that accommodation becomes available for his occupation (s 192(2)). In addition, there is a power to secure that accommodation becomes available for the applicant's occupation (s 192(3)). Since this is only a power and not a duty, it is exercisable at the authority's discretion.

Where an applicant is not in priority need and is intentionally homeless, there is only the right to advice and assistance (HA 1996, s 190(3)), and no corresponding power to secure accommodation.

11.7.7 Duties towards applicants who are intentionally homeless

An applicant found to be intentionally homeless and not in priority need has only the limited right to obtain advice and assistance contained in the HA 1996, s 190(3), as discussed at **11.7.6** above.

An applicant found to be intentionally homeless and in priority need is entitled to advice and assistance in any attempt he may make to secure accommodation (HA 1996, s 190(2)(b)). Additionally, there is a duty, in such cases, to secure that accommodation is made available for the applicant's occupation for such period as the authority considers will give him a reasonable opportunity of securing accommodation for his occupation (s 190(2)(a)). This duty applies equally to restricted cases.

In R (Conville) v Richmond upon Thames LBC [2006] 1 WLR 2808, CA, it was held that the LHA was not entitled to have regard to considerations peculiar to it, such as the extent of its resources and other demands upon it. The LHA had to consider what was reasonable from the applicant's standpoint, having regard to the applicant's circumstances and in the context of the accommodation potentially available.

11.7.8 Other legislative provisions

Where applicants are unable to rely upon Pt VII of the HA 1996, it may be possible for them to obtain assistance under other legislative provisions. These include:

(a) the National Assistance Act 1948, s 21;
(b) the Children Act 1989, ss 17 and 20; and
(c) the Local Government Act 2000, s 2.

Further consideration of these provisions is beyond the scope of this chapter.

11.8 FURTHER READING

J Luba and L Davies, *Housing Allocations and Homelessness* (3rd edn, 2012)

SUMMARY

LHAs have a duty to secure that accommodation is available for any applicant who is:

- eligible for assistance;
- homeless;
- a priority need; and
- not intentionally homeless.

This is subject to possible referral to another LHA if the applicant has no local connection with the LHA to which the application is made, but does have a local connection with another LHA.

CHAPTER 12

HOMELESSNESS II – PROCEDURE

12.1	Applications	197
12.2	Enquiries	198
12.3	Decisions	199
12.4	Statutory reviews	199
12.5	Appeals to the county court	202
12.6	Judicial review	205
12.7	Commissioners for Local Administration	209
12.8	Further reading	211
	Summary	211

LEARNING OUTCOMES

After reading this chapter you will be able to:

- understand the different stages in the homelessness process
- describe the review procedure
- explain the basis upon which appeals can be made to the county court
- outline the procedure for a judicial review application
- describe the role of the ombudsman.

12.1 APPLICATIONS

This chapter outlines the procedure for making a homeless application and for reviewing an adverse decision made by a LHA. The first step in the process is the making of an application. This is dealt with by s 183 of the HA 1996.

12.1.1 When is an application made?

An application is commenced when an applicant approaches an LHA for assistance under Pt VII of the HA 1996. Section 183(1) provides that the statutory provisions will be applicable where a person applies to an LHA for accommodation, or for assistance in obtaining accommodation, and the authority has reason to believe that he may be homeless or threatened with homelessness.

There is no statutory requirement to make the application in writing or in any particular form. For example, in the case of *R v Chiltern DC, ex p Roberts* (1991) 23 HLR 387, QBD, the applicants' solicitors wrote a letter to the council in an attempt to commence an application. The letter contained details of the applicants and stated that they wished to make an application under the relevant legislation in force at the time. The council contended that the letter did not constitute an application, which, it claimed, was begun only when the applicants personally presented themselves at the council offices two months later. The court disagreed with this approach, finding that the letter was sufficient to commence the application and that personal attendance at the council offices was unnecessary. (Note, however, that personal attendance will almost always be necessary during the course of the council's enquiries into the application (see **12.2**), so that the applicant can be asked relevant questions and provide the information necessary to enable the council to reach a decision.)

12.1.2 Who may apply?

An applicant must be eligible for assistance within the meaning of s 185 of the HA 1996 (see **11.2** above). Furthermore, the courts have held that an applicant must not be a dependent child (see the case of *R v Oldham MBC, ex p Garlick* [1993] AC 509, HL, where the court rejected applications made on behalf of 4-year-old children following a finding of intentional homelessness against their parents). Similarly, an applicant must have the mental capacity to understand what it means to make an application and must understand what is involved in being made an offer of accommodation. This would exclude mentally disabled adults who lacked this level of comprehension (*R v Tower Hamlets LBC, ex p Begum* [1993] AC 509, HL).

12.2 ENQUIRIES

Section 184(1) of the HA 1996 provides that if the LHA has reason to believe that an applicant may be homeless or threatened with homelessness, it shall make such enquiries as are necessary to satisfy itself:

(a) whether he is eligible for assistance; and

(b) if so, whether any duty, and if so what duty, is owed to him under Pt VII of the HA 1996.

Section 184(2) goes on to provide that the LHA may also make enquiries as to whether the applicant has a local connection with another LHA.

The threshold for triggering a duty to make enquiries is clearly set at quite a low level. The authority needs only to have 'reason to believe' that the applicant 'may be homeless or threatened with homelessness'. If this duty has arisen, the authority then needs to make adequate enquiries to enable it to satisfy itself as to whether the applicant is eligible and, if so, what, if any, duty is owed.

There are no set procedural requirements laid down as to the scope of enquiries, but the authority clearly needs to make sufficient enquiries to reach a proper decision, and needs to have regard to all relevant considerations. However, an authority's decision will be struck down due to inadequate enquiries only if no reasonable authority could have supposed that the enquiries already made were sufficient (*R v Nottingham CC, ex p Costello* (1989) 21 HLR 301, QBD).

The Homelessness Code of Guidance provides that enquiries should be carried out as quickly as possible and must be sufficiently thorough to enable the authority to establish the facts of the case. Furthermore, the applicant should be given an opportunity to explain his circumstances in full, particularly in relation to matters that could lead to an adverse decision (para 6.15).

Housing authorities may seek information from other departments, such as social services or health authorities, and may approach another housing authority, for example to obtain information about previous applications (para 6.20).

In cases where medical issues arise (including mental health issues), the authority should seek appropriate medical evidence as part of its enquiries. This is particularly relevant in vulnerability cases (see **11.4.4**). However, the decision as to whether or not an applicant is vulnerable is ultimately one which the housing authority must make. The authority cannot simply accept the decision of its medical officer (see *R v Lambeth LBC, ex p Carroll* (1988) 20 HLR 142, where a decision which automatically adopted the findings of the medical adviser was quashed).

Any medical evidence provided by the applicant should also be properly considered, although, so long as the authority has considered the evidence, it is not bound to accept it (see *Noh v Hammersmith and Fulham LBC* [2002] HLR 54, CA).

12.3 DECISIONS

12.3.1 Time limits

There is no statutory time limit within which applications must be dealt with. Each case will be different, depending upon the complexity of the situation. However, the Homelessness Code of Guidance provides that, wherever possible, housing authorities should aim to carry out their initial assessment on the day of application, and complete their inquiries and notify the applicant, within 33 working days (para 6.16). All applicants must be notified of the outcome of their application, including those who the authority decides are not homeless or not in priority need (para 6.21). For the statutory duty to notify applicants, see **12.3.2** below.

The 33-day limit is often exceeded by LHAs, due to pressure of work or the need to obtain evidence from third parties, such as medical reports. For some applicants this does not present a problem, for example where they are adequately housed in temporary accommodation or where their application is likely to fail and they are not keen to know the outcome. However, where authorities fail to reach a decision after a reasonable time, it would be open to the applicant to seek judicial review of the authority's failure (see **12.6**).

The case of R v Lambeth LBC, ex p Weir [2001] EWHC Admin 121; (2001) June 2001 *Legal Action* 26, is an example of a case where an applicant sought judicial review to obtain a decision on an outstanding application. The applicant had applied as homeless in June 1999, but was still awaiting a decision in February 2001. The applicant sought judicial review, which was granted. It was ordered that the authority must notify the applicant of the outcome of his application within 14 days.

12.3.2 Notification

There is a statutory duty to notify applicants of the outcome of their application. Section 184(3) of the HA 1996 provides that, on completing its enquiries, the authority shall notify the applicant of its decision and, so far as any issue is decided against his interests, inform him of the reasons for the decision.

Notice must be given in writing and, if not received by the applicant, shall be treated as having been given to him if it is made available at the authority's office for a reasonable period for collection by him or on his behalf (HA 1996, s 184(6)). This provision is necessary because of the temporary nature of applicants' accommodation (including some applicants who will be of no fixed abode) and the inherent difficulties in ensuring that they receive their post.

Any notice given must also inform the applicant of his right to request a review of the decision and the time within which such a request must be made (HA 1996, s 184(5)). The reasons given in the decision letter must be 'proper, adequate and intelligible' (R v Islington LBC, ex p Hinds (1996) 28 HLR 302, CA). The letter sent to an applicant notifying him of the outcome of his case is often referred to as a 's 184 decision letter'.

12.4 STATUTORY REVIEWS

If an applicant receives an adverse decision he has the right to seek a review. The review is carried out by the LHA to which the applicant has applied. Section 202 of the HA 1996 sets out the decisions that may be reviewed, and s 203 sets out the review procedure.

Statutory reviews were introduced by the HA 1996 as a means of providing applicants with a right of 'appeal' in place of challenging LHA decisions in court. If an applicant is unsuccessful on review, it may still be possible for him to appeal to the county court, but only in limited circumstances and only if he has already exercised his right of review.

12.4.1 Decisions that may be reviewed

Section 202(1) of the HA 1996 provides that an applicant may seek a review of:

(a) any decision as to his eligibility for assistance;
(b) any decision as to what duty is owed to him under ss 190 to 193 and ss 195 and 196;
(c) any decision regarding a local connection referral; or
(d) any decision as to the suitability of accommodation offered in discharge of the authority's duty under s 190, s 193 or s 200.

12.4.1.1 Eligibility

Decisions on eligibility that may be reviewed include:

(a) whether an applicant is a person from abroad (HA 1996, s 185); or
(b) where the applicant is an eligible asylum seeker, whether he is excluded because he has any accommodation available to him, however temporary (HA 1996, s 186(1)).

12.4.1.2 Duties towards homeless persons

Decisions on the question of duties that may be reviewed include:

(a) duties towards intentionally homeless applicants (HA 1996, s 190);
(b) whether an applicant is homeless, in priority need and unintentionally homeless (HA 1996, ss 190–192);
(c) whether a duty under s 193 has come to an end (HA 1996, s 193); and
(d) duties towards those threatened with homelessness (including those threatened with homelessness intentionally) (HA 1996, ss 195 and 196).

12.4.1.3 Local connection

Decisions on local connection that may be reviewed include:

(a) a decision to notify another LHA (HA 1996, s 198(1));
(b) whether the conditions for a local connection referral have been met (HA 1996, s 198(5)); and
(c) duties owed to applicants whose case is considered for referral or is referred (HA 1996, s 200(3) and (4)).

12.4.1.4 Accommodation offered in discharge of duty

Decisions on accommodation offered in discharge of duty that may be reviewed include:

(a) the suitability of accommodation offered under s 190 of the HA 1996 to an intentionally homeless applicant;
(b) the suitability of accommodation offered under s 193 of the Act to those in priority need and not intentionally homeless; and
(c) the suitability of accommodation offered under s 200 to applicants who are referred under local connection provisions.

12.4.2 Time limit for seeking a review

Section 202(3) of the HA 1996 provides that a request for review must be made within 21 days of the day on which the applicant is notified of the authority's decision (under s 184(3), see **12.3.2** above), or such longer period as the authority may allow in writing. For the avoidance of doubt, s 202(2) makes it clear that there is no right to seek a review of a review decision.

12.4.3 Review procedure

The procedure to be followed on review is governed by s 203 of the HA 1996 and by the Allocation of Housing and Homelessness (Review Procedure) Regulations 1999 (SI 1999/71).

The review is carried out by the LHA to which the applicant applied, except in the case of a review against a local connection referral (reg 1(2)(b)). In that situation, the review is carried out jointly by the notifying authority and the notified authority where they were in agreement about the referral, or by a person appointed to conduct such reviews in the case of a disputed referral.

The Regulations provide that the review shall be carried out by someone who was not involved in the original decision and who is senior to the officer who made the original decision (reg 2). The applicant must be notified that he, or someone acting on his behalf, may make representations in writing to the authority (reg 6(2)(a)), and the authority shall notify the applicant of the procedure to be followed (reg 6(2)(b)).

The review officer is required to consider any representations made by the applicant (reg 8(1)), and may need to make further enquiries in the light of any new evidence.

Where the review officer considers that the original decision was deficient or irregular in some way (for example because of failure to take into account relevant information), but is nevertheless minded to make a decision against the applicant, the officer must notify the applicant of this and of his reasons, and must inform the applicant that he, or someone acting on his behalf, has the right to make representations either orally, or in writing or both (reg 8(2)). This is usually the only situation in which oral representations are likely to be considered by an LHA. In *Makisi v Birmingham City Council* [2011] EWCA Civ 355, it was held that reg 8(2) gives an applicant the right to demand a face-to-face oral hearing, not just to make representations over the telephone.

The obligation to notify the applicant where a reviewing officer is 'minded to make' an adverse decision is not a discretionary one. In *Lambeth LBC v Johnston* [2008] EWCA Civ 690, the applicant had already made oral representations to the reviewing officer in relation to a review of the LHA's decision. The reviewing officer did not send a 'minded to make' letter to the applicant prior to making an adverse decision as she felt all relevant representations had already been made. The review decision was quashed on the basis that reg 8(2) had not been complied with (see also *Gibbons v Bury MBC* [2010] EWCA Civ 327).

In the jointly considered cases of *Hall v Wandsworth LBC; Carter v Wandsworth LBC* [2005] 2 All ER 192, CA, guidance was given on the meaning of the word 'deficiency'. It was held that the word had no particular legal meaning and simply meant 'something lacking' which was of sufficient importance to the fairness of the procedure to justify an extra procedural safeguard. The reviewing officer should apply reg 8(2) not merely when there was some significant legal or procedural error in the decision, but whenever, looking at the matter broadly and untechnically, he considered that an important aspect of the case had either not been addressed, or not addressed adequately by the original decision maker.

The review decision can be taken in the light of all relevant information available at the time the review is decided (*Mohamed v Hammersmith and Fulham LBC* [2002] 1 AC 547).

However, the question as to what facts should be taken into account at a review decision will depend on what is being reviewed. This must be dictated in the light of what fairness and common sense requires. Later facts may not be relevant in a given case. In *Omar v Westminster CC* [2008] EWCA Civ 421, a homeless applicant refused the offer of accommodation because it was some distance from a hospital and other support network needed for his sick child. On review of the LHA's decision that it had discharged its duty to the applicant, the reviewing officer obtained an updated medical report which stated that the child no longer needed that level of support. The reviewing officer decided that the offer of accommodation had been unreasonably refused. It was held that the reviewing officer took irrelevant matters into account. The relevant facts should have been those at the date the applicant refused the offer of accommodation, not at the review date.

Section 203(3) of the HA 1996 provides that the LHA shall notify the applicant of the decision reached on review. Notification is required to be given in writing (s 203(8)). The applicant must usually be notified of the decision within eight weeks of his request for a review, or such longer period as the applicant and the officer may agree in writing (reg 9(1) and (2)). There are slightly different time scales for local connection reviews.

Where the decision is against the interests of the applicant, he shall be notified of the reasons for that decision (s 203(4)) and of his right to appeal to a county court on a point of law, including details of the time limits for appealing to the court (s 203(5); see also **12.5** below).

12.4.4 Accommodation pending review

Under s 188(3) of the HA 1996, the LHA may provide temporary accommodation pending the outcome of the applicant's review, but is not obliged to do so. If the LHA refuses to exercise its discretion, the applicant may have grounds to seek judicial review.

It has been held that it is lawful for an LHA to provide accommodation pending review only in exceptional circumstances (R v Camden LBC, ex p Mohammed (1997) 30 HLR 315, QBD). However, the authority should take into account all material considerations, including the applicant's personal circumstances and the consequences of refusing housing pending review. It should have regard to the merits of the case and to any new material, information or argument put forward by the applicant (ex p Mohammed, above).

12.5 APPEALS TO THE COUNTY COURT

Section 204(1) of the HA 1996 provides that where an applicant has requested a review under s 202 and is:

(a) dissatisfied with the decision on review; or
(b) is not notified of the decision within the time prescribed,

he may appeal to the county court on any point of law arising from the review decision, or, in the case of (b), from the original decision.

12.5.1 Appeal on a point of law

It is important to note that an appeal to the county court can be brought only on a point of law. This is the same basis on which an application for judicial review may be brought (see **12.6**), and involves consideration of the legality of the decision rather than a rehearing of the applicant's case. In order to bring an appeal, the applicant must identify some point of law, such as illegality, irrationality or procedural impropriety. In the absence of a point of law, the applicant will be unable to appeal.

12.5.2 Time limits

Section 204(2) of the HA 1996 provides that any appeal must be brought within 21 days of the applicant being notified of the review decision, or of the date on which he should have been notified of the review decision.

Section 204(2A) provides that the court may give permission for an appeal outside the 21-day period. The applicant may apply to the court for an extension of time within the 21-day period. Permission will be granted only if the court is satisfied that there is a good reason for the applicant to be unable to bring the appeal in time (s 204(2A)(a)). The applicant may also apply to the court after the expiry of the 21-day period, but an extension will be granted only if there was a good reason for the applicant's failure to bring the appeal in time and for any delay in applying for permission (s 204(2A)(b)).

12.5.3 Grounds of appeal

In order to establish the basis for an appeal, the applicant must show that one or more of the following public law grounds of challenge apply.

12.5.3.1 Illegality

A decision of an LHA will be illegal if the decision maker has:

(a) acted without legal authority (*A-G v Fulham Corporation* [1921] 1 Ch 440);

(b) fettered his discretion either by acting under the dictation of another (*Lavender (H) & Son v Minister of Housing and Local Government* [1970] 3 All ER 871), or by applying self-created rules of policy without consideration of the applicant's personal circumstances (*British Oxygen v Minister of Technology* [1971] AC 610);

(c) used his powers for an improper purpose (*Congreve v Home Office* [1976] 1 QB 629) or for dual purposes, one of which is unlawful (*Westminster Corp v LNWR* [1905] AC 426 and *R v ILEA, ex p Westminster City Council* [1986] 1 WLR 28);

(d) failed to take into account all relevant considerations (*Roberts v Hopwood* [1925] AC 578; *Shala v Birmingham City Council* [2007] EWCA Civ 624);

(e) taken into account irrelevant considerations (*Padfield v Minister of Agriculture* [1968] AC 997);

(f) made an error of law (*Anisminic Ltd v Foreign Compensation Commission* [1969] 2 AC 147);

(g) made an error of fact that affected the basis of his jurisdiction (*Secretary of State for the Home Department, ex p Khawaja* [1984] AC 74);

(h) wrongly delegated his powers to another (*Vine v National Dock Labour Board* [1957] AC 488);

(i) acted contrary to EU law (*R v Chief Constable of Sussex, ex p International Trader's Ferry Ltd* [1998] QB 477); or

(j) acted incompatibly with a right in the European Convention on Human Rights, contrary to s 6 of the Human Rights Act 1998 (*Begum (Runa) v Tower Hamlets LBC* [2002] 2 All ER 668).

12.5.3.2 Irrationality

A decision of an LHA may also be challenged if it is irrational. This has been held to mean a decision that is 'so unreasonable that no reasonable authority could ever have come to it' (*Associated Provincial Picture Houses Ltd v Wednesbury Corporation* [1948] 1 KB 223; *R (Paul-Coker) v Southwark LBC* [2006] HLR 32 and *R (Joseph) v Newham LBC* [2009] EWHC 2983) or 'outrageous in its defiance of logic' (*CCSU v Minister for the Civil Service* [1985] AC 374).

12.5.3.3 Procedural impropriety

A decision may also be open to challenge on procedural grounds. This concerns the manner in which the decision has been reached and whether any common law or statutory procedural requirements have been breached. The common law requirements are known as the rules of natural justice, otherwise referred to as the rules of procedural fairness. Statutory requirements are known as rules of procedural ultra vires (see *Hall v Wandsworth LBC* at **12.4.3**).

Rules of procedural fairness

There are two basic rules of procedural fairness:

(a) the rule against bias; and
(b) the right to a fair hearing.

Bias may be direct, eg a financial or other interest (*Dimes v Grand Junction Canal Proprietors* (1852) 10 ER 301), or indirect, eg something which gives rise to a real possibility of bias to the fair minded observer (*Magill v Porter and Another* [2002] 1 All ER 645).

The right to a fair hearing includes the right of the applicant to know the case against him and to have the opportunity to put his side of the story (*Fairmount Investments Ltd v Secretary of State for the Environment* [1976] 1 WLR 1255).

Procedural ultra vires

This rule requires the decision maker to comply with any statutory requirements set out in the relevant Act governing the decision-making process. Requirements may be mandatory (*Bradbury v London Borough of Enfield* [1967] 1 WLR 1311) or directory (*Coney v Choyce* [1975] 1 All ER 979). Failure to comply with a mandatory requirement will render a decision ultra vires, whereas failure to comply with a directory requirement will not.

12.5.3.4 Proportionality

Where a decision concerns a human rights issue under the Convention, there is a further requirement for the decision maker to act proportionately (*R v Secretary of State for the Home Department, ex p Daly* [2001] 3 All ER 433). This essentially requires that the means used should not be disproportionate to the objective to be achieved. In a human rights context it requires that, where interference is allowed with a Convention right for some aim set out in the relevant Article of the Convention, the interference should be no more than is necessary to achieve that aim. In colloquial terms it is often referred to as the requirement that the decision maker should not 'use a sledge hammer to crack a nut'.

12.5.4 Remedies

Where an applicant can establish one or more of the above grounds, he will be able to seek 'relief' (or a remedy) from the county court. Section 204(3) of the HA 1996 provides that the county court may make such order confirming, quashing or varying the decision as it thinks fit (see *Slater v Lewisham LBC* [2006] HLR 37, CA).

12.5.5 Accommodation pending appeal

Under s 204(4) of the HA 1996, the LHA has power to secure that accommodation is available to the applicant pending the outcome of the appeal. If the LHA refuses to exercise this power, the applicant can apply to the county court, which may order accommodation pending appeal (s 204A).

When deciding whether to order accommodation pending appeal, the county court is required to apply the principles used by the High Court on an application for judicial review (s 204A(4)) (see **12.6.6**). Furthermore, the county court may order accommodation pending appeal only if satisfied that the failure to do so would substantially prejudice the applicant's ability to pursue the main appeal (s 204A(6)).

12.5.6 Appeal procedure

The procedure for an appeal to the county court is regulated by CPR Part 52 and the accompanying Practice Direction. Regard should also be had to the relevant guidance on public funding and the related (but not binding) Judicial Review Pre-action Protocol (see **12.6.3**).

12.5.6.1 Public funding

Before an applicant can commence proceedings, he will need to obtain funding for the case. Usually this is legal aid. This funding is means tested, and is also subject to the Merits Regulations for public law claims (regs 53–56) (see **5.2.3.3**).

Since the appeal must be filed within 21 days, it is usual for solicitors to use their 'delegated functions' (formerly 'devolved powers') to grant emergency public funding limited to filing and service of the appeal. A full application is then submitted to the LAA for its consideration.

The certificate of public funding may be limited to certain steps in the proceedings. If this is the case, the scope of the certificate will need to be amended as the case progresses. The certificate may also have a financial limitation, which must be kept under review at all times to ensure that it is not exceeded. It is possible to apply to the LAA for an uplift in the costs limitation as the case progresses.

12.5.6.2 Pre-action steps

Unlike an application for judicial review, there is no pre-action protocol to be followed in relation to county court appeals. However, as a matter of good practice (and to prevent incurring unnecessary costs), the requirement to send a letter before action contained in the Judicial Review Protocol should be followed in appeal cases.

The letter before action should be sent to the relevant LHA and to its legal department. It should set out the grounds of appeal and ask for a response within a reasonable period of time (usually seven days, although this will depend to some extent on the deadline for lodging the appeal at court). Failure to send a letter before action may result in adverse costs consequences for the applicant if he is seen as having initiated unnecessary litigation. It could also result in a wasted costs order against the applicant's solicitor.

12.5.6.3 Notice of Appeal

If the letter before action does not resolve the case, the applicant (now the appellant) must file three copies of his Notice of Appeal (Form N161) at the county court within the 21-day deadline. The Notice must be supported by a copy of the appellant's skeleton argument, a copy of the decision being appealed, any witness statements and a bundle of other relevant documents, including, if available, the certificate of public funding. A fee is payable when the Notice is filed.

The Notice must set out the grounds of appeal. A sealed copy of the Notice and supporting documents must be served on the respondent LHA within seven days. The respondent authority need reply to the Notice only where it seeks to uphold its decision for reasons different from or additional to those already given.

The appeal will then usually be listed for a short case management hearing and then for trial in due course. Any appeal from the decision of the county court is to the Court of Appeal. Permission to appeal is required.

12.5.6.4 Costs

The successful party will usually be awarded costs. Where an applicant is publicly funded, his solicitor must account to the LAA for the costs to ensure that the LAA is reimbursed for any monies it has paid to the solicitor by way of public funding. Costs awarded against an unsuccessful publicly funded litigant are not normally enforceable without leave of the court. This means that a litigant with the benefit of a certificate of public funding is largely protected against a costs order, unless his financial position changes significantly (see **5.7** for further details on costs).

12.6 JUDICIAL REVIEW

The introduction of the statutory review scheme in the HA 1996 (see **12.4**) was clearly intended to remove homelessness cases from the scope of judicial review by creating an alternative remedy in the county court. As a general principle of administrative law, it is usually not possible to apply for judicial review where there is an alternative remedy that might be used. However, there is still a number of situations in which the applicant can apply only for judicial review in respect of certain homelessness matters, and there may be very limited situations where he would wish to do so, notwithstanding the availability of an alternative remedy by way of appeal.

Examples of decisions in respect of which judicial review is still available because there is no right of appeal include:

(a) the provision of accommodation pending the outcome of a s 202 review (*R v Camden LBC, ex p Mohammed* (1998) 30 HLR 315, QBD); and

(b) the failure of an LHA to discharge its s 193 duty by the provision of suitable accommodation (*R (on the application of Mohamed Ishaque) v Newham LBC*, (2002) December 2002 *Legal Action* 22).

Examples of where there may be a right of appeal, but where, exceptionally, it may be appropriate to apply for judicial review, include:

(a) a challenge to the legality of a policy (*R v Kensington and Chelsea RLBC, ex p Byfield* (1999) 31 HLR 913, QBD); and

(b) where the application raises an important point of law that should properly be considered by a superior court (*R v Brent LBC, ex p Sadiq* (2001) 33 HLR 525, QBD).

12.6.1 Basis of judicial review

A claim for judicial review is essentially an application to the Administrative Court (a branch of the High Court of Justice) to challenge the lawfulness of a decision. The Administrative Court's jurisdiction is termed 'supervisory' rather than 'appellate'. This means that judicial review is not an appeal. Rather it is an application to ask the court to review the legality of executive action, in this context, a decision made by an LHA in respect of a homelessness application. Judicial review is available only against public bodies, which includes LHAs.

One important distinction between a claim for judicial review and an appeal to the county court on a point of law, is the requirement to obtain permission. Whereas an applicant can appeal to the county court as of right if he can establish one or more grounds of appeal, a claim for judicial review cannot proceed unless permission is first given by the Administrative Court. The requirement to obtain permission is considered in more detail at **12.6.3** below.

12.6.2 Time limits

There are two relevant provisions governing the time limit for an application for judicial review. Section 31(6) of the Senior Courts Act 1981 provides that a claim for judicial review must be brought 'without undue delay'. The CPR, r 54.5 further provides that the claim must be made 'promptly', and in any event not later than three months after the grounds of review first arose.

The combined effect of these two provisions is that a claimant must commence his claim for judicial review as quickly as possible. It is not advisable to assume that a claim will be 'in time' if it is made within the three-month time limit. This is because the court may take the view that, even if an applicant applies within the three-month period, he has not acted promptly or without undue delay. A client considering judicial review should therefore be advised to commence the claim as soon as possible.

It is clear that the time limit for making a claim for judicial review is longer than the 21-day time limit for appealing to the county court (see **12.5.2**). If an applicant were to miss the 21-day appeal deadline and then seek judicial review instead, this would not be considered appropriate by the Administrative Court in the absence of very exceptional circumstances.

An example of where an applicant was allowed to bring an application for judicial review after missing the 21-day county court deadline was the case of *R v Lambeth LBC, ex p Alleyne* (1999) June 1999 *Legal Action* 23, CA. Here, the Court of Appeal held that the applicant should be allowed to proceed. The Court expressed its view that the jurisdiction of the High Court was to be used sparingly in such cases, but where there was an arguable case the claimant ought to have the opportunity to demonstrate that the circumstances were 'exceptional'.

Contrast this with the case of *R v Brent LBC, ex p O'Connor* (1999) 31 HLR 923, QBD, where the applicant was not allowed to seek judicial review after missing the county court deadline. The court found that there was an arguable case, but held that the applicant had to show 'some really exceptional circumstances' to justify not exercising her right of appeal within the time limit. On the facts of the case she was unable to do so.

This situation has now been alleviated to some extent by s 204(2A) of the HA 1996 (introduced by the Homelessness Act 2002), which provides for the extension of the 21-day period in limited circumstances (see **12.5.2** above).

It is also possible to apply for judicial review outside the three-month period in exceptional circumstances. The Administrative Court has a general power to extend the time limit (CPR, r 3.1(2)(a)) where the court considers there is good reason for the delay. This power is likely to be used in very limited circumstances and is at the discretion of the court.

In the case of R v Stratford-upon-Avon DC, ex p Jackson [1985] 1 WLR 1319, the plaintiff was allowed to seek judicial review some seven months after the decision on a planning application because of a delay by the Legal Aid Board (now the LAA) in granting public funding. The court regarded this as a good reason for the delay and extended the time limit. However, delays in public funding are now less likely to provide a good reason for delay, as solicitors should usually be able to exercise their delegated functions to grant emergency funding to claimants to enable the application to be commenced at once (see **5.4.1**).

12.6.3 Judicial review procedure

Judicial review is often referred to as a two-stage procedure. The first stage is obtaining permission. If the claimant is successful in obtaining the court's permission, he may then proceed to the second stage, ie the full hearing of the substantive claim. The purpose of the permission stage is to filter cases, to ensure that only those with arguable grounds proceed to the full hearing stage. However, there is a now a preliminary stage to be complied with prior to the commencement of proceedings. This is the Judicial Review Pre-action Protocol.

12.6.3.1 Pre-action Protocol

The Pre-action Protocol for Judicial Review (PRO 7) is contained in the CPR 1998. The purpose of the Pre-action Protocol is to ensure that the defendant is aware of the potential claim and to give the parties an opportunity to try to resolve the matter before resorting to legal action. It should be used in all but the most urgent of cases. Even where a case is deemed urgent, the claimant should still inform the defendant of the fact that a claim is about to be issued, for example by faxing a copy of the claim form to the defendant before filing at court. Failure to comply with the Protocol could have adverse costs consequences for the claimant.

The Protocol requires the claimant to send a letter before action to the defendant setting out the basis of the claim. The letter should request a reply within a reasonable period, which is usually 14 days (subject to the urgency of the matter, which may require a shorter period). The LHA should usually respond within the given period and indicate whether it intends to contest the claim. If the claim is not conceded, the claimant may then commence his claim.

12.6.3.2 Making the claim

The procedure for making a claim for judicial review is governed by Part 54 of the CPR 1998. The claim is commenced by the issue of a claim form (Form N461) at the Administrative Court. This must contain the information required by CPR, r 8.2, together with details of the names and addresses of interested parties, a request for permission and details of any remedy sought.

Where the claimant is asking for the matter to be considered as a matter of urgency, he must also complete a Request for Urgent Consideration on Form N463, which states the need for the urgency and the timescale within which the permission application should be considered (eg 72 hours, or sooner if necessary). Where an interim injunction is sought, the claimant must also provide a draft order and the grounds for the injunction. The claimant must serve (by fax and post) the claim form and application for urgency on the defendant, advising it of the application and informing the defendant that it may make representations (PD 54, para 21).

Rule 8.2 of the CPR provides that the claim form must state the question that the claimant wants the court to decide, the remedy he is seeking and the enactment under which the claim is being made (if any).

Paragraph 5.6 of PD 54 provides that the claim form must include, or be accompanied by:

(a) a detailed statement of the claimant's grounds for bringing the claim;
(b) a statement of the facts relied on;
(c) any application to extend the time limit for filing the claim form; and
(d) any application for directions.

Paragraph 5.7 provides that, in addition, the claim form must be accompanied by:

(a) any written evidence in support of the claim or application to extend time;
(b) a copy of the order (or decision) that the claimant seeks to have quashed;
(c) an approved copy of the reasons of the court who made the decision, if applicable;
(d) copies of the documents on which the claimant wishes to rely;
(e) copies of any relevant statutory material; and
(f) a list of essential reading for the court.

The claimant must file two copies of a paginated and indexed bundle containing all of the documents referred to in paras 5.6 and 5.7 (para 5.9).

Once the claim form has been issued, upon payment of the current fee, it must be served on the defendant within seven days (CPR, r 54.7), together with an acknowledgement of service form which must be filed by the defendant within 21 days of service (CPR, r 54.8).

The court will then consider the application for permission, usually without a hearing. Following the consideration of the permission application, the parties will be served with an order giving or refusing permission, and giving any directions made by the court (CPR, r 54.11). If permission is refused without a hearing, the claimant may request that the permission application be reconsidered at a hearing, unless the court has recorded that the application is totally without merit (CPR, r 54.12).

If permission is granted, a further fee is payable by the claimant. The defendant must then file its response to the claim and any evidence on which it intends to rely, within 35 days of service of the order granting permission (CPR, r 54.14). The case will be listed for hearing in due course.

12.6.4 Grounds of judicial review

The grounds of judicial review are the same as those considered at **12.5.3** in respect of an appeal to the county court on a point of law.

12.6.5 Remedies

It is important to note that remedies in judicial review cases are discretionary. This means that the court may refuse to grant a remedy even though the LHA has acted unlawfully. This may arise where, for example, the error made no difference to the outcome of the decision.

An appeal against a final decision of the Administrative Court is to the Court of Appeal. Permission to appeal is required.

The following remedies are available in judicial review proceedings (CPR, r 54.2).

12.6.5.1 Public law remedies

These remedies are available only in judicial review proceedings:

(a) A *quashing order*, which quashes the decision in question. This type of order invalidates a decision that has been taken unlawfully.

(b) A *prohibiting order*, which orders the public body to refrain from illegal action. This type of order is very similar to an injunction and is used to prevent unlawful action from being taken. It is not available as an interim remedy (contrast this with an injunction, considered at **12.6.5.2** below).

(c) A *mandatory order*, which enforces the performance by public bodies of their duties. This type of order is used where a public body has failed to carry out a duty imposed on it, usually by statute. It requires the public body to comply with that duty.

12.6.5.2 Private law remedies

These remedies are generally available in litigation, including judicial review cases:

(a) A *declaration*, which declares the correct legal position in relation to an issue. This type of remedy is used to clarify the law where the position is unclear.

(b) An *injunction*, which performs essentially the same function as a prohibiting order (see **12.6.5.1**). An injunction may be used at an interim stage, in contrast to a prohibiting order, which is available only at the end of the case.

(c) *Damages*, which may be claimed only if the claimant can also show a breach of contract or a tort, which will very rarely be the case in a homelessness context. A claim for judicial review can include a claim for damages, but the claimant may not seek damages alone (CPR, r 54.3). Damages may also be available where the public body has committed a breach of the applicant's human rights (Human Rights Act 1998, s 8).

12.6.6 Accommodation pending the hearing

It is possible to seek an interim injunction to secure temporary accommodation pending the hearing of the application for judicial review. In the case of *De Falco v Crawley BC* [1980] QB 460, CA, it was held that it would be necessary to show a strong prima facie case in order to be granted interim relief. In the case of *R v Camden LBC, ex p Mohammed* (1997) 30 HLR 315, QBD, the court gave general guidance on housing pending review, which may be applied by analogy. The LHA should take into account all material considerations, including the applicant's personal circumstances and the consequences of refusing interim housing. It should have regard to the merits of the case and to any new material, information or argument put forward by the applicant.

12.6.7 Public funding

The funding considerations in respect of judicial review are essentially the same as those considered above at **12.5.6.1** in connection with appeals to the county court. Even though the time limit in judicial review cases is theoretically longer than that for appeal, the funding application should still be dealt with on an urgent basis, as proceedings must be commenced as expeditiously as possible.

12.6.8 Costs

The successful party will usually be awarded costs. Where a claimant is publicly funded, his solicitor must account to the LAA for the costs to ensure that the LAA is reimbursed for any monies it has paid to the solicitor by way of public funding. Costs awarded against an unsuccessful publicly funded litigant are not normally enforceable without leave of the court. This means that a litigant with the benefit of a certificate of public funding is largely protected against a costs order, unless his financial position changes significantly (see **5.7.1**).

12.7 COMMISSIONERS FOR LOCAL ADMINISTRATION

A final means of challenge to an LHA decision is a complaint to the Commissioners for Local Administration, also known as 'Ombudsmen'. There are various Ombudsmen schemes, set up to deal with the scrutiny of government departments and public bodies. The Commissioners for Local Administration are empowered under the Local Government Act 1974 to consider complaints of maladministration by LHAs on a regional basis. Although provisions in ss 180–182 of the Localism Act 2011 have transferred some of the areas of housing law previously dealt with by the Ombudsmen to the Housing Ombudsman (see **7.5.4**), complaints relating to allocation and homelessness matters are still within the remit of the local government Ombudsmen. The complainant must demonstrate the he has suffered injustice in consequence of the maladministration (see below).

There is no charge for making a complaint to the Commissioners and the procedure is relatively straightforward. It is intended that complainants should pursue the matter without the assistance of a solicitor, although solicitors are often involved in complex complaints.

The Commissioners have investigatory powers, and may recommend that compensation be paid to the complainant if injustice as a result of maladministration is found.

Maladministration is concerned with the manner in which a decision is reached rather than with the merits of the decision itself. In a homelessness context it could include such issues as:

(a) delay in reaching a decision on an application;
(b) failure to offer accommodation in discharge of duty;
(c) administrative mistakes in dealing with an application.

An investigation by the Commissioners typically takes a number of months. For this reason, it is not considered suitable for urgent matters. Where the applicant could either take court action or make a complaint to the Commissioners, the determining factors will be the urgency and complexity of the case. If the case is not urgent, or raises no significant or complex legal issues, it may be appropriate to make a complaint to the Commissioners. However, since an appeal to the county court is available by way of right, this would usually be the preferred remedy where the applicant can establish grounds of appeal. The only circumstances in which the applicant might prefer to use the Ombudsman's scheme is where he is ineligible for public funding and cannot afford to fund the appeal privately.

A complaint to the Commissioners should usually be made within 12 months of the date on which the grounds for complaint arose, although the deadline may be extended if it is considered reasonable to do so. The complainant must have exhausted the landlord's internal complaint procedure.

Although the Commissioners can recommend that the LHA compensate the complainant, they cannot compel the authority to do so. However, LHAs generally do comply with the Commissioner's recommendations.

Following the completion of an investigation into a complaint, the relevant Commissioner issues a report. The LHA is obliged to consider the report and advise the Commissioner within three months of any action taken to comply with the findings. If the Commissioner is dissatisfied with the response of the LHA, he may issue a further report; and if the LHA is proposing not to take any action in relation to the complaint, the matter must be referred to a meeting of the full council. In practice, adverse political consequences and the effect of publicity usually secure compliance with a Commissioner's report and recommendations.

Housing cases (including homelessness) account for approximately 40% of the complaints to the Commissioners for Local Administration, who therefore have significant expertise in dealing with matters of this type.

12.8 FURTHER READING

J Luba and L Davies, *Housing Allocations and Homelessness* (3rd edn, 2012)

> **SUMMARY**
> - Homelessness procedure begins with an application.
> - The LHA then has a duty to investigate and give written notice to the applicant of its decision.
> - If the decision is adverse, the LHA must give the applicant reasons and notice of the right to review.
> - The applicant has 21 days to request a review.
> - If the review decision is adverse, the applicant has 21 days to appeal to the county court on a point of law.
> - Judicial review is possible for certain challenges to LHA decisions.
> - The ombudsman procedure may be another alternative in non-urgent challenges.

Summaries – Housing Law and Practice

PART I SUMMARY – SECURITY OF TENURE

Topic	Summary	References
Security	Security of tenure for residential tenants can arise under three different statutory regimes. They are assured tenancies under the Housing Act 1988, regulated tenancies under the Rent Act 1977, and secure tenancies under the Housing Act 1985.	
Assured tenancies	To have protection under the 1988 Act a tenant must be an individual to whom a dwelling is let as a separate dwelling, and the tenant or, if it is a joint tenancy, at least one tenant occupies the dwelling as his only or principal home. Some tenancies are excluded from this category of protection, eg tenants with residential landlords.	2.2, 2.3
Assured tenancies – terms	The parties are free to agree a market rent for the property as there is no rent control.	2.4
	The tenant cannot assign the tenancy without the landlord's consent.	
	If the tenancy was a periodic tenancy granted to a sole tenant, there may be a right to succession on his death. The right will arise if there was a spouse or civil partner, or a person living with the tenant as such, in occupation of the premises at the time of the tenant's death.	
Assured tenancies – security	Security is obtained by restricting the basis on which the landlord can obtain possession. Only a court order can terminate an assured tenancy, and the court will not grant such an order unless the appropriate procedure is followed and the landlord satisfies the court on one or more grounds for possession listed in Sch 2 to the Act.	2.5, 2.6
Assured tenants of RSLs and PRPs	Assured tenants who have a registered social landlord (RSL) or private registered provider (PRP) are generally in a better position than those of private landlords. RSLs and PRPs charge below market rents for their properties and the tenancy terms are more generous to the tenant. However, RSLs and PRPs have wider statutory powers to control the behaviour of their tenants, particularly anti-social behaviour. RSLs and PRPs can obtain demotion orders to take away a tenant's security. Anti-social behaviour injunctions and orders can be obtained, and parenting contracts and orders may be used.	2.9
Assured shorthold tenancies	Assured shorthold tenancies are a sub-species of assured tenancies which have less security, as the the landlord can obtain possession simply by serving an appropriate notice requiring possession at least two months after the date of service. Since 2007, however, new assured shorthold tenants have benefited from the Tenancy Deposit Schemes.	2.7, 2.8

Topic	Summary	References
Regulated tenancies	To have a regulated tenancy under the Rent Act 1977, the tenant, who could be an individual or a legal person, must have a let of a separate dwelling. No new regulated tenancy can be created after 15 January 1989 when the assured tenancy regime came into existence. Some tenancies are excluded from this category of protection, eg tenants with resident landlords.	3.2, 3.3
Regulated tenancies – security	On the expiry of a fixed-term tenancy, or the termination by notice to quit of a periodic tenancy if an individual is still in occupation of the property as his home, he can become a statutory tenant and can continue to occupy the dwelling until death, unless the landlord is able to offer suitable alternative accommodation or obtains possession on one of the grounds listed in Sch 15 to the Act. There are also rights of succession to a spouse (as a statutory tenant) or family member (as an assured tenant). Regulated tenants enjoy below-market rents.	3.4, 3.5
Secure tenancies	To have a secure tenancy under the Housing Act 1985, a tenant or licensee must be an individual who has a let of a separate dwelling. He must occupy the dwelling as his only or principal home. The landlord must be a public sector landlord. Some tenancies are excluded from this category of protection, eg introductory tenancies.	6.3, 6.4, 6.5
Secure tenancies – security	Security is obtained by restricting the basis on which the landlord can terminate the secure tenancy or obtain possession of the property. Only a court order can terminate a secure tenancy, and the court will not grant such an order unless the appropriate procedure is followed and the landlord satisfies the court on one or more grounds for possession listed in Sch 2 to the Act or makes out a case for a demotion order which would terminate the secure tenancy.	6.6, 6.7
Secure tenancies – rights	Secure tenants enjoy many rights, including succession rights and the right to buy.	6.8

PART II SUMMARY – DISREPAIR AND UNLAWFUL EVICTION AND HARASSMENT

Topic	Summary	References
Disrepair – meaning	The obligation in a tenancy agreement to repair or keep in repair will be breached only if there is some physical deterioration in the state of the premises.	7.2
Disrepair – contractual obligation	There could be express contractual terms, or terms implied by common law or statute. The most important statutory implied term in a residential lease is that in s 11 of the Landlord and Tenant Act 1985.	7.3
Disrepair – tort obligations	Obligations in relation to disrepair arise in tort law and may make a landlord liable to compensate the tenant under common law and statute, in particular under the Defective Premises Act 1972.	7.4
Disrepair – civil remedies and procedure	There are various options open to a tenant whose landlord is in breach of his repairing obligations. These include self-help, applying for an injunction, specific performance and/or damages. If the repairing obligation is on the tenant, the landlord may have similar remedies, or he could forfeit the tenancy if there is a right reserved in the tenancy agreement. In any court action brought by a tenant, the Pre-action Protocol for Housing Disrepair Cases needs to be followed.	7.5, 7.6
Disrepair – public law obligations	Local authorities have an obligation to deal with properties which are prejudicial to health or a nuisance under the Environmental Protection Act 1990. They can effectively serve an abatement notice on the party responsible for the state of the property. If the local authority fails to act, the occupier could apply to a magistrates' court to serve an order to abate the nuisance. In extreme cases, premises may be made subject to improvement notices or their use prohibited for residential purposes under the provisions in Part 1 of the Housing Act 2004.	7.8
Unlawful eviction and harassment – civil cause	A landlord who unlawfully evicts or harasses his tenant may be sued under various heads of claim. In contract the tenant can pursue claims for breach of the covenant of quiet enjoyment and derogation from grant. In tort, in addition to any trespass and nuisance claims, the tenant may have statutory claims for breach of statute under s 3 of the Protection from Eviction Act 1977 and the tort of eviction under s 27 of the Housing Act 1988. Some tenants are excluded from the statutory remedies, eg tenants who share accommodation with resident landlords.	9.2, 9.3
Unlawful eviction and harassment – criminal sanctions	There are various statutory provisions under which it will be an offence to harass or evict a residential occupier.	9.6

PART III SUMMARY – POSSESSION CLAIMS

Topic	Summary	References
Procedure	CPR 1998, Part 55 is applicable to residential possession claims. Most possession claims arise as a result of rent arrears, and there is a Pre-action Protocol for Possession Claims based on Rent Arrears to be followed by social landlords when bringing possession claims based solely on rent arrears.	10.2, 10.3, 10.7
	There are prescribed forms to be used for the claim and particulars depending on whom possession is being sought against.	
	There is an accelerated procedure to obtain possession against assured shorthold tenants where the landlord is relying on possession based on the service of a valid notice under s 21 of the Housing Act 1988.	
Possession orders	Possession orders can be immediate, outright, suspended or postponed. Which order is made will depend on the nature of the defendant's occupancy and whether the judge has a discretion in whether or not an order can be made.	10.8
	In some situations, once the landlord has made out the ground for possession, the court must grant the possession order, eg Ground 8 for assured tenants.	
	However, a social landlord's legal right to possession may be open to challenge under Article 8 of the Convention, as an unlawful interference with the tenant's right to a home.	
Tolerated trespassers	The status of a tenant who remains in occupation after an order for possession has been made could change to that of tolerated trespasser. The tenant effectively ceases to be a tenant and loses most of the rights that goes with that, eg the ability to sue for breach of the repairing covenant. However, statutory reforms have changed this situation for secure and assured tenants. Now a court order for possession will not terminate the tenancy until the tenant voluntarily vacates or the order is executed.	10.9
Challenging possession orders	There are several ways in which a possession order can be challenged: by way of an application to set aside; by way of appeal; or by applying for a stay or suspension of the order. In some instances the tenancy may be revived if an application to postpone the date of possession of an order is granted.	10.10

PART IV SUMMARY – HOMELESSNESS

Topic	Summary	References
	Part VII of the Housing Act 1996, as amended, puts an obligation on local housing authorities (LHAs) to provide assistance to certain people in need of accommodation. Whether or not a duty arises and the extent of that duty will depend on four principles being applied to an applicant: (a) eligibility; (b) homeless or threatened with homelessness; (c) priority need; (d) intentional homelessness.	
Eligibility	Only persons who are eligible will be able to get assistance under the provisions for homeless applicants contained in Part VII. Persons from abroad may not be eligible if subject to immigration controls, or if the Secretary of State has passed regulations which make them ineligible.	11.2
Homelessness	LHAs have a duty towards those eligible applicants who are homeless or threatened with homelessness. A person will be homeless if he has no accommodation which he can occupy himself or with his family if they would normally reside or could reasonably be expected to reside with him. A person does not need to be literally roofless to be homeless. People living in overcrowded or unfit conditions may be homeless, as may people who may be exposed to domestic violence in their home.

A person is threatened with homelessness if he will become homeless within 28 days. | 11.3 |
Priority need	If an applicant has a priority need, the LHA will have a greater duty to assist. Priority is given to a wide range of applicants. These include pregnant applicants; those with dependent children who reside with them; vulnerable persons such as the disabled; and applicants who face emergency or disaster such as floods or fire.	11.4
Intentional homelessness	The duty towards an eligible applicant who is intentionally homeless will be considerably reduced. An applicant will be intentionally homeless if he has deliberately done something or failed to do something which led to the loss of accommodation.	11.5
Local connection	If an applicant is found to be unintentionally homeless and in priority need, the LHA will have a full housing duty towards him. If, however, the applicant has no local connection with the local area in which he has applied as homeless, the LHA may be able to refer the applicant to another authority with which the applicant does have a local connection. An applicant will have a local connection with an area where he was normally resident or employed or has family associations.	11.6

Topic	Summary	References
Duties	The duty that an LHA has towards an applicant may range from simple advice and assistance, eg to a homeless applicant who is not in priority need, through to a full housing duty to secure that suitable accommodation is available for an applicant who is unintentionally homeless and in priority need.	11.7
Procedure	Once an application is made, the LHA has several obligations to perform. It has a duty to make enquiries, to notify the applicant of the decision and, if the decision is unfavourable, conduct a review if requested by the applicant. In some cases the LHA may have to provide temporary accommodation while it carries out enquiries. If the applicant is unhappy with the performance of the LHA at any stage, he may be able to challenge the actions of the LHA by way of appeal to a county court or, in some cases, by way of an application for judicial review.	Chapter 12

Appendix – Legislation

Defective Premises Act 1972 — 221
    ss 4, 6

Protection from Eviction Act 1977 — 223
    ss 1–3A, 5, 6, 8

Housing Act 1985 — 228
    ss 79–106A, 107A–107E, 112, 113, Schs 1–3

Landlord and Tenant Act 1985 — 259
    ss 8, 11–27A, Sch

Housing Act 1988 — 272
    ss 1, 5–9A, 11, 13, 15–22, 27, 28, Schs 1–2

Environmental Protection Act 1990 — 300
    ss 79–82

Housing Act 1996 — 311
    ss 81, 124–125B, 127–129, 131–137A, 143A, 143B, 143D–143F, 153A–153E, 154, 159, 160ZA, 160A, 166A, 167, 170, 175–177, 182–186, 188–193, 195, 196, 198–200, 202–204A, 206, 208, 210, 211, 218

DEFECTIVE PREMISES ACT 1972
(1972, c. 35)

4. **Landlord's duty of care in virtue of obligation or right to repair premises demised**

    (1) Where premises are let under a tenancy which puts on the landlord an obligation to the tenant for the maintenance or repair of the premises, the landlord owes to all persons who might reasonably be expected to be affected by defects in the state of the premises a duty to take such care as is reasonable in all the circumstances to see that they are reasonably safe from personal injury or from damage to their property caused by a relevant defect.

    (2) The said duty is owed if the landlord knows (whether as the result of being notified by the tenant or otherwise) or if he ought in all the circumstances to have known of the relevant defect.

    (3) In this section 'relevant defect' means a defect in the state of the premises existing at or after the material time and arising from, or continuing because of, an act or omission by the landlord which constitutes or would if he had had notice of the defect, have constituted a failure by him to carry out his obligation to the tenant for the maintenance or repair of the premises; and for the purposes of the foregoing provision 'the material time' means—

        (a) where the tenancy commenced before this Act, the commencement of this Act; and

        (b) in all other cases, the earliest of the following times, that is to say—

            (i) the time when the tenancy commences;

            (ii) the time when the tenancy agreement is entered into;

            (iii) the time when possession is taken of the premises in contemplation of the letting.

    (4) Where premises are let under a tenancy which expressly or impliedly gives the landlord the right to enter the premises to carry out any description of maintenance or repair of the premises, then, as from the time when he first is, or by notice or otherwise can put himself, in a position to exercise the right and so long as he is or can put himself in that position, he shall be treated for the purposes of subsections (1) to (3) above (but for no other purpose) as if he were under an obligation to the tenant for that description of maintenance or repair of the premises; but the landlord shall not owe the tenant any duty by virtue of this subsection in respect of any defect in the state of the premises arising from, or continuing because of, a failure to carry out an obligation expressly imposed on the tenant by the tenancy.

    (5) For the purposes of this section obligations imposed or rights given by any enactment in virtue of a tenancy shall be treated as imposed or given by the tenancy.

    (6) This section applies to a right of occupation given by contract or any enactment and not amounting to a tenancy as if the right were a tenancy, and 'tenancy' and cognate expressions shall be construed accordingly.

6. **Supplemental**

    (1) In this Act—

    'disposal', in relation to premises, includes a letting, and an assignment or surrender of a tenancy, of the premises and the creation by contract of any other right to occupy the premises, and 'dispose' shall be construed accordingly;

    'personal injury' includes any disease and any impairment of a person's physical or mental condition;

    'tenancy' means—

        (a) a tenancy created either immediately or derivatively out of the freehold, whether by a lease or underlease, by an agreement for a lease or underlease or by a tenancy agreement, but not including a mortgage term or any interest arising in favour of a mortgagor by his attorning tenant to his mortgagee; or

        (b) a tenancy at will or a tenancy on sufferance; or

        (c) a tenancy, whether or not constituting a tenancy at common law, created by or in pursuance of any enactment;

    and cognate expressions shall be construed accordingly.

    (2) Any duty imposed by or enforceable by virtue of any provision of this Act is in addition to any duty a person may owe apart from that provision.

(3) Any term of an agreement which purports to exclude or restrict, or has the effect of excluding or restricting, the operation of any of the provisions of this Act, or any liability arising by virtue of any such provision, shall be void.

PROTECTION FROM EVICTION ACT 1977
(1977, c. 43)

PART I
UNLAWFUL EVICTION AND HARASSMENT

1. **Unlawful eviction and harassment of occupier**

    (1) In this section 'residential occupier', in relation to any premises, means a person occupying the premises as a residence, whether under a contract or by virtue of any enactment or rule of law giving him the right to remain in occupation or restricting the right of any other person to recover possession of the premises.

    (2) If any person unlawfully deprives the residential occupier of any premises of his occupation of the premises or any part thereof, or attempts to do so, he shall be guilty of an offence unless he proves that he believed, and had reasonable cause to believe, that the residential occupier had ceased to reside in the premises.

    (3) If any person with intent to cause the residential occupier of any premises—

    (a) to give up the occupation of the premises or any part thereof; or

    (b) to refrain from exercising any right or pursuing any remedy in respect of the premises or part thereof;

    does acts likely to interfere with the peace or comfort of the residential occupier or members of his household, or persistently withdraws or withholds services reasonably required for the occupation of the premises as a residence he shall be guilty of an offence.

    (3A) Subject to subsection (3B) below, the landlord of a residential occupier or an agent of the landlord shall be guilty of an offence if—

    (a) he does acts likely to interfere with the peace or comfort of the residential occupier or members of his household, or

    (b) he persistently withdraws or withholds services reasonably required for the occupation of the premises in question as a residence,

    and (in either case) he knows, or has reasonable cause to believe, that the conduct is likely to cause the residential occupier to give up the occupation of the whole or part of the premises or to refrain from exercising any right or pursuing any remedy in respect of the whole or part of the premises.

    (3B) A person shall not be guilty of an offence under subsection (3A) above if he proves that he had reasonable grounds for doing the acts or withdrawing or withholding the services in question.

    (3C) In subsection (3A) above 'landlord', in relation to a residential occupier of any premises, means the person who, but for—

    (a) the residential occupier's right to remain in occupation of the premises, or

    (b) a restriction on the person's right to recover possession of the premises,

    would be entitled to occupation of the premises and any superior landlord under whom that person derives title.

    (4) A person guilty of an offence under this section shall be liable—

    (a) on summary conviction, to a fine not exceeding the prescribed sum or to imprisonment for a term not exceeding six months or to both;

    (b) on conviction on indictment, to a fine or to imprisonment for a term not exceeding two years or to both.

    (5) Nothing in this section shall be taken to prejudice any liability or remedy to which a person guilty of an offence thereunder may be subject in civil proceedings.

    (6) Where an offence under this section committed by a body corporate is proved to have been committed with the consent or connivance of, or to be attributable to any neglect on the part of, any director, manager or secretary or other similar officer of the body corporate or any person who was purporting to act in any such capacity, he as well as the body corporate shall be guilty of that offence and shall be liable to be proceeded against and punished accordingly.

2. **Restriction on re-entry without due process of law**

    Where any premises are let as a dwelling on a lease which is subject to a right of re-entry or forfeiture it shall not be lawful to enforce that right otherwise than by proceedings in the court while any person is lawfully residing in the premises or part of them.

3. **Prohibition of eviction without due process of law**
    (1) Where any premises have been let as a dwelling under a tenancy which is neither a statutorily protected tenancy nor an excluded tenancy and—
        (a) the tenancy (in this section referred to as the former tenancy) has come to an end, but
        (b) the occupier continues to reside in the premises or part of them,
        it shall not be lawful for the owner to enforce against the occupier, otherwise than by proceedings in the court, his right to recover possession of the premises.
    (2) In this section 'the occupier', in relation to any premises, means any person lawfully residing in the premises or part of them at the termination of the former tenancy.
    (2A) Subsections (1) and (2) above apply in relation to any restricted contract (within the meaning of the Rent Act 1977) which—
        (a) creates a licence; and
        (b) is entered into after the commencement of section 69 of the Housing Act 1980;
        as they apply in relation to a restricted contract which creates a tenancy.
    (2B) Subsections (1) and (2) above apply in relation to any premises occupied as a dwelling under a licence, other than an excluded licence, as they apply in relation to premises let as a dwelling under a tenancy, and in those subsections the expressions 'let' and 'tenancy' shall be construed accordingly.
    (2C) References in the preceding provisions of this section and section 4(2A) below to an excluded tenancy do not apply to—
        (a) a tenancy entered into before the date on which the Housing Act 1988 came into force, or
        (b) a tenancy entered into on or after that date but pursuant to a contract made before that date,
        but, subject to that, 'excluded tenancy' and 'excluded licence' shall be construed in accordance with section 3A below.
    (3) This section shall, with the necessary modifications, apply where the owner's right to recover possession arises on the death of the tenant under a statutory tenancy within the meaning of the Rent Act 1977 or the Rent (Agriculture) Act 1976.

3A. **Excluded tenancies and licences**
    (1) Any reference in this Act to an excluded tenancy or an excluded licence is a reference to a tenancy or licence which is excluded by virtue of any of the following provisions of this section.
    (2) A tenancy or licence is excluded if—
        (a) under its terms the occupier shares any accommodation with the landlord or licensor; and
        (b) immediately before the tenancy or licence was granted and also at the time it comes to an end, the landlord or licensor occupied as his only or principal home premises of which the whole or part of the shared accommodation formed part.
    (3) A tenancy or licence is also excluded if—
        (a) under its terms the occupier shares any accommodation with a member of the family of the landlord or licensor;
        (b) immediately before the tenancy or licence was granted and also at the time it comes to an end, the member of the family of the landlord or licensor occupied as his only or principal home premises of which the whole or part of the shared accommodation formed part; and
        (c) immediately before the tenancy or licence was granted and also at the time it comes to an end, the landlord or licensor occupied as his only or principal home premises in the same building as the shared accommodation and that building is not a purpose-built block of flats.
    (4) For the purposes of subsections (2) and (3) above, an occupier shares accommodation with another person if he has the use of it in common with that person (whether or not also in common with others) and any reference in those subsections to shared accommodation shall be construed accordingly, and if, in relation to any tenancy or licence, there is at any time more than one person who is the landlord or licensor, any reference in those subsections to the landlord or licensor shall be construed as a reference to any one of those persons.
    (5) In subsections (2) to (4) above—
        (a) 'accommodation' includes neither an area used for storage nor a staircase, passage, corridor or other means of access;

- (b) 'occupier' means, in relation to a tenancy, the tenant and, in relation to a licence, the licensee; and
- (c) 'purpose-built block of flats' has the same meaning as in Part III of Schedule 1 to the Housing Act 1988;

and section 113 of the Housing Act 1985 shall apply to determine whether a person is for the purposes of subsection (3) above a member of another's family as it applies for the purposes of Part IV of that Act.

(6) A tenancy or licence is excluded if it was granted as a temporary expedient to a person who entered the premises in question or any other premises as a trespasser (whether or not, before the beginning of that tenancy or licence, another tenancy or licence to occupy the premises or any other premises had been granted to him).

(7) A tenancy or licence is excluded if—
- (a) it confers on the tenant or licensee the right to occupy the premises for a holiday only; or
- (b) it is granted otherwise than for money or money's worth.

(7A) A tenancy or licence is excluded if it is granted in order to provide accommodation under section 4 or Part VI of the Immigration and Asylum Act 1999.

(7C) A tenancy or licence is excluded if it is granted in order to provide accommodation under the Displaced Persons (Temporary Protection) Regulations 2005.

(8) A licence is excluded if it confers rights of occupation in a hostel, within the meaning of the Housing Act 1985, which is provided by—
- (a) the council of a county, county borough, district or London Borough, the Common Council of the City of London, the Council of the Isles of Scilly, the Inner London Education Authority, the London Fire and Emergency Planning Authority, a joint authority within the meaning of the Local Government Act 1985 or a residuary body within the meaning of that Act;
- (aa) an economic prosperity board established under section 88 of the Local Democracy, Economic Development and Construction Act 2009;
- (ab) a combined authority established under section 103 of that Act;
- (b) a development corporation within the meaning of the New Towns Act 1981;
- (c) the new towns residuary body;
- (d) an urban development corporation established by an order under section 135 of the Local Government, Planning and Land Act 1980;
- (e) a housing action trust established under Part III of the Housing Act 1988;
- (g) the Regulator of Social Housing;
- (ga) the Secretary of State under section 89 of the Housing Associations Act 1985;
- (h) a housing trust (within the meaning of the Housing Associations Act 1985) which is a charity, a private registered provider of social housing or a registered social landlord (within the meaning of the Housing Act 1985); or
- (i) any other person who is, or who belongs to a class of person which is, specified in an order made by the Secretary of State.

(8A) In subsection (8)(c) above 'new towns residuary body' means—
- (a) in relation to England, the Homes and Communities Agency so far as exercising functions in relation to anything transferred (or to be transferred) to it as mentioned in section 52(1)(a) to (d) of the Housing and Regeneration Act 2008 or the Greater London Authority so far as exercising its new towns and urban development functions; and
- (b) in relation to Wales, means the Welsh Ministers so far as exercising functions in relation to anything transferred (or to be transferred) to them as mentioned in section 36(1)(a)(i) to (iii) of the New Towns Act 1981.

(9) The power to make an order under subsection (8)(i) above shall be exercisable by statutory instrument which shall be subject to annulment in pursuance of a resolution of either House of Parliament.

PART II
NOTICE TO QUIT

5. **Validity of notices to quit**

(1) Subject to subsection (1B) below no notice by a landlord or a tenant to quit any premises let (whether before or after the commencement of this Act) as a dwelling shall be valid unless—

(a) it is in writing and contains such information as may be prescribed, and

(b) it is given not less than four weeks before the date on which it is to take effect.

(1A) Subject to subsection (1B) below, no notice by a licensor or a licensee to determine a periodic licence to occupy premises as a dwelling (whether the licence was granted before or after the passing of this Act) shall be valid unless—

(a) it is in writing and contains such information as may be prescribed, and

(b) it is given not less than four weeks before the date on which it is to take effect.

(1B) Nothing in subsection (1) or subsection (1A) above applies to—

(a) premises let on an excluded tenancy which is entered into on or after the date on which the Housing Act 1988 came into force unless it is entered into pursuant to a contract made before that date; or

(b) premises occupied under an excluded licence.

(2) In this section 'prescribed' means prescribed by regulations made by the Secretary of State by statutory instrument, and a statutory instrument containing any such regulations shall be subject to annulment in pursuance of a resolution of either House of Parliament.

(3) Regulations under this section may make different provision in relation to different descriptions of lettings and different circumstances.

PART III
SUPPLEMENTAL PROVISIONS

6. Prosecution of offences

Proceedings for an offence under this Act may be instituted by any of the following authorities—

(a) councils of districts and London boroughs;

(aa) councils of Welsh counties and county boroughs;

(b) the Common Council of the City of London;

(c) the Council of the Isles of Scilly.

8. Interpretation

(1) In this Act 'statutorily protected tenancy' means—

(a) a protected tenancy within the meaning of the Rent Act 1977 or a tenancy to which Part I of the Landlord and Tenant Act 1954 applies;

(b) a protected occupancy or statutory tenancy as defined in the Rent (Agriculture) Act 1976;

(c) a tenancy to which Part II of the Landlord and Tenant Act 1954 applies;

(d) a tenancy of an agricultural holding within the meaning of the Agricultural Holdings Act 1986 which is a tenancy in relation to which that Act applies;

(e) an assured tenancy or assured agricultural occupancy under Part I of the Housing Act 1988;

(f) a tenancy to which Schedule 10 to the Local Government and Housing Act 1989 applies;

(g) a farm business tenancy within the meaning of the Agricultural Tenancies Act 1995.

(2) For the purposes of Part I of this Act a person who, under the terms of his employment, had exclusive possession of any premises other than as a tenant shall be deemed to have been a tenant and the expressions 'let' and 'tenancy' shall be construed accordingly.

(3) In Part I of this Act 'the owner', in relation to any premises, means the person who, as against the occupier, is entitled to possession thereof.

(4) In this Act 'excluded tenancy' and 'excluded licence' have the meaning assigned by section 3A of this Act.

(5) If, on or after the date on which the Housing Act 1988 came into force, the terms of an excluded tenancy or excluded licence entered into before that date are varied, then—

(a) if the variation affects the amount of the rent which is payable under the tenancy or licence, the tenancy or licence shall be treated for the purposes of sections 3(2C) and 5(1B) above as a new tenancy or licence entered into at the time of the variation; and

(b) if the variation does not affect the amount of the rent which is so payable, nothing in this Act shall affect the determination of the question whether the variation is such as to give rise to a new tenancy or licence.

(6) Any reference in subsection (5) above to a variation affecting the amount of the rent which is payable under a tenancy or licence does not include a reference to—

(a) a reduction or increase effected under Part III or Part VI of the Rent Act 1977 (rents under regulated tenancies and housing association tenancies), section 78 of that Act (power of rent tribunal in relation to restricted contracts) or sections 11 to 14 of the Rent (Agriculture) Act 1976; or

(b) a variation which is made by the parties and has the effect of making the rent expressed to be payable under the tenancy or licence the same as a rent for the dwelling which is entered in the register under Part IV or section 79 of the Rent Act 1977.

HOUSING ACT 1985
(1985, c. 68)

public sector tenancies

PART IV

SECURE TENANCIES AND RIGHTS OF SECURE TENANTS

Security of tenure

79. Secure tenancies

(1) A tenancy under which a dwelling-house is let as a separate dwelling is a secure tenancy at any time when the conditions described in sections 80 and 81 as the landlord condition and the tenant condition are satisfied.

(2) Subsection (1) has effect subject to—

    (a) the exceptions in Schedule 1 (tenancies which are not secure tenancies),

    (b) sections 89(3) and (4) and 90(3) and (4) (tenancies ceasing to be secure after death of tenant), and

    (c) sections 91(2) and 93(2) (tenancies ceasing to be secure in consequence of assignment or subletting).

(3) The provisions of this Part apply in relation to a licence to occupy a dwelling-house (whether or not granted for a consideration) as they apply in relation to a tenancy.

(4) Subsection (3) does not apply to a licence granted as a temporary expedient to a person who entered the dwelling-house or any other land as a trespasser (whether or not, before the grant of that licence, another licence to occupy that or another dwelling-house had been granted to him).

80. The landlord condition

(1) The landlord condition is that the interest of the landlord belongs to one of the following authorities or bodies—

a local authority,

a development corporation,

a housing action trust,

an urban development corporation in the case of a tenancy falling within subsections (2A) to (2E), the Homes and Communities Agency, the Greater London Authority or the Welsh Ministers (as the case may be),

a housing association to which this section applies by virtue of subsection (2) or housing co-operative to which this section applies.

(2A) A tenancy falls within this subsection if the interest of the landlord is transferred to—

    (a) the Homes and Communities Agency as mentioned in section 52(1)(a) to (d) of the Housing and Regeneration Act 2008,

    (aa) the Greater London Authority as mentioned in section 333ZI(2)(a) to (d) of the Greater London Authority Act 1999, or

    (b) the Welsh Ministers as mentioned in section 36(1)(a)(i) to (iii) of the New Towns Act 1981.

(2B) A tenancy falls within this subsection if it is entered into pursuant to a contract under which the rights and liabilities of the prospective landlord are transferred to the Homes and Communities Agency, the Greater London Authority or the Welsh Ministers as mentioned in subsection (2A)(a), (aa) or (b) (as the case may be).

(2C) A tenancy falls within this subsection if it is granted by the Homes and Communities Agency, the Greater London Authority or the Welsh Ministers to a person (alone or jointly with others) who, immediately before it was entered into, was a secure tenant of the Homes and Communities Agency, the Greater London Authority or the Welsh Ministers (as the case may be).

(2D) A tenancy falls within this subsection if—

    (a) it is granted by the Homes and Communities Agency, the Greater London Authority or the Welsh Ministers to a person (alone or jointly with others),

    (b) before the grant of the tenancy, an order for possession of a dwelling-house let under a secure tenancy was made against the person (alone or jointly with others) and in favour of the Homes and Communities Agency, the Greater London Authority or the Welsh Ministers (as the case may be) on the court being satisfied as mentioned in section 84(2)(b) or (c), and

(c) the tenancy is of the premises which constitute the suitable accommodation as to which the court was so satisfied.

(2E) A tenancy falls within this subsection if it is granted by the Homes and Communities Agency, the Greater London Authority or the Welsh Ministers pursuant to an obligation under section 554(2A).

(3) If a co-operative housing association ceases to be a private registered provider of social housing or a registered social landlord, it shall, within the period of 21 days beginning with the date on which it ceases to be such a body, notify each of its tenants who thereby becomes a secure tenant, in writing, that he has become a secure tenant.

(4) This section applies to a housing co-operative within the meaning of section 27B (agreements under certain superseded provisions) where the dwelling-house is comprised in a housing co-operative agreement within the meaning of that section.

(5) In this Act and in any provision made under this Act, or made by or under any other enactment, a reference to—
   (a) a person within section 80 or 80(1) of this Act, or
   (b) a person who satisfies the landlord condition under this section,
   includes a reference to the Homes and Communities Agency, to the Greater London Authority or to the Welsh Ministers so far as acting in their capacity as landlord (or, in the case of disposals, former landlord) in respect of a tenancy which falls within subsections (2A) to (2E) above but, subject to this, does not include the Homes and Communities Agency, the Greater London Authority or the Welsh Ministers.

(6) Subsection (5)—
   (a) applies whether the person is described as an authority, body or landlord or in any other way and whether the reference is otherwise expressed in a different way, and
   (b) is subject to any provision to the contrary.

81. The tenant condition

The tenant condition is that the tenant is an individual and occupies the dwelling-house as his only or principal home; or, where the tenancy is a joint tenancy, that each of the joint tenants is an individual and at least one of them occupies the dwelling-house as his only or principal home.

82. Security of tenure

(1) A secure tenancy which is either—
   (a) a weekly or other periodic tenancy, or
   (b) a tenancy for a term certain but subject to termination by the landlord,
   cannot be brought to an end by the landlord except as mentioned in subsection (1A).

(1A) The tenancy may be brought to an end by the landlord—
   (a) obtaining—
      (i) an order of the court for the possession of the dwelling-house, and
      (ii) the execution of the order,
   (b) obtaining an order under subsection (3), or
   (c) obtaining a demotion order under section 82A.

(2) In the case mentioned in subsection (1A)(a), the tenancy ends when the order is executed.

(3) Where a secure tenancy is a tenancy for a term certain but with a provision for re-entry or forfeiture, the court shall not order possession of the dwelling-house in pursuance of that provision, but in a case where the court would have made such an order it shall instead make an order terminating the tenancy on a date specified in the order and section 86 (periodic tenancy arising on termination of fixed term) shall apply.

(4) Section 146 of the Law of Property Act 1925 (restriction on and relief against forfeiture), except subsection (4) (vesting in under-lessee), and any other enactment or rule of law relating to forfeiture, shall apply in relation to proceedings for an order under subsection (3) of this section as if they were proceedings to enforce a right of re-entry or forfeiture.

82A. Demotion because of anti-social behaviour

(1) This section applies to a secure tenancy if the landlord is—
   (a) a local housing authority;

(b) a housing action trust;
(ba) a private registered provider of social housing;
(c) a registered social landlord.

(2) The landlord may apply to a county court for a demotion order.

(3) A demotion order has the following effect—
   (a) the secure tenancy is terminated with effect from the date specified in the order;
   (b) if the tenant remains in occupation of the dwelling-house after that date a demoted tenancy is created with effect from that date;
   (c) it is a term of the demoted tenancy that any arrears of rent payable at the termination of the secure tenancy become payable under the demoted tenancy;
   (d) it is also a term of the demoted tenancy that any rent paid in advance or overpaid at the termination of the secure tenancy is credited to the tenant's liability to pay rent under the demoted tenancy.

(4) The court must not make a demotion order unless it is satisfied—
   (a) that the tenant or a person residing in or visiting the dwelling-house has engaged or has threatened to engage in—
      (i) housing-related anti-social conduct, or
      (ii) conduct to which section 153B of the Housing Act 1996 (use of premises for unlawful purposes) applies, and
   (b) that it is reasonable to make the order.

(5) Each of the following has effect in respect of a demoted tenancy at the time it is created by virtue of an order under this section as it has effect in relation to the secure tenancy at the time it is terminated by virtue of the order—
   (a) the parties to the tenancy;
   (b) the period of the tenancy;
   (c) the amount of the rent;
   (d) the dates on which the rent is payable.

(6) Subsection (5)(b) does not apply if the secure tenancy was for a fixed term and in such a case the demoted tenancy is a weekly periodic tenancy.

(7) If the landlord of the demoted tenancy serves on the tenant a statement of any other express terms of the secure tenancy which are to apply to the demoted tenancy such terms are also terms of the demoted tenancy.

(7A) In subsection (4)(a) 'housing-related anti-social conduct' has the same meaning as in section 153A of the Housing Act 1996.

(8) For the purposes of this section a demoted tenancy is—
   (a) a tenancy to which section 143A of the Housing Act 1996 applies if the landlord of the secure tenancy is a local housing authority or a housing action trust;
   (b) a tenancy to which section 20B of the Housing Act 1988 applies if the landlord of the secure tenancy is a private registered provider of social housing or a registered social landlord.

83. Proceedings for possession or termination: notice requirements

(1) The court shall not entertain proceedings for an order mentioned in section 82(1A), other than proceedings under section 107D (recovery of possession on expiry of flexible tenancy), unless—
   (a) the landlord has served a notice on the tenant complying with the provisions of this section, or
   (b) the court considers it just and equitable to dispense with the requirement of such a notice.

(2) A notice under this section shall—
   (a) be in a form prescribed by regulations made by the Secretary of State,
   (b) specify the ground on which the court will be asked to make the order, and
   (c) give particulars of that ground.

(3) Where the tenancy is a periodic tenancy and the ground or one of the grounds specified in the notice is Ground 2 in Schedule 2 (nuisance or other anti-social behaviour), the notice—
   (a) shall also—

(i) state that proceedings for the possession of the dwelling-house may be begun immediately, and

(ii) specify the date sought by the landlord as the date on which the tenant is to give up possession of the dwelling-house, and

(b) ceases to be in force twelve months after the date so specified.

(4) Where the tenancy is a periodic tenancy and Ground 2 in Schedule 2 is not specified in the notice, the notice—

(a) shall also specify the date after which proceedings for the possession of the dwelling-house may be begun, and

(b) ceases to be in force twelve months after the date so specified.

(4A) If the proceedings are for a demotion order under section 82A the notice—

(a) must specify the date after which the proceedings may be begun;

(b) ceases to be in force twelve months after the date so specified.

(5) The date specified in accordance with subsection (3), (4) or (4A) must not be earlier than the date on which the tenancy could, apart from this Part, be brought to an end by notice to quit given by the landlord on the same date as the notice under this section.

(6) Where a notice under this section is served with respect to a secure tenancy for a term certain, it has effect also with respect to any periodic tenancy arising on the termination of that tenancy by virtue of section 86; and subsections (3) to (5) of this section do not apply to the notice.

(7) Regulations under this section shall be made by statutory instrument and may make different provision with respect to different cases or descriptions of case, including different provision for different areas.

83A. Additional requirements in relation to certain proceedings for possession

(1) Where a notice under section 83 has been served on a tenant containing the information mentioned in subsection (3)(a) of that section, the court shall not entertain proceedings for the possession of the dwelling-house unless they are begun at a time when the notice is still in force.

(2) Where—

(a) a notice under section 83 has been served on a tenant, and

(b) a date after which proceedings maybe begun has been specified in the notice in accordance with subsection (4)(a) of that section,

the court shall not entertain proceedings for the possession of the dwelling-house unless they are begun after the date so specified and at a time when the notice is still in force.

(3) Where—

(a) the ground or one of the grounds specified in a notice under section 83 is Ground 2A in Schedule 2 (domestic violence), and

(b) the partner who has left the dwelling-house as mentioned in that ground is not a tenant of the dwelling-house,

the court shall not entertain proceedings for the possession of the dwelling-house unless it is satisfied that the landlord has served a copy of the notice on the partner who has left or has taken all reasonable steps to serve a copy of the notice on that partner.

This subsection has effect subject to subsection (5).

(4) Where—

(a) Ground 2A in Schedule 2 is added to a notice under section 83 with the leave of the court after proceedings for possession are begun, and

(b) the partner who has left the dwelling-house as mentioned in that ground is not a party to the proceedings,

the court shall not continue to entertain the proceedings unless it is satisfied that the landlord has served a notice under subsection (6) on the partner who has left or has taken all reasonable steps to serve such a notice on that partner.

This subsection has effect subject to subsection (5).

(5) Where subsection (3) or (4) applies and Ground 2 in Schedule 2 (nuisance or other anti-social behaviour) is also specified in the notice under section 83, the court may dispense with the

requirements as to service in relation to the partner who has left the dwelling-house if it considers it just and equitable to do so.

(6) A notice under this subsection shall—

(a) state that proceedings for the possession of the dwelling-house have begun,

(b) specify the ground or grounds on which possession is being sought, and

(c) give particulars of the ground or grounds.

84. Grounds and orders for possession

(1) The court shall not make an order for the possession of a dwelling-house let under a secure tenancy except on one or more of the grounds set out in Schedule 2 or in accordance with section 107D (recovery of possession on expiry of flexible tenancy).

(2) The court shall not make an order for possession—

(a) on the grounds set out in Part I of that Schedule (grounds 1 to 8), unless it considers it reasonable to make the order,

(b) on the grounds set out in Part II of that Schedule (grounds 9 to 11), unless it is satisfied that suitable accommodation will be available for the tenant when the order takes effect,

(c) on the grounds set out in Part III of that Schedule (grounds 12 to 16), unless it both considers it reasonable to make the order and is satisfied that suitable accommodation will be available for the tenant when the order takes effect;

and Part IV of the Schedule has effect for determining whether suitable accommodation will be available for a tenant.

(3) Where a notice under section 83 has been served on the tenant, the court shall not make such an order on any of those grounds above unless the ground is specified in the notice; but the grounds so specified may be altered or added to with the leave of the court.

(4) Where a date is specified in a notice under section 83 in accordance with subsection (3) of that section, the court shall not make an order which requires the tenant to give up possession of the dwelling-house in question before the date so specified.

85. Extended discretion of court in certain proceedings for possession

(1) Where proceedings are brought for possession of a dwelling-house let under a secure tenancy on any of the grounds set out in Part I or Part III of Schedule 2 (grounds 1 to 8 and 12 to 16: cases in which the court must be satisfied that it is reasonable to make a possession order), the court may adjourn the proceedings for such period or periods as it thinks fit.

(2) On the making of an order for possession of such a dwelling-house on any of those grounds, or at any time before the execution of the order, the court may—

(a) stay or suspend the execution of the order, or

(b) postpone the date of possession,

for such period or periods as the court thinks fit.

(3) On such an adjournment, stay, suspension or postponement the court—

(a) shall impose conditions with respect to the payment by the tenant of arrears of rent (if any) and rent unless it considers that to do so would cause exceptional hardship to the tenant or would otherwise be unreasonable, and

(b) may impose such other conditions as it thinks fit.

(4) If the conditions are complied with, the court may, if it thinks fit, discharge or rescind the order for possession.

Note: This section is amended by the Housing and Regeneration Act 2008, s. 299, Sch. 11, Pt. 1, paras. 1, 3, as from a day to be appointed: subsection (4) is substituted as follows:

(4) The court may discharge or rescind the order for possession if it thinks it appropriate to do so having had regard to—

(a) any conditions imposed under subsection (3), and

(b) the conduct of the tenant in connection with those conditions.

85A. Proceedings for possession: anti-social behaviour

(1) This section applies if the court is considering under section 84(2)(a) whether it is reasonable to make an order for possession on ground 2 set out in Part 1 of Schedule 2 (conduct of tenant or other person).

(2) The court must consider, in particular—
- (a) the effect that the nuisance or annoyance has had on persons other than the person against whom the order is sought;
- (b) any continuing effect the nuisance or annoyance is likely to have on such persons;
- (c) the effect that the nuisance or annoyance would be likely to have on such persons if the conduct is repeated.

86. Periodic tenancy arising on termination of fixed term

(1) Where a secure tenancy ('the first tenancy') is a tenancy for a term certain and comes to an end—
- (a) by effluxion of time, or
- (b) by an order of the court under section 82(3) (termination in pursuance of provision for re-entry or forfeiture),

a periodic tenancy of the same dwelling-house arises by virtue of this section, unless the tenant is granted another secure tenancy of the same dwelling-house (whether a tenancy for a term certain or a periodic tenancy) to begin on the coming to an end of the first tenancy.

(2) Where a periodic tenancy arises by virtue of this section—
- (a) the periods of the tenancy are the same as those for which rent was last payable under the first tenancy, and
- (b) the parties and the terms of the tenancy are the same as those of the first tenancy at the end of it;

except that the terms are confined to those which are compatible with a periodic tenancy and do not include any provision for re-entry or forfeiture.

Succession on death of tenant

86A. Persons qualified to succeed tenant: England

(1) A person ('P') is qualified to succeed the tenant under a secure tenancy of a dwelling-house in England if—
- (a) P occupies the dwelling-house as P's only or principal home at the time of the tenant's death, and
- (b) P is the tenant's spouse or civil partner.

(2) A person ('P') is qualified to succeed the tenant under a secure tenancy of a dwelling-house in England if—
- (a) at the time of the tenant's death the dwelling-house is not occupied by a spouse or civil partner of the tenant as his or her only or principal home,
- (b) an express term of the tenancy makes provision for a person other than such a spouse or civil partner of the tenant to succeed to the tenancy, and
- (c) P's succession is in accordance with that term.

(3) Subsection (1) or (2) does not apply if the tenant was a successor as defined in section 88.

(4) In such a case, a person ('P') is qualified to succeed the tenant if—
- (a) an express term of the tenancy makes provision for a person to succeed a successor to the tenancy, and
- (b) P's succession is in accordance with that term.

(5) For the purposes of this section—
- (a) a person who was living with the tenant as the tenant's wife or husband is to be treated as the tenant's spouse, and
- (b) a person who was living with the tenant as if they were civil partners is to be treated as the tenant's civil partner.

(6) Subsection (7) applies if, on the death of the tenant, there is by virtue of subsection (5) more than one person who fulfils the condition in subsection (1)(b).

(7) Such one of those persons as may be agreed between them or as may, where there is no such agreement, be selected by the landlord is for the purpose of this section to be treated (according to whether that one of them is of the opposite sex to, or of the same sex as, the tenant) as the tenant's spouse or civil partner.

87. Persons qualified to succeed tenant: Wales

A person is qualified to succeed the tenant under a secure tenancy of a dwelling-house in Wales if he occupies the dwelling-house as his only or principal home at the time of the tenant's death and either—

(a) he is the tenant's spouse or civil partner, or

(b) he is another member of the tenant's family and has resided with the tenant throughout the period of twelve months ending with the tenant's death;

unless, in either case, the tenant was himself a successor, as defined in section 88.

88. Cases where the tenant is a successor

(1) The tenant is himself a successor if—

    (a) the tenancy vested in him by virtue of section 89 (succession to a periodic tenancy), or

    (b) he was a joint tenant and has become the sole tenant, or

    (c) the tenancy arose by virtue of section 86 (periodic tenancy arising on ending of term certain) and the first tenancy there mentioned was granted to another person or jointly to him and another person, or

    (d) he became the tenant on the tenancy being assigned to him (but subject to subsections (2) to (3)), or

    (e) he became the tenant on the tenancy being vested in him on the death of the previous tenant, or

    (f) the tenancy was previously an introductory tenancy and he was a successor to the introductory tenancy.

(2) A tenant to whom the tenancy was assigned in pursuance of an order under section 24 of the Matrimonial Causes Act 1973 (property adjustment orders in connection with matrimonial proceedings) or section 17(1) of the Matrimonial and Family Proceedings Act 1984 (property adjustment orders after overseas divorce &c.) is a successor only if the other party to the marriage was a successor.

(2A) A tenant to whom the tenancy was assigned in pursuance of an order under Part 2 of Schedule 5, or paragraph 9(2) or (3) of Schedule 7, to the Civil Partnership Act 2004 (property adjustment orders in connection with civil partnership proceedings or after overseas dissolution of civil partnership, etc.) is a successor only if the other civil partner was a successor.

(3) A tenant to whom the tenancy was assigned by virtue of section 92 (assignments by way of exchange) is a successor only if he was a successor in relation to the tenancy which he himself assigned by virtue of that section.

(4) Where within six months of the coming to an end of a secure tenancy which is a periodic tenancy ('the former tenancy') the tenant becomes a tenant under another secure tenancy which is a periodic tenancy, and—

    (a) the tenant was a successor in relation to the former tenancy, and

    (b) under the other tenancy either the dwelling-house or the landlord, or both, are the same as under the former tenancy,

the tenant is also a successor in relation to the other tenancy unless the agreement creating that tenancy otherwise provides.

89. Succession to periodic tenancy

(1) This section applies where a secure tenant dies and the tenancy is a periodic tenancy.

(1A) Where there is a person qualified to succeed the tenant under section 86A, the tenancy vests by virtue of this section—

    (a) in that person, or

    (b) if there is more than one such person, in such one of them as may be agreed between them or as may, where there is no agreement, be selected by the landlord.

(2) Where there is a person qualified to succeed the tenant under section 87, the tenancy vests by virtue of this section in that person, or if there is more than one such person in the one to be preferred in accordance with the following rules—

    (a) the tenant's spouse or civil partner is to be preferred to another member of the tenant's family;

    (b) of two or more other members of the tenant's family such of them is to be preferred as may be agreed between them or as may, where there is no such agreement, be selected by the landlord.

(3) Where there is no person qualified to succeed the tenant, the tenancy ceases to be a secure tenancy—

(a) when it is vested or otherwise disposed of in the course of the administration of the tenant's estate, unless the vesting or other disposal is in pursuance of an order made under—
  (i) section 24 of the Matrimonial Causes Act 1973 (property adjustment orders made in connection with matrimonial proceedings),
  (ii) section 17(1) of the Matrimonial and Family Proceedings Act 1984 (property adjustment orders after overseas divorce, &c.),
  (iii) paragraph 1 of Schedule 1 to the Children Act 1989 (orders for financial relief against parents), or
  (iv) Part 2 of Schedule 5, or paragraph 9(2) or (3) of Schedule 7, to the Civil Partnership Act 2004 (property adjustment orders in connection with civil partnership proceedings or after overseas dissolution of civil partnership, etc.);
(b) when it is known that when the tenancy is so vested or disposed of it will not be in pursuance of such an order.

(4) A tenancy which ceases to be a secure tenancy by virtue of this section cannot subsequently become a secure tenancy.

90. Devolution of term certain

(1) This section applies where a secure tenant dies and the tenancy is a tenancy for a term certain.

(2) The tenancy remains a secure tenancy until—
(a) it is vested or otherwise disposed of in the course of the administration of the tenant's estate, as mentioned in subsection (3), or
(b) it is known that when it is so vested or disposed of it will not be a secure tenancy.

(3) The tenancy ceases to be a secure tenancy on being vested or otherwise disposed of in the course of administration of the tenant's estate, unless—
(a) the vesting or other disposal is in pursuance of an order made under—
  (i) section 24 of the Matrimonial Causes Act 1973 (property adjustment orders in connection with matrimonial proceedings),
  (ii) section 17(1) of the Matrimonial and Family Proceedings Act 1984 (property adjustment orders after overseas divorce, &c.),
  (iii) paragraph 1 of Schedule 1 to the Children Act 1989 (orders for financial relief against parents), or
  (iv) Part 2 of Schedule 5, or paragraph 9(2) or (3) of Schedule 7, to the Civil Partnership Act 2004 (property adjustment orders in connection with civil partnership proceedings or after overseas dissolution of civil partnership, etc.), or
(b) the vesting or other disposal is to a person qualified to succeed the tenant.

(4) A tenancy which ceases to be a secure tenancy by virtue of this section cannot subsequently become a secure tenancy.

(5) The following provisions apply where a tenancy that was a secure tenancy of a dwelling-house in England—
(a) has been vested or otherwise disposed of in the course of the administration of the secure tenant's estate, and
(b) has ceased to be a secure tenancy by virtue of this section.

(6) Subject as follows, the landlord may apply to the court for an order for possession of the dwelling-house let under the tenancy.

(7) The court may not entertain proceedings for an order for possession under this section unless—
(a) the landlord has served notice in writing on the tenant—
  (i) stating that the landlord requires possession of the dwelling-house, and
  (ii) specifying a date after which proceedings for an order for possession may be begun, and
(b) that date has passed without the tenant giving up possession of the dwelling-house.

(8) The date mentioned in subsection (7)(a)(ii) must fall after the end of the period of four weeks beginning with the date on which the notice is served on the tenant.

(9) On an application to the court for an order for possession under this section, the court must make such an order if it is satisfied that subsection (5) applies to the tenancy.

(10) The tenancy ends when the order is executed.

Assignment, lodgers and subletting

91. Assignment in general prohibited

(1) A secure tenancy which is—

(a) a periodic tenancy, or

(b) a tenancy for a term certain granted on or after 5th November 1982,

is not capable of being assigned except in the cases mentioned in subsection (3).

(2) If a secure tenancy for a term certain granted before 5th November 1982 is assigned, then, except in the cases mentioned in subsection (3), it ceases to be a secure tenancy and cannot subsequently become a secure tenancy.

(3) The exceptions are—

(a) an assignment in accordance with section 92 (assignment by way of exchange);

(b) an assignment in pursuance of an order made under—

(i) section 24 of the Matrimonial Causes Act 1973 (property adjustment orders in connection with matrimonial proceedings),

(ii) section 17(1) of the Matrimonial and Family Proceedings Act 1984 (property adjustment orders after overseas divorce, &c.),

(iii) paragraph 1 of Schedule 1 to the Children Act 1989 (orders for financial relief against parents), or

(iv) Part 2 of Schedule 5, or paragraph 9(2) or (3) of Schedule 7, to the Civil Partnership Act 2004 (property adjustment orders in connection with civil partnership proceedings or after overseas dissolution of civil partnership, etc.);

(c) an assignment to a person who would be qualified to succeed the tenant if the tenant died immediately before the assignment.

92. Assignments by way of exchange

(1) It is a term of every secure tenancy that the tenant may, with the written consent of the landlord, assign the tenancy to another secure tenant who satisfies the condition in subsection (2) or to an assured tenant who satisfies the conditions in subsection (2A).

(2) The condition is that the other secure tenant has the written consent of his landlord to an assignment of his tenancy either to the first-mentioned tenant or to another secure tenant who satisfies the condition in this subsection.

(2A) The conditions to be satisfied with respect to an assured tenant are—

(a) that the landlord under his assured tenancy is the Regulator of Social Housing, a private registered provider of social housing, ... a registered social landlord or a housing trust which is a charity; and

(b) that he intends to confirm his assured tenancy to the secure tenant referred to in subsection (1) or to another secure tenant who satisfies the condition in subsection (2).

(3) The consent required by virtue of this section shall not be withheld except on one or more of the grounds set out in Schedule 3, and if withheld otherwise than on one of those grounds shall be treated as given.

(4) The landlord may not rely on any of the grounds set out in Schedule 3 unless he has, within 42 days of the tenant's application for the consent, served on the tenant a notice specifying the ground and giving particulars of it.

(5) Where rent lawfully due from the tenant has not been paid or an obligation of the tenancy has been broken or not performed, the consent required by virtue of this section may be given subject to a condition requiring the tenant to pay the outstanding rent, remedy the breach or perform the obligation.

(6) Except as provided by subsection (5), a consent required by virtue of this section cannot be given subject to a condition, and a condition imposed otherwise than as so provided shall be disregarded.

93. Lodgers and subletting

(1) It is a term of every secure tenancy that the tenant—

(a) may allow any persons to reside as lodgers in the dwelling-house, but

(b) will not, without the written consent of the landlord, sublet or part with possession of part of the dwelling-house.

(2) If the tenant under a secure tenancy parts with the possession of the dwelling-house or sublets the whole of it (or sublets first part of it and then the remainder), the tenancy ceases to be a secure tenancy and cannot subsequently become a secure tenancy.

94. Consent to subletting

(1) This section applies to the consent required by virtue of section 93(1)(b) (landlord's consent to subletting of part of dwelling-house).

(2) Consent shall not be unreasonably withheld (and if unreasonably withheld shall be treated as given), and if a question arises whether the withholding of consent was unreasonable it is for the landlord to show that it was not.

(3) In determining that question the following matters, if shown by the landlord, are among those to be taken into account—

(a) that the consent would lead to overcrowding of the dwelling-house within the meaning of Part X (overcrowding);

(b) that the landlord proposes to carry out works on the dwelling-house, or on the building of which it forms part, and that the proposed works will affect the accommodation likely to be used by the sub-tenant who would reside in the dwelling-house as a result of the consent.

(4) Consent may be validly given notwithstanding that it follows, instead of preceding, the action requiring it.

(5) Consent cannot be given subject to a condition (and if purporting to be given subject to a condition shall be treated as given unconditionally).

(6) Where the tenant has applied in writing for consent, then—

(a) if the landlord refuses to give consent, it shall give the tenant a written statement of the reasons why consent was refused, and

(b) if the landlord neither gives nor refuses to give consent within a reasonable time, consent shall be taken to have been withheld.

95. Assignment or subletting where tenant condition not satisfied

(1) This section applies to a tenancy which is not a secure tenancy but would be if the tenant condition referred to in section 81 (occupation by the tenant) were satisfied.

(2) Sections 91 and 93(2) (restrictions on assignment or subletting of whole dwelling-house) apply to such a tenancy as they apply to a secure tenancy, except that—

(a) section 91(3)(b) and (c) (assignments excepted from restrictions) do not apply to such a tenancy for a term certain granted before 5th November 1982, and

(b) references to the tenancy ceasing to be secure shall be disregarded, without prejudice to the application of the remainder of the provisions in which those references occur.

Repairs and improvements

96. Right to have repairs carried out

(1) The Secretary of State may make regulations for entitling secure tenants whose landlords are local housing authorities, subject to and in accordance with the regulations, to have qualifying repairs carried out, at their landlords' expense, to the dwelling-houses of which they are such tenants.

(2) The regulations may make all or any of the following provisions, namely—

(a) provision that, where a secure tenant makes an application to his landlord for a qualifying repair to be carried out, the landlord shall issue a repair notice—

(i) specifying the nature of the repair, the listed contractor by whom the repair is to be carried out and the last day of any prescribed period; and

(ii) containing such other particulars as may be prescribed;

(b) provision that, if the contractor specified in a repair notice fails to carry out the repair within a prescribed period, the landlord shall issue a further repair notice specifying such other listed contractor as the tenant may require; and

(c) provision that, if the contractor specified in a repair notice fails to carry out the repair within a prescribed period, the landlord shall pay to the tenant such sum by way of compensation as may be determined by or under the regulations.

(3) The regulations may also make such procedural, incidental, supplementary and transitional provisions as may appear to the Secretary of State necessary or expedient, and may in particular—

(a) require a landlord to take such steps as may be prescribed to make its secure tenants aware of the provisions of the regulations;

(b) require a landlord to maintain a list of contractors who are prepared to carry out repairs for which it is responsible under the regulations;

(c) provide that, where a landlord issues a repair notice, it shall give to the tenant a copy of the notice and the prescribed particulars of at least two other listed contractors who are competent to carry out the repair;

(d) provide for questions arising under the regulations to be determined by the county court; and

(e) enable the landlord to set off against any compensation payable under the regulations any sums owed to it by the tenant.

(4) Nothing in subsection (2) or (3) shall be taken as prejudicing the generality of subsection (1).

(5) Regulations under this section—

(a) may make different provision with respect to different cases or descriptions of case, including different provision for different areas, and

(b) shall be made by statutory instrument which shall be subject to annulment in pursuance of a resolution of either House of Parliament.

(6) In this section—

'listed contractor', in relation to a landlord, means any contractor (which may include the landlord) who is specified in the landlord's list of contractors;

'qualifying repair', in relation to a dwelling-house, means any repair of a prescribed description which the landlord is obliged by a repairing covenant to carry out;

'repairing covenant', in relation to a dwelling-house, means a covenant, whether express or implied, obliging the landlord to keep in repair the dwelling-house or any part of the dwelling-house;

and for the purposes of this subsection a prescribed description may be framed by reference to any circumstances whatever.

97. Tenant's improvements require consent

(1) It is a term of every secure tenancy that the tenant will not make any improvement without the written consent of the landlord.

(2) In this Part 'improvement' means any alteration in, or addition to, a dwelling-house, and includes—

(a) any addition to or alteration in landlord's fixtures and fittings,

(b) any addition or alteration connected with the provision of services to the dwelling-house,

(c) the erection of a wireless or television aerial, and

(d) the carrying out of external decoration.

(3) The consent required by virtue of subsection (1) shall not be unreasonably withheld, and if unreasonably withheld shall be treated as given.

(4) The provisions of this section have effect, in relation to secure tenancies, in place of section 19(2) of the Landlord and Tenant Act 1927 (general provisions as to covenants, &c. not to make improvements without consent).

(5) In this section 'secure tenancy' does not include a secure tenancy that is a flexible tenancy.

98. Provisions as to consents required by s 97

(1) If a question arises whether the withholding of a consent required by virtue of section 97 (landlord's consent to improvements) was unreasonable, it is for the landlord to show that it was not.

(2) In determining that question the court shall, in particular, have regard to the extent to which the improvement would be likely—

(a) to make the dwelling-house, or any other premises, less safe for occupiers,

(b) to cause the landlord to incur expenditure which it would be unlikely to incur if the improvement were not made, or

(c) to reduce the price which the dwelling-house would fetch if sold on the open market or the rent which the landlord would be able to charge on letting the dwelling-house.

(3) A consent required by virtue of section 97 may be validly given notwithstanding that it follows, instead of preceding, the action requiring it.

(4) Where a tenant has applied in writing for a consent which is required by virtue of section 97—

(a) the landlord shall if it refuses consent give the tenant a written statement of the reason why consent was refused, and

(b) if the landlord neither gives nor refuses to give consent within a reasonable time, consent shall be taken to have been withheld.

99. Conditional consent to improvements

(1) Consent required by virtue of section 97 (landlord's consent to improvements) may be given subject to conditions.

(2) If the tenant has applied in writing for consent and the landlord gives consent subject to an unreasonable condition, consent shall be taken to have been unreasonably withheld.

(3) If a question arises whether a condition was reasonable, it is for the landlord to show that it was.

(4) A failure by a secure tenant to satisfy a reasonable condition imposed by his landlord in giving consent to an improvement which the tenant proposes to make, or has made, shall be treated for the purposes of this Part as a breach by the tenant of an obligation of his tenancy.

99A. Right to compensation for improvements

(1) The powers conferred by this section shall be exercisable as respects cases where a secure tenant has made an improvement and—

(a) the work on the improvement was begun not earlier than the commencement of section 122 of the Leasehold Reform Housing and Urban Development Act 1993,

(b) the landlord, or a predecessor in title of the landlord (being a local authority), has given its written consent to the improvement or is to be treated as having given its consent, and

(c) at the time when the tenancy comes to an end the landlord is a local authority and the tenancy is a secure tenancy.

(2) The Secretary of State may make regulations for entitling the qualifying person or persons (within the meaning given by section 99B)—

(a) at the time when the tenancy comes to an end, and

(b) subject to and in accordance with the regulations,

to be paid compensation by the landlord in respect of the improvement.

(3) The regulations may provide that compensation shall be not payable if—

(a) the improvement is not of a prescribed description,

(b) the tenancy comes to an end in prescribed circumstances,

(c) compensation has been paid under section 100 in respect of the improvement, or

(d) the amount of any compensation which would otherwise be payable in less than a prescribed amount;

and for the purposes of this subsection a prescribed description may be framed by reference to any circumstances whatever.

(4) The regulations may provide that the amount of any compensation payable shall not exceed a prescribed amount but, subject to that, shall be determined by the landlord, or calculated, in such manner, and taking into account such matters, as may be prescribed.

(5) The regulations may also make such procedural, incidental, supplementary and transitional provisions as may appear to the Secretary of State necessary or expedient, and may in particular—

(a) provide for the manner in which and the period within which claims for compensation under the regulations are to be made and for the procedure to be followed in determining such claims,

(b) prescribe the form of any document required to be used for the purposes of or in connection with such claims,

(c) provide for questions arising under the regulations to be determined by the district valuer or the county court, and

(d) enable the landlord to set off against any compensation payable under the regulations any sums owed to it by the qualifying person or persons.

(6) Nothing in subsections (3) to (5) shall be taken as prejudicing the generality of subsection (2).

(7) Regulations under this section—

(a) may make different provision with respect to different cases or descriptions of case, including different provision for different areas, and

(b) shall be made by statutory instrument which (except in the case of regulations making only such provision as is mentioned in subsection (5)(b)) shall be subject to annulment in pursuance of a resolution of either House of Parliament.

(8) For the purposes of this section and section 99B, a tenancy shall be treated as coming to an end if—

(a) it ceases to be a secure tenancy by reason of the landlord condition no longer being satisfied, or

(b) it is assigned, with the consent of the landlord—

(i) to another secure tenant who satisfies the condition in subsection (2) of section 92 (assignments by way of exchange), or

(ii) to an assured tenant who satisfies the conditions in subsection (2A) of that section.

(9) In this section—

(a) 'secure tenancy' does not include a secure tenancy that is a flexible tenancy, and

(b) 'secure tenant' does not include a tenant under a secure tenancy that is a flexible tenancy.

99B. Persons qualifying for compensation

(1) A person is a qualifying person for the purposes of section 99A(2) if—

(a) he is, at the time when the tenancy comes to an end, the tenant or, in the case of a joint tenancy at that time, one of the tenants, and

(b) he is a person to whom subsection (2) applies.

(2) This subsection applies to—

(a) the improving tenant;

(b) a person who became a tenant jointly with the improving tenant;

(c) a person in whom the tenancy was vested, or to whom the tenancy was disposed of, under section 89 (succession to periodic tenancy) or section 90 (devolution of term certain) on the death of the improving tenant or in the course of the administration of his estate;

(d) a person to whom the tenancy was assigned by the improving tenant and who would have been qualified to succeed him if he had died immediately before the assignment;

(e) a person to whom the tenancy was assigned by the improving tenant in pursuance of an order made under—

(i) section 24 of the Matrimonial Causes Act 1973 (property adjustment orders in connection with matrimonial proceedings),

(ii) section 17(1) of the Matrimonial and Family Proceedings Act 1984 (property adjustment orders after overseas divorce, &c.),

(iii) paragraph 1 of Schedule 1 to the Children Act 1989 (orders for financial relief against parents), or

(iv) Part 2 of Schedule 5, or paragraph 9(2) or (3) of Schedule 7, to the Civil Partnership Act 2004 (property adjustment orders in connection with civil partnership proceedings or after overseas dissolution of civil partnership, etc.);

(f) a spouse, former spouse, civil partner, former civil partner, cohabitant or former cohabitant of the improving tenant to whom the tenancy has been transferred by an order made under Schedule 1 to the Matrimonial Homes Act 1983 or Schedule 7 to the Family Law Act 1996.

(3) Subsection (2)(c) does not apply in any case where the tenancy ceased to be a secure tenancy by virtue of section 89(3) or, as the case may be, section 90(3).

(4) Where, in the case of two or more qualifying persons, one of them ('the missing person') cannot be found—

(a) a claim under regulations made under section 99A may be made by, and compensation under those regulations may be paid to, the other qualifying person or persons; but

(b) the missing person shall be entitled to recover his share of any compensation so paid from that person or those persons.

(5) In this section 'the improving tenant' means—

(a) the tenant by whom the improvement mentioned in section 99A(1) was made, or

(b) in the case of a joint tenancy at the time when the improvement was made, any of the tenants at that time.

100. Power to reimburse cost of tenant's improvements

(1) Where a secure tenant has made an improvement and—

(a) the work on the improvement was begun on or after 3rd October 1980,

(b) the landlord, or a predecessor in title of the landlord, has given its written consent to the improvement or is treated as having given its consent, and

(c) the improvement has materially added to the price which the dwelling-house may be expected to fetch if sold on the open market, or the rent which the landlord may be expected to be able to charge on letting the dwelling-house,

the landlord may, at or after the end of the tenancy, make to the tenant (or his personal representatives) such payment in respect of the improvement as the landlord considers to be appropriate.

(3) The power conferred by this section to make such payments as are mentioned in subsection (1) is in addition to any other power of the landlord to make such payments.

101. Rent not to be increased on account of tenant's improvements

(1) This section applies where a person (the 'improving tenant') who is or was the secure tenant of a dwelling-house has lawfully made an improvement and has borne the whole or part of its cost; and for the purposes of this section a person shall be treated as having borne any cost which he would have borne but for any renovation grant or common parts grant under Chapter I of Part I of the Housing Grants, Construction and Regeneration Act 1996 (grants for renewal of private sector housing).

(2) In determining, at any time whilst the improving tenant or his qualifying successor is a secure tenant of the dwelling-house, whether or to what extent to increase the rent, the landlord shall treat the improvement as justifying only such part of an increase which would otherwise be attributable to the improvement as corresponds to the part of the cost which was not borne by the tenant (and accordingly as not justifying an increase if he bore the whole cost).

(3) The following are qualifying successors of an improving tenant—

(a) a person in whom the tenancy was vested, or to whom the tenancy was disposed of, under section 89 (succession to periodic tenancy) or section 90 (devolution of term certain) on the death of the tenant or in the course of the administration of his estate;

(b) a person to whom the tenancy was assigned by the tenant and who would have been qualified to succeed him if he had died immediately before the assignment;

(c) a person to whom the tenancy was assigned by the tenant in pursuance of an order made under—

(i) section 24 of the Matrimonial Causes Act 1973 (property adjustment orders in connection with matrimonial proceedings),

(ii) section 17(1) of the Matrimonial and Family Proceedings Act 1984 (property adjustment orders after overseas divorce, &c.),

(iii) paragraph 1 of Schedule 1 to the Children Act 1989 (orders for financial relief against parents), or

(iv) Part 2 of Schedule 5, or paragraph 9(2) or (3) of Schedule 7, to the Civil Partnership Act 2004 (property adjustment orders in connection with civil partnership proceedings or after overseas dissolution of civil partnership, etc.);

(d) a spouse, former spouse, civil partner, former civil partner, cohabitant or former cohabitant of the tenant to whom the tenancy has been transferred by an order made under Schedule 1 to the Matrimonial Homes Act 1983 or Schedule 7 to the Family Law Act 1996.

(4) This section does not apply to an increase of rent attributable to rates or to council tax.

Variation of terms of tenancy

102. Variation of terms of secure tenancy

(1) The terms of a secure tenancy may be varied in the following ways, and not otherwise—

    (a) by agreement between the landlord and the tenant;

    (b) to the extent that the variation relates to rent or to payments in respect of rates, council tax or services, by the landlord or the tenant in accordance with a provision in the lease or agreement creating the tenancy, or in an agreement varying it;

    (c) in accordance with section 103 (notice of variation of periodic tenancy).

(2) References in this section and section 103 to variation include addition and deletion; and for the purposes of this section the conversion of a monthly tenancy into a weekly tenancy, or a weekly tenancy into a monthly tenancy, is a variation of a term of the tenancy, but a variation of the premises let under a tenancy is not.

(3) This section and section 103 do not apply to a term of a tenancy which—

    (a) is implied by an enactment, or

    (b) may be varied under section 93 of the Rent Act 1977 (housing association and other tenancies: increase of rent without notice to quit).

(4) This section and section 103 apply in relation to the terms of a periodic tenancy arising by virtue of section 86 (periodic tenancy arising on termination of a fixed term) as they would have applied to the terms of the first tenancy mentioned in that section had that tenancy been a periodic tenancy.

103. Notice of variation of periodic tenancy

(1) The terms of a secure tenancy which is a periodic tenancy may be varied by the landlord by a notice of variation served on the tenant.

(2) Before serving a notice of variation on the tenant the landlord shall serve on him a preliminary notice—

    (a) informing the tenant of the landlord's intention to serve a notice of variation,

    (b) specifying the proposed variation and its effect, and

    (c) inviting the tenant to comment on the proposed variation within such time, specified in the notice, as the landlord considers reasonable;

and the landlord shall consider any comments made by the tenant within the specified time.

(3) Subsection (2) does not apply to a variation of the rent, or of payments in respect of services or facilities provided by the landlord or of payments in respect of rates.

(4) The notice of variation shall specify—

    (a) the variation effected by it, and

    (b) the date on which it takes effect;

and the period between the date on which it is served and the date on which it takes effect must be at least four weeks or the rental period, whichever is the longer.

(5) The notice of variation, when served, shall be accompanied by such information as the landlord considers necessary to inform the tenant of the nature and effect of the variation.

(6) If after the service of a notice of variation the tenant, before the date on which the variation is to take effect, gives a valid notice to quit, the notice of variation shall not take effect unless the tenant, with the written agreement of the landlord, withdraws his notice to quit before that date.

Provision of information and consultation

104. Provision of information about tenancies

(1) Every body which lets dwelling-houses under secure tenancies shall from time to time publish information about its secure tenancies in such form as it considers best suited to explain in simple terms, and so far as it considers it appropriate, the effect of—

    (a) the express terms of its secure tenancies,

    (b) the provisions of this Part, and

    (c) the provisions of sections 11 to 16 of the Landlord and Tenant Act 1985 (landlord's repairing obligations),

and shall ensure that so far as is reasonably practicable the information so published is kept up to date.

(2) The landlord under a secure tenancy shall supply the tenant with—
- (a) a copy of the information for secure tenants published by it under subsection (1), and
- (b) a written statement of the terms of the tenancy, so far as they are neither expressed in the lease or written tenancy agreement (if any) nor implied by law;

and the statement required by paragraph (b) shall be supplied when the secure tenancy arises or as soon as practicable afterwards.

(3) A local authority which is the landlord under a secure tenancy shall supply the tenant, at least once in every relevant year, with a copy of such information relating to the provisions mentioned in subsection (1)(b) and (c) as was last published by it; and in this subsection 'relevant year' means any period of twelve months beginning with an anniversary of the date of such publication.

105. Consultation on matters of housing management

(1) A landlord authority shall maintain such arrangements as it considers appropriate to enable those of its secure tenants who are likely to be substantially affected by a matter of housing management to which this section applies—
- (a) to be informed of the authority's proposals in respect of the matter, and
- (b) to make their views known to the authority within a specified period;

and the authority shall, before making any decision on the matter, consider any representations made to it in accordance with those arrangements.

(2) For the purposes of this section, a matter is one of housing management if, in the opinion of the landlord authority, it relates to—
- (a) the management, maintenance, improvement or demolition of dwelling-houses let by the authority under secure tenancies, or
- (b) the provision of services or amenities in connection with such dwelling-houses;

but not so far as it relates to the rent payable under a secure tenancy or to charges for services or facilities provided by the authority.

(3) This section applies to matters of housing management which, in the opinion of the landlord authority, represent—
- (a) a new programme of maintenance, improvement or demolition, or
- (b) a change in the practice or policy of the authority,

and are likely substantially to affect either its secure tenants as a whole or a group of them who form a distinct social group or occupy dwelling-houses which constitute a distinct class (whether by reference to the kind of dwelling-house, or the housing estate or other larger area in which they are situated).

(4) In the case of a landlord authority which is a local housing authority, the reference in subsection (2) to the provision of services or amenities is a reference only to the provision of services or amenities by the authority acting in its capacity as landlord of the dwelling-houses concerned.

(5) A landlord authority shall publish details of the arrangements which it makes under this section, and a copy of the documents published under this subsection shall—
- (a) be made available at the authority's principal office for inspection at all reasonable hours, without charge, by members of the public, and
- (b) be given, on payment of a reasonable fee, to any member of the public who asks for one.

(6) A landlord authority which is a private registered provider of social housing or a registered social landlord shall, instead of complying with paragraph (a) of subsection (5), send a copy of any document published under that subsection—
- (a) to the Relevant Authority, and
- (b) to the council of any district, Welsh county or county borough or London borough in which there are dwelling-houses let by the landlord authority under secure tenancies;

and a council to whom a copy is sent under this subsection shall make it available at its principal office for inspection at all reasonable hours, without charge, by members of the public.

(7) For the purposes of this section—
- (a) secure tenants include demoted tenants within the meaning of section 143A of the Housing Act 1996;
- (b) secure tenancies include demoted tenancies within the meaning of that section.

106. Information about housing allocation

(1) A landlord authority shall publish a summary of its rules—

(a) for determining priority as between applicants in the allocation of its housing accommodation, and

(b) governing cases where secure tenants wish to move (whether or not by way of exchange of dwelling-houses) to other dwelling-houses let under secure tenancies by that authority or another body.

(2) A landlord authority shall—

(a) maintain a set of the rules referred to in subsection (1) and of the rules which it has laid down governing the procedure to be followed in allocating its housing accommodation, and

(b) make them available at its principal office for inspection at all reasonable hours, without charge, by members of the public.

(3) A landlord authority which is a private registered provider of social housing or a registered social landlord shall, instead of complying with paragraph (b) of subsection (2), send a set of the rules referred to in paragraph (a) of that subsection—

(a) to the Relevant Authority, and

(b) to the council of any district, Welsh county or county borough or London borough in which there are dwelling-houses let or to be let by the landlord authority under secure tenancies;

and a council to whom a set of rules is sent under this subsection shall make it available at its principal office for inspection at all reasonable hours, without charge, by members of the public.

(4) A copy of the summary published under subsection (1) shall be given without charge, and a copy of the set of rules maintained under subsection (2) shall be given on payment of a reasonable fee, to any member of the public who asks for one.

(5) At the request of a person who has applied to it for housing accommodation, a landlord authority shall make available to him, at all reasonable times and without charge, details of the particulars which he has given to the authority about himself and his family and which the authority has recorded as being relevant to his application for accommodation.

(6) The provisions of this section do not apply to a landlord authority which is a local housing authority so far as they impose requirements corresponding to those to which such an authority is subject under section 168 of the Housing Act 1996 (provision of information about allocation schemes).

106A. Consultation before disposal to private sector landlord

(1) The provisions of Schedule 3A have effect with respect to the duties of—

(a) a local authority proposing to dispose of dwelling-houses subject to secure tenancies or introductory tenancies, and

(b) the Secretary of State in considering whether to give his consent to such a disposal,

to have regard to the views of tenants liable as a result of the disposal to cease to be secure tenants or introductory tenants.

(2) In relation to a disposal to which that Schedule applies, the provisions of that Schedule apply in place of the provisions of section 105 (consultation on matters of housing management) in the case of secure tenants and section 137 of the Housing Act 1996 (consultation on matters of housing management) in the case of introductory tenants.

(3) That Schedule, and this section, do not apply in relation to any disposal of an interest in land by a local authority if—

(a) the interest has been acquired by the authority (whether compulsorily or otherwise) following the making of an order for compulsory purchase under any enactment, other than section 290 (acquisition of land for clearance),

(b) the order provides that the interest is being acquired for the purpose of disposal to a private registered provider of social housing or a registered social landlord, and

(c) such a disposal is made within one year of the acquisition.

(4) In this section 'registered social landlord' has the same meaning as in Part I of the Housing Act 1996.

Flexible tenancies

107A. Flexible tenancies
(1) For the purposes of this Act, a flexible tenancy is a secure tenancy to which any of the following subsections applies.
(2) This subsection applies to a secure tenancy if—
   (a) it is granted by a landlord in England for a term certain of not less than two years, and
   (b) before it was granted the person who became the landlord under the tenancy served a written notice on the person who became the tenant under the tenancy stating that the tenancy would be a flexible tenancy.
(3) This subsection applies to a secure tenancy if—
   (a) it becomes a secure tenancy by virtue of a notice under paragraph 4ZA(2) of Schedule 1 (family intervention tenancies becoming secure tenancies),
   (b) the landlord under the family intervention tenancy in question was a local housing authority in England,
   (c) the family intervention tenancy was granted to a person on the coming to an end of a flexible tenancy under which the person was a tenant,
   (d) the notice states that the tenancy is to become a secure tenancy that is a flexible tenancy for a term certain of the length specified in the notice, and sets out the other express terms of the tenancy, and
   (e) the length of the term specified in the notice is at least two years.
(4) The length of the term of a flexible tenancy that becomes such a tenancy by virtue of subsection (3) is that specified in the notice under paragraph 4ZA(2) of Schedule 1.
(5) The other express terms of the flexible tenancy are those set out in the notice, so far as those terms are compatible with the statutory provisions relating to flexible tenancies; and in this subsection 'statutory provision' means any provision made by or under an Act.
(6) This subsection applies to a secure tenancy if—
   (a) it is created by virtue of section 137A of the Housing Act 1996 (introductory tenancies becoming flexible tenancies), or
   (b) it arises by virtue of section 143MA of that Act (demoted tenancies becoming flexible tenancies).

107B. Review of decisions relating to flexible tenancies
(1) This section applies if a person ('the prospective landlord')—
   (a) offers to grant a flexible tenancy (whether or not on the coming to an end of an existing tenancy of any kind), or
   (b) serves a notice under section 137A of the Housing Act 1996 stating that, on the coming to an end of an introductory tenancy, it will become a flexible tenancy.
(2) A person to whom the offer is made or on whom the notice is served ('the person concerned') may request a review of the prospective landlord's decision about the length of the term of the tenancy.
(3) The review may only be requested on the basis that the length of the term does not accord with a policy of the prospective landlord as to the length of the terms of the flexible tenancies it grants.
(4) A request for a review must be made before the end of—
   (a) the period of 21 days beginning with the day on which the person concerned first receives the offer or notice, or
   (b) such longer period as the prospective landlord may in writing allow.
(5) On a request being duly made to it, the prospective landlord must review its decision.
(6) The Secretary of State may by regulations make provision about the procedure to be followed in connection with a review under this section.
(7) The regulations may, in particular, make provision—
   (a) requiring the decision on the review to be made by a person of appropriate seniority who was not involved in the original decision, and
   (b) as to the circumstances in which the person concerned is entitled to an oral hearing, and whether and by whom the person may be represented at such a hearing.

(8) The prospective landlord must notify the person concerned in writing of the decision on the review.

(9) If the decision is to confirm the original decision, the prospective landlord must also notify the person of the reasons for the decision.

(10) Regulations under this section—

(a) may contain transitional or saving provision;

(b) are to be made by statutory instrument which is subject to annulment in pursuance of a resolution of either House of Parliament.

107C. Termination of flexible tenancy by tenant

(1) It is a term of every flexible tenancy that the tenant may terminate the tenancy in accordance with the following provisions of this section.

(2) The tenant must serve a notice in writing on the landlord stating that the tenancy will be terminated on the date specified in the notice.

(3) That date must be after the end of the period of four weeks beginning with the date on which the notice is served.

(4) The landlord may agree with the tenant to dispense with the requirement in subsection (2) or (3).

(5) The tenancy is terminated on the date specified in the notice or (as the case may be) determined in accordance with arrangements made under subsection (4) only if on that date—

(a) no arrears of rent are payable under the tenancy, and

(b) the tenant is not otherwise materially in breach of a term of the tenancy.

107D. Recovery of possession on expiry of flexible tenancy

(1) Subject as follows, on or after the coming to an end of a flexible tenancy a court must make an order for possession of the dwelling-house let on the tenancy if it is satisfied that the following conditions are met.

(2) Condition 1 is that the flexible tenancy has come to an end and no further secure tenancy (whether or not a flexible tenancy) is for the time being in existence, other than a secure tenancy that is a periodic tenancy (whether or not arising by virtue of section 86).

(3) Condition 2 is that the landlord has given the tenant not less than six months' notice in writing—

(a) stating that the landlord does not propose to grant another tenancy on the expiry of the flexible tenancy,

(b) setting out the landlord's reasons for not proposing to grant another tenancy, and

(c) informing the tenant of the tenant's right to request a review of the landlord's proposal and of the time within which such a request must be made.

(4) Condition 3 is that the landlord has given the tenant not less than two months' notice in writing stating that the landlord requires possession of the dwelling-house.

(5) A notice under subsection (4) may be given before or on the day on which the tenancy comes to an end.

(6) The court may refuse to grant an order for possession under this section if—

(a) the tenant has in accordance with section 107E requested a review of the landlord's proposal not to grant another tenancy on the expiry of the flexible tenancy, and

(b) the court is satisfied that the landlord has failed to carry out the review in accordance with provision made by or under that section or that the decision on the review is otherwise wrong in law.

(7) If a court refuses to grant an order for possession by virtue of subsection (6) it may make such directions as to the holding of a review or further review under section 107E as it thinks fit.

(8) This section has effect notwithstanding that, on the coming to an end of the flexible tenancy, a periodic tenancy arises by virtue of section 86.

(9) Where a court makes an order for possession of a dwelling-house by virtue of this section, any periodic tenancy arising by virtue of section 86 on the coming to an end of the flexible tenancy comes to an end (without further notice and regardless of the period) in accordance with section 82(2).

(10) This section is without prejudice to any right of the landlord under a flexible tenancy to recover possession of the dwelling-house let on the tenancy in accordance with this Part.

107E. Review of decision to seek possession

(1) A request for a review of a landlord's decision to seek an order for possession of a dwelling-house let under a flexible tenancy must be made before the end of the period of 21 days beginning with the day on which the notice under section 107D(3) is served.

(2) On a request being duly made to it, the landlord must review its decision.

(3) The review must, in particular, consider whether the decision is in accordance with any policy of the landlord as to the circumstances in which it will grant a further tenancy on the coming to an end of an existing flexible tenancy.

(4) The Secretary of State may by regulations make provision about the procedure to be followed in connection with a review under this section.

(5) The regulations may, in particular, make provision—

(a) requiring the decision on the review to be made by a person of appropriate seniority who was not involved in the original decision, and

(b) as to the circumstances in which the person concerned is entitled to an oral hearing, and whether and by whom the person may be represented at such a hearing.

(6) The landlord must notify the tenant in writing of the decision on the review.

(7) If the decision is to confirm the original decision, the landlord must also notify the tenant of the reasons for the decision.

(8) The review must be carried out, and the tenant notified, before the date specified in the notice of proceedings as the date after which proceedings for the possession of the dwelling-house may be begun.

(9) Regulations under this section—

(a) may contain transitional or saving provision;

(b) are to be made by statutory instrument which is subject to annulment in pursuance of a resolution of either House of Parliament.

Supplementary provisions

112. Meaning of 'dwelling-house'

(1) For the purposes of this Part a dwelling-house may be a house or a part of a house.

(2) Land let together with a dwelling-house shall be treated for the purposes of this Part as part of the dwelling-house unless the land is agricultural land (as defined in section 26(3)(a) of the General Rate Act 1967) exceeding two acres.

113. Members of a person's family

(1) A person is a member of another's family within the meaning of this Part if—

(a) he is the spouse or civil partner of that person, or he and that person live together as husband and wife or as if they were civil partners, or

(b) he is that person's parent, grandparent, child, grandchild, brother, sister, uncle, aunt, nephew or niece.

(2) For the purpose of subsection (1)(b)—

(a) a relationship by marriage or civil partnership shall be treated as a relationship by blood,

(b) a relationship of the half-blood shall be treated as a relationship of the whole blood,

(c) the stepchild of a person shall be treated as his child, and

(d) an illegitimate child shall be treated as the legitimate child of his mother and reputed father.

SCHEDULES

SCHEDULE 1
TENANCIES WHICH ARE NOT SECURE TENANCIES

Long leases

1. A tenancy is not a secure tenancy if it is a long tenancy.

Introductory tenancies

1A. A tenancy is not a secure tenancy if it is an introductory tenancy or a tenancy which has ceased to be an introductory tenancy—

(a) by virtue of section 133(3) of the Housing Act 1996 (disposal on death to non-qualifying person), or

(b) by virtue of the tenant, or in the case of a joint tenancy every tenant, ceasing to occupy the dwelling-house as his only or principal home.

1B. A tenancy is not a secure tenancy if it is a demoted tenancy within the meaning of section 143A of the Housing Act 1996.

Premises occupied in connection with employment

2. (1) Subject to sub-paragraph (4B) a tenancy is not a secure tenancy if the tenant is an employee of the landlord or of—

    a local authority,

    a new town corporation,

    a housing action trust,

    an urban development corporation, or

    the governors of an aided school,

and his contract of employment requires him to occupy the dwelling-house for the better performance of his duties.

(2) Subject to sub-paragraph (4B) a tenancy is not a secure tenancy if the tenant is a member of a police force and the dwelling-house is provided for him free of rent and rates in pursuance of regulations made under section 50 of the Police Act 1996 (general regulations as to government, administration and conditions of service of police forces).

(3) Subject to sub-paragraph (4B) a tenancy is not a secure tenancy if the tenant is an employee of a fire and rescue authority and—

(a) his contract of employment requires him to live in close proximity to a particular fire station, and

(b) the dwelling-house was let to him by the authority in consequence of that requirement.

(4) Subject to sub-paragraphs (4A) and (4B) a tenancy is not a secure tenancy if—

(a) within the period of three years immediately preceding the grant the conditions mentioned in sub-paragraph (1), (2) or (3) have been satisfied with respect to a tenancy of the dwelling-house, and

(b) before the grant the landlord notified the tenant in writing of the circumstances in which this exception applies and that in its opinion the proposed tenancy would fall within this exception.

(4A) Except where the landlord is a local housing authority, a tenancy under sub-paragraph (4) shall become a secure tenancy when the periods during which the conditions mentioned in sub-paragraph (1), (2) or (3) are not satisfied with respect to the tenancy amount in aggregate to more than three years.

(4B) Where the landlord is a local housing authority, a tenancy under sub-paragraph (1), (2), (3) or (4) shall become a secure tenancy if the authority notify the tenant that the tenancy is to be regarded as a secure tenancy.

(5) In this paragraph 'contract of employment' means a contract of service or apprenticeship, whether express or implied and (if express) whether oral or in writing.

Land acquired for development

3. (1) A tenancy is not a secure tenancy if the dwelling-house is on land which has been acquired for development and the dwelling-house is used by the landlord, pending development of the land, as temporary housing accommodation.

(2) In this paragraph 'development' has the meaning given by section 55 of the Town and Country Planning Act 1990 (general definition of development for purposes of that Act).

Accommodation for homeless persons

4. A tenancy granted in pursuance of any function under Part VII of the Housing Act 1996 (homelessness) is not a secure tenancy unless the local housing authority concerned have notified the tenant that the tenancy is to be regarded as a secure tenancy.

Family intervention tenancies

4ZA. (1) A tenancy is not a secure tenancy if it is a family intervention tenancy.

(2) But a tenancy mentioned in sub-paragraph (1) becomes a secure tenancy if the landlord notifies the tenant that it is to be regarded as a secure tenancy.

(3) In this paragraph 'a family intervention tenancy' means, subject to sub-paragraph (4), a tenancy granted by a local housing authority in respect of a dwelling-house—
- (a) to a person ('the new tenant') against whom a possession order under section 84 in respect of another dwelling-house—
  - (i) has been made, in relation to a secure tenancy, on ground 2 or 2A of Part 1 of Schedule 2;
  - (ii) could, in the opinion of the authority, have been so made in relation to such a tenancy; or
  - (iii) could, in the opinion of the authority, have been so made if the person had had such a tenancy; and
- (b) for the purposes of the provision of behaviour support services.

(4) A tenancy is not a family intervention tenancy for the purposes of this paragraph if the local housing authority has failed to serve a notice under sub-paragraph (5) on the new tenant before the new tenant entered into the tenancy.

(5) A notice under this sub-paragraph is a notice stating—
- (a) the reasons for offering the tenancy to the new tenant;
- (b) the dwelling-house in respect of which the tenancy is to be granted;
- (c) the other main terms of the tenancy (including any requirements on the new tenant in respect of behaviour support services);
- (d) the security of tenure available under the tenancy and any loss of security of tenure which is likely to result from the new tenant agreeing to enter into the tenancy;
- (e) that the new tenant is not obliged to enter into the tenancy or (unless otherwise required to do so) to surrender any existing tenancy or possession of a dwelling-house;
- (f) any likely action by the local housing authority if the new tenant does not enter into the tenancy or surrender any existing tenancy or possession of a dwelling-house.

(6) The appropriate national authority may by regulations made by statutory instrument amend sub-paragraph (5).

(7) A notice under sub-paragraph (5) must contain advice to the new tenant as to how the new tenant may be able to obtain assistance in relation to the notice.

(8) The appropriate national authority may by regulations made by statutory instrument make provision about the type of advice to be provided in such notices.

(9) Regulations under this paragraph may contain such transitional, transitory or saving provision as the appropriate national authority considers appropriate.

(10) A statutory instrument containing (whether alone or with other provision) regulations under this paragraph which amend or repeal any of paragraphs (a) to (f) of sub-paragraph (5) may not be made—
- (a) by the Secretary of State unless a draft of the instrument has been laid before, and approved by a resolution of, each House of Parliament; and
- (b) by the Welsh Ministers unless a draft of the instrument has been laid before, and approved by a resolution of, the National Assembly for Wales.

(11) Subject to this, a statutory instrument containing regulations made under this paragraph—
- (a) by the Secretary of State is subject to annulment in pursuance of a resolution of either House of Parliament; and
- (b) by the Welsh Ministers is subject to annulment in pursuance of a resolution of the National Assembly for Wales.

(12) In this paragraph—

'appropriate national authority'—
- (a) in relation to England, means the Secretary of State; and
- (b) in relation to Wales, means the Welsh Ministers;

'behaviour support agreement' means an agreement in writing about behaviour and the provision of support services made between the new tenant and the local housing authority concerned (or between persons who include those persons);

'behaviour support services' means relevant support services to be provided by any person to—
- (a) the new tenant; or

(b) any person who is to reside with the new tenant;

for the purpose of addressing the kind of behaviour which led to the new tenant falling within sub-paragraph (3)(a);

'family intervention tenancy' has the meaning given by sub-paragraph (3);

'the new tenant' has the meaning given by sub-paragraph (3)(a);

'relevant support services' means support services of a kind identified in a behaviour support agreement and designed to meet such needs of the recipient as are identified in the agreement.

Accommodation for asylum-seekers

4A. (1) A tenancy is not a secure tenancy if it is granted in order to provide accommodation under section 4 or Part VI of the Immigration and Asylum Act 1999.

(2) A tenancy mentioned in sub-paragraph (1) becomes a secure tenancy if the landlord notifies the tenant that it is to be regarded as a secure tenancy.

Accommodation for persons with Temporary Protection

4B. A tenancy is not a secure tenancy if it is granted in order to provide accommodation under the Displaced Persons (Temporary Protection) Regulations 2005.

Temporary accommodation for persons taking up employment

5. (1) Subject to sub-paragraphs (1A) and (1B), a tenancy is not a secure tenancy if—

(a) the person to whom the tenancy was granted was not, immediately before the grant, resident in the district in which the dwelling-house is situated,

(b) before the grant of the tenancy, he obtained employment, or an offer of employment, in the district or its surrounding area,

(c) the tenancy was granted to him for the purpose of meeting his need for temporary accommodation in the district or its surrounding area in order to work there, and of enabling him to find permanent accommodation there, and

(d) the landlord notified him in writing of the circumstances in which this exception applies and that in its opinion the proposed tenancy would fall within this exception.

(1A) Except where the landlord is a local housing authority, a tenancy under sub-paragraph (1) shall become a secure tenancy on the expiry of one year from the grant or on earlier notification by the landlord to the tenant that the tenancy is to be regarded as a secure tenancy.

(1B) Where the landlord is a local housing authority, a tenancy under sub-paragraph (1) shall become a secure tenancy if at any time the authority notify the tenant that the tenancy is to be regarded as a secure tenancy.

(2) In this paragraph—

'district' means district of a local housing authority; and

'surrounding area', in relation to a district, means the area consisting of each district that adjoins it.

Short-term arrangements

6. A tenancy is not a secure tenancy if—

(a) the dwelling-house has been leased to the landlord with vacant possession for use as temporary housing accommodation,

(b) the terms on which it has been leased include provision for the lessor to obtain vacant possession from the landlord on the expiry of a specified period or when required by the lessor,

(c) the lessor is not a body which is capable of granting secure tenancies, and

(d) the landlord has no interest in the dwelling-house other than under the lease in question or as a mortgagee.

Temporary accommodation during works

7. A tenancy is not a secure tenancy if—

(a) the dwelling-house has been made available for occupation by the tenant (or a predecessor in title of his) while works are carried out on the dwelling-house which he previously occupied as his home, and

(b) the tenant or predecessor was not a secure tenant of that other dwelling-house at the time when he ceased to occupy it as his home.

Agricultural holdings etc.

8. A tenancy is not a secure tenancy if—

    (a) the dwelling-house is comprised in an agricultural holding and is occupied by the person responsible for the control (whether as tenant or as servant or agent of the tenant) of the farming of the holding, or

    (b) the dwelling-house is comprised in the holding held under a farm business tenancy and is occupied by the person responsible for the control (whether as tenant or as servant or agent of the tenant) of the management of the holding.

    (2) In sub-paragraph (1) above—

    'agricultural holding' means any agricultural holding within the meaning of the Agricultural Holdings Act 1986 held under a tenancy in relation to which that Act applies, and

    'farm business tenancy', and 'holding' in relation to such a tenancy, have the same meaning as in the Agricultural Tenancies Act 1995.

Licensed premises

9. A tenancy is not a secure tenancy if the dwelling-house consists of or includes premises which, by virtue of a premises licence under the Licensing Act 2003, may be used for the supply of alcohol (within the meaning of section 14 of that Act) for consumption on the premises.

Student lettings

10. (1) Subject to sub-paragraphs (2A) and (2B), a tenancy of a dwelling-house is not a secure tenancy if—

    (a) it is granted for the purpose of enabling the tenant to attend a designated course at an educational establishment, and

    (b) before the grant of the tenancy the landlord notified him in writing of the circumstances in which this exception applies and that in its opinion the proposed tenancy would fall within this exception.

    (2) A landlord's notice under sub-paragraph (1)(b) shall specify the educational establishment which the person concerned proposes to attend.

    (2A) Except where the landlord is a local housing authority, a tenancy under sub-paragraph (1) shall become a secure tenancy on the expiry of the period specified in sub-paragraph (3) or on earlier notification by the landlord to the tenant that the tenancy is to be regarded as a secure tenancy.

    (2B) Where the landlord is a local housing authority, a tenancy under sub-paragraph (1) shall become a secure tenancy if at any time the authority notify the tenant that the tenancy is to be regarded as a secure tenancy.

    (3) The period referred to in sub-paragraph (2A) is—

    (a) in a case where the tenant attends a designated course at the educational establishment specified in the landlord's notice, the period ending six months after the tenant ceases to attend that (or any other) designated course at that establishment;

    (b) in any other case, the period ending six months after the grant of the tenancy.

    (4) In this paragraph—

    'designated course' means a course of any kind designated by regulations made by the Secretary of State for the purposes of this paragraph;

    'educational establishment' means a university or institution which provides higher education or further education (or both); and for the purposes of this definition 'higher education' and 'further education' have the same meaning as in the Education Act 1996.

    (5) Regulations under sub-paragraph (4) shall be made by statutory instrument and may make different provision with respect to different cases or descriptions of case, including different provision for different areas.

1954 Act tenancies

11. A tenancy is not a secure tenancy if it is one to which Part II of the Landlord and Tenant Act 1954 applies (tenancies of premises occupied for business purposes).

Almshouses

12. A licence to occupy a dwelling-house is not a secure tenancy if—

(a) the dwelling-house is an almshouse, and

(b) the licence was granted by or on behalf of a charity which—

(i) is authorised under its trusts to maintain the dwelling-house as an almshouse, and

(ii) has no power under its trusts to grant a tenancy of the dwelling-house;

and in this paragraph 'almshouse' means any premises maintained as an almshouse, whether they are called an almshouse or not; and 'trusts', in relation to a charity, means the provisions establishing it as a charity and regulating its purposes and administration, whether those provisions take effect by way of trust or not.

SCHEDULE 2

GROUNDS FOR POSSESSION OF DWELLING-HOUSES LET UNDER SECURE TENANCIES

PART I

GROUNDS ON WHICH COURT MAY ORDER POSSESSION IF IT CONSIDERS IT REASONABLE

Ground 1

Rent lawfully due from the tenant has not been paid or an obligation of the tenancy has been broken or not performed.

Ground 2

The tenant or a person residing in or visiting the dwelling-house—

(a) has been guilty of conduct causing or likely to cause a nuisance or annoyance to a person residing, visiting or otherwise engaging in a lawful activity in the locality, or

(b) has been convicted of—

(i) using the dwelling-house or allowing it to be used for immoral or illegal purposes, or

(ii) an indictable offence committed in, or in the locality of, the dwelling-house.

Ground 2A

The dwelling-house was occupied (whether alone or with others) by a married couple, a couple who are civil partners of each other, or a couple living together as husband and wife or a couple living together as if they were civil partners and—

(a) one or both of the partners is a tenant of the dwelling-house,

(b) one partner has left because of violence or threats of violence by the other towards—

(i) that partner, or

(ii) a member of the family of that partner who was residing with that partner immediately before the partner left, and

(c) the court is satisfied that the partner who has left is unlikely to return.

Ground 3

The condition of the dwelling-house or of any of the common parts has deteriorated owing to acts of waste by, or the neglect or default of, the tenant or a person residing in the dwelling-house and, in the case of an act of waste by, or the neglect or default of, a person lodging with the tenant or a sub-tenant of his, the tenant has not taken such steps as he ought reasonably to have taken for the removal of the lodger or sub-tenant.

Ground 4

The condition of furniture provided by the landlord for use under the tenancy, or for use in the common parts, has deteriorated owing to ill-treatment by the tenant or a person residing in the dwelling-house and, in the case of ill-treatment by a person lodging with the tenant or a sub-tenant of his, the tenant has not taken such steps as he ought reasonably to have taken for the removal of the lodger or sub-tenant.

Ground 5

The tenant is the person, or one of the persons, to whom the tenancy was granted and the landlord was induced to grant the tenancy by a false statement made knowingly or recklessly by—

(a) the tenant, or

(b) a person acting at the tenant's instigation.

Ground 6

The tenancy was assigned to the tenant, or to a predecessor in title of his who is a member of his family and is residing in the dwelling-house, by an assignment made by virtue of section 92 (assignments by way of exchange) and a premium was paid either in connection with that assignment or the assignment which the tenant or predecessor himself made by virtue of that section.

In this paragraph 'premium' means any fine or other like sum and any other pecuniary consideration in addition to rent.

Ground 7

The dwelling-house forms part of, or is within the curtilage of, a building which, or so much of it as is held by the landlord, is held mainly for purposes other than housing purposes and consists mainly of accommodation other than housing accommodation, and—

(a) the dwelling-house was let to the tenant or a predecessor in title of his in consequence of the tenant or predecessor being in the employment of the landlord, or of—

a local authority,

a development corporation,

a housing action trust,

an urban development corporation, or

the governors of an aided school, and

(b) the tenant or a person residing in the dwelling-house has been guilty of conduct such that, having regard to the purpose for which the building is used, it would not be right for him to continue in occupation of the dwelling-house.

Ground 8

The dwelling-house was made available for occupation by the tenant (or a predecessor in title of his) while works were carried out on the dwelling-house which he previously occupied as his only or principal home and—

(a) the tenant (or predecessor) was a secure tenant of the other dwelling-house at the time when he ceased to occupy it as his home,

(b) the tenant (or predecessor) accepted the tenancy of the dwelling-house of which possession is sought on the understanding that he would give up occupation when, on completion of the works, the other dwelling-house was again available for occupation by him under a secure tenancy, and

(c) the works have been completed and the other dwelling-house is so available.

PART II
GROUNDS ON WHICH THE COURT MAY ORDER POSSESSION IF SUITABLE ALTERNATIVE ACCOMMODATION IS AVAILABLE

Ground 9

The dwelling-house is overcrowded, within the meaning of Part X, in such circumstances as to render the occupier guilty of an offence.

Ground 10

The landlord intends, within a reasonable time of obtaining possession of the dwelling-house—

(a) to demolish or reconstruct the building or part of the building comprising the dwelling-house, or

(b) to carry out work on that building or on land let together with, and thus treated as part of, the dwelling-house,

and cannot reasonably do so without obtaining possession of the dwelling-house.

Ground 10A

The dwelling-house is in an area which is the subject of a redevelopment scheme approved by the Secretary of State or the Regulator of Social Housing or Scottish Homes in accordance with Part V of this Schedule and the landlord intends within a reasonable time of obtaining possession to dispose of the dwelling-house in accordance with the scheme.

or

Part of the dwelling-house is in such an area and the landlord intends within a reasonable time of obtaining possession to dispose of that part in accordance with the scheme and for that purpose reasonably requires possession of the dwelling-house.

Ground 11

The landlord is a charity and the tenant's continued occupation of the dwelling-house would conflict with the objects of the charity.

PART III
GROUNDS ON WHICH THE COURT MAY ORDER POSSESSION IF IT CONSIDERS IT REASONABLE AND SUITABLE ALTERNATIVE ACCOMMODATION IS AVAILABLE

Ground 12

The dwelling-house forms part of, or is within the curtilage of, a building which, or so much of it as is held by the landlord, is held mainly for purposes other than housing purposes and consists mainly of accommodation other than housing accommodation, or is situated in a cemetery, and—

(a) the dwelling-house was let to the tenant or a predecessor in title of his in consequence of the tenant or predecessor being in the employment of the landlord or of—

a local authority,

a development corporation,

a housing action trust,

an urban development corporation, or

the governors of an aided school,

and that employment has ceased, and

(b) the landlord reasonably requires the dwelling-house for occupation as a residence for some person either engaged in the employment of the landlord, or of such a body, or with whom a contract for such employment has been entered into conditional on housing being provided.

Ground 13

The dwelling-house has features which are substantially different from those of ordinary dwelling-houses and which are designed to make it suitable for occupation by a physically disabled person who requires accommodation of a kind provided by the dwelling-house and—

(a) there is no longer such a person residing in the dwelling-house, and

(b) the landlord requires it for occupation (whether alone or with members of his family) by such a person.

Ground 14

The landlord is a housing association or housing trust which lets dwelling-houses only for occupation (whether alone or with others) by persons whose circumstances (other than merely financial circumstances) make it especially difficult for them to satisfy their need for housing, and—

(a) either there is no longer such a person residing in the dwelling-house or the tenant has received from a local housing authority an offer of accommodation in premises which are to be let as a separate dwelling under a secure tenancy, and

(b) the landlord requires the dwelling-house for occupation (whether alone or with members of his family) by such a person.

Ground 15

The dwelling-house is one of a group of dwelling-houses which it is the practice of the landlord to let for occupation by persons with special needs and—

(a) a social service or special facility is provided in close proximity to the group of dwelling-houses in order to assist persons with those special needs,

(b) there is no longer a person with those special needs residing in the dwelling-house, and

(c) the landlord requires the dwelling-house for occupation (whether alone or with members of his family) by a person who has those special needs.

Ground 15A

The dwelling-house is in England, the accommodation afforded by it is more extensive than is reasonably required by the tenant and—

(a) the tenancy vested in the tenant by virtue of section 89 (succession to periodic tenancy) or 90 (devolution of term certain) in a case where the tenant was not the previous tenant's spouse or civil partner, and

(b) notice of the proceedings for possession was served under section 83 (or, where no such notice was served, the proceedings for possession were begun) more than six months but less than twelve months after the relevant date.

For this purpose 'the relevant date' is—

(a) the date of the previous tenant's death, or

(b) if the court so directs, the date on which, in the opinion of the court, the landlord (or, in the case of joint landlords, any one of them) became aware of the previous tenant's death.

The matters to be taken into account by the court in determining whether it is reasonable to make an order on this ground include—

(a) the age of the tenant,

(b) the period (if any) during which the tenant has occupied the dwelling-house as the tenant's only or principal home, and

(c) any financial or other support given by the tenant to the previous tenant.

Ground 16

The dwelling-house is in Wales, the accommodation afforded by it is more extensive than is reasonably required by the tenant and—

(a) the tenancy vested in the tenant by virtue of section 89 (succession to periodic tenancy) or 90 (devolution of term certain), the tenant being qualified to succeed by virtue of section 87(b) (members of family other than spouse), and

(b) notice of the proceedings for possession was served under section 83 (or, where no such notice was served, the proceedings for possession were begun) more than six months but less than twelve months after the relevant date.

For this purpose 'the relevant date' is—

(a) the date of the previous tenant's death, or

(b) if the court so directs, the date on which, in the opinion of the court, the landlord (or, in the case of joint landlords, any one of them) became aware of the previous tenant's death.

The matters to be taken into account by the court in determining whether it is reasonable to make an order on this ground include—

(a) the age of the tenant,

(b) the period during which the tenant has occupied the dwelling-house as his only or principal home, and

(c) any financial or other support given by the tenant to the previous tenant.

PART IV
SUITABILITY OF ACCOMMODATION

1. For the purposes of section 84(2)(b) and (c) (case in which court is not to make an order for possession unless satisfied that suitable accommodation will be available) accommodation is suitable if it consists of premises—

    (a) which are to be let as a separate dwelling under a secure tenancy, or

    (b) which are to be let as a separate dwelling under a protected tenancy, not being a tenancy under which the landlord might recover possession under one of the Cases in Part II of Schedule 15 to the Rent Act 1977 (cases where court must order possession), or

    (c) which are to be let as a separate dwelling under an assured tenancy which is neither an assured shorthold tenancy, within the meaning of Part I of the Housing Act 1988, nor a tenancy under which the landlord might recover possession under any of Grounds 1 to 5 in Schedule 2 to that Act,

    and, in the opinion of the court, the accommodation is reasonably suitable to the needs of the tenant and his family.

2. In determining whether the accommodation is reasonably suitable to the needs of the tenant and his family, regard shall be had to—

    (a) the nature of the accommodation which it is the practice of the landlord to allocate to persons with similar needs;

    (b) the distance of the accommodation available from the place of work or education of the tenant and of any members of his family;

(c) its distance from the home of any member of the tenant's family if proximity to it is essential to that member's or the tenant's well-being;

(d) the needs (as regards extent of accommodation) and means of the tenant and his family;

(e) the terms on which the accommodation is available and the terms of the secure tenancy;

(f) if furniture was provided by the landlord for use under the secure tenancy, whether furniture is to be provided for use in the other accommodation, and if so the nature of the furniture to be provided.

3. Where possession of a dwelling-house is sought on ground 9 (overcrowding such as to render occupier guilty of offence), other accommodation may be reasonably suitable to the needs of the tenant and his family notwithstanding that the permitted number of persons for that accommodation, as defined in section 326(3) (overcrowding: the space standard), is less than the number of persons living in the dwelling-house of which possession is sought.

4. (1) A certificate of the appropriate local housing authority that they will provide suitable accommodation for the tenant by a date specified in the certificate is conclusive evidence that suitable accommodation will be available for him by that date.

(2) The appropriate local housing authority is the authority for the district in which the dwelling-house of which possession is sought is situated.

(3) This paragraph does not apply where the landlord is a local housing authority.

PART V
APPROVAL OF REDEVELOPMENT SCHEMES FOR PURPOSES OF GROUND 10A

1. (1) The Secretary of State may, on the application of the landlord, approve for the purposes of ground 10A in Part II of this Schedule a scheme for the disposal and redevelopment of an area of land consisting of or including the whole or part of one or more dwelling-houses.

(2) For this purpose—

(a) 'disposal' means a disposal of any interest in the land (including the grant of an option), and

(b) 'redevelopment' means the demolition or reconstruction of buildings or the carrying out of other works to buildings or land;

and it is immaterial whether the disposal is to precede or follow the redevelopment.

(3) The Secretary of State may on the application of the landlord approve a variation of a scheme previously approved by him and may, in particular, approve a variation adding land to the area subject to the scheme.

2. (1) Where a landlord proposes to apply to the Secretary of State for the approval of a scheme or variation it shall serve a notice in writing on any secure tenant of a dwelling-house affected by the proposal stating—

(a) the main features of the proposed scheme or, as the case may be, the scheme as proposed to be varied,

(b) that the landlord proposes to apply to the Secretary of State for approval of the scheme or variation, and

(c) the effect of such approval, by virtue of section 84 and ground 10A in Part II of this Schedule, in relation to proceedings for possession of the dwelling-house,

and informing the tenant that he may, within such period as the landlord may allow (which shall be at least 28 days from service of the notice), make representations to the landlord about the proposal.

(2) The landlord shall not apply to the Secretary of State until it has considered any representations made to it within that period.

(3) In the case of a landlord to which section 105 applies (consultation on matters of housing management) the provisions of this paragraph apply in place of the provisions of that section in relation to the approval or variation of a redevelopment scheme.

3. (1) In considering whether to give his approval to a scheme or variation the Secretary of State shall take into account, in particular—

(a) the effect of the scheme on the extent and character of housing accommodation in the neighbourhood,

(b) over what period of time it is proposed that the disposal and redevelopment will take place in accordance with the scheme, and

(c) to what extent the scheme includes provision for housing provided under the scheme to be sold or let to existing tenants or persons nominated by the landlord;

and he shall take into account any representations made to him and, so far as they are brought to his notice, any representations made to the landlord.

(2) The landlord shall give to the Secretary of State such information as to the representations made to it, and other relevant matters, as the Secretary of State may require.

4. The Secretary of State shall not approve a scheme or variation so as to include in the area subject to the scheme—

(a) part only of one or more dwelling-houses, or

(b) one or more dwelling-houses not themselves affected by the works involved in redevelopment but which are proposed to be disposed of along with other land which is so affected,

unless he is satisfied that the inclusion is justified in the circumstances.

5. (1) Approval may be given subject to conditions and may be expressed to expire after a specified period.

(2) The Secretary of State, on the application of the landlord or otherwise, may vary an approval so as to—

(a) add, remove or vary conditions to which the approval is subject; or

(b) extend or restrict the period after which the approval is to expire.

(3) Where approval is given subject to conditions, the landlord may serve a notice under section 83 (notice of proceedings for possession) specifying ground 10A notwithstanding that the conditions are not yet fulfilled but the court shall not make an order for possession on that ground unless satisfied that they are or will be fulfilled.

6. Where the landlord is a private registered provider of social housing or a housing association registered in the register maintained by Scottish Homes under section 3 of the Housing Associations Act 1985, the Regulator of Social Housing, or Scottish Homes (and not the Secretary of State), has the functions conferred by this Part of this Schedule.

7. In this Part of this Schedule references to the landlord of a dwelling-house include any authority or body within section 80 (the landlord condition for secure tenancies) having an interest of any description in the dwelling-house.

SCHEDULE 3
GROUNDS FOR WITHHOLDING CONSENT TO ASSIGNMENT BY WAY OF EXCHANGE

Ground 1

The tenant or the proposed assignee is subject to an order of the court for the possession of the dwelling-house of which he is the secure tenant.

Ground 2

Proceedings have been begun for possession of the dwelling-house of which the tenant or the proposed assignee is the secure tenant on one or more of grounds 1 to 6 in Part I of Schedule 2 (grounds on which possession may be ordered despite absence of suitable alternative accommodation), or there has been served on the tenant or the proposed assignee a notice under section 83 (notice of proceedings for possession) which specifies one or more of those grounds and is still in force.

Ground 2A

Either—

(a) a relevant order or suspended Ground 2 or 14 possession order is in force, or

(b) an application is pending before any court for a relevant order, a demotion order or a Ground 2 or 14 possession order to be made,

in respect of the tenant or the proposed assignee or a person who is residing with either of them.

A 'relevant order' means—

an injunction under section 152 of the Housing Act 1996 (injunctions against anti-social behaviour);

an injunction to which a power of arrest is attached by virtue of section 153 of that Act (other injunctions against anti-social behaviour);

an injunction under section 153A, 153B or 153D of that Act (injunctions against anti-social behaviour on application of certain social landlords);

an anti-social behaviour order under section 1 of the Crime and Disorder Act 1998; or

an injunction to which a power of arrest is attached by virtue of section 91 of the Anti-social Behaviour Act 2003.

A 'demotion order' means a demotion order under section 82A of this Act or section 6A of the Housing Act 1988.

A 'Ground 2 or 14 possession order' means an order for possession under Ground 2 in Schedule 2 to this Act or Ground 14 in Schedule 2 to the Housing Act 1988.

Where the tenancy of the tenant or the proposed assignee is a joint tenancy, any reference to that person includes (where the context permits) a reference to any of the joint tenants.

Ground 3

The accommodation afforded by the dwelling-house is substantially more extensive than is reasonably required by the proposed assignee.

Ground 4

The extent of the accommodation afforded by the dwelling-house is not reasonably suitable to the needs of the proposed assignee and his family.

Ground 5

The dwelling-house—

(a) forms part of or is within the curtilage of a building which, or so much of it as is held by the landlord, is held mainly for purposes other than housing purposes and consists mainly of accommodation other than housing accommodation, or is situated in a cemetery, and

(b) was let to the tenant or a predecessor in title of his in consequence of the tenant or predecessor being in the employment of—

the landlord,

a local authority,

a development corporation,

a housing action trust,

an urban development corporation, or

the governors of an aided school.

Ground 6

The landlord is a charity and the proposed assignee's occupation of the dwelling-house would conflict with the objects of the charity.

Ground 7

The dwelling-house has features which are substantially different from those of ordinary dwelling-houses and which are designed to make it suitable for occupation by a physically disabled person who requires accommodation of the kind provided by the dwelling-house and if the assignment were made there would no longer be such a person residing in the dwelling-house.

Ground 8

The landlord is a housing association or housing trust which lets dwelling-houses only for occupation (alone or with others) by persons whose circumstances (other than merely financial circumstances) make it especially difficult for them to satisfy their need for housing and if the assignment were made there would no longer be such a person residing in the dwelling-house.

Ground 9

The dwelling-house is one of a group of dwelling-houses which it is the practice of the landlord to let for occupation by persons with special needs and a social service or special facility is provided in close proximity to the group of dwelling-houses in order to assist persons with those special needs and if the assignment were made there would no longer be a person with those special needs residing in the dwelling-house.

Ground 10

The dwelling-house is the subject of a management agreement under which the manager is a housing association of which at least half the members are tenants of dwelling-houses subject to the agreement, at least half the tenants of the dwelling-houses are members of the association and the proposed assignee is not, and is not willing to become, a member of the association. Reference to a management agreement includes a section 247 or 249 arrangement, as defined by section 250A(6) of the Housing and Regeneration Act 2008.

LANDLORD AND TENANT ACT 1985
(1985, c. 70)

Implied terms as to fitness for human habitation

8. Implied terms as to fitness for human habitation

(1) In a contract to which this section applies for the letting of a house for human habitation there is implied, notwithstanding any stipulation to the contrary—

    (a) a condition that the house is fit for human habitation at the commencement of the tenancy, and

    (b) an undertaking that the house will be kept by the landlord fit for human habitation during the tenancy.

(2) …

(3) This section applies to a contract if—

    (a) the rent does not exceed the figure applicable in accordance with subsection (4), and

    (b) the letting is not on such terms as to the tenant's responsibility as are mentioned in subsection (5).

(4) The rent limit for the application of this section is shown by the following Table, by reference to the date of making of the contract and the situation of the premises:

TABLE

Date of making of contract	Rent limit
Before 31st July 1923	In London: £40
	Elsewhere: £26 or £16 (see Note 1)
On or after 31st July 1923 and before 6th July 1957	In London: £40
	Elsewhere: £26
On or after 6th July 1957	In London: £80
	Elsewhere: £52

Notes

1. The applicable figure for contracts made before 31st July 1923 is £26 in the case of premises situated in a borough or urban district which at the date of the contract had according to the last published census a population of 50,000 or more. In the case of a house situated elsewhere, the figure is £16.

2. The references to 'London' are, in relation to contracts made before 1st April 1965, to the administrative county of London and, in relation to contracts made on or after that date, to Greater London exclusive of the outer London boroughs.

(5) This section does not apply where a house is let for a term of three years or more (the lease not being determinable at the option of either party before the expiration of three years) upon terms that the tenant puts the premises into a condition reasonably fit for human habitation.

(6) In this section 'house' includes—

    (a) a part of a house, and

    (b) any yard, garden, outhouses and appurtenances belonging to the house or usually enjoyed with it.

Repairing obligations

11. Repairing obligations in short leases

(1) In a lease to which this section applies (as to which, see sections 13 and 14) there is implied a covenant by the lessor—

    (a) to keep in repair the structure and exterior of the dwelling-house (including drains, gutters and external pipes),

    (b) to keep in repair and proper working order the installations in the dwelling-house for the supply of water, gas and electricity and for sanitation (including basins, sinks, baths and sanitary conveniences, but not other fixtures, fittings and appliances for making use of the supply of water, gas or electricity), and

    (c) to keep in repair and proper working order the installations in the dwelling-house for space heating and heating water.

(1A) If a lease to which this section applies is a lease of a dwelling-house which forms part only of a building, then, subject to subsection (1B), the covenant implied by subsection (1) shall have effect as if—

(a) the reference in paragraph (a) of that subsection to the dwelling-house included a reference to any part of the building in which the lessor has an estate or interest; and

(b) any reference in paragraphs (b) and (c) of that subsection to an installation in the dwelling-house included a reference to an installation which, directly or indirectly, serves the dwelling-house and which either—

(i) forms part of any part of a building in which the lessor has an estate or interest; or

(ii) is owned by the lessor or under his control.

(1B) Nothing in subsection (1A) shall be construed as requiring the lessor to carry out any works or repairs unless the disrepair (or failure to maintain in working order) is such as to affect the lessee's enjoyment of the dwelling-house or of any common parts, as defined in section 60(1) of the Landlord and Tenant Act 1987, which the lessee, as such, is entitled to use.

(2) The covenant implied by subsection (1) ('the lessor's repairing covenant') shall not be construed as requiring the lessor—

(a) to carry out works or repairs for which the lessee is liable by virtue of his duty to use the premises in a tenant-like manner, or would be so liable but for an express covenant on his part,

(b) to rebuild or reinstate the premises in the case of destruction or damage by fire, or by tempest, flood or other inevitable accident, or

(c) to keep in repair or maintain anything which the lessee is entitled to remove from the dwelling-house.

(3) In determining the standard of repair required by the lessor's repairing covenant, regard shall be had to the age, character and prospective life of the dwelling-house and the locality in which it is situated.

(3A) In any case where—

(a) the lessor's repairing covenant has effect as mentioned in subsection (1A), and

(b) in order to comply with the covenant the lessor needs to carry out works or repairs otherwise than in, or to an installation in, the dwelling-house, and

(c) the lessor does not have a sufficient right in the part of the building or the installation concerned to enable him to carry out the required works or repairs,

then, in any proceedings relating to a failure to comply with the lessor's repairing covenant, so far as it requires the lessor to carry out the works or repairs in question, it shall be a defence for the lessor to prove that he used all reasonable endeavours to obtain, but was unable to obtain, such rights as would be adequate to enable him to carry out the works or repairs.

(4) A covenant by the lessee for the repair of the premises is of no effect so far as it relates to the matters mentioned in subsection (1)(a) to (c), except so far as it imposes on the lessor any of the requirements mentioned in subsection (2)(a) or (c).

(5) The reference in subsection (4) to a covenant by the lessee for the repair of the premises includes a covenant—

(a) to put in repair or deliver up in repair,

(b) to paint, point or render,

(c) to pay money in lieu of repairs by the lessee, or

(d) to pay money on account of repairs by the lessor.

(6) In a lease in which the lessor's repairing covenant is implied there is also implied a covenant by the lessee that the lessor, or any person authorised by him in writing, may at reasonable times of the day and on giving 24 hours' notice in writing to the occupier, enter the premises comprised in the lease for the purpose of viewing their condition and state of repair.

12. Restriction on contracting out of s 11

(1) A covenant or agreement, whether contained in a lease to which section 11 applies or in an agreement collateral to such a lease, is void in so far as it purports—

(a) to exclude or limit the obligations of the lessor or the immunities of the lessee under that section, or

(b) to authorise any forfeiture or impose on the lessee any penalty, disability or obligation in the event of his enforcing or relying upon those obligations or immunities,

unless the inclusion of the provision was authorised by the county court.

(2) The county court may, by order made with the consent of the parties, authorise the inclusion in a lease, or in an agreement collateral to a lease, of provisions excluding or modifying in relation to the lease, the provisions of section 11 with respect to the repairing obligations of the parties if it appears to the court that it is reasonable to do so, having regard to all the circumstances of the case, including the other terms and conditions of the lease.

13. Leases to which s 11 applies: general rule

(1) Section 11 (repairing obligations) applies to a lease of a dwelling-house granted on or after 24th October 1961 for a term of less than seven years.

(1A) Section 11 also applies to a lease of a dwelling-house in England granted on or after the day on which section 166 of the Localism Act 2011 came into force which is—

(a) a secure tenancy for a fixed term of seven years or more granted by a person within section 80(1) of the Housing Act 1985 (secure tenancies: the landlord condition), or

(b) an assured tenancy for a fixed term of seven years or more that—

(i) is not a shared ownership lease, and

(ii) is granted by a private registered provider of social housing.

(1B) In subsection (1A)—

'assured tenancy' has the same meaning as in Part 1 of the Housing Act 1988;

'secure tenancy' has the meaning given by section 79 of the Housing Act 1985; and

'shared ownership lease' means a lease—

(a) granted on payment of a premium calculated by reference to a percentage of the value of the dwelling-house or of the cost of providing it, or

(b) under which the lessee (or the lessee's personal representatives) will or may be entitled to a sum calculated by reference, directly or indirectly, to the value of the dwelling-house.

(2) In determining whether a lease is one to which section 11 applies—

(a) any part of the term which falls before the grant shall be left out of account and the lease shall be treated as a lease for a term commencing with the grant,

(b) a lease which is determinable at the option of the lessor before the expiration of seven years from the commencement of the term shall be treated as a lease for a term of less than seven years, and

(c) a lease (other than a lease to which paragraph (b) applies) shall not be treated as a lease for a term of less than seven years if it confers on the lessee an option for renewal for a term which, together with the original term, amounts to seven years or more.

(3) This section has effect subject to—

section 14 (leases to which section 11 applies: exceptions), and

section 32(2) (provisions not applying to tenancies within Part II of the Landlord and Tenant Act 1954).

14. Leases to which s 11 applies: exceptions

(1) Section 11 (repairing obligations) does not apply to a new lease granted to an existing tenant, or to a former tenant still in possession, if the previous lease was not a lease to which section 11 applied (and, in the case of a lease granted before 24th October 1961, would not have been if it had been granted on or after that date).

(2) In subsection (1)—

'existing tenant' means a person who is when, or immediately before, the new lease is granted, the lessee under another lease of the dwelling-house;

'former tenant still in possession' means a person who—

(a) was the lessee under another lease of the dwelling-house which terminated at some time before the new lease was granted, and

(b) between the termination of that other lease and the grant of the new lease was continuously in possession of the dwelling-house or of the rents and profits of the dwelling-house; and

'the previous lease' means the other lease referred to in the above definitions.

(3) Section 11 does not apply to a lease of a dwelling-house which is a tenancy of an agricultural holding within the meaning of the Agricultural Holdings Act 1986 and in relation to which that Act applies or to a farm business tenancy within the meaning of the Agricultural Tenancies Act 1995.

(4) Section 11 does not apply to a lease granted on or after 3rd October 1980 to—

a local authority,

a National Park authority,

a new town corporation,

an urban development corporation,

the Development Board for Rural Wales,

a non-profit registered provider of social housing,

a registered social landlord,

a co-operative housing association,

an educational institution or other body specified, or of a class specified, by regulations under section 8 of the Rent Act 1977 or paragraph 8 of Schedule 1 to the Housing Act 1988 (bodies making student lettings), or

a housing action trust established under Part III of the Housing Act 1988.

(5) Section 11 does not apply to a lease granted on or after 3rd October 1980 to—

(a) Her Majesty in right of the Crown (unless the lease is under the management of the Crown Estate Commissioners), or

(b) a government department or a person holding in trust for Her Majesty for the purposes of a government department.

15. Jurisdiction of county court

The county court has jurisdiction to make a declaration that section 11 (repairing obligations) applies, or does not apply, to a lease—

(a) whatever the net annual value of the property in question, and

(b) notwithstanding that no other relief is sought than a declaration.

16. Meaning of 'lease' and related expressions

In sections 11 to 15 (repairing obligations in short leases)—

(a) 'lease' does not include a mortgage term;

(b) 'lease of a dwelling-house' means a lease by which a building or part of a building is let wholly or mainly as a private residence, and 'dwelling-house' means that building or part of a building;

(c) 'lessee' and 'lessor' mean, respectively, the person for the time being entitled to the term of a lease and to the reversion expectant on it.

17. Specific performance of landlord's repairing obligations

(1) In proceedings in which a tenant of a dwelling alleges a breach on the part of his landlord of a repairing covenant relating to any part of the premises in which the dwelling is comprised, the court may order specific performance of the covenant whether or not the breach relates to a part of the premises let to the tenant and notwithstanding any equitable rule restricting the scope of the remedy, whether on the basis of a lack of mutuality or otherwise.

(2) In this section—

(a) 'tenant' includes a statutory tenant,

(b) in relation to a statutory tenant the reference to the premises let to him is to the premises of which he is a statutory tenant,

(c) 'landlord', in relation to a tenant, includes any person against whom the tenant has a right to enforce a repairing covenant, and

(d) 'repairing covenant' means a covenant to repair, maintain, renew, construct or replace any property.

Service charges

18. Meaning of 'service charge' and 'relevant costs'

(1) In the following provisions of this Act 'service charge' means an amount payable by a tenant of a dwelling as part of or in addition to the rent—

(a) which is payable, directly or indirectly, for services, repairs, maintenance, improvements or insurance or the landlord's costs of management, and

(b) the whole or part of which varies or may vary according to the relevant costs.

(2) The relevant costs are the costs or estimated costs incurred or to be incurred by or on behalf of the landlord, or a superior landlord, in connection with the matters for which the service charge is payable.

(3) For this purpose—

(a) 'costs' includes overheads, and

(b) costs are relevant costs in relation to a service charge whether they are incurred, or to be incurred, in the period for which the service charge is payable or in an earlier or later period.

19. Limitation of service charges: reasonableness

(1) Relevant costs shall be taken into account in determining the amount of a service charge payable for a period—

(a) only to the extent that they are reasonably incurred, and

(b) where they are incurred on the provision of services or the carrying out of works, only if the services or works are of a reasonable standard;

and the amount payable shall be limited accordingly.

(2) Where a service charge is payable before the relevant costs are incurred, no greater amount than is reasonable is so payable, and after the relevant costs have been incurred any necessary adjustment shall be made by repayment, reduction or subsequent charges or otherwise.

20. Limitation of service charges: consultation requirements

(1) Where this section applies to any qualifying works or qualifying long term agreement, the relevant contributions of tenants are limited in accordance with subsection (6) or (7) (or both) unless the consultation requirements have been either—

(a) complied with in relation to the works or agreement, or

(b) dispensed with in relation to the works or agreement by (or on appeal from) a leasehold valuation tribunal.

(2) In this section 'relevant contribution', in relation to a tenant and any works or agreement, is the amount which he may be required under the terms of his lease to contribute (by the payment of service charges) to relevant costs incurred on carrying out the works or under the agreement.

(3) This section applies to qualifying works if relevant costs incurred on carrying out the works exceed an appropriate amount.

(4) The Secretary of State may by regulations provide that this section applies to a qualifying long term agreement—

(a) if relevant costs incurred under the agreement exceed an appropriate amount, or

(b) if relevant costs incurred under the agreement during a period prescribed by the regulations exceed an appropriate amount.

(5) An appropriate amount is an amount set by regulations made by the Secretary of State; and the regulations may make provision for either or both of the following to be an appropriate amount—

(a) an amount prescribed by, or determined in accordance with, the regulations, and

(b) an amount which results in the relevant contribution of any one or more tenants being an amount prescribed by, or determined in accordance with, the regulations.

(6) Where an appropriate amount is set by virtue of paragraph (a) of subsection (5), the amount of the relevant costs incurred on carrying out the works or under the agreement which may be taken into account in determining the relevant contributions of tenants is limited to the appropriate amount.

(7) Where an appropriate amount is set by virtue of paragraph (b) of that subsection, the amount of the relevant contribution of the tenant, or each of the tenants, whose relevant contribution would otherwise exceed the amount prescribed by, or determined in accordance with, the regulations is limited to the amount so prescribed or determined.

20ZA. Consultation requirements: supplementary

(1) Where an application is made to a leasehold valuation tribunal for a determination to dispense with all or any of the consultation requirements in relation to any qualifying works or qualifying long term

agreement, the tribunal may make the determination if satisfied that it is reasonable to dispense with the requirements.

(2) In section 20 and this section—

'qualifying works' means works on a building or any other premises, and

'qualifying long term agreement' means (subject to subsection (3)) an agreement entered into, by or on behalf of the landlord or a superior landlord, for a term of more than twelve months.

(3) The Secretary of State may by regulations provide that an agreement is not a qualifying long term agreement—

(a) if it is an agreement of a description prescribed by the regulations, or

(b) in any circumstances so prescribed.

(4) In section 20 and this section 'the consultation requirements' means requirements prescribed by regulations made by the Secretary of State.

(5) Regulations under subsection (4) may in particular include provision requiring the landlord—

(a) to provide details of proposed works or agreements to tenants or the recognised tenants' association representing them,

(b) to obtain estimates for proposed works or agreements,

(c) to invite tenants or the recognised tenants' association to propose the names of persons from whom the landlord should try to obtain other estimates,

(d) to have regard to observations made by tenants or the recognised tenants' association in relation to proposed works or agreements and estimates, and

(e) to give reasons in prescribed circumstances for carrying out works or entering into agreements.

(6) Regulations under section 20 or this section—

(a) may make provision generally or only in relation to specific cases, and

(b) may make different provision for different purposes.

(7) Regulations under section 20 or this section shall be made by statutory instrument which shall be subject to annulment in pursuance of a resolution of either House of Parliament.

20A. Limitation of service charges: grant-aided works

(1) Where relevant costs are incurred or to be incurred on the carrying out of works in respect of which a grant has been or is to be paid under section 523 of the Housing Act 1985 (assistance for provision of separate service pipe for water supply) or any provision of Part I of the Housing Grants, Construction and Regeneration Act 1996 (grants, &c. for renewal of private sector housing) or any corresponding earlier enactment or article 3 of the Regulatory Reform (Housing Assistance) (England and Wales) Order 2002 (power of local housing authorities to provide assistance), the amount of the grant shall be deducted from the costs and the amount of the service charge payable shall be reduced accordingly.

(2) In any case where—

(a) relevant costs are incurred or to be incurred on the carrying out of works which are included in the external works specified in a group repair scheme, within the meaning of Part I of the Housing Grants, Construction and Regeneration Act 1996, and

(b) the landlord participated or is participating in that scheme as an assisted participant,

the amount which, in relation to the landlord, is the balance of the cost determined in accordance with section 69(3) of the Housing Grants, Construction and Regeneration Act 1996 shall be deducted from the costs, and the amount of the service charge payable shall be reduced accordingly.

20B. Limitation of service charges: time limit on making demands

(1) If any of the relevant costs taken into account in determining the amount of any service charge were incurred more than 18 months before a demand for payment of the service charge is served on the tenant, then (subject to subsection (2)), the tenant shall not be liable to pay so much of the service charge as reflects the costs so incurred.

(2) Subsection (1) shall not apply if, within the period of 18 months beginning with the date when the relevant costs in question were incurred, the tenant was notified in writing that those costs had been incurred and that he would subsequently be required under the terms of his lease to contribute to them by the payment of a service charge.

20C. **Limitation of service charges: costs of proceedings**

(1) A tenant may make an application for an order that all or any of the costs incurred, or to be incurred, by the landlord in connection with proceedings before a court, residential property tribunal or leasehold valuation tribunal, or the Upper Tribunal, or in connection with arbitration proceedings, are not to he regarded as relevant costs to be taken into account in determining the amount of any service charge payable by the tenant or any other person or persons specified in the application.

(2) The application shall be made—

   (a) in the case of court proceedings; to the court before which the proceedings are taking place or, if the application is made after the proceedings are concluded, to a county court;

   (aa) in the case of proceedings before a residential property tribunal, to a leasehold valuation tribunal;

   (b) in the case of proceedings before a leasehold valuation tribunal, to the tribunal before which the proceedings are taking place or if the application is made after the proceedings are concluded, to any leasehold valuation tribunal;

   (c) in the case of proceedings before the Upper Tribunal, to the tribunal;

   (d) in the case of arbitration proceedings, to the arbitral tribunal or, if the application is made after the proceedings are concluded, to a county court.

(3) The court or tribunal to which the application is made may make such order on the application as it considers just and equitable in the circumstances.

21. **Service charge information**

(1) The appropriate national authority may make regulations about the provision, by landlords of dwellings to each tenant by whom service charges are payable, of information about service charges.

(2) The regulations must, subject to any exceptions provided for in the regulations, require the landlord to provide information about—

   (a) the service charges of the tenant,

   (b) any associated service charges, and

   (c) relevant costs relating to service charges falling within paragraph (a) or (b).

(3) The regulations must, subject to any exceptions provided for in the regulations, require the landlord to provide the tenant with a report by a qualified person on information which the landlord is required to provide by virtue of this section.

(4) The regulations may make provision about—

   (a) information to be provided by virtue of subsection (2),

   (b) other information to be provided (whether in pursuance of a requirement or otherwise),

   (c) reports of the kind mentioned in subsection (3),

   (d) the period or periods in relation to which information or reports are to be provided,

   (e) the times at or by which information or reports are to be provided,

   (f) the form and manner in which information or reports are to be provided (including in particular whether information is to be contained in a statement of account),

   (g) the descriptions of persons who are to be qualified persons for the purposes of subsection (3).

(5) Subsections (2) to (4) do not limit the scope of the power conferred by subsection (1).

(6) Regulations under this section may—

   (a) make different provision for different cases or descriptions of case or for different purposes,

   (b) contain such supplementary, incidental, consequential, transitional, transitory or saving provision as the appropriate national authority considers appropriate.

(7) Regulations under this section are to be made by statutory instrument which, subject to subsections (8) and (9)—

   (a) in the case of regulations made by the Secretary of State, is to be subject to annulment in pursuance of a resolution of either House of Parliament, and

   (b) in the case of regulations made by the Welsh Ministers, is to be subject to annulment in pursuance of a resolution of the National Assembly for Wales.

(8) The Secretary of State may not make a statutory instrument containing the first regulations made by the Secretary of State under this section unless a draft of the instrument has been laid before, and approved by a resolution of, each House of Parliament.

(9) The Welsh Ministers may not make a statutory instrument containing the first regulations made by the Welsh Ministers under this section unless a draft of the instrument has been laid before, and approved by a resolution of, the National Assembly for Wales.

(10) In this section—

'the appropriate national authority'—

(a) in relation to England, means the Secretary of State, and

(b) in relation to Wales, means the Welsh Ministers,

'associated service charges', in relation to a tenant by whom a contribution to relevant costs is payable as a service charge, means service charges of other tenants so far as relating to the same costs.

21B. Notice to accompany demands for service charges

(1) A demand for the payment of a service charge must be accompanied by a summary of the rights and obligations of tenants of dwellings in relation to service charges.

(2) The Secretary of State may make regulations prescribing requirements as to the form and content of such summaries of rights and obligations.

(3) A tenant may withhold payment of a service charge which has been demanded from him if subsection (1) is not complied with in relation to the demand.

(4) Where a tenant withholds a service charge under this section, any provisions of the lease relating to non-payment or late payment of service charges do not have effect in relation to the period for which he so withholds it.

(5) Regulations under subsection (2) may make different provision for different purposes.

(6) Regulations under subsection (2) shall be made by statutory instrument which shall be subject to annulment in pursuance of a resolution of either House of Parliament.

22. Request to inspect supporting accounts, etc

(1) This section applies where a tenant, or the secretary of a recognised tenant's association, has obtained such a summary as is referred to in section 21(1) (summary of relevant costs), whether in pursuance of that section or otherwise.

(2) The tenant, or the secretary with the consent of the tenant, may within six months of obtaining the summary require the landlord in writing to afford him reasonable facilities—

(a) for inspecting the accounts, receipts and other documents supporting the summary, and

(b) for taking copies or extracts from them.

(3) A request under this section is duly served on the landlord if it is served on—

(a) an agent of the landlord named as such in the rent book or similar document, or

(b) the person who receives the rent on behalf of the landlord;

and a person on whom a request is so served shall forward it as soon as may be to the landlord.

(4) The landlord shall make such facilities available to the tenant or secretary for a period of two months beginning not later than one month after the request is made.

(5) The landlord shall—

(a) where such facilities are for the inspection of any documents, make them so available free of charge;

(b) where such facilities are for the taking of copies or extracts, be entitled to make them so available on payment of such reasonable charge as he may determine.

(6) The requirement imposed on the landlord by subsection (5)(a) to make any facilities available to a person free of charge shall not be construed as precluding the landlord from treating as part of his costs of management any costs incurred by him in connection with making those facilities so available.

23. Request relating to information held by superior landlord

(1) If a request under section 21 (request for summary of relevant costs) relates in whole or in part to relevant costs incurred by or on behalf of a superior landlord, and the landlord to whom the request is made is not in possession of the relevant information—

(a) he shall in turn make a written request for the relevant information to the person who is his landlord (and so on, if that person is not himself the superior landlord),

(b) the superior landlord shall comply with that request within a reasonable time, and

(c) the immediate landlord shall then comply with the tenant's or secretary's request, or that part of it which relates to the relevant costs incurred by or on behalf of the superior landlord, within the time allowed by section 21 or such further time, if any, as is reasonable in the circumstances.

(2) If a request under section 22 (request for facilities to inspect supporting accounts, &c) relates to a summary of costs incurred by or on behalf of a superior landlord—

(a) the landlord to whom the request is made shall forthwith inform the tenant or secretary of that fact and of the name and address of the superior landlord, and

(b) section 22 shall then apply to the superior landlord as it applies to the immediate landlord.

24. Effect of assignment

The assignment of a tenancy does not affect the validity of a request made under section 21, 22 or 23 before the assignment; but a person is not obliged to provide a summary or make facilities available more than once for the same dwelling and for the same period.

25. Failure to comply with ss. 21 to 23A an offence

(1) It is a summary offence for a person to fail, without reasonable excuse, to perform a duty imposed on him by or by virtue of any of sections 21, 22 or 23.

(2) A person committing such an offence is liable on conviction to a fine not exceeding level 4 on the standard scale.

26. Exception: tenants of certain public authorities

(1) Sections 18 to 25 (limitation on service charges and requests for information about costs) do not apply to a service charge payable by a tenant of—

a local authority,

a National Park authority, or

a new town corporation,

unless the tenancy is a long tenancy, in which case sections 18 to 24 apply but section 25 (offence of failure to comply) does not.

(2) The following are long tenancies for the purposes of subsection (1), subject to subsection (3)—

(a) a tenancy granted for a term certain exceeding 21 years, whether or not it is (or may become) terminable before the end of that term by notice given by the tenant or by re-entry or forfeiture;

(b) a tenancy for a term fixed by law under a grant with a covenant or obligation for perpetual renewal, other than a tenancy by sub-demise from one which is not a long tenancy;

(c) any tenancy granted in pursuance of Part V of the Housing Act 1985 (the right to buy), including any tenancy granted in pursuance of that Part as it has effect by virtue of section 17 of the Housing Act 1996 (the right to acquire).

(3) A tenancy granted so as to become terminable by notice after a death is not a long tenancy for the purposes of subsection (1), unless—

(a) it is granted by a housing association which at the time of the grant is a private registered provider of social housing or a registered social landlord,

(b) it is granted at a premium calculated by reference to a percentage of the value of the dwelling-house or the cost of providing it, and

(c) at the time it is granted it complies with the requirements of the regulations then in force under section 140(4)(b) of the Housing Act 1980 or paragraph 4(2)(b) of Schedule 4A to the Leasehold Reform Act 1967 (conditions for exclusion of shared ownership leases from Part I of Leasehold Reform Act 1967) or, in the case of a tenancy granted before any such regulations were brought into force, with the first such regulations to be in force.

27. Exception: rent registered and not entered as variable

Sections 18 to 25 (limitation on service charges and requests for information about costs) do not apply to a service charge payable by the tenant of a dwelling the rent of which is registered under Part IV of the Rent Act 1977, unless the amount registered is, in pursuance of section 71(4) of that Act, entered as a variable amount.

27A. Liability to pay service charges: jurisdiction

(1) An application may be made to a leasehold valuation tribunal for a determination whether a service charge is payable and, if it is, as to—

(a) the person by whom it is payable,

(b) the person to whom it is payable,

(c) the amount which is payable,

(d) the date at or by which it is payable, and

(e) the manner in which it is payable.

(2) Subsection (1) applies whether or not any payment has been made.

(3) An application may also be made to a leasehold valuation tribunal for a determination whether, if costs were incurred for services, repairs, maintenance, improvements, insurance or management of any specified description, a service charge would be payable for the costs and, if it would, as to—

(a) the person by whom it would be payable,

(b) the person to whom it would be payable,

(c) the amount which would be payable,

(d) the date at or by which it would be payable, and

(e) the manner in which it would be payable.

(4) No application under subsection (1) or (3) may be made in respect of a matter which—

(a) has been agreed or admitted by the tenant,

(b) has been, or is to be, referred to arbitration pursuant to a post-dispute arbitration agreement to which the tenant is a party,

(c) has been the subject of determination by a court, or

(d) has been the subject of determination by an arbitral tribunal pursuant to a post-dispute arbitration agreement.

(5) But the tenant is not to be taken to have agreed or admitted any matter by reason only of having made any payment.

(6) An agreement by the tenant of a dwelling (other than a post-dispute arbitration agreement) is void in so far as it purports to provide for a determination—

(a) in a particular manner, or

(b) on particular evidence,

of any question which may be the subject of an application under subsection (1) or (3).

(7) The jurisdiction conferred on a leasehold valuation tribunal in respect of any matter by virtue of this section is in addition to any jurisdiction of a court in respect of the matter.

SCHEDULE
RIGHTS OF TENANTS WITH RESPECT TO INSURANCE

Construction

1. In this Schedule—

'landlord', in relation to a tenant by whom a service charge is payable which includes an amount payable directly or indirectly for insurance includes any person who has a right to enforce payment of that service charge;

'relevant policy', in relation to a dwelling, means any policy of insurance under which the dwelling is insured (being, in the case of a flat, a policy covering the building containing it); and

'tenant' includes a statutory tenant.

Summary of insurance cover

2. (1) Where a service charge is payable by the tenant of a dwelling which consists of or includes an amount payable directly or indirectly for insurance, the tenant may by notice in writing require the landlord to supply him with a written summary of the insurance for the time being effected in relation to the dwelling.

(2) If the tenant is represented by a recognised tenants' association and he consents, the notice may be served by the secretary of the association instead of by the tenant and may then be for the supply of the summary to the secretary.

(3) A notice under this paragraph is duly served on the landlord if it is served on—
- (a) an agent of the landlord named as such in the rent book or similar document, or
- (b) the person who receives the rent on behalf of the landlord;

and a person on whom such a notice is so served shall forward it as soon as may be to the landlord.

(4) The landlord shall, within the period of twenty-one days beginning with the day on which he receives the notice, comply with it by supplying to the tenant or the secretary of the recognised tenants' association (as the case may require) such a summary as is mentioned in sub-paragraph (1), which shall include—
- (a) the insured amount or amounts under any relevant policy, and
- (b) the name of the insurer under any such policy, and
- (c) the risks in respect of which the dwelling or (as the case may be) the building containing it is insured under any such policy.

(5) In sub-paragraph (4)(a) 'the insured amount or amounts', in relation to a relevant policy, means—
- (a) in the case of a dwelling other than a flat, the amount for which the dwelling is insured under the policy; and
- (b) in the case of a flat, the amount for which the building containing it is insured under the policy and, if specified in the policy, the amount for which the flat is insured under it.

(6) The landlord shall be taken to have complied with the notice if, within the period mentioned in sub-paragraph (4), he instead supplies to the tenant or the secretary (as the case may require) a copy of every relevant policy.

(7) In a case where two or more buildings are insured under any relevant policy, the summary or copy supplied under sub-paragraph (4) or (6) so far as relating to that policy need only be of such parts of the policy as relate—
- (a) to the dwelling, and
- (b) if the dwelling is a flat, to the building containing it.

Inspection of insurance policy etc.

3. (1) Where a service charge is payable by the tenant of a dwelling which consists of or includes an amount payable directly or indirectly for insurance, the tenant may by notice in writing require the landlord—
- (a) to afford him reasonable facilities for inspecting any relevant policy or associated documents and for taking copies of or extracts from them, or
- (b) to take copies of or extracts from any such policy or documents and either send them to him or afford him reasonable facilities for collecting them (as he specifies).

(2) If the tenant is represented by a recognised tenants' association and he consents, the notice may be served by the secretary of the association instead of by the tenant (and in that case any requirement imposed by it is to afford reasonable facilities, or to send copies or extracts, to the secretary).

(3) A notice under this paragraph is duly served on the landlord if it is served on—
- (a) an agent of the landlord named as such in the rent book or similar document, or
- (b) the person who receives the rent on behalf of the landlord;

and a person on whom such a notice is so served shall forward it as soon as may be to the landlord.

(4) The landlord shall comply with a requirement imposed by a notice under this paragraph within the period of twenty-one days beginning with the day on which he receives the notice.

(5) To the extent that a notice under this paragraph requires the landlord to afford facilities for inspecting documents—
- (a) he shall do so free of charge, but
- (b) he may treat as part of his costs of management any costs incurred by him in doing so.

(6) The landlord may make a reasonable charge for doing anything else in compliance with a requirement imposed by a notice under this paragraph.

(7) In this paragraph—

'relevant policy' includes a policy of insurance under which the dwelling was insured for the period of insurance immediately preceding that current when the notice is served (being, in the case of a flat, a policy covering the building containing it), and 'associated documents' means accounts, receipts or other documents which provide evidence of payment of any premiums due under a relevant policy in respect of the period of insurance which is current when the notice is served or the period of insurance immediately preceding that period.

Insurance effected by superior landlord

4. (1) If a notice is served under paragraph 2 in a case where a superior landlord has effected, in whole or in part, the insurance of the dwelling in question and the landlord on whom the notice is served is not in possession of the relevant information—
   (a) he shall in turn by notice in writing require the person who is his landlord to give him the relevant information (and so on, if that person is not himself the superior landlord),
   (b) the superior landlord shall comply with the notice within a reasonable time, and
   (c) the immediate landlord shall then comply with the tenants' or secretary's notice in the manner provided by sub-paragraphs (4) to (7) of paragraph 2 within the time allowed by that paragraph or such further time, if any, as is reasonable in the circumstances.

   (2) If, in a case where a superior landlord has effected, in whole or in part, the insurance of the dwelling in question, a notice under paragraph 3 imposes a requirement relating to any policy of insurance effected by the superior landlord—
   (a) the landlord on whom the notice is served shall forthwith inform the tenant or secretary of that fact and of the name and address of the superior landlord, and
   (b) that paragraph shall then apply to the superior landlord in relation to that policy as it applies to the immediate landlord.

Effect of change of landlord

4A. (1) This paragraph applies where, at a time when a duty imposed on the landlord or a superior landlord by virtue of any of paragraphs 2 to 4 remains to be discharged by him, he disposes of the whole or part of his interest as landlord or superior landlord).

   (2) If the landlord or superior landlord is, despite the disposal, still in a position to discharge the duty to any extent, he remains responsible for discharging it to that extent.

   (3) If the other person is in a position to discharge the duty to any extent, he is responsible for discharging it to that extent.

   (4) Where the other person is responsible for discharging the duty to any extent (whether or not the landlord or superior landlord is also responsible for discharging it to that or any other extent)—
   (a) references to the landlord or superior landlord in paragraphs 2 to 4 are to, or include, the other person so far as is appropriate to reflect his responsibility for discharging the duty to that extent, but
   (b) in connection with its discharge by that person, paragraphs 2(4) and 3(4) apply as if the reference to the day on which the landlord receives the notice were to the date of the disposal referred to in sub-paragraph (1).

Effect of assignment

5. The assignment of a tenancy does not affect any duty imposed by virtue of any of paragraphs 2 to 4A; but a person is not required to comply with more than a reasonable number of requirements imposed by any one person.

Offence of failure to comply

6. (1) It is a summary offence for a person to fail, without reasonable excuse, to perform a duty imposed on him by or by virtue of any of paragraphs 2 to 4A.
   (2) A person committing such an offence is liable on conviction to a fine not exceeding level 4 on the standard scale.

Tenants' right to notify insurers of possible claim

7. (1) This paragraph applies to any dwelling in respect of which the tenant pays to the landlord a service charge consisting of or including an amount payable directly or indirectly for insurance.
   (2) Where—
   (a) it appears to the tenant of any such dwelling that damage has been caused—
       (i) to the dwelling, or

(ii) if the dwelling is a flat, to the dwelling or to any other part of the building containing it,

in respect of which a claim could be made under the terms of a policy of insurance, and

(b) it is a term of that policy that the person insured under the policy should give notice of any claim under it to the insurer within a specified period,

the tenant may, within that specified period, serve on the insurer a notice in writing stating that it appears to him that damage has been caused as mentioned in paragraph (a) and describing briefly the nature of the damage.

(3) Where—
- (a) any such notice is served on an insurer by a tenant in relation to any such damage, and
- (b) the specified period referred to in sub-paragraph (2)(b) would expire earlier than the period of six months beginning with the date on which the notice is served,

the policy in question shall have effect as regards any claim subsequently made in respect of that damage by the person insured under the policy as if for the specified period there were substituted that period of six months.

(4) Where the tenancy of a dwelling to which this paragraph applies is held by joint tenants, a single notice under this paragraph may be given by any one or more of those tenants.

(6) Any such regulations—
- (a) may make different provision with respect to different cases or descriptions of case, including different provision for different areas, and
- (b) shall be made by statutory instrument.

Right to challenge landlord's choice of insurers

8. (1) This paragraph applies where a tenancy of a dwelling requires the tenant to insure the dwelling with an insurer nominated or approved by the landlord.

(2) The tenant or landlord may apply to a county court or leasehold valuation tribunal for a determination whether—
- (a) the insurance which is available from the nominated or approved insurer for insuring the tenant's dwelling is unsatisfactory in any respect, or
- (b) the premiums payable in respect of any such insurance are excessive.

(3) No such application may be made in respect of a matter which—
- (a) has been agreed or admitted by the tenant,
- (b) under an arbitration agreement to which the tenant is a party is to be referred to arbitration, or
- (c) has been the subject of determination by a court or arbitral tribunal.

(4) On an application under this paragraph the court or tribunal may make—
- (a) an order requiring the landlord to nominate or approve such other insurer as is specified in the order, or
- (b) an order requiring him to nominate or approve another insurer who satisfies such requirements in relation to the insurance of the dwelling as are specified in the order.

(6) An agreement by the tenant of a dwelling (other than an arbitration agreement) is void in so far as it purports to provide for a determination in a particular manner, or on particular evidence, of any question which may be the subject of an application under this paragraph.

Exception for tenants of certain public authorities

9. (1) Paragraphs 2 to 8 do not apply to a tenant of—

a local authority,

a National Park authority, or

a new town corporation,

unless the tenancy is a long tenancy, in which case paragraphs 2 to 5 and 7 and 8 apply but paragraph 6 does not.

(2) Subsections (2) and (3) of section 26 shall apply for the purposes of subparagraph (1) as they apply for the purposes of subsection (1) of that section.

HOUSING ACT 1988
(1988, c. 50)

PART I
RENTED ACCOMMODATION

CHAPTER I
ASSURED TENANCIES

Meaning of assured tenancy etc.

1. Assured tenancies

(1) A tenancy under which a dwelling-house is let as a separate dwelling is for the purposes of this Act an assured tenancy if and so long as—

(a) the tenant or, as the case may be, each of the joint tenants is an individual; and

(b) the tenant or, as the case may be, at least one of the joint tenants occupies the dwelling-house as his only or principal home; and

(c) the tenancy is not one which, by virtue of subsection (2) or subsection (6) below, cannot be an assured tenancy.

(2) Subject to subsection (3) below, if and so long as a tenancy falls within any paragraph in Part I of Schedule 1 to this Act, it cannot be an assured tenancy; and in that Schedule—

(a) 'tenancy' means a tenancy under which a dwelling-house is let as a separate dwelling;

(b) Part II has effect for determining the rateable value of a dwelling-house for the purposes of Part I; and

(c) Part III has effect for supplementing paragraph 10 in Part I.

(2A) The Secretary of State may by order replace any amount referred to in paragraphs 2 and 3A of Schedule 1 to this Act by such amount as is specified in the order; and such an order shall be made by statutory instrument which shall be subject to annulment in pursuance of a resolution of either House of Parliament.

(3) Except as provided in Chapter V below, at the commencement of this Act, a tenancy—

(a) under which a dwelling-house was then let as a separate dwelling, and

(b) which immediately before that commencement was an assured tenancy for the purposes of sections 56 to 58 of the Housing Act 1980 (tenancies granted by approved bodies),

shall become an assured tenancy for the purposes of this Act.

(4) In relation to an assured tenancy falling within subsection (3) above—

(a) Part I of Schedule 1 to this Act shall have effect subject to subsection (5) below as if it consisted only of paragraphs 11 and 12; and

(b) sections 56 to 58 of the Housing Act 1980 (and Schedule 5 to that Act) shall not apply after the commencement of this Act.

(5) In any case where—

(a) immediately before the commencement of this Act the landlord under a tenancy is a fully mutual housing association, and

(b) at the commencement of this Act the tenancy becomes an assured tenancy by virtue of subsection (3) above,

then, so long as that association remains the landlord under that tenancy (and under any statutory periodic tenancy which arises on the coming to an end of that tenancy), paragraph 12 of Schedule 1 to this Act shall have effect in relation to that tenancy with the omission of sub-paragraph (1)(h).

Security of tenure

5. Security of tenure

(1) An assured tenancy cannot be brought to an end by the landlord except by—

(a) obtaining—

(i) an order of the court for possession of the dwelling-house under section 7 or 21, and

(ii) the execution of the order,

(b) obtaining an order of the court under section 6A (demotion order), or

(c) in the case of a fixed term tenancy which contains power for the landlord to determine the tenancy in certain circumstances, by the exercise of that power,

and, accordingly, the service by the landlord of a notice to quit is of no effect in relation to a periodic assured tenancy.

(1A) Where an order of the court for possession of the dwelling-house is obtained, the tenancy ends when the order is executed.

(2) If an assured tenancy which is a fixed term tenancy comes to an end otherwise than by virtue of—

(a) an order of the court of the kind mentioned in subsection (1)(a) or (b) or any other order of the court, or

(b) a surrender or other action on the part of the tenant,

then, subject to section 7 and Chapter II below, the tenant shall be entitled to remain in possession of the dwelling-house let under that tenancy and, subject to subsection (4) below, his right to possession shall depend upon a periodic tenancy arising by virtue of this section.

(3) The periodic tenancy referred to in subsection (2) above is one—

(a) taking effect in possession immediately on the coming to an end of the fixed term tenancy;

(b) deemed to have been granted by the person who was the landlord under the fixed term tenancy immediately before it came to an end to the person who was then the tenant under that tenancy;

(c) under which the premises which are let are the same dwelling-house as was let under the fixed term tenancy;

(d) under which the periods of the tenancy are the same as those for which rent was last payable under the fixed term tenancy; and

(e) under which, subject to the following provisions of this Part of this Act, the other terms are the same as those of the fixed term tenancy immediately

before it came to an end, except that any term which makes provision for determination by the landlord or the tenant shall not have effect while the tenancy remains an assured tenancy.

(4) The periodic tenancy referred to in subsection (2) above shall not arise if, on the coming to an end of the fixed term tenancy, the tenant is entitled, by virtue of the grant of another tenancy, to possession of the same or substantially the same dwelling-house as was let to him under the fixed term tenancy.

(5) If, on or before the date on which a tenancy is entered into or is deemed to have been granted as mentioned in subsection (3)(b) above, the person who is to be the tenant under that tenancy—

(a) enters into an obligation to do any act which (apart from this subsection) will cause the tenancy to come to an end at a time when it is an assured tenancy, or

(b) executes, signs or gives any surrender, notice to quit or other document which (apart from this subsection) has the effect of bringing the tenancy to an end at a time when it is an assured tenancy,

the obligation referred to in paragraph (a) above shall not be enforceable or, as the case may be, the surrender, notice to quit or other document referred to in paragraph (b) above shall be of no effect.

(5A) Nothing in subsection (5) affects any right of pre-emption—

(a) which is exercisable by the landlord under a tenancy in circumstances where the tenant indicates his intention to dispose of the whole of his interest under the tenancy, and

(b) in pursuance of which the landlord would be required to pay, in respect of the acquisition of that interest, an amount representing its market value.

'Dispose' means dispose by assignment or surrender, and 'acquisition' has a corresponding meaning.

(6) If, by virtue of any provision of this Part of this Act, Part I of Schedule 1 to this Act has effect in relation to a fixed term tenancy as if it consisted only of paragraphs 11 and 12, that Part shall have the like effect in relation to any periodic tenancy which arises by virtue of this section on the coming to an end of the fixed term tenancy.

(7) Any reference in this Part of this Act to a statutory periodic tenancy is a reference to a periodic tenancy arising by virtue of this section.

6. Fixing of terms of statutory periodic tenancy

(1) In this section, in relation to a statutory periodic tenancy,—

(a) 'the former tenancy' means the fixed term tenancy on the coming to an end of which the statutory periodic tenancy arises; and

(b) 'the implied terms' means the terms of the tenancy which have effect by virtue of section 5(3)(e) above, other than terms as to the amount of the rent;

but nothing in the following provisions of this section applies to a statutory periodic tenancy at a time when, by virtue of paragraph 11 or paragraph 12 in Part I of Schedule 1 to this Act, it cannot be an assured tenancy.

(2) Not later than the first anniversary of the day on which the former tenancy came to an end, the landlord may serve on the tenant, or the tenant may serve on the landlord, a notice in the prescribed form proposing terms of the statutory periodic tenancy different from the implied terms and, if the landlord or the tenant considers it appropriate, proposing an adjustment of the amount of the rent to take account of the proposed terms.

(3) Where a notice has been served under subsection (2) above,—

(a) within the period of three months beginning on the date on which the notice was served on him, the landlord or the tenant, as the case may be, may, by an application in the prescribed form, refer the notice to a rent assessment committee under subsection (4) below; and

(b) if the notice is not so referred, then, with effect from such date, not falling within the period referred to in paragraph (a) above, as may be specified in the notice, the terms proposed in the notice shall become terms of the tenancy in substitution for any of the implied terms dealing with the same subject matter and the amount of the rent shall be varied in accordance with any adjustment so proposed.

(4) Where a notice under subsection (2) above is referred to a rent assessment committee, the committee shall consider the terms proposed in the notice and shall determine whether those terms, or some other terms (dealing with the same subject matter as the proposed terms), are such as, in the committee's opinion, might reasonably be expected to be found in an assured periodic tenancy of the dwelling-house concerned, being a tenancy—

(a) which begins on the coming to an end of the former tenancy; and

(b) which is granted by a willing landlord on terms which, except in so far as they relate to the subject matter of the proposed terms, are those of the statutory periodic tenancy at the time of the committee's consideration.

(5) Whether or not a notice under subsection (2) above proposes an adjustment of the amount of the rent under the statutory periodic tenancy, where a rent assessment committee determine any terms under sub-section (4) above, they shall, if they consider it appropriate, specify such an adjustment to take account of the terms so determined.

(6) In making a determination under subsection (4) above, or specifying an adjustment of an amount of rent under subsection (5) above, there shall be disregarded any effect on the terms or the amount of the rent attributable to the granting of a tenancy to a sitting tenant.

(7) Where a notice under subsection (2) above is referred to a rent assessment committee, then, unless the landlord and the tenant otherwise agree, with effect from such date as the committee may direct—

(a) the terms determined by the committee shall become terms of the statutory periodic tenancy in substitution for any of the implied terms dealing with the same subject matter; and

(b) the amount of the rent under the statutory periodic tenancy shall be altered to accord with any adjustment specified by the committee;

but for the purposes of paragraph (b) above the committee shall not direct a date earlier than the date specified, in accordance with subsection (3)(b) above, in the notice referred to them.

(8) Nothing in this section requires a rent assessment committee to continue with a determination under subsection (4) above if the landlord and tenant give notice in writing that they no longer require such a determination or if the tenancy has come to an end.

6A. Demotion because of anti-social behaviour

(1) This section applies to an assured tenancy if—

(a) the landlord is a non-profit registered provider of social housing,

(b) the landlord is a profit-making registered provider of social housing and the dwelling-house let on the tenancy is social housing within the meaning of Part 2 of the Housing and Regeneration Act 2008, or the landlord is a registered social landlord.

(2) The landlord may apply to a county court for a demotion order.

(3) A demotion order has the following effect—
- (a) the assured tenancy is terminated with effect from the date specified in the order;
- (b) if the tenant remains in occupation of the dwelling-house after that date a demoted tenancy is created with effect from that date;
- (c) it is a term of the demoted tenancy that any arrears of rent payable at the termination of the assured tenancy become payable under the demoted tenancy;
- (d) it is also a term of the demoted tenancy that any rent paid in advance or overpaid at the termination of the assured tenancy is credited to the tenant's liability to pay rent under the demoted tenancy.

(4) The court must not make a demotion order unless it is satisfied—
- (a) that the tenant or a person residing in or visiting the dwelling-house has engaged or has threatened to engage in conduct to which section 153A or 153B of the Housing Act 1996 (anti-social behaviour or use of premises for unlawful purposes) applies, and
- (b) that it is reasonable to make the order.

(5) The court must not entertain proceedings for a demotion order unless—
- (a) the landlord has served on the tenant a notice under subsection (6), or
- (b) the court thinks it is just and equitable to dispense with the requirement of the notice.

(6) The notice must—
- (a) give particulars of the conduct in respect of which the order is sought;
- (b) state that the proceedings will not begin before the date specified in the notice;
- (c) state that the proceedings will not begin after the end of the period of twelve months beginning with the date of service of the notice.

(7) The date specified for the purposes of subsection (6)(b) must not be before the end of the period of two weeks beginning with the date of service of the notice.

(8) Each of the following has effect in respect of a demoted tenancy at the time it is created by virtue of an order under this section as it has effect in relation to the assured tenancy at the time it is terminated by virtue of the order—
- (a) the parties to the tenancy;
- (b) the period of the tenancy;
- (c) the amount of the rent;
- (d) the dates on which the rent is payable.

(9) Subsection (8)(b) does not apply if the assured tenancy was for a fixed term and in such a case the demoted tenancy is a weekly periodic tenancy.

(10) If the landlord of the demoted tenancy serves on the tenant a statement of any other express terms of the assured tenancy which are to apply to the demoted tenancy such terms are also terms of the demoted tenancy.

(11) For the purposes of this section a demoted tenancy is a tenancy to which section 20B of the Housing Act 1988 applies.

7. **Orders for possession**

(1) The court shall not make an order for possession of a dwelling-house let on an assured tenancy except on one or more of the grounds set out in Schedule 2 to this Act; but nothing in this Part of this Act relates to proceedings for possession of such a dwelling-house which are brought by a mortgagee, within the meaning of the Law of Property Act 1925, who has lent money on the security of the assured tenancy.

(2) The following provisions of this section have effect, subject to section 8 below, in relation to proceedings for the recovery of possession of a dwelling-house let on an assured tenancy.

(3) If the court is satisfied that any of the grounds in Part I of Schedule 2 to this Act is established then, subject to subsections (5A) and (6) below, the court shall make an order for possession.

(4) If the court is satisfied that any of the grounds in Part II of Schedule 2 to this Act is established, then, subject to subsections (5A) and (6) below, the court may make an order for possession if it considers it reasonable to do so.

(5) Part III of Schedule 2 to this Act shall have effect for supplementing Ground 9 in that Schedule and Part IV of that Schedule shall have effect in relation to notices given as mentioned in Grounds 1 to 5 of that Schedule.

(5A) The court shall not make an order for possession of a dwelling-house let on an assured periodic tenancy arising under Schedule 10 to the Local Government and Housing Act 1989 on any of the following grounds, that is to say,—

(a) Grounds 1, 2 and 5 in Part I of Schedule 2 to this Act;

(b) Ground 16 in Part II of that Schedule; and

(c) if the assured periodic tenancy arose on the termination of a former 1954 Act tenancy, within the meaning of the said Schedule 10, Ground 6 in Part I of Schedule 2 to this Act.

(6) The court shall not make an order for possession of a dwelling-house to take effect at a time when it is let on an assured fixed term tenancy unless—

(a) the ground for possession is Ground 2 or Ground 8 in Part I of Schedule 2 to this Act or any of the grounds in Part II of that Schedule, other than Ground 9 or Ground 16; and

(b) the terms of the tenancy make provision for it to be brought to an end on the ground in question (whether that provision takes the form of a provision for re-entry, for forfeiture, for determination by notice or otherwise).

(6A) In the case of a dwelling-house in England, subsection (6)(a) has effect as if it also referred to Ground 7 in Part 1 of Schedule 2 to this Act.

(7) Subject to the preceding provisions of this section, the court may make an order for possession of a dwelling-house on grounds relating to a fixed term tenancy which has come to an end; and where an order is made in such circumstances, any statutory periodic tenancy which has arisen on the ending of the fixed term tenancy shall end (without any notice and regardless of the period) in accordance with section 5(1A).

8. Notice of proceedings for possession

(1) The court shall not entertain proceedings for possession of a dwelling-house let on an assured tenancy unless—

(a) the landlord or, in the case of joint landlords, at least one of them has served on the tenant a notice in accordance with this section and the proceedings are begun within the time limits stated in the notice in accordance with subsections (3) to (4B) below; or

(b) the court considers it just and equitable to dispense with the requirement of such a notice.

(2) The court shall not make an order for possession on any of the grounds in Schedule 2 to this Act unless that ground and particulars of it are specified in the notice under this section; but the grounds specified in such a notice may be altered or added to with the leave of the court.

(3) A notice under this section is one in the prescribed form informing the tenant that—

(a) the landlord intends to begin proceedings for possession of the dwelling-house on one or more of the grounds specified in the notice; and

(b) those proceedings will not begin earlier than a date specified in the notice in accordance with subsections (4) to (4B) below; and

(c) those proceedings will not begin later than twelve months from the date of service of the notice.

(4) If a notice under this section specifies in accordance with subsection (3)(a) above Ground 14 in Schedule 2 to this Act (whether with or without other grounds), the date specified in the notice as mentioned in subsection (3)(b) above shall not be earlier than the date of the service of the notice.

(4A) If a notice under this section specifies in accordance with subsection (3)(a) above, any of Grounds 1, 2, 5 to 7, 9 and 16 in Schedule 2 to this Act (whether without other grounds or with any ground other than Ground 14), the date specified in the notice as mentioned in subsection (3)(b) above shall not be earlier than—

(a) two months from the date of service of the notice, and

(b) if the tenancy is a periodic tenancy, the earliest date on which, apart from section 5(1) above, the tenancy could be brought to an end by a notice to quit given by the landlord on the same date as the date of service of the notice under this section.

(4B) In any other case, the date specified in the notice as mentioned in subsection (3)(b) above shall not be earlier than the expiry of the period of two weeks from the date of service of the notice.

(5) The court may not exercise the power conferred by subsection (1)(b) above if the landlord seeks to recover possession on Ground 8 in Schedule 2 to this Act.

(6) Where a notice under this section—

   (a) is served at a time when the dwelling-house is let on a fixed term tenancy, or

   (b) is served after a fixed term tenancy has come to an end but relates (in whole or in part) to events occurring during that tenancy,

   the notice shall have effect notwithstanding that the tenant becomes or has become tenant under a statutory periodic tenancy arising on the coming to an end of the fixed term tenancy.

8A. Additional notice requirements: ground of domestic violence

(1) Where the ground specified in a notice under section 8 (whether with or without other grounds) is Ground 14A in Schedule 2 to this Act and the partner who has left the dwelling-house as mentioned in that ground is not a tenant of the dwelling-house, the court shall not entertain proceedings for possession of the dwelling-house unless—

   (a) the landlord or, in the case of joint landlords, at least one of them has served on the partner who has left a copy of the notice or has taken all reasonable steps to serve a copy of the notice on that partner, or

   (b) the court considers it just and equitable to dispense with such requirements as to service.

(2) Where Ground 14A in Schedule 2 to this Act is added to a notice under section 8 with the leave of the court after proceedings for possession are begun and the partner who has left the dwelling-house as mentioned in that ground is not a party to the proceedings, the court shall not continue to entertain the proceedings unless—

   (a) the landlord or, in the case of joint landlords, at least one of them has served a notice under subsection (3) below on the partner who has left or has taken all reasonable steps to serve such a notice on that partner, or

   (b) the court considers it just and equitable to dispense with the requirement of such a notice.

(3) A notice under this subsection shall—

   (a) state that proceedings for the possession of the dwelling-house have begun,

   (b) specify the ground or grounds on which possession is being sought, and

   (c) give particulars of the ground or grounds.

9. Extended discretion of court in possession claims

(1) Subject to subsection (6) below, the court may adjourn for such period or periods as it thinks fit proceedings for possession of a dwelling-house let on an assured tenancy.

(2) On the making of an order for possession of a dwelling-house let on an assured tenancy or at any time before the execution of such an order, the court, subject to subsection (6) below, may—

   (a) stay or suspend execution of the order, or

   (b) postpone the date of possession,

   for such period or periods as the court thinks just.

(3) On any such adjournment as is referred to in subsection (1) above or on any such stay, suspension or postponement as is referred to in subsection (2) above, the court, unless it considers that to do so would cause exceptional hardship to the tenant or would otherwise be unreasonable, shall impose conditions with regard to payment by the tenant of arrears of rent (if any) and rent and may impose such other conditions as it thinks fit.

(4) If any such conditions as are referred to in subsection (3) above are complied with, the court may, if it thinks fit, discharge or rescind any such order as is referred to in subsection (2) above.

(5), (5A) ...

(6) This section does not apply if the court is satisfied that the landlord is entitled to possession of the dwelling-house—

   (a) on any of the grounds in Part I of Schedule 2 to this Act; or

   (b) by virtue of subsection (1) or subsection (4) of section 21 below.

9A. Proceedings for possession: anti-social behaviour

(1) This section applies if the court is considering under section 7(4) whether it is reasonable to make an order for possession on ground 14 set out in Part 2 of Schedule 2 (conduct of tenant or other person).

(2) The court must consider, in particular—
  (a) the effect that the nuisance or annoyance has had on persons other than the person against whom the order is sought;
  (b) any continuing effect the nuisance or annoyance is likely to have on such persons;
  (c) the effect that the nuisance or annoyance would be likely to have on such persons if the conduct is repeated.

11. Payment of removal expenses in certain cases
  (1) Where a court makes an order for possession of a dwelling-house let on an assured tenancy on Ground 6 or Ground 9 in Schedule 2 to this Act (but not on any other ground), the landlord shall pay to the tenant a sum equal to the reasonable expenses likely to be incurred by the tenant in removing from the dwelling-house.
  (2) Any question as to the amount of the sum referred in subsection (1) above shall be determined by agreement between the landlord and the tenant or, in default of agreement, by the court.
  (3) Any sum payable to a tenant by virtue of this section shall be recoverable as a civil debt due from the landlord.

Rent and other terms

13. Increase of rent under assured periodic tenancies
  (1) This section applies to—
    (a) a statutory periodic tenancy other than one which, by virtue of paragraph 11 or paragraph 12 in Part I of Schedule 1 to this Act, cannot for the time being be an assured tenancy; and
    (b) any other periodic tenancy which is an assured tenancy, other than one in relation to which there is a provision, for the time being binding on the tenant, under which the rent for a particular period of the tenancy will or may be greater than the rent for an earlier period.
  (2) For the purpose of securing an increase in the rent under a tenancy to which this section applies, the landlord may serve on the tenant a notice in the prescribed form proposing a new rent to take effect at the beginning of a new period of the tenancy specified in the notice, being a period beginning not earlier than—
    (a) the minimum period after the date of the service of the notice; and
    (b) except in the case of a statutory periodic tenancy—
      (i) in the case of an assured agricultural occupancy, the first anniversary of the date on which the first period of the tenancy began;
      (ii) in any other case, on the date that falls 52 weeks after the date on which the first period of the tenancy began; and
    (c) if the rent under the tenancy has previously been increased by virtue of a notice under this subsection or a determination under section 14 below—
      (i) in the case of an assured agricultural occupancy, the first anniversary of the date on which the increased rent took effect;
      (ii) in any other case, the appropriate date.
  (3) The minimum period referred to in subsection (2) above is—
    (a) in the case of a yearly tenancy, six months;
    (b) in the case of a tenancy where the period is less than a month, one month; and
    (c) in any other case, a period equal to the period of the tenancy.
  (3A) The appropriate date referred to in subsection (2)(c)(ii) above is—
    (a) in a case to which subsection (3B) below applies, the date that falls 53 weeks after the date on which the increased rent took effect;
    (b) in any other case, the date that falls 52 weeks after the date on which the increased rent took effect.
  (3B) This subsection applies where—
    (a) the rent under the tenancy has been increased by virtue of a notice under this section or a determination under section 14 below on at least one occasion after the coming into force of the Regulatory Reform (Assured Periodic Tenancies) (Rent Increases) Order 2003; and
    (b) the fifty-third week after the date on which the last such increase took effect begins more than six days before the anniversary of the date on which the first such increase took effect.

(4) Where a notice is served under subsection (2) above, a new rent specified in the notice shall take effect as mentioned in the notice unless, before the beginning of the new period specified in the notice,—
- (a) the tenant by an application in the prescribed form refers the notice to a rent assessment committee; or
- (b) the landlord and the tenant agree on a variation of the rent which is different from that proposed in the notice or agree that the rent should not be varied.

(5) Nothing in this section (or in section 14 below) affects the right of the landlord and the tenant under an assured tenancy to vary by agreement any term of the tenancy (including a term relating to rent).

15. Limited prohibition on assignment etc. without consent

(1) Subject to subsection (3) below, it shall be an implied term of every assured tenancy which is a periodic tenancy that, except with the consent of the landlord, the tenant shall not—
- (a) assign the tenancy (in whole or in part); or
- (b) sub-let or part with possession of the whole or any part of the dwelling-house let on the tenancy.

(2) Section 19 of the Landlord and Tenant Act 1927 (consents to assign not to be unreasonably withheld etc.) shall not apply to a term which is implied into an assured tenancy by subsection (1) above.

(3) In the case of a periodic tenancy which is not a statutory periodic tenancy or an assured periodic tenancy arising under Schedule 10 to the Local Government and Housing Act 1989 subsection (1) above does not apply if—
- (a) there is a provision (whether contained in the tenancy or not) under which the tenant is prohibited (whether absolutely or conditionally) from assigning or sub-letting or parting with possession or is permitted (whether absolutely or conditionally) to assign, sub-let or part with possession; or
- (b) a premium is required to be paid on the grant or renewal of the tenancy.

(4) In subsection (3)(b) above 'premium' includes—
- (a) any fine or other like sum;
- (b) any other pecuniary consideration in addition to rent; and
- (c) any sum paid by way of deposit, other than one which does not exceed one-sixth of the annual rent payable under the tenancy immediately after the grant or renewal in question.

16. Access for repairs

It shall be an implied term of every assured tenancy that the tenant shall afford to the landlord access to the dwelling-house let on the tenancy and all reasonable facilities for executing therein any repairs which the landlord is entitled to execute.

Miscellaneous

17. Succession to assured tenancy

(1) Subject to subsection (1D), in any case where—
- (a) the sole tenant under an assured periodic tenancy dies, and
- (b) immediately before the death, the tenant's spouse or civil partner was occupying the dwelling-house as his or her only or principal home, and
- (c) ...

then, on the death, the tenancy vests by virtue of this section in the spouse or civil partner (and, accordingly, does not devolve under the tenant's will or intestacy).

(1A) Subject to subsection (1D), in any case where—
- (a) there is an assured periodic tenancy of a dwelling-house in England under which—
  - (i) the landlord is a private registered provider of social housing, and
  - (ii) the tenant is a sole tenant,
- (b) the tenant under the tenancy dies,
- (c) immediately before the death, the dwelling-house was not occupied by a spouse or civil partner of the tenant as his or her only or principal home,
- (d) an express term of the tenancy makes provision for a person other than such a spouse or civil partner of the tenant to succeed to the tenancy, and
- (e) there is a person whose succession is in accordance with that term,

then, on the death, the tenancy vests by virtue of this section in that person (and, accordingly, does not devolve under the tenant's will or intestacy).

(1B) Subject to subsection (1D), in any case where—
  (a) there is an assured tenancy of a dwelling-house in England for a fixed term of not less than two years under which—
    (i) the landlord is a private registered provider of social housing, and
    (ii) the tenant is a sole tenant,
  (b) the tenant under the tenancy dies, and
  (c) immediately before the death, the tenant's spouse or civil partner was occupying the dwelling-house as his or her only or principal home,
then, on the death, the tenancy vests by virtue of this section in the spouse or civil partner (and, accordingly, does not devolve under the tenant's will or intestacy).

(1C) Subject to subsection (1D), in any case where—
  (a) there is an assured tenancy of a dwelling-house in England for a fixed term of not less than two years under which—
    (i) the landlord is a private registered provider of social housing, and
    (ii) the tenant is a sole tenant,
  (b) the tenant under the tenancy dies,
  (c) immediately before the death, the dwelling-house was not occupied by a spouse or civil partner of the tenant as his or her only or principal home,
  (d) an express term of the tenancy makes provision for a person other than such a spouse or civil partner of the tenant to succeed to the tenancy, and
  (e) there is a person whose succession is in accordance with that term,
then, on the death, the tenancy vests by virtue of this section in that person (and accordingly does not devolve under the tenant's will or intestacy).

(1D) Subsection (1), (1A), (1B) or (1C) does not apply if the tenant was himself a successor as defined in subsection (2) or subsection (3).

(1E) In such a case, on the death, the tenancy vests by virtue of this section in a person ('P') (and, accordingly, does not devolve under the tenant's will or intestacy) if, and only if—
  (a) (in a case within subsection (1)) the tenancy is of a dwelling-house in England under which the landlord is a private registered provider of social housing,
  (b) an express term of the tenancy makes provision for a person to succeed a successor to the tenancy, and
  (c) P's succession is in accordance with that term.

(2) For the purposes of this section, a tenant is a successor in relation to a tenancy if—
  (a) the tenancy became vested in him either by virtue of this section or under the will or intestacy of a previous tenant; or
  (b) at some time before the tenant's death the tenancy was a joint tenancy held by himself and one or more other persons and, prior to his death, he became the sole tenant by survivorship; or
  (c) he became entitled to the tenancy as mentioned in section 39(5) below.

(3) For the purposes of this section, a tenant is also a successor in relation to a tenancy (in this subsection referred to as 'the new tenancy') which was granted to him (alone or jointly with others) if—
  (a) at some time before the grant of the new tenancy, he was, by virtue of subsection (2) above, a successor in relation to an earlier tenancy of the same or substantially the same dwelling-house as is let under the new tenancy; and
  (b) at all times since he became such a successor he has been a tenant (alone or jointly with others) of the dwelling-house which is let under the new tenancy or of a dwelling-house which is substantially the same as that dwelling-house.

(4) For the purposes of this section—
  (a) a person who was living with the tenant as his or her wife or husband shall be treated as the tenant's spouse, and
  (b) a person who was living with the tenant as if they were civil partners shall be treated as the tenant's civil partner.

(5) If, on the death of the tenant, there is, by virtue of subsection (4) above, more than one person who fulfils the condition in subsection (1)(b) or (1B)(c) above, such one of them as may be decided by agreement or, in default of agreement, by the county court shall for the purposes of this section be treated (according to whether that one of them is of the opposite sex to, or of the same sex as, the tenant) as the tenant's spouse or the tenant's civil partner.

(6) If, on the death of the tenant, there is more than one person in whom the tenancy would otherwise vest by virtue of subsection (1A), (1C) or (1E), the tenancy vests in such one of them as may be agreed between them or, in default of agreement, as is determined by the county court.

(7) This section does not apply to a fixed term assured tenancy that is a lease of a dwelling-house—
 (a) granted on payment of a premium calculated by reference to a percentage of the value of the dwelling-house or of the cost of providing it, or
 (b) under which the lessee (or the lessee's personal representatives) will or may be entitled to a sum calculated by reference, directly or indirectly, to the value of the dwelling-house.

18. Provisions as to reversions on assured tenancies

(1) If at any time—
 (a) a dwelling-house is for the time being lawfully let on an assured tenancy, and
 (b) the landlord under the assured tenancy is himself a tenant under a superior tenancy; and
 (c) the superior tenancy comes to an end,

then, subject to subsection (2) below, the assured tenancy shall continue in existence as a tenancy held of the person whose interest would, apart from the continuance of the assured tenancy, entitle him to actual possession of the dwelling-house at that time.

(2) Subsection (1) above does not apply to an assured tenancy if the interest which, by virtue of that subsection, would become that of the landlord, is such that, by virtue of Schedule 1 to this Act, the tenancy could not be an assured tenancy.

(3) Where, by virtue of any provision of this Part of this Act, an assured tenancy which is a periodic tenancy (including a statutory periodic tenancy) continues beyond the beginning of a reversionary tenancy which was granted (whether before, on or after the commencement of this Act) so as to begin on or after—
 (a) the date on which the previous contractual assured tenancy came to an end, or
 (b) a date on which, apart from any provision of this Part, the periodic tenancy could have been brought to an end by the landlord by notice to quit,

the reversionary tenancy shall have effect as if it had been granted subject to the periodic tenancy.

(4) The reference in subsection (3) above to the previous contractual assured tenancy applies only where the periodic tenancy referred to in that subsection is a statutory periodic tenancy and is a reference to the fixed term tenancy which immediately preceded the statutory periodic tenancy.

19. Restriction on levy of distress for rent

(1) Subject to subsection (2) below, no distress for the rent of any dwelling-house let on an assured tenancy shall be levied except with the leave of the county court; and, with respect to any application for such leave, the court shall have the same powers with respect to adjournment, stay, suspension, postponement and otherwise as are conferred by section 9 above in relation to proceedings for possession of such a dwelling-house.

(2) Nothing in subsection (1) above applies to distress levied under section 102 of the County Courts Act 1984.

CHAPTER II
ASSURED SHORTHOLD TENANCIES

19A. Assured shorthold tenancies: post-Housing Act 1996 tenancies.

An assured tenancy which—
(a) is entered into on or after the day on which section 96 of the Housing Act 1996 comes into force (otherwise than pursuant to a contract made before that day), or
(b) comes into being by virtue of section 5 above on the coming to an end of an assured tenancy within paragraph (a) above,

is an assured shorthold tenancy unless it falls within any paragraph in Schedule 2A to this Act.

20. **Assured shorthold tenancies: pre-Housing Act 1996 tenancies**
 (1) Subject to subsection (3) below, an assured tenancy which is not one to which section 19A above applies is an assured shorthold tenancy if—
 (a) it is a fixed term tenancy granted for a term certain of not less than six months,
 (b) there is no power for the landlord to determine the tenancy at any time earlier than six months from the beginning of the tenancy, and
 (c) a notice in respect of it is served as mentioned in subsection (2) below.
 (2) The notice referred to in subsection (1)(c) above is one which—
 (a) is in such form as may be prescribed;
 (b) is served before the assured tenancy is entered into;
 (c) is served by the person who is to be the landlord under the assured tenancy on the person who is to be the tenant under that tenancy; and
 (d) states that the assured tenancy to which it relates is to be a shorthold tenancy.
 (3) Notwithstanding anything in subsection (1) above, where—
 (a) immediately before a tenancy (in this subsection referred to as 'the new tenancy') is granted, the person to whom it is granted or, as the case may be, at least one of the persons to whom it is granted was a tenant under an assured tenancy which was not a shorthold tenancy, and
 (b) the new tenancy is granted by the person who, immediately before the beginning of the tenancy, was the landlord under the assured tenancy referred to in paragraph (a) above,
 the new tenancy cannot be an assured shorthold tenancy.
 (4) Subject to subsection (5) below, if, on the coming to an end of an assured shorthold tenancy (including a tenancy which was an assured shorthold but ceased to be assured before it came to an end), a new tenancy of the same or substantially the same premises comes into being under which the landlord and the tenant are the same as at the coming to an end of the earlier tenancy, then, if and so long as the new tenancy is an assured tenancy, it shall be an assured shorthold tenancy, whether or not it fulfils the conditions in paragraphs (a) to (c) of subsection (1) above.
 (5) Subsection (4) above does not apply if, before the new tenancy is entered into (or, in the case of a statutory periodic tenancy, takes effect in possession), the landlord serves notice on the tenant that the new tenancy is not to be a shorthold tenancy.
 (5A) Subsections (3) and (4) above do not apply where the new tenancy is one to which section 19A above applies.
 (6) In the case of joint landlords—
 (a) the reference in subsection (2)(c) above to the person who is to be the landlord is a reference to at least one of the persons who are to be joint landlords; and
 (b) the reference in subsection (5) above to the landlord is a reference to at least one of the joint landlords.

20A. **Post-Housing Act 1996 tenancies: duty of landlord to provide statement as to terms of tenancy**
 (1) Subject to subsection (3) below, a tenant under an assured shorthold tenancy to which section 19A above applies may, by notice in writing, require the landlord under that tenancy to provide him with a written statement of any term of the tenancy which—
 (a) falls within subsection (2) below, and
 (b) is not evidenced in writing.
 (2) The following terms of a tenancy fall within this subsection, namely—
 (a) the date on which the tenancy began or, if it is a statutory periodic tenancy or a tenancy to which section 39(7) below applies, the date on which the tenancy came into being,
 (b) the rent payable under the tenancy and the dates on which that rent is payable,
 (c) any term providing for a review of the rent payable under the tenancy, and
 (d) in the case of a fixed term tenancy, the length of the fixed term.
 (3) No notice may be given under subsection (1) above in relation to a term of the tenancy if—
 (a) the landlord under the tenancy has provided a statement of that term in response to an earlier notice under that subsection given by the tenant under the tenancy, and

(b) the term has not been varied since the provision of the statement referred to in paragraph (a) above.

(4) A landlord who fails, without reasonable excuse, to comply with a notice under subsection (1) above within the period of 28 days beginning with the date on which he received the notice is liable on summary conviction to a fine not exceeding level 4 on the standard scale.

(5) A statement provided for the purposes of subsection (1) above shall not be regarded as conclusive evidence of what was agreed between the parties to the tenancy in question.

(6) Where—

(a) a term of a statutory periodic tenancy is one which has effect by virtue of section 5(3)(e) above, or

(b) a term of a tenancy to which subsection (7) of section 39 below applies is one which has effect by virtue of subsection (6)(e) of that section,

subsection (1) above shall have effect in relation to it as if paragraph (b) related to the term of the tenancy from which it derives.

(7) In subsections (1) and (3) above—

(a) references to the tenant under the tenancy shall, in the case of joint tenants, be taken to be references to any of the tenants, and

(b) references to the landlord under the tenancy shall, in the case of joint landlords, be taken to be references to any of the landlords.

20B. Demoted assured shorthold tenancies

(1) An assured tenancy is an assured shorthold tenancy to which this section applies (a demoted assured shorthold tenancy) if—

(a) the tenancy is created by virtue of an order of the court under section 82A of the Housing Act 1985 or section 6A of this Act (a demotion order), and

(b) the landlord is a private registered provider of social housing or a registered social landlord.

(2) At the end of the period of one year starting with the day when the demotion order takes effect a demoted assured shorthold tenancy ceases to be an assured shorthold tenancy unless subsection (3) applies, but see section 20C.

(3) This subsection applies if before the end of the period mentioned in subsection (2) the landlord gives notice of proceedings for possession of the dwelling house.

(4) If subsection (3) applies the tenancy continues to be a demoted assured shorthold tenancy until the end of the period mentioned in subsection (2) or (if later) until one of the following occurs—

(a) the notice of proceedings for possession is withdrawn;

(b) the proceedings are determined in favour of the tenant;

(c) the period of six months beginning with the date on which the notice is given ends and no proceedings for possession have been brought.

(5) Registered social landlord has the same meaning as in Part 1 of the Housing Act 1996.

20C. Assured shorthold tenancies following demoted tenancies

(1) Subsection (2) applies if—

(a) section 20B applies to an assured shorthold tenancy of a dwelling-house in England ('the demoted tenancy'),

(b) the landlord is a private registered provider of social housing,

(c) the demoted tenancy was created by an order under section 6A made after the coming into force of section 163(2) of the Localism Act 2011,

(d) the assured tenancy that was terminated by that order was an assured shorthold tenancy that, whether or not it was a fixed term tenancy when terminated by the order, was granted for a term certain of not less than two years,

(e) apart from subsection (2), the demoted tenancy would cease to be an assured shorthold tenancy by virtue of section 20B(2) or (4), and

(f) the landlord has served a notice within subsection (3) on the tenant before the demoted tenancy ceases to be an assured shorthold tenancy by virtue of section 20B(2) or (4).

(2) The demoted tenancy does not cease to be an assured shorthold tenancy by virtue of section 20B(2) or (4), and at the time when it would otherwise cease to be an assured shorthold tenancy by virtue of section 20B(2) to (4)—

    (a) it becomes an assured shorthold tenancy which is a fixed term tenancy for a term certain, and

    (b) section 20B ceases to apply to it.

(3) The notice must—

    (a) state that, on ceasing to be a demoted assured shorthold tenancy, the tenancy will become an assured shorthold tenancy which is a fixed term tenancy for a term certain of the length specified in the notice,

    (b) specify a period of at least two years as the length of the term of the tenancy, and

    (c) set out the other express terms of the tenancy.

(4) Where an assured shorthold tenancy becomes a fixed term tenancy by virtue of subsection (2)—

    (a) the length of its term is that specified in the notice under subsection (3), and

    (b) its other express terms are those set out in the notice.

20D. Assured shorthold tenancies following family intervention tenancies

(1) An assured tenancy that arises by virtue of a notice under paragraph 12ZA(2) of Schedule 1 in respect of a family intervention tenancy is an assured shorthold tenancy if—

    (a) the landlord under the assured tenancy is a private registered provider of social housing,

    (b) the dwelling-house is in England,

    (c) the family intervention tenancy was granted to a person on the coming to an end of an assured shorthold tenancy under which the person was a tenant, and

    (d) the notice states that the family intervention tenancy is to be regarded as an assured shorthold tenancy.

(2) This section does not apply if the family intervention tenancy was granted before the coming into force of section 163(3) of the Localism Act 2011.

21. Recovery of possession on expiry or termination of assured shorthold tenancy

(1) Without prejudice to any right of the landlord under an assured shorthold tenancy to recover possession of the dwelling-house let on the tenancy in accordance with Chapter I above, on or after the coming to an end of an assured shorthold tenancy which was a fixed term tenancy, a court shall make an order for possession of the dwelling-house if it is satisfied—

    (a) that the assured shorthold tenancy has come to an end and no further assured tenancy (whether shorthold or not) is for the time being in existence, other than an assured shorthold periodic tenancy (whether statutory or not); and

    (b) the landlord or, in the case of joint landlords, at least one of them has given to the tenant not less than two months' notice in writing stating that he requires possession of the dwelling-house.

(1A) Subsection (1B) applies to an assured shorthold tenancy of a dwelling-house in England if—

    (a) it is a fixed term tenancy for a term certain of not less than two years, and

    (b) the landlord is a private registered provider of social housing.

(1B) The court may not make an order for possession of the dwelling-house let on the tenancy unless the landlord has given to the tenant not less than six months' notice in writing—

    (a) stating that the landlord does not propose to grant another tenancy on the expiry of the fixed term tenancy, and

    (b) informing the tenant of how to obtain help or advice about the notice and, in particular, of any obligation of the landlord to provide help or advice.

(2) A notice under paragraph (b) of subsection (1) above may be given before or on the day on which the tenancy comes to an end; and that subsection shall have effect notwithstanding that on the coming to an end of the fixed term tenancy a statutory periodic tenancy arises.

(3) Where a court makes an order for possession of a dwelling-house by virtue of subsection (1) above, any statutory periodic tenancy which has arisen on the coming to an end of the assured shorthold tenancy shall end (without further notice and regardless of the period) in accordance with section 5(1A).

(4) Without prejudice to any such right as is referred to in subsection (1) above, a court shall make an order for possession of a dwelling-house let on an assured shorthold tenancy which is a periodic tenancy if the court is satisfied—

    (a) that the landlord or, in the case of joint landlords, at least one of them has given to the tenant a notice in writing stating that, after a date specified in the notice, being the last day of a period of the tenancy and not earlier than two months after the date the notice was given, possession of the dwelling-house is required by virtue of this section; and

    (b) that the date specified in the notice under paragraph (a) above is not earlier than the earliest day on which, apart from section 5(1) above, the tenancy could be brought to an end by a notice to quit given by the landlord on the same date as the notice under paragraph (a) above.

(4A) Where a court makes an order for possession of a dwelling-house by virtue of subsection (4) above, the assured shorthold tenancy shall end in accordance with section 5(1A).

(5) Where an order for possession under subsection (1) or (4) above is made in relation to a dwelling-house let on a tenancy to which section 19A above applies, the order may not be made so as to take effect earlier than—

    (a) in the case of a tenancy which is not a replacement tenancy, six months after the beginning of the tenancy, and

    (b) in the case of a replacement tenancy, six months after the beginning of the original tenancy.

(5A) Subsection (5) above does not apply to an assured shorthold tenancy to which section 20B (demoted assured shorthold tenancies) applies.

(6) In subsection (5)(b) above, the reference to the original tenancy is—

    (a) where the replacement tenancy came into being on the coming to an end of a tenancy which was not a replacement tenancy, to the immediately preceding tenancy, and

    (b) where there have been successive replacement tenancies, to the tenancy immediately preceding the first in the succession of replacement tenancies.

(7) For the purposes of this section, a replacement tenancy is a tenancy—

    (a) which comes into being on the coming to an end of an assured shorthold tenancy, and

    (b) under which, on its coming into being—

        (i) the landlord and tenant are the same as under the earlier tenancy as at its coming to an end, and

        (ii) the premises let are the same or substantially the same as those let under the earlier tenancy as at that time.

22. Reference of excessive rents to rent assessment committee

(1) Subject to section 23 and subsection (2) below, the tenant under an assured shorthold tenancy may make an application in the prescribed form to a rent assessment committee for a determination of the rent which, in the committee's opinion, the landlord might reasonably be expected to obtain under the assured shorthold tenancy.

(2) No application may be made under this section if—

    (a) the rent payable under the tenancy is a rent previously determined under this section;

    (aa) the tenancy is one to which section 19A above applies and more than six months have elapsed since the beginning of the tenancy or, in the case of a replacement tenancy, since the beginning of the original tenancy; or

    (b) the tenancy is an assured shorthold tenancy falling within subsection (4) of section 20 above (and, accordingly, is one in respect of which notice need not have been served as mentioned in subsection (2) of that section).

(3) Where an application is made to a rent assessment committee under subsection (1) above with respect to the rent under an assured shorthold tenancy, the committee shall not make such a determination as is referred to in that subsection unless they consider—

    (a) that there is a sufficient number of similar dwelling-houses in the locality let on assured tenancies (whether shorthold or not); and

    (b) that the rent payable under the assured shorthold tenancy in question is significantly higher than the rent which the landlord might reasonably be expected to be able to obtain under the tenancy, having regard to the level of rents payable under the tenancies referred to in paragraph (a) above.

(4) Where, on an application under this section, a rent assessment committee make a determination of a rent for an assured shorthold tenancy—

(a) the determination shall have effect from such date as the committee may direct, not being earlier than the date of the application;

(b) if, at any time on or after the determination takes effect, the rent which, apart from this paragraph, would be payable under the tenancy exceeds the rent so determined, the excess shall be irrecoverable from the tenant; and

(c) no notice may be served under section 13(2) above with respect to a tenancy of the dwelling-house in question until after the first anniversary of the date on which the determination takes effect.

(5) Subsections (4), (5) and (8) of section 14 above apply in relation to a determination of rent under this section as they apply in relation to a determination under that section and, accordingly, where subsection (5) of that section applies, any reference in subsection (4)(b) above to rent is a reference to rent exclusive of the amount attributable to rates.

(5A) Where—

(a) an assured tenancy ceases to be an assured shorthold tenancy by virtue of falling within paragraph 2 of Schedule 2A to this Act, and

(b) at the time when it so ceases to be an assured shorthold tenancy there is pending before a rent assessment committee an application in relation to it under this section,

the fact that it so ceases to be an assured shorthold tenancy shall, in relation to that application, be disregarded for the purposes of this section.

(6) In subsection (2)(aa) above, the references to the original tenancy and to a replacement tenancy shall be construed in accordance with subsections (6) and (7) respectively of section 21 above.

CHAPTER IV
PROTECTION FROM EVICTION

27. Damages for unlawful eviction

(1) This section applies if, at any time after 9 June 1988, a landlord (in this section referred to as 'the landlord in default') or any person acting on behalf of the landlord in default unlawfully deprives the residential occupier of any premises of his occupation of the whole or part of the premises.

(2) This section also applies if, at any time after 9 June 1988, a landlord (in this section referred to as 'the landlord in default') or any person acting on behalf of the landlord in default—

(a) attempts unlawfully to deprive the residential occupier of any premises of his occupation of the whole or part of the premises, or

(b) knowing or having reasonable cause to believe that the conduct is likely to cause the residential occupier of any premises—

(i) to give up his occupation of the premises or any part thereof, or

(ii) to refrain from exercising any right or pursuing any remedy in respect of the premises or any part thereof,

does acts likely to interfere with the peace or comfort of the residential occupier or members of his household, or persistently withdraws or withholds services reasonably required for the occupation of the premises as a residence,

and, as a result, the residential occupier gives up his occupation of the premises as a residence.

(3) Subject to the following provisions of this section, where this section applies, the landlord in default shall, by virtue of this section, be liable to pay to the former residential occupier, in respect of his loss of the right to occupy the premises in question as his residence, damages assessed on the basis set out in section 28 below.

(4) Any liability arising by virtue of subsection (3) above—

(a) shall be in the nature of a liability in tort; and

(b) subject to subsection (5) below, shall be in addition to any liability arising apart from this section (whether in tort, contract, or otherwise).

(5) Nothing in this section affects the right of a residential occupier to enforce any liability which arises apart from this section in respect of his loss of the right to occupy premises as his residence; but damages shall not be awarded both in respect of such a liability and in respect of a liability arising by virtue of this section on account of the same loss.

(6) No liability shall arise by virtue of subsection (3) above if—
   (a) before the date on which proceedings to enforce the liability are finally disposed of, the former residential occupier is reinstated in the premises in question in such circumstances that he becomes again the residential occupier of them; or
   (b) at the request of the former residential occupier, a court makes an order (whether in the nature of an injunction or otherwise) as a result of which he is reinstated as mentioned in paragraph (a) above;

and, for the purposes of paragraph (a) above, proceedings to enforce a liability are finally disposed of on the earliest date by which the proceedings (including any proceedings on or in consequence of an appeal) have been determined and any time for appealing or further appealing has expired, except that if any appeal is abandoned, the proceedings shall be taken to be disposed of on the date of the abandonment.

(7) If, in proceedings to enforce a liability arising by virtue of subsection (3) above, it appears to the court—
   (a) that, prior to the event which gave rise to the liability, the conduct of the former residential occupier or any person living with him in the premises concerned was such that it is reasonable to mitigate the damages for which the landlord in default would otherwise be liable, or
   (b) that, before the proceedings were begun, the landlord in default offered to reinstate the former residential occupier in the premises in question and either it was unreasonable of the former residential occupier to refuse that offer or, if he had obtained alternative accommodation before the offer was made, it would have been unreasonable of him to refuse that offer if he had not obtained that accommodation,

the court may reduce the amount of damages which would otherwise be payable by such amount as it thinks appropriate.

(8) In proceedings to enforce a liability arising by virtue of subsection (3) above, it shall be a defence for the defendant to prove that he believed, and had reasonable cause to believe—
   (a) that the residential occupier had ceased to reside in the premises in question at the time when he was deprived of occupation as mentioned in subsection (1) above or, as the case may be, when the attempt was made or the acts were done as a result of which he gave up his occupation of those premises; or
   (b) that, where the liability would otherwise arise by virtue only of the doing of acts or the withdrawal or withholding of services, he had reasonable grounds for doing the acts or withdrawing or withholding the services in question.

(9) In this section—
   (a) 'residential occupier', in relation to any premises, has the same meaning as in section 1 of the 1977 Act;
   (b) 'the right to occupy', in relation to a residential occupier, includes any restriction on the right of another person to recover possession of the premises in question;
   (c) 'landlord', in relation to a residential occupier, means the person who, but for the occupier's right to occupy, would be entitled to occupation of the premises and any superior landlord under whom that person derives title;
   (d) 'former residential occupier', in relation to any premises, means the person who was the residential occupier until he was deprived of or gave up his occupation as mentioned in subsection (1) or subsection (2) above (and, in relation to a former residential occupier, 'the right to occupy' and 'landlord' shall be construed accordingly).

28. **The measure of damages**

(1) The basis for the assessment of damages referred to in section 27(3) above is the difference in value, determined as at the time immediately before the residential occupier ceased to occupy the premises in question as his residence, between—

(a) the value of the interest of the landlord in default determined on the assumption that the residential occupier continues to have the same right to occupy the premises as before that time; and

(b) the value of that interest determined on the assumption that the residential occupier has ceased to have the right.

(2) In relation to any premises, any reference in this section to the interest of the landlord in default is a reference to his interest in the building in which the premises in question are comprised (whether or not that building contains any other premises) together with its curtilage.

(3) For the purposes of the valuations referred to in subsection (1) above, it shall be assumed—

(a) that the landlord in default is selling his interest on the open market to a willing buyer;

(b) that neither the residential occupier nor any member of his family wishes to buy; and

(c) that it is unlawful to carry out any substantial development of any of the land in which the landlord's interest subsists or to demolish the whole or part of any building on that land.

(4) In this section 'the landlord in default' has the same meaning as in section 27 above and subsection (9) of that section applies in relation to this section as it applies in relation to that.

(5) Section 113 of the Housing Act 1985 (meaning of 'members of a person's family') applies for the purposes of subsection (3)(b) above.

(6) The reference in subsection (3)(c) above to substantial development of any of the land in which the landlord's interest subsists is a reference to any development other than—

(a) development for which planning permission is granted by a general development order for the time being in force and which is carried out so as to comply with any condition or limitation subject to which planning permission is so granted; or

(b) a change of use resulting in the building referred to in subsection (2) above or any part of it being used as, or as part of, one or more dwelling-houses;

and in this subsection 'general development order' has the meaning given in section 56(6) of the Town and Country Planning Act 1990 and other expressions have the same meaning as in that Act.

SCHEDULES

SCHEDULE 1

TENANCIES WHICH CANNOT BE ASSURED TENANCIES

PART I
THE TENANCIES

Tenancies entered into before commencement

1. A tenancy which is entered into before, or pursuant to a contract made before, the commencement of this Act.

Tenancies of dwelling-houses with high rateable values

2. (1) A tenancy—

(a) which is entered into on or after 1 April 1990 (otherwise than, where the dwelling-house had a rateable value on 31 March 1990, in pursuance of a contract made before 1 April 1990), and

(b) under which the rent payable for the time being is payable at a rate exceeding £100,000 a year,

(2) In sub-paragraph (1) 'rent' does not include any sum payable by the tenant as is expressed (in whatever terms) to be payable in respect of rates, council tax, services, management, repairs, maintenance or insurance, unless it could not have been regarded by the parties to the tenancy as a sum so payable.

2A. A tenancy—

(a) which was entered into before 1 April 1990, or on or after that date in pursuance of a contract made before that date, and

(b) under which the dwelling-house had a rateable value on 31 March 1990 which, if it is in Greater London, exceeded £1,500 and, if it is elsewhere, exceeded £750.

Tenancies at a low rent

3. A tenancy under which for the time being no rent is payable.

3A. A tenancy—

(a) which is entered into on or after 1 April 1990 (otherwise than, where the dwelling-house had a rateable value on 31 March 1990, in pursuance of a contract made before 1 April 1990, and

(b) under which the rent payable for the time being is payable at a rate of, if the dwelling-house is in Greater London, £1,000 or less a year and, if it is elsewhere, £250 or less a year.

3B. A tenancy—

(a) which was entered into before 1 April 1990 or, where the dwelling-house had a rateable value on 31 March 1990, on or after 1 April 1990 in pursuance of a contract made before that date, and

(b) under which the rent for the time being payable is less than two-thirds of the rateable value of the dwelling-house on 31 March 1990.

3C. Paragraph 2(2) above applies for the purposes of paragraphs 3, 3A and 3B as it applies for the purposes of paragraph 2(1).

Business tenancies

4. A tenancy to which Part II of the Landlord and Tenant Act 1954 applies (business tenancies).

Licensed premises

5. A tenancy under which the dwelling-house consists of or comprises premises which, by virtue of a premises licence under the Licensing Act 2003, may be used for the supply of alcohol (within the meaning of section 14 of that Act) for consumption on the premises.

Tenancies of agricultural land

6. (1) A tenancy under which agricultural land, exceeding two acres, is let together with the dwelling-house.

(2) In this paragraph 'agricultural land' has the meaning set out in section 26(3)(a) of the General Rate Act 1967 (exclusion of agricultural land and premises from liability for rating).

Tenancies of agricultural holdings etc.

7. (1) A tenancy under which the dwelling-house—

(a) is comprised in an agricultural holding, and

(b) is occupied by the person responsible for the control (whether as tenant or as servant or agent of the tenant) of the farming of the holding.

(2) A tenancy under which the dwelling-house—

(a) is comprised in the holding held under a farm business tenancy, and

(b) is occupied by the person responsible for the control (whether as tenant or as servant or agent of the tenant) of the management of the holding.

(3) In this paragraph—

'agricultural holding' means any agricultural holding within the meaning of the Agricultural Holdings Act 1986 held under a tenancy in relation to which that Act applies, and

'farm business tenancy' and 'holding', in relation to such a tenancy, have the same meaning as in the Agricultural Tenancies Act 1995.

Lettings to students

8. (1) A tenancy which is granted to a person who is pursuing, or intends to pursue, a course of study provided by a specified educational institution and is so granted either by that institution or by another specified institution or body of persons.

(2) In sub-paragraph (1) above 'specified' means specified, or of a class specified, for the purposes of this paragraph by regulations made by the Secretary of State by statutory instrument.

(3) A statutory instrument made in the exercise of the power conferred by sub-paragraph (2) above shall be subject to annulment in pursuance of a resolution of either House of Parliament.

Holiday lettings

9. A tenancy the purpose of which is to confer on the tenant the right to occupy the dwelling-house for a holiday.

Resident landlords

10. (1) A tenancy in respect of which the following conditions are fulfilled—

(a) that the dwelling-house forms part only of a building and, except in a case where the dwelling-house also forms part of a flat, the building is not a purpose-built block of flats; and

(b) that, subject to Part III of this Schedule, the tenancy was granted by an individual who, at the time when the tenancy was granted, occupied as his only or principal home another dwelling-house which,—

(i) in the case mentioned in paragraph (a) above, also forms part of the flat; or

(ii) in any other case, also forms part of the building; and

(c) that, subject to Part III of this Schedule, at all times since the tenancy was granted the interest of the landlord under the tenancy has belonged to an individual who, at the time he owned that interest, occupied as his only or principal home another dwelling-house which,—

(i) in the case mentioned in paragraph (a) above, also formed part of the flat; or

(ii) in any other case, also formed part of the building; and

(d) that the tenancy is not one which is excluded from this sub-paragraph by sub-paragraph (3) below.

(2) If a tenancy was granted by two or more persons jointly, the reference in sub-paragraph (1)(b) above to an individual is a reference to any one of those persons and if the interest of the landlord is for the time being held by two or more persons jointly, the reference in sub-paragraph (1)(c) above to an individual is a reference to any one of those persons.

(3) A tenancy (in this sub-paragraph referred to as 'the new tenancy') is excluded from sub-paragraph (1) above if—

(a) it is granted to a person (alone, or jointly with others) who, immediately before it was granted, was a tenant under an assured tenancy (in this sub-paragraph referred to as 'the former tenancy') of the same dwelling-house or of another dwelling-house which forms part of the building in question; and

(b) the landlord under the new tenancy and under the former tenancy is the same person or, if either of those tenancies is or was granted by two or more persons jointly, the same person is the landlord or one of the landlords under each tenancy.

Crown tenancies

11. (1) A tenancy under which the interest of the landlord belongs to Her Majesty in right of the Crown or to a government department or is held in trust for Her Majesty for the purpose of a government department.

(2) The reference in sub-paragraph (1) above to the case where the interest of the landlord belongs to Her Majesty in right of the Crown does not include the case where that interest is under the management of the Crown Estate commissioners or it is held by the Secretary of State as the result of the exercise by him of functions under Part III of the Housing Associations Act 1985.

Local authority tenancies etc.

12. (1) A tenancy under which the interest of the landlord belongs to—

(a) a local authority, as defined in sub-paragraph (2) below;

(b) the Commission for the New Towns;

(d) an urban development corporation established by an order under section 135 of the Local Government, Planning and Land Act 1980;

(e) a development corporation, within the meaning of the New Towns Act 1981;

(f) an authority established under section 10 of the Local Government Act 1985 (waste disposal authorities);

(fa) an authority established for an area in England by an order under section 207 of the Local Government and Public Involvement in Health Act 2007 (joint waste authorities);

(g) a residuary body, within the meaning of the Local Government Act 1985;

(gg) The Residuary Body for Wales (Corff Gweddilliol Cymru);

(h) a fully mutual housing association; or

(i) a housing action trust established under Part III of this Act.

(2) The following are local authorities for the purposes of sub-paragraph (1)(a) above—

(a) the council of a county, county borough, district or London borough;

(b) the Common Council of the City of London;

(c) the Council of the Isles of Scilly;

(d) the Broads Authority;

(da) a National Park Authority;

(e) the Inner London Education Authority;

(ee) the London Fire and Emergency Planning Authority;

(f) a joint authority, within the meaning of the Local Government Act 1985;

(fa) an economic prosperity board established under section 88 of the Local Democracy, Economic Development and Construction Act 2009;

(fb) a combined authority established under section 103 of that Act; and

(g) a police and crime commissioner.

Family intervention tenancies

12ZA. (1) A family intervention tenancy.

(2) But a family intervention tenancy becomes an assured tenancy if the landlord notifies the tenant that it is to be regarded as an assured tenancy.

(3) In this paragraph 'a family intervention tenancy' means, subject to sub-paragraph (4), a tenancy granted by a private registered provider of social housing or a registered social landlord ('the landlord') in respect of a dwelling-house—

(a) to a person ('the new tenant') against whom a possession order under section 7 in respect of another dwelling-house—

(i) has been made, in relation to an assured tenancy, on ground 14 or 14A of Part 2 of Schedule 2;

(ii) could, in the opinion of the landlord, have been so made in relation to such a tenancy; or

(iii) could, in the opinion of the landlord, have been so made if the person had had such a tenancy; and

(b) for the purposes of the provision of behaviour support services.

(4) A tenancy is not a family intervention tenancy for the purposes of this paragraph if the landlord has failed to serve a notice under sub-paragraph (5) on the new tenant before the new tenant entered into the tenancy.

(5) A notice under this sub-paragraph is a notice stating—

(a) the reasons for offering the tenancy to the new tenant;

(b) the dwelling-house in respect of which the tenancy is to be granted;

(c) the other main terms of the tenancy (including any requirements on the new tenant in respect of behaviour support services);

(d) the security of tenure available under the tenancy and any loss of security of tenure which is likely to result from the new tenant agreeing to enter into the tenancy;

(e) that the new tenant is not obliged to enter into the tenancy or (unless otherwise required to do so) to surrender any existing tenancy or possession of a dwelling-house;

(f) any likely action by the landlord if the new tenant does not enter into the tenancy or surrender any existing tenancy or possession of a dwelling-house.

(6) The appropriate national authority may by regulations made by statutory instrument amend sub-paragraph (5).

(7) A notice under sub-paragraph (5) must contain advice to the new tenant as to how the new tenant may be able to obtain assistance in relation to the notice.

(8) The appropriate national authority may by regulations made by statutory instrument make provision about the type of advice to be provided in such notices.

(9) Regulations under this paragraph may contain such transitional, transitory or saving provision as the appropriate national authority considers appropriate.

(10) A statutory instrument containing (whether alone or with other provision) regulations under this paragraph which amend or repeal any of paragraphs (a) to (f) of sub-paragraph (5) may not be made—

(a) by the Secretary of State unless a draft of the instrument has been laid before, and approved by a resolution of, each House of Parliament; and

(b) by the Welsh Ministers unless a draft of the instrument has been laid before, and approved by a resolution of, the National Assembly for Wales.

(11) Subject to this, a statutory instrument containing regulations made under this paragraph—
 (a) by the Secretary of State is subject to annulment in pursuance of a resolution of either House of Parliament; and
 (b) by the Welsh Ministers is subject to annulment in pursuance of a resolution of the National Assembly for Wales.

(12) In this paragraph—

'appropriate national authority'—
 (a) in relation to England, means the Secretary of State; and
 (b) in relation to Wales, means the Welsh Ministers;

'behaviour support agreement' means an agreement in writing about behaviour and the provision of support services made between the new tenant, the landlord and the local housing authority for the district in which the dwelling-house which is to be subject to the new tenancy is situated (or between persons who include those persons);

'behaviour support services' means relevant support services to be provided by any person to—
 (a) the new tenant; or
 (b) any person who is to reside with the new tenant;
for the purpose of addressing the kind of behaviour which led to the new tenant falling within sub-paragraph (3)(a);

'family intervention tenancy' has the meaning given by sub-paragraph (3);

'landlord' has the meaning given by sub-paragraph (3);

'local housing authority' (and the reference to its district) has the same meaning as in the Housing Act 1985 (see sections 1 and 2(1) of that Act);

'the new tenant' has the meaning given by sub-paragraph (3)(a);

'registered social landlord' has the same meaning as in Part 1 of the Housing Act 1996;

'relevant support services' means support services of a kind identified in a behaviour support agreement and designed to meet such needs of the recipient as are identified in the agreement.

Accommodation for asylum-seekers

12A. (1) A tenancy granted by a private landlord under arrangements for the provision of support for asylum-seekers or dependants of asylum-seekers made under section 4 or Part VI of the Immigration and Asylum Act 1999.

(2) 'Private landlord' means a landlord who is not within section 80(1) of the Housing Act 1985.

Accommodation for persons with Temporary Protection

12B. (1) A tenancy granted by a private landlord under arrangements for the provision of accommodation for persons with temporary protection made under the Displaced Persons (Temporary Protection) Regulations 2005.

(2) 'Private landlord' means a landlord who is not within section 80(1) of the Housing Act 1985.

Transitional cases

13. (1) A protected tenancy, within the meaning of the Rent Act 1977.
 (2) A housing association tenancy, within the meaning of Part VI of that Act.
 (3) A secure tenancy.
 (4) Where a person is a protected occupier of a dwelling-house, within the meaning of the Rent (Agriculture) Act 1976, the relevant tenancy, within the meaning of that Act, by virtue of which he occupies the dwelling-house.

PART II
RATEABLE VALUES

14. (1) The rateable value of a dwelling-house at any time shall be ascertained for the purposes of Part I of this Schedule as follows—
 (a) if the dwelling-house is a hereditament for which a rateable value is then shown in the valuation list, it shall be that rateable value;

(b) if the dwelling-house forms part only of such a hereditament or consists of or forms part of more than one such hereditament, its rateable value shall be taken to be such value as is found by a proper apportionment or aggregation of the rateable value or values so shown.

(2) Any question arising under this Part of this Schedule as to the proper apportionment or aggregation of any value or values shall be determined by the county court and the decision of that court shall be final.

15. Where, after the time at which the rateable value of a dwelling-house is material for the purposes of any provision of Part I of this Schedule, the valuation list is altered so as to vary the rateable value of the hereditament of which the dwelling-house consists (in whole or in part) or forms part and the alteration has effect from that time or from an earlier time, the rateable value of the dwelling-house at the material time shall be ascertained as if the value shown in the valuation list at the material time had been the value shown in the list as altered.

16. Paragraphs 14 and 15 above apply in relation to any other land which, under section 2 of this Act, is treated as part of a dwelling-house as they apply in relation to the dwelling-house itself.

PART III
PROVISIONS FOR DETERMINING APPLICATION OF PARAGRAPH 10 (RESIDENT LANDLORDS)

17. (1) In determining whether the condition in paragraph 10(1)(c) above is at any time fulfilled with respect to a tenancy, there shall be disregarded—

(a) any period of not more than twenty-eight days, beginning with the date on which the interest of the landlord under the tenancy becomes vested at law and in equity in an individual who, during that period, does not occupy as his only or principal home another dwelling-house which forms part of the building or, as the case may be, flat concerned;

(b) if, within a period falling within paragraph (a) above, the individual concerned notifies the tenant in writing of his intention to occupy as his only or principal home another dwelling-house in the building or, as the case may be, flat concerned, the period beginning with the date on which the interest of the landlord under the tenancy becomes vested in that individual as mentioned in that paragraph and ending—

(i) at the expiry of the period of six months beginning on that date, or

(ii) on the date on which that interest ceases to be so vested, or

(iii) on the date on which that interest becomes again vested in such an individual as is mentioned in paragraph 10(1)(c) or the condition in that paragraph becomes deemed to be fulfilled by virtue of paragraph 18(1) or paragraph 20 below,

whichever is the earlier; and

(c) any period of not more than two years beginning with the date on which the interest of the landlord under the tenancy becomes, and during which it remains, vested—

(i) in trustees as such; or

(ii) by virtue of section 9 of the Administration of Estates Act 1925, in the Probate Judge or the Public Trustee.

(2) Where the interest of the landlord under a tenancy becomes vested at law and in equity in two or more persons jointly, of whom at least one was an individual, sub-paragraph (1) above shall have effect subject to the following modifications—

(a) in paragraph (a) for the words from 'an individual' to 'occupy' there shall be substituted 'the joint landlords if, during that period none of them occupies'; and

(b) in paragraph (b) for the words 'the individual concerned' there shall be substituted 'any of the joint landlords who is an individual' and for the words 'that individual' there shall be substituted 'the joint landlords'.

18. (1) During any period when—

(a) the interest of the landlord under the tenancy referred to in paragraph 10 above is vested in trustees as such, and

(b) that interest is held on trust for any person who or for two or more persons of whom at least one occupies as his only or principal home a dwelling-house which forms part of the building or, as the case may be, flat referred to in paragraph 10(1)(a),

the condition in paragraph 10(1)(c) shall be deemed to be fulfilled and accordingly, no part of that period shall be disregarded by virtue of paragraph 17 above.

(2) If a period during which the condition in paragraph 10(1)(c) is deemed to be fulfilled by virtue of sub-paragraph (1) above comes to an end on the death of a person who was in occupation of a dwelling-house as mentioned in paragraph (b) of that sub-paragraph, then, in determining whether that condition is at any time thereafter fulfilled, there shall be disregarded any period—

(a) which begins on the date of the death;

(b) during which the interest of the landlord remains vested as mentioned in sub-paragraph (1)(a) above; and

(c) which ends at the expiry of the period of two years beginning on the date of the death or on any earlier date on which the condition in paragraph 10(1)(c) becomes again deemed to be fulfilled by virtue of sub-paragraph (1) above.

19. In any case where—

(a) immediately before a tenancy comes to an end the condition in paragraph 10(1)(c) is deemed to be fulfilled by virtue of paragraph 18(1) above, and

(b) on the coming to an end of that tenancy the trustees in whom the interest of the landlord is vested grant a new tenancy of the same or substantially the same dwelling-house to a person (alone or jointly with others) who was the tenant or one of the tenants under the previous tenancy,

the condition in paragraph 10(1)(b) above shall be deemed to be fulfilled with respect to the new tenancy.

20. (1) The tenancy referred to in paragraph 10 above falls within this paragraph if the interest of the landlord under the tenancy becomes vested in the personal representatives of a deceased person acting in that capacity.

(2) If the tenancy falls within this paragraph, the condition in paragraph 10(1)(c) shall be deemed to be fulfilled for any period, beginning with the date on which the interest becomes vested in the personal representatives and not exceeding two years, during which the interest of the landlord remains so vested.

21. Throughout any period which, by virtue of paragraph 17 or paragraph 18(2) above, falls to be disregarded for the purpose of determining whether the condition in paragraph 10(1)(c) is fulfilled with respect to a tenancy, no order shall be made for possession of the dwelling-house subject to that tenancy, other than an order which might be made if that tenancy were or, as the case may be, had been an assured tenancy.

22. For the purposes of paragraph 10 above, a building is a purpose-built block of flats if as constructed it contained, and it contains, two or more flats; and for this purpose 'flat' means a dwelling-house which—

(a) forms part only of a building; and

(b) is separated horizontally from another dwelling-house which forms part of the same building.

SCHEDULE 2
GROUNDS FOR POSSESSION OF DWELLING-HOUSES LET ON ASSURED TENANCIES

PART I
GROUNDS ON WHICH COURT MUST ORDER POSSESSION

Ground 1

Not later than the beginning of the tenancy the landlord gave notice in writing to the tenant that possession might be recovered on this ground or the court is of the opinion that it is just and equitable to dispense with the requirement of notice and (in either case)—

(a) at some time before the beginning of the tenancy, the landlord who is seeking possession or, in the case of joint landlords seeking possession, at least one of them occupied the dwelling-house as his only or principal home; or

(b) the landlord who is seeking possession or, in the case of joint landlords seeking possession, at least one of them requires the dwelling-house as his, his spouse's or his civil partner's only or principal home and neither the landlord (or, in the case of joint landlords, any one of them) nor any other person who, as landlord, derived title under the landlord who gave the notice mentioned above acquired the reversion on the tenancy for money or money's worth.

Ground 2

The dwelling-house is subject to a mortgage granted before the beginning of the tenancy and—

(a) the mortgagee is entitled to exercise a power of sale conferred on him by the mortgage or by section 101 of the Law of Property Act 1925; and

(b) the mortgagee requires possession of the dwelling-house for the purpose of disposing of it with vacant possession in exercise of that power; and

(c) either notice was given as mentioned in Ground 1 above or the court is satisfied that it is just and equitable to dispense with the requirement of notice;

and for the purposes of this ground 'mortgage' includes a charge and 'mortgagee' shall be construed accordingly.

Ground 3

The tenancy is a fixed term tenancy for a term not exceeding eight months and—

(a) not later than the beginning of the tenancy the landlord gave notice in writing to the tenant that possession might be recovered on this ground; and

(b) at some time within the period of twelve months ending with the beginning of the tenancy, the dwelling-house was occupied under a right to occupy it for a holiday.

Ground 4

The tenancy is a fixed term tenancy for a term not exceeding twelve months and—

(a) not later than the beginning of the tenancy the landlord gave notice in writing to the tenant that possession might be recovered on this ground; and

(b) at some time within the period of twelve months ending with the beginning of the tenancy, the dwelling-house was let on a tenancy falling within paragraph 8 of Schedule 1 to this Act.

Ground 5

The dwelling-house is held for the purpose of being available for occupation by a minister of religion as a residence from which to perform the duties of his office and—

(a) not later than the beginning of the tenancy the landlord gave notice in writing to the tenant that possession might be recovered on this ground; and

(b) the court is satisfied that the dwelling-house is required for occupation by a minister of religion as such a residence.

Ground 6

The landlord who is seeking possession or, if that landlord is a non-profit registered provider of social housing, registered social landlord or charitable housing trust, or (where the dwelling-house is social housing within the meaning of Part 2 of the Housing and Regeneration Act 2008) a profit-making registered provider of social housing, a superior landlord intends to demolish or reconstruct the whole or a substantial part of the dwelling-house or to carry out substantial works on the dwelling-house or any part thereof or any building of which it forms part and the following conditions are fulfilled—

(a) the intended work cannot reasonably be carried out without the tenant giving up possession of the dwelling-house because—

(i) the tenant is not willing to agree to such a variation of the terms of the tenancy as would give such access and other facilities as would permit the intended work to be carried out, or

(ii) the nature of the intended work is such that no such variation is practicable, or

(iii) the tenant is not willing to accept an assured tenancy of such part only of the dwelling-house (in this sub-paragraph referred to as 'the reduced part') as would leave in the possession of his landlord so much of the dwelling-house as would be reasonable to enable the intended work to be carried out and, where appropriate, as would give such access and other facilities over the reduced part as would permit the intended work to be carried out, or

(iv) the nature of the intended work is such that such a tenancy is not practicable; and

(b) either the landlord seeking possession acquired his interest in the dwelling-house before the grant of the tenancy or that interest was in existence at the time of that grant and neither that landlord (or, in the case of joint landlords, any of them) nor any other person who, alone or jointly with others, has acquired that interest since that time acquired it for money or money's worth; and

(c) the assured tenancy on which the dwelling-house is let did not come into being by virtue of any provision of Schedule 1 to the Rent Act 1977, as amended by Part I of Schedule 4 to this Act or, as the case may be, section 4 of the Rent (Agriculture) Act 1976, as amended by Part II of that Schedule.

For the purposes of this ground, if, immediately before the grant of the tenancy, the tenant to whom it was granted or, if it was granted to joint tenants, any of them was the tenant or one of the joint tenants of the dwelling-house concerned under an earlier assured tenancy or, as the case may be, under a tenancy to which Schedule 10 to the Local Government and Housing Act 1989 applied, any reference in paragraph (b) above to the grant of the tenancy is a reference to the grant of the earlier assured tenancy or, as the case may be, to the grant of the tenancy to which the said Schedule 10 applied.

For the purposes of this ground 'registered social landlord' has the same meaning as in the Housing Act 1985 (see section 5(4) and (5) of that Act) and 'charitable housing trust' means a housing trust, within the meaning of the Housing Associations Act 1985, which is a charity, …

Ground 7

The tenancy is a periodic tenancy (including a statutory periodic tenancy), or a fixed term tenancy of a dwelling-house in England, which has devolved under the will or intestacy of the former tenant and the proceedings for the recovery of possession are begun not later than twelve months after the death of the former tenant or, if the court so directs, after the date on which, in the opinion of the court, the landlord or, in the case of joint landlords, any one of them became aware of the former tenant's death.

For the purposes of this ground, the acceptance by the landlord of rent from a new tenant after the death of the former tenant shall not be regarded as creating a new … tenancy, unless the landlord agrees in writing to a change (as compared with the tenancy before the death) in the amount of the rent, the period or length of term of the tenancy, the premises which are let or any other term of the tenancy.

This ground does not apply to a fixed term tenancy that is a lease of a dwelling-house—

(a) granted on payment of a premium calculated by reference to a percentage of the value of the dwelling-house or of the cost of providing it, or

(b) under which the lessee (or the lessee's personal representatives) will or may be entitled to a sum calculated by reference, directly or indirectly, to the value of the dwelling-house.

Ground 8

Both at the date of the service of the notice under section 8 of this Act relating to the proceedings for possession and at the date of the hearing—

(a) if rent is payable weekly or fortnightly, at least eight weeks' rent is unpaid;

(b) if rent is payable monthly, at least two months' rent is unpaid;

(c) if rent is payable quarterly, at least one quarter's rent is more than three months in arrears; and

(d) if rent is payable yearly, at least three months' rent is more than three months in arrears;

and for the purpose of this ground 'rent' means rent lawfully due from the tenant.

PART II

GROUNDS ON WHICH COURT MAY ORDER POSSESSION

Ground 9

Suitable alternative accommodation is available for the tenant or will be available for him when the order for possession takes effect.

Ground 10

Some rent lawfully due from the tenant—

(a) is unpaid on the date on which the proceedings for possession are begun; and

(b) except where subsection (1)(b) of section 8 of this Act applies, was in arrears at the date of the service of the notice under that section relating to those proceedings.

Ground 11

Whether or not any rent is in arrears on the date on which proceedings for possession are begun, the tenant has persistently delayed paying rent which has become lawfully due.

Ground 12

Any obligation of the tenancy (other than one related to the payment of rent) has been broken or not performed.

Ground 13

The condition of the dwelling-house or any of the common parts has deteriorated owing to acts of waste by, or the neglect or default of, the tenant or any other person residing in the dwelling-house and, in the case of an act of waste by, or the neglect or default of, a person lodging with the tenant or a sub-tenant of his, the tenant has not taken such steps as he ought reasonably to have taken for the removal of the lodger or sub-tenant.

For the purposes of this ground, 'common parts' means any part of a building comprising the dwelling-house and any other premises which the tenant is entitled under the terms of the tenancy to use in common with the occupiers of other dwelling-houses in which the landlord has an estate or interest.

Ground 14

The tenant or a person residing in or visiting the dwelling-house—

- (a) has been guilty of conduct causing or likely to cause a nuisance or annoyance to a person residing, visiting or otherwise engaging in a lawful activity in the locality, or
- (b) has been convicted of—
    - (i) using the dwelling-house or allowing it to be used for immoral or illegal purposes, or
    - (ii) an indictable offence committed in, or in the locality of, the dwelling-house.

Ground 14A

The dwelling-house was occupied (whether alone or with others) by a married couple, a couple who are civil partners of each other, a couple living together as husband and wife or a couple living together as if they were civil partners and—

- (a) one or both of the partners is a tenant of the dwelling-house,
- (b) the landlord who is seeking possession is a non-profit registered provider of social housing, a registered social landlord or a charitable housing trust, or, where the dwelling-house is social housing within the meaning of Part 2 of the Housing and Regeneration Act 2008, a profit-making registered provider of social housing,
- (c) one partner has left the dwelling-house because of violence or threats of violence by the other towards—
    - (i) that partner, or
    - (ii) a member of the family of that partner who was residing with that partner immediately before the partner left, and
- (d) the court is satisfied that the partner who has left is unlikely to return.

For the purposes of this ground 'registered social landlord' and 'member of the family' have the same meaning as in Part I of the Housing Act 1996 and 'charitable housing trust' means a housing trust, within the meaning of the Housing Associations Act 1985, which is a charity ...

Ground 15

The condition of any furniture provided for use under the tenancy has, in the opinion of the court, deteriorated owing to ill-treatment by the tenant or any other person residing in the dwelling-house and, in the case of ill-treatment by a person lodging with the tenant or by a sub-tenant of his, the tenant has not taken such steps as he ought reasonably to have taken for the removal of the lodger or sub-tenant.

Ground 16

The dwelling-house was let to the tenant in consequence of his employment by the landlord seeking possession or a previous landlord under the tenancy and the tenant has ceased to be in that employment.

For the purposes of this ground, at a time when the landlord is or was the Secretary of State, employment by a health services body, as defined in section 60(7) of the National Health Service and Community Care Act 1990, or by a Local Health Board, shall be regarded as employment by the Secretary of State.

Ground 17

The tenant is the person, or one of the persons, to whom the tenancy was granted and the landlord was induced to grant the tenancy by a false statement made knowingly or recklessly by—

- (a) the tenant, or
- (b) a person acting at the tenant's instigation.

PART III
SUITABLE ALTERNATIVE ACCOMMODATION

1. For the purposes of Ground 9 above, a certificate of the local housing authority for the district in which the dwelling-house in question is situated, certifying that the authority will provide suitable alternative

accommodation for the tenant by a date specified in the certificate, shall be conclusive evidence that suitable alternative accommodation will be available for him by that date.

2. Where no such certificate as is mentioned in paragraph 1 above is produced to the court, accommodation shall be deemed to be suitable for the purposes of Ground 9 above if it consists of either—

   (a) premises which are to be let as a separate dwelling such that they will then be let on an assured tenancy, other than—

   (i) a tenancy in respect of which notice is given not later than the beginning of the tenancy that possession might be recovered on any of Grounds 1 to 5 above, or

   (ii) an assured shorthold tenancy, within the meaning of Chapter II of Part I of this Act, or

   (b) premises to be let as a separate dwelling on terms which will, in the opinion of the court, afford to the tenant security of tenure reasonably equivalent to the security afforded by Chapter 1 of Part I of this Act in the case of an assured tenancy of a kind mentioned in sub-paragraph (a) above,

   and, in the opinion of the court, the accommodation fulfils the relevant conditions as defined in paragraph 3 below.

3. (1) For the purposes of paragraph 2 above, the relevant conditions are that the accommodation is reasonably suitable to the needs of the tenant and his family as regards proximity to place of work, and either—

   (a) similar as regards rental and extent to the accommodation afforded by dwelling-houses provided in the neighbourhood by any local housing authority for persons whose needs as regards extent are, in the opinion of the court, similar to those of the tenant and of his family; or

   (b) reasonably suitable to the means of the tenant and to the needs of the tenant and his family as regards extent and character; and

   that if any furniture was provided for use under the assured tenancy in question, furniture is provided for use in the accommodation which is either similar to that so provided or is reasonably suitable to the needs of the tenant and his family.

   (2) For the purposes of sub-paragraph (1)(a) above, a certificate of a local housing authority stating—

   (a) the extent of the accommodation afforded by dwelling-houses provided by the authority to meet the needs of tenants with families of such number as may be specified in the certificate, and

   (b) the amount of the rent charged by the authority for dwelling-houses affording accommodation of that extent,

   shall be conclusive evidence of the facts so stated.

4. Accommodation shall not be deemed to be suitable to the needs of the tenant and his family if the result of their occupation of the accommodation would be that it would be an overcrowded dwelling-house for the purposes of Part X of the Housing Act 1985.

5. Any document purporting to be a certificate of a local housing authority named therein issued for the purposes of this Part of this Schedule and to be signed by the proper officer of that authority shall be received in evidence and, unless the contrary is shown, shall be deemed to be such a certificate without further proof.

6. In this Part of this Schedule 'local housing authority' and 'district', in relation to such an authority, have the same meaning as in the Housing Act 1985.

PART IV
NOTICES RELATING TO RECOVERY OF POSSESSION

7. Any reference in Grounds 1 to 5 in Part I of this Schedule or in the following provisions of this Part to the landlord giving a notice in writing to the tenant is, in the case of joint landlords, a reference to at least one of the joint landlords giving such a notice.

8. (1) If, not later than the beginning of a tenancy (in this paragraph referred to as 'the earlier tenancy'), the landlord gives such a notice in writing to the tenant as is mentioned in any of Grounds 1 to 5 in Part I of this Schedule, then, for the purposes of the ground in question and any further application of this paragraph, that notice shall also have effect as if it has been given immediately before the beginning of any later tenancy falling within sub-paragraph (2) below.

   (2) Subject to sub-paragraph (3) below, sub-paragraph (1) above applies to a later tenancy—

   (a) which takes effect immediately on the coming to an end of the earlier tenancy; and

   (b) which is granted (or deemed to be granted) to the person who was the tenant under the earlier tenancy immediately before it came to an end; and

(c) which is of substantially the same dwelling-house as the earlier tenancy.

(3) Sub-paragraph (1) above does not apply in relation to a later tenancy if, not later than the beginning of the tenancy, the landlord gave notice in writing to the tenant that the tenancy is not one in respect of which possession can be recovered on the ground in question.

9. Where paragraph 8(1) above has effect in relation to a notice given as mentioned in Ground 1 in Part I of this Schedule, the reference in paragraph (b) of that ground to the reversion on the tenancy is a reference to the reversion on the earlier tenancy and on any later tenancy falling within paragraph 8(2) above.

10. Where paragraph 8(1) above has effect in relation to a notice given as mentioned in Ground 3 or Ground 4 in Part I of this Schedule, any second or subsequent tenancy in relation to which the notice has effect shall be treated for the purpose of that ground as beginning at the beginning of the tenancy in respect of which the notice was actually given.

11. Any reference in Grounds 1 to 5 in Part I of this Schedule to a notice being given not later than the beginning of the tenancy is a reference to its being given not later than the day on which the tenancy is entered into and, accordingly, section 45(2) of this Act shall not apply to any such reference.

ENVIRONMENTAL PROTECTION ACT 1990
(1990, c. 43)

PART III
STATUTORY NUISANCES AND CLEAN AIR

Statutory nuisances: England and Wales

79. Statutory nuisances and inspections therefor

(1) Subject to subsections (1ZA) to (6A) below, the following matters constitute 'statutory nuisances' for the purposes of this Part, that is to say—

    (a) any premises in such a state as to be prejudicial to health or a nuisance;

    (b) smoke emitted from premises so as to be prejudicial to health or a nuisance;

    (c) fumes or gases emitted from premises so as to be prejudicial to health or a nuisance;

    (d) any dust, steam, smell or other effluvia arising on industrial, trade or business premises and being prejudicial to health or a nuisance;

    (e) any accumulation or deposit which is prejudicial to health or a nuisance;

    (ea) any water covering land or land covered with water which is in such a state as to be prejudicial to health or a nuisance;

    (f) any animal kept in such a place or manner as to be prejudicial to health or a nuisance;

    (fa) any insects emanating from relevant industrial, trade or business premises and being prejudicial to health or a nuisance;

    (faa) any insects emanating from premises and being prejudicial to health or a nuisance;

    (fb) artificial light emitted from premises so as to be prejudicial to health or a nuisance;

    (fba) artificial light emitted from—

        (i) premises;

        (ii) any stationary object,

    so as to be prejudicial to health or a nuisance;

    (g) noise emitted from premises so as to be prejudicial to health or a nuisance;

    (ga) noise that is prejudicial to health or a nuisance and is emitted from or caused by a vehicle, machinery or equipment in a street;

    (h) any other matter declared by any enactment to be a statutory nuisance;

and it shall be the duty of every local authority to cause its area to be inspected from time to time to detect any statutory nuisances which ought to be dealt with under section 80 below or sections 80 and 80A below and, where a complaint of a statutory nuisance is made to it by a person living within its area, to take such steps as are reasonably practicable to investigate the complaint.

(1ZA) The Scottish Ministers may by regulations—

    (a) amend this section so as to—

        (i) prescribe additional matters which constitute statutory nuisances for the purposes of this Part;

        (ii) vary the description of any matter which constitutes a statutory nuisance;

    (b) in relation to an amendment under paragraph (a), amend this Act and any other enactment to make such incidental, supplementary, consequential, transitory, transitional or saving provision as the Scottish Ministers consider appropriate.

(1ZB) Before making regulations under subsection (1ZA) above, the Scottish Ministers must consult, in so far as it is reasonably practicable to do so, the persons mentioned in subsection (1ZC) below.

(1ZC) Those persons are—

    (a) such associations of local authorities; and

    (b) such other persons,

as the Scottish Ministers consider appropriate.

(1A) No matter shall constitute a statutory nuisance to the extent that it consists of, or is caused by, any land being in a contaminated state.

(1B) Land is in a 'contaminated state' for the purposes of subsection (1A) above if, and only if, it is in such a condition, by reason of substances in, on or under the land, that—

(a) harm is being caused or there is a possibility of harm being caused; or

(b) pollution of controlled waters is being, or is likely to be, caused;

and in this subsection 'harm', 'pollution of controlled waters' and 'substance' have the same meaning as in Part IIA of this Act.

(2) Subsection (1)(b), (fb), (fba) and (g) above do not apply in relation to premises (or, in respect of paragraph (fba)(ii) above, a stationary object located on premises)—

(a) occupied on behalf of the Crown for naval, military or air force purposes or for the purposes of the department of the Secretary of State having responsibility for defence, or

(b) occupied by or for the purposes of a visiting force.

(3) Subsection (1)(b) above does not apply to—

(i) smoke emitted from a chimney of a private dwelling within a smoke control area,

(ii) dark smoke emitted from a chimney of a building or a chimney serving the furnace of a boiler or industrial plant attached to a building or for the time being fixed to or installed on any land,

(iii) smoke emitted from a railway locomotive steam engine, or

(iv) dark smoke emitted otherwise than as mentioned above from industrial or trade premises.

(4) Subsection (1)(c) above does not apply in relation to premises other than private dwellings.

(5) Subsection (1)(d) above does not apply to steam emitted from a railway locomotive engine.

(5ZA) For the purposes of subsection (1)(ea) above, 'land'—

(a) includes structures (other than buildings) in, on or over land;

(b) does not include—

(i) mains or other pipes used for carrying a water supply;

(ii) any part of the public sewerage system;

(iii) any other sewers, drains or other pipes used for carrying sewage;

(iv) the foreshore, that is to say, the land between the high and low water marks of ordinary spring tides;

(v) the seabed.

(5ZB) In subsection (5ZA) above—

'drain', 'sewage' and 'sewer' have the meanings given by section 59 of the Sewerage (Scotland) Act 1968 (c 47);

'main' has the meaning given by section 109(1) of the Water (Scotland) Act 1980 (c 45);

'pipe' includes a service pipe within the meaning of that section of that Act;

'public sewerage system' has the meaning given by section 29 of the Water Services etc (Scotland) Act 2005 (asp 3).

(5A) Subsection (1)(fa) does not apply to insects that are wild animals included in Schedule 5 to the Wildlife and Countryside Act 1981 (animals which are protected), unless they are included in respect of section 9(5) of that Act only.

(5AA) Subsection (1)(faa) above does not apply to insects that are wild animals included in Schedule 5 to the Wildlife and Countryside Act 1981 (c 69).

(5AB) For the purposes of subsection (1)(faa) above, 'premises' does not include—

(a) a site of special scientific interest (within the meaning of section 3(6) of the Nature Conservation (Scotland) Act 2004 (asp 6));

(b) such other place (or type of place) as may be prescribed in regulations made by the Scottish Ministers.

(5AC) Before making regulations under subsection (5AB)(b) above, the Scottish Ministers must consult, in so far as it is reasonably practicable to do so, the persons mentioned in subsection (5AD) below.

(5AD) Those persons are—

(a) such associations of local authorities; and

(b) such other persons,

as the Scottish Ministers consider appropriate.

(5B) Subsection (1)(fb) does not apply to artificial light emitted from—

(a) an airport;

(b) harbour premises;

(c) railway premises, not being relevant separate railway premises;

(d) tramway premises;

(e) a bus station and any associated facilities;

(f) a public service vehicle operating centre;

(g) a goods vehicle operating centre;

(h) a lighthouse;

(i) a prison.

(5BA) Subsection (1)(fba) above does not apply to artificial light emitted from a lighthouse (within the meaning of Part 8 of the Merchant Shipping Act 1995).

(6) Subsection (1)(g) above does not apply to noise caused by aircraft other than model aircraft.

(6A) Subsection (1)(ga) above does not apply to noise made—

(a) by traffic,

(b) by any naval, military or air force of the Crown or by a visiting force (as defined in subsection (2) above), or

(c) by a political demonstration or a demonstration supporting or opposing a cause or campaign.

(7) In this Part—

'airport' has the meaning given by section 95 of the Transport Act 2000;

'appropriate person' means—

(a) in relation to England, the Secretary of State;

(b) in relation to Wales, the National Assembly for Wales;

'associated facilities', in relation to a bus station, has the meaning given by section 83 of the Transport Act 1985;

'bus station' has the meaning given by section 83 of the Transport Act 1985;

'chimney' includes structures and openings of any kind from or through which smoke may be emitted;

'dust' does not include dust emitted from a chimney as an ingredient of smoke;

'equipment' includes a musical instrument;

'fumes' means any airborne solid matter smaller than dust;

'gas' includes vapour and moisture precipitated from vapour;

'goods vehicle operating centre', in relation to vehicles used under an operator's licence, means a place which is specified in the licence as an operating centre for those vehicles, and for the purposes of this definition 'operating centre' and 'operator's licence' have the same meaning as in the Goods Vehicles (Licensing of Operators) Act 1995;

'harbour premises' means premises which form part of a harbour area and which are occupied wholly or mainly for the purposes of harbour operations, and for the purposes of this definition 'harbour area' and 'harbour operations' have the same meaning as in Part 3 of the Aviation and Maritime Security Act 1990;

'industrial, trade or business premises' means premises used for any industrial, trade or business purposes or premises not so used on which matter is burnt in connection with any industrial, trade or business process, and premises are used for industrial purposes where they are used for the purposes of any treatment or process as well as where they are used for the purposes of manufacturing;

'lighthouse' has the same meaning as in Part 8 of the Merchant Shipping Act 1995;

'local authority' means, subject to subsection (8) below,—

(a) in Greater London, a London borough council, the Common Council of the City of London and, as respects the Temples, the Sub-Treasurer of the Inner Temple and the Under-Treasurer of the Middle Temple respectively;

(b) in England outside Greater London, a district council;

(bb) in Wales, a county council or county borough council;

(c) the Council of the Isles of Scilly; and

(d) in Scotland, a district or islands council or a council constituted under section 2 of the Local Government etc (Scotland) Act 1994;

'noise' includes vibration;

'person responsible'—

(a) in relation to a statutory nuisance, means the person to whose act, default or sufferance the nuisance is attributable;

(b) in relation to a vehicle, includes the person in whose name the vehicle is for the time being registered under the Vehicle Excise and Registration Act 1994 and any other person who is for the time being the driver of the vehicle;

(c) in relation to machinery or equipment, includes any person who is for the time being the operator of the machinery or equipment;

'prejudicial to health' means injurious, or likely to cause injury, to health;

'premises' includes land (subject to subsection (5AB) above) and, subject to subsection (12) and, in relation to England and Wales, section 81A(9) below, any vessel;

'prison' includes a young offender institution;

'private dwelling' means any building, or part of a building, used or intended to be used, as a dwelling;

'public service vehicle operating centre', in relation to public service vehicles used under a PSV operator's licence, means a place which is an operating centre of those vehicles, and for the purposes of this definition 'operating centre', 'PSV operator's licence' and 'public service vehicle' have the same meaning as in the Public Passenger Vehicles Act 1981;

'railway premises' means any premises which fall within the definition of 'light maintenance depot', 'network', 'station' or 'track' in section 83 of the Railways Act 1993;

'relevant separate railway premises' has the meaning given by subsection (7A);

'road' has the same meaning as in Part IV of the New Roads and Street Works Act 1991;

'smoke' includes soot, ash, grit and gritty particles emitted in smoke;

'street' means a highway and any other road, footway, square or court that is for the time being open to the public;

'tramway premises' means any premises which, in relation to a tramway, are the equivalent of the premises which, in relation to a railway, fall within the definition of 'light maintenance depot', 'network', 'station' or 'track' in section 83 of the Railways Act 1993;

and any expressions used in this section and in the Clean Air Act 1993 have the same meaning in this section as in that Act and section 3 of the Clean Air Act 1993 shall apply for the interpretation of the expression 'dark smoke' and the operation of this Part in relation to it.

(7A) Railway premises are relevant separate railway premises if—

(a) they are situated within—

(i) premises used as a museum or other place of cultural, scientific or historical interest, or

(ii) premises used for the purposes of a funfair or other entertainment, recreation or amusement, and

(b) they are not associated with any other railway premises.

(7B) For the purposes of subsection (7A)—

(a) a network situated as described in subsection (7A)(a) is associated with other railway premises if it is connected to another network (not being a network situated as described in subsection (7A)(a));

(b) track that is situated as described in subsection (7A)(a) but is not part of a network is associated with other railway premises if it is connected to track that forms part of a network (not being a network situated as described in subsection (7A)(a));

(c) a station or light maintenance depot situated as described in subsection (7A)(a) is associated with other railway premises if it is used in connection with the provision of railway services other than services provided wholly within the premises where it is situated.

In this subsection 'light maintenance depot', 'network', 'railway services', 'station' and 'track' have the same meaning as in Part 1 of the Railways Act 1993.

(7C) In this Part 'relevant industrial, trade or business premises' means premises that are industrial, trade or business premises as defined in subsection (7), but excluding—

(a) land used as arable, grazing, meadow or pasture land,

(b) land used as osier land, reed beds or woodland,

(c) land used for market gardens, nursery grounds or orchards,

(d) land forming part of an agricultural unit, not being land falling within any of paragraphs (a) to (c), where the land is of a description prescribed by regulations made by the appropriate person, and

(e) land included in a site of special scientific interest (as defined in section 52(1) of the Wildlife and Countryside Act 1981),

and excluding land covered by, and the waters of, any river or watercourse, that is neither a sewer nor a drain, or any lake or pond.

(7D) For the purposes of subsection (7C)—

'agricultural' has the same meaning as in section 109 of the Agriculture Act 1947;

'agricultural unit' means land which is occupied as a unit for agricultural purposes;

'drain' has the same meaning as in the Water Resources Act 1991;

'lake or pond' has the same meaning as in section 104 of that Act;

'sewer' has the same meaning as in that Act.

(8) Where, by an order under section 2 of the Public Health (Control of Disease) Act 1984, a port health authority has been constituted for any port health district, the port health authority shall have by virtue of this subsection, as respects its district, the functions conferred or imposed by this Part in relation to statutory nuisances other than a nuisance falling within paragraph (fb), (g) or (ga) of subsection (1) above and no such order shall be made assigning those functions; and 'local authority' and 'area' shall be construed accordingly.

(9) In this Part 'best practicable means' is to be interpreted by reference to the following provisions—

(a) 'practicable' means reasonably practicable having regard among other things to local conditions and circumstances, to the current state of technical knowledge and to the financial implications;

(b) the means to be employed include the design, installation, maintenance and manner and periods of operation of plant and machinery, and the design, construction and maintenance of buildings and structures;

(c) the test is to apply only so far as compatible with any duty imposed by law;

(d) the test is to apply only so far as compatible with safety and safe working conditions, and with the exigencies of any emergency or unforeseeable circumstances;

and, in circumstances where a code of practice under section 71 of the Control of Pollution Act 1974 (noise minimisation) is applicable, regard shall also be had to guidance given in it.

(10) A local authority shall not without the consent of the Secretary of State institute summary proceedings under this Part in respect of a nuisance falling within paragraph (b), (d), (e), (fb) or (g) and, in relation to Scotland, paragraph (ga), of subsection (1) above if proceedings in respect thereof might be instituted under Part I or under regulations under section 2 of the Pollution Prevention and Control Act 1999.

(11) The area of a local authority which includes part of the seashore shall also include for the purposes of this Part the territorial sea lying seawards from that part of the shore; and subject to subsection (12) and, in relation to England and Wales, section 81A below, this Part shall have effect, in relation to any area included in the area of a local authority by virtue of this subsection—

(a) as if references to premises and the occupier of premises included respectively a vessel and the master of a vessel; and

(b) with such other modifications, if any, as are prescribed in regulations made by the Secretary of State.

(12) A vessel powered by steam reciprocating machinery is not a vessel to which this Part of this Act applies.

80. Summary proceedings for statutory nuisances

(1) Subject to subsection (2A) where a local authority is satisfied that a statutory nuisance exists, or is likely to occur or recur, in the area of the authority, the local authority shall serve a notice ('an abatement notice') imposing all or any of the following requirements—

(a) requiring the abatement of the nuisance or prohibiting or restricting its occurrence or recurrence;

(b) requiring the execution of such works, and the taking of such other steps, as may be necessary for any of those purposes, and the notice shall specify the time or times within which the requirements of the notice are to be complied with.

(2) Subject to section 80A(1) below, the abatement notice shall be served—

   (a) except in a case falling within paragraph (b) or (c) below, on the person responsible for the nuisance;

   (b) where the nuisance arises from any defect of a structural character, on the owner of the premises;

   (c) where the person responsible for the nuisance cannot be found or the nuisance has not yet occurred, on the owner or occupier of the premises.

(2A) Where a local authority is satisfied that a statutory nuisance falling within paragraph (g) of section 79(1) above exists, or is likely to occur or recur, in the area of the authority, the authority shall—

   (a) serve an abatement notice in respect of the nuisance in accordance with subsections (1) and (2) above; or

   (b) take such other steps as it thinks appropriate for the purpose of persuading the appropriate person to abate the nuisance or prohibit or restrict its occurrence or recurrence.

(2B) If a local authority has taken steps under subsection (2A)(b) above and either of the conditions in subsection (2C) below is satisfied, the authority shall serve an abatement notice in respect of the nuisance.

(2C) The conditions are—

   (a) that the authority is satisfied at any time before the end of the relevant period that the steps taken will not be successful in persuading the appropriate person to abate the nuisance or prohibit or restrict its occurrence or recurrence;

   (b) that the authority is satisfied at the end of the relevant period that the nuisance continues to exist, or continues to be likely to occur or recur, in the area of the authority.

(2D) The relevant period is the period of seven days starting with the day on which the authority was first satisfied that the nuisance existed, or was likely to occur or recur.

(2E) The appropriate person is the person on whom the authority would otherwise be required under subsection (2A)(a) above to serve an abatement notice in respect of the nuisance.

(3) A person served with an abatement notice may appeal against the notice to a magistrates' court or in Scotland, the sheriff within the period of twenty-one days beginning with the date on which he was served with the notice.

(4) If a person on whom an abatement notice is served, without reasonable excuse, contravenes or fails to comply with any requirement or prohibition imposed by the notice, he shall be guilty of an offence.

(4A) Where a local authority have reason to believe that a person has committed an offence under subsection (4) above, the local authority may give that person a notice (a 'fixed penalty notice') in accordance with section 80ZA offering the person the opportunity of discharging any liability to conviction for that offence by payment of a fixed penalty.

(5) Except in a case falling within subsection (6) below, a person who commits an offence under subsection (4) above shall be liable on summary conviction to a fine not exceeding level 5 on the standard scale together with a further fine of an amount equal to one-tenth of that level for each day on which the offence continues after the conviction.

(6) A person who commits an offence under subsection (4) above on industrial, trade or business premises shall be liable on summary conviction to a fine not exceeding £20,000.

(7) Subject to subsection (8) below, in any proceedings for an offence under subsection (4) above in respect of a statutory nuisance it shall be a defence to prove that the best practicable means were used to prevent, or to counteract the effects of, the nuisance.

(8) The defence under subsection (7) above is not available—

   (a) in the case of a nuisance falling within paragraph (a), (d), (e), (f), (fa) or (g) of section 79(1) above except where the nuisance arises on industrial, trade or business premises;

   (aza) in the case of a nuisance falling within paragraph (fb) of section 79(1) above except where—

      (i) the artificial light is emitted from industrial, trade or business premises, or

      (ii) the artificial light (not being light to which sub-paragraph (i) applies) is emitted by lights used for the purpose only of illuminating an outdoor relevant sports facility;

(aa) in the case of a nuisance falling within paragraph (ga) of section 79(1) above except where the noise is emitted from or caused by a vehicle, machinery or equipment being used for industrial, trade or business purposes;

(b) in the case of a nuisance falling within paragraph (b) of section 79(1) above except where the smoke is emitted from a chimney; and

(c) in the case of a nuisance falling within paragraph (c) or (h) of section 79(1) above.

(8A) For the purposes of subsection (8)(aza) a relevant sports facility is an area, with or without structures, that is used when participating in a relevant sport, but does not include such an area comprised in domestic premises.

(8B) For the purposes of subsection (8A) 'relevant sport' means a sport that is designated for those purposes by order made by the Secretary of State, in relation to England, or the National Assembly for Wales, in relation to Wales.

A sport may be so designated by reference to its appearing in a list maintained by a body specified in the order.

(8C) In subsection (8A) 'domestic premises' means—

(a) premises used wholly or mainly as a private dwelling, or

(b) land or other premises belonging to, or enjoyed with, premises so used.

(9) In proceedings for an offence under subsection (4) above in respect of a statutory nuisance falling within paragraph (g) or (ga) of section 79(1) above where the offence consists in contravening requirements imposed by virtue of subsection (1)(a) above it shall be a defence to prove—

(a) that the alleged offence was covered by a notice served under section 60 or a consent given under section 61 or 65 of the Control of Pollution Act 1974 (construction sites, etc); or

(b) where the alleged offence was committed at a time when the premises were subject to a notice under section 66 of that Act (noise reduction notice), that the level of noise emitted from the premises at that time was not such as to a constitute a contravention of the notice under that section; or

(c) where the alleged offence was committed at a time when the premises were not subject to a notice under section 66 of that Act, and when a level fixed under section 67 of that Act (new buildings liable to abatement order) applied to the premises, that the level of noise emitted from the premises at that time did not exceed that level.

(10) Paragraphs (b) and (c) of subsection (9) above apply whether or not the relevant notice was subject to appeal at the time when the offence was alleged to have been committed.

80ZA. Fixed penalty notice: supplemental

(1) This section applies to a fixed penalty notice given under section 80(4A).

(2) A fixed penalty notice must give reasonable particulars of the circumstances alleged to constitute the offence.

(3) A fixed penalty notice must also state—

(a) the amount of the fixed penalty;

(b) the period within which it may be paid;

(c) the—

(i) person to whom; and

(ii) address at which,

payment may be made;

(d) the method or methods by which payment may be made;

(e) the consequences of not making a payment within the period for payment.

(4) The amount of the fixed penalty under section 80(4A) is—

(a) in the case of a nuisance relating to industrial, trade or business premises, £400;

(b) in any other case, £150.

(5) The period for payment of the fixed penalty is 14 days beginning with the day after the day on which the notice is given.

(6) The local authority may extend the period for paying the fixed penalty in any particular case if they consider it appropriate to do so by sending notice to the person to whom the fixed penalty notice was given.

(7) No proceedings for an offence under section 80(4) may be commenced before the end of the period for payment of the fixed penalty.

(8) In proceedings for an offence under section 80(4), a certificate which—
- (a) purports to be signed by or on behalf of a person having responsibility for the financial affairs of the local authority; and
- (b) states that payment of the amount specified in the fixed penalty notice was or was not received by the expiry of the period within which that fixed penalty may be paid,

is sufficient evidence of the facts stated.

(9) Where proceedings for an offence in respect of which a fixed penalty notice has been given are commenced, the notice is to be treated as withdrawn.

(10) Any sum received by a local authority under section 80(4A) accrues to that authority.

(11) The Scottish Ministers may, by regulations—
- (a) provide that fixed penalty notices may not be given in such circumstances as may be prescribed;
- (b) provide for the form of a fixed penalty notice;
- (c) provide for the method or methods by which fixed penalties may be paid;
- (d) modify subsection (4)(a) or (b) above so as to substitute a different amount (not exceeding level 2 on the standard scale) for the amount for the time being specified there;
- (e) provide for the amount of the fixed penalty to be different in different cases or descriptions of case;
- (f) modify subsection (5) above so as to substitute a different period for the period for the time being specified there;
- (g) provide for the keeping of accounts, and the preparation and publication of statements of account relating to fixed penalties under section 80(4A).

(12) Before making regulations under subsection (11) above, the Scottish Ministers must consult, in so far as it is reasonably practicable to do so, the persons mentioned in subsection (13) below.

(13) Those persons are—
- (a) such associations of local authorities; and
- (b) such other persons,

as the Scottish Ministers consider appropriate.

81. Supplementary provisions

(1) Subject to subsection (1A) below, where more than one person is responsible for a statutory nuisance section 80 above shall apply to each of those persons whether or not what any one of them is responsible for would by itself amount to a nuisance.

(1A) In relation to a statutory nuisance within section 79(1)(ga) above for which more than one person is responsible (whether or not what any one of those persons is responsible for would by itself amount to such a nuisance), section 80(2)(a) above shall apply with the substitution of 'any one of the persons' for 'the person'.

(1B) In relation to a statutory nuisance within section 79(1)(ga) above caused by noise emitted from or caused by an unattended vehicle or unattended machinery or equipment for which more than one person is responsible, section 80A above shall apply with the substitution—
- (a) in subsection (2)(a), of 'any of the persons' for 'the person' and of 'one such person' for 'that person',
- (b) in subsection (2)(b), of 'such a person' for 'that person',
- (c) in subsection (3), of 'any of the persons' for 'the person' and of 'one such person' for 'that person',
- (d) in subsection (5), of 'any person' for 'the person', and
- (e) in subsection (7), of 'a person' for 'the person' and of 'such a person' for 'that person'.

(2) Where a statutory nuisance which exists or has occurred within the area of a local authority, or which has affected any part of that area, appears to the local authority to be wholly or partly caused by some

act or default committed or taking place outside the area, the local authority may act under section 80 above as if the act or default were wholly within that area, except that any appeal shall be heard by a magistrates' court or in Scotland, the sheriff having jurisdiction where the act or default is alleged to have taken place.

(3) Where an abatement notice has not been complied with, the local authority may, whether or not—

(a) proceedings have been taken for an offence under section 80(4); or

(b) a fixed penalty notice has been given under section 80(4A) in respect of that offence (regardless of whether the fixed penalty notice is accepted),

abate the nuisance and do whatever may be necessary in execution of the abatement notice.

(3A) The power under subsection (3) above shall, where the matter to be abated is a statutory nuisance by virtue of section 79(1)(g) above, include power to seize and remove any equipment which it appears to the authority is being or has been used in the emission of the noise in question.

(3B) A person who wilfully obstructs any person exercising, by virtue of subsection (3A) above, the power conferred by subsection (3) above shall be liable, on summary conviction, to a fine not exceeding level 3 on the standard scale.

(3C) Schedule 1 to the Antisocial Behaviour etc (Scotland) Act 2004 shall have effect in relation to equipment seized by virtue of subsection (3A) above as it does in relation to equipment seized under section 47(2) of that Act, subject to the following modifications—

(a) in paragraph 1(a), 'noise offence' means an offence under section 80(4) above in respect of a statutory nuisance falling within section 79(1)(g) above; and

(b) in paragraph 1(b), 'seized equipment' means equipment seized by virtue of subsection (3A) above.

(4) Any expenses reasonably incurred by a local authority in abating, or preventing the recurrence of, a statutory nuisance under subsection (3) above may be recovered by them from the person by whose act or default the nuisance was caused and, if that person is the owner of the premises, from any person who is for the time being the owner thereof; and the court or sheriff may apportion the expenses between persons by whose acts or defaults the nuisance is caused in such manner as the court consider or sheriff considers fair and reasonable.

(5) If a local authority is of opinion that proceedings for an offence under section 80(4) above would afford an inadequate remedy in the case of any statutory nuisance , they may, subject to subsection (6) below, take proceedings in the High Court or, in Scotland, in any court of competent jurisdiction for the purpose of securing the abatement, prohibition or restriction of the nuisance, and the proceedings shall be maintainable notwithstanding the local authority have suffered no damage from the nuisance.

(6) In any proceedings under subsection (5) above in respect of a nuisance falling within paragraph (g) or (ga) of section 79(1) above, it shall be a defence to prove that the noise was authorised by a notice under section 60 or a consent under section 61 (construction sites) of the Control of Pollution Act 1974.

(7) The further supplementary provisions in Schedule 3 to this Act shall have effect.

82. Summary proceedings by persons aggrieved by statutory nuisances

(1) A magistrates' court may act under this section on a complaint or, in Scotland, the sheriff may act under this section on a summary application, made by any person on the ground that he is aggrieved by the existence of a statutory nuisance.

(2) If the magistrates' court or, in Scotland, the sheriff is satisfied that the alleged nuisance exists, or that although abated it is likely to recur on the same premises or, in the case of a nuisance within section 79(1)(ga) above, in the same street or, in Scotland, road, the court or the sheriff shall make an order for either or both of the following purposes—

(a) requiring the defendant or, in Scotland, defender to abate the nuisance, within a time specified in the order, and to execute any works necessary for that purpose;

(b) prohibiting a recurrence of the nuisance, and requiring the defendant or defender, within a time specified in the order, to execute any works necessary to prevent the recurrence;

and, in England and Wales, may also impose on the defendant a fine not exceeding level 5 on the standard scale.

(3) If the magistrates' court or the sheriff is satisfied that the alleged nuisance exists and is such as, in the opinion of the court or of the sheriff, to render premises unfit for human habitation, an order under

subsection (2) above may prohibit the use of the premises for human habitation until the premises are, to the satisfaction of the court or of the sheriff, rendered fit for that purpose.

(4) Proceedings for an order under subsection (2) above shall be brought—

(a) except in a case falling within paragraph (b), (c) or (d) below, against the person responsible for the nuisance;

(b) where the nuisance arises from any defect of a structural character, against the owner of the premises;

(c) where the person responsible for the nuisance cannot be found, against the owner or occupier of the premises;

(d) in the case of a statutory nuisance within section 79(1)(ga) above caused by noise emitted from or caused by an unattended vehicle or unattended machinery or equipment, against the person responsible for the vehicle, machinery or equipment.

(5) Subject to subsection (5A) below, where more than one person is responsible for a statutory nuisance, subsections (1) to (4) above shall apply to each of those persons whether or not what any one of them is responsible for would by itself amount to a nuisance.

(5A) In relation to a statutory nuisance within section 79(1)(ga) above for which more than one person is responsible (whether or not what any one of those persons is responsible for would by itself amount to a nuisance), subsection (4)(a) above shall apply with the substitution of 'each person responsible for the nuisance who can be found' for 'the person responsible for the nuisance'.

(5B) In relation to a statutory nuisance within section 79(1)(ga) above caused by noise emitted from or caused by an unattended vehicle or unattended machinery or equipment for which more than one person is responsible, subsection (4)(d) above shall apply with the substitution of 'any person' for 'the person'.

(6) Before instituting proceedings for an order under subsection (2) above against any person, the person aggrieved by the nuisance shall give to that person such notice in writing of his intention to bring the proceedings as is applicable to proceedings in respect of a nuisance of that description and the notice shall specify the matter complained of.

(7) The notice of the bringing of proceedings in respect of a statutory nuisance required by subsection (6) above which is applicable is—

(a) in the case of a nuisance falling within paragraph (g) or (ga) of section 79(1) above, not less than three days' notice; and

(b) in the case of a nuisance of any other description, not less than twenty-one days' notice;

but the Secretary of State may, by order, provide that this subsection shall have effect as if such period as is specified in the order were the minimum period of notice applicable to any description of statutory nuisance specified in the order.

(8) A person who, without reasonable excuse, contravenes any requirement or prohibition imposed by an order under subsection (2) above shall be guilty of an offence and liable on summary conviction to a fine not exceeding level 5 on the standard scale together with a further fine of an amount equal to one-tenth of that level for each day on which the offence continues after the conviction.

(9) Subject to subsection (10) below, in any proceedings for an offence under subsection (8) above in respect of a statutory nuisance it shall be a defence to prove that the best practicable means were used to prevent, or to counteract the effects of, the nuisance.

(10) The defence under subsection (9) above is not available—

(a) in the case of a nuisance falling within paragraph (a), (d), (e), (f), (fa) or (g) of section 79(1) above except where the nuisance arises on industrial, trade or business premises;

(aza) in the case of a nuisance falling within paragraph (fb) of section 79(1) above except where—

(i) the artificial light is emitted from industrial, trade or business premises, or

(ii) the artificial light (not being light to which sub-paragraph (i) applies) is emitted by lights used for the purpose only of illuminating an outdoor relevant sports facility;

(aa) in the case of a nuisance falling within paragraph (ga) of section 79(1) above except where the noise is emitted from or caused by a vehicle, machinery or equipment being used for industrial, trade or business purposes;

(b) in the case of a nuisance falling within paragraph (b) of section 79(1) above except where the smoke is emitted from a chimney;

(c) in the case of a nuisance falling within paragraph (c) or (h) of section 79(1) above; and

(d) in the case of a nuisance which is such as to render the premises unfit for human habitation.

(10A) For the purposes of subsection (10)(aza) 'relevant sports facility' has the same meaning as it has for the purposes of section 80(8)(aza).

(11) If a person is convicted of an offence under subsection (8) above, a magistrates' court or the sheriff may, after giving the local authority in whose area the nuisance has occurred an opportunity of being heard, direct the authority to do anything which the person convicted was required to do by the order to which the conviction relates.

(12) Where on the hearing of proceedings for an order under subsection (2) above it is proved that the alleged nuisance existed at the date of the making of the complaint or summary application, then, whether or not at the date of the hearing it still exists or is likely to recur, the court or the sheriff shall order the defendant or defender (or defendants or defenders in such proportions as appears fair and reasonable) to pay to the person bringing the proceedings such amount as the court or the sheriff considers reasonably sufficient to compensate him for any expenses properly incurred by him in the proceedings.

(13) If it appears to the magistrates' court or to the sheriff that neither the person responsible for the nuisance nor the owner or occupier of the premises or (as the case may be) the person responsible for the vehicle, machinery or equipment can be found the court or the sheriff may, after giving the local authority in whose area the nuisance has occurred an opportunity of being heard, direct the authority to do anything which the court or the sheriff would have ordered that person to do.

HOUSING ACT 1996
(1996, c. 52)

PART III
LANDLORD AND TENANT

CHAPTER I
TENANTS' RIGHTS

Forfeiture

81. Restriction on termination of tenancy for failure to pay service charge

(1) A landlord may not, in relation to premises let as a dwelling, exercise a right of re-entry or forfeiture for failure by a tenant to pay a service charge or administration charge unless—

    (a) it is finally determined by (or on appeal from) a leasehold valuation tribunal or by a court, or by an arbitral tribunal in proceedings pursuant to a post-dispute arbitration agreement, that the amount of the service charge or administration charge is payable by him, or

    (b) the tenant has admitted that it is so payable.

(2) The landlord may not exercise a right of re-entry or forfeiture by virtue of subsection (1)(a) until after the end of the period of 14 days beginning with the day after that on which the final determination is made.

(3) For the purposes of this section it is finally determined that the amount of a service charge or administration charge is payable—

    (a) if a decision that it is payable is not appealed against or otherwise challenged, at the end of the time for bringing an appeal or other challenge, or

    (b) if such a decision is appealed against or otherwise challenged and not set aside in consequence of the appeal or other challenge, at the time specified in subsection (3A).

(3A) The time referred to in subsection (3)(b) is the time when the appeal or other challenge is disposed of—

    (a) by the determination of the appeal or other challenge and the expiry of the time for bringing a subsequent appeal (if any), or

    (b) by its being abandoned or otherwise ceasing to have effect.

(4) The reference in subsection (1) to premises let as a dwelling does not include premises let on—

    (a) a tenancy to which Part II of the Landlord and Tenant Act 1954 applies (business tenancies),

    (b) a tenancy of an agricultural holding within the meaning of the Agricultural Holdings Act 1986 in relation to which that Act applies, or

    (c) a farm business tenancy within the meaning of the Agricultural Tenancies Act 1995.

(4A) References in this section to the exercise of a right of re-entry or forfeiture include the service of a notice under section 146(1) of the Law of Property Act 1925 (restriction on re-entry or forfeiture).

(5) In this section—

    (a) 'administration charge' has the meaning given by Part 1 of Schedule 11 to the Commonhold and Leasehold Reform Act 2002,

    (b) 'arbitration agreement' and 'arbitral tribunal' have the same meaning as in

Part 1 of the Arbitration Act 1996 and 'post-dispute arbitration agreement', in relation to any matter, means an arbitration agreement made after a dispute about the matter has arisen,

    (c) 'dwelling' has the same meaning as in the Landlord and Tenant Act 1985, and

    (d) 'service charge' means a service charge within the meaning of section 18(1) of the Landlord and Tenant Act 1985, other than one excluded from that section by section 27 of that Act (rent of dwelling registered and not entered as variable).

(5A) Any order of a court to give effect to a determination of a leasehold valuation tribunal shall be treated as a determination by the court for the purposes of this section.

(6) Nothing in this section affects the exercise of a right of re-entry or forfeiture on other grounds.

PART V
CONDUCT OF TENANTS

CHAPTER I
INTRODUCTORY TENANCIES

General provisions

124. Introductory tenancies

(1) A local housing authority or a housing action trust may elect to operate an introductory tenancy regime.

(2) When such an election is in force, every periodic tenancy of a dwelling-house entered into or adopted by the authority or trust shall, if it would otherwise be a secure tenancy, be an introductory tenancy, unless immediately before the tenancy was entered into or adopted the tenant or, in the case of joint tenants, one or more of them was—

 (a) a secure tenant of the same or another dwelling-house, or

 (b) a tenant under a relevant assured tenancy, other than an assured shorthold tenancy, of the same or another dwelling-house.

(2A) In subsection (2)(b) 'relevant assured tenancy' means—

 (a) an assured tenancy in respect of social housing under which the landlord is a private registered provider of social housing, or

 (b) an assured tenancy under which the landlord is a registered social landlord;

 and for these purposes "social housing" has the same meaning as in Part 2 of the Housing and Regeneration Act 2008.

(3) Subsection (2) does not apply to a tenancy entered into or adopted in pursuance of a contract made before the election was made.

(4) For the purposes of this Chapter a periodic tenancy is adopted by a person if that person becomes the landlord under the tenancy, whether on a disposal or surrender of the interest of the former landlord.

(5) An election under this section may be revoked at any time, without prejudice to the making of a further election.

125. Duration of introductory tenancy

(1) A tenancy remains an introductory tenancy until the end of the trial period, unless one of the events mentioned in subsection (5) occurs before the end of that period.

(2) The 'trial period' is the period of one year beginning with—

 (a) in the case of a tenancy which was entered into by a local housing authority or housing action trust—

  (i) the date on which the tenancy was entered into, or

  (ii) if later, the date on which a tenant was first entitled to possession under the tenancy; or

 (b) in the case of a tenancy which was adopted by a local housing authority or housing action trust, the date of adoption;

 but this is subject to subsections (3) and (4) and to section 125A (extension of trial period by 6 months).

(3) Where the tenant under an introductory tenancy was formerly a tenant under another introductory tenancy, or a relevant assured shorthold tenancy, any period or periods during which he was such a tenant shall count towards the trial period, provided—

 (a) if there was one such period, it ended immediately before the date specified in subsection (2), and

 (b) if there was more than one such period, the most recent period ended immediately before that date and each period succeeded the other without interruption.

(3A) In subsection (3) 'relevant assured shorthold tenancy' means—

 (a) an assured shorthold tenancy in respect of social housing under which the landlord is a private registered provider of social housing, or

 (b) an assured shorthold tenancy under which the landlord is a registered social landlord;

 and for these purposes 'social housing' has the same meaning as in Part 2 of the Housing and Regeneration Act 2008.

(4) Where there are joint tenants under an introductory tenancy, the reference in subsection (3) to the tenant shall be construed as referring to the joint tenant in whose case the application of that subsection produces the earliest starting date for the trial period.

(5) A tenancy ceases to be an introductory tenancy if, before the end of the trial period—
   (a) the circumstances are such that the tenancy would not otherwise be a secure tenancy,
   (b) a person or body other than a local housing authority or housing action trust becomes the landlord under the tenancy,
   (c) the election in force when the tenancy was entered into or adopted is revoked, or
   (d) the tenancy ceases to be an introductory tenancy by virtue of section 133(3) (succession).

(6) A tenancy does not come to an end merely because it ceases to be an introductory tenancy, but a tenancy which has once ceased to be an introductory tenancy cannot subsequently become an introductory tenancy.

(7) This section has effect subject to section 130 (effect of beginning proceedings for possession).

125A. Extension of trial period by 6 months

(1) If both of the following conditions are met in relation to an introductory tenancy, the trial period is extended by 6 months.

(2) The first condition is that the landlord has served a notice of extension on the tenant at least 8 weeks before the original expiry date.

(3) The second condition is that either—
   (a) the tenant has not requested a review under section 125B in accordance with subsection (1) of that section, or
   (b) if he has, the decision on the review was to confirm the landlord's decision to extend the trial period.

(4) A notice of extension is a notice—
   (a) stating that the landlord has decided that the period for which the tenancy is to be an introductory tenancy should be extended by 6 months, and
   (b) complying with subsection (5).

(5) A notice of extension must—
   (a) set out the reasons for the landlord's decision, and
   (b) inform the tenant of his right to request a review of the landlord's decision and of the time within which such a request must be made.

(6) In this section and section 125B 'the original expiry date' means the last day of the period of one year that would apply as the trial period apart from this section.

125B. Review of decision to extend trial period

(1) A request for review of the landlord's decision that the trial period for an introductory tenancy should be extended under section 125A must be made before the end of the period of 14 days beginning with the day on which the notice of extension is served.

(2) On a request being duly made to it, the landlord shall review its decision.

(3) The Secretary of State may make provision by regulations as to the procedure to be followed in connection with a review under this section.

Nothing in the following provisions affects the generality of this power.

(4) Provision may be made by regulations—
   (a) requiring the decision on review to be made by a person of appropriate seniority who was not involved in the original decision, and
   (b) as to the circumstances in which the person concerned is entitled to an oral hearing, and whether and by whom he may be represented at such a hearing.

(5) The landlord shall notify the tenant of the decision on the review.

If the decision is to confirm the original decision, the landlord shall also notify him of the reasons for the decision.

(6) The review shall be carried out and the tenant notified before the original expiry date.

127. Proceedings for possession

(1) The landlord may only bring an introductory tenancy to an end by obtaining—

    (a) an order of the court for the possession of the dwelling-house, and

    (b) the execution of the order.

(1A) In such a case, the tenancy ends when the order is executed.

(2) The court shall make an order of the kind mentioned in subsection (1)(a) unless the provisions of section 128 apply.

128. Notice of proceedings for possession

(1) The court shall not entertain proceedings for the possession of a dwelling-house let under an introductory tenancy unless the landlord has served on the tenant a notice of proceedings complying with this section.

(2) The notice shall state that the court will be asked to make an order for the possession of the dwelling-house.

(3) The notice shall set out the reasons for the landlord's decision to apply for such an order.

(4) The notice shall specify a date after which proceedings for the possession of the dwelling-house may be begun.

The date so specified must not be earlier than the date on which the tenancy could, apart from this Chapter, be brought to an end by notice to quit given by the landlord on the same date as the notice of proceedings.

(5) The court shall not entertain any proceedings for possession of the dwelling-house unless they are begun after the date specified in the notice of proceedings.

(6) The notice shall inform the tenant of his right to request a review of the landlord's decision to seek an order for possession and of the time within which such a request must be made.

(7) The notice shall also inform the tenant that if he needs help or advice about the notice, and what to do about it, he should take it immediately to a Citizens' Advice Bureau, a housing aid centre, a law centre or a solicitor.

129. Review of decision to seek possession

(1) A request for review of the landlord's decision to seek an order for possession of a dwelling-house let under an introductory tenancy must be made before the end of the period of 14 days beginning with the day on which the notice of proceedings is served.

(2) On a request being duly made to it, the landlord shall review its decision.

(3) The Secretary of State may make provision by regulations as to the procedure to be followed in connection with a review under this section.

Nothing in the following provisions affects the generality of this power.

(4) Provision may be made by regulations—

    (a) requiring the decision on review to be made by a person of appropriate seniority who was not involved in the original decision, and

    (b) as to the circumstances in which the person concerned is entitled to an oral hearing, and whether and by whom he may be represented at such a hearing.

(5) The landlord shall notify the person concerned of the decision on the review.

If the decision is to confirm the original decision, the landlord shall also notify him of the reasons for the decision.

(6) The review shall be carried out and the tenant notified before the date specified in the notice of proceedings as the date after which proceedings for the possession of the dwelling-house may be begun.

Succession on death of tenant

131. Persons qualified to succeed tenant

A person is qualified to succeed the tenant under an introductory tenancy if he occupies the dwelling-house as his only or principal home at the time of the tenant's death and either—

(a) he is the tenant's spouse or civil partner, or

(b) he is another member of the tenant's family and has resided with the tenant throughout the period of twelve months ending with the tenant's death;

unless, in either case, the tenant was himself a successor, as defined in section 132.

132. **Cases where the tenant is a successor**
- (1) The tenant is himself a successor if—
  - (a) the tenancy vested in him by virtue of section 133 (succession to introductory tenancy),
  - (b) he was a joint tenant and has become the sole tenant,
  - (c) he became the tenant on the tenancy being assigned to him (but subject to subsections (2) and (3)), or
  - (d) he became the tenant on the tenancy being vested in him on the death of the previous tenant.
- (2) A tenant to whom the tenancy was assigned in pursuance of an order under section 24 of the Matrimonial Causes Act 1973 (property adjustment orders in connection with matrimonial proceedings) or section 17(1) of the Matrimonial and Family Proceedings Act 1984 (property adjustment orders after overseas divorce, &c.) is a successor only if the other party to the marriage was a successor.
- (2A) A tenant to whom the tenancy was assigned in pursuance of an order under Part 2 of Schedule 5, or paragraph 9(2) or (3) of Schedule 7, to the Civil Partnership Act 2004 (property adjustment orders in connection with civil partnership proceedings or after overseas dissolution of civil partnership, etc.) is a successor only if the other civil partner was a successor.
- (3) Where within six months of the coming to an end of an introductory tenancy ('the former tenancy') the tenant becomes a tenant under another introductory tenancy, and—
  - (a) the tenant was a successor in relation to the former tenancy, and
  - (b) under the other tenancy either the dwelling-house or the landlord, or both, are the same as under the former tenancy,

  the tenant is also a successor in relation to the other tenancy unless the agreement creating that tenancy otherwise provides.

133. **Succession to introductory tenancy**
- (1) This section applies where a tenant under an introductory tenancy dies.
- (2) Where there is a person qualified to succeed the tenant, the tenancy vests by virtue of this section in that person, or if there is more than one such person in the one to be preferred in accordance with the following rules—
  - (a) the tenant's spouse or civil partner is to be preferred to another member of the tenant's family;
  - (b) of two or more other members of the tenant's family such of them is to be preferred as may be agreed between them or as may, where there is no such agreement, be selected by the landlord.
- (3) Where there is no person qualified to succeed the tenant, the tenancy ceases to be an introductory tenancy—
  - (a) when it is vested or otherwise disposed of in the course of the administration of the tenant's estate, unless the vesting or other disposal is in pursuance of an order made under—
    - (i) section 24 of the Matrimonial Causes Act 1973 (property adjustment orders made in connection with matrimonial proceedings),
    - (ii) section 17(1) of the Matrimonial and Family Proceedings Act 1984 (property adjustment orders after overseas divorce, &c.),
    - (iii) paragraph 1 of Schedule 1 to the Children Act 1989 (orders for financial relief against parents), or
    - (iv) Part 2 of Schedule 5, or paragraph 9(2) or (3) of Schedule 7, to the Civil Partnership Act 2004 (property adjustment orders in connection with civil partnership proceedings or after overseas dissolution of civil partnership, etc.); or
  - (b) when it is known that when the tenancy is so vested or disposed of it will not be in pursuance of such an order.

Assignment

134. **Assignment in general prohibited**
- (1) An introductory tenancy is not capable of being assigned except in the cases mentioned in subsection (2).
- (2) The exceptions are—

(a) an assignment in pursuance of an order made under—

    (i) section 24 of the Matrimonial Causes Act 1973 (property adjustment orders in connection with matrimonial proceedings),

    (ii) section 17(1) of the Matrimonial and Family Proceedings Act 1984 (property adjustment orders after overseas divorce, &c.),

    (iii) paragraph 1 of Schedule 1 to the Children Act 1989 (orders for financial relief against parents), or

    (iv) Part 2 of Schedule 5, or paragraph 9(2) or (3) of Schedule 7, to the Civil Partnership Act 2004 (property adjustment orders in connection with civil partnership proceedings or after overseas dissolution of civil partnership, etc.);

(b) an assignment to a person who would be qualified to succeed the tenant if the tenant died immediately before the assignment.

(3) Subsection (1) also applies to a tenancy which is not an introductory tenancy but would be if the tenant, or where the tenancy is a joint tenancy, at least one of the tenants, were occupying or continuing to occupy the dwelling-house as his only or principal home.

Repairs

135. Right to carry out repairs

The Secretary of State may by regulations under section 96 of the Housing Act 1985 (secure tenants: right to carry out repairs) apply to introductory tenants any provision made under that section in relation to secure tenants.

Provision of information and consultation

136. Provision of information about tenancies

(1) Every local housing authority or housing action trust which lets dwelling-houses under introductory tenancies shall from time to time publish information about its introductory tenancies, in such form as it considers best suited to explain in simple terms, and, so far as it considers it appropriate, the effect of—

    (a) the express terms of its introductory tenancies,

    (b) the provisions of this Chapter, and

    (c) the provisions of sections 11 to 16 of the Landlord and Tenant Act 1985 (landlord's repairing obligations),

and shall ensure that so far as is reasonably practicable the information so published is kept up to date.

(2) The landlord under an introductory tenancy shall supply the tenant with—

    (a) a copy of the information for introductory tenants published by it under subsection (1), and

    (b) a written statement of the terms of the tenancy, so far as they are neither expressed in the lease or written tenancy agreement (if any) nor implied by law;

and the statement required by paragraph (b) shall be supplied on the grant of the tenancy or as soon as practicable afterwards.

137. Consultation on matters of housing management

(1) This section applies in relation to every local housing authority and housing action trust which lets dwelling-houses under introductory tenancies and which is a landlord authority for the purposes of Part IV of the Housing Act 1985 (secure tenancies).

(2) The authority or trust shall maintain such arrangements as it considers appropriate to enable those of its introductory tenants who are likely to be substantially affected by a relevant matter of housing management—

    (a) to be informed of the proposals of the authority or trust in respect of the matter, and

    (b) to make their views known to the authority or trust within a specified period;

and the authority or trust shall, before making a decision on the matter, consider any representations made to it in accordance with those arrangements.

(3) A matter is one of housing management if, in the opinion of the authority or trust concerned, it relates to—

    (a) the management, improvement, maintenance or demolition of dwelling-houses let by the authority or trust under introductory or secure tenancies, or

(b) the provision of services or amenities in connection with such dwelling-houses;

but not so far as it relates to the rent payable under an introductory or secure tenancy or to charges for services or facilities provided by the authority or trust.

(4) A matter is relevant if, in the opinion of the authority or trust concerned, it represents—
  (a) a new programme of maintenance, improvement or demolition, or
  (b) a change in the practice or policy of the authority or trust,

and is likely substantially to affect either its introductory tenants as a whole or a group of them who form a distinct social group or occupy dwelling-houses which constitute a distinct class (whether by reference to the kind of dwelling-house, or the housing estate or other larger area in which they are situated).

(5) In the case of a local housing authority, the reference in subsection (3) to the provision of services or amenities is a reference only to the provision of services or amenities by the authority acting in its capacity as landlord of the dwelling-houses concerned.

(6) The authority or trust shall publish details of the arrangements which it makes under this section, and a copy of the documents published under this subsection shall—
  (a) be made available at its principal office for inspection at all reasonable hours, without charge, by members of the public, and
  (b) be given, on payment of a reasonable fee, to any member of the public who asks for one.

Introductory tenancies that are to become flexible tenancies

137A. Introductory tenancies that are to become flexible tenancies

(1) Where this section applies, a tenancy of a dwelling-house in England that ceases to be an introductory tenancy and becomes a secure tenancy in accordance with this Chapter becomes a flexible tenancy for a term certain.

(2) This section applies if, before entering into or adopting the introductory tenancy, the person who became the landlord under the tenancy served a written notice on the person who was or became the tenant under the tenancy—
  (a) stating that, on ceasing to be an introductory tenancy, the tenancy would become a secure tenancy that would be a flexible tenancy for a term certain of the length specified in the notice,
  (b) specifying a period of at least two years as the length of the term of the tenancy, and
  (c) setting out the other express terms of the tenancy.

(3) The length of the term of a flexible tenancy that becomes such a tenancy by virtue of this section is that specified in the notice under subsection (2).

(4) The other express terms of the flexible tenancy are those set out in the notice, so far as those terms are compatible with the statutory provisions relating to flexible tenancies; and in this subsection 'statutory provision' means any provision made by or under an Act.

CHAPTER 1A
DEMOTED TENANCIES

General provisions

143A. Demoted tenancies

(1) This section applies to a periodic tenancy of a dwelling-house if each of the following conditions is satisfied.

(2) The first condition is that the landlord is either a local housing authority or a housing action trust.

(3) The second condition is that the tenant condition in section 81 of the Housing Act 1985 is satisfied.

(4) The third condition is that the tenancy is created by virtue of a demotion order under section 82A of that Act.

(5) In this Chapter—
  (a) a tenancy to which this section applies is referred to as a demoted tenancy;
  (b) references to demoted tenants must be construed accordingly.

143B. Duration of demoted tenancy

(1) A demoted tenancy becomes a secure tenancy at the end of the period of one year (the demotion period) starting with the day the demotion order takes effect; but this is subject to subsections (2) to (5).

(2) A tenancy ceases to be a demoted tenancy if any of the following paragraphs applies—

(a) either of the first or second conditions in section 143A ceases to be satisfied;

(b) the demotion order is quashed;

(c) the tenant dies and no one is entitled to succeed to the tenancy.

(3) If at any time before the end of the demotion period the landlord serves a notice of proceedings for possession of the dwelling-house subsection (4) applies.

(4) The tenancy continues as a demoted tenancy until the end of the demotion period or (if later) until any of the following occurs—

(a) the notice of proceedings is withdrawn by the landlord;

(b) the proceedings are determined in favour of the tenant;

(c) the period of 6 months beginning with the date on which the notice is served ends and no proceedings for possession have been brought.

(5) A tenancy does not come to an end merely because it ceases to be a demoted tenancy.

Proceedings for possession

143D. Proceedings for possession

(1) The landlord may only bring a demoted tenancy to an end by obtaining—

(a) an order of the court for the possession of the dwelling-house, and

(b) the execution of the order.

(1A) In such a case, the tenancy ends when the order is executed.

(2) The court must make an order for possession unless it thinks that the procedure under sections 143E and 143F has not been followed.

143E. Notice of proceedings for possession

(1) Proceedings for possession of a dwelling-house let under a demoted tenancy must not be brought unless the landlord has served on the tenant a notice of proceedings under this section.

(2) The notice must—

(a) state that the court will be asked to make an order for the possession of the dwelling-house;

(b) set out the reasons for the landlord's decision to apply for the order;

(c) specify the date after which proceedings for the possession of the dwelling-house may be begun;

(d) inform the tenant of his right to request a review of the landlord's decision and of the time within which the request must be made.

(3) The date specified under subsection (2)(c) must not be earlier than the date on which the tenancy could (apart from this Chapter) be brought to an end by notice to quit given by the landlord on the same date as the notice of proceedings.

(4) The court must not entertain proceedings begun on or before the date specified under subsection (2)(c).

(5) The notice must also inform the tenant that if he needs help or advice—

(a) about the notice, or

(b) about what to do about the notice,

he must take the notice immediately to a Citizen's Advice Bureau, a housing aid centre, a law centre or a solicitor.

143F. Review of decision to seek possession

(1) Before the end of the period of 14 days beginning with the date of service of a notice for possession of a dwelling-house let under a demoted tenancy the tenant may request the landlord to review its decision to seek an order for possession.

(2) If a request is made in accordance with subsection (1) the landlord must review the decision.

(3) The Secretary of State may by regulations make provision as to the procedure to be followed in connection with a review under this section.

(4) The regulations may include provision—
   (a) requiring the decision on review to be made by a person of appropriate seniority who was not involved in the original decision;
   (b) as to the circumstances in which the tenant is entitled to an oral hearing, and whether and by whom he may be represented at the hearing.

(5) The landlord must notify the tenant—
   (a) of the decision on the review;
   (b) of the reasons for the decision.

(6) The review must be carried out and notice given under subsection (5) before the date specified in the notice of proceedings as the date after which proceedings for possession of the dwelling-house may be begun.

CHAPTER III

INJUNCTIONS AGAINST ANTI-SOCIAL BEHAVIOUR

153A. Anti-social behaviour injunction

(1) In this section—

'anti-social behaviour injunction' means an injunction that prohibits the person in respect of whom it is granted from engaging in housing-related anti-social conduct of a kind specified in the injunction;

'anti-social conduct' means conduct capable of causing nuisance or annoyance to some person (who need not be a particular identified person);

'conduct' means conduct anywhere;

'housing-related means directly or indirectly relating to or affecting the housing management functions of a relevant landlord.

(2) The court on the application of a relevant landlord may grant an anti-social behaviour injunction if the condition in subsection (3) is satisfied.

(3) The condition is that the person against whom the injunction is sought is engaging, has engaged or threatens to engage in housing-related conduct capable of causing a nuisance or annoyance to—
   (a) a person with a right (of whatever description) to reside in or occupy housing accommodation owned or managed by a relevant landlord,
   (b) a person with a right (of whatever description) to reside in or occupy other housing accommodation in the neighbourhood of housing accommodation mentioned in paragraph (a),
   (c) a person engaged in lawful activity in, or in the neighbourhood of, housing accommodation mentioned in paragraph (a), or
   (d) a person employed (whether or not by a relevant landlord) in connection with the exercise of a relevant landlord's housing management functions.

(4) Without prejudice to the generality of the court's power under subsection (2), a kind of conduct may be described in an anti-social behaviour injunction by reference to a person or persons and, if it is, may (in particular) be described by reference—
   (a) to persons generally,
   (b) to persons of a description specified in the injunction, or
   (c) to persons, or a person, specified in the injunction.

153B. Injunction against unlawful use of premises

(1) This section applies to conduct which consists of or involves using or threatening to use housing accommodation owned or managed by a relevant landlord for an unlawful purpose.

(2) The court on the application of the relevant landlord may grant an injunction prohibiting the person in respect of whom the injunction is granted from engaging in conduct to which this section applies.

153C. Injunctions: exclusion order and power of arrest

(1) This section applies if the court grants an injunction under subsection (2) of section 153A or 153B and it thinks that either of the following paragraphs applies—
   (a) the conduct consists of or includes the use or threatened use of violence;

(b) there is a significant risk of harm to a person mentioned in any of paragraphs (a) to (d) of section 153A(3).

(2) The court may include in the injunction a provision prohibiting the person in respect of whom it is granted from entering or being in—

(a) any premises specified in the injunction;

(b) any area specified in the injunction.

(3) The court may attach a power of arrest to any provision of the injunction.

153D. Injunction against breach of tenancy agreement

(1) This section applies if a relevant landlord applies for an injunction against a tenant in respect of the breach or anticipated breach of a tenancy agreement on the grounds that the tenant—

(a) is engaging or threatening to engage in conduct that is capable of causing nuisance or annoyance to any person, or

(b) is allowing, inciting or encouraging any other person to engage or threaten to engage in such conduct.

(2) The court may proceed under subsection (3) or (4) if it is satisfied—

(a) that the conduct includes the use or threatened use of violence, or

(b) that there is a significant risk of harm to any person.

(3) The court may include in the injunction a provision prohibiting the person in respect of whom it is granted from entering or being in—

(a) any premises specified in the injunction;

(b) any area specified in the injunction.

(4) The court may attach a power of arrest to any provision of the injunction.

(5) Tenancy agreement includes any agreement for the occupation of residential accommodation owned or managed by a relevant landlord.

153E. Injunctions: supplementary

(1) This section applies for the purposes of sections 153A to 153D.

(2) An injunction may—

(a) be made for a specified period or until varied or discharged;

(b) have the effect of excluding a person from his normal place of residence.

(3) An injunction may be varied or discharged by the court on an application by—

(a) the person in respect of whom it is made;

(b) the relevant landlord.

(4) If the court thinks it just and convenient it may grant or vary an injunction without the respondent having been given such notice as is otherwise required by rules of court.

(5) If the court acts under subsection (4) it must give the person against whom the injunction is made an opportunity to make representations in relation to the injunction as soon as it is practicable for him to do so.

(6) The court is the High Court or a county court.

(7) Each of the following is a relevant landlord—

(a) a housing action trust;

(b) a local authority (within the meaning of the Housing Act 1985);

(ba) a non-profit registered provider of social housing;

(c) a registered social landlord.

(8) A charitable housing trust which does not fall within subsection (7)(ba) or (c) is also a relevant landlord for the purposes of section 153D.

(9) Housing accommodation includes—

(a) flats, lodging-houses and hostels;

(b) any yard, garden, outhouses and appurtenances belonging to the accommodation or usually enjoyed with it;

(c) in relation to a neighbourhood, the whole of the housing accommodation owned or managed by a relevant landlord in the neighbourhood and any common areas used in connection with the accommodation.

(10) A landlord owns housing accommodation if either of the following paragraphs applies to him—

(a) he is a person (other than a mortgagee not in possession) who is for the time being entitled to dispose of the fee simple in the premises, whether in possession or in reversion;

(b) he is a person who holds or is entitled to the rents and profits of the premises under a lease which (when granted) was for a term of not less than three years.

(11) The housing management functions of a relevant landlord include—

(a) functions conferred by or under any enactment;

(b) the powers and duties of the landlord as the holder of an estate or interest in housing accommodation.

(12) Harm includes serious ill-treatment or abuse (whether physical or not).

154. Powers of arrest: ex-parte applications for injunctions

(1) In determining whether to exercise its power under section 153C(3) or 153D(4) to attach a power of arrest to an injunction which it intends to grant on an ex-parte application, the High Court or a county court shall have regard to all the circumstances including—

(a) whether it is likely that the applicant will be deterred or prevented from seeking the exercise of the power if the power is not exercised immediately, and

(b) whether there is reason to believe that the respondent is aware of the proceedings for the injunction but is deliberately evading service and that the applicant or any person of a description mentioned in any of paragraphs (a) to (d) of section 153A(3) (as the case may be) will be seriously prejudiced if the decision as to whether to exercise the power were delayed until substituted service is effected.

(2) Where the court exercises its power as mentioned in subsection (1), it shall afford the respondent an opportunity to make representations relating to the exercise of the power as soon as just and convenient at a hearing of which notice has been given to all the parties in accordance with rules of court.

PART VI
ALLOCATION OF HOUSING ACCOMMODATION

Introductory

159. Allocation of housing accommodation

(1) A local housing authority shall comply with the provisions of this Part in allocating housing accommodation.

(2) For the purposes of this Part a local housing authority allocate housing accommodation when they—

(a) select a person to be a secure or introductory tenant of housing accommodation held by them,

(b) nominate a person to be a secure or introductory tenant of housing accommodation held by another person, or

(c) nominate a person to be an assured tenant of housing accommodation held by a private registered provider of social housing or a registered social landlord.

(3) The reference in subsection (2)(a) to selecting a person to be a secure tenant includes deciding to exercise any power to notify an existing tenant or licensee that his tenancy or licence is to be a secure tenancy.

(4) The references in subsection (2)(b) and (c) to nominating a person include nominating a person in pursuance of any arrangements (whether legally enforceable or not) to require that housing accommodation, or a specified amount of housing accommodation, is made available to a person or one of a number of persons nominated by the authority.

(4A) Subject to subsection (4B), the provisions of this Part do not apply to an allocation of housing accommodation by a local housing authority in England to a person who is already—

(a) a secure or introductory tenant, or

(b) an assured tenant of housing accommodation held by a private registered provider of social housing or a registered social landlord.

(4B) The provisions of this Part apply to an allocation of housing accommodation by a local housing authority in England to a person who falls within subsection (4A)(a) or (b) if—

(a) the allocation involves a transfer of housing accommodation for that person,

(b) the application for the transfer is made by that person, and

(c) the authority is satisfied that the person is to be given reasonable preference under section 166A(3).

(5) The provisions of this Part do not apply to an allocation of housing accommodation by a local housing authority in Wales to a person who is already a secure or introductory tenant unless the allocation involves a transfer of housing accommodation for that person and is made on his application.

(7) Subject to the provisions of this Part, a local housing authority may allocate housing accommodation in such manner as they consider appropriate.

Eligibility for allocation of housing accommodation

160ZA. Allocation only to eligible and qualifying persons: England

(1) A local housing authority in England shall not allocate housing accommodation--

(a) to a person from abroad who is ineligible for an allocation of housing accommodation by virtue of subsection (2) or (4), or

(b) to two or more persons jointly if any of them is a person mentioned in paragraph (a).

(2) A person subject to immigration control within the meaning of the Asylum and Immigration Act 1996 is ineligible for an allocation of housing accommodation by a local housing authority in England unless he is of a class prescribed by regulations made by the Secretary of State.

(3) No person who is excluded from entitlement to universal credit or housing benefit by section 115 of the Immigration and Asylum Act 1999 (exclusion from benefits) shall be included in any class prescribed under subsection (2).

(4) The Secretary of State may by regulations prescribe other classes of persons from abroad who are ineligible to be allocated housing accommodation by local housing authorities in England.

(5) Nothing in subsection (2) or (4) affects the eligibility of a person who falls within section 159(4B).

(6) Except as provided by subsection (1), a person may be allocated housing accommodation by a local housing authority in England (whether on his application or otherwise) if that person—

(a) is a qualifying person within the meaning of subsection (7), or

(b) is one of two or more persons who apply for accommodation jointly, and one or more of the other persons is a qualifying person within the meaning of subsection (7).

(7) Subject to subsections (2) and (4) and any regulations under subsection (8), a local housing authority may decide what classes of persons are, or are not, qualifying persons.

(8) The Secretary of State may by regulations—

(a) prescribe classes of persons who are, or are not, to be treated as qualifying persons by local housing authorities in England, and

(b) prescribe criteria that may not be used by local housing authorities in England in deciding what classes of persons are not qualifying persons.

(9) If a local housing authority in England decide that an applicant for housing accommodation—

(a) is ineligible for an allocation by them by virtue of subsection (2) or (4), or

(b) is not a qualifying person,

they shall notify the applicant of their decision and the grounds for it.

(10) That notice shall be given in writing and, if not received by the applicant, shall be treated as having been given if it is made available at the authority's office for a reasonable period for collection by him or on his behalf.

(11) A person who is not being treated as a qualifying person may (if he considers that he should be treated as a qualifying person) make a fresh application to the authority for an allocation of housing accommodation by them.

160A. Allocation only to eligible persons: Wales

(1) A local housing authority in Wales shall not allocate housing accommodation—

(a) to a person from abroad who is ineligible for an allocation of housing accommodation by virtue of subsection (3) or (5);

(b) to a person who the authority have decided is to be treated as ineligible for such an allocation by virtue of subsection (7); or

(c) to two or more persons jointly if any of them is a person mentioned in paragraph (a) or (b).

(2) Except as provided by subsection (1), any person may be allocated housing accommodation by a local housing authority in Wales (whether on his application or otherwise).

(3) A person subject to immigration control within the meaning of the Asylum and Immigration Act 1996 is (subject to subsection (6)) ineligible for an allocation of housing accommodation by a local housing authority in Wales unless he is of a class prescribed by regulations made by the Secretary of State.

(4) No person who is excluded from entitlement to universal credit or housing benefit by section 115 of the Immigration and Asylum Act 1999 (exclusion from benefits) shall be included in any class prescribed under subsection (3).

(5) The Secretary of State may by regulations prescribe other classes of persons from abroad who are (subject to subsection (6)) ineligible for an allocation of housing accommodation, either in relation to local housing authorities in Wales generally or any particular local housing authority in Wales.

(6) Nothing in subsection (3) or (5) affects the eligibility of a person who is already—

(a) a secure or introductory tenant;

(b) an assured tenant of housing accommodation allocated to him by a local housing authority in Wales.

(7) A local housing authority in Wales may decide that an applicant is to be treated as ineligible for an allocation of housing accommodation by them if they are satisfied that—

(a) he, or a member of his household, has been guilty of unacceptable behaviour serious enough to make him unsuitable to be a tenant of the authority; and

(b) in the circumstances at the time his application is considered, he is unsuitable to be a tenant of the authority by reason of that behaviour.

(8) The only behaviour which may be regarded by the authority as unacceptable for the purposes of subsection (7)(a) is—

(a) behaviour of the person concerned which would (if he were a secure tenant of the authority) entitle the authority to a possession order under section 84 of the Housing Act 1985 (c. 68) on any ground mentioned in Part 1 of Schedule 2 to that Act (other than ground 8); or

(b) behaviour of a member of his household which would (if he were a person residing with a secure tenant of the authority) entitle the authority to such a possession order.

(9) If a local housing authority in Wales decide that an applicant for housing accommodation—

(a) is ineligible for an allocation by them by virtue of subsection (3) or (5); or

(b) is to be treated as ineligible for such an allocation by virtue of subsection (7),

they shall notify the applicant of their decision and the grounds for it.

(10) That notice shall be given in writing and, if not received by the applicant, shall be treated as having been given if it is made available at the authority's office for a reasonable period for collection by him or on his behalf.

(11) A person who is being treated by a local housing authority in Wales as ineligible by virtue of subsection (7) may (if he considers that he should no longer be treated as ineligible by the authority) make a fresh application to the authority for an allocation of housing accommodation by them.

Allocation schemes

166A. Allocation in accordance with allocation scheme: England

(1) Every local housing authority in England must have a scheme (their 'allocation scheme') for determining priorities, and as to the procedure to be followed, in allocating housing accommodation.

For this purpose 'procedure' includes all aspects of the allocation process, including the persons or descriptions of persons by whom decisions are taken.

(2) The scheme must include a statement of the authority's policy on offering people who are to be allocated housing accommodation—

(a) a choice of housing accommodation; or

(b) the opportunity to express preferences about the housing accommodation to be allocated to them.

(3) As regards priorities, the scheme shall, subject to subsection (4), be framed so as to secure that reasonable preference is given to—

(a) people who are homeless (within the meaning of Part 7);

(b) people who are owed a duty by any local housing authority under section 190(2), 193(2) or 195(2) (or under section 65(2) or 68(2) of the Housing Act 1985) or who are occupying accommodation secured by any such authority under section 192(3);

(c) people occupying insanitary or overcrowded housing or otherwise living in unsatisfactory housing conditions;

(d) people who need to move on medical or welfare grounds (including any grounds relating to a disability); and

(e) people who need to move to a particular locality in the district of the authority, where failure to meet that need would cause hardship (to themselves or to others).

The scheme may also be framed so as to give additional preference to particular descriptions of people within one or more of paragraphs (a) to (e) (being descriptions of people with urgent housing needs).

The scheme must be framed so as to give additional preference to a person with urgent housing needs who falls within one or more of paragraphs (a) to (e) and who—

(i) is serving in the regular forces and is suffering from a serious injury, illness or disability which is attributable (wholly or partly) to the person's service,

(ii) formerly served in the regular forces,

(iii) has recently ceased, or will cease to be entitled, to reside in accommodation provided by the Ministry of Defence following the death of that person's spouse or civil partner who has served in the regular forces and whose death was attributable (wholly or partly) to that service, or

(iv) is serving or has served in the reserve forces and is suffering from a serious injury, illness or disability which is attributable (wholly or partly) to the person's service.

For this purpose 'the regular forces' and 'the reserve forces' have the meanings given by section 374 of the Armed Forces Act 2006.

(4) People are to be disregarded for the purposes of subsection (3) if they would not have fallen within paragraph (a) or (b) of that subsection without the local housing authority having had regard to a restricted person (within the meaning of Part 7).

(5) The scheme may contain provision for determining priorities in allocating housing accommodation to people within subsection (3); and the factors which the scheme may allow to be taken into account include—

(a) the financial resources available to a person to meet his housing costs;

(b) any behaviour of a person (or of a member of his household) which affects his suitability to be a tenant;

(c) any local connection (within the meaning of section 199) which exists between a person and the authority's district.

(6) Subject to subsection (3), the scheme may contain provision about the allocation of particular housing accommodation—

(a) to a person who makes a specific application for that accommodation;

(b) to persons of a particular description (whether or not they are within subsection (3)).

(7) The Secretary of State may by regulations—

(a) specify further descriptions of people to whom preference is to be given as mentioned in subsection (3), or

(b) amend or repeal any part of subsection (3).

(8) The Secretary of State may by regulations specify factors which a local housing authority in England must not take into account in allocating housing accommodation.

(9) The scheme must be framed so as to secure that an applicant for an allocation of housing accommodation—

(a) has the right to request such general information as will enable him to assess—

(i) how his application is likely to be treated under the scheme (including in particular whether he is likely to be regarded as a member of a group of people who are to be given preference by virtue of subsection (3)); and

(ii) whether housing accommodation appropriate to his needs is likely to be made available to him and, if so, how long it is likely to be before such accommodation becomes available for allocation to him;

(b) has the right to request the authority to inform him of any decision about the facts of his case which is likely to be, or has been, taken into account in considering whether to allocate housing accommodation to him; and

(c) has the right to request a review of a decision mentioned in paragraph (b), or in section 160ZA(9), and to be informed of the decision on the review and the grounds for it.

(10) As regards the procedure to be followed, the scheme must be framed in accordance with such principles as the Secretary of State may prescribe by regulations.

(11) Subject to the above provisions, and to any regulations made under them, the authority may decide on what principles the scheme is to be framed.

(12) A local housing authority in England must, in preparing or modifying their allocation scheme, have regard to—

(a) their current homelessness strategy under section 1 of the Homelessness Act 2002,

(b) their current tenancy strategy under section 150 of the Localism Act 2011, and

(c) in the case of an authority that is a London borough council, the London housing strategy.

(13) Before adopting an allocation scheme, or making an alteration to their scheme reflecting a major change of policy, a local housing authority in England must—

(a) send a copy of the draft scheme, or proposed alteration, to every private registered provider of social housing and registered social landlord with which they have nomination arrangements (see section 159(4)), and

(b) afford those persons a reasonable opportunity to comment on the proposals.

(14) A local housing authority in England shall not allocate housing accommodation except in accordance with their allocation scheme.

167. **Allocation in accordance with allocation scheme: Wales**

(1) Every local housing authority in Wales shall have a scheme (their 'allocation scheme') for determining priorities, and as to the procedure to be followed, in allocating housing accommodation.

For this purpose 'procedure' includes all aspects of the allocation process, including the persons or descriptions of persons by whom decisions are to be taken.

(1A) The scheme shall include a statement of the authority's policy on offering people who are to be allocated housing accommodation—

(a) a choice of housing accommodation; or

(b) the opportunity to express preferences about the housing accommodation to be allocated to them.

(2) As regards priorities, the scheme shall, subject to subsection (2ZA), be framed so as to secure that reasonable preference is given to—

(a) people who are homeless (within the meaning of Part 7);

(b) people who are owed a duty by any local housing authority under section 190(2), 193(2) or 195(2) (or under section 65(2) or 68(2) of the Housing Act 1985) or who are occupying accommodation secured by any such authority under section 192(3);

(c) people occupying insanitary or overcrowded housing or otherwise living in unsatisfactory housing conditions;

(d) people who need to move on medical or welfare grounds (including grounds relating to a disability); and

(e) people who need to move to a particular locality in the district of the authority, where failure to meet that need would cause hardship (to themselves or to others).

The scheme may also be framed so as to give additional preference to particular descriptions of people within this subsection (being descriptions of people with urgent housing needs).

(2ZA) People are to be disregarded for the purposes of subsection (2) if they would not have fallen within paragraph (a) or (b) of that subsection without the local housing authority having had regard to a restricted person (within the meaning of Part 7).

(2A) The scheme may contain provision for determining priorities in allocating housing accommodation to people within subsection (2); and the factors which the scheme may allow to be taken into account include—

(a) the financial resources available to a person to meet his housing costs;

(b) any behaviour of a person (or of a member of his household) which affects his suitability to be a tenant;

(c) any local connection (within the meaning of section 199) which exists between a person and the authority's district.

(2B) Nothing in subsection (2) requires the scheme to provide for any preference to be given to people the authority have decided are people to whom subsection (2C) applies.

(2C) This subsection applies to a person if the authority are satisfied that—

(a) he, or a member of his household, has been guilty of unacceptable behaviour serious enough to make him unsuitable to be a tenant of the authority; and

(b) in the circumstances at the time his case is considered, he deserves by reason of that behaviour not to be treated as a member of a group of people who are to be given preference by virtue of subsection (2).

(2D) Subsection (8) of section 160A applies for the purposes of subsection (2C)(a) above as it applies for the purposes of subsection (7)(a) of that section.

(2E) Subject to subsection (2), the scheme may contain provision about the allocation of particular housing accommodation—

(a) to a person who makes a specific application for that accommodation;

(b) to persons of a particular description (whether or not they are within subsection (2)).

(3) The Secretary of State may by regulations—

(a) specify further descriptions of people to whom preference is to be given as mentioned in subsection (2), or

(b) amend or repeal any part of subsection (2).

(4) The Secretary of State may by regulations specify factors which a local housing authority in Wales shall not take into account in allocating housing accommodation.

(4A) The scheme shall be framed so as to secure that an applicant for an allocation of housing accommodation—

(a) has the right to request such general information as will enable him to assess—

(i) how his application is likely to be treated under the scheme (including in particular whether he is likely to be regarded as a member of a group of people who are to be given preference by virtue of subsection (2)); and

(ii) whether housing accommodation appropriate to his needs is likely to be made available to him and, if so, how long it is likely to be before such accommodation becomes available for allocation to him;

(b) is notified in writing of any decision that he is a person to whom subsection (2C) applies and the grounds for it;

(c) has the right to request the authority to inform him of any decision about the facts of his case which is likely to be, or has been, taken into account in considering whether to allocate housing accommodation to him; and

(d) has the right to request a review of a decision mentioned in paragraph (b) or (c), or in section 160A(9), and to be informed of the decision on the review and the grounds for it.

(5) As regards the procedure to be followed, the scheme shall be framed in accordance with such principles as the Secretary of State may prescribe by regulations.

(6) Subject to the above provisions, and to any regulations made under them, the authority may decide on what principles the scheme is to be framed.

(7) Before adopting an allocation scheme, or making an alteration to their scheme reflecting a major change of policy, a local housing authority in Wales shall—

(a) send a copy of the draft scheme, or proposed alteration, to every private registered provider of social housing and registered social landlord with which they have nomination arrangements (see section 159(4)), and

(b) afford those persons a reasonable opportunity to comment on the proposals.

(8) A local housing authority in Wales shall not allocate housing accommodation except in accordance with their allocation scheme.

Supplementary

170. Co-operation between certain social landlords and local housing authorities

Where a local housing authority so request, a private registered provider of social housing or registered social landlord shall co-operate to such extent as is reasonable in the circumstances in offering accommodation to people with priority under the authority's allocation scheme.

PART VII
HOMELESSNESS

Homelessness and threatened homelessness

175. Homelessness and threatened homelessness

(1) A person is homeless if he has no accommodation available for his occupation, in the United Kingdom or elsewhere, which he—

    (a) is entitled to occupy by virtue of an interest in it or by virtue of an order of a court,

    (b) has an express or implied licence to occupy, or

    (c) occupies as a residence by virtue of any enactment or rule of law giving him the right to remain in occupation or restricting the right of another person to recover possession.

(2) A person is also homeless if he has accommodation but—

    (a) he cannot secure entry to it, or

    (b) it consists of a moveable structure, vehicle or vessel designed or adapted for human habitation and there is no place where he is entitled or permitted both to place it and to reside in it.

(3) A person shall not be treated as having accommodation unless it is accommodation which it would be reasonable for him to continue to occupy.

(4) A person is threatened with homelessness if it is likely that he will become homeless within 28 days.

176. Meaning of accommodation available for occupation

Accommodation shall be regarded as available for a person's occupation only if it is available for occupation by him together with—

(a) any other person who normally resides with him as a member of his family, or

(b) any other person who might reasonably be expected to reside with him.

References in this Part to securing that accommodation is available for a person's occupation shall be construed accordingly.

177. Whether it is reasonable to continue to occupy accommodation

(1) It is not reasonable for a person to continue to occupy accommodation if it is probable that this will lead to domestic violence or other violence against him, or against—

    (a) a person who normally resides with him as a member of his family, or

    (b) any other person who might reasonably be expected to reside with him.

(1A) For this purpose 'violence' means—

    (a) violence from another person; or

    (b) threats of violence from another person which are likely to be carried out;

and violence is 'domestic violence' if it is from a person who is associated with the victim.

(2) In determining whether it would be, or would have been, reasonable for a person to continue to occupy accommodation, regard may be had to the general circumstances prevailing in relation to housing in the district of the local housing authority to whom he has applied for accommodation or for assistance in obtaining accommodation.

(3) The Secretary of State may by order specify—

    (a) other circumstances in which it is to be regarded as reasonable or not reasonable for a person to continue to occupy accommodation, and

    (b) other matters to be taken into account or disregarded in determining whether it would be, or would have been, reasonable for a person to continue to occupy accommodation.

182. Guidance by the Secretary of State

(1) In the exercise of their functions relating to homelessness and the prevention of homelessness, a local housing authority or social services authority shall have regard to such guidance as may from time to time be given by the Secretary of State.

(2) The Secretary of State may give guidance either generally or to specified descriptions of authorities.

Application for assistance in case of homelessness or threatened homelessness

183. Application for assistance

(1) The following provisions of this Part apply where a person applies to a local housing authority for accommodation, or for assistance in obtaining accommodation, and the authority have reason to believe that he is or may be homeless or threatened with homelessness.

(2) In this Part—

'applicant' means a person making such an application,

'assistance under this Part' means the benefit of any function under the following provisions of this Part relating to accommodation or assistance in obtaining accommodation, and

'eligible for assistance' means not excluded from such assistance by section 185 (persons from abroad not eligible for housing assistance) or section 186 (asylum seekers and their dependants).

(3) Nothing in this section or the following provisions of this Part affects a person's entitlement to advice and information under section 179 (duty to provide advisory services).

184. Inquiry into cases of homelessness or threatened homelessness

(1) If the local housing authority have reason to believe that an applicant may be homeless or threatened with homelessness, they shall make such inquiries as are necessary to satisfy themselves—

(a) whether he is eligible for assistance, and

(b) if so, whether any duty, and if so what duty, is owed to him under the following provisions of this Part.

(2) They may also make inquiries whether he has a local connection with the district of another local housing authority in England, Wales or Scotland.

(3) On completing their inquiries the authority shall notify the applicant of their decision and, so far as any issue is decided against his interests, inform him of the reasons for their decision.

(3A) If the authority decide that a duty is owed to the applicant under section 193(2) or 195(2) but would not have done so without having had regard to a restricted person, the notice under subsection (3) must also—

(a) inform the applicant that their decision was reached on that basis,

(b) include the name of the restricted person,

(c) explain why the person is a restricted person, and

(d) explain the effect of section 193(7AD) or (as the case may be) section 195(4A).

(4) If the authority have notified or intend to notify another local housing authority under section 198 (referral of cases), they shall at the same time notify the applicant of that decision and inform him of the reasons for it.

(5) A notice under subsection (3) or (4) shall also inform the applicant of his right to request a review of the decision and of the time within which such a request must be made (see section 202).

(6) Notice required to be given to a person under this section shall be given in writing and, if not received by him, shall be treated as having been given to him if it is made available at the authority's office for a reasonable period for collection by him or on his behalf.

(7) In this Part 'a restricted person' means a person—

(a) who is not eligible for assistance under this Part,

(b) who is subject to immigration control within the meaning of the Asylum and Immigration Act 1996, and

(c) either—

(i) who does not have leave to enter or remain in the United Kingdom, or

(ii) whose leave to enter or remain in the United Kingdom is subject to a condition to maintain and accommodate himself, and any dependants, without recourse to public funds.

Eligibility for assistance

185. Persons from abroad not eligible for housing assistance

(1) A person is not eligible for assistance under this Part if he is a person from abroad who is ineligible for housing assistance.

(2) A person who is subject to immigration control within the meaning of the Asylum and Immigration Act 1996 is not eligible for housing assistance unless he is of a class prescribed by regulations made by the Secretary of State.

(2A) No person who is excluded from entitlement to universal credit or housing benefit by section 115 of the Immigration and Asylum Act 1999 (exclusion from benefits) shall be included in any class prescribed under subsection (2).

(3) The Secretary of State may make provision by regulations as to other descriptions of persons who are to be treated for the purposes of this Part as persons from abroad who are ineligible for housing assistance.

(4) A person from abroad who is not eligible for housing assistance shall be disregarded in determining for the purposes of this Part whether a person falling within subsection (5)—

(a) is homeless or threatened with homelessness, or

(b) has a priority need for accommodation.

(5) A person falls within this subsection if the person—

(a) falls within a class prescribed by regulations made under subsection (2); but

(b) is not a national of an EEA State or Switzerland.

186. Asylum-seekers and their dependants

(1) An asylum-seeker, or a dependant of an asylum-seeker who is not by virtue of section 185 a person from abroad who is ineligible for housing assistance, is not eligible for assistance under this Part if he has any accommodation in the United Kingdom, however temporary, available for his occupation.

(2) For the purposes of this section a person who makes a claim for asylum—

(a) becomes an asylum-seeker at the time when his claim is recorded by the Secretary of State as having been made, and

(b) ceases to be an asylum-seeker at the time when his claim is recorded by the Secretary of State as having been finally determined or abandoned.

(3) For the purposes of this section a person—

(a) becomes a dependant of an asylum-seeker at the time when he is recorded by the Secretary of State as being a dependant of the asylum-seeker, and

(b) ceases to be a dependant of an asylum-seeker at the time when the person whose dependant he is ceases to be an asylum-seeker or, if it is earlier, at the time when he is recorded by the Secretary of State as ceasing to be a dependant of the asylum-seeker.

(4) In relation to an asylum-seeker, 'dependant' means a person—

(a) who is his spouse or a child of his under the age of eighteen, and

(b) who has neither a right of abode in the United Kingdom nor indefinite leave under the Immigration Act 1971 to enter or remain in the United Kingdom.

(5) In this section a 'claim for asylum' means a claim made by a person that it would be contrary to the United Kingdom's obligations under the Convention relating to the Status of Refugees done at Geneva on 28th July 1951 and the Protocol to that Convention for him to be removed from, or required to leave, the United Kingdom.

Interim duty to accommodate

188. Interim duty to accommodate in case of apparent priority need

(1) If the local housing authority have reason to believe that an applicant may be homeless, eligible for assistance and have a priority need, they shall secure that accommodation is available for his occupation pending a decision as to the duty (if any) owed to him under the following provisions of this Part.

(1A) But if the local housing authority have reason to believe that the duty under section 193(2) may apply in relation to an applicant in the circumstances referred to in section 195A(1), they shall secure that accommodation is available for the applicant's occupation pending a decision of the kind referred to in subsection (1) regardless of whether the applicant has a priority need.

(2) The duty under this section arises irrespective of any possibility of the referral of the applicant's case to another local housing authority (see sections 198 to 200).

(3) The duty ceases when the authority's decision is notified to the applicant, even if the applicant requests a review of the decision (see section 202).

The authority may secure that accommodation is available for the applicant's occupation pending a decision on a review.

189. Priority need for accommodation

(1) The following have a priority need for accommodation—

(a) a pregnant woman or a person with whom she resides or might reasonably be expected to reside;

(b) a person with whom dependent children reside or might reasonably be expected to reside;

(c) a person who is vulnerable as a result of old age, mental illness or handicap or physical disability or other special reason, or with whom such a person resides or might reasonably be expected to reside;

(d) a person who is homeless or threatened with homelessness as a result of an emergency such as flood, fire or other disaster.

(2) The Secretary of State may by order—

(a) specify further descriptions of persons as having a priority need for accommodation, and

(b) amend or repeal any part of subsection (1).

(3) Before making such an order the Secretary of State shall consult such associations representing relevant authorities, and such other persons, as he considers appropriate.

(4) No such order shall be made unless a draft of it has been approved by resolution of each House of Parliament.

Duties to persons found to be homeless or threatened with homelessness

190. Duties to persons becoming homeless intentionally

(1) This section applies where the local housing authority are satisfied that an applicant is homeless and is eligible for assistance but are also satisfied that he became homeless intentionally.

(2) If the authority are satisfied that the applicant has a priority need, they shall—

(a) secure that accommodation is available for his occupation for such period as they consider will give him a reasonable opportunity of securing accommodation for his occupation, and

(b) provide him with (or secure that he is provided with) advice and assistance in any attempts he may make to secure that accommodation becomes available for his occupation.

(3) If they are not satisfied that he has a priority need, they shall provide him with (or secure that he is provided with) advice and assistance in any attempts he may make to secure that accommodation becomes available for his occupation.

(4) The applicant's housing needs shall be assessed before advice and assistance is provided under subsection (2)(b) or (3).

(5) The advice and assistance provided under subsection (2)(b) or (3) must include information about the likely availability in the authority's district of types of accommodation appropriate to the applicant's housing needs (including, in particular, the location and sources of such types of accommodation).

191. Becoming homeless intentionally

(1) A person becomes homeless intentionally if he deliberately does or fails to do anything in consequence of which he ceases to occupy accommodation which is available for his occupation and which it would have been reasonable for him to continue to occupy.

(2) For the purposes of subsection (1) an act or omission in good faith on the part of a person who was unaware of any relevant fact shall not be treated as deliberate.

(3) A person shall be treated as becoming homeless intentionally if—

(a) he enters into an arrangement under which he is required to cease to occupy accommodation which it would have been reasonable for him to continue to occupy, and

(b) the purpose of the arrangement is to enable him to become entitled to assistance under this Part,

and there is no other good reason why he is homeless.

192. Duty to persons not in priority need who are not homeless intentionally

(1) This section applies where the local housing authority—
　(a) are satisfied that an applicant is homeless and eligible for assistance, and
　(b) are not satisfied that he became homeless intentionally,
but are not satisfied that he has a priority need.

(2) The authority shall provide the applicant with (or secure that he is provided with) advice and assistance in any attempts he may make to secure that accommodation becomes available for his occupation.

(3) The authority may secure that accommodation is available for occupation by the applicant.

(4) The applicant's housing needs shall be assessed before advice and assistance is provided under subsection (2).

(5) The advice and assistance provided under subsection (2) must include information about the likely availability in the authority's district of types of accommodation appropriate to the applicant's housing needs (including, in particular, the location and sources of such types of accommodation).

193. Duty to persons with priority need who are not homeless intentionally

(1) This section applies where the local housing authority are satisfied that an applicant is homeless, eligible for assistance and has a priority need, and are not satisfied that he became homeless intentionally.

(2) Unless the authority refer the application to another local housing authority (see section 198), they shall secure that accommodation is available for occupation by the applicant.

(3) The authority are subject to the duty under this section until it ceases by virtue of any of the following provisions of this section.

(3A) ...

(3B) In this section 'a restricted case' means a case where the local housing authority would not be satisfied as mentioned in subsection (1) without having had regard to a restricted person.

(5) The local housing authority shall cease to be subject to the duty under this section if—
　(a) the applicant, having been informed by the authority of the possible consequence of refusal or acceptance and of the right to request a review of the suitability of the accommodation, refuses an offer of accommodation which the authority are satisfied is suitable for the applicant,
　(b) that offer of accommodation is not an offer of accommodation under Part 6 or a private rented sector offer, and
　(c) the authority notify the applicant that they regard themselves as ceasing to be subject to the duty under this section.

(6) The local housing authority shall cease to be subject to the duty under this section if the applicant—
　(a) ceases to be eligible for assistance,
　(b) becomes homeless intentionally from the accommodation made available for his occupation,
　(c) accepts an offer of accommodation under Part VI (allocation of housing),
　(cc) accepts an offer of an assured tenancy (other than an assured shorthold tenancy) from a private landlord, or
　(d) otherwise voluntarily ceases to occupy as his only or principal home the accommodation made available for his occupation.

(7) The local housing authority shall also cease to be subject to the duty under this section if the applicant, having been informed of the possible consequence of refusal or acceptance and of his right to request a review of the suitability of the accommodation, refuses a final offer of accommodation under Part 6.

(7A) An offer of accommodation under Part 6 is a final offer for the purposes of subsection (7) if it is made in writing and states that it is a final offer for the purposes of subsection (7).

(7AA) The authority shall also cease to be subject to the duty under this section if the applicant, having been informed in writing of the matters mentioned in subsection (7AB)—
　(a) accepts a private rented sector offer, or
　(b) refuses such an offer.

(7AB) The matters are—
- (a) the possible consequence of refusal or acceptance of the offer, and
- (b) that the applicant has the right to request a review of the suitability of the accommodation, and
- (c) in a case which is not a restricted case, the effect under section 195A of a further application to a local housing authority within two years of acceptance of the offer.

(7AC) For the purposes of this section an offer is a private rented sector offer if—
- (a) it is an offer of an assured shorthold tenancy made by a private landlord to the applicant in relation to any accommodation which is, or may become, available for the applicant's occupation,
- (b) it is made, with the approval of the authority, in pursuance of arrangements made by the authority with the landlord with a view to bringing the authority's duty under this section to an end, and
- (c) the tenancy being offered is a fixed term tenancy (within the meaning of Part 1 of the Housing Act 1988) for a period of at least 12 months.

(7AD) In a restricted case the authority shall, so far as reasonably practicable, bring their duty under this section to an end as mentioned in subsection (7AA).

(7B)–(7E) ...

(7F) The local housing authority shall not—
- (a) make a final offer of accommodation under Part 6 for the purposes of subsection (7); or
- (ab) approve a private rented sector offer; or
- (b) ...

unless they are satisfied that the accommodation is suitable for the applicant and that subsection (8) does not apply to the applicant.

(8) This subsection applies to an applicant if—
- (a) the applicant is under contractual or other obligations in respect of the applicant's existing accommodation, and
- (b) the applicant is not able to bring those obligations to an end before being required to take up the offer.

(9) A person who ceases to be owed the duty under this section may make a fresh application to the authority for accommodation or assistance in obtaining accommodation.

(10) The appropriate authority may provide by regulations that subsection (7AC)(c) is to have effect as if it referred to a period of the length specified in the regulations.

(11) Regulations under subsection (10)—
- (a) may not specify a period of less than 12 months, and
- (b) may not apply to restricted cases.

(12) In subsection (10) 'the appropriate authority'—
- (a) in relation to local housing authorities in England, means the Secretary of State;
- (b) in relation to local housing authorities in Wales, means the Welsh Ministers.

195. Duties in case of threatened homelessness

(1) This section applies where the local housing authority are satisfied that an applicant is threatened with homelessness and is eligible for assistance.

(2) If the authority—
- (a) are satisfied that he has a priority need, and
- (b) are not satisfied that he became threatened with homelessness intentionally,

they shall take reasonable steps to secure that accommodation does not cease to be available for his occupation.

(3) Subsection (2) does not affect any right of the authority, whether by virtue of a contract, enactment or rule of law, to secure vacant possession of any accommodation.

(3A) ...

(4) Where, in a case which is not a restricted threatened homelessness case, in pursuance of the duty under subsection (2) the authority secure that accommodation other than that occupied by the applicant when he made his application is available for occupation by him, the provisions of section

193(3) to (9) (period for which duty owed) apply, with any necessary modifications, in relation to the duty under this section as they apply in relation to the duty under section 193 in a case which is not a restricted case (within the meaning of that section).

(4A) Where, in a restricted threatened homelessness case, in pursuance of the duty under subsection (2) the authority secure that accommodation other than that occupied by the applicant when he made his application is available for occupation by him, the provisions of section 193(3) to (9) (period for which duty owed) apply, with any necessary modifications, in relation to the duty under this section as they apply in relation to the duty under section 193 in a restricted case (within the meaning of that section).

(4B) In subsections (4) and (4A) 'a restricted threatened homelessness case' means a case where the local housing authority would not be satisfied as mentioned in subsection (1) without having had regard to a restricted person.

(5) If the authority—
   (a) are not satisfied that the applicant has a priority need, or
   (b) are satisfied that he has a priority need but are also satisfied that he became threatened with homelessness intentionally,

   they shall provide him with (or secure that he is provided with) advice and assistance in any attempts he may make to secure that accommodation does not cease to be available for his occupation.

(6) The applicant's housing needs shall be assessed before advice and assistance is provided under subsection (5).

(7) The advice and assistance provided under subsection (5) must include information about the likely availability in the authority's district of types of accommodation appropriate to the applicant's housing needs (including, in particular, the location and sources of such types of accommodation).

(8) If the authority decide that they owe the applicant the duty under subsection (5) by virtue of paragraph (b) of that subsection, they may, pending a decision on a review of that decision—
   (a) secure that accommodation does not cease to be available for his occupation; and
   (b) if he becomes homeless, secure that accommodation is so available.

(9) If the authority—
   (a) are not satisfied that the applicant has a priority need; and
   (b) are not satisfied that he became threatened with homelessness intentionally,

   the authority may take reasonable steps to secure that accommodation does not cease to be available for the applicant's occupation.

195A. Re-application after private rented sector offer

(1) If within two years beginning with the date on which an applicant accepts an offer under section 193(7AA) (private rented sector offer), the applicant re-applies for accommodation, or for assistance in obtaining accommodation, and the local housing authority—
   (a) is satisfied that the applicant is homeless and eligible for assistance, and
   (b) is not satisfied that the applicant became homeless intentionally,

   the duty under section 193(2) applies regardless of whether the applicant has a priority need.

(2) For the purpose of subsection (1), an applicant in respect of whom a valid notice under section 21 of the Housing Act 1988 (orders for possession on expiry or termination of assured shorthold tenancy) has been given is to be treated as homeless from the date on which that notice expires.

(3) If within two years beginning with the date on which an applicant accepts an offer under section 193(7AA), the applicant re-applies for accommodation, or for assistance in obtaining accommodation, and the local housing authority—
   (a) is satisfied that the applicant is threatened with homelessness and eligible for assistance, and
   (b) is not satisfied that the applicant became threatened with homelessness intentionally,

   the duty under section 195(2) applies regardless of whether the applicant has a priority need.

(4) For the purpose of subsection (3), an applicant in respect of whom a valid notice under section 21 of the Housing Act 1988 has been given is to be treated as threatened with homelessness from the date on which that notice is given.

(5) Subsection (1) or (3) does not apply to a case where the local housing authority would not be satisfied as mentioned in that subsection without having regard to a restricted person.

(6) Subsection (1) or (3) does not apply to a re-application by an applicant for accommodation, or for assistance in obtaining accommodation, if the immediately preceding application made by that applicant was one to which subsection (1) or (3) applied.

196. Becoming threatened with homelessness intentionally

(1) A person becomes threatened with homelessness intentionally if he deliberately does or fails to do anything the likely result of which is that he will be forced to leave accommodation which is available for his occupation and which it would have been reasonable for him to continue to occupy.

(2) For the purposes of subsection (1) an act or omission in good faith on the part of a person who was unaware of any relevant fact shall not be treated as deliberate.

(3) A person shall be treated as becoming threatened with homelessness intentionally if—

(a) he enters into an arrangement under which he is required to cease to occupy accommodation which it would have been reasonable for him to continue to occupy, and

(b) the purpose of the arrangement is to enable him to become entitled to assistance under this Part,

and there is no other good reason why he is threatened with homelessness.

Referral to another local housing authority

198. Referral of case to another local housing authority

(1) If the local housing authority would be subject to the duty under section 193 (accommodation for those with priority need who are not homeless intentionally) but consider that the conditions are met for referral of the case to another local housing authority, they may notify that other authority of their opinion.

(2) The conditions for referral of the case to another authority are met if—

(a) neither the applicant nor any person who might reasonably be expected to reside with him has a local connection with the district of the authority to whom his application was made,

(b) the applicant or a person who might reasonably be expected to reside with him has a local connection with the district of that other authority, and

(c) neither the applicant nor any person who might reasonably be expected to reside with him will run the risk of domestic violence in that other district.

(2ZA) The conditions for referral of the case to another authority are also met if—

(a) the application is made within the period of two years beginning with the date on which the applicant accepted an offer from the other authority under section 193(7AA) (private rented sector offer), and

(b) neither the applicant nor any person who might reasonably be expected to reside with the applicant will run the risk of domestic violence in the district of the other authority.

(2A) But the conditions for referral mentioned in subsection (2) or (2ZA) are not met if—

(a) the applicant or any person who might reasonably be expected to reside with him has suffered violence (other than domestic violence) in the district of the other authority; and

(b) it is probable that the return to that district of the victim will lead to further violence of a similar kind against him.

(3) For the purposes of subsections (2), (2ZA) and (2A) 'violence' means—

(a) violence from another person; or

(b) threats of violence from another person which are likely to be carried out;

and violence is 'domestic violence' if it is from a person who is associated with the victim.

(4) The conditions for referral of the case to another authority are also met if—

(a) the applicant was on a previous application made to that other authority placed (in pursuance of their functions under this Part) in accommodation in the district of the authority to whom his application is now made, and

(b) the previous application was within such period as may be prescribed of the present application.

(5) The question whether the conditions for referral of a case are satisfied shall be decided by agreement between the notifying authority and the notified authority or, in default of agreement, in accordance with such arrangements as the Secretary of State may direct by order.

(6) An order may direct that the arrangements shall be—

(a) those agreed by any relevant authorities or associations of relevant authorities, or

(b) in default of such agreement, such arrangements as appear to the Secretary of State to be suitable, after consultation with such associations representing relevant authorities, and such other persons, as he thinks appropriate.

(7) No such order shall be made unless a draft of the order has been approved by a resolution of each House of Parliament.

199. Local connection

(1) A person has a local connection with the district of a local housing authority if he has a connection with it—

(a) because he is, or in the past was, normally resident there, and that residence is or was of his own choice,

(b) because he is employed there,

(c) because of family associations, or

(d) because of special circumstances.

(2) ...

(3) Residence in a district is not of a person's own choice if—

(a) ...

(b) he, or a person who might reasonably be expected to reside with him, becomes resident there because he is detained under the authority of an Act of Parliament.

(4) ...

(5) The Secretary of State may by order specify ... circumstances in which—

(a) a person is not to be treated as employed in a district, or

(b) residence in a district is not to be treated as of a person's own choice.

(6) A person has a local connection with the district of a local housing authority if he was (at any time) provided with accommodation in that district under section 95 of the Immigration and Asylum Act 1999 (support for asylum seekers).

(7) But subsection (6) does not apply—

(a) to the provision of accommodation for a person in a district of a local housing authority if he was subsequently provided with accommodation in the district of another local housing authority under section 95 of that Act, or

(b) to the provision of accommodation in an accommodation centre by virtue of section 22 of the Nationality, Immigration and Asylum Act 2002 (use of accommodation centres for section 95 support).

200. Duties to applicant whose case is considered for referral or referred

(1) Where a local housing authority notify an applicant that they intend to notify or have notified another local housing authority of their opinion that the conditions are met for the referral of his case to that other authority—

(a) they cease to be subject to any duty under section 188 (interim duty to accommodate in case of apparent priority need), and

(b) they are not subject to any duty under section 193 (the main housing duty),

but they shall secure that accommodation is available for occupation by the applicant until he is notified of the decision whether the conditions for referral of his case are met.

(2) When it has been decided whether the conditions for referral are met, the notifying authority shall notify the applicant of the decision and inform him of the reasons for it.

The notice shall also inform the applicant of his right to request a review of the decision and of the time within which such a request must be made.

(3) If it is decided that the conditions for referral are not met, the notifying authority are subject to the duty under section 193 (the main housing duty).

(4) If it is decided that those conditions are met, the notified authority are subject to the duty under section 193 (the main housing duty).

(5) The duty under subsection (1) ceases as provided in that subsection even if the applicant requests a review of the authority's decision (see section 202).

The authority may secure that accommodation is available for the applicant's occupation pending the decision on a review.

(6) Notice required to be given to an applicant under this section shall be given in writing and, if not received by him, shall be treated as having been given to him if it is made available at the authority's office for a reasonable period for collection by him or on his behalf.

Right to request review of decision

202. Right to request review of decision

(1) An applicant has the right to request a review of—

    (a) any decision of a local housing authority as to his eligibility for assistance,

    (b) any decision of a local housing authority as to what duty (if any) is owed to him under sections 190 to 193 and 195 and 196 (duties to persons found to be homeless or threatened with homelessness),

    (c) any decision of a local housing authority to notify another authority under section 198(1) (referral of cases),

    (d) any decision under section 198(5) whether the conditions are met for the referral of his case,

    (e) any decision under section 200(3) or (4) (decision as to duty owed to applicant whose case is considered for referral or referred),

    (f) any decision of a local housing authority as to the suitability of accommodation offered to him in discharge of their duty under any of the provisions mentioned in paragraph (b) or (e) or as to the suitability of accommodation offered to him as mentioned in section 193(7), or

    (g) any decision of a local housing authority as to the suitability of accommodation offered to him by way of a private rented sector offer (within the meaning of section 193).

(1A) An applicant who is offered accommodation as mentioned in section 193(5), (7) or (7A) may under subsection (1)(f) or (as the case may be) (g) request a review of the suitability of the accommodation offered to him whether or not he has accepted the offer.

(2) There is no right to request a review of the decision reached on an earlier review.

(3) A request for review must be made before the end of the period of 21 days beginning with the day on which he is notified of the authority's decision or such longer period as the authority may in writing allow.

(4) On a request being duly made to them, the authority or authorities concerned shall review their decision.

203. Procedure on a review

(1) The Secretary of State may make provision by regulations as to the procedure to be followed in connection with a review under section 202.

Nothing in the following provisions affects the generality of this power.

(2) Provision may be made by regulations—

    (a) requiring the decision on review to be made by a person of appropriate seniority who was not involved in the original decision, and

    (b) as to the circumstances in which the applicant is entitled to an oral hearing, and whether and by whom he may be represented at such a hearing.

(3) The authority, or as the case may be either of the authorities, concerned shall notify the applicant of the decision on the review.

(4) If the decision is—

    (a) to confirm the original decision on any issue against the interests of the applicant, or

    (b) to confirm a previous decision—

        (i) to notify another authority under section 198 (referral of cases), or

        (ii) that the conditions are met for the referral of his case,

    they shall also notify him of the reasons for the decision.

(5) In any case they shall inform the applicant of his right to appeal to a county court on a point of law, and of the period within which such an appeal must be made (see section 204).

(6) Notice of the decision shall not be treated as given unless and until subsection (5), and where applicable subsection (4), is complied with.

(7) Provision may be made by regulations as to the period within which the review must be carried out and notice given of the decision.

(8) Notice required to be given to a person under this section shall be given in writing and, if not received by him, shall be treated as having been given if it is made available at the authority's office for a reasonable period for collection by him or on his behalf.

204. Right of appeal to county court on point of law

(1) If an applicant who has requested a review under section 202—

   (a) is dissatisfied with the decision on the review, or

   (b) is not notified of the decision on the review within the time prescribed under section 203,

   he may appeal to the county court on any point of law arising from the decision or, as the case may be, the original decision.

(2) An appeal must be brought within 21 days of his being notified of the decision or, as the case may be, of the date on which he should have been notified of a decision on review.

(2A) The court may give permission for an appeal to be brought after the end of the period allowed by subsection (2), but only if it is satisfied—

   (a) where permission is sought before the end of that period, that there is a good reason for the applicant to be unable to bring the appeal in time; or

   (b) where permission is sought after that time, that there was a good reason for the applicant's failure to bring the appeal in time and for any delay in applying for permission.

(3) On appeal the court may make such order confirming, quashing or varying the decision as it thinks fit.

(4) Where the authority were under a duty under section 188, 190 or 200 to secure that accommodation is available for the applicant's occupation, or had the power under section 195(8) to do so, they may secure that accommodation is so available—

   (a) during the period for appealing under this section against the authority's decision, and

   (b) if an appeal is brought, until the appeal (and any further appeal) is finally determined.

204A. Section 204(4): appeals

(1) This section applies where an applicant has the right to appeal to the county court against a local housing authority's decision on a review.

(2) If the applicant is dissatisfied with a decision by the authority—

   (a) not to exercise their power under section 204(4) ('the section 204(4) power') in his case;

   (b) to exercise that power for a limited period ending before the final determination by the county court of his appeal under section 204(1) ('the main appeal'); or

   (c) to cease exercising that power before that time,

   he may appeal to the county court against the decision.

(3) An appeal under this section may not be brought after the final determination by the county court of the main appeal.

(4) On an appeal under this section the court—

   (a) may order the authority to secure that accommodation is available for the applicant's occupation until the determination of the appeal (or such earlier time as the court may specify); and

   (b) shall confirm or quash the decision appealed against,

   and in considering whether to confirm or quash the decision the court shall apply the principles applied by the High Court on an application for judicial review.

(5) If the court quashes the decision it may order the authority to exercise the section 204(4) power in the applicant's case for such period as may be specified in the order.

(6) An order under subsection (5) —

   (a) may only be made if the court is satisfied that failure to exercise the section 204(4) power in accordance with the order would substantially prejudice the applicant's ability to pursue the main appeal;

   (b) may not specify any period ending after the final determination by the county court of the main appeal.

206. Discharge of functions by local housing authorities

(1) A local housing authority may discharge their housing functions under this Part only in the following ways—

   (a) by securing that suitable accommodation provided by them is available,

   (b) by securing that he obtains suitable accommodation from some other person, or

   (c) by giving him such advice and assistance as will secure that suitable accommodation is available from some other person.

(2) A local housing authority may require a person in relation to whom they are discharging such functions—

   (a) to pay such reasonable charges as they may determine in respect of accommodation which they secure for his occupation (either by making it available themselves or otherwise), or

   (b) to pay such reasonable amount as they may determine in respect of sums payable by them for accommodation made available by another person.

208. Discharge of functions: out-of-area placements

(1) So far as reasonably practicable a local housing authority shall in discharging their housing functions under this Part secure that accommodation is available for the occupation of the applicant in their district.

(2) If they secure that accommodation is available for the occupation of the applicant outside their district, they shall give notice to the local housing authority in whose district the accommodation is situated.

(3) The notice shall state—

   (a) the name of the applicant,

   (b) the number and description of other persons who normally reside with him as a member of his family or might reasonably be expected to reside with him,

   (c) the address of the accommodation,

   (d) the date on which the accommodation was made available to him, and

   (e) which function under this Part the authority was discharging in securing that the accommodation is available for his occupation.

(4) The notice must be in writing, and must be given before the end of the period of 14 days beginning with the day on which the accommodation was made available to the applicant.

210. Suitability of accommodation

(1) In determining for the purposes of this Part whether accommodation is suitable for a person, the local housing authority shall have regard to Parts 9 and 10 of the Housing Act 1985 (slum clearance and overcrowding) and Parts 1 to 4 of the Housing Act 2004.

(2) The Secretary of State may by order specify—

   (a) circumstances in which accommodation is or is not to be regarded as suitable for a person, and

   (b) matters to be taken into account or disregarded in determining whether accommodation is suitable for a person.

211. Protection of property of homeless persons and persons threatened with homelessness

(1) This section applies where a local housing authority have reason to believe that—

   (a) there is danger of loss of, or damage to, any personal property of an applicant by reason of his inability to protect it or deal with it, and

   (b) no other suitable arrangements have been or are being made.

(2) If the authority have become subject to a duty towards the applicant under—

   section 188 (interim duty to accommodate),

   section 190, 193 or 195 (duties to persons found to be homeless or threatened with homelessness), or

   section 200 (duties to applicant whose case is considered for referral or referred),

   then, whether or not they are still subject to such a duty, they shall take reasonable steps to prevent the loss of the property or prevent or mitigate damage to it.

(3) If they have not become subject to such a duty, they may take any steps they consider reasonable for that purpose.

(4) The authority may decline to take action under this section except upon such conditions as they consider appropriate in the particular case, which may include conditions as to—
   (a) the making and recovery by the authority of reasonable charges for the action taken, or
   (b) the disposal by the authority, in such circumstances as may be specified, of property in relation to which they have taken action.

(5) References in this section to personal property of the applicant include personal property of any person who might reasonably be expected to reside with him.

(6) Section 212 contains provisions supplementing this section.

218. **Index of defined expressions: Part VII**

The following Table shows provisions defining or otherwise explaining expressions used in this Part (other than provisions defining or explaining an expression used in the same section)—

• accommodation available for occupation	• section 176
• applicant	• section 183(2)
• assistance under this Part	• section 183(2)
• associated (in relation to a person)	• section 178
• assured tenancy and assured shorthold tenancy	• section 230
• district (of local housing authority)	• section 217(3)
• eligible for assistance	• section 183(2)
• homeless	• section 175(1)
• housing functions under this Part (in sections 206 and 208)	• section 205(2)
• intentionally homeless	• section 191
• intentionally threatened with homelessness	• section 196
• local connection	• section 199
• local housing authority — in England and Wales — in Scotland	• section 230 section 217(2)(a)
• prescribed	• section 215(1)
• priority need	• section 189
• private landlord	• section 217(1)
• reasonable to continue to occupy accommodation	• section 177
• registered social landlord	• section 230
• relevant authority	• section 217(1)
• restricted person	• section 184(7)
• social services authority	• section 217(1) and (2)(b)
• threatened with homelessness	• section 175(4)

Index

accelerated possession claims
   assured shorthold tenants 157–8
   defence 158
administration charges 127
   reasonableness 127
agricultural employee
   recovery of regulated tenancy for 42
agricultural holdings
   assured tenancy exclusion 12
   protected tenancy exclusion 36
agricultural land
   assured tenancy exclusion 12
   protected tenancy exclusion 36
allocation of housing, local housing authorities 72
   additional preference 74
   challenging 75–6
   choice-based schemes 73
   Code of Guidance 72–3
   discrimination issues 76
   eligibility of applicants 74–5
   factors taken into account 74
   former service personnel 74
   homelessness and 72–3
   housing need 73
   immigration controls and 74, 75
   priority need 73
   reasonable preference 73–4
   review of decisions 76
   statement of policy 73, 75
   see also **homelessness**
alternative dispute resolution
   disrepair 112
annoyance
   recovery of assured tenancy 22–3
   recovery of regulated tenancy 39–40
anti-social behaviour
   assured shorthold tenancies 31–3
   demoted tenancies 30–1, 83
   discretionary possession ground 160–1
   family intervention tenancy 33, 84
   injunctions 31–2, 83
   parenting contracts and orders 32–3, 83
   private sector tenants 33
   recovery of assured tenancy 20
   secure tenancy
     assignment objection 93
     recovery 86
   selective licensing 8
anti-social behaviour orders 32
   harassment remedy 144
appeals, homelessness claims
   accommodation pending 204
   costs 205
   funding 204–5
   grounds 202–4
   illegality ground 203
   irrationality ground 203

appeals, homelessness claims – *continued*
   notice of appeal 205
   point of law ground 202
   pre-action steps 205
   procedural impropriety ground 203–4
   procedural *ultra vires* 204
   procedure 204–5
   proportionality 204
   remedies 204
   time limits 202
   to county court 202–5
approved redevelopment scheme
   recovery of secure tenancy 87
armed forces personnel
   homelessness 183
   recovery of regulated tenancy for 43
assignment
   periodic assured tenants 14
   regulated tenancies 40
   secure tenancies
     anti-social behaviour objection 93
     by way of exchange 92–3
     property adjustment order 93
     to person qualified to succeed 93
     unlawful 87
   without consent 40
assured shorthold tenancies 24–6
   accelerated possession claims 157–8
   expiry of fixed-term tenancy 26
   last date of tenancy 26
   legislation 24
   no security of tenure 24, 25
   notice requirement 24
   notice of termination 26
   periodic tenancies 26
   post-HA 1996 25
   pre-HA 1996 24–5
   recovery of possession 25
   rent assessment committee 26
   tenancy deposit scheme 26–8
   termination of tenancy 26
assured tenancies
   access to repair 15
   anti-social behaviour
     demoted tenancies 30–1
     family intervention tenancy 12, 33, 84
     ground for possession 20
     injunctions 31–2
     orders 32
     parenting contracts and orders 32–3
   assignment 14
   definition 10
   demoted tenancies 30–1
   dwelling-house 10–11
   exclusions 11–13
   exclusive use 11
   fixed-term 16

assured tenancies – *continued*
  grounds for possession 17
    anti-social behaviour 20
    breach of obligation 21
    death of periodic tenant 19
    deterioration of dwelling 21–2
    deterioration of furniture 24
    discretionary 20–4
    domestic violence 23
    false statements 24
    former employee 24
    furniture deterioration 24
    mandatory 17–20
    ministers of religion 18
    mortgagees 18
    nuisance, annoyance or criminal activity 22–3
    out-of-season holiday lettings 18
    owner occupier 17–18
    reasonableness 20
    redevelopment 18–19
    rent arrears 21
      persistent delay in paying 21
      serious 19–20
    student accommodation 18
    suitable alternative accommodation 21
    termination of employment 24
  HA 1988 9–10
  let as dwelling-house 10
  matrimonial home 11
  only or principal home 11
  periodic tenants
    assignment 14
    rent increases 13–14
    sub-letting 14
    succession rights 14–15
  private sector landlords 33
  registered social landlords 28
    advantages 29
    demoted tenancies 30–1
    disadvantages 29–30
  security of tenure 16–17
    fixed-term tenancy 16
    notice period 17
    notice provisions 16–17
    section 8 notice 16
  separate dwelling-house 10–11
  sub-letting 14
    continuation in tenancy 15–16
  terms 13–16
asylum seekers
  assured tenancy exclusion 12
  homelessness 175
  public sector housing 55

board and lodgings
  protected tenancy exclusion 36
  secure tenancies 94
breach of obligation
  recovery of assured tenancy 21
  recovery of regulated tenancy 39
business tenancies
  assured tenancy exclusion 12
  protected tenancy exclusion 36

charity landlord
  occupation conflicting with objectives of 87
civil partners
  assured tenancy 11
    succession 14, 15
  secure tenancy succession 90, 91
  statutory tenancy succession 38
  succession 14, 15, 54, 90, 91
collective enfranchisement 124
Commissioners for Local Administration 209–10
commonhold ownership
  registration 125
consultation
  secure tenancy management 94–5
  service charges 126
controlled work contracts (public funding) 60, 65
  delegated functions 65
  devolved powers 65
  help at court 65
  legal help 65
  Lexcel standard 65
  quality mark person 65
  specialist quality mark 65
costs
  general rules 69
  homelessness appeals 205
  homelessness judicial review 209
  public funding 69–70
  see also **public funding**
criminal activity
  recovery of assured tenancy 22–3
  recovery of regulated tenancy 39–40
Crown lets
  assured tenancy exclusion 12

damages
  disrepair remedy
    contractual measure 110–11
    distress and inconvenience 110
    mitigation duty 111
    tort measure 111
  homelessness judicial review remedy 209
  unlawful eviction/harassment
    aggravated 142
    double recovery 144
    exemplary 142
    general 141
    mitigation 143
    nominal 141
    reduction 143
    s 27 and 28 HA 1988 142–4
    s 27 defence 142
    s 28 measure of damages 142–3
    security lost 143–4
    special 141
damp 105, 115
death of tenant
  recovery of assured tenancy 19
declaration remedy
  homelessness judicial review 209
defective premises
  duties from repair obligation 106–7
  duties from right to repair 106–7

demolition
   recovery of secure tenancy 87
demoted tenancies 81
   anti-social behaviour and 83
   assured tenants 30–1
   demotion order 30–1
   effect of order 83
   grounds 82–3
   possession claims 155
Deposit Protection Service 27
deposits
   tenancy deposit scheme 26–8
deterioration of dwelling
   recovery of assured tenancy 21–2
   recovery of regulated tenancy 40
deterioration of furniture
   recovery of assured tenancy 24
   recovery of regulated tenancy 40
Director of Legal Aid Casework 59
disabled person's accommodation
   recovery of secure tenancy 88
discrimination prohibition 48, 54–5
   allocation of secure tenancies 76
displaced persons
   assured tenancy exclusion 12
disrepair
   access to repair 15
   alternative dispute resolution 112
   assured tenancy 15
   business efficacy to agreement 102
   civil remedies
      complaint to ombudsman 109
      damages 110–11
      interim injunction 109–10
      landlord's remedies 111
      manager appointment 109
      public sector scheme 108
      receiver appointment 109
      self-help 108, 111
      set-off against rent 108
      specific performance 110, 111
      tenant's remedies 107–11
   commencing proceedings 113
   common parts 102
   costs penalties 112
   damages
      contractual measure 110–11
      distress and inconvenience 110
      mitigation duty 111
      tort measure 111
   damp 105, 115
   defective premises
      duties from repair obligation 106–7
      duties from right to repair 106–7
   early notification letter 112
   environmental matters 115–16
      abatement notice 116
      damp 105, 115
   flowchart 118
   implied terms
      common law 102
      on landlord 102–5
      statutory 102–5

disrepair – *continued*
   on tenant 102
   improvement notices 116–17
   improvements distinguished 100–1
   injury to tenant 105, 106
   inspection 112
   installations 104
   interim injunction 109–10
   landlord's obligation
      common law implied terms 102
      damp 105
      extension beyond dwelling-house 104–5
      fitness for occupation 101, 102
      installations 104
      standard of repair 104
      statutory implied terms 102–5
      structure and exterior 103
      to keep in proper working order 102, 103
      to keep in repair 102, 103
   landlord's remedies 111
   letter of claim 112
   limitation period 113
   manager appointment 109
   meaning 99–100
   mitigation duty 111
   notice requirement 101
   obligations 99
      express terms 101
      implied terms *see* implied terms
      on landlord 102–5
      on tenant 102, 105
      in tort 106–7
   occupiers' liability 105–6
   Pre-action Protocol 112–13
   procedure for claim
      commencing proceedings 113
      costs 113
      early notification letter 112
      expert inspection 112, 113
      letter of claim 112
      limitation period 113
      Part 36 offers 113
      Pre-action Protocol 112–13
      public funding 114–15
   prohibition orders 116–17
   public funding of claim 114–15
   public law obligations
      enforcement by local authority 116
      enforcement in magistrates' court 116
      environmental matters 115–16
      health and safety 115
      improvement notices 116–17
      prohibition orders 116–17
      public funding 116–17
   receiver appointment 109
   redecoration after 101
   repair meaning 100
   secure tenant repairs 94
   self-help remedy 108, 111
   single joint expert 113
   specific performance remedy 110, 111
   standard of repair 104
   structure and exterior 103–4

disrepair – continued
  tenant's obligations
    access for landlord 102, 105
    common law implied terms 102
    statutory implied terms 105
    use in tenant-like manner 102
  tenant's remedies 107–11
    see also individual remedies
  tortious obligations
    common law 105–6
    defective premises 106–7
    injury to tenant 105, 106
    occupiers' liability 106

domestic violence
  homelessness 179
    priority need 183
  recovery of assured tenancy 23
  recovery of secure tenancy 86

dwelling
  assured tenancies 10–11
  deterioration 21–2, 40
  separate 10–11, 36, 76, 77
  upkeep 4

early notification letter
  disrepair 112

employee, former
  possession grounds 88
  recovery of assured tenancy from 24
  recovery of regulated tenancy from 40

enfranchisement
  collective 124
  conditions for 121–2
  freehold of house 121–2
  human rights challenge 122
  purchase price 122

environmental matters
  abatement notice 116
  damp 115
  disrepair 115–16

EU nationals
  homelessness 176

eviction
  unlawful *see* **unlawful eviction**

exclusive possession
  leasehold estates 3
  protected tenancies 36

exclusive use
  assured tenancies 11

experts
  single joint expert 113

fair trial right 47, 157
false statements
  recovery of assured tenancy 24
  recovery of secure tenancy 86–7
family intervention tenancy
  anti-social behaviour 33, 84
  assured tenancy exclusion 12
family, respect for 47–8, 54–5
financial eligibility (public funding)
  capital and income limits 66
  disposable capital 66

financial eligibility (public funding) – continued
  disposable income 66
  guide to assessing 66–8
  passporting arrangement 66
fit for occupation
  disrepair 101, 102
  homelessness and 179
  housing condition 54
  landlord's repair obligation 101, 102
fixed-term tenancies
  assured tenancy 16
  effluxion of time 82
  secure tenancy 81
  statutory tenancy arising 82
  termination 81–2
flats (long leases)
  appointment of manager 123
  collective enfranchisement 124
  commonhold ownership registration 125
  compulsory acquisition of landlord's interest 123
  extended lease 124–5
  first refusal right 122–3
  leasehold valuation tribunal 123
  management of building 123
  qualifying tenants 122–3
flexible tenancies 77, 78
  review 78
  termination 82
forfeiture, long leases
  failure to pay service charges 128
  failure to pay for short periods 128
  failure to pay small amounts 128
  long leases 162–3
  notification of due rent 128–9
  s 146 notice procedure 129
  s 146 notice restriction 129
  statutory protection 128–9
former employee, recovery of tenancy from
  assured tenancy 24
  regulated tenancy 40
  secure tenancy 88
furniture deterioration
  assured tenancy 24
  regulated tenancy 40

Guidance (OFT)
  unfair terms in tenancy agreements 6

harassment
  breach of statutory duty 138–9
    excluded tenancies and licences 139
    statutorily protected tenancies 138–9
  civil causes of action 136–40
  civil procedure
    commencing proceedings *see* commencement of proceedings
    Part 7 claims 145–6
    public funding 146
  civil remedies
    anti-social behaviour orders 144
    damages *see* damages
    injunctions 140–1
    interim injunctions 141

harassment – *continued*
- commencement of proceedings 146–8
  - claim form N1 146
  - defence 148
  - form N16A 147–8
  - further information 146–7
  - interim injunction application 147–8
  - particulars of claim 146–7
  - service of injunction order 147–8
  - urgent or without notice applications 147
- contract claims
  - derogation from grant 136–7
  - other contractual terms breach 137
  - quiet enjoyment breach 136
- criminal sanctions 135–6
  - compensation orders 150
  - Criminal Law Act 1977 149–50
  - dealing with offences 149
  - landlord meaning 149
  - Protection from Eviction Act 1977 148–9
  - Protection from Harassment Act 1997 150
  - residential occupier meaning 149
  - violent entry to premises 149–50
- damages
  - aggravated 142
  - double recovery 144
  - exemplary 142
  - general 141
  - mitigation 143
  - nominal 141
  - reduction 143
  - s 27 and 28 HA 1988 142–4
  - s 27 defence 142
  - s 28 measure of damages 142–3
  - security lost 143–4
  - special 141
- injunctions 140–1
- interim injunctions 141
- legal representation 146
- legislation 135
- nuisance 138
- Protection from Harassment Act 1997 140
  - remedies 144
- public funding 146
- tort claims 137–40
  - s 27 of HA 1988 140
- trespass to goods 138
- trespass to land 137–8
- trespass to person 138
- unlawfully to attempt to deprive 140
- unlawfully to deprive 140

help at court 61–2
- controlled work 65
- controlled work contracts 65
- legal representation 61
- need for representation 61
- specialist quality mark 65

high value premises
- assured tenancy exclusion 11
- protected tenancy exclusion 36

holiday lets
- assured tenancy exclusion 12
- protected tenancy exclusion 36

holiday lets – *continued*
- recovery of assured tenancy 18
- recovery of regulated tenancy 42

homelessness
- accommodation
  - meaning 177
  - offered, review of 200
  - pending appeal 204
  - pending judicial review 209
  - pending review 202
  - suitability 174, 192–4
  - temporary 174
- act or omission
  - in good faith 187
  - intentional homelessness 185
- allocation of secure tenancies 73
- appeals
  - accommodation pending appeal 204
  - costs 205
  - funding 204–5
  - grounds 202–4
  - illegality ground 203
  - irrationality ground 203
  - notice of appeal 205
  - point of law 202
  - pre-action steps 205
  - procedural impropriety ground 203–4
  - procedural *ultra vires* 204
  - procedure 204–5
  - proportionality 204
  - remedies 204
  - time limits 202
  - to county court 202–5
- applications
  - applicants 198
  - when made 197
- asylum seekers 55, 175
- Code of Guidance 177
- Commissioners for Local Administration 209–10
- decisions
  - notification 199
  - time limits 199
- definition 176–7
- discrimination claims 50
- domestic violence 179, 183
- duties towards homeless person 50–1, 190–6
  - accommodation pending enquiries 191
  - assistance under other provisions 196
  - cessation of duty 194–5
  - decisions, to make and notify 191
  - enquiries 191, 198
  - intentionally homeless persons 195–6
  - no priority need 195
  - protection of property 191
  - review of 200
  - successful applicants 192–6
  - suitability of accommodation 192–4
- eligibility for assistance 174–6
- emergency or other disaster 182
- enquiries 191, 198
  - accommodation pending 191
- EU nationals 176
- former prisoners

homelessness – *continued*
    local connection 189
    priority need 183
  habitual residence 175–6
  homeless persons 173–4
  housing circumstances in area 179
  human rights and 50
  immigration controls 175
  initial application 174
  intentional homelessness
    act or omission in good faith 187
    collusive arrangement 186
    conduct of parties 186–7
    consequence of act 185–6
    deliberate act or omission 185
    duties of LHA 195–6
    meaning of intentional 184–5
  judicial review
    accommodation pending hearing 209
    basis of 206
    claim form 207–8
    costs 209
    damages 209
    declaration remedy 209
    documents supporting claim 208
    examples of decisions 205–6
    funding 209
    grounds 208
    injunction 209
    mandatory order 209
    Pre-action Protocol 207
    private law remedies 209
    procedure 207–8
    prohibiting order 209
    public law remedies 208–9
    quashing order 209
    remedies 208–9
    service of claim 208
    time limits 206–7
  legislation 72–3, 174
  licence to occupy 178
  local connection 187–90
    employment 188
    family associations 188–9
    former prisoners 189
    meaning 188
    no local connection 189
    normal residence 188
    special circumstances 189
    statutory review 200
    time of referral 189–90
    to two or more authorities 189
  medical evidence 198
  member of family 177
  moveable structures 178
  occupancy
    basis 178
    reasonableness of continuing to occupy 178–9
  ombudsman 209–10
  overcrowding 179
  partially eligible households 176
  persons from abroad 175–6
    EU nationals 176

homelessness – *continued*
    habitual residence 175–6
    subject to immigration control 175
  priority need
    applicants without 195
    armed forces personnel 183
    asylum seekers 183
    children or young people 182
    dependent with children 181
    disabilities, learning or physical 182
    fleeing domestic violence 183
    former prisoners 183
    human rights challenge 183–4
    institutional background vulnerability 182
    mental illness 182
    non-eligible persons 183
    old age 181
    other special reason 182
    persons with 180
    pregnant women 180
    restricted persons 183
    vulnerabilities 181–2
  refugees 175
  refusal
    initial 174
    on review 174
  reviews, statutory *see* statutory review
  right to occupy 178
    statutory 178
  role of lawyer 174
  securing entry 178
  statutory definition 176–7
  statutory review 199–202
    accommodation offered 200
    accommodation pending 202
    duties 200
    eligibility 200
    local connection 200
    procedure 200–2
    review officer 201
    reviewable decisions 199–200
    time limit 200
  suitability of accommodation 192–4
  temporary accommodation 174
  threatened with 179
  time limits
    appeals 202
    decision 199
    judicial review 206–7
    statutory review 200
  unfit for human occupation 179
Homes and Communities Agency 28
houseboats 11
houses in multiple occupation (HMO)
  definition 6–7
  disrepair claims 117
  failure to obtain licence 7–8
  licensing provisions 6–7
  management orders 8
  mandatory licensing 7
housing associations
  protected tenancy exclusion 37
  registered rents 44

housing condition
    fitness for occupation 54, 101, 102, 179
    human rights and 54
    see also **disrepair**
housing cooperatives
    protected tenancy exclusion 37
housing disputes
    public funding *see* **public funding**
Housing Health and Safety Rating System 115
housing law
    property law 1–2
    public law 2
Housing Possession Court Duty scheme 64
human rights 2
    compatibility with Convention Rights 48–9
    county court proceedings 55–6
    discrimination prohibition 48, 54–5
        homelessness and 50
    duty to provide home 50–1
    enfranchisement and 122
    European Convention rights 47–8
    fair trial right 47, 157
    homelessness 50
    housing conditions 54
    interpretation by courts 48–9
    introductory tenancies 81
    legal challenges to housing law 49–55
    legislation 47–8
    local housing authority as public authority 48
    margin of appreciation 49
    possession claims 51–4
        discretionary grounds 51
        hearing 157
        notice to quit 51
        warrants for possession 53–4
    procedure for claims 55–6
    protection of property 48
    public authority meaning 48
    registered social landlord as public authority 48–9
    respect for family and private life 47–8, 54–5
    succession claims 54, 91–2

immigration controls
    homelessness 175
improvement notices
    disrepair claims 116–17
improvements
    by secure tenants 94
    repairs distinguished 100–1
initial trespassers 5
injunctions
    anti-social behaviour 31–2
    homelessness judicial review remedy 209
    interim 141
    unlawful eviction/harassment 140–1, 147–8
inspection
    disrepair claim 112, 113
intentional homelessness
    act or omission in good faith 187
    collusive arrangement 186
    conduct of parties 186–7
    consequence of act 185–6
    deliberate act or omission 185

intentional homelessness – *continued*
    duties of LHA 195–6
    meaning of intentional 184–5
interim injunctions
    repairs 109–10
    unlawful eviction/harassment 141
introductory tenancies 79
    behaviour of tenant 80
    extension 80
    human rights 81
    landlord condition 80
    possession proceedings 81
    rights of tenant 80
    tenant condition 80
    termination 80–1
    trial period 80
investigative representation 62, 63

judicial review, homelessness claims
    accommodation pending hearing 209
    basis of 206
    claim form 207–8
    costs 209
    damages 209
    declaration remedy 209
    documents supporting claim 208
    examples of decisions 205–6
    funding 209
    grounds 208
    injunction 209
    mandatory order 209
    Pre-action Protocol 207
    private law remedies 209
    procedure 207–8
    prohibiting order 209
    public law remedies 208–9
    quashing order 209
    remedies 208–9
    service of claim 208
    time limits 206–7

landlord occupation
    recovery of regulated tenancy for 40–1
landlords
    local authorities *see* **local housing authorities**
    private 8
leasehold estates
    exclusive possession 3
    loan secured on property 3
    owner occupation 3
leasehold valuation tribunal
    appointment of manager 123
    service charges 127–8
leaseholder 3
leases
    contract legislation and 5–6
    HA 2004 6
    unfair contract terms 5–6
    see also **tenancies**
Legal Aid Agency 59
legal help 60
    controlled work contracts 65
    reasonableness 61

legal help – *continued*
  specialist quality mark 65
  sufficient benefit test 61
legal representation
  criteria for
    special, for housing disputes 63–4
    standard 63
  full representation 62, 63
  harassment 146
  homelessness 64
  investigative representation 62, 63
  judicial review claims 64
  licensed work contracts 65
  public funding 62–4
  unlawful eviction 146
lessee 3
letter of claim
  disrepair 112
licence to occupy 178
licences 4
  houses in multiple occupation 6–7
  selective licensing 8
licensed premises
  assured tenancy exclusion 12
  protected tenancy exclusion 36
licensed work contracts (public funding) 60
  legal representation 65
limitation period
  disrepair claim 113
local authority lets
  assured tenancy exclusion 12
local connection, homelessness claims 187–90
  employment 188
  family associations 188–9
  former prisoners 189
  meaning 188
  no local connection 189
  normal residence 188
  special circumstances 189
  statutory review 200
  time of referral 189–90
  to two or more authorities 189
local housing authorities
  allocation of housing 72
    additional preference 74
    challenging 75–6
    Code of Guidance 72
    discrimination issues 76
    eligibility of applicants 74–5
    factors taken into account 74
    former service personnel 74
    homelessness and 73
    housing need 73
    immigration controls and 74, 75
    priority need 73
    reasonable preference 73–4
    review of decisions 76
    statement of policy 73, 75
  asylum seekers 55
  homelessness *see* **homelessness**
  housing conditions 54
  human rights
    housing conditions 54

local housing authorities – *continued*
  other areas of challenge 55
  possession claims 51–4
  procedure for claims 55–6
  social services 55
  succession claims 54
  introductory tenancies *see* **introductory tenancies**
  legislation 72
  non-secure tenancies
    ceasing to be secure 78–9
    exclusion for secure status 79–80
  possession claims
    discretionary grounds 51
    non-discretionary grounds 51–3
    notice to quit 51
    warrant for possession 53–4
  public authority for human rights claims 48
  Right to Buy scheme 71
  right to repair scheme 108
  secure tenants *see* **secure tenancies**
  succession claims 54
  tenancy strategy 71–2
  see also **homelessness**
lodgers
  protected tenancy exclusion 36
  in secure tenancies 94
long leases
  administration charges 127
    reasonableness 127
  assured tenant security 120
    limits 120–1
    when does not arise 121
  collective enfranchisement 124
  commonhold ownership registration 125
  definition 119
  enfranchisement
    collective 124
    conditions for 121–2
    freehold of house 121–2
    human rights challenge 122
    purchase price 122
  flats
    appointment of manager 123
    collective enfranchisement 124
    commonhold ownership registration 125
    compulsory acquisition of landlord's interest 123
    extended lease 124–5
    first refusal right 122–3
    leasehold valuation tribunal 123
    management of building 123
    qualifying tenants 122–3
  forfeiture 162–3
    failure to pay service charges 128
    failure to pay for short periods 128
    failure to pay small amounts 128
    notification of due rent 128–9
    s 146 notice procedure 129
    s 146 notice restriction 129
  mortgage default
    case law 130–2
    challenge to lender's rights 130–2
    matrimonial homes 130–2
    new mortgages 130

long leases – *continued*
    new procedures 130
    possession order 129
    Pre-action Protocol 130
    public funding 132
    regulated mortgage contracts 130
    unauthorised tenants 130
    undue influence 130–2
  registration as legal estates 3
  security on expiry of lease 120–1
  service charges 125–8
    administration charges 127
    consultation 126
    definition 126
    demand 126
    disputes 127–8
    exclusion from protection 126
    failure to pay 128
    leasehold valuation tribunal 127–8
    legislation 126
    reasonableness 126
  summary 132–3
low or no rent tenancies
  assured tenancy exclusion 11
  protected tenancy exclusion 36

management orders
  houses in multiple occupation 8
  selective licensing and 8
management, secure tenancies
  consultation right 94–5
  right to manage 95–6
manager appointment
  disrepair 109
mandatory order
  homelessness judicial review 209
matrimonial homes
  assured tenancies 11
  undue influence 130–2
ministers of religion
  assured tenancies 18
  regulated tenancies 42
misconduct of employee occupier
  recovery of secure tenancy 87
mortgage default
  case law 130–2
  challenge to lender's rights 130–2
  long leases 129–32
  matrimonial homes 130–2
  new mortgages 130
  new procedures 130
  possession order 129
  Pre-action Protocol 130
  public funding 132
  regulated mortgage contracts 130
  unauthorised tenants 130
  undue influence 130–2
mortgagees
  possession claims 153, 154–5
  possession grounds 162
  recovery of assured tenancy by 18

notice
  periodic tenancies 4
notice of appeal
  homelessness appeals 205
notice of termination
  assured tenancies 16–17
  notice period 17
  prescribed form 17
  section 8 notice 16
notice to quit
  ineffective 144
  length 144–5
  prescribed information 145
  tenant's 145
  unlawful eviction 144–5
nuisance
  anti-social behaviour possession ground 160–1
  recovery of assured tenancy 22–3
  recovery of regulated tenancy 39–40
  unlawful eviction/harassment and 138

occupation
  licences 4
  owner occupiers 3
    leasehold estates 3
  tenancies 3–4
  trespassers 4–5
occupiers' liability
  disrepair and 105–6
Office of Fair Trading
  unfair terms in tenancy agreements guidance 6
ombudsman
  disrepair complaints 109
  homelessness 209–10
overcrowding
  homelessness 179
  recovery of secure tenancy 87–8
owner occupiers 3
  leasehold estates 3
  recovery of assured tenancy 17–18
  recovery of regulated tenancy 42

parenting contracts 32–3, 83
parenting orders 32–3, 83
particulars of claim
  possession claims 153–4
  unlawful eviction/harassment 146–7
periodic assured tenancies
  assignment 14
  rent increases 13–14
  sub-letting 14
  succession rights 14–15
periodic tenancies
  assured shorthold tenancies 26
  notice requirement 4
possession claims 151–72
  accelerated
    assured shorthold tenants 157–8
    defence 158
    postponement of possession 158
  after notice to quit 51

possession claims – *continued*
   assured shorthold tenants 157–8
   checklist for claims 168–9
   Civil Procedure Rules 152–3
   claim form 153
   commencement of claim 153–5
     against trespassers 155
     claim form 153, 155
     demoted tenancies 155
     hearing date 155
     mortgagee claims 153, 154–5
     particulars of claim 153–4
   defendant's response 156
   demoted tenancies 155
   forfeiture of long lease 162–3
   forms N11, N11B, N11M and N11R 156
   hearing
     date 155
     human rights 157
     track allocation 157
   human rights 51–3
   local housing authority 51–3
   mortgagee claims 153, 154–5
   non-discretionary grounds 51–3
   particulars of claim 153–4
     residential property requirements 154
   Protocol
     mortgage or home purchase plan arrears 153
     rent arrears 152
   public funding 168
   rent arrears 152
   service of claims 156
   termination on discretionary grounds 51
   track allocation 157
   trespassers 155
   warrants for possession 53–4
possession grounds
   agricultural employee 42
   anti-social behaviour 86
     discretion 160–1
   armed forces personnel 43
   assignment without consent 40
   assured tenancies
     breach of obligation 21
     deterioration 21–2
     discretionary 20–4
     domestic violence 23
     false statements 24
     former employee 24
     furniture deterioration 24
     mandatory 17–20
     ministers of religion 18
     mortgagees 18
     nuisance, annoyance or criminal activity 22–3
     out-of-season holiday lettings 18
     owner occupier 17–18
     reasonableness 20
     redevelopment 18–19
     registered social landlords 28
     rent arrears 21
       persistent delay in paying 21
       serious 19–20
     student accommodation 18

possession grounds – *continued*
     suitable alternative accommodation 21
     termination of employment 24
   breach of obligation 21, 39
   charity landlord's objectives 87
   demolition or reconstruction of premises 87
   deterioration of dwelling 21–2, 40
   deterioration of furniture 24, 40
   disabled persons accommodation 88
   discretionary 20–4
     anti-social behaviour 160–1
     rent arrears 160, 162
   domestic violence 23, 86
   employee misconduct 87
   false statements 24, 86–7
   former employee 24, 40, 88
   furniture deterioration 24, 40
   landlord occupation 40–1
   mandatory 17–20, 161–2
   ministers of religion 18, 42
   misconduct 87
   mortgagees 18, 162
   non-spouse successor 88
   notice to quit 40
   nuisance, annoyance or criminal activity 22–3, 39–40
   occupation as retirement home 42
   out-of-season holiday lets 18, 42
   over-charging of sub-tenant 41
   overcrowding 87–8
   owner occupation 17–18, 42
   protected shorthold tenant 42–3
   reasonableness 20, 39
   redevelopment 18–19, 87
   regulated tenancies
     agricultural employee 42
     armed forces personnel 43
     assignment without consent 40
     breach of obligation 39
     deterioration of dwelling house 40
     deterioration of furniture 40
     former employee 40
     landlord occupation 40–1
     minister of religion 42
     notice to quit 40
     nuisance, annoyance or criminal activity 39–40
     occupation as retirement home 42
     out-of-season holiday lets 42
     over-charging of sub-tenant 41
     owner occupation 42
     protected shorthold tenant 42–3
     reasonableness test 39
     rent arrears 39
     student accommodation 42
     suitable alternative accommodation 39
   rent arrears 21, 39, 85–6
     discretion 160
     persistent delay in paying 21
     postponed orders 162
     serious 19–20
     suspended orders 163, 164
   secure tenancies 85–9
     anti-social behaviour 86
     approved redevelopment scheme 87

possession grounds – *continued*
    charity landlord's objectives 87
    demolition or reconstruction of premises 87
    disabled persons accommodation 88
    domestic violence 86
    employee misconduct 87
    false statements 86–7
    former employee 88
    misconduct 87
    non-spouse successor 88
    overcrowding 87–8
    rent arrears 85–6
    special housing needs occupant 88
    suitable alternative accommodation 89
    unlawful assignment 87
  special housing needs occupant 88
  student accommodation 18, 42
  suitable alternative accommodation 21, 39, 89
  termination of employment 24
  unlawful assignment 87
possession orders 158–64
  against mortgagors 162
  against trespassers 163
    tolerated trespassers 164–5
  appeal against 166–7
  breach 164
  challenging 166–7
    appeal 166–7
    application to set aside 166
    stay 167
    suspension 167
  discretionary grounds 159–61
  flowchart 169–72
  forfeiture of long lease 162–3
  mandatory grounds 161–2
  postponement 162, 163–4
  set aside 166
  stay 167
  suspended 163, 164, 167
  unauthorised tenants 162
Prevention of Social Housing Fraud Act 2013 30
priority need, homelessness claims
  applicants without 195
  armed forces personnel 183
  asylum seekers 183
  children or young people 182
  dependent children 181
  disabilities, learning or physical 182
  fleeing domestic violence 183
  former prisoners 183
  human rights challenge 183–4
  institutional background vulnerability 182
  mental illness 182
  non-eligible persons 183
  old age 181
  other special reason 182
  persons with 180
  pregnant women 180
  restricted persons 183
  vulnerabilities 181–2
private landlords
  selective licensing 8
private life, respect for 47–8, 54–5

private registered providers *see* **registered social landlords**
private sector tenants
  anti-social behaviour 33
prohibiting order
  homelessness judicial review 209
prohibition orders
  disrepair claims 116–17
property adjustment order
  assignment of secure tenancy 93
property law 1–2
protected shorthold tenant
  recovery of regulated tenancy from 42–3
protected tenancies
  assured tenancy exclusion 12
  exclusions 36–7
  exclusive possession 36
  only or principal home 36
  recovery of possession *see* **regulated tenancies**, grounds for possession
  rent *see* **regulated tenancies**
  security of tenure 37
    see also statutory tenancies
  separate dwelling 36
  shared accommodation 36
  shared ownership schemes 36
  sub-letting 36
  succession 38
Protection from Eviction Act 1977
  criminal sanctions 148–9
Protection from Harassment Act 1997 140, 144, 150
protection of property
  European Convention right 48
public bodies lettings
  assured tenancy exclusion 12
  protected tenancy exclusion 36
public funding
  civil legal advice 64
  contracts *see* controlled work contracts; licensed work contracts
  controlled work contracts 60, 65
    delegated functions 65
    devolved powers 65
    help at court 65
    legal help 65
    Lexcel standard 65
    quality mark person 65
    specialist quality mark 65
  costs 69–70
  disrepair claims 114–15
    public law obligations 116–17
  financial eligibility
    capital and income limits 66
    disposable capital 66
    disposable income 66
    guide to assessing 66–8
    passporting arrangement 66
  Funding Code 59
  help at court 61–2
    controlled work contracts 65
    legal representation 61
    need for representation 61
    specialist quality mark 65

public funding – continued
  homelessness
    appeals 204–5
    judicial review 209
  Housing Possession Court Duty scheme 64
  LASPO provisions 59–60
  legal help 61
    controlled work contracts 65
    reasonableness 61
    specialist quality mark 65
    sufficient benefit test 61
  legal representation
    criteria for 61–4
    full representation 62, 63
    harassment 146
    homelessness 64
    investigative representation 62, 63
    judicial review claims 64
    licensed work contracts 65
    unlawful eviction 146
  licensed work contracts 60, 65
    legal representation 65
  limits in housing matters 60
  merits criteria regulations 59–60
  possession claims 168
  procedure regulations 60
  procedures regulations 65
  specialist quality mark 65
  standard civil contract 65
  statutory charge 69
  Telephone Gateway Service 64
  undue influence claims 132
public law 2
public sector housing
  allocation 72
    additional preference 74
    challenging 75–6
    Code of Guidance 72
    discrimination issues 76
    eligibility of applicants 74–5
    factors taken into account 74
    former service personnel 74
    homelessness and 73
    housing need 73
    immigration controls and 74, 75
    priority need 73
    reasonable preference 73–4
    review of decisions 76
    statement of policy 73, 75
  asylum seekers 55
  introductory tenancies *see* **introductory tenancies**
  non-secure tenancies
    ceasing to be secure 78–9
    exclusion for secure status 79–80
  right to repair scheme 108
  secure tenants *see* **secure tenancies**
  see also **local housing authorities**

quashing order
  homelessness judicial review 209
quiet enjoyment
  unlawful eviction/harassment and 136

Rachmanism *see* **unlawful eviction**
reasonableness
  administration charges 127
  recovery of assured tenancy 20
  recovery of regulated tenancy 39
  service charges 126
receiver appointment
  disrepair 109
reconstruction
  recovery of secure tenancy 87
redecoration 101
redevelopment
  recovery of assured tenancy 18–19
  recovery of secure tenancy 87
registered social landlords
  assured tenancies
    advantages 29
    demoted tenancies 30–1
    disadvantages 29–30
  as public authority 48–9
  secure tenancies 72, 77
registration of rent
  housing association tenants 44
  re-registration 44
  regulated tenancies 44
regulated tenancies
  grounds for possession
    agricultural employee 42
    armed forces personnel 43
    assignment without consent 40
    breach of obligation 39
    deterioration of dwelling house 40
    deterioration of furniture 40
    former employee 40
    landlord occupation 40–1
    minister of religion 42
    notice to quit 40
    nuisance, annoyance or criminal activity 39–40
    occupation as retirement home 42
    out-of-season holiday lets 42
    over-charging of sub-tenant 41
    owner occupation 42
    protected shorthold tenant 42–3
    reasonableness test 39
    rent arrears 39
    student accommodation 42
    suitable alternative accommodation 39
  rent
    determination of fair rent 43–4
    fair rent 43
    housing association tenants 44
    market rent 43
    maximum rent increase 43
    re-registration 44
    registration 44
    scarcity value 43
  statutory *see* **statutory tenancies**
  succession 38
rent
  arrears *see* **rent arrears**
  fair rent 43
  housing association tenants 44

Index

rent – *continued*
    increases, periodic assured tenants 13–14
    market rent 43
    maximum rent increase 43
    re-registration 44
    registration 44
    regulated tenancies 43–4
    rent review clause 13–14
    scarcity value 43
rent arrears
    assured tenancy 21
        persistent delay in paying 21
        serious 19–20
    possession ground
        discretion 160
            suspended orders 163, 164
    regulated tenancy 39
    secure tenancy 85–6
    serious 19–20
rent assessment committees
    assured shorthold tenancies 26
    scarcity value 43
repairs *see* **disrepair**
resident landlord
    assured tenancy exclusion 12–13
    continuous residence requirement 13
    dwelling in same flat or building 12–13
    only or principal home 13
    protected tenancy exclusion 36
respect for family and private life 47–8, 54–5
retirement home
    recovery of regulated tenancy for 42
right to buy
    discount 97
        repayment on early sale 97
    eligibility to exercise right 96
    exercise of right 97
    first refusal right 98
    legislation 96
    secure tenancies 71, 96–8
    suspension 96
right to manage *see* **management, secure tenancies**

secure tenancies
    absence from home 77
    allocation 72
        additional preference 74
        challenging 75–6
        Code of Guidance 72–3
        discrimination issues 76
        eligibility of applicants 74–5
        factors taken into account 74
        former services personnel 74
        homelessness and 73
        housing need 73
        immigration controls and 74, 75
        priority need 73
        reasonable preference 73–4
        review of decisions 76
        statement of policy 73, 75
    assignment
        anti-social behaviour objection 93
        by way of exchange 92–3

secure tenancies – *continued*
        property adjustment order 93
        to person qualified to succeed 93
    asylum seekers 55
    ceasing to be secure 78–9
    consultation on housing management matters 94–5
    demoted tenancies 81
        anti-social behaviour and 83
        effect of demotion order 83
        grounds 82–3
    exclusion from secure status 79–80
    fixed-term tenancy
        statutory tenancy arising 82
        termination 81–2
    flexible tenancies 77, 78
        review 78
        termination 82
    grounds for possession 85–9
        anti-social behaviour 86
        approved redevelopment scheme 87
        charity landlord's objectives 87
        demolition or reconstruction of premises 87
        disabled persons accommodation 88
        domestic violence 86
        employee misconduct 87
        false statements 86–7
        former employee 88
        misconduct 87
        non-spouse successor 88
        overcrowding 87
        rent arrears 85–6
        special housing needs occupant 88
        suitable alternative accommodation 89
        unlawful assignment 87
    improvements by tenant 94
    landlord condition 78
    let as separate dwelling 76, 77
    lodgers 94
    management
        consultation right 94–5
        right of tenant to manage 95–6
    matrimonial disputes 89–90
    only or principal home 77
    provision of 72–3
    registered social landlords 72, 77
    repair right 94
    right to buy 71
        discount 97
            repayment on early sale 97
        eligibility to exercise right 96
        exercise of right 97
        first refusal right 98
        legislation 96
        suspension 96
    rights of tenant
        assignment 92–3
        consultation on housing management matters 94–5
        improvements 94
        lodgers 94
        management 95–6
        repair 94
        right to buy *see* right to buy
        sub-letting 94

secure tenancies – *continued*
    succession *see* succession
    termination of tenancy 89–90
    security of tenure 81–3
        demoted tenancies 81, 82–3
        fixed-term tenancy 81–2
        notice requirements 84–5
        possession order 81, 82
        termination by tenant 81
    sub-letting 94
    succession
        before 2 Apr 2012 90–1
        after 2 Apr 2012 90
        civil partners 90, 91
        family definition 91–2
        period of residence 91
        right to succeed 90–2
        'successor' defined 92
    tenant condition 77–8
    termination by tenant 89–90
    unlawfully sub-letting 79
    see also **introductory tenancies**
security of tenure
    assured shorthold tenancies 24, 25
    assured tenancies
        fixed-term tenancy 16
        notice period 17
        notice provisions 16–17
        section 8 notice 16
    secure tenancies
        demoted tenancies 82–3
        fixed-term tenancy 81–2
        notice requirements 84–5
        possession order 81
        termination by tenant 81
selective licensing
    designated areas 8
    management orders 8
self-help remedy
    repairs 108, 111
service charges 125–8
    administration charges 127
        reasonableness 127
    consultation 126
    definition 126
    demand 126
    disputes 127–8
    exclusion from protection 126
    failure to pay 128
    leasehold valuation tribunal 127–8
    legislation 126
    reasonableness 126
service of claim
    possession claim 156
shared ownership leases
    protected tenancy exclusion 36
single joint expert 113
special housing needs occupation
    recovery of secure tenancy 88
specific performance
    repairs 110, 111
statutory charge
    public funding 69

statutory tenancies
    recovery of possession *see* **regulated tenancies**, grounds for possession
    rent *see* **regulated tenancies**
    statutory tenant status 37–8
    succession 38
    termination of fixed-term secure tenancy 82
    terms of tenancy 38
student accommodation
    recovery of assured tenancy 18
    recovery of regulated tenancy 42
student lets
    assured tenancy exclusion 12
    protected tenancy exclusion 36
sub-letting
    overcharging of sub-tenant 41
    periodic assured tenants 14
    protected tenancies 36
    regulated tenancy 40, 41
    secure tenancies 94
    without consent 40
subletting
    unlawfully 79
succession
    civil partners 14, 15, 54, 90, 91
    human rights 54, 91
    periodic assured tenants 14–15
    secure tenancies
        before 2 Apr 2012 90–1
        after 2 Apr 2012 90
        civil partners 90, 91
        family definition 91–2
        period of residence 91
        right to succeed 90–2
        'successor' defined 92
suitable alternative accommodation
    recovery of assured tenancy 21
    recovery of regulated tenancy 39
    recovery of secure tenancy 89

Telephone Gateway Service 64
tenancies
    fixed period 3
    leasehold estates in land 3–4
    periodic, notice requirement 4
    registration as legal estates 3
    upkeep of dwelling 4
    see also individual types eg **protected tenancies**; **secure tenancies**
tenancy deposit scheme
    assured shorthold tenancies 26–8
    authorised schemes 27
    insurance schemes 27
    non-compliance 27–8
Tenancy Deposit Solutions Ltd 27
tenant 3
Tenant Services Authority 28
tolerated trespassers 5, 164–5
    effect of being 165
    reform of law 165
tort claims
    disrepair
        common law 105–6

tort claims – *continued*
    defective premises 106–7
    injury to tenant 105, 106
    occupiers' liability 106
  unlawful eviction/harassment
    breach of statutory duty 138–9
    nuisance 138
    s 27 of HA 1988 140
    trespass to goods 138
    trespass to land 137–8
    trespass to person 138
    unlawfully to attempt to deprive 140
    unlawfully to deprive 140
trespass to goods 138
trespass to land 137–8
trespass to person 138
trespassers
  initial trespassers 5
  occupation by 4–5
  possession claims against 155
  possession orders against 163
  tolerated 5, 164–5

undue influence
  matrimonial homes 130–2
  public funding 132
unfair contract terms
  effect of term 5–6
  Office of Fair Trading Guidance 6
  residential leases 5–6
unfit for occupation 54, 101, 179
unlawful assignment
  recovery of secure tenancy 87
unlawful eviction
  breach of statutory duty 138–9
    excluded tenancies and licences 139
    statutorily protected tenancies 138–9
  civil causes of action 136–40
  civil procedure
    commencing proceedings *see* commencement of proceedings
    Part 7 claims 145–6
    public funding 146
  civil remedies
    injunctions 140–1
    interim injunctions 141
    see also damages
  commencement of proceedings 146–8
    claim form N1 146
    defence 148
    form N16A 147–8
    further information 146–7
    interim injunction application 147–8

unlawful eviction – *continued*
    particulars of claim 146–7
    service of injunction order 147–8
    urgent or without notice applications 147
  contract claims
    derogation from grant 136–7
    other contractual terms breach 137
    quiet enjoyment breach 136
  criminal sanctions 135–6
    compensation orders 150
    Criminal Law Act 1977 149–50
    dealing with offences 149
    landlord meaning 149
    Protection from Eviction Act 1977 148–9
    residential occupier meaning 149
    violent entry to premises 149–50
  damages
    aggravated 142
    double recovery 144
    exemplary 142
    general 141
    mitigation 143
    nominal 141
    reduction 143
    s 27 and 28 HA 1988 142–3
    s 27 defence 142
    s 28 measure of damages 142–3
    security lost 143–4
    special 141
  injunctions 140–1
  interim injunctions 141
  legal representation, information on property 146
  legislation 135
  notice to quit
    ineffective 144
    length of notice 144–5
    prescribed information 145
  nuisance 138
  public funding 146
  tort claims
    breach of statutory duty 138–9
    nuisance 138
    s 27 of HA 1988 140
    trespass to goods 138
    trespass to land 137–8
    trespass to person 138
    unlawfully to attempt to deprive 140
    unlawfully to deprive 140
  trespass to goods 137
  trespass to land 137–8

warrant for possession 53–4, 167–8
  oppression in execution of 168